Guitar
ALL-IN-ONE

FOR DUMMIES®
A Wiley Brand

2nd Edition

by Jon Chappell, Mark Phillips, and Desi Serna

Guitar All-In-One For Dummies,® 2nd Edition

Published by: **John Wiley & Sons, Inc.,** 111 River Street, Hoboken, NJ 07030-5774, www.wiley.com

Copyright © 2014 by John Wiley & Sons, Inc., Hoboken, New Jersey

Media and software compilation copyright © 2014 by John Wiley & Sons, Inc. All rights reserved.

Published simultaneously in Canada

For general information on our other products and services, please contact our Customer Care Department within the U.S. at 877-762-2974, outside the U.S. at 317-572-3993, or fax 317-572-4002. For technical support, please visit www.wiley.com/techsupport.

Wiley publishes in a variety of print and electronic formats and by print-on-demand. Some material included with standard print versions of this book may not be included in e-books or in print-on-demand. If this book refers to media such as a CD or DVD that is not included in the version you purchased, you may download this material at http://booksupport.wiley.com. For more information about Wiley products, visit www.wiley.com.

Library of Congress Control Number: 2014931922

ISBN 978-1-118-87202-4 (pbk); ISBN 978-1-118-87210-9 (ePub); ISBN 978-1-118-87206-2 (ePDF)

Manufactured in the United States of America

C10007756_012219

Contents at a Glance

Introduction **1**

Book I: Guitar 101 .... **5**
Chapter 1: Guitar Anatomy and Tuning 7
Chapter 2: Getting Ready to Play 21
Chapter 3: Buying and Stringing a Guitar 33
Chapter 4: Deciphering Music Notation and Tablature 59

Book II: Sounds and Techniques **75**
Chapter 1: Basic Major and Minor Chords 77
Chapter 2: Adding Spice: Basic 7th Chords 95
Chapter 3: Power Chords and Barre Chords 109
Chapter 4: Right-Hand Rhythm Guitar Techniques 123
Chapter 5: Playing Melodies in Position and in Double-Stops 147

Book III: Getting to Know Guitar Theory **163**
Chapter 1: Navigating the Fretboard and Building Triads 165
Chapter 2: Getting to Know the CAGED System 189
Chapter 3: Playing Snazzier Chords with Chord Tones and Extensions 211
Chapter 4: Playing Chord Progressions by Numbers 229
Chapter 5: Identifying Tonics, Keys, and Modes 241
Chapter 6: Dominant Function and Voice Leading 271

Book IV: Rock Guitar **283**
Chapter 1: I Know, It's Only Rock Guitar, but I Like It 285
Chapter 2: Playing Lead 301
Chapter 3: Groovin' on Riffs 323
Chapter 4: Going Up the Neck and Playing the Fancy Stuff 333
Chapter 5: The Care and Feeding of Your Electric Guitar 355

Book V: Blues Guitar **377**
Chapter 1: Introducing the Blues and Playing Blues Rhythm 379
Chapter 2: Blues Progressions, Song Forms, and Moves 405
Chapter 3: Musical Riffs: Bedrock of the Blues 427

Book VI: Classical Guitar 443

Chapter 1: Introducing the Classical Guitar 445
Chapter 2: Playing Easy Pieces in Open Position 467
Chapter 3: Combining Arpeggios and Melody 481

Book VII: Exercises: Practice, Practice, Practice 501

Chapter 1: Putting the Major Scales to Use in Your Playing 503
Chapter 2: Adding Major Scale Sequences to Your Repertoire 517
Chapter 3: Tackling the Three Minor Scales 531
Chapter 4: Building Finger Independence with Chord Exercises 561

Appendix A: 96 Common Chords 587

Appendix B: Accessing the Video Clips and Audio Tracks 591

Index 599

Table of Contents

Introduction *1*
   About This Book 1
   Foolish Assumptions 2
   Icons Used in This Book 3
   Beyond the Book 4
   Where to Go from Here 4

Book I: Guitar 101 .... *5*

Chapter 1: Guitar Anatomy and Tuning. 7
   The Parts and Workings of a Guitar 7
   How Guitars Make Sound 11
      Strings doing their thing 11
      Using left and right hands together 11
      Notes on the neck: Half steps and frets 12
      Comparing how acoustics and electrics generate sound 12
   Tuning Your Guitar 13
   Tuning Your Guitar to Itself 14
   Tuning Your Guitar to an External Source 16
      Keying in to the piano 17
      Putting that pitch pipe to work 18
      Getting a taste of the tuning fork 18
      Employing the electronic tuner 18
      Using the audio tracks 19

Chapter 2: Getting Ready to Play. 21
   Assuming the Positions 21
      Sitting down and playing a spell 22
      Standing up and delivering 23
      Fretting with your left hand 24
      Picking with your right hand 26
   Getting Your Head Around Guitar Notation 28
      Understanding chord diagrams 28
      Taking in tablature... 30
      Reading rhythm slashes 30
   Discovering How to Play a Chord 31

Chapter 3: Buying and Stringing a Guitar 33

First Things First: Developing a Purchasing Plan.....................34
Noting Some Considerations for Your First Guitar 35
Sifting through Models to Match Your Style..........................36
Looking for Quality...38
    Construction and body type.................................39
    Woods, hardware, and other goodies 41
    Workmanship 42
    Appointments (cosmetic extras) 43
Before You Buy: Walking through the Buying Process.................44
    Online or bricks-and-mortar?...............................44
    Seeking expert advice......................................44
    Negotiating with the salesperson 45
    Closing the deal...45
Changing Your Strings 47
    Surveying string-changing strategies 47
    Removing old strings.......................................48
Stringing an Acoustic Guitar 48
    Changing strings step by step 48
    Tuning up 52
Stringing a Nylon-String Guitar 52
    Changing strings step by step 52
    Tuning up 55
Stringing an Electric Guitar 55
    Changing strings step by step 55
    Tuning up 57
    Setting up a floating bridge...............................57

Chapter 4: Deciphering Music Notation and Tablature 59

Knowing the Ropes of Standard Music Notation......................59
    The composer's canvas: The staff, clef, measures, and bar lines....60
    Pitch: The highs and lows of music.........................61
    Duration: How long to hold a note, what determines
      rhythm, and so on 63
    Expression, articulation, and other symbols 66
Relating the Notes on the Staff to the Fretboard...................69
Relishing the Usefulness of Guitar-Specific Notation...............70
    Fingering indications for the right and left hands 70
    Stepping up to the barre...................................72
    Taking on tablature, a nice complement to standard notation 73

Book II: Sounds and Techniques.................................. 75

Chapter 1: Basic Major and Minor Chords 77

Chords in the A Family...78
    Fingering A-family chords..................................78
    Strumming A-family chords..................................79

Chords in the D Family 81
   Fingering D-family chords 81
   Strumming D-family chords 83
Chords in the G Family 84
   Fingering G-family chords 84
   Strumming G-family chords 84
Chords in the C Family 85
   Fingering C-family chords 85
   Strumming C-family chords 86
Songs with Basic Major and Minor Chords 87
Fun with the "Oldies" Progression 94

Chapter 2: Adding Spice: Basic 7th Chords 95
Dominant 7th Chords 95
   D7, G7, and C7 96
   E7 (the two-finger version) and A7 97
   E7 (the four-finger version) and B7 98
Minor 7th Chords — Dm7, Em7, and Am7 98
Major 7th Chords — Cmaj7, Fmaj7, Amaj7, and Dmaj7 99
Playing Songs with 7th Chords 101

Chapter 3: Power Chords and Barre Chords .109
Reviewing Open-position Chords 110
Putting Power Chords into Play 111
   Moving power chords 113
   Pulling the power together 114
Getting Behind the Barre 114
   Getting a grip on barre chords 115
   Playing E-based barre chords 116
   Moving the E-form barre chord around the neck 117
   Other E forms: Minor, dominant 7, minor 7, and 7sus ... 117
   Playing A-based barre chords 119
   Moving the A-form barre chord 121
   A forms: Minor, dominant 7, minor 7, 7sus, and major 7 ... 121

Chapter 4: Right-Hand Rhythm Guitar Techniques 123
Strumming Along 123
   Downstrokes 124
   Upstrokes 125
   Combining downstrokes and upstrokes 126
Mixing Single Notes and Strums 131
   The pick-strum 131
   Boom-chick 131
   Moving bass line 132
Disrupting Your Sound: Syncopated Strumming 133
   Syncopated notation: Dots and ties 133
   Playing syncopated figures 134

Giving Your Left Hand a Break..135
  Left-hand muting..136
  Implying syncopation..136
Suppressing the Right Hand..137
  Right-hand muting..137
Left-hand Movement within a Right-hand Strum...........................138
Giving Your Fingers Some Style...139
Getting Into Rhythm Styles...141
  Straight-four feel...142
  Two-beat feel..143
  16-feel..143
  Heavy metal gallop...144
  Reggae rhythm..144
  Three feel...144

Chapter 5: Playing Melodies in Position and in Double-Stops 147

Playing Scales and Exercises in Position.................................147
  Playing in position versus open strings..............................148
  Playing exercises in position..148
  Shifting positions 150
  Creating your own exercises to build strength and dexterity 151
Practicing Songs in Position...152
Double-Stop Basics...156
  Defining double-stops..156
  Trying exercises in double-stops.....................................156
Playing Songs in Double-Stops..158

Book III: Getting to Know Guitar Theory.................. 163

Chapter 1: Navigating the Fretboard and Building Triads 165

Tracing Back to Strings 6 and 5..166
  Moving whole steps and half steps...................................168
  Sharps and flats...168
  Grouping notes...170
Tracking Notes and Playing Octaves.....................................172
  Shaping octaves with your 1st finger on strings 6 and 5.............173
  Octaves starting on strings 4 and 3.................................174
  Octaves that are three strings apart 175
  Repeating octaves beyond the 12th fret.............................175
Measuring the Space between Pitches with Intervals 176
  Playing intervals 1 through 7...177
  Filling in the gaps with flats and sharps 181
Harmonizing the Major Scale to Build Triads and Chords............182
  Major triad: Building from the 1st scale degree of the major scale ...183
  Minor triad: Building from the 2nd scale degree of
    the major scale...184
The Seven Triads of the Major Scale......................................186
Playing the Chord Sequence of the Major Scale.........................187

Chapter 2: Getting to Know the CAGED System **189**

Chord Inversions and Chord Voicings 190
Using the C Form 191
The C form as a moveable barre chord 191
Playing a C form arpeggio pattern 192
Playing C form chord voicings 195
Using the A Form 198
Using the G Form 201
Using the E Form 202
Using the D Form 205
Playing Minor CAGED Forms 207
Playing the C minor form 207
Playing the A minor form 208
Playing the G minor form 208
Playing the E minor form 209
Playing the D minor form 209

**Chapter 3: Playing Snazzier Chords with Chord Tones
and Extensions** **211**

About Chord Tones and Extensions 211
Adding 7ths to the Major Scale Chords 213
Playing major and minor 7th chords 217
Playing dominant 7th chords 219
Playing minor 7th flat 5 chords 220
Working with 2nds and 9ths 221
Sus2 chords 221
Add9 chords 221
Minor chords with 2nds and 9ths 222
9th chords 224
Working with 4ths and 11ths 225
Sus4 chords 225
Add4 chords 225
Playing 6th Chords and Blues Shuffles 226

Chapter 4: Playing Chord Progressions by Numbers **229**

Drawing Chord Progressions from the Major Scale 230
Using Roman Numerals to Represent Chords 230
Visualizing Numbers on the Fretboard 231
Transposing to New Keys 232
Playing Common Chord Progressions 233
Playing I-IV-V chord progressions 234
Playing major chord progressions 234
Adding minor chords ii, iii, and vi 235
Playing minor chord progressions 235
Starting Numbers on the 5th String 236
Playing Chord Progressions with Open Chords 239

Chapter 5: Identifying Tonics, Keys, and Modes 241

Understanding the Relationship between Major and Minor Scales......242
Numbering the Relative Minor..243
    Accounting for any interval changes...................................244
    Looking at a few minor key song examples 246
Identifying the Modes of the Major Scale......................................248
    Ionian (I)...249
    Dorian (ii)..250
    Phrygian (iii)..254
    Lydian (IV)...257
    Mixolydian (V)...261
    Aeolian (vi)..264
    Locrian (vii♭5)...264
Key Signatures and Common Discrepancies 265
    Looking past the key signature to figure out a song's mode.......265
    Considering some common discrepancies in music notation 266
Comparing Scale Formulas and Structures....................................268

Chapter 6: Dominant Function and Voice Leading 271

Chord Function and the Dominant Chord.....................................271
    Leading with the leading tone...273
    Tension rises with a tritone...273
    Playing songs with dominant function..................................273
Secondary Dominants..275
    Drawing attention to some common secondary dominants 275
    Thinking of secondary dominants as mini key changes...............277
    Songs that use secondary dominants 279
Voice Leading...280

Book IV: Rock Guitar 283

Chapter 1: I Know, It's Only Rock Guitar, but I Like It 285

Differentiating Between Rock and Acoustic Guitar . . .
    It Ain't Just Volume...286
    Sound quality, or timbre...287
    Signal...287
    Distortion and sustain...288
    Oh yes, and volume...289
    Listening examples 290
Knowing the Essentials: The Power Trio..290
    The electric guitar 291
    The amplifier 295
    Effects..297

Accessorizing Your Guitar...298
    Picks 299
    Straps...299
    Cords 300
    Tuners 300

Chapter 2: Playing Lead..301

Taking the Lead 301
    Holding the pick 304
    Attacking the problem..304
Playing Single Notes 304
    Single-note technique..305
    Alternate picking in downstrokes and upstrokes.........308
    Using scales 308
    Skips 311
    Combining steps and skips..311
Starting at the Bottom: Low-Note Melodies 311
Going to the Top: High-Note Melodies 312
Playing in Position 313
    Open position 313
    Moveable, or closed, position 314
Jamming on Lower Register Riffs 315
Making It Easy: The Pentatonic Scale 316
Playing the Pentatonic Scale: Three Ways to Solo 317
    Pentatonics over a major key..318
    Pentatonics over a minor key..319
    Pentatonics over a blues progression..........................319
Improvising Leads 321

Chapter 3: Groovin' on Riffs 323

Getting Your Groove On: Basic Riffs 324
    Half-note and whole-note riffs......................................324
    Eighth-note and quarter-note riffs 324
    Sixteenth-note riffs...327
    Eighth-note syncopation..328
Playing Two Notes Can be Better than One: Double-Stops...330
Combining Single-Note Riffs and Chords...............................331

Chapter 4: Going Up the Neck and Playing the Fancy Stuff.......333

Going Up the Neck...334
    Choking up on the neck 334
    Playing double-stops on the move 335
Playing in Position 337
    Positions defined 337
    A firm position...337

Using the Moveable Pentatonic Scale 338
    Staying at home position 338
    Going above home position 339
    Dropping below home position 340
Changing Your Position 341
    Licks that transport 341
    From the depths to the heights 342
Knowing Where to Play 343
    Associating keys with positions 343
    Placing positions 345
    Putting the five positions into play 347
Bringing Down the Hammer-ons 347
Having Pull with Pull-offs 348
Slippin' into Slides 349
Bending to Your Will 351
    Bend and release 352
    Pre-bend 353
Sounding a Vibrato That Makes You Quiver 354

Chapter 5: The Care and Feeding of Your Electric Guitar 355

Using the Tools of the Trade 356
    The basics 356
    Power user tools 357
Changing Strings 359
    Choosing the right strings 359
    Removing the old strings 360
    Putting on the new strings 363
Cleaning the Parts of Your Guitar 366
    The strings 367
    The body, fingerboard, and hardware 367
    The frets 367
    The electronics 368
Setting Up Your Guitar to Optimize Performance 368
    Warning signs 369
    Bridge spring tension 371
    Fixing minor wiring problems 373
Troubleshooting Guide 373
Storing Your Guitar 374

Book V: Blues Guitar **377**

Chapter 1: Introducing the Blues and Playing Blues Rhythm 379

Beyond the Delta: Defining the Blues Guitar Sound 380
    The method to the music: Chord progressions 381
    The guitarist's language of melody 381
    Playing blues expressively 382
    The groove that sets the pace 383

Strumming Along 383
   Stroking down 384
   . . . And stroking up 384
   Combining down and up 384
   Striking to a beat 385
Mixing Single Notes and Strumming 386
   Separating bass and treble: The pick-strum 387
   Playing common pick-strum patterns 387
Shuffling the Beats with Syncopated Strumming 389
   A bit of notation: Dots that extend and ties that bind ... 390
   Syncopation: Playing with dots and ties 390
Muting: Stopping the String from Ringing 391
   Muting the sound between two chords (left hand) 391
   Simulating syncopation with left-hand muting 392
   Muting the sound of a note (right hand) 392
Copying the Classics: Plucking Fingerstyle Blues 394
The Right Hand's Bliss: Different Rhythm Styles to Play ... 394
   The shuffle groove 395
   The driving straight-four 397
   The slow 12/8, with groups of three 399
   The two-beat feel 402
   The slow and funky 16 feel 403

Chapter 2: Blues Progressions, Song Forms, and Moves .... .405
Blues by the Numbers 405
Recognizing the Big Dogs: Primary Key Families and Their Chords 406
The Structure of a Blues Song, Baby 407
   Playing the 12-bar blues 408
   The quick four 409
   The turnaround 410
   Slow blues 411
   The 8-bar blues 413
   Straight-four (or rock blues) 414
Applying Structures to Keys 415
   A move with many chords: The Jimmy Reed move 416
   The sound of sadness: Minor blues 420
Accessorizing the 12-Bar Blues: Intros, Turnarounds, and Endings 421
   Intros 421
   Turnarounds 421
   Endings 423
High Moves 423

Chapter 3: Musical Riffs: Bedrock of the Blues .... .427
Basic Single-Note Riffs 427
   For the low-down bass notes: Quarter-note riffs 428
   The big daddy of riffs: Eighth-note riffs 429
   Adding a little funk: 16th-note riffs 430
   Throwing rhythm for a loop: Syncopated eighth-note riffs 430

Double the Strings, Double the Fun: Two-Note Riffs (or Double-Stops).....431
Straight feel.. 432
Shuffle, or swing, eighths 433
High-Note Riffs, the Bridge to Lead Guitar 434
Keith Richards's borrowed trademark: Quick-four riffs 435
Intro, turnaround, and ending riffs 435
Mastering the Rhythm Figure 440

Book VI: Classical Guitar 443

Chapter 1: Introducing the Classical Guitar 445

Classical Guitar: One Term, Two Meanings, and a Bit of History.......... 446
How a Classical Guitar Is Physically Different from Its Peers 447
Beyond Physique: Other Unique Attributes of Classical Guitar 450
Player's form and technique 450
Musical knowledge and skills 451
Situating Yourself to Play 452
Taking your seat.. 454
Supporting the guitar: Leg position.. 454
Embracing the guitar: Arm support.. 456
Placing your hands correctly.. 456
Approaching the Strings with Your Hands... 459
Fretting the strings: Left-hand form 460
Preparing to pluck: Right-hand form 462
Stroking the strings: Basic right-hand technique 462

Chapter 2: Playing Easy Pieces in Open Position 467

Coordinating Contrapuntal Music: Layered Melodies........................... 468
Playing two melodies in sync rhythmically................................. 468
Opposing forces: Separating the thumb
and fingers rhythmically 470
Thickening the upper part by adding double-stops..................... 471
Melody and Accompaniment: Using All Your Fingers 472
Matching rhythm between accompaniment and melody............. 472
Getting creative with the flow: Two parts, two rhythms.............. 473
Playing Easy Pieces in Different Textural Styles.................................... 474

Chapter 3: Combining Arpeggios and Melody 481

Grasping the Combination in Context 481
Going Downtown: Melody in the Bass 482
Playing a bass melody within arpeggios..................................... 483
Practicing making a bass melody stand out................................ 484
Moving Uptown: Melody in the Treble 485
Playing a treble melody within arpeggios 487
Practicing making a treble melody stand out 488

Mixing Up Your Melodic Moves: The Thumb and Fingers Take Turns 488
Playing a shifting treble-and-bass melody within arpeggios........489
Practicing making a shifting melody stand out............490
Playing Pieces That Combine Arpeggios and Melodies........491

Book VII: Exercises: Practice, Practice, Practice 501

Chapter 1: Putting the Major Scales to Use in Your Playing 503

Practicing Five Major Scale Patterns 504
Major scale pattern #1 504
Major scale pattern #2 507
Major scale pattern #3 508
Major scale pattern #4 510
Major scale pattern #5 512
Applying Your Scale Work to Actual Pieces of Music......................513
"The First Noël"..............................514

Chapter 2: Adding Major Scale Sequences to Your Repertoire 517

Practicing Major Scale Sequences.......................518
Major scale sequences using pattern #1................518
Major scale sequences using pattern #2................519
Major scale sequences using pattern #3................522
Major scale sequences using pattern #4................523
Major scale sequences using pattern #5................524
Putting Your Sequence Skills to Work with a Few Songs 526
"Oh, Them Golden Slippers".......................527
"We Wish You a Merry Christmas".......................527

Chapter 3: Tackling the Three Minor Scales 531

Familiarizing Yourself with Natural Minor Scales 532
Natural minor scale pattern #1 532
Natural minor scale pattern #2 534
Natural minor scale pattern #3 536
Natural minor scale pattern #4 537
Natural minor scale pattern #5 539
Raising the Bar with Melodic Minor Scales....................540
Melodic minor scale pattern #1........................540
Melodic minor scale pattern #2........................542
Melodic minor scale pattern #3........................544
Melodic minor scale pattern #4........................545
Melodic minor scale pattern #5........................547
Harmonizing with Harmonic Minor Scales....................549
Harmonic minor scale pattern #1 549
Harmonic minor scale pattern #2 551
Harmonic minor scale pattern #3 552
Harmonic minor scale pattern #4 552
Harmonic minor scale pattern #5 555

Playing Pieces Using the Three Minor Scales 557
"God Rest Ye Merry, Gentlemen" 557
Handel's "Allegro" 557
"The Three Ravens" 559

Chapter 4: Building Finger Independence with Chord Exercises . . .561

Practicing Inversion Patterns 562
Patterns using outside chords 563
Patterns using inside chords 571
Playing Chord Progressions 580
Progressions using outside chords 580
Progressions using inside chords 581
Practicing Pieces that Use Chord Progressions 582
Putting outside chords to use with "Danny Boy" 582
Playing inside chords in "Look for the Silver Lining" 584

Appendix A: 96 Common Chords *587*

*Appendix B: Accessing the Video Clips and
Audio Tracks* *591*

Index *599*

Introduction

•••

So, you want to play guitar, eh? No one can blame you. The guitar isn't just a beautiful, soulful, and versatile instrument. For about 80 years now, it has also set the standard for coolness in the music world. Not a bad combination.

Though the guitar as we know it is only about a century and a half old, its roots as a plucked stringed instrument go back deep into history. Many ancient folk instruments have followed the basic strings-stretched-over-fretboard-and-played-with-fingers design for thousands of years, and the guitar is in some ways the culmination of that legacy. It seems humans have always had something like the guitar in mind.

After the guitar was electrified in the 1930s — that is, when it went from soft backup instrument to a forceful and expressive vehicle for soloing — its popularity skyrocketed, and its intrinsic qualities and sound changed popular music forever. But its softer side didn't go away. When Bob Dylan famously "plugged in" at the 1965 Newport Folk Festival and was booed by outraged folk fans, it became clear that the electric guitar had entered its own universe.

Guitar All-in-One For Dummies, 2nd Edition covers both the acoustic and the electric universes — as well as the older classical guitar one, which has its own language, techniques, and musical pedigree.

About This Book

First, here's what this book is not: It's not a textbook, nor a long-winded history, nor a rote learning tool. Lots of those kinds of books are on the market, if that's what you're looking for — but beware, they're often dry and assume underlying knowledge.

Guitar All-in-One For Dummies, 2nd Edition is a generous conglomeration of material from several *For Dummies* guitar and music books. It aims to cover the guitar gamut, from what those thingies are called that wind the strings (tuning machines) to how Stevie Ray Vaughan got his incredible sound (by tuning lower, among other tricks) to how to employ the insights of guitar theory in your playing.

Much of the material is relevant to any style of guitar playing. But three popular guitar genres each get their own sections, called *books*: rock guitar, blues guitar, and classical guitar. You'll also find chapters on learning to read music, on building your chord repertoire, on practicing, scales, riffs, and how to play the fancy stuff . . . let's just say there's a lot here. And don't forget, the book is accompanied by 30 video clips and more than 120 audio tracks that can help you on your way to sounding just like the pros.

In this book, important words are defined in italics. Key words in lists that bring important ideas to your attention are in bold. And Web addresses are in monofont to set them apart.

Here are a few other conventions to help you navigate this book:

✔ **Right hand and left hand:** Instead of using "strumming hand" and "fretting hand," this book uses "right hand" for the hand that picks or strums the strings and "left hand" for the hand that frets the strings (it's easier and shorter that way). Sincere apologies to those left-handed readers who are using this book; you folks should read "right hand" to mean "left hand" and vice versa. You're probably used to stuff like that.

✔ **Up and down, higher and lower, and so on:** If you're asked to move a note or chord up the guitar neck or to play it higher on the neck, it means higher in pitch, or toward the body of the guitar. If you're asked to go down or lower on the neck, it means toward the headstock, or lower in pitch. (Those who hold a guitar with the headstock tilted upward may need to do a bit of mental adjustment whenever you see these terms. Just remember that these terms are about pitch, not position, and you'll do just fine.)

✔ **Dual music notation:** Some songs and exercises are arranged with the standard music staff and guitar tablature. You can use either of these methods, but you don't need to look at both at the same time. In many cases, the music under scrutiny also is on the free audio files for the book, so look for the Play This! icon that points you to specific tracks.

Foolish Assumptions

This book doesn't assume you know anything about playing guitar or reading music. It starts from zero and builds from the ground up — and then keeps going and going. It contains straightforward, informal explanations of how guitars work, what the different kinds are, how to get started playing, and how to form chords and strum and fingerpick. It then proceeds to help deepen your knowledge in several directions.

This book is designed for just about anyone who loves guitar. It's as useful for people who have barely touched a guitar as it is for those who have fiddled around with one for years but would like to get more serious. Even advanced players — those who would like to try a different genre than they're used to, or who specifically need to work on, say, their outside chord inversion patterns — will find plenty of valuable information in these pages.

No matter your situation, experience, or motives, this book's goal is to give you enough information so that ultimately you can explore the guitar on your own. Many of the best guitar players describe themselves as "self-taught." You can use this book to teach yourself. Discovering what the instrument can do, finding ways to make new sounds, suddenly grasping a better way to fret notes or chords that just minutes ago seemed impossible — these are tremendously exciting and satisfying experiences. Such magic awaits you if you're willing to put in some time and effort. That's a big *if*, though. It really is up to you.

Icons Used in This Book

As you go through the chapters of this book, you'll find friendly icons scattered here and there. They're designed to draw your attention to different kinds of information, from helpful guidance to pleasant diversions.

Be sure to pay attention to anything that has this icon attached. As you may guess, it's something important that you shouldn't forget. Tuck this info in the back of your mind.

When you see this icon, you know that some handy-dandy information follows that can save you time, trouble, money, energy, and more.

There's an occasional step into the swamp of technical jargon or complex discussion, and this icon gives you fair warning. It's not essential stuff. Feel free to flip past it if you just don't care.

Pay attention to text featuring this icon. It can help you avoid mistakes and problems.

This means there's an audio track or video clip that relates to what you're reading. The video and audio examples that appear throughout the text bring a lot of the music in this book to life. You can find these tracks and clips at www.dummies.com/go/guitaraio.

Beyond the Book

In addition to the book content, you can find a free online Cheat Sheet that includes handy info on fingerboard diagrams and tablature, 24 common guitar chords, and all the notes on the first nine frets. Go to www.dummies.com/ cheatsheet/guitaraio to access this handy reference material, and then print it out and keep it handy.

This book comes with additional free articles that cover information that simply couldn't fit into the book. Check them out at www.dummies.com/extras/ guitaraio.

Finally, remember that www.dummies.com/go/guitaraio is home to the video clips and audio tracks that accompany this book. Head there for demonstrations of notes, riffs, scales, chords, songs, exercises, the sounds of instruments, and various guitar features — and much more.

Where to Go from Here

The book is organized into parts (called books) with chapters grouped according to broad, related topics. But you sure don't have to read it from front to back — or in any particular order. The idea is that you can skim through the table of contents and pick and choose whatever's interesting to you, based on where you are currently in your musical journey. Then go directly to that section and get cracking.

Still, if you really want some tips about where to begin, here are a few:

✔ If you've never touched a guitar before, definitely start with Book I (and if looking at printed music gives you heart palpitations, you really should think about heading to Chapter 4 in Book I).

✔ If you're okay on the very basics, try Book II, which covers chord and note fundamentals and basic techniques.

✔ If you're okay strumming along by a campfire, but get wobbly in the knees whenever you think of playing anything higher than the 5th fret, check out the chapters in Book III.

✔ If you're already not bad at playing but would like to dig deeper into some particular styles, such as rock, blues, or classical guitar, head to Books IV–VI.

✔ And if you're actually pretty good but could use some terrific warmups to get your fingers even more limber (limberer?), head for Book VII for lots (and lots) of practice material.

Bottom line: Every person's musical journey is unique. Don't feel like you have to learn this or that. Let yourself be attracted to the kind of guitar music and styles that truly speak to you. Have fun! That's really the whole point.

Book I
Guitar 101

getting started with

guitar

Contents at a Glance

Chapter 1: Guitar Anatomy and Tuning **7**

The Parts and Workings of a Guitar 7

How Guitars Make Sound 11

Tuning Your Guitar..13

Tuning Your Guitar to Itself 14

Tuning Your Guitar to an External Source 16

Chapter 2: Getting Ready to Play **21**

Assuming the Positions 21

Getting Your Head Around Guitar Notation..28

Discovering How to Play a Chord 31

Chapter 3: Buying and Stringing a Guitar **33**

First Things First: Developing a Purchasing Plan.......................................34

Noting Some Considerations for Your First Guitar 35

Sifting through Models to Match Your Style...36

Looking for Quality...38

Before You Buy: Walking through the Buying Process................................44

Changing Your Strings 47

Stringing an Acoustic Guitar...48

Stringing a Nylon-String Guitar 52

Stringing an Electric Guitar...55

Chapter 4: Deciphering Music Notation and Tablature **59**

Knowing the Ropes of Standard Music Notation...59

Relating the Notes on the Staff to the Fretboard..69

Relishing the Usefulness of Guitar-Specific Notation.................................70

Chapter 1

Guitar Anatomy and Tuning

In This Chapter

▶ Identifying the different parts of the guitar

▶ Understanding how the guitar works

▶ Counting strings and frets

▶ Tuning the guitar relatively (to itself)

▶ Tuning to a fixed source

▶ Access the audio track and video clip at www.dummies.com/go/guitaraio/

A ll guitars — whether painted purple with airbrushed skulls and lightning bolts or finished in a natural-wood pattern with a fine French lacquer — share certain physical characteristics that make them behave like guitars and not violins or tubas. If you're confused about the difference between a headstock and a pickup or you're wondering which end of the guitar to hold under your chin, this chapter is for you.

This chapter describes the differences among the various parts of the guitar and tell you what those parts do. It also tells you how to hold the instrument and why the guitar sounds the way it does. You *don't* hold the guitar under your chin — unless, of course, you're Jimi Hendrix.

One of the great injustices of life is that before you can even play music on the guitar, you must endure the painstaking process of getting your instrument in tune. Fortunately for guitarists, you have only six strings to tune, as opposed to the couple hundred strings in a piano. Also encouraging is the fact that you can use several different methods to get your guitar in tune, as this chapter describes.

The Parts and Workings of a Guitar

Guitars come in two basic flavors: *acoustic* and *electric*. From a hardware standpoint, electric guitars have more components and doohickeys than acoustic guitars. Guitar makers generally agree, however, that making an acoustic guitar is harder than making an electric guitar. That's why, pound for pound, acoustic guitars cost just as much or more than their electric counterparts. (When you're ready to go guitar or guitar accessory shopping, check out Book I Chapter 3.) But both types follow the same basic approach to such principles as neck construction and string tension. That's why both acoustic and electric guitars have similar shapes and features, despite a sometimes radical difference in tone production. Figures 1-1 and 1-2 show the various parts of acoustic and electric guitars.

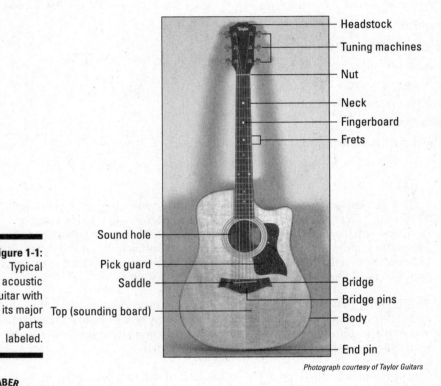

Headstock

Tuning machines

Nut

Neck

Fingerboard

Frets

Sound hole

Pick guard

Saddle

Bridge

Bridge pins

Top (sounding board)

Body

End pin

Figure 1-1: Typical acoustic guitar with its major parts labeled.

Photograph courtesy of Taylor Guitars

Here are the names and functions of the various parts of a guitar:

- **Back (acoustic only):** The part of the body that holds the sides in place; made of two or three pieces of wood.

- **Bar (electric only):** A metal rod attached to the bridge that varies the string tension by tilting the bridge back and forth. Also called the tremolo bar, whammy bar, vibrato bar, and wang bar.

- **Body:** The box that provides an anchor for the neck and bridge and creates the playing surface for the right hand. On an acoustic, the body includes the amplifying sound chamber that produces the guitar's tone. On an electric, it consists of the housing for the bridge assembly and electronics (pickups as well as volume and tone controls).

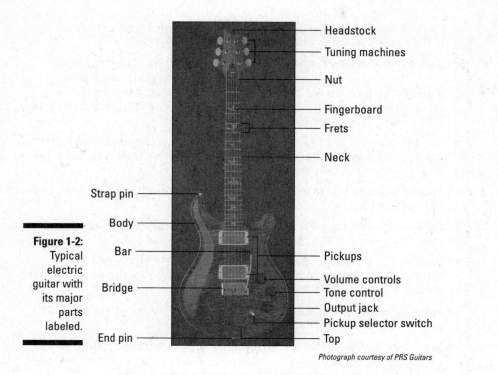

Headstock
Tuning machines
Nut
Fingerboard
Frets
Neck
Strap pin
Body
Bar
Pickups
Volume controls
Tone control
Bridge
Output jack
Pickup selector switch
End pin
Top

Figure 1-2:
Typical electric guitar with its major parts labeled.

Photograph courtesy of PRS Guitars

✔ **Bridge:** The metal (electric) or wooden (acoustic) plate that anchors the strings to the body.

✔ **Bridge pins (acoustic only):** Plastic or wooden dowels that insert through bridge holes and hold the strings securely to the bridge.

✔ **End pin:** A post where the rear end of the strap connects. On *acoustic-electrics* (acoustic guitars with built-in pickups and electronics), the pin often doubles as the *output jack* where you plug in.

✔ **Fingerboard:** A flat, plank-like piece of wood that sits atop the neck, where you place your left-hand (or right-hand, if you're playing a left-handed guitar) fingers to produce notes and chords. The fingerboard is also known as the *fretboard,* because the frets are embedded in it.

✔ **Frets:** Thin metal wires or bars running perpendicular to the strings that shorten the effective vibrating length of a string when you press down on it, enabling it to produce different pitches.

✔ **Headstock:** The section that holds the tuning machines (hardware assembly) and provides a place for the manufacturer to display its logo.

✔ **Neck:** The long, clublike wooden piece that connects the headstock to the body and holds the fretboard.

✔ **Nut:** A grooved sliver of stiff nylon or other synthetic substance that stops the strings from vibrating beyond the neck. The strings pass through the grooves on their way to the tuning machines in the headstock. The nut is one of the two points at which the vibrating area of the string ends. (The other is the bridge.)

✔ **Output jack:** The insertion point for the cord that connects the electric guitar (or acoustic guitar that has been fitted with a pickup) to an amplifier or other electronic device.

✔ **Pickup selector (electric only):** A switch that determines which pickups are currently active.

✔ **Pickups:** Barlike magnets that create the electrical current, which the amplifier converts into musical sound.

✔ **Saddle:** For acoustic, a thin plastic strip that sits inside a slot in the bridge; for electric, separate metal pieces that provide the contact point for the strings and the bridge.

✔ **Sides (acoustic only):** Separate curved wooden pieces on the body that join the top to the back.

✔ **Strap pin:** Metal post where the front, or top, end of the strap connects. (*Note:* Not all acoustics have a strap pin. If the guitar is missing one, tie the top of the strap around the headstock, above the nut.)

✔ **Strings:** The six metal (for electric and steel-string acoustic guitars) or nylon (for classical guitars) wires that, drawn taut, produce the notes of the guitar. Although not strictly part of the actual guitar (you attach and remove them at will on top of the guitar), strings are an integral part of the whole system, and a guitar's entire design and structure revolves around making the strings ring out with a joyful noise. (See Book I Chapter 3 for info on changing strings.)

✔ **Top:** The face of the guitar. On an acoustic, this piece is also the *sounding board,* which produces almost all the guitar's acoustic qualities. On an electric, the top is merely a cosmetic or decorative cap that overlays the rest of the body material.

✔ **Tuning machines:** Geared mechanisms that raise and lower the tension of the strings, drawing them to different pitches. The string wraps tightly around a post that sticks out through the top, or face, of the headstock. The post passes through to the back of the headstock, where gears connect it to a tuning key. Also known as tuners, tuning pegs, tuning keys, and tuning gears.

✔ **Volume and tone controls (electric only):** Knobs that vary the loudness of the guitar's sound and its bass and treble frequencies.

How Guitars Make Sound

After you can recognize the basic parts of the guitar, you may also want to understand how those parts work together to make sound. The following sections cover this just so you know why your guitar sounds the way it does, instead of like a kazoo or an accordion. The important thing to remember is that a guitar makes the sound, but *you* make the music.

Strings doing their thing

Any instrument must have some part of it moving in a regular, repeated motion to create vibration that moves air molecules to produce musical sound (a sustained tone, or *pitch*). In a guitar, this part is the vibrating string. A string that you bring to a certain tension and then set in motion (by a plucking action) produces a predictable sound — for example, the note A. If you tune a string of your guitar to different tensions, you get different tones. The greater the tension of a string, the higher the pitch.

You couldn't do very much with a guitar, though, if the only way to change pitches was to frantically adjust the tension on the strings every time you pluck a string. So guitarists resort to the other way to change a string's pitch — by shortening its effective vibrating length. They do so by fretting — pacing back and forth and mumbling to themselves. (Just kidding; guitarists never do *that* kind of fretting unless they haven't held their guitars for a couple of days.) In guitar-speak, *fretting* refers to pushing the string against the fretboard so the string vibrates only between the fingered fret (metal wire) and the bridge. This way, by moving the left hand up and down the neck (toward the bridge and the nut, respectively), you shorten the effective string length and change pitches comfortably and easily.

The fact that smaller instruments, such as mandolins and violins, are higher in pitch than cellos and basses (and guitars, for that matter) is no accident. Their pitch is higher because their strings are shorter. The string tension of all these instruments may be closely related, making them feel somewhat consistent in response to the hands and fingers, but the drastic difference in string lengths is what results in the wide differences of pitch among them. This principle holds true in animals, too. A Chihuahua has a higher-pitched bark than a St. Bernard because its vocal cords are much shorter.

Using left and right hands together

The guitar normally requires two hands working together to create music. If you want to play, say, middle C on the piano, all you do is take your index finger, position it above the appropriate white key under the piano's logo, and drop it down: *donnnng.* A preschooler can sound just like Elton John if playing only middle C, because just one finger of one hand, pressing one key, makes the sound.

The guitar is somewhat different. To play middle C on the guitar, you must take your left-hand index finger and *fret* the 2nd string (that is, press it down to the fingerboard) at the 1st fret. This action, however, doesn't itself produce a sound. You must then strike or pluck that 2nd string with your right hand to actually produce the note middle C audibly.

Music readers take note: The guitar sounds an octave lower than its written notes. For example, playing a written, third-space C on the guitar actually produces a middle C.

Notes on the neck: Half steps and frets

The smallest *interval* (unit of musical distance in pitch) of the musical scale is the *half step.* On the piano, the alternating white and black keys represent this interval (as do the places where you find two adjacent white keys with no black key in between). To proceed by half steps on a keyboard instrument, you move your finger up or down to the next available key, white or black. On the guitar, *frets* — the horizontal metal wires (or bars) that you see embedded in the fretboard, running perpendicular to the strings — represent these half steps. To go up or down by half steps on a guitar means to move your left hand one fret at a time, higher or lower on the neck.

Each fret represents one half step. Two frets make a whole step.

Comparing how acoustics and electrics generate sound

Vibrating strings produce the different tones on a guitar. But you must be able to *hear* those tones, or you face one of those if-a-tree-falls-in-a-forest questions. For an acoustic guitar, that's no problem, because an acoustic instrument provides its own amplifier in the form of the hollow sound chamber that boosts its sound . . . well, acoustically.

But an electric guitar makes virtually no acoustic sound at all. (Well, a tiny bit, like a buzzing mosquito, but nowhere near enough to fill a stadium or anger your next-door neighbors.) An electric instrument creates its tones entirely through electronic means. The vibrating string is still the source of the sound, but a hollow wood chamber isn't what makes those vibrations audible. Instead, the vibrations disturb, or *modulate*, the magnetic field that the *pickups* — wire-wrapped magnets positioned underneath the strings — produce. As the vibrations of the strings modulate the pickup's magnetic field, the pickup produces a tiny electric current that exactly reflects that modulation.

Guitars, therefore, make sound by amplifying string vibrations either acoustically (by passing the sound waves through a hollow chamber) or electronically (by amplifying and outputting a current through a speaker). That's the physical process anyway. How a guitar produces *different* sounds — and the ones that you want it to make — is up to you and how you control the pitches that those strings produce. Left-hand fretting is what changes these pitches. Your right-hand motions not only help produce the sound by setting the string in motion, but they also determine the *rhythm* (the beat or pulse), *tempo* (the speed of the music), and *feel* (interpretation, style, spin, magic, mojo, *je ne sais quoi,* whatever) of those pitches. Put both hand motions together, and they spell music. *Guitar* music.

Tuning Your Guitar

Tuning is to guitarists what parallel parking is to city drivers: an everyday and necessary activity that can be vexingly difficult to master. Unlike the piano, which is tuned by a professional once in a while, the guitar is normally tuned by its owner — and it needs constant adjusting.

Before you can tune your guitar, you need to know how to refer to the two main players — strings and frets.

✔ **Strings:** Strings are numbered consecutively 1 through 6, from skinniest to fattest. The 1st string is the skinniest, located closest to the floor (when you hold the guitar in playing position). Working your way up, the 6th string is the fattest, closest to the ceiling.

   The 6th string may seem like it should be called string 1, because it's the first one you see when you look down and play. It's not. Get it through your head: The skinniest, highest-sounding string is the 1st string.

   You should memorize the letter names of the open strings (E, A, D, G, B, E, from 6th to 1st) so you're not limited to referring to them by number. An easy way to memorize the open strings in order is to remember the phrase *Eddie Ate Dynamite; Good Bye, Eddie.*

✔ **Frets:** *Fret* can actually refer to either the space where you put your left-hand finger or to the thin metal bar running across the fingerboard. When fingering, *fret* means the space in between the metal bars — where you can comfortably fit a left-hand finger.

The 1st fret is the region between the *nut* (the thin, grooved strip that separates the headstock from the neck) and the first metal bar. The 5th fret, then, is the fifth space up from the nut — technically, the region between the fourth and fifth metal fret bars.

Most guitars have a marker on the 3rd and 5th frets (and others up the neck), either a decorative design embedded in the fingerboard or a dot on the side of the neck, or both.

One more point of business to square away. You'll come across the terms *open strings* and *fretted strings* from this point on in this book. Here's what those terms mean:

- **Open string:** A string that's not fretted at all. You play without pressing down on any frets.
- **Fretted string:** A string you play while pressing down on a particular fret.

Tuning Your Guitar to Itself

Relative tuning is so named because you don't need any outside reference to which you tune the instrument. As long as the strings are in tune with each other, you can create sonorous and harmonious tones. Those same tones may turn into sounds resembling those of a catfight if you try to play along with another instrument, however; but as long as you tune the strings *relative to one another*, the guitar is in tune with itself.

To tune a guitar by using the relative method, choose one string — say, the 6th string — as the starting point. Leave the pitch of that string as is; then tune all the other strings relative to that 6th string.

The *5th-fret method* derives its name from the fact that you almost always play a string at the 5th fret and then compare the sound of that note to that of the next open string. You need to be careful, though, because the 4th fret (the 5th fret's jealous understudy) puts in a cameo appearance toward the end of the process.

Here's how to get your guitar in tune by using the 5th-fret method (check out the diagram in Figure 1-3, which outlines all five steps):

1. **Play the 5th fret of the 6th (low E) string (the fattest one, closest to the ceiling) and then play the open 5th (A) string (the one next to it).**

    Let both notes ring together (in other words, allow the 6th string to continue vibrating while you play the 5th string). Their pitches should match exactly. If they don't seem quite right, determine whether the 5th string is lower or higher than the fretted 6th string.

- If the 5th string seems lower, or *flat,* turn its tuning key with your left hand (in a counterclockwise direction as you look directly at the tuning key) to raise the pitch.

- If the 5th string seems *sharp,* or higher sounding, use its tuning key to lower the pitch (by turning it in a clockwise direction as you look directly at the tuning key).

You may go too far with the tuning key if you're not careful; if so, you need to reverse your motions. In fact, if you *can't* tell whether the 5th string is higher or lower, tune it flat intentionally (that is, tune it too low) and then come back to the desired pitch.

2. **Play the 5th fret of the 5th (A) string and then play the open 4th (D) string.**

   Let both of these notes ring together. If the 4th string seems flat or sharp relative to the fretted 5th string, use the tuning key of the 4th string to adjust its pitch accordingly. Again, if you're not sure whether the 4th string is higher or lower, "overtune" it in one direction — flat, or lower, is better — and then come back.

3. **Play the 5th fret of the 4th (D) string and then play the open 3rd (G) string.**

   Let both notes ring together again. If the 3rd string seems flat or sharp relative to the fretted 4th string, use the tuning key of the 3rd string to adjust the pitch accordingly.

4. **Play the 4th — *not* the 5th! — fret of the 3rd (G) string and then play the open 2nd (B) string.**

   Let both strings ring together. If the 2nd string seems flat or sharp, use its tuning key to adjust the pitch accordingly.

5. **Play the 5th (yes, back to the 5th for this one) fret of the 2nd (B) string and then play the open 1st (high E) string.**

   Let both notes ring together. If the 1st string seems flat or sharp, use its tuning key to adjust the pitch accordingly. If you're satisfied that both strings produce the same pitch, you've now tuned the upper (that is, *upper* as in higher-pitched) five strings of the guitar relative to the fixed (untuned) 6th string. Your guitar's now in tune with itself.

You may want to go back and repeat the process, because some strings may have slipped out of tune. To get the hang of the 5th-fret tuning method and matching fretted strings against open ones, check out Video Clip 1.

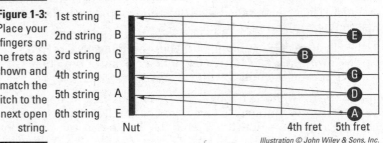

Figure 1-3:
Place your
fingers on
the frets as
shown and
match the
pitch to the
next open
string.

1st string   E
2nd string   B
3rd string   G
4th string   D
5th string   A
6th string   E

Nut   4th fret   5th fret

Illustration © John Wiley & Sons, Inc.

When you tune in the normal way, you use your left hand to turn the tuning peg. But after you remove your finger from the string that you're fretting, it stops ringing; therefore, you can no longer hear the string you're trying to tune to (the fretted string) as you adjust the open string. However, you can tune the open string while keeping your left-hand finger on the fretted string. Simply use your right hand! After you strike the two strings in succession (the fretted string and the open string), take your right hand and reach over your left hand (which remains stationary as you fret the string) and turn the tuning peg of the appropriate string until both strings sound exactly the same.

Note: This book assumes you're right-handed. No offense to lefties. As always, and as you are no doubt used to, simply switch your reading of *left* and *right* everywhere if you're playing a left-handed guitar.

Tuning Your Guitar to an External Source

Getting the guitar in tune with itself through the 5th-fret method in the preceding section is good for your ear, but it isn't very practical if you need to play with other instruments or voices that are accustomed to standard tuning references (see the section "Getting a taste of the tuning fork," a little later in this chapter). If you want to bring your guitar into the world of other people or instruments, you need to know how to tune to a fixed source, such as a piano, pitch pipe, tuning fork, or electronic tuner. Doing so ensures that everyone is playing by the same tuning rules. Besides, your guitar and strings are built for optimal tone production if you tune to standard pitch.

The following sections describe some typical ways to tune your guitar by using fixed references. These methods enable you to not only get in tune but also make nice with all the other instruments in the neighborhood.

Book I

Guitar 101

Keying in to the piano

Because it holds its pitch so well (needing only biannual or annual tunings, depending on conditions), a piano is a great tool to use for tuning a guitar, and a keyboard may be even better. Assuming you have an electronic keyboard or a well-tuned piano around, all you need to do is match the open strings of the guitar to the appropriate keys on the piano. Figure 1-4 shows a piano keyboard and the corresponding open guitar strings.

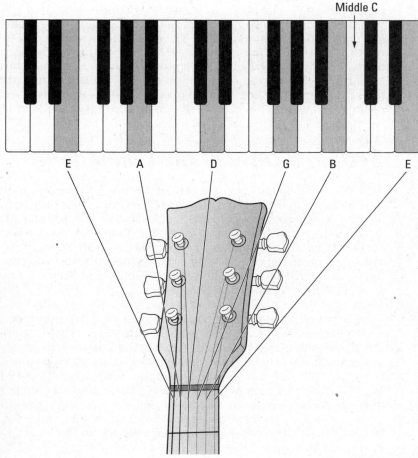

Figure 1-4:
A view of the piano keyboard, highlighting the keys that correspond to the open strings of the guitar.

Illustration © John Wiley & Sons, Inc.

Putting that pitch pipe to work

Obviously, if you're off to the beach with your guitar, you're not going to want to put a piano in the back of your car, even if you're really fussy about tuning. So you need a smaller and more practical device that supplies standard-tuning reference pitches. Enter the *pitch pipe*. The pitch pipe evokes images of stern, matronly chorus leaders who purse their prunelike lips around a circular harmonica to deliver an anemic squeak that instantly marshals together the reluctant voices of the choir. Yet pitch pipes serve their purpose.

For guitarists, special pitch pipes exist consisting of pipes that play only the notes of the open strings of the guitar (but sounding in a higher range) and none of the in-between notes. The advantage of a pitch pipe is that you can hold it firmly in your mouth while blowing, keeping your hands free for tuning. The disadvantage to a pitch pipe is that you sometimes take a while getting used to hearing a wind-produced pitch against a struck-string pitch. But with practice, you can tune with a pitch pipe as easily as you can with a piano. And a pitch pipe certainly fits much more easily into your shirt pocket.

Getting a taste of the tuning fork

After you get good enough at discerning pitches, you need only one single-pitched tuning reference to get your whole guitar in tune. The tuning fork offers only one pitch, and it usually comes in only one flavor: A. More specifically, it's the A note above middle C, and it vibrates at 440 cycles per second, commonly known as *A-440*). If you tune your open 5th string (A) to the tuning fork's A, you can tune every other string to that string by using the relative tuning method discussed in the section "Tuning Your Guitar to Itself with the 5th-Fret Method" earlier in this chapter.

Using a tuning fork requires a little finesse. You must strike the fork against something firm, such as a tabletop or kneecap, and then hold it close to your ear or place the stem (or handle) — and *not* the tines (or fork prongs) — against something that resonates. This resonator can be the tabletop again or the top of the guitar. (You can even hold it between your teeth, which leaves your hands free! It really works, too!) At the same time, you must somehow play an A and tune it to the fork's tone. The process is kind of like pulling your house keys out of your pocket while you're loaded down with an armful of groceries. It may not be easy, but if you do it enough, you eventually become an expert.

Employing the electronic tuner

The quickest and most accurate way to get in tune is to employ an *electronic tuner.* This handy device seems to possess spooky powers. Newer electronic tuners made especially for guitars can usually sense what string you're playing, tell you what pitch you're nearest, and indicate whether you're flat (too low) or sharp (too high). About the only thing these devices don't do is turn the tuning keys for you (although they're probably working on that). Some older, graph-type tuners feature a switch that selects which string you want to tune. Figure 1-5 shows a typical electronic tuner.

Figure 1-5:
An electronic tuner makes tuning a snap.

Photograph courtesy of KORG USA, Inc.

You can either plug your guitar into the tuner (if you're using an electric instrument) or you can use the tuner's built-in microphone to tune an acoustic. In both types of tuners — the ones where you select the strings and the ones that automatically sense the string — the display indicates two things: what note you're closest to (E, A, D, G, B, E) and whether you're flat or sharp of that note.

Electronic tuners are usually powered by 9-volt batteries or two AAs that can last for a year with regular usage (up to two or even three years with only occasional usage). Many electronic tuners are inexpensive (as low as $20 or so) and are well worth the money. You can also find tuners in the form of apps for your smartphone and other handheld devices on the web. (Tuners are also mentioned in Book I Chapter 3.)

Using the audio tracks

PLAY THIS!

For your tuning convenience, you can also tune to Track 1 of this book. Track 1 plays the open strings. Listen to the tone of each open string as it sounds slowly, one at a time (1st to the 6th, or skinniest to fattest) and tune your guitar's open strings to those on the track. Go back to the beginning of Track 1 to repeat the tuning notes as often as necessary to get your strings exactly in tune with the strings on the audio tracks.

The benefit of using Track 1 to help you tune is that it always plays back the exact pitch and never goes sharp or flat, not even a little bit. So you can use Track 1 at any time to get perfectly tuned notes.

Chapter 2

Getting Ready to Play

In This Chapter

▶ Positioning your body and hands before you play

▶ Reading chord diagrams, tablature, and rhythm slashes

▶ Playing chords

▶ Access the video clips at www.dummies.com/go/guitaraio/

Guitars are user-friendly instruments. They fit comfortably into the arms of most humans, and the way your two hands fall on the strings naturally is pretty much the position from which you should play. This chapter tells you all about good posture techniques and how to hold your hands — just as if you were a young socialite at a finishing school.

Just remember that good posture and position, at the very least, prevent strain and fatigue and, at best, help develop good concentration habits and tone. After you get positioned correctly with the guitar, the chapter goes over some basic music-deciphering skills and shows you how to play a chord.

Assuming the Positions

You can either sit or stand while playing the guitar, and the position you choose makes virtually no difference whatsoever to your tone or technique. Most people prefer to sit while practicing but stand while performing publicly. (**Note:** The one exception to the sit or stand option is the classical guitar, which you normally play in a sitting position. The orthodox practice is to play in a seated position only. This practice doesn't mean that you *can't* play a classical-style guitar or classical music while standing, but the serious pursuit of the classical guitar requires that you sit while playing. See the chapters in Book VI for full details.)

The following sections describe sitting and standing postures for playing the guitar and show you how to position both of your hands.

Sitting down and playing a spell

To hold the guitar in a sitting position, rest the *waist* of the guitar on your right leg. (The waist is the indented part between the guitar's upper and lower *bouts,* which are the protruding curved parts that look like shoulders and hips.) Place your feet slightly apart. Balance the guitar by lightly resting your right forearm on the bass bout, as shown in Figure 2-1. Don't use the left hand to support the neck. You should be able to take your left hand completely off the fretboard without the guitar dipping toward the floor. You can also put on a strap to help you (see next section).

Figure 2-1:
Typical
sitting
position.

Photograph courtesy of Cherry Lane Music

Classical-guitar technique, on the other hand, requires you to hold the instrument on your *left* leg, not on your right. This position puts the center of the guitar closer to the center of your body, making the instrument easier to play, especially with the left hand, because you can better execute the difficult fingerings of the classical-guitar music in that position.

You must also elevate the classical guitar, which you can do either by raising the left leg with a specially made *guitar foot stool* (the traditional way) or by using a *support arm,* which goes between your left thigh and the guitar's lower side (the modern way). This device enables your left foot to remain on the floor and instead pushes the guitar up in the air.

Standing up and delivering

Book I

Guitar 101

To stand and play the guitar, you need to securely fasten (or tie) a strap to both strap pins on the guitar. Then you can stand in a normal way and check out how cool you look in the mirror with that guitar slung over your shoulders. You may need to adjust the strap to get the guitar at a comfortable playing height.

If your strap slips off a pin while you're playing in a standing position, you have about a 50-50 chance of catching your guitar before it hits the floor (and that's if you're quick and experienced with slipping guitars). So don't risk damaging your guitar by using an old or worn strap or one with holes that are too large for the pins to hold securely. Guitars aren't built to bounce, as Pete Townshend has demonstrated so many times.

Your body makes a natural adjustment in going from a sitting position to a standing position. So don't try to overanalyze where your arms fall, relative to your sitting position. Just stay relaxed and, above all, *look cool.* (You're a guitar player now! Looking cool is just as important as knowing how to play . . . well, *almost* as important.) Figure 2-2 shows a typical standing position.

Figure 2-2:
Typical
standing
position.

Photograph courtesy of Cherry Lane Music

Fretting with your left hand

To get an idea of correct left-hand positioning on the guitar, extend your left hand, palm up, and make a loose fist, placing your thumb roughly between your 1st and 2nd fingers. All your knuckles should be bent. Your hand should look about the same after you stick a guitar neck in there. The thumb glides along the back of the neck, straighter than if you were making a fist but not rigid. The finger knuckles stay bent whether they're fretting or relaxed. Again, the left hand should fall in place very naturally on the guitar neck — as if you're picking up a tool you've been using all your life.

To fret a note, press the tip of your finger down on a string, keeping your knuckles bent. Try to get the fingertip to come down vertically on the string rather than at an angle. This position exerts the greatest pressure on the string and also prevents the sides of the finger from touching adjacent strings — which may cause either buzzing or *muting* (deadening the string or preventing it from ringing). Use your thumb from its position underneath the neck to help *squeeze* the fingerboard for a tighter grip. Video Clip 2 shows you how to apply your left-hand fingers to the fingerboard to fret correctly.

When playing a particular fret, keep in mind that you don't place your finger directly on the metal fret wire but in between the two frets (or between the nut and 1st fret wire). For example, if you're playing the 5th fret, place your finger in the square between the 4th and 5th fret wires. Don't place it exactly in the center of the square (midway between the fret wires) but closer to the higher fret wire (in this case, the 5th). This technique gives you the clearest sound and prevents buzzing.

Left-hand fretting requires strength, but don't be tempted to try speeding up the process of strengthening your hands through artificial means. Building up the strength in your left hand takes time and practice, period. You may see advertisements for hand-strengthening devices and believe that these products may expedite your left-hand endurance. Sure, these devices may work (and the same goes for the home-grown method of squeezing a racquet ball or tennis ball), but one thing's for sure: Nothing helps you build your left-hand fretting strength better or faster than simply playing guitar. Often.

Because of the strength your left hand exerts while fretting, other parts of your body may tense up to compensate. At periodic intervals, make sure you relax your left shoulder, which has a tendency to rise as you work on your fretting. Take frequent "drop-shoulder" breaks. You want to keep your upper arm and forearm parallel to the side of your body. Relax your elbow so it stays at your side.

To maintain a good left-hand position, you need to keep it comfortable and natural. If your hand starts to hurt or ache, *stop playing and take a rest*. As with any other activity that requires muscular development, resting enables your body to catch up.

The following sections give you additional, specific details on left-hand fretting for electric and classical guitars.

Electric endeavours

Electric necks are both narrower (from the 1st string to the 6th) and shallower (from the fingerboard to the back of the neck) than acoustic necks. Electric guitars are, therefore, easier to fret. But the space between each string is smaller, so you're more likely to touch and deaden an adjacent string with your fretting finger. The biggest difference, however, between fretting on an electric and on a nylon- or steel-string acoustic is the action.

A guitar's *action* refers to how high above the frets the strings ride and, to a lesser extent, how easy the strings are to fret. On an electric guitar, fretting strings is like passing a hot knife through butter. The easier action of an electric enables you to use a more relaxed left-hand position than you normally would on an acoustic, with the palm of the left hand facing slightly outward. Figure 2-3 shows a photo of the left hand resting on the fingerboard of an electric guitar, fretting a string.

Figure 2-3: The electric guitar neck lies comfortably between the thumb and the 1st finger as the 1st finger frets a note.

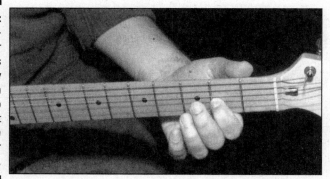

Photograph courtesy of Cherry Lane Music

Classical conditions

Because nylon-string guitars have a wide fingerboard and are the model of choice for classical music, their necks require a slightly more (ahem) formal left-hand approach. Try to get the palm-side of your knuckles (the ones that connect your fingers to your hand) to stay close to and parallel to the side of the neck so the fingers run perpendicular to the strings and all the fingers are the same distance away from the neck. (If your hand isn't perfectly parallel, the little finger "falls away" or is farther from the neck than your index finger.) Figure 2-4 shows the left-hand position for nylon-string guitars.

Figure 2-4:
Correct
left-hand
position for
a classical
guitar.

Photograph courtesy of Cherry Lane Music

Picking with your right hand

If you hold a guitar in your lap and drape your right arm over the upper bout, your right hand, held loosely outstretched, crosses the strings at about a 60 degree angle. This position is good for playing with a pick. For fingerstyle playing, you want to turn your right hand more perpendicular to the strings. For classical guitar, you want to keep the right hand as close to a 90 degree angle as possible.

The following sections provide guidelines on right-hand picking with a pick and with your fingers. Refer to Video Clip 3 to double-check that you're picking correctly.

If you're using a pick

You do almost all your electric guitar playing with a pick, whether you're belting out rock and roll, blues, jazz, country, or pop. On acoustic, you can play either with a pick or with your fingers. On both electric and acoustic, you play most *rhythm* (chord-based accompaniment) and virtually all *lead* (single-note melodies) by holding the pick, or *plectrum* (the old-fashioned term), between the thumb and index finger. Figure 2-5 shows the correct way to hold a pick — with just the tip sticking out, perpendicular to the thumb.

Figure 2-5:
Correct
pick-holding
technique.

Photograph courtesy of Cherry Lane Music

If you're *strumming* (playing rhythm), you strike the strings with the pick by using wrist and elbow motion. The more vigorous the strum, the more elbow you must put into the mix. For playing lead, you use only the more economical wrist motion. Don't grip the pick too tightly as you play — and plan on dropping it a lot for the first few weeks that you use it.

Picks come in various *gauges.* The gauge indicates how stiff, or thick, it is.

✔ Thinner picks are easier to manage for the beginner.

✔ Medium picks are the most popular, because they're flexible enough for comfortable rhythm playing yet stiff enough for leads.

✔ Heavy-gauge picks may seem unwieldy at first, but they're the choice for pros, and eventually all skilled instrumentalists graduate to them (although a few famous holdouts exist — such as Neil Young).

If you're using your fingers

If you eschew such paraphernalia as picks and want to go *au naturel* with your right hand, you're fingerpicking (although you can fingerpick with special individual, wraparound picks that attach to your fingers — called, confusingly enough, *fingerpicks*). *Fingerpicking* means that you play the guitar by plucking the strings with the individual right-hand fingers. The thumb plays the *bass,* or low, strings, and the fingers play the *treble,* or high, strings. In fingerpicking, you use the tips of the fingers to play the strings, positioning the hand over the sound hole (if you're playing acoustic) and keeping the wrist stationary but not rigid. Maintaining a slight arch in the wrist so the fingers come down more vertically on the strings also helps.

Because of the special right-hand strokes that you use in playing classical guitar (the *free stroke* and the *rest stroke*), you must hold your fingers almost perfectly perpendicular to the strings to execute the correct technique. A perpendicular approach enables your fingers to draw against the strings with maximum strength. See the chapters in Book VI for a lot more information on playing classical guitar.

Getting Your Head Around Guitar Notation

Although you don't need to read music to play the guitar, musicians have developed a few simple tricks through the years that aid in communicating such basic ideas as song structure, chord construction, chord progressions, and important rhythmic figures. Pick up on the shorthand devices for *chord diagrams, tablature,* and *rhythm slashes* (described in the following sections), and you're sure to start coppin' licks faster than Vince Gill pickin' after three cups of coffee.

You really *don't* need to read music to play the guitar. Many guitar pros do not read music. With the help of the chord diagrams, tablature, and rhythm slashes explained in this section, plus hearing what all this stuff sounds like through the magic of the companion audio tracks and video clips for this book (see the Introduction for how to access those), you can pick up on everything you need to understand and play the guitar. And the chapters in Book III are all about *guitar theory* — which is much more valuable to know about for most guitarists than knowing how to read sheet music.

Understanding chord diagrams

Don't worry — reading a chord diagram is *not* like reading music; it's far simpler. All you need to do is understand where to put your fingers to form a chord. A *chord* is the simultaneous sounding of three or more notes.

Figure 2-6 shows the anatomy of a chord chart, and the following list briefly explains what the different parts of the diagram mean:

✔ *The grid of six vertical lines and five horizontal ones* represents the guitar fretboard, as if you stood the guitar up on the floor or chair and looked straight at the upper part of the neck from the front.

✔ The *vertical lines* represent the guitar strings. The line at the far left is the low 6th string, and the right-most vertical line is the high 1st string.

✔ The *horizontal lines* represent frets. The thick horizontal line at the top is the *nut* of the guitar, where the fretboard ends. So the 1st fret is actually the second vertical line from the top.

✔ The *dots* that appear on vertical string lines between horizontal fret lines represent notes that you fret.

✔ The *numerals* directly below each string line (just below the last fret line) indicate which left-hand finger you use to fret that note. On the left hand, 1 = index finger; 2 = middle finger; 3 = ring finger; and 4 = little finger. You don't use the thumb to fret, except in unusual circumstances.

✔ The *X* or *O* symbols directly above some string lines indicate strings that you leave open (unfretted) or that you don't play. An *X* (not shown in Figure 2-6) above a string means that you don't pick or strike that string with your right hand. An *O* indicates an open string that you *do* play.

If a chord starts on a fret *other* than the 1st fret, a numeral appears to the right of the diagram, next to the top fret line, to indicate in which fret you actually start. (In such cases, the top line is *not* the nut.) In most cases, however, you deal primarily with chords that fall within only the first four frets of the guitar. Chords that fall within the first four frets typically use open strings, so they're referred to as *open* chords.

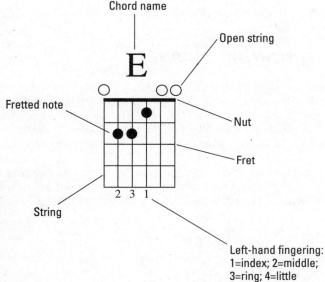

Figure 2-6:
A standard chord diagram for an E chord.

Illustration © John Wiley & Sons, Inc.

Taking in tablature

REMEMBER

Tablature (or just *tab,* for short) is a notation system that graphically represents the frets and strings of the guitar. Whereas chord diagrams do so in a static way, tablature shows how you play music over a period of time. For most of the musical examples that appear in this book, you'll see a *tablature staff* (or *tab staff,* for short) beneath the standard notation staff. This second staff reflects exactly what's going on in the regular musical staff above it but in *guitar language.* Tab is guitar-specific — in fact, many call it *guitar tab.* Tab doesn't tell you what *note* to play (such as C or F♯ or E♭). It does, however, tell you what *string* to fret and where exactly on the fingerboard to *fret* that string.

Figure 2-7 shows you the tab staff and some sample notes and a chord. The top line of the tab staff represents the 1st string of the guitar — high E. The bottom line of the tab corresponds to the 6th string on the guitar, low E. The other lines represent the other four strings in between — the second line from the bottom is the 5th string, and so on. A number appearing on any given line tells you to fret that string in that numbered fret. For example, if you see the numeral 2 on the second line from the top, you need to press down the 2nd string in the 2nd fret above the nut (actually, the space between the 1st and 2nd metal frets, right?). A 0 on a line means that you play the open string.

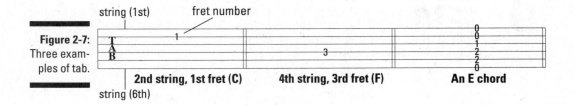

Figure 2-7:
Three examples of tab.

Reading rhythm slashes

Musicians use a variety of shorthand tricks to indicate certain musical directions because, although a particular musical concept itself is often simple enough, to notate that idea in standard written music form may prove unduly complicated and cumbersome. So musicians use a road map that gets the point across yet avoids the issue of reading (or writing) music.

Rhythm slashes are slash marks (/) that simply tell you *how* to play rhythmically but not *what* to play. The chord in your left hand determines what you play. Say, for example, you see the diagram shown in Figure 2-8.

Figure 2-8:
One
measure of
an E chord.

If you see such a chord symbol with four slashes beneath it, as shown in the figure, you know to finger an E chord and strike it four times. What you don't see, however, is a number of differently pitched notes clinging to various lines of a music staff, including several hole-in-the-center half notes and a slew of solid quarter notes — in short, any of that junk that you needed to memorize in grade school just to play "Mary Had a Little Lamb" on the recorder. All you need to remember on seeing this particular diagram is to "play an E chord four times." Simple, isn't it?

Discovering How to Play a Chord

Chords are the basic building blocks of songs. You can play a chord (the simultaneous sounding of three or more notes) several ways on the guitar — by *strumming* (dragging a pick or the back of your fingernails across the strings in a single, quick motion), *plucking* (with the right-hand fingers), or even smacking the strings with your open hand or fist. (Okay, that's rare, unless you're in a heavy metal band.) But you can't just strike *any* group of notes; you must play a group of notes organized in some musically meaningful arrangement. That means learning left-hand chord forms.

After you think you understand (somewhat) the guitar notation described in the preceding sections, your best bet is to jump right in and play your first chord. Start with E major, because it's a particularly guitar-friendly chord and one that you use a lot. And it's pretty easy.

After you get the hang of playing chords, you'll eventually find that you can move several fingers into position simultaneously. For now, though, just place your fingers one at a time on the frets and strings, as the following instructions indicate (you can also refer to Figure 2-6):

1. **Place your 1st (index) finger on the 3rd string, 1st fret (actually between the nut and 1st fret wire but closer to the fret wire).**

   Don't press down hard until you have your other fingers in place. Apply just enough pressure to keep your finger from moving off the string.

2. **Place your 2nd (middle) finger on the 5th string, 2nd fret.**

   Again, apply just enough pressure to keep your fingers in place. You now have two fingers on the guitar, on the 3rd and 5th strings, with an as-yet unfretted string (the 4th) in between.

3. **Place your 3rd (ring) finger on the 4th string, 2nd fret.**

   You may need to wriggle your ring finger a bit to get it to fit in there between the 1st and 2nd fingers and below the fret wire.

Figure 2-9 shows a photo of how your E chord should look after all your fingers are positioned correctly. Now that your fingers are in position, strike down through all six strings with your right hand to hear your first chord, E. To see how to form an E chord step by step, check out Video Clip 4.

Figure 2-9: Notice how the fingers curve and the knuckles bend on an E chord.

Photograph courtesy of Jon Chappell

One of the hardest things to do in playing chords is to avoid *buzzing*. Buzzing results if you're not pressing down quite hard enough when you fret. A buzz can also result if a fretting finger accidentally comes in contact with an adjacent string, preventing that string from ringing freely. Without removing your fingers from the frets, try "rocking and rolling" your fingers around on their tips to eliminate any buzzes when you strum the chord.

Chapter 3

Buying and Stringing a Guitar

In This Chapter

▶ Creating a buying strategy

▶ Knowing what you want in your guitar

▶ Matching music styles to guitar models

▶ Following a few guidelines before you make the big buy

▶ Understanding string-changing basics

*B*uying a new guitar is exciting. You go to the music store and immediately face a world of possibilities — a supermarket of tantalizing choices. Every guitar on the wall seems to scream, "Pick me! Pick me!" Should you exercise restraint and avoid the models you know you can't afford?

Heck no. Be bold and just try any model that strikes your fancy. After all, you're not test driving a Ferrari; you're simply asking the salesperson to see how different guitars feel and sound. And you're not being frivolous, either. Playing a range of guitars helps you understand the differences between high-quality, expensive guitars and acceptable but affordable guitars.

So indulge yourself. Even if you don't have enough experience to recognize the subtle distinctions between a good guitar and a great guitar, at least expose yourself to them. And don't wait until the day you decide to buy an instrument to pick one up for the first time. Make several visits to the music store before you're ready to buy and then take the time to absorb your experiences. Try to visit a few different music stores if you can. Some stores may be the exclusive dealer of a specific brand in your region; other retailers may not be able to sell that brand of guitar. Also, you pick up far more knowledge about what makes a good, playable guitar than you may think just by handling several different instruments.

Buying a guitar can be a similar experience to thinking you have the basics of a foreign language down pat and then visiting the country where it's spoken: You practice for weeks, but the first time a native starts speaking to you, you're completely flustered. But don't rush it; hang in there. You're just buying a guitar; you're not in a strange land trying to find the restroom. You're eventually going to sort it all out — with the help of this chapter.

First Things First: Developing a Purchasing Plan

Before you walk into your local music store ready to plop down your hard-earned dough on a new guitar, you need to take stock of what you're doing. You need to ask yourself some tough questions about your pending purchase — and you need to do so *now*. Don't wait until you get to the store to develop a buying strategy (which, by that time, usually translates into no strategy at all). The two most important factors in making any purchasing decision — especially concerning a guitar, where passions tend to run high — are to develop a plan and to gather all the information you need to make the best choice.

Start developing your purchasing plan by answering some specific questions about exactly what you want in a guitar — and how much you can spend to attain it. Narrowing your scope doesn't mean you can't change your mind after you get to the store and see all the nifty instruments available or that you can't let on-the-spot inspiration and whim play a significant part in your final decision. ("I just *can't* decide between these two guitars . . . oh, what the heck! Just give me *both* of them!") But you *do* need a point of departure.

Ask yourself the following questions:

- **What's my level of commitment?** Regardless of your current ability, do you realistically envision yourself practicing every day for the next five years, pursuing a dedicated program of guitar excellence? Or do you first want to see whether this whole "guitar thing" is going to stick? Just because you can *afford* a $1,000 guitar doesn't mean that you should necessarily buy it. Before plunking down any cash, honestly determine the importance of the guitar in your life and then act responsibly according to that priority.

- **What's my spending limit?** The answer to this question is critical because usually, the more expensive the guitar, the greater its appeal. So you need to balance your level of commitment and your available resources. You don't want to have to give up food for six months and live in a cardboard box just because you got carried away in a moment of buying fever at the music store. You can very easily overextend yourself. If you don't set a limit on how much you can spend, you can't know whether you exceed that limit . . . or by how much.

- **Am I a new-guitar person or a used-guitar person?** You're going to have a much easier time comparing attributes among new guitars. And all the retail and discount prices of new instruments are pretty much standardized — which isn't, to say, however, that all the prices are the same; stores usually discount at different rates. Expect to pay between 10 and 35 percent off the *list price* (manufacturer's suggested retail price) at a music store and pay slightly less if you're buying online. Big chains offer better discounts than smaller mom-and-pop stores because they buy in quantity and get a better price from the manufacturer.

Both retail and online operations also offer a warranty against any manufacturer defects on new instruments. You won't find comparable protection if you're buying a guitar from a newspaper ad (although music stores also sell used instruments, usually with warranties). On the other hand, you *can* sometimes get a really good deal on a used instrument . . . *if you know what to look for.* And, of course, if you want a vintage instrument, you're looking at a used guitar by definition.

As a rule, most asking prices in newspaper ads are too high. Be ready to dicker to get a better price for such a guitar — even if it's exactly what you're looking for.

After you feel you have satisfactory answers to those questions, proceed to the second prong of your guitar-purchasing attack plan: *gathering information on the specific guitar for you.* The following section helps you become more knowledgeable about guitar construction, materials, and workmanship. Remember, being an informed buyer is the best defense against making a bad deal in the retail arena.

Noting Some Considerations for Your First Guitar

If you're just starting out as a novice guitarist, you may ask, "What's the minimum I need to spend to avoid winding up with a piece of junk?" That's a good question, because modern manufacturing practices now enable *luthiers* (the fancy term for guitar makers) to turn out some pretty good stuff for around $200 — and even less sometimes.

If you're an adult (that is, older than 14), and you're looking to grow with an instrument, plan to spend between $200 and $250 for an acoustic guitar and a little less for an electric. (Electric guitars are a little easier to build than acoustics are, so they usually cost a bit less than comparable acoustics.) Not bad for something that can provide years of entertainment and help you develop musical skills, is it?

In trying to decide on a prospective guitar, consider the following criteria:

✔ **Appearance:** You must like the way a particular guitar looks, or you're never really happy with it. So use your eye and your sense of taste (your sense of aesthetics — don't lick the guitar) to select possible candidates. A red guitar isn't inherently better or worse than a green one, but you're perfectly free to base your decision to buy simply on whether you like the look of the guitar.

✔ **Playability:** Just because a guitar is relatively inexpensive doesn't necessarily mean it's difficult to play (although this correlation was often the case in the past). You should be able to press the strings down to the fretboard with relative ease. And you shouldn't find the up-the-neck frets unduly difficult either, although they're usually harder to play than the lower frets are.

Go back to that Ferrari — er, more expensive guitar — at the other end of the rack and see how a high-quality guitar plays. Then return to the more affordable instrument you're considering. Is the playability wildly different? It shouldn't be. If it doesn't feel comfortable to you, move on.

✔ **Intonation:** Besides being relatively easy to play, a guitar must play in tune. Test the intonation by playing a 12th-fret harmonic on the 1st string (place your finger lightly on the string — don't press — at the 12th fret and pluck the string) and match that to playing the fretted note at the 12th fret. Although the notes are of a different tonal quality, the pitch should be exactly the same. Apply this test to all six strings. Listen especially to the 3rd and 6th strings. On a guitar that's not set up correctly, these strings are likely to go out of tune first. If you don't trust your ears to tell the difference, enlist the aid of an experienced guitarist on this issue; it's *crucial.*

✔ **Solid construction:** If you're checking out an acoustic, rap gently on the top of the instrument (like your doctor does to check your ribs and chest) to make sure it's rattle free. Peer inside the hole, looking for gobs of glue and other evidence of sloppy workmanship. (Rough-sanded braces are a big tip-off to a hastily constructed instrument.) On an electric, test that the metal hardware is all tightly secured and rattle free. Strum the open strings hard and listen for any rattling. Running your hand along the edge of the neck to check that the frets are smooth and filed correctly is another good test. If you're not sure what you should be feeling, consult an experienced guitarist on this "fret check."

Sifting through Models to Match Your Style

Asking for a type of guitar by musical style is completely legitimate. Ask for a heavy-metal guitar, and the salesperson nods knowingly and leads you to the corner of the store with all the scary-looking stuff. If you request a jazz guitar, you and the salesperson trundle off in a different direction. Figure 3-1 shows some popular models. Note the variety in shape and style.

Figure 3-1:
Different
axes for
various
styles.

Photographs courtesy of Charvel Guitars, Epiphone Guitar Corp., Fender Musical Instruments Corporation, Gibson Guitar Corp., Guild Guitars, PRS Guitars, and Taylor Guitars

Now, some musical styles do share guitar models. You can play both blues and rock, for example, with equal success on a Fender Stratocaster (or Strat, for short). And a Gibson Les Paul is just as capable of playing a wailing lead as a Strat. (As a rule, however, the tone of a Les Paul is going to be fatter and less jangly than that of a Strat.) Making your own kind of music on the guitar of your choice is part of the fun.

Following are some popular music styles and classic guitars that many people associate with those styles. (Although many of these models are beyond the price range of a first-time buyer, familiarity with them will help you associate models with styles and vice versa. Often, lower-priced guitars are based on the higher-end iconic models.) This list is by no means exhaustive but does include recognized standard-bearers of the respective genres:

- **Acoustic blues:** National Steel, Gibson J-200
- **Bluegrass:** Martin Dreadnought, Taylor Dreadnought, Collings Dreadnought, Santa Cruz Dreadnought, Gallagher Dreadnought
- **Classical:** Ramirez, Hopf, Khono, Humphrey, Hernandez, Alvarez
- **Country:** Fender Telecaster, Gretsch 6120, Fender Stratocaster
- **Electric blues:** Gibson ES-355, Fender Telecaster, Fender Stratocaster, Gibson Les Paul
- **Folk:** Dreadnoughts and Grand Concerts by Martin, Taylor, Collings, Larrivée, Lowden, Yamaha, Alvarez, Epiphone, Ibanez, and Guild; Gibson J-200; Ovation Adamas

- ✔ **Heavy metal:** Gibson Explorer, Flying V, and SG; Fender Stratocaster; Dean; Ibanez Iceman; Charvel San Dimas; Jackson Soloist

- ✔ **Jazz:** Gibson ES-175, Super 400 L-5, and Johnny Smith; archtops by D'Angelico, D'Aquisto, and Benedetto; Epiphone Emperor Regent; Ibanez signature models

- ✔ **New age, new acoustic:** Taylor Grand Concert, Ovation Balladeer, Takamine nylon-electric

- ✔ **R&B:** Fender Stratocaster, Gibson ES-335

- ✔ **Rock:** Fender Stratocaster, Gibson Les Paul and SG, Ibanez RG and signature series, Paul Reed Smith, Tom Anderson

Although the preceding list contains guitars that people generally associate with given styles, don't let that limit your creativity. Play the music you want to play on the guitar you want to play it on, no matter what some chart tells you. These guitars are all super sweet, and the price tag reflects the quality as well as the heritage of these guitars.

Looking for Quality

Maybe you already have a "starter guitar" and are ready move upgrade. If you haven't already developed gear lust for a certain model but are hankering for a new toy just the same, consider the following three common approaches to choosing a second guitar:

- ✔ **The contrasting and complementary approach:** If you own an acoustic, you may want to consider getting an electric (or vice versa), because having an array of different guitars in your arsenal is always nice. Diversity is healthy for a person seeking to bolster a collection.

- ✔ **The clone approach:** Some people just want to acquire as many, say, Les Pauls as they can in a lifetime: old ones, new ones, red ones, blue ones . . . hey — it's *your* money. Buy as many as you want (and can afford).

- ✔ **The upgrade approach:** If all you ever want to do is master the Stratocaster, just get a better version of what you had before. That way, you can use the new guitar for important occasions.

How much should you spend on your second (or later) instrument? One guideline is to go into the next spending bracket from your old guitar. This way, you don't end up with many similar guitars. Plan on spending about $200 more than the current value (not what you paid) of the guitar you own. That ensures that even if you stick with a certain model line, you're getting a guitar that's categorically different from your initial instrument.

When should you stop buying guitars? Why, as soon as the money runs out, of course. Actually, no hard-and-fast rules dictate how many guitars are "enough." These days, however, a reasonably well-appointed guitar arsenal includes a single-coil electric (such as a Fender Strat), a humbucker electric (such as a Gibson Les Paul), a semihollow-body electric, a hollow-body jazz (electric), an acoustic steel-string, an acoustic 12-string, and a nylon-string classical. Then maybe you can add one or two more guitars in a given specialty, such as a steel-bodied guitar set up especially for playing slide, a 12-string electric, or an electric bass.

Then, of course, you can start collecting non-guitar fretted instruments, such as ukuleles, mandolins, banjos, and *dobros* (a type of resonator guitar that's played with a slide and not fretted) . . . but that's another story.

When upgrading, the issue again becomes one of *quality.* But this time, instead of just making sure you have an instrument that plays in tune, frets easily, and doesn't collapse if you breathe on it, you also need to *make informed decisions.* Don't worry — that's not as grave as it sounds. Consider the following four pillars for judging quality in an instrument:

- ✔ **Construction and body type:** How the guitar is designed and put together
- ✔ **Materials:** The woods, metals (used in hardware, pickups, electronics), and other substances used
- ✔ **Workmanship:** The quality of the building
- ✔ **Appointments:** The aesthetic additions and other doodads

Not sure just what all those terms mean in determining the quality of a guitar? The following sections clue you in.

Construction and body type

How a guitar is built defines what type of guitar it is and (to some extent) what type of music it's used for. Consider just two examples:

- ✔ A *solid-body electric guitar* is used for rock. It has no holes in the body — which adds to its *sustain* (the guitar's ability to increase the amount of time a plucked note rings).
- ✔ An *acoustic archtop* is used for traditional jazz, because it has a carved, contoured top, which produces mellow tones associated with that style.

This section covers the three most important issues regarding guitar construction: solid versus laminated wood, body caps, and neck construction.

Solid wood versus laminated wood

A solid-wood acoustic guitar is more desirable than a *laminated* one (where the guitar maker uses layers of inexpensive wood pressed together and covered with a veneer). Guitars made completely out of solid wood are more expensive — costing about $500 or more.

The guitar's top is the most critical element in sound production; the back and sides primarily reflect the sound back through the top. So if you can't afford a solid-wood acoustic guitar, look to various configurations in which the top is solid and various other parts are laminated. A good choice is a solid-top guitar with laminated back and sides, which is much less expensive than an all-solid-wood model.

If you're unsure as to whether a guitar has solid or laminated wood, ask the dealer or consult the manufacturer.

Body caps

In the electric realm, one big determinant of price is whether the top has a cap. A *cap* is a decorative layer of fine wood — usually a variety of *figured* maple (one having a naturally occurring decorative grain pattern) — that sits on top of the body without affecting the sound. Popular cap woods include flame maple and quilted maple. Figured-wood tops usually come with clear, or see-through, finishes to show off the wood's attractive grain pattern.

Neck construction

Here are the three most common types of neck construction, from the least expensive to the most expensive:

- ✔ **Bolt-on:** The neck attaches to the back of the guitar with large bolts (although a plate sometimes covers the bolt holes). Fender Stratocasters and Telecasters are examples of guitars with bolt-on necks.

- ✔ **Set-in (or glued-in):** The neck joins the body with an unbroken surface covering the connection, creating a seamless effect from neck to body. The joint is glued. Les Pauls and Paul Reed Smiths have set-in necks.

- ✔ **Neck-through-body:** A high-end construction where the neck is one long unit (although usually consisting of several pieces of wood glued together) that doesn't stop at the body but continues all the way through to the tail of the guitar. This type of neck is great for getting maximum sustain. A Jackson Soloist is an example.

Just because a construction technique is more advanced or expensive doesn't mean that it's necessarily better than other techniques. Could you "improve" the sound of Jimi Hendrix's Strat by modifying its neck to a glued-in configuration? *Sacrilege!*

Woods, hardware, and other goodies

A guitar isn't limited by what it's made of any more than a sculpture is. Michelangelo's *David* and your aunt Agnes's candy dish are both made of marble, but which one would you travel to Florence to see? So don't judge a guitar *only* by its materials, but a guitar with better materials (abalone inlays as opposed to plastic ones) tends to have commensurately better workmanship — and is, therefore, a better guitar — than a model that uses inexpensive materials. Here are some important guitar materials to consider.

Woods

As you may expect, the more expensive or rare a wood, the more expensive the guitar you construct from that wood. Guitar makers break woods down into categories, and each category has a bearing on the guitar's expense.

Following are the three criteria used for classifying wood:

- ✔ **Type:** This category simply determines whether a piece of wood is mahogany, maple, or rosewood. Rosewood tends to be the most expensive wood used in the construction of acoustic-guitar bodies, followed by maple and then mahogany.

- ✔ **Style:** You can classify woods further by looking at the wood's region or grain style. For example, the figured maples, such as quilted and flame, are more expensive than rock or bird's-eye maples.

- ✔ **Grade:** Guitar makers use a grading system, from A to AAA (the highest), to evaluate woods based on grain, color, and consistency. High-quality guitars get the highest-grade wood.

Hardware

In more expensive instruments, you see upgrades on all components, including the *hardware,* or the metal parts of the guitar. Chrome-plated hardware is usually the cheapest, so if you begin looking at more expensive guitars, you start to see gold-plated and black-matte-finished knobs, switches, and tuning machines in place of chrome.

The actual hardware the manufacturer uses — not just the finishes on it — changes, too, on more expensive instruments. High-quality, name-brand hardware often replaces the guitar maker's less prestigious, generic brand of hardware on high-end axes. For example, manufacturers may use a higher-grade product for the tuning machines on an upscale guitar — such as *locking Sperzels* (a popular third-party tuner type and brand), which lock the string in place as opposed to forcing the user to tie the string off at the post.

The bridge is an important upgrade area as well. The so-called *floating bridge* (so designated because you can move it up and down by means of the whammy bar) is a complicated affair of springs, fine-tuning knobs, and anchors. The better floating assemblies, such as the Floyd Rose system or systems manufactured under a Floyd Rose license, operate much more smoothly and reliably than do the simple three-spring varieties found on low-cost guitars. (The strings spring right back to pitch on a Floyd Rose system, even after the most torturous whammy bar abuse.)

Pickups and electronics

Unless a guitar manufacturer is also known for making great pickups, you see more and more use of third-party pickups as you go up the quality ladder. In the electric arena, Seymour Duncan, DiMarzio, Bartolini, Bill Lawrence, Lace, and EMG are examples of high-quality pickup brands that guitar makers piggy-back onto their models. Fishman and L.R. Baggs are two popular acoustic pickup systems found on many well-known guitars.

Although they're not known by name brands, the electronics in electric guitars also improve along with the other components as you venture into more expensive territory. You can see a greater variety, for example, in pickup manipulation. Manufacturers can provide circuitry that changes double-coil, or humbucker, pickups into single-coils, enabling them to emulate the behavior of Stratlike pickups. Having one guitar that can imitate the pickup behavior of other guitar types provides you with a tonally versatile instrument. You also see more manipulation in wiring schemes. For example, guitar makers may reverse the *polarity* of a pickup — the direction the signal flows — to make the guitar sound softer and swirlier.

With more expensive guitars, you may also encounter improved volume and tone controls, resulting in better *taper*. Taper is the gradualness or abruptness of change (also called *response*) of a signal's characteristics (in this case, volume and tone) as you turn a knob from its minimum value to its maximum. A knob exhibiting a smoother taper is evidence of a higher grade of electronics. Really cheap guitars give you no sound at all until turned up to 3; then you get a swell of sound from about 4 to about 7 and no change at all between 7 and the knob's maximum value, 10 — or, on those really rare, loud guitars, 11. (And if you don't get that last joke, watch *This Is Spinal Tap*. It's required viewing for all guitarists.)

Workmanship

For more expensive guitars, you can really bring out the white glove and get fussy. Some people even bring in a dentist's mirror to inspect the interior of an acoustic guitar.

For acoustic guitars in the mid-priced to expensive range, you should expect to find *gapless joints* — solid wood-to-wood connections between components, especially where the neck meets the body. You should also expect clean and glob-free gluing (in the top and back bracing), a smooth and even finish application, and a good setup: the strings at the right height with no buzzing, the neck warp- and twist-free, and the intonation true.

Look at the places on a guitar where different surfaces meet — particularly where the neck joins the body and the edge of the fingerboard where the metal frets embed into the fret slots. You should see no trace of excess glue, and the surfaces should be uniformly mated to each other.

You can glean all this information by simply playing the guitar and noting your impressions. Like traveling in a Rolls-Royce or Bentley, playing a quality guitar should be one smooth ride.

Appointments (cosmetic extras)

Appointments are the fancy stuff that have no acoustic or structural effect on the guitar. They exist solely as decorative elements. Some people find fancy appointments showy or pretentious, but a great guitar is a work of art to behold with the eye as well as the ear.

Typical appointments include intricate neck inlays (such as abalone figures countersunk into the fretboard), a fancy headstock design, and, on an acoustic guitar, the *rosette*, or lining around the edges of the body and the sound hole.

One subtle aspect about appointments: You may think that the only difference between two guitars is in the appointments — for example, a fancy inlay job may seem to be the only thing that distinguishes between a certain company's Grand Deluxe and Deluxe models. But the truth is that the more expensive guitar — although nominally the same in materials and construction — often gets the choicest materials and enjoys higher quality-control standards.

This situation is just a Darwinian reality. If 12 pieces of wood, all destined to become guitar tops, come into the factory, slated for six Grand Deluxes and six Deluxes (fictitious titles, by the way, bearing no resemblance to actual guitar models, living or deceased), the six best pieces of wood go to the Grand Deluxes and the six next-best pieces to the Deluxe models.

Before You Buy: Walking through the Buying Process

Buying a guitar is similar to buying a car or house (okay, it's a *little* less monumental than buying a house) in that it's an exciting endeavor and lots of fun, but you must exercise caution and be a savvy customer, too. Only you know the right guitar for you, what the right price is for your budget and commitment level, and whether a deal feels right. Don't deny your natural instincts as a shopper, even if you're new to guitar shopping. Look, listen, consider, go have lunch before the big buy, and talk it over with your sweetie.

Keep in mind that you're *shopping*. And the whole shopping experience is no different with guitars than with any other commodity. Do your research and get differing opinions *before* you buy. And trust your instincts.

Online or bricks-and-mortar?

With many purchases these days, you face the question, "Do I buy from a store or online?" For a musical instrument, a good rule is this: If you know *exactly* what you want — down to the color and options — you may consider buying an instrument online. You often get the best available price for your chosen instrument by going this route, and you may even avoid paying sales tax (if the music company is out of state), though you may pay shipping. (Some online sellers offer free shipping under certain conditions.)

Buying sight unseen is common with many products, such as electronic gadgets, automobiles, and computers. But if you can't cotton to buying something as personal as a guitar without falling in love with it first — and you want to "date" your guitar before "marrying" it — stick with the traditional storefront approach. A guitar bought from a store usually comes with an official service agreement and unofficial, friendly cooperation from the staff that's worth its weight in gold. Music stores know they're competing with online sellers, and they make up for it in spades with service.

Seeking expert advice

A certain saying goes, "An expert is someone who knows more than you do." If you have such a friend — whose knowledge and experience in guitars exceeds your own — bring the friend along, by all means. This friend not only knows about guitars but also knows *you*. A salesperson doesn't know you, nor does he necessarily have your best interests in mind. But a friend does. And another opinion never hurts, if only to help articulate your own.

Enlist your guitar teacher (if you have one) to help you navigate through the guitar buyer's jungle, especially if she's been with you a while and knows your tastes and playing style. Your teacher may know things about you that you may not even realize about yourself — for example, that you've gotten sidetracked in the steel-string section although your principal interests lie in nylon-string guitar music. A good teacher asks questions, listens to your answers, and gently guides you to where *you* want to go.

Negotiating with the salesperson

Dealing with a salesperson doesn't need to be a stressful, adversarial affair, but some people get pretty anxious about the entire situation. If you establish your priorities before you enter the store, you don't come off as vague and unprepared as he begins his salvo of questions.

A typical first question from a salesperson may be "How much do you want to spend?" In essence, "What price range are you looking at so I know which end of the store to take you to?" It's a fair question, and if you can answer directly, you end up saving a lot of time. They may also ask about your playing ability and style preferences, so be ready to answer.

Be prepared to answer the salesperson's questions succinctly — for example, "I prefer Strat-style guitars, although not necessarily by Fender, and I'm an intermediate blues player — not a shredder — and I'd like to keep costs at less than $600." Answers such as these make you sound decisive and thoughtful. The salesperson should have plenty to go on from that kind of information. But if you say, "Oh, for the right guitar, price is no object; I like the one that what's-his-name plays on MTV," you're not going to be taken seriously — nor are you likely to end up with the instrument you need.

As the salesperson speaks, listen carefully and ask questions. You're there to observe and absorb, not impress. If you decide you're not ready to buy at this point, say that. Thank them for their time and get a card. You're certainly free to go elsewhere and investigate another store. It's actually your duty!

Closing the deal

Find out the *retail,* or *list,* price of an instrument before you walk into the store. The manufacturer presets these numbers, and they're public knowledge. Visit the websites of popular online sellers (such as Guitar Center and Sweetwater) to determine the manufacturer's suggested retail price on a particular product. As of this writing, a Gibson Les Paul Standard *lists* for well more than $3,000, and a Fender American Standard Stratocaster *lists* for more than $1,500. Figure 3-2 shows these two industry stalwarts.

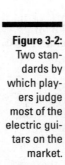

Figure 3-2:
Two stan-
dards by
which play-
ers judge
most of the
electric gui-
tars on the
market.

Gibson Les Paul   Fender Stratocaster

*Photographs courtesy of Gibson Guitar Corp. and Fender Musical
Instruments Corporation*

Another common pricing standard, one that's well below the list price, is the *minimum advertised price*, or MAP. The MAP was developed as an agreement between manufacturers and sellers to prevent larger stores from undercutting smaller ones by advertising rock-bottom sale prices. All music stores offer discounts, and the range can vary greatly. Big, urban-based stores that buy mass quantities of instruments can usually offer greater discounts than smaller (mom-and-pop) stores can in remote areas. Online sellers can match and sometimes beat big-store prices because they don't have the overhead of maintaining a storefront or showroom facility.

Don't neglect the value of service. Retail stores — unlike online sellers — are in a better position to devote close, personal service to a new guitar customer. Perhaps as a result of facing stiff competition from the booming online biz, many stores are upping their service incentives. Service includes anything from fixing minor problems and making adjustments to providing periodic *setups* (sort of like a tune-up and oil change for your guitar).

Note, though, that list prices are public knowledge, and salespeople from all types of vendors must tell you *their* selling price *with no strings attached* (meaning with no conditions). The vendor can rightfully charge up to list price, although in practice no one ever does. The advertised selling price is typically the lowest the seller can go. If you're going to compare online prices to bricks-and-mortar prices, make sure your online prices are from reputable and established sellers, and try to be sympathetic to the slightly higher prices you may find in a store.

Changing Your Strings

Many people consider their guitars to be delicate, precious, and fragile instruments: They seem reluctant to tune their strings, let alone change them. Although you should be careful not to drop or scratch your guitar (and setting guitars afire à la Jimi Hendrix generally causes significant damage), you needn't worry about causing damage by changing, tuning, or overtightening guitar strings. The fact is that guitars are incredibly rugged and can deal with hundreds of pounds of string tension while enduring the playing styles of even the most heavy-handed guitarists.

Changing strings isn't something you should be shy about: You can jump into it with both feet. Changing your guitar strings has few drawbacks — it improves the sound of the guitar, helps prevent broken strings at inopportune moments, and aids you in identifying other maintenance problems. During periodic string changing, for example, you may discover a gouged bridge slot or a loose or rattling tuning post.

Surveying string-changing strategies

Old guitars improve with age, but old strings just get worse. The first time you play new strings is the best they will ever sound. Strings gradually deteriorate until they either break or you can't take the dreary sounds they produce. Old strings sound dull and lifeless, and they lose their *tensility* (ability to hold tension), becoming brittle. This condition makes the strings feel stiffer and harder to fret, and because the strings no longer stretch to reach the fret, they get tighter, causing your notes to go sharp, particularly up the neck.

You should replace all the strings at once, unless you break one and must replace it quickly. The strings tend to wear at the same rate, so if you replace all the old strings with new ones simultaneously, the strings start the race against time on equal footing.

Here are the conditions under which you should replace your strings:

- ✔ They exhibit visible signs of corrosion or caked-on dirt or grime.
- ✔ They don't play in tune, usually fretting sharp, especially in the upper register.
- ✔ You can't remember the last time you changed them and you have an important gig (and don't want to chance any breakage).

Removing old strings

Obviously, to put on a new string, you have to remove the old one. Unless you're really in a hurry (such as when you're in the middle of the first verse, trying to get your new string on and tuned before the guitar solo), you can take off any string by turning the tuning peg to loosen the string so much that you can grab the string from the center and pull it off the post. You don't need to wind it completely off the post by using the peg.

A quicker method is to simply snip off the old string with wire cutters. Snipping off a string may seem weird and brutal, but neither the sudden release of tension nor the cutting itself hurts the guitar. It does a number on the old string, but you don't need to concern yourself with that.

The only reason *not* to cut the string is to save it as a spare, in case the new one breaks while putting it on (rare, but it happens). An old B string is better than no B string.

A common misconception is that you should maintain constant string tension on the guitar neck at all times. Therefore, you may hear that you should replace the strings one at a time because removing all the strings is bad for the guitar, but this simply isn't true. Replacing strings one at a time is *convenient* for tuning but is no healthier for the guitar. Guitars are made of tougher stuff than that.

Changing strings one at a time does make sense if the guitar has a vibrato (whammy) bar. If you take all the strings off, it will take longer to equalize the tension on the whammy contraption when you retune.

However you remove the old string, after it's off, you're ready to put on a new one. The methods for stringing a guitar diverge slightly, depending on whether you're stringing a steel-string acoustic, a classical, or an electric guitar. The rest of this chapter covers all these methods.

Stringing an Acoustic Guitar

Generally, steel-string acoustic guitars are probably easier to string than classicals or electrics (covered later). The following sections walk you through changing an acoustic's strings and tuning it up.

Changing strings step by step

You have two places to attach your new string: the bridge and the headstock. Start by attaching the string to the bridge, which is a pretty straightforward task.

Step 1: Attaching the string to the bridge

Acoustic guitars have a bridge with six holes leading to the inside of the guitar. To attach a new string to the bridge, follow these steps:

1. **Remove the old string (see the earlier section "Removing old strings") and pop out the bridge pin.**

   Bridge pins sometimes stick, so you may need to use a table knife to pry it out, but be careful not to ding the wood. A better alternative is the notched edge in a peg winder or needle-nose pliers.

2. **Place the end of the new string that has a little brass ring (called a *ball*) inside the hole that held the bridge pin.**

   Just stuff it down the hole a couple of inches. (How far isn't critical, because you're going to pull it up soon.)

3. **Wedge the bridge pin firmly back in the hole with the slot facing forward (toward the nut).**

   The slot provides a channel for the string to get out. Figure 3-3 shows the correct disposition for the new string and the bridge pin.

4. **Pull gently on the string until the ball rests against the bottom of the pin. Keep your thumb or finger on the pin so it doesn't pop out and disappear into the abyss.**

   Be careful not to kink the string as you pull it.

5. **Test the string by gently tugging on it.**

   If you don't feel the string shift, the ball is snug against the bridge pin, and you're ready to secure the string to the tuning post, which is the focus of the following section.

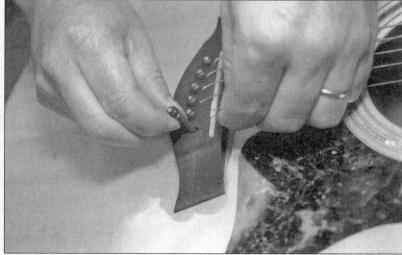

Figure 3-3: How to place the new string in the bridge and position the bridge pin.

Photograph courtesy of Jon Chappell

Step 2: Securing the string to the tuning post

After securely attaching the string to the bridge pin, you can focus your attention on the headstock. The steps are slightly different for the treble strings (G, B, E) and the bass strings (E, A, D). You wind treble strings clockwise and bass strings counterclockwise.

To attach a treble string to the tuning post, follow these steps:

1. **Pass the string through the hole in the post.**

   Leave enough slack between the bridge pin and the tuning post to enable you to wind the string around the post several times.

2. **Kink (or crease) the metal wire toward the inside of the guitar.**

   Figure 3-4 shows how to kink the string to prepare it for winding.

3. **While keeping the string tight against the post with one hand, wind the tuning peg clockwise with the other hand.**

   This step is a bit tricky and requires some manual dexterity (but so does playing the guitar). Keep your eye on the post to ensure that as the string wraps around the post, it winds *down, toward the headstock surface.* Figure 3-5 shows how the strings wrap around the posts. Be sure the strings go into the correct slot in the nut. Don't get discouraged if you can't get your windings to look exactly like the strings shown in Figure 3-5. Getting everything to go smoothly takes a bit of practice.

   Winding the string downward on the post increases what's called the *breaking angle.* The breaking angle is the angle between the post and the nut. A sharper angle brings more tension down onto the nut and creates better *sustain,* the length of time the note continues. To get the maximum angle, wind the string so it sits as low as possible on the post. (This fact is true for all guitars, not just acoustics.)

To attach a bass string, follow the preceding steps *except* that you wind the strings *counterclockwise* in Step 3 so the string goes up the middle and goes over the post to the left (as you face the headstock).

If you find that you've left too much slack, unwind the string and start again, kinking the string farther down. If you don't leave enough slack, your winding doesn't go all the way down the post, which may result in slipping if the string doesn't have enough length to grab firmly around the post. Neither situation is tragic. You simply undo what you've done and try again. As may happen in trying to get the two ends of a necktie the same length, you may need a couple tries to get it right.

Figure 3-4:
String kinked to the inside of the head-stock, with slack for winding.

Photograph courtesy of Jon Chappell

Figure 3-5:
The treble strings wrap clockwise; the bass strings wrap counter-clockwise.

Photograph courtesy of Jon Chappell

Tuning up

After you secure the string around the post and start winding it with the tuning key, you can begin to hear the string come up to pitch. As the string tightens, place it in its correct nut slot. If you're changing strings one at a time, you can just tune the new one to the old ones, which, presumably, are relatively in tune. Check out Book I Chapter 1 for the nuts and bolts (or was that nuts and posts?) of tuning your guitar.

After you get the string to the correct pitch, tug on it (by pulling it out and away from the fingerboard) in various places up and down its length to stretch it out a bit. Doing so can cause the string to go flat — sometimes drastically if you left any loose windings on the post — so tune it back up to pitch by winding the peg. Repeat the tune-stretch process two or three times to help the new strings hold their pitch.

Using a *peg winder* to quickly turn the tuning pegs reduces your string-winding time considerably. A peg winder also features a notch in one side of the sleeve that can help you pop a stuck bridge pin. You can find them online or in almost any music store

After the string is up to pitch and stretched out, you're ready to remove the excess string that sticks out from the post. You can snip this excess off with wire cutters (if you have them) or bend the string back and forth over the same crease until it breaks off.

Whatever you do, don't leave the straight string length protruding. It could poke you or someone standing next to you (such as the bass player) in the eye or give you a sharp jab in your fingertip.

Stringing a Nylon-String Guitar

Stringing a nylon-string guitar is different from stringing a steel-string acoustic because both the bridge and the posts are different. Nylon-string guitars don't use bridge pins (strings are tied off instead), and their headstocks are slotted and have rollers, as opposed to posts.

Changing strings step by step

In one sense, nylon strings are easier to deal with than steel strings are, because nylon isn't as springy as steel. Attaching the string to the tuning post, however, can be a bit trickier. As you do with the steel-string acoustic mentioned earlier in this chapter, begin by securing the bridge end of the string first and then turn your attention to the headstock.

Step 1: Attaching the string to the bridge

Whereas steel-string acoustic strings have a ball at one end, nylon strings have no such ball: Both ends are loose. (Well, you *can* buy ball-ended nylon-string sets, but they're not what you normally use.) You can, therefore, attach either end of the string to the bridge. If the ends look different, however, use the one that looks like the middle of the string, not the one that has the loosely coiled appearance. Just follow these steps:

Book I

Guitar 101

1. **Remove the old string described in the section "Removing old strings," earlier in this chapter.**

2. **Pass one end of the new string through the hole in the top of the bridge, in the direction away from the soundhole, leaving about an inch and a half sticking out the rear of the hole.**

3. **Secure the string by bringing the short end over the bridge and passing it under the long part of the string, as shown in Figure 3-6a. Then pass the short end under, over, and then under itself, on the top of the bridge, as shown in Figure 3-6b.**

   You may need a couple tries to get the end at just the right length, where not too much excess is dangling off the top of the bridge. (You can always cut the excess away, too.)

4. **Pull on the long end of the string with one hand and move the knot with the other to remove excess slack and cause the knot to lie flat against the bridge.**

Figure 3-6:
Tying off the bridge end of the string.

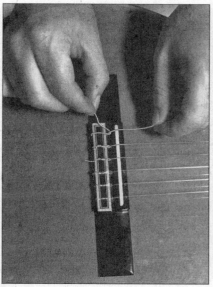

a

b

Photographs courtesy of Jon Chappell

Step 2: Securing the string to the tuning post

On a nylon-string guitar, the tuning posts (called *rollers*) pass through the headstock sideways instead of going through perpendicularly as on a steel-string acoustic or electric guitar. This is known as a *slotted headstock*. To attach the string to the tuning post in a slotted headstock, follow these steps:

1. **Pass the string through the hole in the tuning post. Bring the end of the string back over the roller toward you; then pass the string under itself in front of the hole. Pull up on the string end so the long part of the string (the part attached to the bridge) sits in the U-shaped loop you just formed, as shown in Figure 3-7a.**

   Make your loop come from the outside (that is, approaching from the left on the lower three bass strings and from the right on the treble strings).

2. **Pass the short end under and over itself, creating two or three wraps.**

   Doing so should hold the loose end firmly in place, as shown in Figure 3-7b, and prevent the string from slipping out of the hole.

3. **Wind the peg so the string wraps on top of the loop you just formed, forcing it down against the post.**

4. **Pull the string length taut with one hand and turn the tuning peg with the other hand.**

   Wrap the windings to the outside of the hole, away from the center of the guitar.

Figure 3-7:
Creating a U-shaped loop with the short end of the string (a). Creating wraps to hold the short end of the string in place (b).

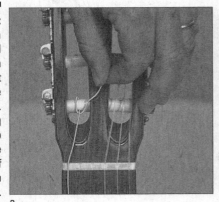

a   b

Photographs courtesy of Jon Chappell

Tuning up

As you continue turning the tuning peg, the string slowly comes nearer to pitch. Nylon strings, like steel strings, require quite a bit of stretching out, so after you get the string initially up to pitch, grab it at various places around its length, pull on it (away from the fingerboard), and then tune it up again. Repeat this process two or three times to keep the guitar in tune longer.

Snip away the excess after you're done with all six strings. Nylon strings aren't as dangerous as steel strings if any excess protrudes, but the extra string hanging out is unsightly, and besides, classical guitarists are a little fussier about how their instruments look than acoustic guitarists are.

Stringing an Electric Guitar

Generally, electric guitarists need to change their strings more often than do steel-string acoustic or nylon-string guitarists. Because changing strings is so common on electric guitars, builders take a more progressive approach to the hardware, often making changing strings very quick and easy. Of the three types of guitars — steel-string acoustic, nylon-string, and electric — you can change the strings on electric guitars most easily by far.

Changing strings step by step

As you would on steel-string acoustic and nylon-string guitars, begin stringing an electric guitar by first securing the string to the bridge and then attaching the string to the headstock. Electric strings are similar to steel-string acoustic strings in that they have ball ends and are made of metal, but electric strings are usually composed of a lighter-gauge wire than steel-string acoustic strings, and the 3rd string is unwound, or plain, whereas a steel-string acoustic guitar's is wound.

Step 1: Attaching the string to the bridge

Most electric guitars use a simple method for securing the string to the bridge. You pass the string through a hole in the bridge (sometimes reinforced with a collar, or *grommet*) that's smaller than the ball at the end of the string — so the ball holds the string just as the knot at the end of a piece of thread holds a stitch in fabric. On some guitars (such as the Fender Telecaster), the collars anchor right into the body, and the strings pass through the back of the instrument and out the top.

Figure 3-8 shows two designs for attaching a string to an electric: from a top-mounted bridge and through the back. The following steps show how to secure the strings to the bridge.

1. **Remove the old string, as described in the section "Removing Old Strings," earlier in this chapter.**

2. **Anchor the string at the bridge by passing the string through the hole (from the back or bottom of the guitar) until the ball stops the movement.**

   Then you're ready to focus on the tuning post. You do this on all but a few guitars (such as those fitted with a Floyd Rose mechanism, discussed later in this chapter).

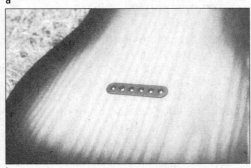

Figure 3-8: Strings pass through the bridge toward the headstock (a). Strings pass through the bridge from the back of the guitar (b).

a

b

Photographs courtesy of Jon Chappell

Step 2: Securing the string to the tuning post

In most cases, the posts on an electric resemble those of a steel-string acoustic. A post protrudes through the headstock, and you pass your string through the post's hole, kink the string to the inside (toward the center of the headstock), and begin winding while holding the long part of the string with one hand for control. Refer to Figure 3-4 to see how to kink the string to prepare it for winding and about how much slack to leave.

Some electric guitars, notably Fender Stratocasters and Telecasters, feature *string retainers,* little rollers or channels screwed into the top of the headstock that pull the top two or four strings down low onto the headstock, sort of like a tent stake. If your guitar has those, pass the strings under them.

Some tuners feature a *locking mechanism* so you don't need to worry about winding, slack, and all that bother. Inside the post hole is a viselike device that clamps down on the string as it passes through. A *knurled* (ridge-covered) dial underneath the headstock or on top of the post loosens and tightens the vise.

Some guitars have tuners with slotted posts instead of a hole. These devices also enable quick string changes, because you simply lay the string in the slot at the top of the post, kink it, and begin winding. You don't even need to leave any slack for winding.

Tuning up

Tuning up an electric guitar isn't much different from tuning an acoustic (see earlier in this chapter), except that the strings will slip out of tune more easily and more often, so they require more tweaking to get all six strings up to pitch. If you have a floating bridge (described in the following section), tuning a string changes the tension on the bridge, causing all the strings that were formerly in tune to go slightly out of tune, so the process takes even longer. But eventually, all the strings "settle down" and the tuning stabilizes.

Setting up a floating bridge

Rock music in the 1980s made extensive use of the whammy bar and *floating bridge* (where the bridge isn't fixed but floats on a spring assembly). Standard floating bridges weren't meant for the kind of abuse that creative guitarists like Steve Vai and Joe Satriani cook up, though, so manufacturers developed better ways to increase the bridges' motion and make sure the bridges returned to their original position and the strings remained in tune.

Floyd Rose invented the most successful of these assemblies. Rose used his own patented design to ensure a highly accurate, movable bridge system and *locking nut* (a clamplike device that replaces the standard nut). Other manufacturers, such as Kahler, have developed similar systems.

The Floyd Rose system takes the strings in a top-mounted approach, instead of through the back, but with one notable difference: Guitarists must snip off the ball end before attaching the string so the end can fit in the tiny viselike mechanism that holds the string in place. If you own a Floyd, you must carry spare strings with the balls snipped off or have wire cutters always ready.

In floating bridge systems that also feature a locking nut, winding the string on the post isn't so critical. After you lock the nut (by using a small hex key or Allen wrench), what you do with the tuning pegs doesn't matter. You then perform all tuning, using small dials, or knobs, on the bridge. These knobs are known as *fine tuners* because their movements are much smaller and more precise than the ones by the tuners on the headstock.

Stringing up and tuning an electric guitar fitted with a floating bridge takes a little longer than it does on a regular electric, but if you plan to do a lot of whammy bar work, it's well worth the effort.

Chapter 4

Deciphering Music Notation and Tablature

In This Chapter

▶ Reading standard music notation

▶ Applying the symbols to guitar playing

▶ Decoding fingering indications and tablature

*L*et's face it. Most guitarists can probably get by without reading music. However, being able to read music opens up opportunities and can increase your understanding of many kinds of music. You can more quickly absorb how to play music if you read music even a little, rather than not at all. And if you want to play classical guitar, reading music really is essential. This chapter, then, is written mainly with classical guitar in mind, although any guitar player can gain from the information in this chapter.

This chapter makes it quick and easy to learn the basics of music notation, as much as possible, and gives you more than one way to approach the written music examples that appear in this book. It gets you familiar with written symbols and notation practices — including tablature — so that you can better understand what you're likely to see once you go out and start encountering printed music.

Knowing the Ropes of Standard Music Notation

Music written for traditional classical guitar uses *standard music notation* — the stuff of clefs, staves (plural of *staff*), and notes — just as you find in music for the violin, flute, piano, trumpet, and saxophone. So let's start off by getting familiar with the symbols you see when looking at "normal music." The following sections show you the blank slate on which composers write music notation and cover the three main elements of music: pitch, duration (rhythm), and expression/articulation.

The composer's canvas: The staff, clef, measures, and bar lines

The current system of writing music has evolved from centuries of different approaches, and it's come a long way since the medieval era. When composers sit down today to write music, they don't write on just any old piece of paper. The blank canvas for a composer isn't really totally blank, as in a solid white sheet of paper. It's a series of horizontal grids that can receive the notes and other music symbols from the composer's pen.

Figure 4-1 shows a blank canvas, according to the way any musician first sees it, just waiting for a masterpiece to be written on it! The following sections explain its components.

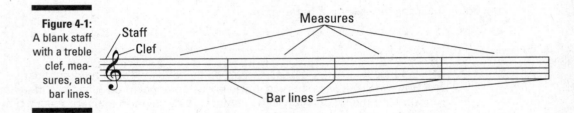

Figure 4-1:
A blank staff with a treble clef, measures, and bar lines.

Staff

The grid of five horizontal lines and four spaces onto which all notes are placed is called a *staff*. The bottom line is called the first line, and the top line is the fifth line. The space between the first and second lines is the first space.

Notes can appear either on a line or in the space between two lines. The placement of a note on the staff designates the note's pitch (how high or low it is) and its letter name.

Clef

The staff appears with a *clef* (the squiggly thing at the beginning of the line), which defines what the pitches are on the lines and spaces. Guitar music uses the *treble clef,* also called the *G clef* because the curlicue of the clef symbol (which looks sort of like a fancy *G*) wraps around the second line from the bottom, which is its way of telling you, "This is G." You can determine any note placed on the staff by counting up or down the lines and spaces starting at G.

Measures and bar lines

Just as you need a staff and a clef to tell you the notes' pitches, you must also have some sort of context in which to place notes in time. Most music has a beat, or pulse, that gives the music a rhythmic unit that the notes play off.

The beat in turn is usually "felt" in larger groups of two, three, or four; you represent this division in written music with vertical lines that separate the music into sections called *measures,* or *bars.* The section between two vertical lines is a *measure* (or *bar*), and the vertical lines themselves are called *bar lines.* Grouping music into measures is a way to keep it manageable by organizing the notes into smaller units — units that support the beat's natural emphasis. Measures allow you to keep your place in the music and to break it down into smaller chunks for easier digestion.

Book I

Guitar 101

Pitch: The highs and lows of music

Pitch is the highness or lowness of a note. Music notation uses the staff, the clef, and the placement of a note on the staff to show pitch. Take a look at Figure 4-2 and Table 4-1 for a breakdown of the various symbols and definitions used for pitch.

Figure 4-2: Music showing the elements of pitch.

Pitch names: G A B C   G F♯ E D   A B C A   G♯ B♭ A♭ B

Table 4-1		Symbols Used to Show Pitch
Number in Figure 4-2	**Symbol Name or Term**	**Description**
1	Note	A musical symbol whose position on the staff indicates its pitch and whose shape indicates its duration. The notes on the five lines of the staff (from bottom to top) are E, G, B, D, and F. You can remember these using the saying "**e**very **g**ood **b**oy **d**oes **f**ine." The notes placed on the four spaces in between the lines (from bottom to top) spell out the word *face* (F, A, C, and E).

(continued)

Table 4-1 *(continued)*

Number in Figure 4-2	Symbol Name or Term	Description
2	**Ledger lines**	Notes can fall above or below the staff as well as within the staff. To indicate a pitch that falls higher or lower than the staff, use ledger lines, which you can think of as short, temporary staff lines. Note names progress up or down the ledger lines (and the spaces between them) the same way they do on the staff lines. So, for example, the first ledger line below the staff is C, and the first ledger line above the staff is A. Try counting down two notes from the bottom line E and up two notes from the top line F to verify this for yourself.
3	**Sharps, flats, naturals, and accidentals**	The first seven letters of the alphabet — A through G — make up the *natural* notes in music. You can easily see these if you look at just the white keys of a piano (or other keyboard instrument). In between some of these natural notes (white keys) are other notes (the black keys) that don't have names of their own. These in-between notes are known as *sharps* or *flats* and are named according to their adjacent, surrounding natural notes, with either an added sharp symbol (♯) or flat symbol (♭) following the letter name. When you see F♯ in music, you play F one half step (one fret) higher than the natural version of the note. A note with a flat symbol next to it, such as D♭, tells you to play the note one half step lower than the natural version. A *natural* sign (♮) restores a note that's been modified by a sharp or flat to its natural pitch state. In effect, it neutralizes the sharp or flat. *Accidentals* are notes outside the key (defined by the *key signature*) and are indicated in the music by the appearance of a sharp, flat, or natural sign modifying a note. Whenever you see an accidental in a measure of music, that sharp, flat, or natural affects all the notes of that pitch following it for the rest of the measure (see the preceding section for the definition of measure).

Number in Figure 4-2	Symbol Name or Term	Description
4	**Key signature**	The listing of flats or sharps at the beginning of the staff, immediately to the right of the clef, tells you which notes to play flat or sharp for the entirety of the piece (or at least a major section of the piece), unless otherwise indicated with an accidental. For example, the music in Figure 4-2 has a *key signature* of one sharp — F♯. That means any time you encounter any F (whether in the staff or on a ledger line), you play it a half step (one fret) higher. In other words, the key signature sends out the loud and clear message: "All Fs are hereby sharped until further notice!"

Duration: How long to hold a note, what determines rhythm, and so on

While the placement of a note on the staff indicates its pitch, the *shape* of the note indicates its length in time, or *duration*, in relation to the beat. The longer in duration the notes are, the more slowly they move, or the more time there is between their respective starting notes. The shorter the notes' values, the faster they come. Without rhythm, the notes have no motion. You need both pitch and rhythm together to make music.

Rests also pertain to duration; these symbols indicate musical silence and have specific values, just as notes do.

Written high, sounds low

Guitar music is written in treble clef, but the actual sound of the pitches you play is an octave lower. For example, when you see a third-space C on the staff, you play the 2nd string, 1st fret. And you'd be playing the note correctly, according to the way guitar players play written notes on the treble clef. But the note you play *actually* sounds middle C (which is the first ledger line below the staff in music for other sound-as-written instruments, such as the piano). So the guitar is kind of a low-pitched instrument (at least compared with other treble clef instruments, such as the flute, violin, and oboe). Why the discrepancy? Well, writing the *actual* sounding pitches would be very awkward to read, as it would put so many of the notes many ledger lines below the staff.

You can increase the length of individual notes or rests by placing a *dot* to the right of the note head or rest. You can also increase the length of a note by adding a *tie*, which connects one note to another of the same pitch immediately following it. All these elements, along with other common symbols used to indicate duration, are covered in Table 4-2; the table corresponds to Figure 4-3, which shows the symbols in the context of a musical excerpt.

Figure 4-3:
Music
showing
duration.

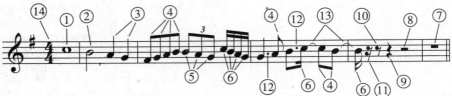

Table 4-2	Symbols Used to Indicate Duration	
Number in Figure 4-3	**Symbol Name or Term**	**Description**
1	Whole note	An open note head with no stem; receives four beats in 4/4 time.
2	Half note	An open note head with a stem; receives two beats in 4/4.
3	Quarter note	A solid note head with a stem; receives one beat in 4/4.
4	Eighth note	A solid note head with a stem and one flag or beam; receives half a beat in 4/4.
5	Eighth-note triplet	A group of three evenly spaced eighth notes appearing with the numeral *3,* to be played in the space of one quarter note in 4/4.
6	Sixteenth note	A solid note head with a stem and two flags or beams; receives one quarter of a beat in 4/4.
7	Whole rest	A small rectangle that hangs down from a staff line indicating an entire measure's rest in any meter.
8	Half rest	A small rectangle that sits on a staff line indicating two beats' rest in 4/4.
9	Quarter rest	A symbol that indicates one beat of rest in 4/4.

Number in Figure 4-3	Symbol Name or Term	Description
10	Eighth rest	A symbol that indicates a half beat's rest in 4/4.
11	Sixteenth rest	A symbol that indicates a quarter beat's rest in 4/4.
12	Augmentation dot	A *dot* appearing to the right of the note head or rest that tells you to increase the note's or rest's length by half of the original value. For example, a quarter note is one beat, so a dotted quarter note equals one and a half beats.
13	Tie	A curved line that joins two notes of the same pitch. You play the first note for its full value, and instead of restriking the second (tied) note, you let the note sustain for the combined value of both notes.
14	Time signature	A two-digit symbol that appears at the beginning of the piece that helps you count the beats in a measure and tells you which beats to stress, or give emphasis to. The top number indicates how many beats are in each measure, and the bottom number tells you what type of note (half, quarter, eighth, and so on) gets one beat. For example, in 3/4 time, you play three beats to the measure, with the quarter note receiving one beat. In 4/4 time, you play four beats to the measure, with the quarter note receiving the pulse or beat. Knowing how to read (and play according to) the time signature helps you to capture the feel of the music.

When you tap your foot to the music on the radio, at a concert, or on your portable music player, you're tapping (or stomping or clapping) along to the beat. If you count to yourself 1-2-3-4, or 1-2-3 — or however many beats logically make up one measure of that song or piece — you can figure out the time signature. Most popular music is in 4/4, as is most of the music in this book. Some song forms are specifically written in a certain time signature. For example, a waltz is written in 3/4. So the next time someone says, "Do I hear a waltz?" listen and tap along in units of three to determine if they're correct.

The different types of note values relate mathematically to the other types of notes. For example, a whole note is equal to two half notes, and a half note equals two quarter notes. Therefore, a whole note is equal in total duration to four quarter notes. Figure 4-4 shows the relative durations of the most common note types.

When "playing" a rest on the guitar, you often have to stop a string from ringing. Be careful not to get into the bad habit that some beginning guitarists do and look only where to play notes rather than where to "play" or observe rests. When you see a rest, make sure that you're not only *not* striking a note during that time but also that you stop any previously struck string or strings from ringing through the rest.

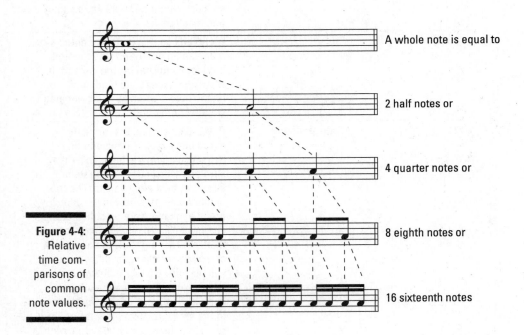

Figure 4-4:
Relative time comparisons of common note values.

A whole note is equal to

2 half notes or

4 quarter notes or

8 eighth notes or

16 sixteenth notes

Expression, articulation, and other symbols

Beyond the primary elements of pitch and duration, you often see other symbols and terms in written music. These additional markings give you a range of instructions, from how to play the music more expressively to how to navigate instructions to repeat a certain passage. Figure 4-5 and Table 4-3 show just some of these expression and *articulation* (how notes are struck) symbols and other markings.

Figure 4-5:
Expression,
articulation,
and miscel-
laneous
symbols and
terms.

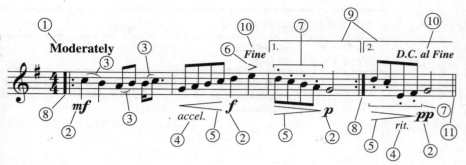

Table 4-3	Expression, Articulation, and Miscellaneous Symbols and Terms	
Number in Figure 4-5	**Symbol Name or Term**	**Description**
1	Tempo heading	A word or phrase that offers guidance on the speed and/or general feel of the piece. In much classical music, tempo headings are written in Italian (such as *Andante, Adagio,* or *Moderato*), but it's also common to see the words written in the composer's or publisher's native language (as in Figure 4-5, with *Moderately*).
2	Dynamic marking	Letters that tell you how loud or soft to play. The letters are the abbreviations of Italian words and terms, such as *mf* for *mezzo-forte* (medium loud), *mp* (*mezzo-piano,* medium soft), *f* (*forte,* loud), *p* (*piano,* soft), *ff* (*fortissimo,* very loud), and *pp* (*pianissimo,* very soft).
3	Slur	A curved line between two notes of different pitch that tells you to connect the second note smoothly to the first. Slurs appear in music requiring a *legato* (*ligado* in Spanish) approach, where the notes blend together in a sustained, uninterrupted fashion.
4	Accelerando and ritardando	Instructions that tell you to play gradually faster (*accelerando,* abbreviated *accel.*) or gradually slower (*ritardando,* abbreviated *ritard.* or *rit.*).

(continued)

Table 4-3 *(continued)*

Number in Figure 4-5	Symbol Name or Term	Description
5	**Crescendo** and **decrescendo (diminuendo)**	Symbols that resemble open wedges (called "hairpins" by some musicians) or the abbreviated versions *cresc.* and *decresc.* (or *dim.*) that tell you to play gradually louder (*crescendo*) or softer (*decrescendo, diminuendo*).
6	**Accent**	A small wedge-shaped or caret-like marking above or below a note that tells you to emphasize the note by striking it harder than normal.
7	**Staccato dot**	A small dot placed above or below the note head that tells you to play the note short and detached.
8	**Repeat signs**	Special bar-line-type symbols that tell you to repeat the measures between the signs.
9	**Ending brackets**	Lines that separate different endings in a repeated section. In Figure 4-5, play the measure under the first ending bracket the first time. On the repeat, play only the second ending, skipping the first ending.
10	**D.C. al Fine**	A score direction that tells you to go back to the beginning (*D.C.* stands for *Da capo,* Italian for "from the top") and play to the part marked *Fine* (Italian for "end"). *D.C. al Coda* tells you to go back to the beginning and play until you see the words *To Coda.* Then skip to the part of the music marked *Coda* (which indicates the final part of the music — *coda* is Italian for "tail") with the coda symbol (which resembles a set of crosshairs or a cross covering an oval). *D.S.* (for *dal segno,* or "from the sign") tells you to go back to the sign (a slanted, stylized *s* with two dots on either side and a slash bisecting the *s*).
11	**Double bar lines**	Two bar lines spaced close together, indicating the end of a section or, if the lines are a combination of a thick and thin pair, the end of a piece.

Relating the Notes on the Staff to the Fretboard

Classical guitarists are no different from other musicians dealing with written music in that after they identify and understand the symbols of standard music notation, they have to correlate them to their instrument. In other words, they have to *play*. At the most basic level — executing the correct pitch and rhythm — you must be able to play the note you see on the staff correctly on the guitar.

Associating a note on the staff with a string and fret location (even if the fret is zero — meaning an open string) is the first step to reading music on the guitar. A good way to begin associating notes on the staff as they relate to the guitar is to consider just the pitches of the open strings, as shown in Figure 4-6. The diagram above the staff shows the guitar neck if you were to hold it upright, facing the headstock, with the low E string appearing at the far left.

Figure 4-6: The pitches of the open strings.

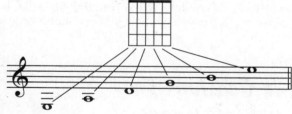

You can use these pitches to help tune your guitar to a piano or other fixed-pitch source. See Book I Chapter 1 for more on tuning your guitar.

To help you correlate the notes of the treble clef with the frets on the guitar, check out Figure 4-7, which shows notes from E to F on the staff as they correspond to the fingerboard. Don't worry about playing anything yet — just get used to the idea that when you see, for example, an E on the 1st (lowest) line of the treble clef, it corresponds to the 4th string, 2nd fret on the guitar.

Figure 4-7: The notes on the staff corresponding to the frets on the fingerboard.

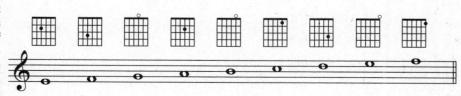

Though the notes can extend off the staff in each direction by at least three ledger lines (see "Ledger lines" in Table 4-1 for more info), in reality you'll encounter far more passages of notes using ledger lines *below* the staff than above it. So be sure you get familiar with those low pitches, as you'll be playing them quite a bit.

Relishing the Usefulness of Guitar-Specific Notation

Guitarists who read standard music notation observe all symbols and practices regarding clefs, *staves*, pitches, and rhythms that other musicians do. But music written for guitar also employs additional symbols that instruct you to perform the music in certain ways that are specific to the instrument. If these symbols appear, observing them helps you perform the music in an easier, more efficient way, or enables you to better realize the intent of the composer or arranger.

These extra symbols don't change anything regarding the pitch or rhythm; their purpose is to instruct you on how to perform the piece in the best way. The following sections explore some symbols you encounter only in music written for guitar.

Fingering indications for the right and left hands

If you see little numbers and letters in the treble staff, it usually means someone (the composer or arranger, a teacher, or the editor) has gone through and thoughtfully provided you with the suggested, the best, or even the *only possible* working fingering indications. *Fingering* is the term guitarists use for the choice, or assignment, of specific fingers to play a given note or passage of notes. In classical guitar, the issue of fingering comes up a lot.

Numbers without circles appearing next to or near note heads tell you which left-hand fingers to use, as follows:

- 1 = Index finger
- 2 = Middle finger
- 3 = Ring finger
- 4 = Little finger

You almost never use the left-hand thumb in fingering. Letters above or below notes indicate right-hand fingers, with the letters signifying the Spanish words for the thumb and the index, middle, and ring fingers:

- ✔ *p* = thumb (*pulgar*)
- ✔ *i* = index (*índice*)
- ✔ *m* = middle (*medio*)
- ✔ *a* = ring (*anular*)

Except for some special percussive techniques and in flamenco style, you don't use the right-hand little finger. Figure 4-8 shows a passage of music with some left- and right-hand fingering indications.

Figure 4-8:
Music with left- and right-hand fingering indications.

Sometimes you have to use the same left-hand finger to fret two consecutive notes on the same string at different frets. This requires you to actually move your left hand up or down the neck. Keeping your finger in contact with the string as you move to the new fret helps to guide your left hand. The guide finger is indicated in notation with a short, straight line appearing to the left of the second of the two finger numbers, slanting in the direction of the left-hand movement (up or down). Figure 4-9 shows the 1st finger acting as a guide finger moving down one fret from A to A♭.

Figure 4-9:
Notation indicating a guide finger.

Unlike the piano, where each note on the staff indicates one and only one piano key, the guitar often provides more than one place to play a given note. For example, you can play the second line G on the open 3rd string or on the

4th string at the 5th fret. If the music requires you to play a note or passage of notes on a certain string, you see a number inside a circle, which indicates the string. For example, if you must play a second-line G on the 4th string (instead of as an open 3rd string), you see a *4* inside a circle. Figure 4-10 shows a passage that's playable only if you take the downstem G on the 4th string, 5th fret.

Figure 4-10:
A number in a circle tells you which string to play a note on.

Stepping up to the barre

You often have to fret more than one string at a time at the same fret, and you do this by taking a finger and flattening it out to form a "bar" — or, as it's known in classical guitar lingo, *barre*. You may see various ways to indicate a barre in guitar music. Here a capital *C* is used (because it stands for the Spanish *ceja* or *cejilla*) for a full barre (all six strings) and a *C* with a vertical line bisecting it for a half or partial barre (fewer than six strings). A roman numeral tells you at which fret to place the barre, and a dotted line indicates how long you must hold the barre in place to successfully execute the passage underneath it. Figure 4-11 shows how barre notation appears in classical guitar music.

Figure 4-11:
What barre indications look like.

Book I

Guitar 101

Taking on tablature, a nice complement to standard notation

Tablature staff (called "tab" for short) is sometimes added to the standard notation staff. *Tablature* is a six-line staff that represents the guitar fretboard (see Figure 4-12). Note that each line represents a string of the guitar, with the top line corresponding to the 1st (high-E) string and the bottom line corresponding to the 6th (low-E) string. A number on a line provides the fret location for that note. (Tablature doesn't tell you which finger to use, but you may be able to get that information from the standard music staff.)

Figure 4-12: The six-line tab staff shows notes as fret numbers on lines.

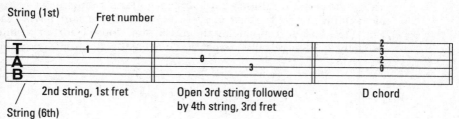

String (1st)
Fret number

String (6th)

2nd string, 1st fret

Open 3rd string followed by 4th string, 3rd fret

D chord

Remember from earlier that all musicians have to be able to understand the symbols of standard music notation and *then* relate them to their instrument? Tablature skips that step! The good news is, you can use tab right away, with no previous experience in reading music. The bad news is, tab is more limited than standard music notation. For one thing, it works only for guitar, so it doesn't teach you the more universal skill of reading music, and it doesn't indicate rhythm.

Tab does, however, work very well in conjunction with the standard music staff. All the notes in the tab staff align vertically with the notes appearing above in the standard music staff. If you're ever unsure as to where to play a note appearing in the music staff, all you need to do is shoot your eyes straight down to the corresponding string-and-fret location in the tab staff. Conversely, if you find yourself in the tab staff and you're uncertain of what's supposed to be happening with regard to rhythms or rests, take a quick trip uptown to see how that passage is displayed in the music staff. Figure 4-13 shows how the notes on the standard music notation staff relate to the tab staff and vice versa.

Figure 4-13: Standard music notation and tab play nicely together in the same system.

Tab staffs aren't traditional for classical guitarists (and may cause some classical guitar purists to raise an eyebrow). That being said, having the additional tab staff accompanying the music staff doesn't hurt anything. Providing as many ways as possible to get you *playing* the guitar is a good thing.

Book II
Sounds and Techniques

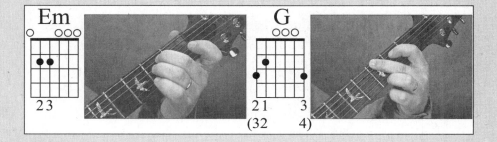

Contents at a Glance

Chapter 1: Basic Major and Minor Chords 77

Chords in the A Family 78
Chords in the D Family 81
Chords in the G Family 84
Chords in the C Family 85
Songs with Basic Major and Minor Chords 87
Fun with the "Oldies" Progression 94

Chapter 2: Adding Spice: Basic 7th Chords 95

Dominant 7th Chords 95
Minor 7th Chords — Dm7, Em7, and Am7 98
Major 7th Chords — Cmaj7, Fmaj7, Amaj7, and Dmaj7 99
Playing Songs with 7th Chords 101

Chapter 3: Power Chords and Barre Chords 109

Reviewing Open-position Chords 110
Putting Power Chords into Play 111
Getting Behind the Barre 114

Chapter 4: Right-Hand Rhythm Guitar Techniques. 123

Strumming Along 123
Mixing Single Notes and Strums...131
Disrupting Your Sound: Syncopated Strumming 133
Giving Your Left Hand a Break 135
Suppressing the Right Hand 137
Left-hand Movement within a Right-hand Strum 138
Giving Your Fingers Some Style 139
Getting Into Rhythm Styles 141

Chapter 5: Playing Melodies in Position and in Double-Stops 147

Playing Scales and Exercises in Position 147
Practicing Songs in Position 152
Double-Stop Basics 156
Playing Songs in Double-Stops 158

Chapter 1

Basic Major and Minor Chords

In This Chapter

▶ Checking out chords in the A, D, G, and C families

▶ Playing songs by using basic major and minor chords

▶ Sweatin' to the oldies

▶ Access the audio tracks and video clips at www.dummies.com/go/guitaraio/

Accompanying yourself as you sing your favorite songs — or as someone else sings them if your voice is less than melodious — is one of the best ways to pick up basic guitar chords. If you know basic chords, you can play lots of popular songs right away, from "Skip to My Lou" to "Louie Louie."

This chapter organizes the major and minor chords into families. A *family* of chords is simply a group of related chords — related because you often use them together to play songs. The concept is sort of like color-coordinating your clothing or assembling a group of foods to create a balanced meal. Chords in a family go together like peanut butter and jelly. Along the way, you'll expand your guitar notation vocabulary as you start to develop your chord-playing and strumming skills.

Or think of a family of chords as a plant. If one of the chords — the one that feels like home base in a song (usually the chord you start and end a song with) — is the plant's root, and the other chords in the family are the different shoots rising up from that same root. In fact, that chord really is called the *root*. Together, the root and "shoots" make up the family. Put 'em all together and you have a lush garden . . . er, song.

By the way, the technical term for a chord family is a *key*. So you can say, "This song uses A-family chords" *or* "This song is in the key of A."

Chords in the A Family

The A family (key of A) is a popular one for playing songs on the guitar because, like the other families in this chapter, its chords are easy to play. That's because A-family chords contain *open* strings (strings that you play without pressing down any notes). Chords that contain open strings are called open chords, or open-position chords. Listen to "Fire and Rain" by James Taylor and "Tears in Heaven" by Eric Clapton to hear songs that use A-family chords.

The basic chords in the A family are A, D, and E. Each of these chords is what's known as a *major* chord. A chord that's named by a letter name alone, such as these (A, D, and E), is always major. The following sections explain how to finger and strum chords in the key of A.

Fingering A-family chords

When fingering chords, you use the "ball" of your fingertip, placing it just behind the fret (on the side toward the tuning pegs). Arch your fingers so the fingertips fall perpendicular to the neck. And make sure your left-hand fingernails are short so they don't prevent you from pressing the strings all the way down to the fingerboard.

Checking out chord qualities

Chords have different qualities, which has nothing to do with whether they're good or bad little chords. You can define *quality* as the *relationship* between the different notes that make up the chord — or simply, what the chord sounds like.

Besides the quality of being major, other chord qualities include *minor, 7th, minor 7th,* and *major 7th.* The following list describes each of these types of chord qualities:

- **Major chords:** These are simple chords that have a stable sound.

- **Minor chords:** These are simple chords that have a soft, sometimes sad sound.

- **7th chords:** These are bluesy, funky-sounding chords.

- **Minor 7th chords:** These chords sound mellow and jazzy.

- **Major 7th chords:** These chords sound bright and jazzy.

Each type of chord, or chord quality, has a different kind of sound, and you can often distinguish the chord type just by hearing it. Listen, for example, to the sound of a major chord by strumming A, D, and E. (For more on 7th, minor 7th, and major 7th chords, check out Book II Chapter 2.)

Figure 1-1 shows the fingering for the A, D, and E chords — the basic chords in the A family. (If you're unclear about reading the chord diagrams, check out Book I Chapter 2.)

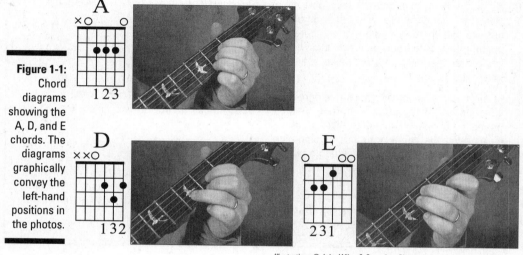

Figure 1-1: Chord diagrams showing the A, D, and E chords. The diagrams graphically convey the left-hand positions in the photos.

Illustrations © John Wiley & Sons, Inc. Photographs courtesy of Jon Chappell

Book II

Sounds and Techniques

Don't play any strings marked with an X (the 6th string on the A chord and the 5th and 6th strings on the D chord, for example). Strike just the top five (5th through 1st) strings in the A chord and the top four (4th through 1st) strings in the D chord. Selectively striking strings may be awkward at first, but keep at it and you'll get the hang of it. If you play a string marked with an X, you'll know because it will sound wrong, if not awful.

Strumming A-family chords

Use your right hand to strum A-family chords with one of the following:

✔ A pick

✔ Your thumb

✔ The back of your fingernails (in a brushing motion toward the floor)

Start strumming from the lowest-pitched string of the chord (the side of the chord toward the ceiling as you hold the guitar) and strum toward the floor.

Playing callus-ly

Playing chords can be a little painful at first. No matter how tough you are, if you've never played the guitar before, your left-hand fingertips are *soft*. Fretting a guitar string, therefore, is going to feel to your fingertips almost as if you're hammering a railroad spike with your bare hand. (Ouch!)

In short, *pressing down on the string hurts*. This situation isn't weird at all — in fact, it's quite normal for beginning guitarists. (Well, it's weird if you *enjoy* the pain.) You must develop nice, thick calluses on your fingertips before playing the guitar can ever feel completely comfortable. It may take weeks or even months to build up those protective layers of dead skin, depending on how much and how often you play. But after you finally earn your calluses, you never lose

them (completely, anyway). Like a Supreme Court justice, you're a guitar player *for life*.

You can develop your calluses by playing the basic chords in this chapter over and over again. As you progress, you also gain strength in your hands and fingers and become more comfortable in general while playing the guitar. Before you know it's happening, fretting a guitar becomes as natural to you as shaking hands with your best friend.

As with any physical-conditioning routine, make sure you stop and rest if you begin to feel tenderness or soreness in your fingers or hands. Building up those calluses takes *time,* and you can't hurry time (or love, for that matter, as Diana Ross would attest).

A *progression* is simply a series of chords that you play one after the other. Figure 1-2 presents a simple progression in the key of A and instructs you to strum each chord — in the order shown (reading from left to right) — four times. Use all downstrokes (dragging your pick across the strings toward the floor) as you play. Listen to the example on Track 2 at 0:00 to hear the rhythm of this progression and try to play along with it. You also can view Video Clip 5 to see and hear Figure 1-2.

Figure 1-2:
A simple chord progression in the key of A.

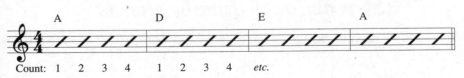

After strumming each chord four times, you come to a vertical line in the music that follows the four strum symbols. This line is a *bar line*. It's not something that you play. Bar lines visually separate the music into smaller sections known as *measures*, or *bars*. Measures make written music easier to grasp, because they break up the music into little, digestible chunks. See Book I Chapter 4 for more information on bar lines and measures.

Don't hesitate or stop at the bar line. Keep your strumming speed the same throughout, even as you play "between the measures" — that is, in the imaginary "space" from the end of one measure to the beginning of the next that the bar line represents. Start out playing as slowly as necessary to help you keep the beat steady. You can always speed up as you get more confident and proficient in your chord fingering and switching.

By playing a progression over and over, you start to develop left-hand strength and calluses on your fingertips. Try it (and try it . . . and try it . . .).

If you want to play a song right away, skip to the section "Songs with Basic Major and Minor Chords," at the end of this chapter. Because you now know the basic open chords in the A family, you can play "Kumbaya." Rock on!

Book II

Sounds and Techniques

Chords in the D Family

The basic chords that make up the D family are D, E minor (written *Em*), G, and A. The D family, therefore, shares two basic open chords with the A family (D and A) and introduces two new ones: Em and G. Because you already know how to play D and A from the preceding section, you need to work on only two more chords to add the entire D family to your repertoire: Em and G. Listen to "Here Comes the Sun" by the Beatles or "Who Says" by John Mayer to hear the sound of a song that uses D-family chords.

Minor describes the quality of a type of chord. A minor chord sounds distinctly different from a major chord. You may characterize the sound of a minor chord as sad, mournful, scary, or even ominous. Note that the relationship of the notes that make up the chord determines a chord's quality. A chord named by a capital letter followed by a small *m* is always minor.

Fingering D-family chords

Figure 1-3 shows you how to finger the two basic chords in the D family that aren't in the A family: Em and G. You may notice that none of the strings in either chord diagram displays an X symbol, so you get to strike all the strings whenever you play a G or Em chord. If you feel like it, go ahead and celebrate by dragging your pick or right-hand fingers across the strings in a big *keraaaang*.

Practicing and getting good

Saying that the more you practice, the better you'll get may sound obvious, but it's true. However, perhaps even more important is this concept: *The more you practice, the faster you'll get good.* Although there's no set amount of practice time for "getting good," a good rule is to practice a minimum of 30 minutes every day. Also, it's generally agreed that practicing at regular intervals is better than jamming a week's worth of time (say, 3 1/2 hours) all into one practice session.

If at first you find a new technique difficult to master, stick with it, and you'll eventually get the hang of it. To get even better on the guitar, try the following:

✔ Set aside a certain time every day for practicing.

✔ Get together with your guitar-playing friends and get them to listen to what you're doing.

✔ Create a practice environment where you have privacy, away from distractions (TV, conversations, your mother bugging you to come to dinner, and so on).

✔ Watch videos of guitar players who play the kind of music you like and that you'd like to learn. Or type in a song title plus the word "guitar" into YouTube — you'll likely find a video of someone playing that song on guitar, maybe even in a lesson-type presentation.

Figure 1-3:
The Em and G chords. All six strings are available for play in each chord.

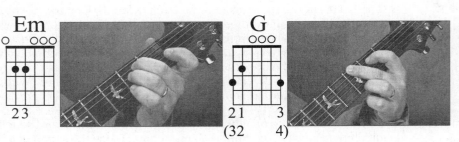

Illustrations © John Wiley & Sons, Inc. Photographs courtesy of Jon Chappell

Try the following trick to quickly pick up how to play Em and to hear the difference between the major and minor chord qualities: Play E, which is a major chord, and then lift your index finger off the 3rd string. Now you're playing Em, the minor-chord version of E. By alternating the two chords, you can easily hear the difference in quality between a major and minor chord.

Notice the alternative fingering for G (2-3-4 instead of 1-2-3). As your hand gains strength and becomes more flexible, you want to switch to the 2-3-4 fingering instead of the initially easier 1-2-3 fingering (the version shown in Figure 1-3). You can switch to other chords with greater ease and efficiency when you're using the 2-3-4 fingering for G.

Strumming D-family chords

In Figure 1-4, you play a simple chord progression, using D-family chords. Notice the difference in the strum in this figure versus that of Figure 1-2.

Book II

Sounds and Techniques

- ✔ In Figure 1-2, you strum each chord four times per measure. Each strum is one pulse, or beat.

- ✔ Figure 1-4 (Track 2 at 0:16) divides the second strum of each measure (or the second beat) into two strums — up and down — both of which together take up the time of one beat, meaning that you must play each strum in beat 2 twice as quickly as you do a regular strum.

Figure 1-4: Progression with chords found in the key of D.

The additional symbol 2 with the strum symbol means that you strum down toward the floor, and 4 means that you strum up toward the ceiling. The term *sim.* is an abbreviation of the Italian word *simile*, which instructs you to keep playing in a *similar* manner — in this case, to keep strumming in a down, down-up, down, down pattern.

You can see the motion of the downstrokes and upstrokes on Video Clip 6.

If you're using only your fingers for strumming, play upstrokes with the back of your thumbnail whenever you see the symbol 4.

Knowing the basic open chords in the D family (D, Em, G, and A) enables you to play a song in the key of D right now. If you skip to the section "Songs with Basic Major and Minor Chords," at the end of this chapter, you can play the song "Swing Low, Sweet Chariot" right now. Go for it!

Chords in the G Family

By tackling related chord families (as A, D, and G are), you carry over your knowledge from family to family in the form of chords that you already know from earlier families. The basic chords that make up the G family are G, Am, C, D, and Em. If you already know G, D, and Em (which we describe in the preceding sections on the A and D families), you can now try Am and C. Listen to "You've Got a Friend" by James Taylor or "Every Rose Has Its Thorn" by Poison to hear the sound of a song that uses G-family chords.

Fingering G-family chords

In Figure 1-5, you see the fingerings for Am and C, the new chords you need to play in the G family. Notice that the fingering of these two chords is similar: Each has finger 1 on the 2nd string, 1st fret, and finger 2 on the 4th string, 2nd fret. (Only finger 3 must change in switching between these two chords.) In moving between these chords, keep these first two fingers in place on the strings. Switching chords is always easier if you don't need to move all your fingers to new positions. The notes that different chords share are known as *common tones*. Notice the X over the 6th string in each of these chords. Don't play that string while strumming either C or Am.

Figure 1-5: The fingering for the Am and C chords.

Illustrations © John Wiley & Sons, Inc. Photographs courtesy of Jon Chappell

Strumming G-family chords

Figure 1-6 shows a simple chord progression you can play by using G-family chords. Play this progression over and over to get accustomed to switching chords and build up those left-hand calluses. It *does* get easier after a while.

Notice that in each measure, you play beats 2 and 3 as "down-up" strums. Listen to Track 2 (at 0:43) to hear this sound; check out Video Clip 7 to see the figure played.

Figure 1-6:
Chord progression using G-family chords.

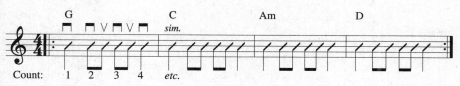

Knowing the basic open chords in the G family (G, Am, C, D, and Em) enables you to play a song in the key of G right now. Skip to the section "Songs with Basic Major and Minor Chords" at the end of this chapter, and you can play "Auld Lang Syne."

Book II

Sounds and Techniques

Chords in the C Family

The last chord family discussed in this chapter is C. Some people say that C is the easiest key to play in. That's because C uses only the white-key notes of the piano in its musical scale and, as such, is sort of the music theory square one — the point at which everything (and, usually, everyone) begins in music. The C family is last in this chapter because it's so easy that it has lots of chords in its family — too many to master all at once.

The basic chords that make up the C family are C, Dm, Em, F, G, and Am. If you practice the preceding sections on the A-, D-, and G-family chords, you know C, Em, G, and Am. So in this section, you need to pick up only two more chords: Dm and F. After you know these two additional chords, you'll have all the basic major and minor chords down pat. Listen to "Dust in the Wind" by Kansas or "Lucky" by Jason Mraz and Colbie Caillat to hear the sound of a song that uses C-family chords.

Fingering C-family chords

In Figure 1-7, you see the new chords you need to play in the C family. Notice that both the Dm and F chords have the 2nd finger on the 3rd string, 2nd fret. Hold down this common tone as you switch between these two chords. Notice the "arch" indication in the F-chord diagram — that tells you to fret (or barre) two strings with one finger.

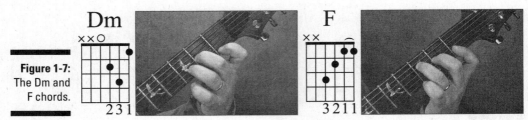

Figure 1-7: The Dm and F chords.

Illustrations © John Wiley & Sons, Inc. Photographs courtesy of Jon Chappell

Many people find the F chord the most difficult chord to play of all the basic major and minor chords. That's because F uses no open strings and it requires a *barre*. A barre is what you're playing whenever you press down two or more strings at once with a single left-hand finger. To play the F chord, for example, you use your 1st finger to press down both the 1st and 2nd strings at the 1st fret simultaneously.

You must exert extra finger pressure to play a barre. At first, you may find that, as you strum the chord (hitting the top four strings only, as the Xs in the chord diagram indicate), you hear some buzzes or muffled strings. Experiment with various placements of your index finger. Try adjusting the angle of your finger or try rotating your finger slightly on its side. Keep trying until you find a position for the 1st finger that enables all four strings to ring clearly as you strike them. You can also play a "full" F chord using your 1st finger to press down all six strings at the first fret, and your remaining fingers to fret the remaining notes. See Book II Chapter 3 for more on barre chords.

Strumming C-family chords

Figure 1-8 (Track 2 at 1:10) shows a simple chord progression you can play by using C-family chords. Play the progression over and over to get used to switching among the chords in this family and, of course, to help build up those calluses. Video Clip 8 shows the right-hand motion for the syncopated figure in the middle of each bar.

Look at Figure 1-8. Notice the small curved line joining the second half of beat 2 to beat 3. This line is known as a *tie*. A tie tells you not to strike the second note of the two tied notes (in this case, the one on beat 3). Instead, just keep holding the chord on that beat (letting it ring) without restriking it with your right hand.

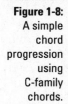

Figure 1-8:
A simple chord progression using C-family chords.

Listen to Track 2 to hear the sound of this strumming pattern. This slightly jarring rhythmic effect is an example of *syncopation*. In syncopation, the musician either strikes a note (or chord) where you don't expect to hear it or fails to strike a note (or chord) where you do expect to hear it.

You probably usually expect to strike notes on the beats (1, 2, 3, and 4). In the example in Figure 1-8, however, you don't strike a chord on beat 3. That variation in the strumming pattern makes the chord on beat 2 1/2 feel as if it's *accentuated* (or, as musicians say, *accented*). This accentuation interrupts the normal (expected) pulse of the music, resulting in the syncopation of the music. Syncopation breaks up the regular pattern of beats and presents an element of surprise in music. The balance between expectation and surprise in music is what holds a listener's interest. (Well, that and the promise of free hors d'oeuvres at the intermission.)

To play a song that uses C-family chords right now, skip to the song "Michael, Row the Boat Ashore," in the next section. Bon voyage!

Songs with Basic Major and Minor Chords

This section is where the real music happens — you know, songs. If the titles here hearken back to those bygone campfire days in the distant recesses of your youth, fear not, young-at-heart campers. These songs, although seemingly simple, illustrate universal principles that carry over into the — shall we say it? — hipper musical genres. Pick up on these songs first, and you're certain to be playing the music of your choice in no time.

You may notice that all the strumming examples provided in this chapter are only four measures long. Must all your exercises be limited this way? No, but songwriters do very commonly write music in four-measure phrases. So the length of these exercises prepares you for actual passages in real songs. You may also notice that each strumming example is in 4/4 time, which means that each measure contains four beats. Any reason? Most popular songs contain four beats per measure, so the 4/4 time signature in the exercises also prepares you to play actual songs. (See Book I Chapter 4 for more on time signatures.)

In the earlier examples in this chapter, you play each chord for one full measure. But in this section of actual songs, you sometimes play a single chord for more than a measure, and sometimes you change chords within a single measure. Listen to the audio track for each song to hear the rhythm of the chord change as you follow the beat numbers (1, 2, 3, and 4) that appear below the guitar staff.

After you can comfortably play your way through these songs, try to memorize them. That way, you don't need to stare into a book as you're trying to develop your rhythm.

If you get bored with these songs — or with the way you play them — show the music to a guitar-playing friend and ask him to play the same songs by using the strumming patterns and chord positions we indicate. Listening to someone else play helps you hear the songs objectively, and if your friend has a little flair, you may pick up a cool trick or two. Work on infusing personality into all your playing, even if it's a simple folk song. You can hear these songs on Tracks 3 through 6:

✔ **Kumbaya (Track 3):** To play "Kumbaya" (the ultimate campfire song), you need to know how to play A, D, and E chords (see the section "Fingering A-family chords," earlier in this chapter); how to strum by using all downstrokes; and how to start a fire.

The first measure in this song is known as a *pickup measure*, which is incomplete; it starts the song with one or more beats missing — in this case, the first two. During the pickup measure, the guitar part shows a rest, or a musical silence. Don't play during the rest; begin playing on the syllable ya on beat 1. Note, too, that the last bar is missing two beats — beats 3 and 4. The missing beats in the last measure enable you to repeat the pickup measure in repeated playings of the song, and to make that measure, combined with the first incomplete measure, total the requisite four beats.

✔ **Swing Low, Sweet Chariot (Track 4):** To play "Swing Low, Sweet Chariot," you need to know how to play D, Em, G, and A chords (see the section "Fingering D-family chords," earlier in this chapter); how to play down and down-up strums; and how to sing like James Earl Jones.

This song starts with a one-beat pickup, and the guitar rests for that beat. Notice that beat 2 of measures 2, 4, and 6 has two strums instead of one. Strum those beats down and then up (2 and 4) with each strum twice as fast as a regular strum.

✔ **Auld Lang Syne (Track 5):** To play "Auld Lang Syne," you need to know how to play G, Am, C, D, and Em chords (see the section "Fingering G-family chords," earlier in this chapter); how to play down and down-up strums; and what *auld lang syne* means in the first place.

Measure 8 is a little tricky, because you play three different chords in the same measure (Em, Am, and D). In the second half of the measure, you change chords on each beat — one stroke per chord. Practice playing only measure 8 slowly, over and over. Then play the song.

In changing between G and C (bars 4 to 6 and 12 to 14), fingering G with fingers 2, 3, and 4 instead of 1, 2, and 3 makes the chord switch easier. If you finger the chord that way, the 2nd and 3rd fingers form a shape that simply moves over one string.

✔ **Michael, Row the Boat Ashore (Track 6):** To play "Michael, Row the Boat Ashore," you need to know how to play C, Dm, Em, F, and G chords (see the earlier section "Fingering C-family chords"); how to play a syncopated eighth-note strum (see the section "Strumming C-family chords"); and the meaning of the word *hootenanny*.

The strumming pattern here is syncopated. The strum that normally occurs on beat 3 is anticipated, meaning that it actually comes half a beat early. This kind of syncopation gives the song a Latin feel. Listen to Track 6 to hear the strumming rhythm.

On the Dm and F chords, you don't strum the lowest two strings (the 6th and 5th). For the C chord, don't strum the bottom string (the 6th).

Book II

Sounds and Techniques

Kumbaya

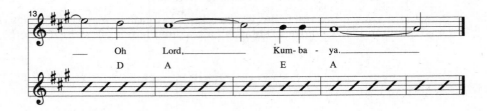

Swing Low, Sweet Chariot

Book II

Sounds and Techniques

Auld Lang Syne

Michael, Row the Boat Ashore

Book II

Sounds and Techniques

Fun with the "Oldies" Progression

As promised in the introduction to this chapter, you can play lots of popular songs right away if you know the basic major and minor chords. One cool thing that you can do right now is play oldies — songs from the late '50s and early '60s, such as "Earth Angel" and "Duke of Earl." These songs are based on what's sometimes called the *oldies progression,* a series of four chords, repeated over and over to form the accompaniment for a song.

You can play the oldies progression in any key, but the best guitar keys for the oldies progression are C and G. In the key of C, the four chords that make up the progression are C-Am-F-G. And in the key of G, the chords are G-Em-C-D. Try strumming the progression in each key by playing four down-strums per chord. Play the four chords over and over, in the sequence given. If you need help with the fingerings for these chords, check out the sections "Chords in the C Family" and "Chords in the G Family," earlier in this chapter.

The fun begins as you sing oldies while accompanying yourself with the oldies progression. As you sing a particular song, you'll find that one of the keys (C or G) better suits your vocal range, so use that key. Playing oldies can become addicting, but the good news is that, if you can't stop, you build up your calluses very quickly.

If you don't know the lyrics or don't have some of these songs in your music collection, try searching for them on YouTube.

For some songs, you play four one-beat strums per chord; for others, you play eight or two. Here are some songs you can play with the oldies progression right now, including how many times you strum each chord. Don't forget to sing. Have fun!

- **All I Have to Do Is Dream:** Two strums per chord
- **Breaking Up Is Hard to Do:** Two strums per chord
- **Duke of Earl:** Four strums per chord
- **Earth Angel:** Two strums per chord
- **Hey Paula:** Two strums per chord
- **Please, Mr. Postman:** Eight strums per chord
- **Runaround Sue:** Eight strums per chord
- **Tears on My Pillow:** Two strums per chord
- **Teenager in Love:** Four strums per chord
- **There's a Moon Out Tonight:** Two strums per chord

Chapter 2

Adding Spice: Basic 7th Chords

In This Chapter

▶ Playing dominant, minor, and major 7th chords

▶ Trying songs that use 7th chords

▶ Access the audio tracks and video clips at www.dummies.com/go/guitaraio/

This chapter shows you how to play what are known as open-position 7th chords. Seventh chords are no more difficult to play than are the simple major or minor chords described in Book II Chapter 1, but their sound is more complex (because they're made up of four different notes instead of three), and their use in music is a little more specialized.

The situation is kind of like that of the knives in your kitchen. Any big, sharp knife can cut both a pizza and a pineapple, but if you spend a lot of time doing either, you figure out that you need to use the circular-bladed gizmo for the pizza and a cleaver for the pineapple. These utensils may not be as versatile or as popular as your general-purpose knives, but if you're making Hawaiian-style pizza, nothing beats 'em. The more your culinary skills develop, the more you appreciate specialized cutlery. Likewise, the more your ear skills develop, the more you understand where to substitute 7th chords for the more ordinary major and minor chords. The different 7th chords can make the blues sound *bluesy* and jazz sound *jazzy*.

Seventh chords come in several varieties, and each type has a different sound, or quality. This chapter introduces you to the three most important types of 7th chords you'll encounter: dominant 7th, minor 7th, and major 7th.

Dominant 7th Chords

Dominant seems a funny, technical name for a chord that's called a plain "seven" if you group it with a letter-name chord symbol. If you say just C7 or A7, for example, you're referring to a dominant 7th chord.

TECHNICAL STUFF

Actually, the term *dominant* refers to the 5th degree of a major scale — which is called the dominant.

The important thing is that you call the chords in the following sections "dominant 7ths" to distinguish them from other types of 7th chords (minor 7ths and major 7ths, discussed later in this chapter). Note, too, that *dominant* has nothing whatsoever to do with leather and studded collars. You can hear the sound of dominant 7ths in such songs as Sam the Sham and the Pharaohs' "Wooly Bully," the Beatles' "I Saw Her Standing There," and Oasis's "Roll with It."

D7, G7, and C7

The D7, G7, and C7 chords are among the most common of the open dominant 7ths. Figure 2-1 shows you diagrams of these three chords that guitarists often use together to play songs.

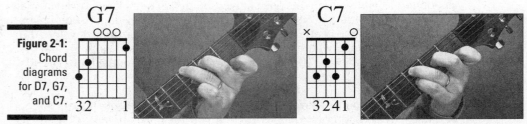

Figure 2-1: Chord diagrams for D7, G7, and C7.

Illustrations © John Wiley & Sons, Inc. Photographs courtesy of Jon Chappell

TIP

If you already know how to play C (introduced in Book II Chapter 1), you can form C7 by simply adding your pinky on the 3rd string at the 3rd fret.

PLAY THIS!

Notice the *X*s above the 5th and 6th strings on the D7 chord. Don't play those strings as you strum. Similarly, for the C7 chord, don't play the 6th string as you strum. Check out the right-hand motion in Video Clip 9 to see what your right hand should look like.

Practice strumming D7, G7, and C7. You don't need written music for this exercise, so you're on the honor system to do it. Try strumming D7 four times, G7 four times, and then C7 four times. You want to accustom your left hand to the feel of the chords themselves and to switching among them.

If you want to play a song right now with these new chords, skip to the section "Playing Songs with 7th Chords," later in this chapter. You can play "Home on the Range" with the chords you know right now.

E7 (the two-finger version) and A7

Two more 7th chords you often use together to play songs are the E7 and A7 chords. Figure 2-2 shows how you play these two open 7th chords.

 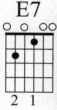   

Figure 2-2: Chord diagrams for E7 and A7.

Illustrations © John Wiley & Sons, Inc. Photographs courtesy of Jon Chappell

If you know how to play E (check out the previous chapter), you can form E7 by simply removing your 3rd finger from the 4th string.

This version of the E7 chord, as Figure 2-2 shows, uses only two fingers. You can also play an open position E7 chord with four fingers (as described in the following section). For now, though, play the two-finger version, because it's easier to fret quickly, especially if you're just starting out.

Practice E7 and A7 by strumming each chord four times, switching back and forth between them. Be sure to avoid striking the 6th string on the A7 chord.

If you want to play a song that uses these two open 7th chords right now, skip to the section "Playing Songs with 7th Chords," later in this chapter, and play "All Through the Night."

E7 (the four-finger version) and B7

Two more popular open-position 7th chords are the four-finger version of E7 and the B7 chord. Figure 2-3 shows you how to finger the four-finger E7 and the B7 chords. Most people think that this E7 has a better *voicing* (vertical arrangement of notes) than does the two-finger E7. You often use the B7 chord along with E7 to play certain songs.

Be sure to avoid striking the 6th string on the B7 chord.

Figure 2-3: Chord diagrams for E7 (the four-finger version) and B7.

Illustrations © John Wiley & Sons, Inc. Photographs courtesy of Jon Chappell

If you already know how to play E (see previous chapter), you can form this E7 by simply adding your pinky on the 2nd string at the 3rd fret.

Practice these chords by strumming each one four times, switching back and forth. As you do so, notice that your 2nd finger plays the same note at the same fret in each chord — the one at the 2nd fret of the 5th string. This note is a *common tone* (that is, it's common to both chords). In switching back and forth between the two chords, keep this finger down on the 5th string — doing so makes switching easier.

Always hold down common tones whenever you're switching chords. They provide an anchor of stability for your left hand.

To use these chords in a song right now, skip to the section "Playing Songs with 7th Chords," later in this chapter, and play "Over the River and Through the Woods."

Minor 7th Chords — Dm7, Em7, and Am7

Minor 7th chords differ from dominant 7th chords in that their character is a little softer and jazzier. Minor 7th chords are the chords you hear in "Moondance" by Van Morrison, the verses of "Light My Fire" by the Doors, and "Box Set" by Barenaked Ladies.

Figure 2-4 shows diagrams for the three open-position minor 7th (m7) chords: Dm7, Em7, and Am7. See Video Clip 10 for more.

Figure 2-4: Chord diagrams for Dm7, Em7, and Am7.

Illustrations © John Wiley & Sons, Inc. Photographs courtesy of Jon Chappell

Notice that the Dm7 uses a two-string *barre* — that is, you press down two strings with a single finger (the 1st finger, in this case) at the 1st fret. Angling your finger slightly or rotating it on its side may help you fret those notes firmly and eliminate any buzzes as you play the chord. Also, the 6th and 5th strings have *X*s above them. Don't strike those strings while strumming.

You finger the Am7 chord much as you do the C chord in the previous chapter; just lift your 3rd finger off a C chord — and you have Am7. In switching between C and Am7 chords, be sure to hold down the two common tones with your 1st and 2nd fingers. This way, you can switch between the chords much more quickly. And if you know how to play an F chord (see Chapter 4), you can form Dm7 simply by removing your 3rd finger.

Major 7th Chords — Cmaj7, Fmaj7, Amaj7, and Dmaj7

Major 7th chords differ from dominant 7th chords and minor 7th chords in that their character is bright and jazzy. You can hear this kind of chord at the beginning of "Ventura Highway" by America, "Don't Let the Sun Catch You Crying" by Gerry and the Pacemakers, and "Take It Easy" by The Eagles.

Figure 2-5 shows four open-position major 7th (maj7) chords: Cmaj7, Fmaj7, Amaj7, and Dmaj7.

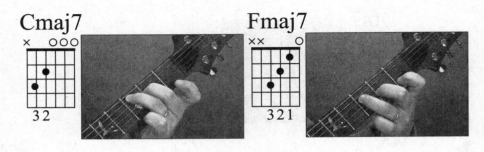

Figure 2-5: Chord diagrams for Cmaj7, Fmaj7, Amaj7, and Dmaj7 chords.

Illustrations © John Wiley & Sons, Inc. Photographs courtesy of Jon Chappell

Notice that the Dmaj7 uses a three-string barre with the 1st finger. Rotating the 1st finger slightly on its side helps make the chord easier to play. Refer to Video Clip 11 to make sure your 1st finger position resembles the one in the video. Don't play the 6th or 5th strings as you strike the Dmaj7 or Fmaj7 (see the *X*s in the diagrams in Figure 2-5). And don't play the 6th string on the Amaj7 or Cmaj7.

In moving between Cmaj7 and Fmaj7, notice that the 2nd and 3rd fingers move as a fixed shape across the strings in switching between these chords. You don't fret any string in a Cmaj7 chord with your 1st finger, but keep it curled and poised above the 1st fret of the 2nd string so you can bring it down quickly for the switch to Fmaj7.

Practice moving back and forth (strumming four times each) between Cmaj7 and Fmaj7 and between Amaj7 and Dmaj7.

To use these chords in a song right now, check out the next section and play "It's Raining, It's Pouring" and "Oh, Susanna."

Playing Songs with 7th Chords

Listen to Tracks 7 through 11 to hear the rhythm of the strums of these songs as you follow the slash notation in the guitar part (flip to Chapter 3 to find out more about rhythm slashes). Don't try to play the vocal line. It's there only as a reference.

Here's some useful information about the songs to help you along:

✔ **Home on the Range (Track 7):** To play "Home on the Range," you need to know how to play C, C7, F, D7, and G7 chords (see Book II Chapter 1 for the C and F chords and the section "Dominant 7th Chords," earlier in this chapter, for the others); how to play a bass-strum-strum pattern; and how to wail like a coyote.

In the music, you see the words *Bass Strum Strum* over the rhythm slashes. Instead of simply strumming the chord for three beats, play only the lowest note of the chord on the first beat and then strum the remaining notes of the chord on beats 2 and 3. The *sim.* means to keep on playing this pattern throughout.

✔ **All Through the Night (Track 8):** To play "All Through the Night," you need to know how to play D, E7 (use the two-finger version for this song), A7, and G chords (see the previous chapter for the D and G chords and the section earlier in this chapter on the E7 and A7 chords); how to read repeat signs; and how to stay awake during this intensely somnolent ditty.

In the music, you see *repeat signs,* which tell you to play certain measures twice (in this case, you play measures 1, 2, 3, 4, and then measures 1, 2, 3, 5). A repeat sign consists of a thick vertical line and a thin vertical line (through the staff) with two dots next to them. A repeat sign that marks the *beginning* of a section to be repeated has its dots to the *right* of the vertical lines. You see this at the beginning of measure 1. A repeat sign that marks the *end* of a section to be repeated has its dots to the *left* of the vertical lines, as at the end of measure 4.

✔ **Over the River and Through the Woods (Track 9):** To play "Over the River and Through the Woods," you need to know how to play A, D, E7 (use the four-finger version), and B7 chords (see previous chapter for the A and D chords and the section on the four-finger version of E7 and B7, earlier in this chapter); how to strum in 6/8 time; and the way to Grandma's house (in case your horse stumbles and you need to shoot it).

The 6/8 time signature has a lilting feel to it — sort of as though the music has a gallop or limp. "When Johnny Comes Marching Home Again" is another familiar song in 6/8 time. Count only two beats per measure — not six — with each group of three eighth notes sounding like one big beat; otherwise, you'll end up sounding like a rabbit that's had three cups of coffee.

✔ **It's Raining, It's Pouring (Track 10):** To play "It's Raining, It's Pouring," you need to know how to play Amaj7 and Dmaj7 chords (see the section, "Major 7th Chords — Cmaj7, Fmaj7, Amaj7, and Dmaj7," earlier in this chapter) and how to sing in a whiny, annoying voice.

This song is a jazzed-up version of the old nursery rhyme "It's Raining, It's Pouring," also known as the childhood taunt "Billy Is a Sissy" (or whichever personal childhood nemesis you plug in to the title). The major 7th chords you play in this song sound jazzy and give any song a modern sound. Use all downstrokes on the strums.

✔ **Oh, Susanna (Track 11):** To play "Oh, Susanna," you need to know how to play Cmaj7, Dm7, Em7, Fmaj7, Am7, D7, G7, and C chords (see previous chapter for C and various sections earlier in this chapter for the different 7th chords) and how to balance a banjo on your knee while traveling the Southern United States.

This arrangement of "Oh, Susanna" uses three types of 7th chords: dominant 7ths (D7 and G7), minor 7ths (Dm7, Em7, and Am7), and major 7ths (Cmaj7 and Fmaj7). Using minor 7ths and major 7ths gives the song a hip sound. Use all downstrokes on the strums.

Lest you think this attempt to "jazz up" a simple folk song comes from out of the blue, listen to James Taylor's beautiful rendition of "Oh, Susanna" on the 1970 album *Sweet Baby James* to hear a similar approach. He actually says "banjo" without sounding corny.

Home on the Range

All Through the Night

Over the River and Through the Woods

It's Raining, It's Pouring

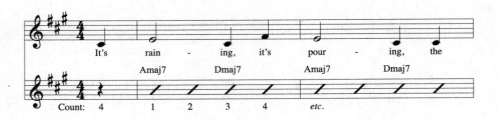

Oh, Susanna

I___ come from Al - a - bam - a with a
Cmaj7   Dm7   Em7   Fmaj7

Count: 1   2   1   2

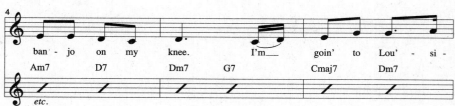

ban - jo on my knee. I'm___ goin' to Lou' - si -
Am7   D7   Dm7   G7   Cmaj7   Dm7

etc.

an - a, my Su - san - na for to see.
Em7   Am7   Dm7   G7   C

Book II

Sounds and Techniques

Chapter 3

Power Chords and Barre Chords

In This Chapter

▶ Trying your hand at open-position chords

▶ Jump-starting with power chords

▶ Mastering barre chords

▶ Access the audio tracks at www.dummies.com/go/guitaraio/

*W*hen rock guitarists play, chords are what they play most of the time. You may have a vision of your favorite guitar hero up on stage wailing away on a single-note lead passage, but the rest of the time, when he's singing or when someone else is singing or when someone else is the featured soloist, he's playing chords. And although the best guitarists are known for their lead playing, between these fleeting moments of immortal glory those guys are churning out chords.

Chords are the workday week of the playing rock guitarist. Leads are Saturday night. And in rock and roll, just as in life, you have to work all week to earn your Saturday night. Because chord playing constitutes what you do for the majority of your rock-guitar-playing life, this chapter shows you some essential chords to master.

Chords are built in the left hand (or right, perhaps, if you're a lefty) and realized as sound by strums from the right hand. But you don't create music on the guitar by strumming something once and letting it sit there ringing indefinitely. Music has to move, and rock music has to move mightily. The two ways to do that are to strum cool rhythms and to play awesome-sounding chords.

Because this chapter focuses on chords and your left hand, don't worry about what your right hand is supposed to do. For now, you can execute the figures and rhythm charts in this chapter by playing one strum (that is, one downward stroke across the strings) per slash. Things get fancier in the next chapter, but playing one strum per slash allows you to concentrate on your left-hand chord work.

Of course you don't *have* to play the figures using only the one-stroke-per-beat approach. If the spirit moves you — and the musical feel allows — try throwing in some in-between, up-and-down strums to get your music moving a bit. Just don't let any right-hand fanciness get in the way of the business of switching chords.

Fingering or "grabbing" chords is the hardest thing beginning guitarists encounter — much harder than anything the right hand has to do. *Facility* is strength combined with speed and accuracy. Playing chords on an electric guitar is fairly undemanding from a strength perspective — unlike on the acoustic guitar, where developing your left-hand strength can be a struggle.

Reviewing Open-position Chords

Open-position chords, so named because they involve unfretted strings, are allowed to ring open, along with the fretted notes. Open-position chords have a "jangly," pleasing quality and are sometimes called "cowboy chords" — probably because you can play simple, plaintive, spur-janglin', chip-kickin' songs with them.

Figure 3-1 is a chart of 24 chords that comprise just about all the useful chords you use for guitar in open position. If you've never tried your hand (pun intended!) at open-position chords before, flip back to Book II Chapter 1 for how to form and play these fundamental chords.

Remember, an "X" over a string means that it is *not* played or sounded; an "O" indicates an open string that *is* sounded when strumming. (Book II Chapter 1 explains chord diagrams.) Note that alternate fingerings appear below the primary ones.

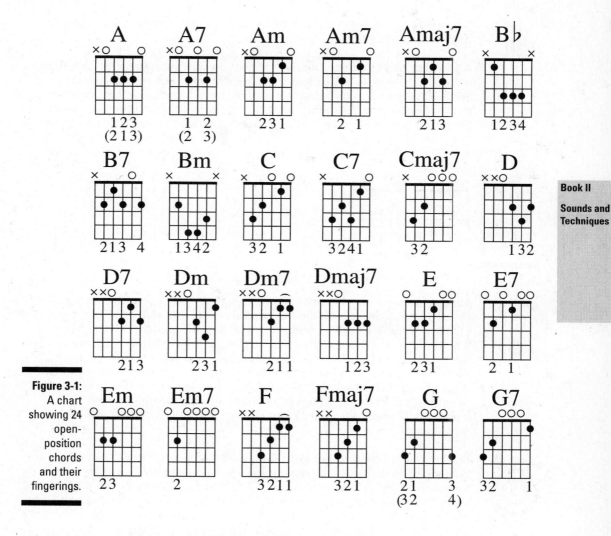

Figure 3-1: A chart showing 24 open-position chords and their fingerings.

Book II

Sounds and Techniques

Putting Power Chords into Play

Now it's time to put the cowpokes out to pasture. While open-position chords are not uncommon in electric guitar, electric players tend to favor their fast-moving, hard-hitting counterparts: *power chords*. Power chords are even easier to finger than open-position chords and they provide a simple means for moving beyond those first three frets. They represent rock guitar playing in all its raw and rugged glory, and once you understand how to use the 6th and 5th strings to name them, placing them on the neck is as easy as A-B-C♯.

A *power chord* is a two- or three-note chord that contains only the root and 5th degree of the chord.

A two-note power chord contains the root on the bottom and the 5th degree on top. A three-note power chord is built (from the bottom up) as root, 5th, octave, so it has a root at the bottom, the 5th on top of that, and then the root again, one octave higher than the chord's lowest note. An open-position A power chord would be either one of the two examples presented in Figure 3-2.

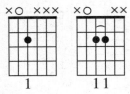

Figure 3-2:
Two ways
to play an
A power
chord.

Missing from power chords is the all-important 3rd degree (in the traditional sense, a *chord* is defined as three or more different notes, so a power chord is something of an exception). The 3rd of a chord is what determines whether the chord is major or minor. The flat 3rd (one-and-a-half steps from the root) makes the chord minor. The major 3rd (two whole steps from the root) makes the chord major. In either chord, though, the root and the 5th don't change. So take away the 3rd and you have a chord that is neither major nor minor: It can function as either, without being "wrong." This ambiguity is precisely what makes power chords so versatile, especially in rock music.

Power chords have another desirable quality, other than their stark construction and open sound: They sound great when played with distortion. This is because distortion imbues tones with *harmonics*, or different high-pitched notes in varying degrees of intensity, that make a sound much more harmonically rich than a non-distorted sound. Heavy distortion doesn't sound as good on full major or minor chords, because the harmonics of those closely spaced intervals (the root, 3rd, and 5th) clash in the upper registers, making the sound brittle and strident. But with just the root and 5th, the upper harmonics get close enough to dance together beautifully without stepping on each other's toes.

Moving power chords

Unlike their open-position brethren, power chords do not incorporate open strings and are therefore *moveable chords*. Any chord that you can move from one position on the neck to another without rearranging your fingers is a moveable chord. Because they're moveable, not to mention minimal, you can switch from any power chord to another without twisting your fingers up like so much linguini. If you can count up to 12 and spell up to the letter G, you can find every power chord. Welcome to Easy Street.

Power chords take their name from the root note, as all chords do. In a G power chord, G is the root. Because power chords incorporate only the root and the 5th, they are often referred to as "5" chords. When you see a chord written "G5," it's a G power chord.

The power chord shown in Figure 3-3 has its root on the 6th string. Because the note on the 6th string at the 5th fret is A, it's an A power chord (A5). Move the whole chord up a whole step (two frets) and it becomes B5. Likewise, move it down a step and it's G5. Move it down one more step and it becomes — any guesses? — F5.

Figure 3-3: A 6th-string-based power chord at the 5th fret, A5.

The 5th-string-based power chord looks almost exactly the same except it's shifted over a set of strings. Figure 3-4 is a 5th-string-based power chord played at the 1st fret.

Figure 3-4: A 5th-string-based power chord at the 1st fret, B♭5.

Like the 6th-string-based power chords, 5th-string-based chords can be moved around with ease. Move the B♭5 up a step (two frets) to get C5, up another step to D5, and so on.

Pulling the power together

Position is the term used to describe where a chord is placed on the neck. A chord's position is named for the fret where you plant your first finger. It doesn't matter which string you're on, just which fret. The 5th-string-based B♭5 is in first position. The first power chord you played — the 6th-string-based A5 at the 5th fret — is in 5th position.

Before you jump onstage with Aerosmith, try mixing up 6th- and 5th-string-based power chords. Because power chords have so few notes and always assume the same shape, it's a breeze to move them around the neck. Figure 3-5 (Track 12) is a typical power-chord progression. You don't have to keep up with the performance you hear on the audio track when trying to finger and strum these chords. Just try switching the chords *in time* — that is, after every four beats.

Figure 3-5:
Mixing
6th- and 5th-
string-based
power
chords in
a single
progression.

Getting Behind the Barre

So now you're slinging power chords all over the neck, and you're thinking that all you need to be a rock god is a pair of leather pants and some friends who don't smell so good. Well, pull your Lear jet back into the hangar for a minute. Although countless songs have been written using only the chord forms already covered — open-position and power chords — your musical vocabulary is about to expand a thousandfold. It's time to belly up to the barre.

The term *barre chord* strikes fear into the hearts of beginning guitarists everywhere. Technically, a barre chord is just a chord where your left-hand 1st (index) finger lies flat across the strings, forming a "bar," with the rest of the chord made up by other fingers. Nevertheless, the term usually carries with it connotations of medieval torture practices.

Beginners have trouble with barre chords, because they seem to require an inordinate amount of strength — strength that you may think is better applied to a stuck lid on a pickle jar, not having fun playing the guitar. Although strength is certainly involved, you don't need quite so much of it after you become good at playing barre chords. Playing barre chords is like riding a bicycle: It's really tough at first, but then it becomes second nature. The difference is that barre chords hurt more when you're on them than when you fall off.

In rock, barre chords separate the men from the boys, the women from the girls, and those who rule from them that drool.

Getting a grip on barre chords

Memorize the Barre Chord Creed for the most important aspects to learning and mastering barre chords: A day without orange juice is like a day without sunshine. Oh, wait, that's not it. Here are the tips to keep in mind:

- ✔ **Press firmly.** You don't need to embed the strings permanently into your flesh, but apply strong, even pressure with your 1st finger. Rotate the finger slightly onto its side — the side away from the 2nd finger.

- ✔ **Thumb it.** Keep your thumb placed directly in the center of the neck's back. This is where the strength comes from. You'll know you're doing it right when the heel of your hand gets sore. Isn't this the greatest?

- ✔ **Keep your arms in.** Don't let your elbow stick out at your side like a chicken wing. Pull your elbow into your side, and keep your left shoulder relaxed and down.

- ✔ **Be fat-free.** Make tiny adjustments so that the fleshy parts of your fingers aren't touching adjacent strings, causing them to muffle. Keep your knuckles rounded and try to press straight down on the strings, rather than from the side. Also make sure that a string isn't running directly under the crease in the knuckle between your 1st and 2nd finger joints.

Barre is the Spanish word for *bar*, and guitarists use this spelling because a lot of guitar notation uses Spanish terms (the same way other terms in music, such as *piano* for "soft," *fortissimo* for "very loud," and *scuza plisa tu pasa di pasta* for "the band is hungry" are in Italian), and because *barre* distinguishes itself from *bar*, the metal arm on the bridge of some guitars.

Book II

Sounds and Techniques

Playing E-based barre chords

Barre chords are formed as open-position-based chords with an added barre (your 1st finger) placed over the top. The first step is to finger an open-position E form (see Book II Chapter 1 for a detailed explanation, if you're a bit rusty). But instead of using your first three fingers, fret the chord with your 2nd, 3rd, and 4th fingers. This leaves your 1st finger free to barre.

With an open chord, the nut — that slotted bar between the headstock and the fretboard — is acting like a barre. You're going to move the whole chord up and take over the nut's job with your 1st finger.

1. **Slide all the fretted notes up (away from the headstock) exactly one fret.**

2. **Lay your index finger down in the 1st fret, across all six strings, parallel to the nut.**

3. **Minding the Barre Chord Creed, apply pressure and strum away.**

Congratulations. You are now playing an F barre chord (see Figure 3-6). And, in a manner of speaking, you are now the nut.

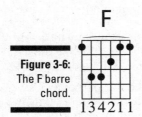

Figure 3-6:
The F barre chord.

Unless you're the type weakened only by kryptonite, you will have trouble getting the F chord to sound good and feel comfortable. In the beginning, playing an F chord will strain your hand, muffle the strings, and cause you to holler at various inanimate objects. This is normal.

Barre chords are harder to play in the first few frets, where the nut offers resistance, and way up the neck, where the action is higher and the frets are narrower. Once you can form the barre F chord immediately, without agonizing through the steps shown earlier, try moving your F chord to the 5th fret (where, by the way, it becomes an A chord). It should be easier to press the strings down here than at the 1st fret.

Moving the E-form barre chord around the neck

All barre chords are moveable chords — that's the beauty of 'em. Now that you've formed a barre chord (and can play it so that the strings, when strummed, ring through clearly), you're ready to move this sucker.

You've already had a glimpse of the thinking involved because you've moved power chords around the neck. (And some brave souls followed the advice in the last section to move the F chord up to the 5th fret.) Apply what you know about moving power chords to barre chords. The only difference is that you're moving *more* notes per chord.

To identify which chords you're playing on the neck as you move around, take the 6th-string shortcut. Because the lowest string of the guitar is called E, you can use the name of the notes on the 6th string to tell you where to play a given E-based form, just as we did with power chords. For example, the 5th fret of the E string is A, so the chord formed at the 5th fret using an E form is A. This shortcut enables guitarists to place chords on the fretboard by using the lowest note of the chord as the guide. The barre chord dubbed the "E-form" can also be called a *6th-string-based chord*. Unless something heavy has fallen on your head in the last few minutes, you probably remember 6th-string-based chords from power chords, too.

Other E forms: Minor, dominant 7, minor 7, and 7sus

So far, you've built and moved only the E-major barre shape. As you know from open-position chords, there are chordal varieties other than major. Chords that are given simple letter names (E, B♭, D) are majors — all others are qualified (E minor, B♭ minor7, D7sus).

Here's where your hard labor on that first barre pays off. Having successfully wrangled the E-major barre-chord form, you can easily start adding other chord qualities. All of these forms can be played with small, easy changes to the E-major barre. And all of them correspond directly with open-position E chords you already know. You are about to be so very happy.

To make things even easier for yourself, try these new forms at the 3rd fret, where it starts getting more reasonable to finger chords *sans* buzz and rattle.

TIP

Using the 6th-string shortcut, you know that an E barre form played at the 3rd fret is a G chord. So if you play these forms in 3rd position, they'll all be G chords of one type or another. But pay attention to the shapes, which you'll move around, rather than the chords' letter names.

To change a G major barre into a G minor barre, lift your 2nd (middle) finger. Let the newly exposed note — 3rd string, 3rd fret — ring out with the rest of the barred notes. Yeah, that's all there is to it! Figure 3-7 shows a 3rd-position G minor barre chord.

Figure 3-7: A G minor barre chord using the E-based form.

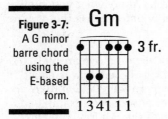

To change an G major into an G7 (also known as G dominant7), lift the 4th finger, as shown in Figure 3-8.

Figure 3-8: A G7 barre chord using the E-based form.

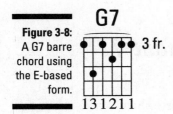

To change an G major into an Gm7 (G minor7), lift the 2nd and 4th fingers, as shown in Figure 3-9.

Figure 3-9: A G minor7 barre chord using the E-based form.

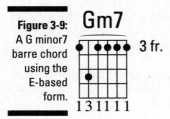

To change a G major into an G7sus — where the 3rd degree is *suspended*, or raised a half step, to the 4th degree — lift the 2nd finger and move the 4th finger over to the 3rd string, as shown in Figure 3-10.

Figure 3-10:
A G7sus
barre chord
using the
E-based
form.

G7sus

3 fr.

1 3 1 4 1 1

You've just learned four new chord forms — which, because they're applicable anywhere from 1st to 12th position, give you 48 new chords. Holy harmony. Go write a song, already.

Create your own exercise by moving these forms all over the neck. Then switch between forms as you move them around: Play a major chord in 1st position, a minor in 3rd, and a dominant 7 in 8th. You might just trip onto the next "Freebird." We could use a new "Freebird."

Playing A-based barre chords

Just as the family of E-based barres have open-position E forms (they are simply open-position shapes with a barre in front of them), A-based barres have open-position A forms. To form these chords, apply the same logic used to get from an open-position E major chord to a 1st position F major barre. No need to reinvent the wheel — save your creativity for your playing or your excuses for practicing at 2 a.m.

To create an A-based barre chord (see Figure 3-11), grab a plain ol' open A major, but use fingers 2, 3, and 4, instead of 1, 2, and 3, and then follow these steps:

1. **Slide all the fretted notes up exactly one fret.**

2. **Lay your index finger down in the first fret, across the top five strings, parallel to the nut.**

3. **Minding the Barre Chord Creed, apply pressure and strum away.**

For A-based barre chords, the barre is shorter: Your first finger needs to span only the top five strings.

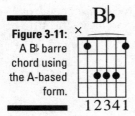

Figure 3-11:
A B♭ barre
chord using
the A-based
form.

1 2 3 4 1

You don't have to barre all six strings for the A-based barre because its root is on the 5th string: it's a 5th-string-based form. If your index finger does lay across the 6th string (which can be hard to avoid), be careful not to strum the 6th string with your right hand. You might want to let your index finger lay limply on that bottom string, which will help mute the sound if you strum it accidentally. Be careful, because the results can be horrific once you start moving the A-based barre chord around the neck. An open low E string against a 6th-fret E♭ major chord? Ick.

The hard part about this chord is pulling up the 3rd-finger knuckle so that the barred 1st string can sound. Because most guitarists find that to be too much trouble, they just end up playing the inner four strings (2 through 5) on the A major form. When they do this, they no longer have to make a barre out of the 1st finger — just the 3rd finger — which makes this a pretty easy chord to play. Try Figure 3-12, compare it with your success on the previous fingering, and choose which form works best for you.

Figure 3-12:
The alterna-
tive way
to finger
an A-form
barre chord.

1 3 3 3

Astute players who are not yet blinded by pain may have spotted something familiar in the bottom strings of the A and E barre forms: power chords. All three lower strings of the A major and E major barres contain the same notes as their power-chord counterparts. Also, you may recall that power chords do not carry a chord's 3rd degree; in keeping, the bottom three strings of the A minor and E minor barre shapes are identical not only to their power-chord counterparts but to their major brethren. Wow. Full circle, dude.

Moving the A-form barre chord

Because you can play a B♭ chord as a barre chord, you can now play all 12 A-based major barre chords (the entire chromatic scale). All A-based chords are moveable and get their name from the 5th string (just as the open A chord does, and similar to how the E-chord form derives its name).

Figure 3-13 uses all A-based major barre chords. Say the names of the chords aloud as you play them at their corresponding frets. All this naming is good for you. Listen to and play along with audio Track 13 to check your work. Don't worry about matching the strumming pattern you hear — just strum along at your own pace and switch between chords after every bar.

Figure 3-13:
A progression using A-based major barre chords.

A forms: Minor, dominant 7, minor 7, 7sus, and major 7

Everything you already know about moving chords around the neck carries over to these other barre-chord forms. Playing the minor, 7, or minor 7 versions is no more physically demanding than playing the major barre forms, it's just a matter of learning the fingering.

You can follow the numbered list in the section "Playing A-based barre chords" for creating the other versions of these A-based forms, or you can just try to form them after placing your 1st-finger barre over the appropriate fret and forming the chords from your remaining three fingers.

Figure 3-14 is a chart of five chord forms in A. The possible chord forms extend beyond these five, but these are the key chord types for playing most music.

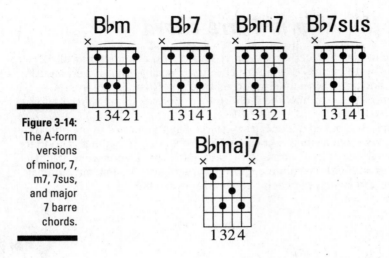

Figure 3-14: The A-form versions of minor, 7, m7, 7sus, and major 7 barre chords.

You can find barre forms that directly correspond with open-position chords. For example, the 5th-string based D minor played in 5th position has all the same notes (though some in different octaves) as the open-position D minor.

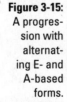

The number of chords you now can play up and down the neck is just plain incalculable (a fancy word for "too dang many"). You are a veritable font of chord knowledge. Dip into the fountain and enjoy this progression, which alternates between E- (6th-string) and A-based (5th-string) forms as the chords descend the neck. The changes in Figure 3-15 fit Bob Dylan's "Lay Lady Lay." You can also listen to this on Track 14.

Figure 3-15: A progression with alternating E- and A-based forms.

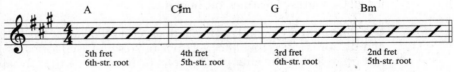

Chapter 4

Right-Hand Rhythm Guitar Techniques

In This Chapter

▶ Strumming with your right hand

▶ Using your palm to mute and accent

▶ Exploring different rhythm feels

▶ Access the audio tracks at www.dummies.com/go/guitaraio/

The right hand marshals the chords and notes you form in the left hand into the syncronized sounds you actually hear. The right hand is the engine that drives rhythm guitar, which weaves together the bass and drums and provides the underpinning for the singer, lead guitar, or other melodic instruments.

Whether it's playing in a steady eighth-note groove, a funky 16 feel, or a hard-swinging shuffle, the rhythm guitar and the right-hand strumming that propels it forge the chords and riffs you learn into a moving musical experience.

This chapter shows you different ways you can strum the guitar to make the rhythm fit a bunch of different styles and feels. These variations help keep your music vital-sounding, and help you to develop your skills as a rhythm guitarist — one who provides the backing and the foundation to support the melody, and who can act as the glue between the other rhythm instruments such as the bass and drums.

Strumming Along

Strumming is defined as dragging a pick (or the fingers) across the strings of the guitar. In doing that, you create rhythm.

If you "pick-drag" in regular, even strokes, one per beat, adhering to a tempo (musical rate), you're strumming the guitar in rhythm. And that's music, whether you mean it to be or not. More specifically, you're strumming a quarter-note rhythm, which is fine for songs such as the Beatles' "Let It Be" and other ballads. For the record, strumming an E chord in quarter notes looks like the notation in Figure 4-1 (Track 15). Rhythm slashes show that you should play the entire chord.

Figure 4-1:
Playing an
E chord in
one bar of
four quarter
notes.

The hardest part of learning rhythm guitar is realizing — and then maintaining — all the repetition involved. It's not what people expect when they pick up the guitar and want to learn a smorgasbord of cool licks and great riffs. But being able to play *in time* with unerring precision and rock-steady consistency is an essential skill and a hallmark of solid musicianship. Most rhythm playing in rock guitar involves a one- or two-bar pattern that gets repeated over and over, varying only where there are accent points that the band plays in unison.

After you learn to play consistently, you can then deviate from the established pattern you lay down and work on your own variations, as long as they're tasteful, appropriate, and not too numerous. Like a rock and roll rebel once said, "You have to know the rules before you can break them."

Downstrokes

A *downstroke* (indicated by the symbol ⊓) is the motion of dragging the pick toward the floor in a downward motion, brushing across multiple strings on the guitar in the process. Because you execute a downstroke quickly (even on slow songs) the separate strings are sounded virtually simultaneously. Playing three or more notes this way produces a chord.

Strumming in eighth-note downstrokes

To get out of the somewhat plodding rhythm of a quarter-note-only strumming pattern, you turn to eighth notes. As the math implies, an eighth note is one half the value of a quarter note, but in musical terms that equates to twice as fast, or more precisely, twice as frequently.

So instead of playing one strum per beat, you now play two strums per beat. This means you must move your hand twice as fast, striking the strings two times per beat, instead of once per beat as you did to produce quarter notes. At moderate and slower tempos, you can do this easily. For faster tempos you use alternating upstrokes and downstrokes (explained later in this chapter). For playing the progression in Figure 4-1, however, simply using repeated downstrokes is easiest.

Figure 4-2 (Track 16) uses eighth notes for the first three beats of each bar and a quarter note for the last beat of each bar. The quarter note allows you a little more time to switch chords between the end of each bar and the beginning of the new bar. Isn't that humane?

Figure 4-2: An eighth-note progression using right-hand downstrokes.

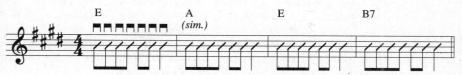

The term *sim.* in the music notation tells you to continue in a *sim*ilar fashion. It's typically used for articulation directions, such as down- and upstrokes.

Reading eighth-note notation

Notice that instead of the previously used slashes, you now have slashes with *stems* (the vertical lines coming down from the note head) and *beams* (the thicker horizontal lines that connect the stems). Quarter notes have single stems attached to them; eighth notes have stems with beams connecting them to each other. An eighth note by itself, or separated by a rest, will have a flag instead of a beam: ♪.

Even though this newly introduced notation denotes specific rhythmic values (quarter notes, eighth notes), the note heads are still elongated and angled — not the same kind of smaller, rounded note heads used to indicate individual pitches. The symbols used in this chapter are still rhythm slashes that tell you *how* (in what rhythm) to play, but not exactly *what* (the individual pitches) to play. Your left-hand chord position determines the pitches.

Upstrokes

An upstroke (indicated by the symbol ∨) is just what it sounds like: the opposite of a downstroke. Instead of dragging your pick down toward the floor, you start from a position below the strings and drag your pick upward across them. Doing this comfortably may seem a little less natural than playing a downstroke. One reason for this is that you're going against gravity. Also, some beginners have a hard time holding on to their pick or preventing it from getting stuck in the strings. With practice, however, you can flow with the ups as easily as you can with the downs.

TIP

You use *up*strokes for the *up*beats (offbeats) in eighth-note playing as the strokes in between the quarter-note beats. And when you start playing, don't worry about hitting all the strings in an upstroke. For example, when playing an E chord with an upstroke, you needn't strum the strings all the way through to the sixth string. Generally, in an upstroke, hitting just the top three or four strings is good enough. You may notice that your right hand naturally arcs away from the strings by that point, to an area above the center of the guitar. This is fine.

Upstrokes don't get equal time with their downwardly mobile counterparts. You typically use upstrokes only *in conjunction* with downstrokes. Whereas you can use downstrokes by themselves just fine — for entire songs, even — very rarely do you use upstrokes in isolation or without surrounding them on either side with downstrokes. (Some situations, such as the "Reggae rhythm" shown in Figure 4-21, do call for just upstrokes.)

So you should first tackle upstrokes in their most natural habitat: in an eighth-note rhythm figure where they provide the in-between notes, or *offbeats*, to the on-the-beat downstrokes.

Combining downstrokes and upstrokes

The easiest way to perform an upstroke smoothly is in its reciprocal response to a downstroke. Play Figure 4-3 (Track 17) with a relaxed, free-swinging up-and-down arm motion, working to get equal emphasis on each stroke, and being aware that your downstrokes will naturally include more (and lower) string-strikes than your upstrokes. The time signature is 4/4, which means the measures contain four beats, and each quarter note receives one beat.

Figure 4-3:
An easy 4/4 strum in eighth notes using down-strokes and upstrokes.

At this easygoing tempo, you can probably play Figure 4-3 with all downstrokes. If you try that, however, you discover that it introduces a tenser, more-frantic motion in your own strumming motion, which is not in character with the song's mellow feel. Frantic motion can be a very good thing in rock, though. (Figure 4-14, for example, shows you how an all-downstroke approach on a faster song is more appropriate than the easy back and forth of alternating downstrokes and upstrokes.)

Whether an eighth-note pattern takes an all-downstroke approach versus a downstroke-upstroke approach is determined more by feel than speed. (And it is physically easier to play eighth notes with alternating strokes.)

Playing a combination figure

Quarter notes and eighth notes make up much of medium-tempo-based music, so Figure 4-4 (Track 18) shows how a progression might use a mixture of quarters and eighths to convey different rhythmic intensity levels in a song.

Figure 4-4:
Strumming in quarter and eighth notes for different intensity levels.

You not only have to control the strums in your down and up picking, but which strings you strike in each chord as well. Don't forget that you play only the top four strings in a D chord and only the top five in a C chord.

Strumming in sixteenths

Sixteenth notes come twice as fast as eighth notes, or four to the beat. That can seem pretty twitchy, so sixteenth notes are almost always played with alternating downstrokes and upstrokes. Some punk and metal bands play fast sixteenth-note-based songs with all downstrokes, but their songs are usually about pain and masochism, so it's understandable, given the circumstances. The acoustic guitar part in the Who's "Pinball Wizard" is a classic example of sixteenth-note strumming.

Let's start off with a progression played at a medium tempo, using a common sixteenth-note figure. Figure 4-5 (Track 19) is based on an R&B progression and uses a repeated sixteenth-note scheme. It leaves true *syncopation* (rhythms employing dots and ties) out of the picture until later in the chapter.

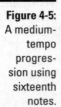

Figure 4-5:
A medium-tempo progression using sixteenth notes.

If the rhythmic notation seems like it's getting a little dense, don't worry too much about understanding the notation thoroughly or being able to play it at sight. What's important is to learn the figure, memorize it, and play it correctly and with confidence. Listening to Track 19 repeatedly to learn this figure is okay, too.

Reading sixteenth-note notation

Sixteenth notes are indicated with two beams connecting their stems (or if they're by themselves, two *flags* (♫)).

Getting a shuffle feel

An important rhythm feel used extensively in rock is the *shuffle*. A shuffle is a lilting eighth-note sound where the beat is divided into two unbalanced halves, a long note followed by a short. Think of the riffs to such songs as Elvis Presley's "Hound Dog," the Beach Boys' "California Girls," Fleetwood Mac's "Don't Stop Thinking About Tomorrow," and the Grateful Dead's "Truckin'." These are all based on a shuffle feel.

The shuffle is formed from triplets, where the beat is first subdivided into three equal parts. Then the first two notes are held together.

Rather than thinking about it too much, try this simple exercise, which can help you hear the difference between straight eighth notes (equally spaced) and triplet eighth notes (the first held twice as long as the second):

1. **Tap your foot in a steady beat and say the following line, matching the bold syllables to your foot taps:**

   Twink-le **twink**-le **lit**-tle **star**.

   That's the sound of normal, equally spaced, straight eighth notes.

2. **Now in the same tempo (that is, keeping your foot tap constant), try saying this line, based in triplets:**

   Fol-low the **yel**-low brick **road**.

That's the sound of triplets. In both cases you should keep your foot tap at exactly the same tempo and change only how you subdivide the beat.

3. **Create shuffle eighth notes by sounding only the first and third notes of the triplet.**

   Do this by sustaining the first note through the second or by leaving out that second note entirely. The new sound is a limping, uneven division that goes l-o-n-g-short, l-o-n-g-short, and so forth.

   A good way to remember the sound of triplet eighth notes (the basis of a shuffle feel) is the song "When Johnny Comes Marching Home Again." If you tap your foot or snap your fingers on the beat and then try saying the lyrics in rhythm, you get:

   When **John**-ny comes **march**-ing **home** a-**gain**, hur-**rah**

   The bold type represents the beat, where the syllables coincide with your foot tap or finger snap. The phrase "Johnny comes" is in triplets, because each syllable falls on one note of the three in between two beats. The rest of the phrase, "marching home again, hurrah," divides each beat into two-syllable pairs, the first syllable longer than the second. This is the sound of eighth notes in a shuffle feel.

Figure 4-6 (Track 20) is a shuffle feel that uses downstrokes and upstrokes. To reward you for saying "twinkle, twinkle little star" out loud while you tapped your foot, you'll get three new bonus chords that are easy to play and will give your shuffle progression a real lift.

Figure 4-6:
Eighth-note
shuffle in
G. Play the
three new
chord forms
by moving
one finger
from the
chord it's
derived
from.

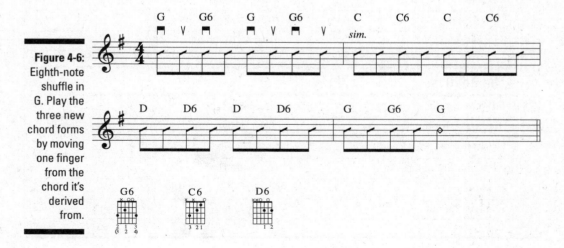

Actually, the chords aren't so much new as they are a one-finger variation of chords you already play. These "new" chords are easily executed by moving one and only one finger, while keeping the others anchored. It's the first step to getting both hands moving on the guitar, a really exciting accomplishment that makes you feel like a real guitar player. Have fun with this one!

The upstrokes still come at the in-between points — within the beats — but because of the unequal rhythm, it may take you a little time to adjust.

Dividing up songs by straight eighths and shuffle feel

If you've never thought of songs by your favorite band as being in a straight-eighth feel or a shuffle feel, it's fun to go down their hits and see in which category their individual songs belong. Here's how some of the Beach Boys' and the Beatles' hits break down:

The Beach Boys

Straight Eighth	Shuffle
Surfin' USA	Good Vibrations
Surfin' Safari	Barbara Ann
Kokomo	California Girls
I Get Around	Wouldn't It Be Nice
Fun, Fun, Fun	Help Me Rhonda

The Beatles

Straight Eighth	Shuffle
Hard Day's Night	Can't Buy Me Love
I Want to Hold Your Hand	Love Me Do
I Saw Her Standing There	Revolution
Yesterday	Got to Get You into My Life
Twist and Shout	Penny Lane

Mixing Single Notes and Strums

Rhythm guitar includes many more approaches than just simultaneously strumming chords. A piano player doesn't plunk down all her fingers at once every time she plays an accompaniment part, and guitarists shouldn't have to strike all the strings every time they bring their pick down.

In fact, guitarists borrow a technique from their keyboard-plunking counterparts, who separate the left and right hands to play bass notes and chords, respectively. When guitarists separate out the components of a chord, they don't use separate hands, but combine both aspects in their right hand. Playing bass notes with chords is called a *pick-strum* pattern.

The pick-strum

Separating the bass and treble so that they play independently in time is a great way to provide rhythmic variety and introduce different chordal textures. Guitarists can even set up an interplay of the different parts — a bass and treble complementarity or counterpoint.

Boom-chick

The simplest accompaniment pattern is known by the way it sounds: *boom-chick.* The boom-chick pattern is very efficient because you don't have to play all the notes of the chord at once. Typically you play the bass note on the *boom,* and the all the notes in the chord except the bass note on the *chick* — but you get sonic credit for playing twice.

Figure 4-7 (Track 21) shows a boom-chick, or bass-chord, pattern in a bouncy country-rock progression.

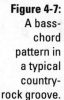

Figure 4-7:
A bass-chord pattern in a typical country-rock groove.

The symbol *C* immediately to the right of the treble clef of Figure 4-7 is a short-hand way to indicate 4/4 time. The examples in this book use *4/4* to indicate music in 4/4 time, but many examples of printed sheet music use *C* to indicate *common*, or 4/4, time.

Separating the bass notes from the treble chord forms can also create a more dynamic and interesting rhythm sound in a straight-ahead rock groove, like Figure 4-8 (Track 22), in a funky, Led Zeppelin-type of feel.

Figure 4-8: The bass-note-and-chord treatment makes things more varied and interesting.

Moving bass line

Another device available to you after you separate the bass from the chord is the moving bass line. Examples of songs with moving bass lines include Neil Young's "Southern Man," Led Zeppelin's "Babe, I'm Gonna Leave You," the Grateful Dead's "Friend of the Devil," and the Nitty Gritty Dirt Band's "Mr. Bojangles." A moving bass line can employ the boom-chick pattern.

Figure 4-9 (Track 23) shows a descending bass line, made more effective by isolating the bass line from the chords. Although this is left-hand movement within a chord form, similar to the shuffle figure in Figure 4-6, you can think of this as new chord forms entirely, if that's conceptually easier for you.

Figure 4-9: A moving bass line over a chord progression.

When a chord symbol features two letters separated by a forward slash, it indicates the chord and the bass note over which that chord sounds. For example, C/G is a C chord with a G in the bass. In this case, the bass note is a chord member (the notes of a C chord are C, E, and G), but it doesn't always have to be that way. In the chord progression C-C/B-C/A, the bass notes B and A are not part of the chord but help to provide motion to another chord.

Disrupting Your Sound: Syncopated Strumming

After you develop a feel for strumming in different combinations of quarters, eighths, and sixteenths, you can increase the rhythmic variation to these various groupings by applying syncopation. *Syncopation* is the disruption or alteration of the expected sounding of notes. In rock and roll right-hand rhythm playing, you do that by staggering your strum and mixing up your up- and downstrokes to strike different parts of the beats. By doing so, you let the vehicles of syncopation — dots and ties — steer your rhythmic strumming to a more driving and interesting course.

Syncopated notation: Dots and ties

A *dot* attached to a note increases its rhythmic value by half its original value. For example, a dot attached to a half note (two beats) makes it three beats long. A dotted quarter note is one and a half beats long, or, a quarter note plus an eighth note. A *tie* is a curved line that connects two notes of the same pitch. The value of the note is the combined values of the two notes together, and only the first note is sounded.

Figure 4-10 shows some common syncopation figures employing dots and ties. The top part of the table deals with dots and shows note values, their new value with a dot and the equivalent expressed in ties, and a typical figure using a dot with that note value. The bottom part of the figure deals with ties and shows note values, their new value when tied to another note, and a typical figure using a tie with that note value.

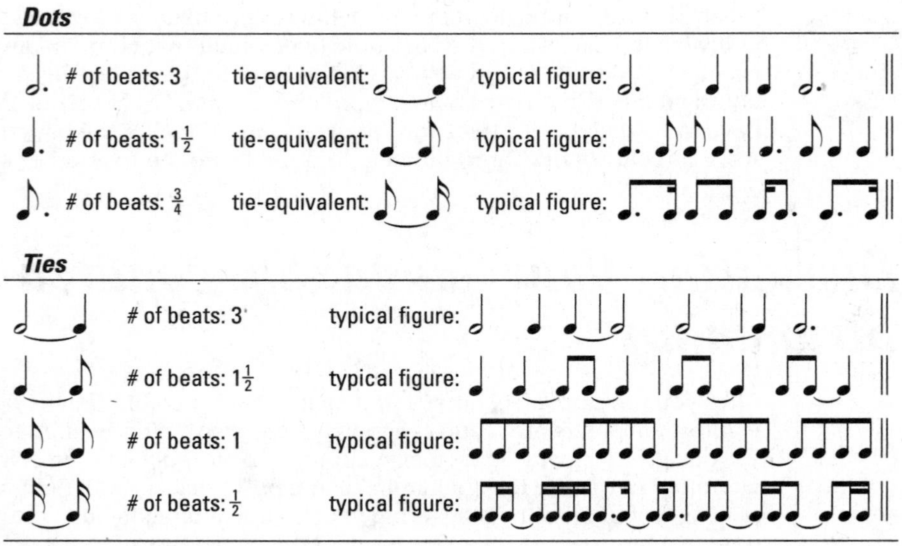

Dots

♩.	# of beats: 3	tie-equivalent:	typical figure:
♩.	# of beats: 1½	tie-equivalent:	typical figure:
♪.	# of beats: ¾	tie-equivalent:	typical figure:

Ties

	# of beats: 3	typical figure:
	# of beats: 1½	typical figure:
	# of beats: 1	typical figure:
	# of beats: ½	typical figure:

Figure 4-10:
Common
syncopation
features.

Playing syncopated figures

So much for the music theory behind syncopation. How do you actually play syncopated figures? Try jumping in and playing two progressions, one using eighth notes and one using sixteenth notes, that employ common syncopation patterns found in rock.

Figure 4-11 (Track 24) shows a useful syncopation scheme for an easy 4/4 rhythm at a moderate tempo. Pay close attention to the downstroke (⊓) and upstroke (∨) indications. Because the normal flow of down- and upstrokes is interrupted in syncopation, it's important to remember which stroke direction to play a note to avoid getting your strums out of sync.

Figure 4-12 (Track 25) uses eighth- as well as sixteenth-note syncopation. It's not particularly difficult to play after you can hear the sound in your head. If it helps, listen to Track 25 first to get the rhythm memorized in your head before attempting to play it on the guitar.

If you're having trouble playing the figures exactly, or you can't quite anticipate where the next strike comes after the dot or tie, try simply saying the rhythm of the figure on the syllable *dah* while tapping your foot or snapping your fingers. The best way to learn a figure is to internalize it and then — and only then — worry about getting your hands to execute what's in your head.

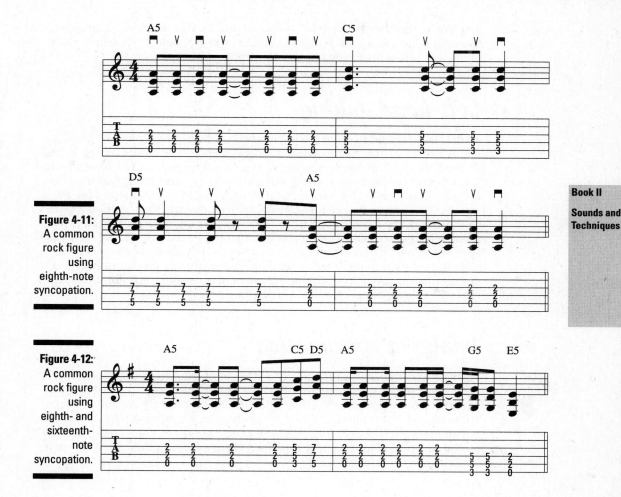

Figure 4-11: A common rock figure using eighth-note syncopation.

Figure 4-12: A common rock figure using eighth- and sixteenth-note syncopation.

Book II

Sounds and Techniques

Giving Your Left Hand a Break

If you listen closely to rhythm guitar in rock songs, you'll hear that strummed figures are not one wall of sound — that minute breaks occur in between the strums. These breaks prevent the chord strums from running into each other and creating sonic mush. The little gaps in sound keep a strumming figure sounding crisp and controlled.

To form these breaks, or slight sonic pauses, you need to stop the strings from ringing momentarily. Talking *very small* moments here — much smaller than those pauses on a greeting card commercial when the daughter realizes she's just like her mother as they sip cocoa and look out the window. Controlling the right hand's gas pedal with the left hand's brake pedal is a useful technique for cutting off the ring-out of the strings.

Left-hand muting

To get the left-hand to mute the in-between sound between any two chords, just relax the fretting fingers enough to release pressure on the fretted strings. These strings will instantly deaden, or muffle, cutting off sound. What's more, if you keep your right-hand going along in the same strumming pattern, you produce a satisfying *thunk* sound as the right hand hits all these deadened strings. This percussive element, intermixed among the ringing notes creates an ideal rock rhythm sound: part percussive, part syncopated, and all driving. If you relax the left hand even further so that it goes limp across all six strings, then no strings will sound, not just the ones the left hand fingers cover. Also, allowing your left-hand to do the muting means you can keep your right hand going, uninterrupted, in alternating down- and upstrokes. The notation indicates a left-hand mute with an *X* note head.

Implying syncopation

Figure 4-13 (Track 26) is technically a straight-ahead, down-and-up eighth-note strum in the right hand. But because you employ left-hand muting, the sound seems to cut off in the just the right places, creating an almost syncopated sound. Your right hand isn't performing true syncopation, because it's playing straight through. It's just that some of the notes don't come through audibly. Left-hand muting provides the guitarist with another means for controlling the strings' sound.

Figure 4-13:
A strum employing left-hand muting to simulate syncopation.

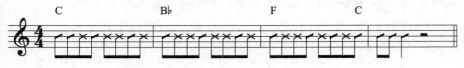

Left-hand muting is one of those rhythm techniques that guitarists just seem to develop naturally, so obvious and useful is its benefit. And like riding a bicycle, left-hand muting is more difficult to execute slowly. So don't analyze it too much as you're learning; just strum and mute in the context of a medium-tempo groove. Your hands will magically sync up, and you won't even have to think about it.

Although left-hand muting belongs to the hand not named in this chapter, its impetus is drawn from right-hand motion. Plus, performing a left-hand mute is impossible without another hand to turn it into sound.

Suppressing the Right Hand

You can also mute with your *right* hand (using the heel of the palm), but this produces a different effect than left-hand muting. In right-hand muting, you still hear the sound of the fretted string, but in a subdued way. You don't use right-hand muting to stop the sound completely, as you do in a left-hand mute; you just want to suppress the string from ringing freely. Like left-hand muting, right-hand muting keeps your tone from experiencing runaway ring-out, but additionally it provides an almost murky, smoldering sound to the notes, which can be quite useful for dramatic effect. You sometimes hear this technique referred to as *chugging*.

Right-hand muting

You perform a right-hand mute by anchoring the heel of your right hand on the strings just above the bridge. Don't place your hand too far forward or you'll completely deaden the strings. Do it just enough so that the strings are dampened (*damping* is a musical term which means to externally stop a string from ringing) slightly, but still ring through. Keep it there through the duration of the strum.

If a *palm mute* (as right-hand muting is known) de-emphasizes a string strike, then its evil twin, the *accent*, draws attention to a string strike. An accent is easy to execute: Just strike the string or strings harder than usual, and lift your right hand palm from the strings as you do, to allow the strings to ring free. The result is that the accented strum stands out above all the rest. An accent is indicated with a > just above or below the note head.

Palm mutes are much easier to perform if only one or two of the strings are struck, due to the restricted movement of the right hand caused by anchoring it to the strings' surface above the bridge. Figure 4-14 (Track 27) is a rhythm figure where you strike only the lowest note of the chord on the palm mutes, and the upper strings on the accents. Strike only the lowest note of the chord when a *P.M.* (palm mute) appears. Play this progression using all downstrokes to add intensity.

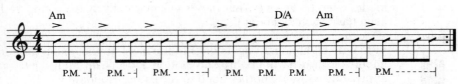

Figure 4-14:
A rhythm
figure
with palm
mutes and
accents.

The interplay between the palm-muted notes and the accented chords creates a sound that makes it seem like two instruments playing.

Left-hand Movement within a Right-hand Strum

When you begin to move the left-hand in conjunction with the right, you uncover an exciting new dimension in rhythm guitar: left-hand movement simultaneous with right-hand rhythm. This "liberating of the left hand" is also the first step in playing single-note riffs and leads on the guitar (see Book IV Chapter 4 for more on the glories of lead guitar).

Figure 4-15 (Track 28) features a classic left-hand figure that fits either a straight-eighth-note groove or a shuffle feel (although it's placed here in a straight-eighth setting). The changing notes in this example are the 5th degrees of each chord, which move briefly to the 6th degree. So in an A chord, the E moves to F♯; in a D chord the A moves to B; and in an E chord the B moves to C♯. You can find this "5-6 move" in songs by Chuck Berry, the Beatles, ZZ Top, and plenty of blues-rock tunes. The 5-6 move fits over any I-IV-V progression. In Figure 4-14 it's in the key of A.

Note that to more easily accommodate the 5-6 move, alternate chords and fingering are supplied to satisfy the A, D, and E chords. In each case the chords use only three strings, all adjacent to each other.

And even though it's in steady eighth notes, this progression should be played using all right-hand downstrokes. If you can throw in some palm muting (as is done on Track 28), so much the better!

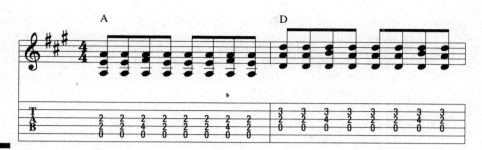

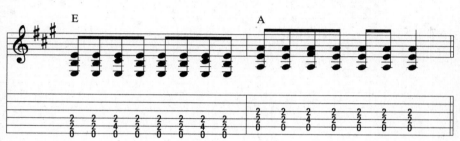

Figure 4-15: An eighth-note 5-6 progression using all down-strokes and a moving left hand.

Giving Your Fingers Some Style

Although more than 99 percent of all rock playing is played with a pick, occasions for fingerstyle do pop up from time to time. *Fingerstyle*, as the name implies, means that you pluck the strings with the right-hand fingertips. For these times you can put the pick down, stick it between your teeth, or tuck it in your palm, whichever allows you to grab it the fastest after the fingerstyle passage is over.

Fingerstyle is especially suited to playing *arpeggios,* or chords played one note at a time in a given pattern. Fingerstyle is a much easier way to play different strings in rapid succession, as you must do for arpeggiated passages. Generally speaking, the thumb plays the bass strings and the fingers play the upper three strings. Think of the opening figure to Kansas's "Dust in the Wind," Fleetwood Mac's "Landslide," or Simon and Garfunkel's "The Boxer," and imagine trying to play those patterns with your pick hopping frantically around the strings.

Position your right hand just above the strings, so your fingers can dangle freely but in reach of the individual strings. In Figure 4-16, the thumb plays the downstem notes and the right-hand fingers play the upper notes. (For you classical guitar aficionados out there: The standard way to notate the right-hand fingers is with the letters *p, i, m,* and *a,* for the Spanish words for the thumb, index, middle and ring fingers — see the chapters in Book VI for much more on classical guitar.)

In the example in Figure 4-16 (Track 29), you don't need to be that careful about which fingers play which strings, so I don't indicate any left-hand fingerings. But a good way to approach is to use the index finger to play the 3rd string, the middle finger to play the 2nd string, and the ring finger to play the 1st string. Work for an even attack in the fingers and a smooth flow between the thumb and the fingers.

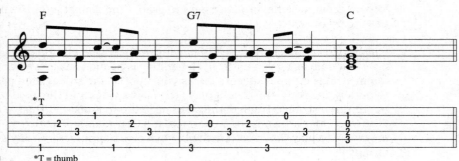

Figure 4-16: Fingerstyle arpeggios played with the right-hand thumb, index, middle, and ring fingers.

*T = thumb

Of course, you don't *have* to play an arpeggiated passage fingerstyle, if it's slow and there's relatively little string skipping involved. But for longer passages, or if the tempo is fairly rapid and the string skipping is relentless, work out the passage as a fingerstyle exercise.

Getting Into Rhythm Styles

To close out this chapter and your study of the right-hand rhythm styles, this section tackles some song-length exercises that illustrate many of the characteristics, both chordal and rhythmic, of standard grooves or feels in rock music.

Rhythm section players often talk to each other in terms of *feel*, and standard terms have developed to describe some of the more common rhythmic accompaniment styles. Table 4-1 provides a list of different feels by their popular name, what time signature they're in, what their characteristics are, and some classic tunes that illustrate that feel.

Table 4-1		Classic Songs in a Variety of Grooves	
Name	**Time Signature**	**Characteristic**	**Tunes**
Straight-four	4/4	Easy, laid-back feel	Tom Petty: "Won't Back Down," Eagles: "New Kid in Town," The Beatles: "Hard Day's Night"
Heavy back-beat	4/4	Like straight-four, but with a heavier back-beat (accent on beats 2 and 4)	Bachman Turner Overdrive: "Taking Care of Business," Bob Seger: "Old Time Rock and Roll," Spencer Davis/Blues Brothers: "Gimme Some Lovin'"
Two-beat	¢ 2/2, or 2/4	jumping boom-chick	Creedence Clearwater Revival: "Bad Moon Rising," The Beatles: "I Feel Fine," Pure Prairie League: "Amie"
16-feel	4/4	Funky or busy accompaniment	James Brown: "I Feel Good," Sam and Dave/Blues Brothers: "Soul Man," Aerosmith: "Walk This Way"
Metal gallop	4/4	Driving sixteenth-note sound like a horse's gallop	Metallica: "Blackened," Led Zeppelin: "The Immigrant Song"

(continued)

Table 4-1 (continued)

Name	Time Signature	Characteristic	Tunes
Shuffle	4/4	Limping lilting eighth notes; swing feel	Fleetwod Mac: "Don't Stop," ZZ Top: "La Grange" and "Tush," The Beatles: "Can't Buy Me Love" and "Revolution"
Three-feel	3/4, 6/8, 12/8	Meter felt in groups of three	The Eagles: "Take It to the Limit," The Beatles: "Norwegian Wood" (6/8) and "You've Got to Hide Your Love Away" (6/8)
Reggae/ska	4/4	Laid-back with syncopation	Eric Clapton: "I Shot the Sheriff," Bob Marley: "No Woman, No Cry," Johnny Nash: "Stir It Up"

Straight-four feel

Figure 4-17 (Track 30) is an easy, laid-back, straight-eighth-note groove in 4/4. It's perfect for songs in the style of The Eagles, Tom Petty, and soft-rock ballads or medium-tempo songs. When you get the rhythm down, try varying the speed of your strum by making the quarter-note strums a little slower and more drawn out than the eighth-note strums. This will give your strings a nice *k-e-r-r-r-a-n-g* sound.

Figure 4-17: A straight-ahead 4/4 groove in the style of The Eagles.

Two-beat feel

Figure 4-18 (Track 31) is in a cut-time, or two-beat, feel using a boom-chick or pick-strum pattern. *Cut time* refers to the time signature, where a vertical line "cuts" the C, the shorthand symbol for 4/4, in half. A two-beat feel features a heavy bass on the first and third beats, and chord fills on beats two and four. Bass runs (single bass notes that connect chords together) are thrown in for some extra left-hand movement.

Book II

Sounds and Techniques

Figure 4-18:
A two-beat country groove with bass runs.

16-feel

The "16" in the title refers to sixteenth notes. In a 16-feel groove, the unit of subdivision is the sixteenth note, and its spirited activity here creates a funky feel (see Figure 4-19 and listen to Track 32). You can play many songs in a 16-feel with the pick-strum approach, where individual bass notes are pitted against chordal figures in a low-high dialog.

Figure 4-19:
A medium tempo funky groove in a 16-feel.

Heavy metal gallop

Heavy metal is an entire subculture in rock music, but it can claim as its own one unique accompaniment figure: the gallop, which is composed of an eighth note followed by two sixteenths, repeated over and over. Figure 4-20 (Track 33) shows a two-bar gallop figure using up- and downstrokes. The palm mutes and accents make this passage sound almost ominous — a desired quality in heavy metal rhythm playing.

Figure 4-20:
A heavy metal gallop using eighths and sixteenths.

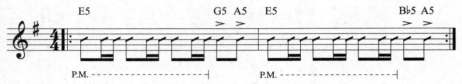

Reggae rhythm

Reggae is a wonderfully laid-back rhythm style that features sparse chordal jabs from the guitar delivered on the offbeat. Reggae can exist either in a straight-eighth or shuffle feel. In Figure 4-21 (Track 34) it's in a medium-slow shuffle. Pay particular attention to the upstroke indications — several of them occur in a row, resulting from the successive offbeat strums.

Figure 4-21:
A typical Reggae backup pattern highlighting the offbeats.

Three feel

A song in a three feel is pretty easy to spot — it's counted in groups of three (not the usual two and four), and you can do the waltz to it. If you played hooky from ballroom dancing lessons as a kid and don't know how to waltz, you can usually hear a strong beat one, followed by the weaker beats two and three. The Eagles' "Take It to the Limit" is in 3/4, and the Beatles' "Norwegian Wood" is in 6/8. Technically, a song in 6/8 is felt in two, because it's separated into two halves each receiving three eighth notes. But in the unfussy world of rock rhythm, anytime a guitarist has to strum in three — whether it's in 3/4 or whether it's in 6/8 or 12/8 (as in some doo-wop-type songs) — he just calls it a "three feel." So "Norwegian Wood" and "House of the Rising Sun," which are in 6/8, and "You Really Got a Hold on Me" and "Nights in White Satin," which are in 12/8, can be described as "three feel" songs. Strum in groups of three or go *boom-chick-chick*, depending on the tempo (it's sometimes easier on faster tempos to go *boom-chick-chick*).

Figure 4-22 (Track 35) is written in 3/4, and features a descending bass line, which is fairly common in songs in three.

Book II

Sounds and Techniques

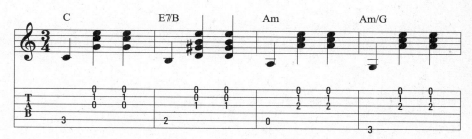

Figure 4-22:
A song in 3/4, featuring a moving bass line.

Chapter 5

Playing Melodies in Position and in Double-Stops

In This Chapter

▶ Practicing single notes in position

▶ Playing songs in position

▶ Playing double-stops up, down, and across the neck

▶ Practicing songs in double-stops

▶ Access the audio tracks and video clips at www.dummies.com/go/guitaraio/

*O*ne of the giveaways of beginning guitar players is that they can play only down the neck, in open position. As you get to know the guitar better, you'll find you can use the whole neck to express your musical ideas. In the first part of this chapter, you venture out of open-position base camp into the higher altitudes of position playing.

The term *double-stop* doesn't refer to going back to the store because you forgot the milk. It's guitar lingo for playing two notes at the same time — something the guitar can do with relative ease but which is impossible on woodwinds. (Actually, guitarists lifted the term from violin playing but quickly made double-stops truly their own.) The second part of this chapter gives you the scoop on how to play double-stops.

Playing Scales and Exercises in Position

As you listen to complicated-sounding guitar music played by virtuoso guitarists, you may imagine their left hands leaping around the fretboard with abandon. But usually, if you watch those guitarists on stage or TV, you discover that their left hands hardly move at all. Those guitarists are playing in position.

Playing in position means that your left hand remains in a fixed location on the neck, with each finger more or less on permanent assignment to a specific fret, and that you fret every note — you don't use any open strings. If you're playing in *5th position,* for example, your 1st finger plays the 5th fret, your 2nd finger plays the 6th fret, your 3rd finger plays the 7th fret, and your 4th finger plays the 8th fret. A *position,* therefore, gets its name from the fret that your 1st finger plays. (What guitarists call *open position* consists of the combination of all the open strings plus the notes in 1st or 2nd position.)

In addition to enabling you to play notes where they feel and sound best on the fingerboard (not just where you can most easily grab available notes, such as the open-string notes in open position), playing in position makes you look cool — like a nonbeginner! Think of it this way: A lay-up and a slam dunk are both worth two points in basketball, but only in the latter case does the announcer scream, "And the crowd goes wild!"

The following sections explain the differences between playing in position and playing with open strings; it also provides plenty of exercises to help you get comfortable with playing in position.

Playing in position versus open strings

Why play in position? Why not use open position and open strings all the time? Two key reasons:

- ✔ **It's easier to play high-note melodies.** Playing in open position allows you to play up to only the 4th or 5th fret. If you want to play higher than that, position playing enables you to play the notes smoothly and economically.

- ✔ **You can instantly transpose any pattern or phrase that you know in position to another key simply by moving your hand to another position.** Because position playing involves no open strings, everything you play in position is *movable.*

People have the idea that playing guitar in lower positions is easier than playing in higher ones. The higher notes actually aren't harder to play; they're just harder to read in standard notation if you don't get too far in a conventional method book (where reading high notes is usually saved for last). But here, you're focusing on guitar playing rather than music reading — so go for the high notes whenever you want.

Playing exercises in position

The major scale — you know, the familiar do-re-me-fa-sol-la-ti-do sound you get by playing the white keys on the piano starting from C (check out Book VII Chapter 1 to get some practice with the major scale) — is a good place to start practicing the skills you need to play in position. Figure 5-1 shows a C major scale in 2nd position. Although you can play this scale in open position, play it as the tab staff in the figure indicates, because you want to start practicing your position playing. If you're unfamiliar with playing scales, play along to Video Clip 12.

Figure 5-1:
A one-octave C-major scale in 2nd position.

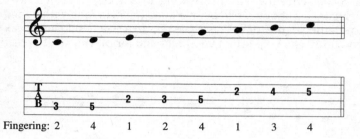

Fingering: 2   4   1   2   4   1   3   4

Book II

Sounds and Techniques

The most important thing about playing in position is the location of your left hand — in particular, the position and placement of the fingers of your left hand. The following list contains tips for positioning your left hand and fingers:

- ✔ **Keep your fingers over the appropriate frets the entire time you're playing.** Because you're in 2nd position for this scale, keep your 1st finger over the 2nd fret, your 2nd finger over the 3rd fret, your 3rd finger over the 4th fret, and your 4th finger over the 5th fret at all times — even if they're not fretting any notes at the moment.

- ✔ **Keep all your fingers close to the fretboard, ready to play.** At first, your fingers may exhibit a tendency to straighten out and rise away from the fretboard. This tendency is natural, so work to keep them curled and to hold them down near the frets where they belong for the position.

- ✔ **Relax!** Although you may think you need to intensely focus all your energy on performing this maneuver correctly or positioning that finger just so, you don't. What you're actually working toward is simply adopting the most natural and relaxed approach to playing the guitar. (You may not think it all that natural right now, but eventually, you'll catch the drift. Honest!) So take things easy, but remain aware of your movements. Is your left shoulder riding up like Quasimodo's? Check it periodically to make sure it stays tension-free. And be sure to take frequent deep breaths, especially if you feel yourself tightening up.

Notice that the score in Figure 5-1 indicates left-hand fingerings under the tab numbers. These indicators aren't essential because the position itself dictates these fingerings. But if you want, you can read the finger numbers (instead of the tab numbers) and play the C scale that way (keeping an eye on the tab staff to check which string you're on). Then, if you memorize the fingerings, you have a *movable pattern* that enables you to play a major scale from any starting note.

Play the *one-octave scale* (one having a range of only eight notes) shown in Figure 5-1 by using both down- and upstrokes — that is, by using alternate (down and up) picking. Try it descending as well. You should practice all scales ascending and descending.

After you practice the one-octave scale for a while, you can move to the next level. Figure 5-2 shows a two-octave C-major scale (one with a range of 15 notes) in the 7th position. This scale requires you to play on all six strings. Video Clip 13 can help orient your left hand for playing in 7th position.

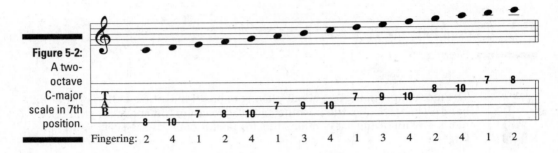

Figure 5-2: A two-octave C-major scale in 7th position.

Fingering: 2 4 1 2 4 1 3 4 1 3 4 2 4 1 2

To help you remember to hold your fingers over the appropriate frets all the time (even if they're not playing at the moment) and keep your fingers close to the fretboard, remember this: Keep your friends close, your enemies closer, and your frets even closer.

Practice playing the scale shown in Figure 5-2 up and down the neck, using alternate picking. If you memorize the fingering pattern (shown under the tab numbers), you can play any major scale simply by moving your hand up or down to a different position. Try it. And then challenge the nearest piano player to a *transposing* (key-changing) contest, using the major scale.

Play scales slowly at first to ensure that your notes sound clean and smooth, and then gradually increase your speed.

Shifting positions

Music isn't so simple that you can play it all in one position, and life would be pretty static if you could. In real-world situations, you must often play an uninterrupted passage that takes you through different positions. To do so successfully, you need to master the *position shift* like an old politician.

Andrés Segovia, legend of the classical guitar, devised fingerings for all 12 major and minor scales. Figure 5-3 shows how Segovia played the two-octave C-major scale. It differs from the two scales in the preceding section in that it requires a position shift in the middle of the scale. Watch and listen to Video Clip 14 to hear the imperceptible movement of the right hand during the shift.

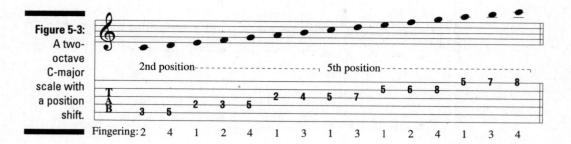

Figure 5-3: A two-octave C-major scale with a position shift.

Book II

Sounds and Techniques

Play the first seven notes in 2nd position and then shift up to 5th position by smoothly gliding your 1st finger up to the 5th fret (3rd string). As you play the scale downward, play the first eight notes in 5th position, and then shift to 2nd position by smoothly gliding your 3rd finger down to the 4th fret (3rd string). The important thing is that the position shift sound seamless. Someone listening shouldn't be able to tell that you shift positions. The trick is in the smooth gliding of the 1st (while ascending) or 3rd (while descending) finger.

You must practice this smooth glide to make it sound uninterrupted and seamless. Isolate just the two notes involved (3rd string, 4th fret, and 3rd string, 5th fret) and play them over and over as shown in the scale until you can make them sound as if you're making no position shift at all.

Creating your own exercises to build strength and dexterity

Some people do all sorts of exercises to develop their position playing. They buy books that contain nothing but position-playing exercises. Some of these books aim to develop sight-reading skills, and others aim to develop left-hand finger strength and dexterity. But you don't really need such books. You can make up your own exercises to build finger strength and dexterity. (And sight reading doesn't concern you now anyway, because you're reading tab numbers.)

To create your own exercises, just take the two-octave major scale shown in Figure 5-2 and number the 15 notes of the scale as 1 through 15. Then make up a few simple mathematical combinations that you can practice playing. Following are some examples:

- 1-2-3-1, 2-3-4-2, 3-4-5-3, 4-5-6-4, and so on. (See Figure 5-4a.)
- 1-3-2-4, 3-5-4-6, 5-7-6-8, 7-9-8-10, and so on. (See Figure 5-4b.)
- 15-14-13, 14-13-12, 13-12-11, 12-11-10, and so on. (See Figure 5-4c.)

Figure 5-4 (Track 36) shows how these numbers look in music and tab. Remember, these are suggested patterns to memorize and help build dexterity.

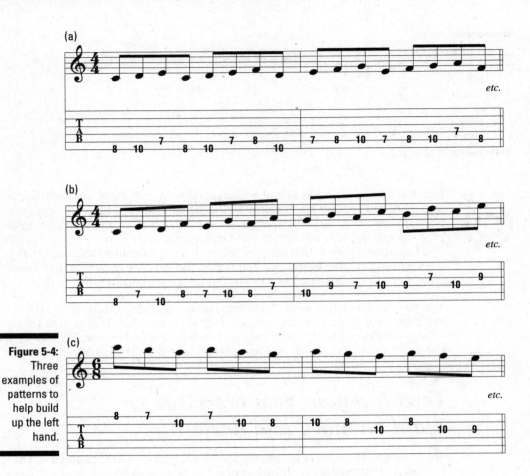

Figure 5-4: Three examples of patterns to help build up the left hand.

You get the idea. You can make up literally hundreds of permutations and practice them endlessly — or until you get bored. Piano students have a book called *Hanon* that contains lots of scale permutations to help develop strength and independence of the fingers. You can check out that book for permutation ideas, but making up your own is probably just as easy.

Practicing Songs in Position

Certain keys fall comfortably into certain positions on the guitar. Songs are based in keys, so if you play a song in a particular key, the song will also fall comfortably into a certain position. Rock, jazz, blues, and country lead playing all demand certain positions in order to render an authentic sound.

Telling you that the melody of a song sounds best if you play it in one position rather than another may seem a bit arbitrary to you. But it's just a fact that playing a Chuck Berry lick in A is almost impossible in anything *but* 5th position. Country licks that you play in A, on the other hand, fall most comfortably in 2nd position, and trying to play them anywhere else is just making things hard on yourself.

That's one of the great things about the guitar: The best position for a certain style not only sounds best to your ears, but also feels best to your hands. And that's what makes playing the guitar so much fun.

Play the following songs by reading the tab numbers and listening to the audio tracks; notice how cool playing up the neck feels instead of playing way down in open position, where those beginners play.

Whenever you're playing in position, be sure to keep your left hand in a fixed position, perpendicular to the neck, with your 1st finger at a given fret and the other fingers following in order, one per fret. Hold the fingers over the appropriate frets, very close to the fretboard, even if they're not fretting notes at the moment. You can hear these two songs on Tracks 37 and 38:

Book II

Sounds and Techniques

- ✔ **Simple Gifts (Track 37):** To play this song, you need to know how to play in 4th position (see the section "Playing Scales and Exercises in Position," earlier in this chapter) and what *'tis* and *'twill* mean.

  This song is in the key of A, making 4th position ideal, because you find all the notes between the 4th and 7th frets. Because you play no open strings in this song, memorize the fingering and then try playing the same melody in other positions and keys. The fingering is the same in every position, even though the tab numbers change. Go on — try it.

- ✔ **Turkey in the Straw (Track 38):** To play this song, you need to know how to play in 7th position (see the section "Playing Scales and Exercises in Position," earlier in this chapter) and what saying "day-day to the wagon tongue" means.

  When you play this song, note that the key of G sits nicely in 7th position (with the notes of the song all falling between the 7th and 10th frets). As with "Simple Gifts" (or any song played without open strings), if you memorize the fingering pattern, you can transpose the song to different keys by moving the pattern to a higher or lower starting fret.

Simple Gifts

Turkey in the Straw

As___ I was a - go - ing on___ down the road with a

Fingering: 1 4 2 2 4 2 1 3 4 1 1 1 2 4

ti - red team___ and a heav - y load, I___ cracked my___ whip___ and the

1 1 1 4 2 4 1 4 4 1 2 2 4 2 1 3 4

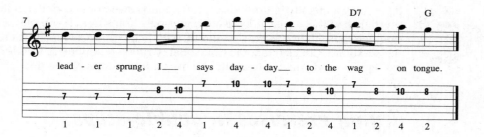

lead - er sprung, I___ says day - day___ to the wag - on tongue.

1 1 1 2 4 1 4 4 1 2 4 1 2 4 2

Book II

Sounds and Techniques

Double-Stop Basics

You experience the guitar's capability to play more than one note simultaneously as you strum a chord, but you can also play more than one note in a melodic context. Playing double-stops is a great way to play in harmony with yourself. So adept is the guitar at playing double-stops, in fact, that some musical forms — such as '50s rock and roll, country, and Mariachi music (you know, the music that Mexican street bands play) — use double-stops as a hallmark of their styles.

The following sections define double-stops and help you get comfortable with them by providing a few exercises.

Defining double-stops

A *double-stop* is nothing more than two notes that you play at the same time. It falls somewhere between a single note (one note) and a chord (three or more notes). You can play a double-stop on adjacent strings or on nonadjacent strings (by skipping strings). The examples and songs in this chapter, however, involve only adjacent-string double-stops, because they're the easiest to play.

If you play a melody in double-stops, it sounds sweeter and richer, fuller and prettier than if you play it by using only single notes. And if you play a *riff* in double-stops, it sounds gutsier and thicker — the double-stops just create a bigger sound. Check out some Chuck Berry riffs — "Johnny B. Goode," for example — and you can hear that he uses double-stops all the time.

Trying exercises in double-stops

You can play double-stops in two general ways: by using only *one* pair of strings (the first two strings, for example) — moving the double-stops up and down the neck — or in one area of the neck by using *different* string pairs and moving the double-stops across the neck (first playing the 5th and 4th strings, for example, and then the 4th and 3rd, and so on).

Playing double-stops up and down the neck

Start with a C-major scale that you play in double-stop *3rds* (notes that are two letter names apart, such as C-E, D-F, and so on), exclusively on the first two strings, moving up the neck. This type of double-stop pattern appears in Figure 5-5 (Track 39). The left-hand fingering doesn't appear below the tab numbers in this score, but that's not difficult to figure out. Start with your 1st finger for the first double-stop. (You need only one finger to fret this first double-stop because the 1st string is open.) Then, for all the other double-stops in the scale, use fingers 1 and 3 if the notes are two frets apart (the second and third double-stops, for example) and use fingers 1 and 2 if the notes are one fret apart (the fourth and fifth double-stops, for example). With your right hand, strike only the 1st and 2nd strings.

View Video Clip 15 to see the ascending motion of the left hand and the correct fingerings. You can hear it too on Track 39, time marker 0:00.

Book II

Sounds and Techniques

Figure 5-5:
A C major scale in double-stops on one pair of strings.

Playing double-stops across the neck

Playing double-stops across the neck is probably more common than playing up and down the neck on a string pair. Figure 5-6 (Track 39, time marker 0:11) shows a C-major scale that you play in 3rds in open position, moving across the neck; Video Clip 16 shows you how it's done. Again, the example doesn't show the fingerings for each double-stop, but you can use fingers 1 and 2 if the notes are one fret apart (the first double-stop, for example) and fingers 1 and 3 if the notes are two frets apart (the second double-stop).

Figure 5-6:
A C-major scale in double-stops moving across the neck.

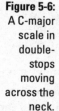

What's especially common in rock and blues songs is playing double-stops across the neck where the two notes that make up the double-stop are on the same fret (which you play as a two-string barre). Check out the chapters in Books IV and V for more info on rock and blues.

To hear double-stops in action, listen to the opening of Jimmy Buffett's "Margaritaville," Leo Kottke's version of the Allman Brothers' "Little Martha," Van Morrison's "Brown Eyed Girl," Chuck Berry's "Johnny B. Goode," the intros to Simon and Garfunkel's "Homeward Bound" and "Bookends," and the intro to Jason Mraz's "I Won't Give Up."

Playing Songs in Double-Stops

Double-stops can make your playing sound very cool (as when Chuck Berry rocks out on "Johnny B. Goode"), or they can make your melodic passages sound extra sweet (as when two singers harmonize with each other). In the songs that follow, you get to sound both cool ("Double-Stop Rock") and sweet ("Aura Lee" and "The Streets of Laredo").

To keep things nice and easy, all the double-stops are on adjacent strings (no muting of "in between" strings necessary). And here's a tip to make things especially easy: When the two notes of a double-stop fall on the same fret (which happens a lot in the Chuck Berry–inspired "Double-Stop Rock"), play them as a small barre (with a single finger). You can listen to these songs on Tracks 40–42:

- **Aura Lee (Track 40):** To play this song — made famous by Elvis Presley as "Love Me Tender" — you need to know how to play double-stops up and down the neck on the 1st and 2nd strings (see the aptly titled section "Playing double-stops up and down the neck," earlier in this chapter) and how to gyrate your pelvis while raising one side of your upper lip.

    You play this arrangement of "Aura Lee" exclusively on the first two strings, moving up and down the neck. The two notes of the double-stop sometimes move in the same direction and sometimes in opposite directions. Other times, one of the notes moves up or down while the other remains stationary. Mixing directions makes an arrangement more interesting.

    Notice that the left-hand fingerings appear under the tab numbers. If the same finger plays successive notes but at different frets, a slanted line indicates the position shift (as in measures 5 and 9). For your right-hand picking, use all downstrokes. Remember to repeat the first four bars (as the repeat signs around them indicate) before continuing to bar 5.

↙ **The Streets of Laredo (Track 41):** To play this song, you need to know how to play double-stops across the neck (see the section "Playing double-stops across the neck," earlier in this chapter) and how to sound light-hearted while playing a song about a conversation with a corpse.

In this arrangement, you play double-stops across the strings, near the bottom of the neck. The double-stops give the song a sweet, pretty sound — just the thing for a tête-à-tête between a passerby and a mummified cowboy. The tab doesn't indicate fingering, but you can use fingers 1 and 2 for double-stops that are one fret apart and 1 and 3 for double-stops two frets apart. For right-hand picking, use all downstrokes.

↙ **Double-Stop Rock (Track 42):** To play this song, you don't have to know how to do the "duck walk," but you do have to be able to play double-stops with a Chuck Berry rock and roll attitude.

In this arrangement, you play double-stops across the neck, mostly in 5th position (see the section "Playing double-stops across the neck," earlier in this chapter). Using only three one-measure phrases, repeated at various times, you play a 12-bar blues in the key of A (see Book V Chapter 3 for more on the 12-bar blues). Note that the fingering for the phrase played against the E7 chord (measure 9) is the same as that of the phrase played against the D7 chord (measure 5); in fact, the two phrases are the same, albeit two frets apart.

Book II

Sounds and Techniques

Aura Lee

The Streets of Laredo

Double-Stop Rock

Book III

Getting to Know Guitar Theory

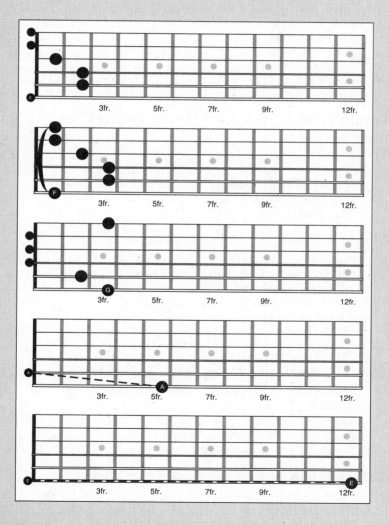

Check out a free online article about putting guitar theory into practice at www. dummies.com/extras/guitaraio.

Contents at a Glance

Chapter 1: Navigating the Fretboard and Building Triads **165**

Tracing Back to Strings 6 and 5 166
Tracking Notes and Playing Octaves 172
Measuring the Space between Pitches with Intervals................................176
Harmonizing the Major Scale to Build Triads and Chords.........................182
The Seven Triads of the Major Scale 186
Playing the Chord Sequence of the Major Scale 187

Chapter 2: Getting to Know the CAGED System **189**

Chord Inversions and Chord Voicings...190
Using the C Form..191
Using the A Form..198
Using the G Form..201
Using the E Form..202
Using the D Form..205
Playing Minor CAGED Forms 207

**Chapter 3: Playing Snazzier Chords with Chord Tones
and Extensions** **211**

About Chord Tones and Extensions..211
Adding 7ths to the Major Scale Chords 213
Working with 2nds and 9ths...221
Working with 4ths and 11ths..225
Playing 6th Chords and Blues Shuffles 226

Chapter 4: Playing Chord Progressions by Numbers.............**229**

Drawing Chord Progressions from the Major Scale....................................230
Using Roman Numerals to Represent Chords 230
Visualizing Numbers on the Fretboard...231
Transposing to New Keys 232
Playing Common Chord Progressions...233
Starting Numbers on the 5th String 236
Playing Chord Progressions with Open Chords..239

Chapter 5: Identifying Tonics, Keys, and Modes **241**

Understanding the Relationship between Major and Minor Scales.............242
Numbering the Relative Minor 243
Identifying the Modes of the Major Scale..248
Key Signatures and Common Discrepancies..265
Comparing Scale Formulas and Structures 268

Chapter 6: Dominant Function and Voice Leading...............**271**

Chord Function and the Dominant Chord...271
Secondary Dominants...275
Voice Leading...280

Chapter 1

Navigating the Fretboard and Building Triads

In This Chapter

▶ Memorizing notes on strings 6 and 5

▶ Getting familiar with whole steps, half steps, sharps, and flats

▶ Using octave shapes and playing intervals

▶ Building a triad and chord on each major scale degree

▶ Access the audio tracks and video clips at www.dummies.com/go/guitaraio/

*B*elieve it or not, mastering the guitar fretboard doesn't require you to memorize every single note on it. Guitar players may play notes all over the neck, but they usually navigate by using shapes and patterns based mainly on the notes on strings 6 and 5.

In the first part of this chapter, you get to know the natural notes along strings 6 and 5 and then use them to track everything else you play on the fretboard with octaves. You see the difference between a half step and a whole step and find out how to fill in the gaps between natural notes with flats and sharps. Finally, you explore intervals and octaves and discover which songs can help you use them. Armed with all that, you can begin to make your way around the guitar neck like a pro and set yourself up for mastering the chord shapes and scale patterns covered in the rest of this book.

Listen to Track 43 to hear notes, steps, octaves, and intervals.

In the second half of this chapter, you get started with basic chord construction by stacking the major scale in 3rds to form triads and then playing the notes of these triads simultaneously to sound chords. The basic chords you form here are the platforms on which other types of chords are built in Book III Chapters 2 and 3. The sequence of major and minor chords that the major scale produces — one of the most important patterns in all of music — is used, among other things, to play chord progressions and chart chord changes (which you begin to explore in Book III Chapter 4).

Listen to Track 44 for some examples of what you encounter in this chapter, including chord construction, triads, chords, and the harmonized major scale.

This chapter builds on the basic chord info covered in Book II Chapters 1 and 2. If you need a refresher, you may want to refer back to those chapters.

Tracing Back to Strings 6 and 5

Guitar players use the notes on strings 6 and 5 (the low E string and the A string) to track other notes on other strings, so the first thing to do memorize the natural notes on strings 6 and 5. The *natural notes* are the letters A through G without any flat or sharp signs next to them. Figure 1-1 shows the natural notes on the 6th string between the open position and the 12th fret.

Figure 1-1: The notes on the 6th string.

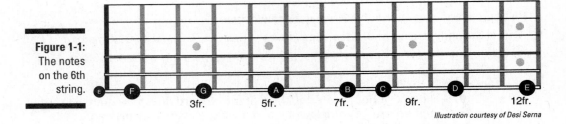

Illustration courtesy of Desi Serna

You may already be familiar with some of these notes because they're used so frequently, especially as *roots* (the primary pitch from which a chord gets its letter name) to common chords. For example, the open 6th string is E, and it serves as the root of all open E chords, including E and E minor. To help you keep track of these natural notes, consider the following five key points as you look at the group of fretboard diagrams in Figure 1-2:

- ✔ The open 6th string is E and the root of an E chord.
- ✔ The 1st fret is F and the root of an F chord.
- ✔ The 3rd fret is G and the root of a G chord.
- ✔ The 5th fret is A, matching the 5th string open, used for relative tuning.
- ✔ The 12th fret is E, an octave higher than the same string open (specially marked by two inlays or dots on the fretboard on most guitars).

Instead of looking at the fretboard empty and trying to remember its notes, connect the notes to something familiar, like common chord shapes and other strings. Try playing through the five notes in the preceding list forward and backward, reviewing the associations laid out for you. Call out the notes as you play them to further cement them into your memory.

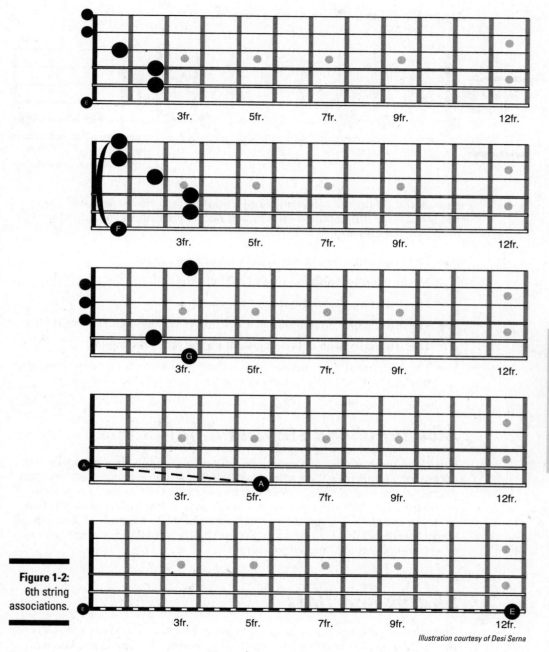

Book III

Getting to Know Guitar Theory

Figure 1-2:
6th string associations.

Illustration courtesy of Desi Serna

Figure 1-3 shows the natural notes on the 5th string.

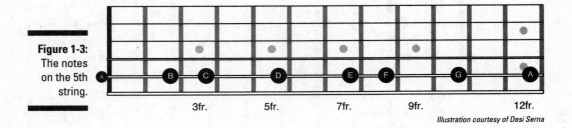

Illustration courtesy of Desi Serna

Figure 1-3:
The notes on the 5th string.

3fr.   5fr.   7fr.   9fr.   12fr.

Just as you do for the 6th string notes, you can associate the notes along the 5th string with common chords and another string, as explained in the following list and shown in Figure 1-4:

- The open 5th string is A and the root of an A chord.
- The 2nd fret is B and the root of a B7 chord.
- The 3rd fret is C and the root of a C chord.
- The 5th fret is D, matching the 4th string open, used for relative tuning.
- The 7th fret is E, an octave higher than the 6th string open.
- The 12th fret is A, an octave higher than the same string open (specially marked by two inlays or dots on the fretboard on most guitars).

Moving whole steps and half steps

Musicians measure the distance between *pitches* (sound frequencies or notes) with intervals called whole and half steps. The distance between one pitch and the next is called a *half step* or *semitone*. On a guitar, a half step is one fret. Two half steps make up a *whole step* or *whole tone,* which is two frets. For example, E-F and B-C are half steps, and F-G-A-B and D-C-E are whole steps. These pitches are always separated by these distances, regardless of where you play them on the fretboard.

Sharps and flats

The pitches between the natural notes are called flats and sharps. A *flat* is one half step lower than its corresponding natural note and is marked with the musical symbol ♭. A *sharp* is a half step higher and is marked with the symbol ♯.

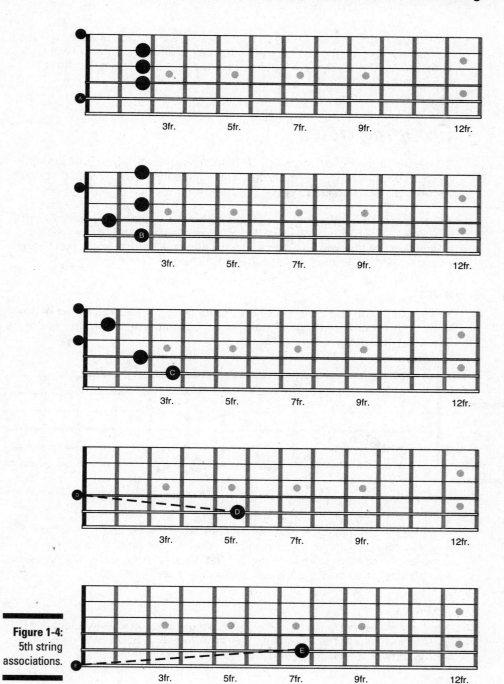

Figure 1-4:
5th string
associations.

Illustration courtesy of Desi Serna

Book III

Getting to Know Guitar Theory

For example, the pitch in between F and G on the 6th string is either F♯, meaning one half step higher than F, or G♭, meaning one half step lower than G. F♯ and G♭ are *enharmonic*, meaning they're two different note names with the same pitch.

Grouping notes

To memorize the remaining notes on both strings, think of the notes in groups. Grouping notes together helps you remember string areas that don't connect easily to a common open chord or open string.

As you review the note groups covered here, take a moment to rehearse all the notes in each group, playing through them forward and backward and calling them out as you go. After you have all these natural notes memorized, you can easily fill in the gaps with flats and sharps.

A-B-C

To start, take the first three notes on the 5th string: A-B-C. You can play this same group of notes with the same spacing beginning at the 5th fret of the 6th string, as shown in Figure 1-5.

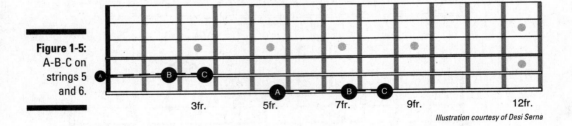

Figure 1-5: A-B-C on strings 5 and 6.

Illustration courtesy of Desi Serna

Wherever you find an A, B is always a whole step higher, and B and C are always a half step apart. If you memorize these notes on the 5th string between the open position and the 3rd fret, then you also know the notes on the 6th string between the 5th and 8th frets — they're the same!

C-D-E

Similarly, you can group the notes C-D-E. These notes are always separated by whole steps. On the 5th string, they're at frets 3, 5, and 7, and on the 6th string, they're at frets 8, 10, and 12 (see Figure 1-6).

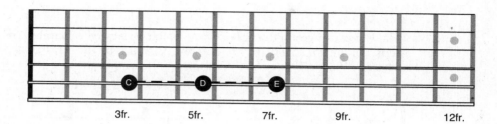

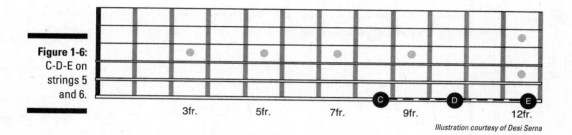

Figure 1-6:
C-D-E on
strings 5
and 6.

Illustration courtesy of Desi Serna

Whenever you're on a C, you can reach up a whole step to D and another whole step to E. Likewise, whenever you're on an E, you can reach *down* a whole step to D and another whole step to C.

E-F-G

You can also group the notes E-F-G on the 6th and 5th strings, as shown in Figure 1-7. On the 6th string, these notes are between the open position and the 3rd fret; on the 5th string, they're between the 7th and 10th frets.

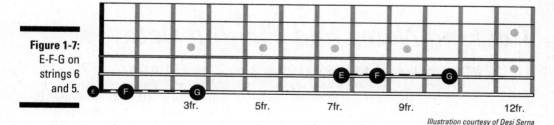

Figure 1-7:
E-F-G on
strings 6
and 5.

Illustration courtesy of Desi Serna

Wherever you find an E, F is always a half step higher, and F and G are always a whole step apart.

Book III

Getting to Know Guitar Theory

F-G-A

Finally, you can group the notes F-G-A, which are always separated by whole steps. On the 6th string, they're at frets 1, 3, and 5; on the 5th string, they're at frets 8, 10, and 12 (see Figure 1-8).

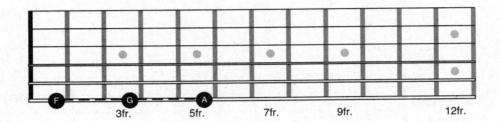

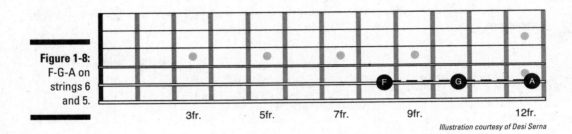

Figure 1-8:
F-G-A on strings 6 and 5.

Illustration courtesy of Desi Serna

Whenever your 1st finger is on F, you can reach up a whole step to G and another whole step to A. Similarly, whenever your 4th finger is on A, you can reach *down* a whole step to G and another whole step to F.

Tracking Notes and Playing Octaves

You can use the notes along strings 6 and 5, covered in the preceding section, to track any note anywhere on the fretboard. How? With octave shapes. An *octave* is the distance between one pitch and another with half or double its frequency. In other words, it's a higher or lower version of the same pitch. You can also think of an octave as the same pitch in a different *register*. Octave pitches are also called *unison pitches*. On the guitar fretboard, octaves follow certain spacings or shapes that you finger in different ways.

In music, the word *unison* can refer to two identical pitches being sounded by separate or different instruments, including voices. For example, two guitar players both playing their 6th strings open produce unison pitches. Unison can also refer to pitches that are the same but separated by an octave or more. For example, one guitarist playing the 6th string open and another playing the 1st string open, both E, produce unison pitches.

Shaping octaves with your 1st finger on strings 6 and 5

The first octave shape you need to know stems off of strings 6 and 5. Place your 1st finger somewhere on the 6th or 5th string and use another finger to reach over two strings and up two frets: You now have the same note an octave higher. Figure 1-9 shows what this octave shape looks like. Notice that you can also play octaves of the open strings.

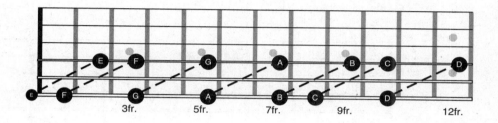

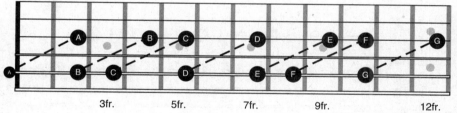

Figure 1-9: Octaves on strings 6 and 5.

Illustration courtesy of Desi Serna

Book III

Getting to Know Guitar Theory

You can finger these octave shapes with either your 1st and 3rd fingers or your 1st and 4th fingers — whichever is more comfortable. Guitar players usually opt to strum octave shapes on strings 6 and 5 by using a pick and leaning their fretting fingers back to touch (but not fret) other strings to prevent them from ringing. This technique creates a raking sound from the muted strings. In fact, jazz guitar legend Wes Montgomery was famous for playing melodies and solos by using octave shapes in this fashion, opting to strum across the strings with the pad of his right thumb for a soft, mellow sound. You hear this technique in his song "Bumpin' on Sunset." Jimi Hendrix strummed the same kind of octave shapes with a pick, using distortion, for his songs "Fire" and "Third Stone from the Sun."

For a demonstration on playing octave shapes, watch Video Clip 17.

If you need to identify a note on string 4 or 3, use octave shapes to trace it back to the notes you have memorized on strings 6 and 5.

Octaves starting on strings 4 and 3

You can play octave shapes with your 1st finger on string 4 or 3 and the octaves on string 2 or 1, although the shapes are slightly different than they are on strings 6 and 5. With the way the 2nd string is tuned (one half step lower), you need to move over two strings and up *three* frets to reach the octave (see Figure 1-10).

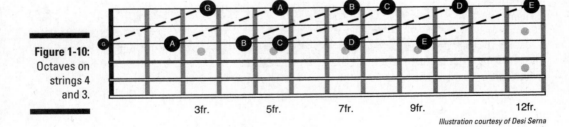

Figure 1-10: Octaves on strings 4 and 3.

Illustration courtesy of Desi Serna

If you have to identify a note on string 2 or 1, use octave shapes to trace it back to strings 4 and 3 and then again to strings 6 and 5. However, keep in mind that the 1st string is E, just as the 6th string is E, and the positions of all the notes on both strings are the same.

Octaves that are three strings apart

Another octave shape that's less common but still good to know reaches over three strings and in the direction opposite the previous shape's direction. You can play these octaves by placing your 1st finger on either string 1 or 2 and then reaching over to either string 4 or 5 with either your 3rd or 4th finger, as shown in Figure 1-11. Notice that you can also use the open strings.

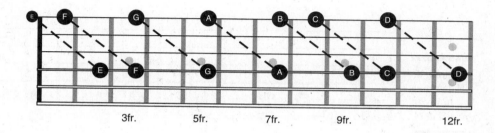

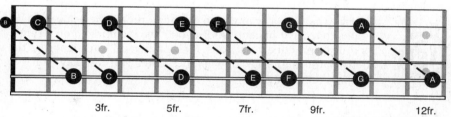

Figure 1-11: Octaves that are three strings apart.

Illustration courtesy of Desi Serna

Book III

Getting to Know Guitar Theory

Repeating octaves beyond the 12th fret

The preceding sections cover notes between the open strings and the 12th fret, but what about the fretboard area beyond that? Fortunately, everything — including notes and spacing — repeats at the 12th fret. Just as strings 6 and 5 open are E and A, the same strings are E and A at the 12th fret. Just as the first inlay marker past the open 6th string is G, the first marker past the 12th fret is also G. As you can see in Figure 1-12, the guitar neck between 0 and 12 is identical to the neck between 12 and 24, though your guitar may not have a full 24 frets. Note the fret numbers indicated below the neck diagrams.

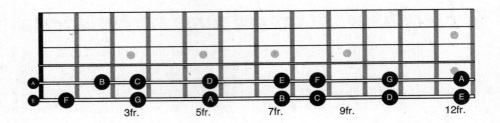

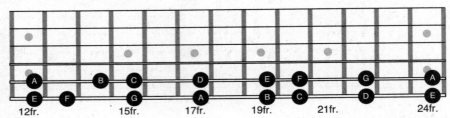

Figure 1-12:
Notes open
to 12 and
from 12 to 24.

Illustration courtesy of Desi Serna

After you can identify any note on the fretboard by using various octave shapes to trace it back to a note you have memorized on string 6 or string 5, it's time to practice your skills. Pick a note and track it across the whole fretboard. For example, see how many E notes you can play.

Measuring the Space between Pitches with Intervals

Just as builders use measurements to identify distances between points, guitarists use *intervals* to identify distances between pitches. You use intervals to build scales and chords and to describe musical movement.

The tape measure used in music is called the *major scale*. The major scale has seven pitches that are separated by a series of intervals known as *whole* and *half steps*. Here's what the major scale formula looks like:

W-W-H-W-W-W-H

The Ws represent whole steps, and the Hs represent half steps. Starting on any note, you can follow this basic step formula to produce the major scale. Figure 1-13 shows what the major scale looks like when you start on G.

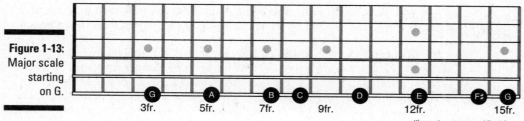

Figure 1-13:
Major scale
starting
on G.

Illustration courtesy of Desi Serna

Note: Before you can look at each interval individually, analyze its steps, and explore how it looks on the fretboard, you need to see the major scale in different positions (see Figure 1-14). You don't have to memorize these scale patterns now; they just provide a visual reference for the rest of this section.

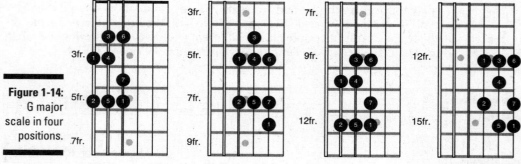

Figure 1-14:
G major
scale in four
positions.

Illustration courtesy of Desi Serna

Book III

**Getting to
Know
Guitar
Theory**

Playing intervals 1 through 7

The distance from the 1st to the 2nd scale degrees in the major scale is called a *second interval,* from the 1st to the 3rd is called a *third,* from the 1st to the 4th is called a *fourth,* and so on. Here's what makes up each interval:

- **2nd:** A whole step above the 1st scale degree.

- **3rd:** Two whole steps or over a string and back one fret.

- **4th:** Two and a half steps or over one string.

- **5th:** Three and a half steps or over a string and up two frets.

- **6th:** Four and a half steps or over two strings and back one fret. (The same note is also over one string and up two whole steps.)

- **7th:** Five and a half steps or over two strings and up one fret. (A 7th is one half step shy of an octave.)

When you move from string 3 to 2 to play an interval, you need to move up an extra fret because the 2nd string is tuned a half step lower than the others.

A 3rd is normally over a string and back one fret, but when moving from string 3 to 2, a 3rd is over a string and in the very same fret. Normally a 4th is over one string, but it's up one fret from string 3 to 2. You see this earlier in the section on octaves where you have to reach up an extra fret between strings 4 and 2 and 3 and 1. Moving from the 6th string to the 1st, everything changes at the 2nd string, and an extra fret is needed. Because the 1st string is tuned to the 2nd string in the same manner that strings 6 to 3 are tuned, intervals between them are normal.

3rds

Guitarists often play *harmonic intervals,* which are really just intervals you play together to create harmony. *Thirds* are a common harmonic interval.

To play thirds, play the 1st and 3rd scale degrees simultaneously and then ascend or descend the scale in groups of two with the notes always 3 scale degrees apart. You can do this in five different positions by following the tab in Figure 1-15. You can also hear and see this example in Video Clip 18.

Figure 1-15: Harmonic 3rds in G.

Illustration courtesy of Desi Serna

Figure 1-15 and Video Clip 18 show just five examples in the G major scale. You can play in 3rds in other keys by starting at a different fret and using the same interval shapes. For example, start on A at the 5th fret of the 6th string to play 3rds in the A major scale.

Many songs feature guitar parts played in 3rds. One of the best examples is the opening to "Brown Eyed Girl" by Van Morrison. The guitar plays the G major scale in 3rds over the G chord and the C major scale in 3rds over the C chord.

6ths (or inverted 3rds)

Sometimes guitarists invert 3rds by moving the 1st degree up an octave. What was 1-3 becomes 3-1. The interval is inverted, get it? For example, G-B would become B-G. Figure 1-16 shows examples of inverting the 3rd G-B.

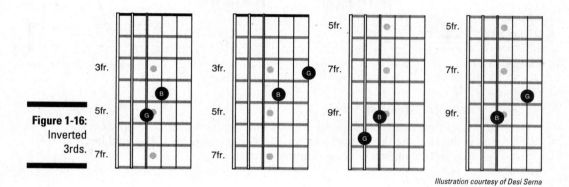

Illustration courtesy of Desi Serna

Figure 1-16:
Inverted
3rds.

With intervals, you always count from the note in the lowest position to the note in the highest position. Thus, inverted 3rds are more commonly called *6ths*. G to B is 3 scale degrees (G-A-B, *one-two-three*), so the interval is called a 3rd. B to G, on the other hand, is 6 scale degrees (B-C-D-E-F♯-G, *one-two-three-four-five-six*), so it's called a 6th.

You can play through the whole scale in 6ths in two different positions by following the tab in Figure 1-17. Because you only want to sound the notes in the tab and not the other strings, and because these interval shapes are two strings apart, you need to either fingerpick or apply some left-hand muting technique (like you do with octave shapes).

Figure 1-17:
Playing in
6ths.

Illustration courtesy of Desi Serna

Book III

Getting to Know Guitar Theory

Harmony-wise, when you play in 6ths, you hear 3rds and roots, but technically, the distance between each pair of notes from low to high is identified as a 6th.

5ths

By far, the most popular harmonic interval among guitar players is the *5th*. After all, a root and a 5th make up the so-called *power chord* that appears in almost every distorted rock song ever recorded. A 5th is written as G5, A5, and so on in a chord chart. Figure 1-18 shows the G scale in 5ths in two different positions. Notice that the 7th scale degree has a 5th that's different from all the rest. It naturally occurs one half step lower in the scale and is called a *flat 5th*.

Figure 1-18:
5ths in G.

Illustration courtesy of Desi Serna

4ths (or inverted 5ths)

Sometimes guitarists invert 5ths by moving the lower note up an octave while keeping the upper note the same. For instance, G-D would become D-G. Figure 1-19 illustrates two examples for you.

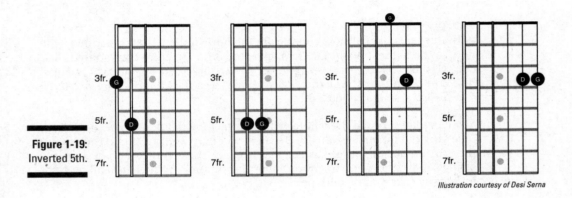

Figure 1-19:
Inverted 5th.

Illustration courtesy of Desi Serna

Inverted 5ths are called *4ths* for the same reason that inverted 3rds are called 6ths. G to D is a 5th (G-A-B-C-D), while D to G is a 4th (D-E-F#-G). You can play the G major scale in 4ths by following the tab in Figure 1-20.

Figure 1-20:
Playing in
4ths.

Illustration courtesy of Desi Serna

In harmony, when you play in 4ths you hear the upper note of the interval as the root and the lower one as the 5th, but technically, the distance between each pair of notes from low to high is a 4th. By far the most famous example of using 4ths is in the song "Smoke on the Water" by Deep Purple. The opening guitar riff uses 4ths in G minor. Other songs include "Money For Nothing" by Dire Straits and "Wish You Were Here" by Pink Floyd.

Filling in the gaps with flats and sharps

Like the spaces between natural notes, the spaces between intervals are filled with flats and sharps. For example, the 1st and 2nd major scale degrees are a whole step apart, meaning they have a pitch in between them. This pitch is called a *flat 2nd* (♭2) because it's one half step lower than a 2nd interval. Here are the rest of the flats between the major scale degrees:

- **Flat 3rd (♭3):** The pitch in between 2 and 3
- **Flat 5th (♭5):** The pitch in between 4 and 5
- **Flat 6th (♭6):** The pitch in between 5 and 6
- **Flat 7th (♭7):** The pitch in between 6 and 7

Figure 1-21 shows flat intervals on the fretboard marked in black.

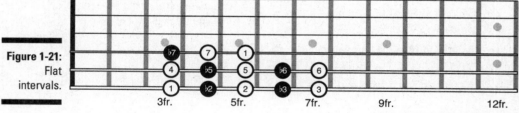

Figure 1-21:
Flat intervals.

3fr.   5fr.   7fr.   9fr.   12fr.

Illustration courtesy of Desi Serna

Book III

Getting to Know Guitar Theory

Some flats can also be considered sharps. For example, you can also call a flat 5th a *sharp 4th* (♯4). However, musicians usually use the term *flat* in these cases because flats are used to identify minor intervals. For example, a flat 3rd is also called a *minor 3rd*, a flat 6th is also called a *minor 6th*, and a flat 7th is also called a *minor 7th*.

While playing in 3rds, you may notice that some 3rds are one half step lower than others. For example, in the G major scale, G and B (G-A-B) are two whole steps apart, while A and C (A-B-C) are only one and a half steps apart. In music, the distance from G to B is major, while the distance from A to C is minor, which is why the same intervals are called major and minor 3rds.

When you play the major scale in 3rds (see Figure 1-15), note that three of the scale degrees have major 3rds, and four have minor 3rds. Specifically, the formula is major-minor-minor-major-major-minor-minor. They each have what's called a *perfect 5th,* except for the last one (which has a flat 5th).

Interval qualities

In music, intervals are classified by one of five qualities. The five interval qualities in music are

✔ **Perfect (P):** The perfect intervals are 5ths, 4ths, and 8ths (better known as *unisons* or *octaves*).

✔ **Major (M):** The major intervals are 3rds, 6ths, and 7ths.

✔ **Minor (m):** The minor intervals are flat 3rds, flat 6ths, and flat 7ths.

✔ **Augmented (A):** When you increase a perfect or major interval by one half step, you get an augmented interval, which is also called a sharp interval. For example, G to C is a 4th, while G to C♯ is a sharp or augmented 4th (A4 or ♯4).

✔ **Diminished (dim):** When you decrease a perfect or minor interval by one half step,

you get a diminished interval, also called a flat interval. For example, G to D is a 5th, while G to D♭ is a flat or diminished 5th (♭5 or dim 5). G to B♭ is a minor 3rd, while G to B♭♭ is a double flat or diminished third (♭♭3 or dim 3).

Decreasing an interval that's already flat, like a minor 3rd, creates a double flat or diminished interval. What's confusing here is that, from a player's perspective, decreasing a minor interval simply puts you on another interval — namely, a 2nd (in the previous example, B♭♭ is enharmonically an A). You may also be wondering whether decreasing a major interval is also considered diminishing. Nope! Decreasing a major interval creates a minor interval.

Harmonizing the Major Scale to Build Triads and Chords

A *triad* is a set of three notes stacked in 3rds. Playing in 3rds means that you start on a scale degree, count it as "1," and then move to the scale degree that is three away, "3." For example, the G major scale is G-A-B-C-D-E-F♯. If you start counting from G, then the 3rd is B (G-A-B, 1-2-3). If you start counting from A, then the 3rd is C (A-B-C, 1-2-3).

A triad is three notes that are all a 3rd apart. For example, in the G major scale, G and B are a 3rd apart and B and D are a 3rd apart. Together all three of these notes are a 3rd apart, called *two consecutive 3rds*. G-B-D make a G triad. You also call the *members* of the triad *root, 3rd,* and *5th* because counting from the starting point, G, B is the 3rd degree and D is the 5th.

G	A	B	C	D	E	F♯
1	2	3	4	5	6	7
G		B		D		
1		3		5		

Harmonizing a root, 3rd, and 5th together (in other words, playing them simultaneously) produces a *chord*. Basically, the difference between any old chord and a triad is that a chord is a group of three or more notes, and a triad is *specifically* a root, 3rd, and 5th.

You build triads on all scale degrees by following a formula of 3rds. Not all triads are the same. Because of the half step and whole step formula of the major scale, some 3rds are closer or farther apart than others. As a result, there are major triads and minor triads. One triad is diminished.

Major triad: Building from the 1st scale degree of the major scale

Building a triad starting from the 1st degree of the major scale produces a major triad. Sounding the triad's notes produces a major chord. In the first diagram in Figure 1-22, you see all 7 degrees of the G major scale in one sample position. In the second diagram, you see just the root, 3rd, and 5th triad. When you strum all three of these triad notes simultaneously, you play a chord. Specifically, this chord is *G major* — *G* because the root is G and *major* because the distance between the root and 3rd is two whole steps, which make up a major 3rd. The third diagram in Figure 1-22 shows you that the actual note names of the G triad are G, B, and D.

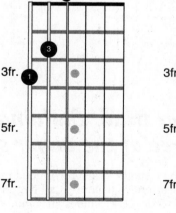

Figure 1-22:
G major scale and G triad.

a   b   c

Illustration courtesy of Desi Serna

Need help building and playing triads? Watch Video Clip 19.

A G major chord is always made from the notes G-B-D; however, you can have more than one occurrence of each note. For example, you can play a G major chord as G-B-D-G or G-B-D-G-B. You can even stack the notes out of order like this: G-D-G-B. Whatever order you play the notes in and however many occurrences of each note you play, all combinations of G-B-D produce harmony that's recognized as a G major chord.

Figure 1-23 shows a handful of common G major chord shapes. Notice that they all use the same notes, although not necessarily in the same number or order. Chords like the ones shown here are considered triads because, technically, they're still based on three pitches even though they vary in the exact number and order of their notes.

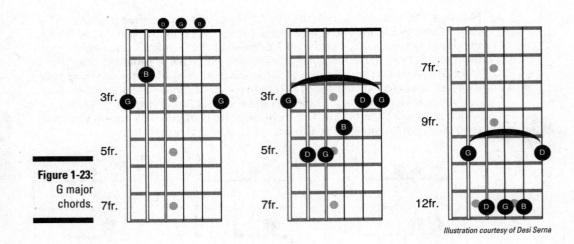

Figure 1-23: G major chords.

Illustration courtesy of Desi Serna

Minor triad: Building from the 2nd scale degree of the major scale

Using the G major scale introduced in the preceding section, count *one-two-three-four-five* from the 2nd degree, A (A-B-C-D-E), and take every other note, 1-3-5 or A-C-E. This is an *A minor triad* — *A* because the root is A and *minor* because the distance from 1 to 3 is a step and a half, which makes up a minor 3rd or flat 3rd (♭3) interval.

Figure 1-24 shows you how to build a triad from the 2nd major scale degree, A. The major scale used here is exactly the same as the one used for the previous triad, G major. The only difference is that you're now counting from the 2nd scale degree, A, to determine its 3rd and 5th. The G note was left at the 3rd fret of the 6th string blank so that you know not to start on it.

You can play the note A either on the open 5th string or at the 5fth fret of the 6th string. You need to do the latter to play the triad as a chord. From the figure, you can see that the notes of this A minor triad are A-C-E.

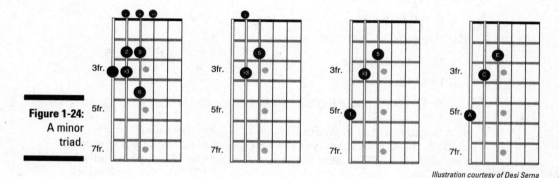

Figure 1-24:
A minor triad.

Illustration courtesy of Desi Serna

Figure 1-25 shows a handful of common A minor chord shapes. Notice that they all use the same notes, although not necessarily in the same number or order. (In case you don't know, an "X" at the top of a string indicates that you don't play that string.)

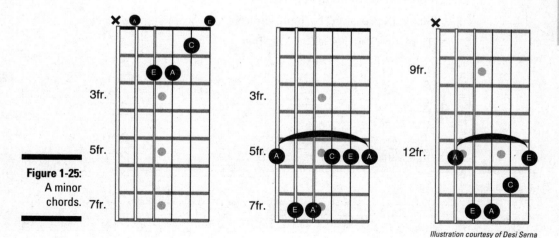

Figure 1-25:
A minor chords.

Illustration courtesy of Desi Serna

Book III

Getting to Know Guitar Theory

The Seven Triads of the Major Scale

After you understand how to build triads (see the preceding section), you can continue to build on each degree in the G major scale (refer to Figure 1-14 in Chapter 2 for G major scale patterns). Try doing this on your own on the fretboard. Here's what the completed scale looks like in triads:

1. **G:** G-B-D, G major

2. **A:** A-C-E, A minor

3. **B:** B-D-F♯, B minor

4. **C:** C-E-G, C major

5. **D:** D-F♯-A, D major

6. **E:** E-B-G, E minor

7. **F♯:** F♯-A-B, F♯ minor ♭5 (also called a *diminished triad*)

By following the tab in Figure 1-26, you can play through all seven major triads in three different ways. The first four measures put each interval on a separate string. The next four measures put the 3rd and 5th on the same string. The last four measures put the root and 3rd on the same string. Remember that the triad notes are exactly the same in all three examples; each version just uses some notes in a different location.

Playing triads one note at a time, as shown in Figure 1-26, is often done in riffs and bass lines. Guitar riff examples include:

"Centerfield" by John Fogerty

"Manic Depression" by Jimi Hendrix

"Tightrope" by Stevie Ray Vaughan

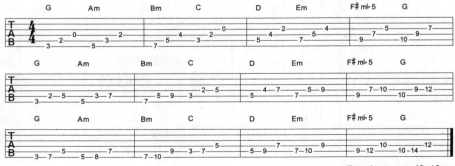

Figure 1-26: Major scale triads in G.

Illustration courtesy of Desi Serna

Bass examples include:

"Ob-La-Di, Ob-La-Da" by The Beatles

"Hound Dog" by Elvis Presley

"Stir It Up" by Bob Marley and the Wailers

Playing the Chord Sequence of the Major Scale

If you take each triad from the major scale and play its notes as a common chord shape, you get the seven chords shown in Figure 1-27. The chords are shown first in the open position and then as barre chords that move up the neck along the 6th and 5th strings.

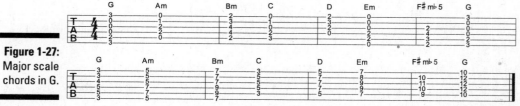

Figure 1-27: Major scale chords in G.

Illustration courtesy of Desi Serna

You can hear and see the G major scale chords by watching Video Clip 20.

Notice how the 1st, 4th, and 5th scale degrees produce major chords, while the 2nd, 3rd, and 6th scale degrees produce minor chords. These six chords are the ones most commonly used in music, so memorize their qualities. From 1 to 6, the sequence is major-minor-minor-major-major-minor.

Say and play that sequence over and over because it's one of the most important patterns in music. After all, you don't just see it in the G major scale. Because you construct every major scale by using the same intervals, all the scales produce the same types of triads and the same major/minor chord sequence. So the 1st degree of every major scale makes a major chord, the 2nd makes a minor, and so on.

Chapter 2

Getting to Know the CAGED System

In This Chapter

▶ Forming and fingering major and minor chord shapes

▶ Playing chord inversions and voicings

▶ Visualizing how chord shapes connect to cover the whole fretboard

▶ Access the audio track and video clips at www.dummies.com/go/guitaraio/

The guitar uses five basic major chord shapes. In the open position, they are C, A, G, E, and D. What does that spell? *CAGED*. The cool thing is that you can play each one as a barre chord and move it around the neck, and you can break these barre chords into smaller chord shapes. Also, each chord is taken from a larger arpeggio pattern that you can use to form additional voicings.

In the guitar world, you can apply the CAGED system in a few different ways. This chapter deals with using it to form and finger chords. You literally play every possible major and minor chord. More than that, you get to know the simple concept used to form these chords so you don't have to memorize a bunch of chord diagrams. You change the ordering and spacing of the pitches by using inversions and voicings. You get away from standard chord shapes and play new chord forms that offer more variety and versatility.

Listen to Track 45 to hear some examples of the CAGED system in action.

Chord Inversions and Chord Voicings

Before you can use the CAGED system to create different chord inversions, you need to familiarize yourself with a few terms and concepts:

✔ A *chord inversion* is a reordering of notes in a chord. A C major chord is C-E-G, root-3rd-5th, with the root, C, placed in the *bass* (lowest) position. If you play the chord with E in the bass as E-G-C (3rd-5th-root), you make what's called the *first inversion*. If you put the 5th in the bass as G-C-E (5th-3rd-root), you make the *second inversion*. In inversions, the chord *members* (the intervals that make up the chord) trade the bottom position. You can see some examples in Figure 2-1.

With chords, if a note other than the root is played in the lowest (bass) position, you specify it with a slash (/). The first letter is the actual chord, and the second letter is the *alternate bass note*. So when you see C/G, for example, you play a C chord but with G as the lowest note.

Figure 2-1: C chord inversions.

Illustration courtesy of Desi Serna

✔ A *chord voicing* refers to the order and spacing of a chord's members. Any combination of C-E-G makes a C chord, but C-E-G sounds different than E-G-C or C-G-C-E. Each inversion in Figure 2-1 is a voicing.

Figure 2-2 includes some additional chord voicings for C. Some examples have spacing between their pitches that require you to either mute strings or fingerpick. The way these chord shapes are *voiced* (the order of and spacing between the notes) gives them their sounds.

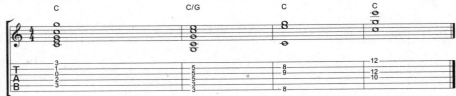

Figure 2-2: C chord voicings.

Illustration courtesy of Desi Serna

Using the C Form

The open C chord is one of the most basic types of chords guitarists play. You probably learned it early on when you first started with guitar. But did you know the C chord shape doesn't have to be confined to the open position? You can move the shape up and play other major chords with it. Just remember if you move your fingers up, you also have to move up the open strings in the chord shape. You accomplish this move either by placing a *capo* (a device clamped on the fingerboard to raise the open strings) on your guitar or by rearranging your fingers and barring across the neck.

When you move the C shape away from the open position and use it to form chords with other notes, the new chords are no longer C. Instead, they take on new names according to the root pitches that they're formed on. For example, move a C shape up one fret and it becomes C♯, up two frets and it becomes D, then D♯, E, and so on. Although you name each chord by its root, it's still a *C form,* (not to be confused with the actual chord name).

In the following sections, you see the open C chord moved up and played as a barre chord, an arpeggio pattern, and then as fragmented chord voicings.

The C form as a moveable barre chord

To use the C form as a moveable barre chord, your 1st finger acts like a capo and lays across (*barres*) the guitar neck while your remaining fingers form the rest of the chord shape. One way to arrive at this fingering is to play an ordinary open C chord, replace fingers 1-2-3 with 2-3-4 (this puts your 4th finger on C at the 3rd fret of the 5th string), slide your fingers up two frets, and then barre across the 2nd fret with your 1st finger. Figure 2-3 shows you what this chord shape looks like. The numbers indicate the fingering.

Book III

Getting to Know Guitar Theory

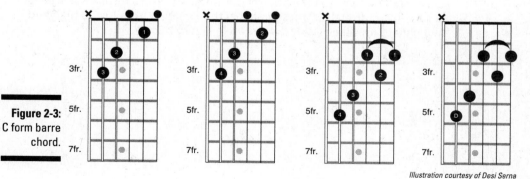

Figure 2-3: C form barre chord.

Illustration courtesy of Desi Serna

How to get started with fingering and playing your first CAGED form, C, is indicated in Video Clip 21.

When everything is in place, this shape actually becomes a D chord. Your 4th finger ends up on the new root D at the 5th fret of the 5th string, as shown in the fourth diagram in Figure 2-3.

Don't fret (no pun intended) if this barre chord is hard to play. This shape is rarely, if ever, used in its entirety. Instead, it's usually broken apart into smaller, more easily fingered pieces. However, to understand where these fragments come from, you need to know the full form. So just focus on visualizing the shape of the C form barre chord. If you're having trouble, don't barre completely across the fingerboard with your 1st finger. The only open strings in a C chord are the 1st and 3rd, so you need to barre only enough to cover those strings when you move the shape up.

Slide this barre chord shape around and play a chord for notes along the 5th string, as shown in Figure 2-4. Note the root is always under your 4th finger.

Playing a C form arpeggio pattern

Before you break down the C form into smaller and more useable chord voicings, add to it in the form of an arpeggio pattern. An *arpeggio* is a technique in which you play the notes of a chord one at a time like a scale rather than simultaneously as a chord. The verb *arpeggiate* describes how players pick through the notes of chords individually rather than strumming them all simultaneously (think of the opening to "The House of the Rising Sun" by The Animals or "Everybody Hurts" by R.E.M.).

For example, a D chord is D-F♯-A. Using the position of a C form D chord, you find these notes in the barre chord shape but also outside of it. For instance, you see an F♯ at the 2nd fret of the 6th string, an A at the 5th fret of the 6th string, and another A at the 5th fret of the 1st string. To form a full arpeggio pattern, play through *all* these notes in this position from low to high and then high to low like a scale, as shown in Figure 2-5.

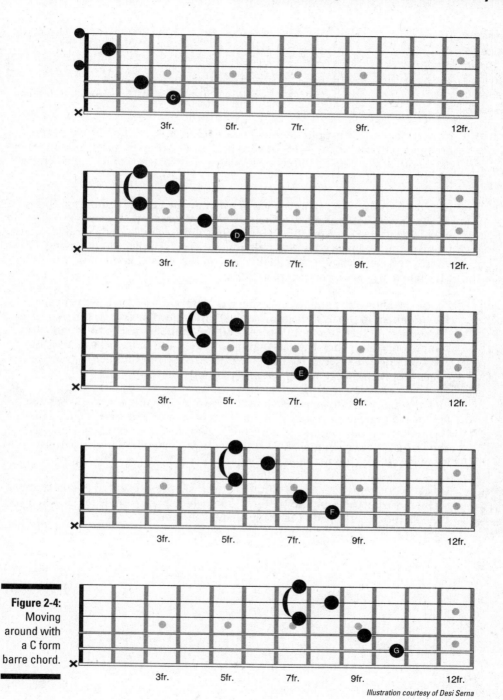

Figure 2-4:
Moving
around with
a C form
barre chord.

Illustration courtesy of Desi Serna

Figure 2-5:
C form
arpeggio
pattern tab.

Illustration courtesy of Desi Serna

Notice that the lowest pitched note available in this position is where the arpeggio pattern begins — on the 3rd of D, or F♯. When mapping out an arpeggio like this, you don't need to start on the root. Instead, touch on all chord members in the position.

Also notice that some strings have more than one chord member on them. When playing notes simultaneously as a chord, you can choose only one note per string, but arpeggios allow you to play multiple notes on a string because you can fret and pick each one individually. For example, when playing a chord, you can use either the F♯ or the A on the 1st string but not both. When playing an arpeggio, you can play both.

Figure 2-6 shows the shape this arpeggio pattern makes on the fretboard. The numbers in the first diagram indicate the chord intervals, the letters in the second indicate the note names, and the numbers in the third indicate a sample fingering. The intervals and note names add more perspective, but you don't need to memorize them. Feel free to try the sample fingering or come up with a different fingering that better suits you.

Play through the C form arpeggio one note at a time like a scale, ascending and descending until you have it completely memorized. You can also use this pattern at different frets to play arpeggios for other pitches. Figure 2-7 shows just three examples, C, D, and E, but you can position the pattern around any note along the 5th string.

Don't try to memorize all the different chord shapes presented. Instead, focus on memorizing the arpeggio patterns from which each form is taken. Then you can use those patterns to build any shape you want.

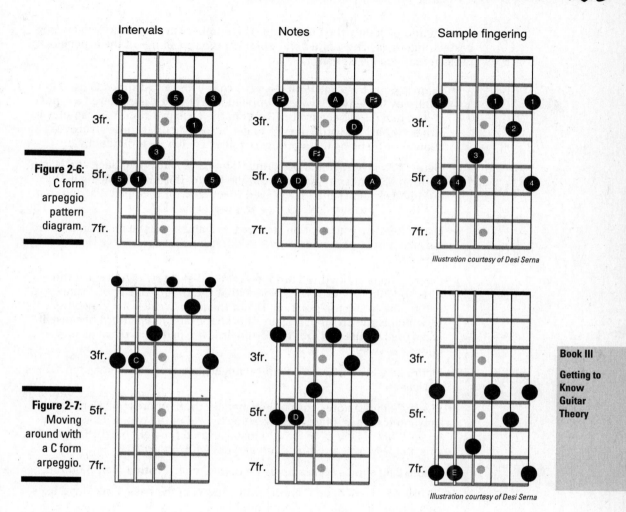

Intervals   Notes   Sample fingering

Figure 2-6:
C form
arpeggio
pattern
diagram.

Illustration courtesy of Desi Serna

Figure 2-7:
Moving
around with
a C form
arpeggio.

Illustration courtesy of Desi Serna

Playing C form chord voicings

Different C form chord voicings are played by breaking down the arpeggio
pattern into smaller, fragmented pieces. Figure 2-8 shows you several ways
to play partial chord shapes based on the full C form. In these examples,

you fret and pick only the black dots. The numbers in the black dots are suggested fingerings. The white dots represent the remainder of the arpeggio pattern that you aren't using:

- Figure 2-8a is a fragment on strings 1 to 4. This chord shape is used in "Stairway to Heaven" by Led Zeppelin as a D/F♯. It's considered a type of first inversion because the 3rd is in the bass position. You can play it either by barring with your 1st finger across the first three strings (as shown) or by using all four fingers to fret each note individually.

- Figure 2-8b is a fragment on strings 2 to 4 and is used in "Jack and Diane" by John Mellencamp. As shown in the figure, this chord voicing is D/F♯, but in "Jack and Diane," it's played together with the open A string as a D/A and moved two frets higher and used as an E/A.

- Figure 2-8c is a fragment on strings 1 to 3 and is part of an open D chord. It's also moved around the neck as different chords in "Hole Hearted" by Extreme.

- Figure 2-8d is an inverted 3rd interval used in "Stay Together for the Kids" by Blink 182 as a D/F♯. Notice that the root of this chord shape is the note in the top position, D, not the note in the bottom position, F♯, which is the 3rd. Technically, this shape isn't a full chord because it lacks the 5th interval, but roots and 3rds are usually written as major chords anyway.

- Figure 2-8e is an E/G♯. Eric Clapton fingerpicks this chord shape in "Tears in Heaven."

- Figure 2-8f uses notes spaced in a manner that requires you to mute the unwanted strings, fingerpick, or some hybrid of the two. It's used in the song "Cliffs of Dover" by Eric Johnson as a G5 (power chord). Technically, this shape is only a root and 5th and not a full chord.

- Figure 2-8g shows you can play an open C chord with a high G on top.

- Figure 2-8h is an open C chord with a low G in the bass. Pink Floyd uses this shape in "Wish You Were Here."

- Figure 2-8i is an open C chord with a low E in the bass. Stone Temple Pilots use it in "Plush."

When you use fragmented chord shapes, make sure you still visualize the unused notes so that you can track what the chord name is.

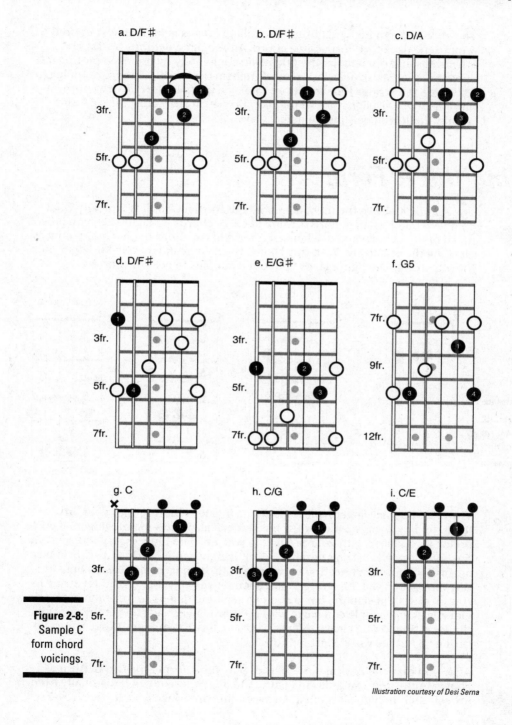

Book III

Getting to Know Guitar Theory

Figure 2-8: Sample C form chord voicings.

Illustration courtesy of Desi Serna

The style of Keith Richards from The Rolling Stones is built almost entirely around the use of a C form barre chord. Although he detunes his 1st and 5th strings and often omits the 6th string completely by not even putting it on, the rest of his strings, 2 through 4, remain the same as standard tuning. These are the strings Richards used to play a partial C form barre chord on so many of his signature songs, like "Brown Sugar," "Start Me Up," and "Honky Tonk Women," just to name a few.

Using the A Form

The *A form* is one of the most commonly used shapes and is typically what comes to mind when guitarists think of barre chords. In Figure 2-9, you move up an open A chord and use it as an A form barre chord to play major chords all along the 5th string. With this shape, the root is under your 1st finger on the 5th string. The figure gives you four examples to get you started.

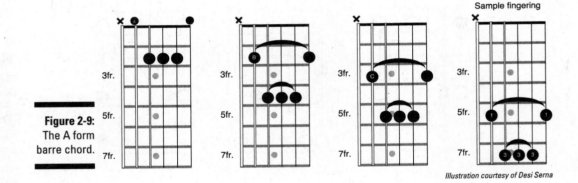

Figure 2-9: The A form barre chord.

Illustration courtesy of Desi Serna

The most popular fingering for this shape includes barring with your 3rd finger to play strings 2 through 4, but you can also use separate fingers if you prefer. If you barre with your 3rd finger, you may find it necessary to leave out the note on the 1st string because it's difficult not to bump into it. This in turn means that you don't need to barre with your 1st finger because it's only fretting the root on the 5th string. If you should need the note on the 1st string to ring clearly, then skip the barre and use separate fingers to fret each note individually. Some people can barre with their 3rd finger and still get the note on the 1st string to ring clearly. Maybe you can, too. Experiment to see which fingering technique works best for you.

After you play the A form barre chord, play the A form arpeggio pattern as shown in the four examples in Figure 2-10. Play these notes individually from lowest pitch to highest pitch in an ascending order like a scale; then reverse direction. Use the diagrams in the figure to play major arpeggios for roots along the 5th string. Numbers show the intervals in the first three diagrams. The fourth example includes a sample fingering.

The A form arpeggio pattern has two additional notes that aren't part of the barre chord. This includes a note on the 6th string and another on the 4th string. Notice that you play two notes in all on the 4th string.

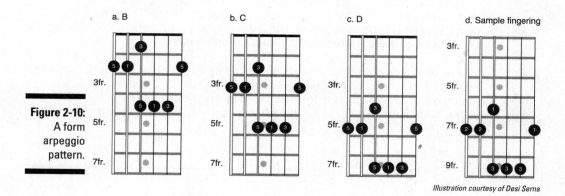

Figure 2-10:
A form
arpeggio
pattern.

Illustration courtesy of Desi Serna

You can break up this arpeggio into various chord voicings, as shown in Figure 2-11. Remember to fret and play only the black dots. The clear dots are only to show where the remainder of the whole form is.

- ✔ Figure 2-11a uses only strings 1 through 3. Led Zeppelin uses this shape in the interlude to "Stairway to Heaven" as both a type of C, as shown here, and a type of D two frets higher.

- ✔ Figure 2-11b features a shape on strings 2 to 4 that's often used together with a C form on the same strings. You can barre these three notes with your 1st finger to play a C and then add your 2nd and 3rd fingers to play an F in C form, as you hear in "Brown Sugar" by The Rolling Stones.

- ✔ Figure 2-11c shows a standard power chord shape that's used on countless songs.

- ✔ Figure 2-11d shows one way to incorporate the extra arpeggio note on the 4th string. John Mayer uses this shape in the chorus of "Daughters."

- ✔ Figure 2-11e is similar to Figure 2-11d, minus the root D on the 5th string. This D/F♯, which is really only a root and 3rd, shows up in the chorus to "All Right Now" by Free.

- ✔ Figure 2-11f uses the extra arpeggio note on the 6th string. It's an F power chord with the 5th, C, in the bass and is used in the opening to "The Wind Cries Mary" by Jimi Hendrix.

Book III

**Getting to
Know
Guitar
Theory**

✔ Figure 2-11g is an F played as only a root and 3rd and is used in "Scar Tissue" by Red Hot Chili Peppers. This interval is often called a *10th* because the 3rd is a register above the root, ten steps in the major scale.

✔ Figure 2-11h is a C and is arpeggiated in the opening to "Cliffs of Dover" by Eric Johnson.

If only the root and 5th are used in a chord, it's considered a *power chord,* and you write it as *C5, F5,* and so on. If only a root and 3rd are used, then you sometimes see it written as *G(no5).* However, most of the time a root and 3rd combo is still considered a major chord and is written as such, even though the absence of the 5th technically makes it incomplete.

Guitarists often combine two sets of chord voicings by barring the A form on strings 2 to 4 with the 1st finger and then adding the 2nd and 3rd fingers to build a partial C form, as is the case in "Jack and Diane," "Funk #49," "All Right Now," and many others. Keith Richards uses the same technique a whole lot.

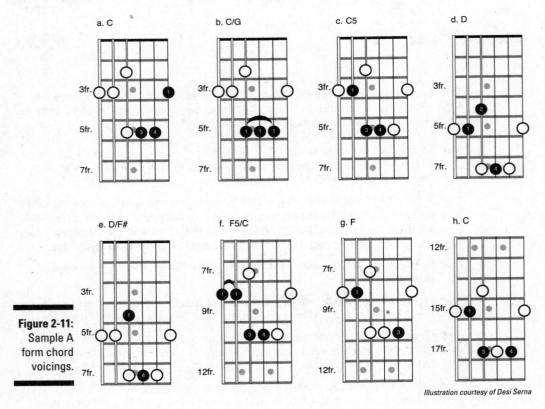

Figure 2-11:
Sample A form chord voicings.

Illustration courtesy of Desi Serna

Using the G Form

Figure 2-12 shows you the *G form*. Like the C form, this barre chord is hard to play and rarely, if ever, used in its entirety. Usually, you break it down into other, more manageable shapes. You use the G form to form major chords for notes along the 6th string.

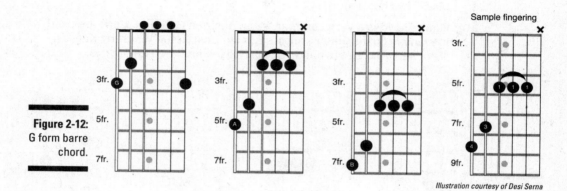

Figure 2-12: G form barre chord.

Sample fingering

Illustration courtesy of Desi Serna

Play the full G form arpeggio pattern shown in Figure 2-13. It includes an additional note on the 2nd string. Play it as a scale. The additional chord tone on the 2nd string explains why you can play an open G chord with either the 2nd string open, B, or the 3rd fret of the 2nd string, D. Both notes are part of the chord.

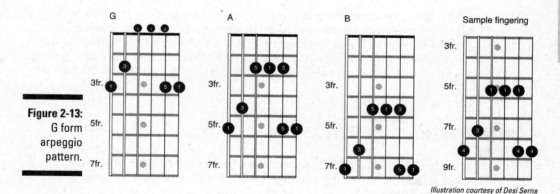

Figure 2-13: G form arpeggio pattern.

Sample fingering

Illustration courtesy of Desi Serna

Figure 2-14 shows you how to play G form chord voicings.

- ✔ Figure 2-14a features a part of the barre chord that's used in the song "Snow (Hey Oh)" by Red Hot Chili Peppers as a B.

- ✔ Figure 2-14b shows the C/G used in the opening to "Stairway to Heaven" by Led Zeppelin.

- ✔ Figure 2-14c shows the F/A used in the opening to "The Wind Cries Mary" by Jimi Hendrix.

- ✔ Figure 2-14d is a very common, open position G/B. Variations are used in many acoustic guitar songs, such as "Dust in the Wind" by Kansas, "Landslide" by Fleetwood Mac, and "Blackbird" by The Beatles.

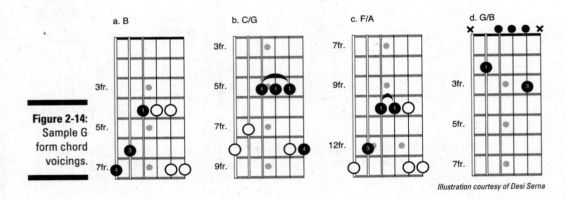

Figure 2-14: Sample G form chord voicings.

Illustration courtesy of Desi Serna

The G form has three notes in a row on strings 2–4 just like the A form. In fact, the two forms are connected by this group of notes. You can fret this group of notes with your 1st finger and use it together with a partial C form to play in the style of Keith Richards, among others. You see that this type of chord change can be viewed as a combination of the G form and C form too.

Using the E Form

Like the A form, the *E form* is a standard barre chord shape. You use it to form major chords for notes along the 6th string, as shown in Figure 2-15. You can form it into some unique chord voicings, especially when you use the extra note found in its arpeggio pattern.

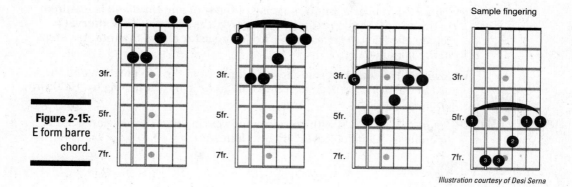

Sample fingering

Figure 2-15:
E form barre
chord.

Illustration courtesy of Desi Serna

You add only one note to the E form shape to complete the arpeggio pattern:
a 3rd interval on the 5th string (see Figure 2-16). Play it as a scale.

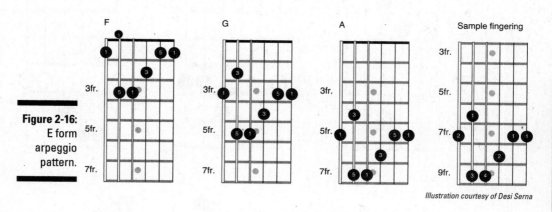

Figure 2-16:
E form
arpeggio
pattern.

Sample fingering

Illustration courtesy of Desi Serna

Book III

**Getting to
Know
Guitar
Theory**

Figure 2-17 shows some of the E form chord voicings heard in popular music.

- ✔ Figure 2-17a is a common F chord that guitarists usually learn with basic
  open chords. You can always play a full E form barre chord partially like
  this and still visually track the root on the 6th string when you do.

- ✔ Figure 2-17b is similar to the preceding F shape, but it's reduced even
  further to include only the first three strings. This E/G♯ is used in
  "Gloria" by Van Morrison. Even though you're fretting and playing only
  strings 1 through 3, track the root E on the 6th string with your eye.

- ✔ Figure 2-17c is the B♭/F used in the opening to "Johnny B. Goode" by
  Chuck Berry.

✔ Figure 2-17d uses a unique spacing of the root and third and is featured in the song "Tripping Billies" by Dave Matthews Band. This interval is often called a *10th* because the 3rd is a register above the root, ten steps in the major scale.

✔ Figure 2-17e is an inverted 3rd with the root in the top position and the 3rd in the bass. It's used as a B/D♯ and an A/C♯ in the opening to "Hold On Loosely" by 38 Special.

✔ Figure 2-17f is a G/B with some unique spacing that's arpeggiated in the opening to "Cliffs of Dover" by Eric Johnson.

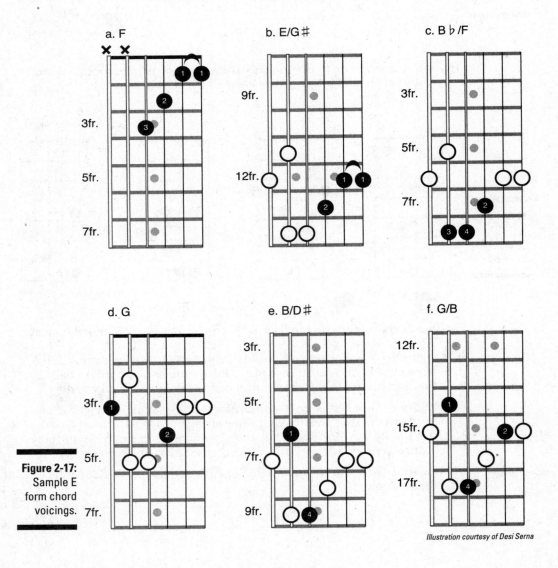

Figure 2-17:
Sample E form chord voicings.

Illustration courtesy of Desi Serna

Using the D Form

The D form is unique in that it's the only CAGED form that isn't rooted to either the 6th or 5th string. Instead, its root is on the 4th string (see Figure 2-18). It's awkward to finger and technically isn't a barre chord. As with some of the other CAGED forms, you don't usually use it in the same way that it appears in the open position.

You may prefer to finger the D form in a different way. For instance, some guitar players swap their 2nd and 3rd fingers. Others can barre the 1st and 3rd strings with their 3rd finger and fret the note on the 2nd string with their 4th finger. You don't need to play this whole chord perfectly.

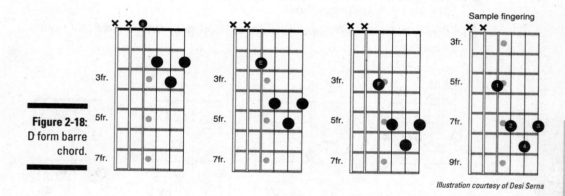

Figure 2-18: D form barre chord.

Illustration courtesy of Desi Serna

Book III

Getting to Know Guitar Theory

Play the full D form arpeggio pattern in Figure 2-19. Notice that you have a lot more to work with here than in the small D form. Three additional chord members on strings 4 through 6 fit with this form. Play it as a scale.

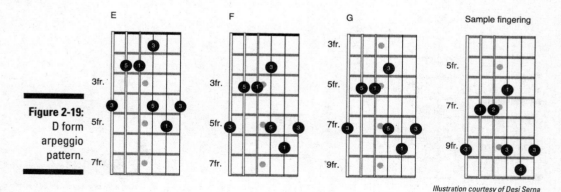

Figure 2-19: D form arpeggio pattern.

Illustration courtesy of Desi Serna

The D form is used less often than the other CAGED forms, but it can still form some unique and useable chord voicings, as you can see in Figure 2-20.

✔ Figure 2-20a is a very common version of an open D that puts the 3rd, F♯, in the bass at the 2nd fret of the 6th string. It's often fingered as a regular D chord with the thumb wrapped around the neck to fret the 6th string. You hear variations of it in "Free Bird" by Lynyrd Skynyrd.

✔ Figure 2-20b is a power chord with the root on the 4th string. This F5 is used in "All the Small Things" by Blink 182.

✔ Figure 2-20c is an E/G♯ and fits into both a D form and a C form. It's used in "Tears in Heaven" by Eric Clapton. Finger this shape with your first three fingers or try using your thumb, as in the figure.

✔ Figure 2-20d is another variation on E/G♯. This one occurs in "Crash into Me" by Dave Matthews Band.

✔ Figure 2-20e is an F♯/A♯ and is used in "Snow (Hey Oh)" by Red Hot Chili Peppers.

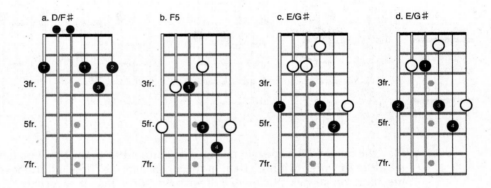

a. D/F♯ b. F5 c. E/G♯ d. E/G♯

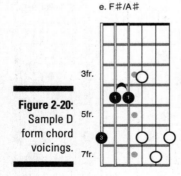

e. F♯/A♯

Figure 2-20: Sample D form chord voicings.

Illustration courtesy of Desi Serna

The triangular D shape on strings 1 through 3 is often moved around the guitar neck. This shape fits into both the D form and the C form. You trace the root back to either the 4th or 5th string by using these forms. Most uses of the D form occur in the open position as a D/F♯, as in "Free Bird."

Playing Minor CAGED Forms

Just as you use the CAGED arpeggios to form major chord voicings, you can do the same with minor arpeggios. In this section, you lower all the 3rds in each arpeggio pattern to minor 3rds (♭3rds). This simple adjustment changes everything from major to minor. You then fret and play different kinds of minor chord voicings with each of the five minor CAGED forms.

Adding the minor CAGED forms to the majors is a lot to pile on your plate, especially if all the major forms haven't yet sunk in completely. Work through this next section slowly, or save the minor forms for another time.

Playing the C minor form

Figure 2-21a shows the original C form (major). Compare that to Figure 2-21b, which shows the Cm form (the *m* stands for minor). As you can see from the figure, the Cm form uses the same arpeggio pattern as the C form except with minor 3rds. Figures 2-21c and 2-21d show some sample minor chord voicings. Notice that the actual chord in this position is Dm. In fact, Figure 2-21d is part of a basic open Dm chord that's a commonly used shape all over the neck. Remember to only play the black dots in examples like this.

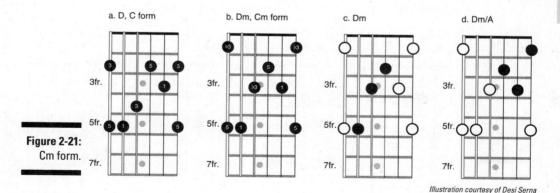

Figure 2-21: Cm form.

a. D, C form   b. Dm, Cm form   c. Dm   d. Dm/A

Illustration courtesy of Desi Serna

Playing the A minor form

Figure 2-22a shows the original A form, while Figure 2-22b shows the same arpeggio pattern with minor 3rds — or the Am form. In this position, the actual chords are C and C minor. Figure 2-22c illustrates a commonly used minor chord voicing. Notice that it's a standard minor barre chord. This barre chord is often reduced to only strings 1 to 3, as shown in Figure 2-22d.

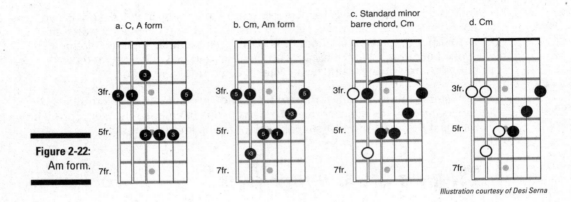

Figure 2-22: Am form.

Illustration courtesy of Desi Serna

Playing the G minor form

In Figure 2-23a, you see the original G form, followed by the same arpeggio pattern with minor 3rds (or Gm form) in Figure 2-23b. In this position, the actual chords are A and A minor. Figure 2-23c shows you one way to get a useable barre chord out of it. Figure 2-23d shows a unique Dm in Gm form that appears in the song "So Much to Say" by Dave Matthews Band.

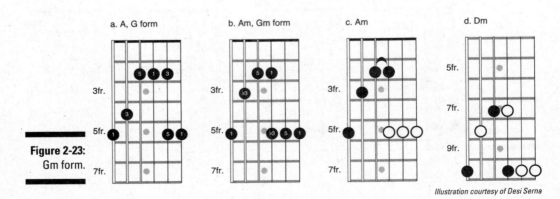

Figure 2-23: Gm form.

Illustration courtesy of Desi Serna

Playing the E minor form

Figure 2-24a illustrates the original E form, while Figure 2-24b shows the same arpeggio pattern with minor 3rds (or Em form). In this position, the actual chords are G and G minor. Figure 2-24c shows a sample minor chord voicing, which is a standard minor barre chord. This barre chord is often reduced to just strings 1 through 3, as shown in Figure 2-24d.

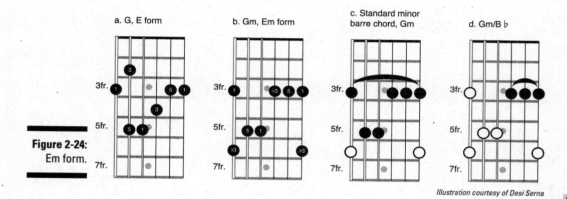

Figure 2-24:
Em form.

Illustration courtesy of Desi Serna

Playing the D minor form

Figure 2-25a illustrates the original D form, followed by the same arpeggio pattern with minor 3rds (Dm form), shown in Figure 2-25b. In this position, the actual chords are F and F minor. Figure 2-25c shows a sample minor chord voicing, which is a full Dm shape when played in the open position. Notice that this shape shares a lot in common with the Cm form (see the earlier section for details on the C form).

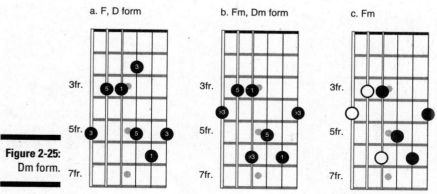

Figure 2-25:
Dm form.

Illustration courtesy of Desi Serna

Book III

Getting to Know Guitar Theory

Chapter 3

Playing Snazzier Chords with Chord Tones and Extensions

In This Chapter

▶ Discovering added chord tones and extensions

▶ Getting to know 2nds, 4ths, 6ths, 7ths, 9ths, 11ths, and 13ths

▶ Playing "sus" and "add" chords

▶ Using 6ths to play blues shuffles

▶ Access the audio track and video clips at www.dummies.com/go/guitaraio/

Chords are made from roots, 3rds, and 5ths. These intervals come from the major scale, where the scale degrees produce different triads, some major and some minor (and one diminished). Guitar players add *chord tones* and *extensions* to triads by incorporating other degrees from the major scale — including 2nds, 4ths, 6ths, 7ths, 9ths, 11ths, and 13ths.

In this chapter, you break away from the standard major and minor chords to play fancier chords with more depth and color. You get to know what the little numbers next to chord names mean and how you can form new chord shapes. Rather than have you play all the chord types that are taught in traditional theory, this chapter focuses on chords that guitarists typically use in popular music. It doesn't cover every single chord type that you may come across, but it gives you enough examples so you can begin to make sense of other types of chords when you encounter them.

Listen to Track 46 to hear some examples of chord tones and extensions (plus sa taste of something not covered here: pedal points).

About Chord Tones and Extensions

Before you get started playing new types of chords, some preliminary information about chord construction and naming convention is in order. This is not a comprehensive explanation of the whole subject, but it's enough to prep you for the rest of the chapter where many more details are revealed.

You go beyond playing triad-based chords by adding in the degrees of the major scale other than 1, 3, and 5. These added *chord tones* are the 2nd, 4th, 6th, and 7th. Sometimes chord tones extend an octave above the 7th. In this case, the chord tones are called *extensions* and are numbered to reflect their position in the register above the first seven degrees of the scale. For example, 2 becomes 9, 4 becomes 11, and 6 becomes 13.

G A B C D E F♯ G A B C D E F♯

1 2 3 4 5 6 7 8 9 10 11 12 13 14

Perhaps a bit confusingly, in music theory, 1, 3, 5, and 7 are always counted the same regardless of register. Only 2, 4, and 6 get renumbered when they extend beyond the 7th. And they only get renumbered once. Transpose them up additional octaves, and their numbers don't increase.

When an extension like 9, 11, or 13 is present in a chord, then the 7th is supposed to be included too, plus any extensions before the one in the chord name. For example:

G major: 1-3-5, G-B-D

Gmaj7: 1-3-5-7, G-B-D-F♯

Gmaj9: 1-3-5-7-9, G-B-D-F♯-A

Gmaj11: 1-3-5-7-9-11, G-B-D-F♯-A-C

Gmaj13: 1-3-5-7-9-11-13, G-B-D-F♯-A-C-E

But this isn't always the way it's done, as you'll soon see.

If an extension is added to a triad, but the 7th and other extensions *aren't* also included, the term *add* is used. For example:

G: 1-3-5, G-B-D

Gadd9: 1-3-5-9, G-B-D-A

Gadd11: 1-3-5-11, G-B-D-C

Gadd13: 1-3-5-13, G-B-D-E

Moving on to sus chords, because of their proximity to the 3rd, 2 and 4 often replace the 3rd. When this happens, the chord becomes *suspended* and the abbreviation *sus* appears in the name. The lack of a 3rd in sus chords creates an open, unresolved sound. For example:

G: 1-3-5, G-B-D

Gsus2: 1-2-5, G-A-D

Gsus4: 1-4-5, G-C-D

If a 2 or 4 is added but the 3rd remains, then the term *add* is used:

> **Gadd2:** 1-2-3-5, G-A-B-D
>
> **Gadd4:** 1-3-4-5, G-B-C-D

But, remember, 2nds and 9ths are the same. So are 4ths and 11ths. So you may see the chords above stacked and written as follows:

> **Gadd9:** 1-3-5-9, G-B-D-A
>
> **Gadd11:** 1-3-5-11, G-B-D-C

Notice that these chords use the very same notes as the chords before them. The only difference is in how the notes are stacked and the chords named. But guitar players often stack chord members out of order anyway, so it's hard to follow a strict convention. As a result, 2nds and 9ths and 4ths and 11ths are often used interchangeably.

Guitarists not only need to rearrange chord members at times but also leave some out in order to make a chord shape physically playable and pleasant sounding. This is especially true as you add more chord tones and extensions. For example, a major 13th chord is supposed to be stacked 1-3-5-7-9-11-13. You don't have enough fingers and strings for that! Obviously, something has to go. In cases like this, you at least try to retain the 3rd, the 7th, and the extension that the chord is named after. So a Gmaj13 might be played 1-3-7-13, 1-7-3-13, or some such combination.

Book III

Getting to Know Guitar Theory

Adding 7ths to the Major Scale Chords

You begin playing new chords by adding 7ths to major scale chords. Adding 7ths is a good place to start because it's in keeping with the consecutive 3rds formula that triads follow (1-3-5-7 are all consecutive 3rds). Plus, you can easily add 7ths without needing to suspend a 3rd or interfere with the rest of the triad. Using the G major scale and its basic triads as a starting place, you add a 7th to each chord by counting up seven from each scale degree.

Figure 3-1 includes seven diagrams, all with the same notes from the G major scale. Each diagram counts from a different starting point so you can see the 7th of each scale degree. Starting points and 7ths are shown in black. The starting points are the roots to each triad/chord in the scale. You add the 7ths to the basic triads to create 7th chords.

A 7th is a 3rd above a 5th and keeps with the 3rds sequence used to build the basic triads. In the major scale, counting 1-2-3 is a 3rd, but so are 3-4-5 and 5-6-7. In all, you build a 7th chord by using the intervals 1-3-5-7, which are all a 3rd apart.

There are two types of 7th intervals. One type — the *major 7th* — is almost an octave, missing it by just a half step and named after the type of 7th that occurs in the major scale. You see major 7ths on G and C in Figure 3-1. The other type — a *minor* or *♭7th* — misses the octave by a whole step and is named by the type of 7th that occurs in a minor scale. You see minor 7ths on A, B, D, and E in the same figure. You may be wondering why the 5th scale degree has a minor 7th when it produces a major triad and chord. More on this in a moment!

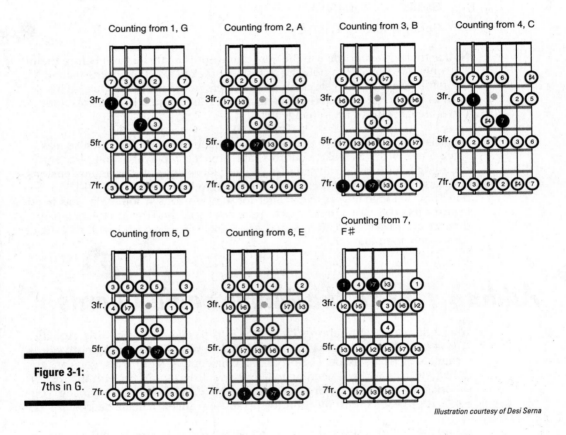

Figure 3-1: 7ths in G.

Illustration courtesy of Desi Serna

The following list shows what the basic major and minor triads in G look like after you add 7ths to create 7th chords. The notations in parentheses illustrate the most common ways to write the chord names. (Find out how to use triads to play plain major and minor chords in Book II Chapter 1.)

✔ **G:** 1-3-5-7, G-B-D-F♯, G major 7 (Gmaj7, GM7, GΔ)

✔ **A:** 1-♭3-5-♭7, A-C-E-G, A minor 7 (Amin7, Am7, A-7)

✔ **B:** 1-♭3-5-♭7, B-D-F♯-A, B minor 7 (Bmin7, Bm7, B-7)

- **C:** 1-3-5-7, C-E-G-B, C major 7 (Cmaj7, CM7, CΔ)
- **D:** 1-3-5-♭7, D-F♯-A-C, D dominant 7 (D7)
- **E:** 1-♭3-5-♭7, E-B-G-D, E minor 7 (Emin7, Em7, E-7)
- **F♯:** 1-♭3-♭5-♭7, F♯-A-C-E, F♯ minor 7♭5, half diminished 7th (F♯min7♭5, F♯m7♭5, F♯-7♭5, F♯°)

When you add the 7ths in the preceding list to standard major and minor barre chords (E form and A form; see Book II Chapter 2), you get the new chord shapes shown in Figure 3-2. In this example and all the rest in this chapter, the numbers represent intervals, which are important to look at so that you see how each chord shape is constructed. You're on your own to work out fingerings, but your fingers will easily fall into place with these chord shapes. Try playing forward and backward through the scale with 7th chords.

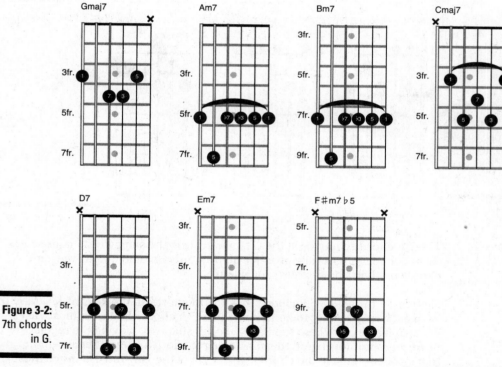

Figure 3-2: 7th chords in G.

Illustration courtesy of Desi Serna

PLAY THIS!

Watch Video Clip 22 to hear and see 7th chords in G.

You can also play through 7th chords in the open position, as shown in Figure 3-3. Again, the numbers represent intervals. Work out your own fingerings.

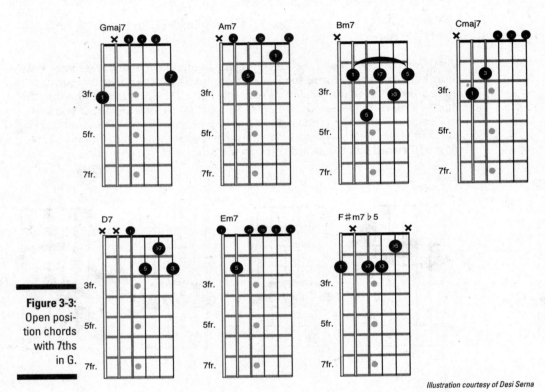

Figure 3-3: Open position chords with 7ths in G.

Illustration courtesy of Desi Serna

The 7th chord sequence in the G major scale is the same in all major scales. All major scales naturally produce maj7 chords on their 1st degrees, m7 chords on their 2nd degrees, and so on.

Figures 3-4 through 3-6 include tab with 7th chords in the keys of A, C, and D. With each key, you get to know some new 7th chord shapes. In most cases, you can figure out where the 7th is in each shape by playing the regular major or minor form first, then switching to the 7th chord. The new note that's added to make the chord shape a 7th is the 7th! You can move these shapes away from the open position and use them as full or partial barre chords to play 7th chords for other notes around the fretboard.

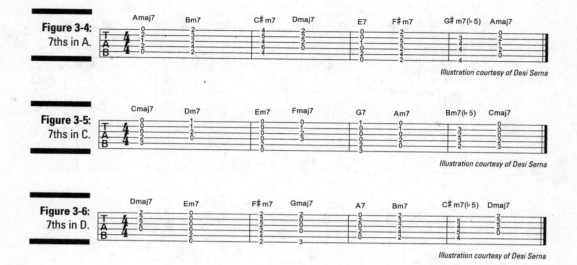

Figure 3-4: 7ths in A.

Illustration courtesy of Desi Serna

Figure 3-5: 7ths in C.

Illustration courtesy of Desi Serna

Figure 3-6: 7ths in D.

Illustration courtesy of Desi Serna

Playing major and minor 7th chords

As you can see in all the previous figures, there's more than one way to put together a 7th chord shape. Figure 3-7 shows a few more m7 examples, namely variations on the open Em7 and Am7 forms. Expect to see these shapes used elsewhere on the fretboard as full or partial barre chords. To understand why these variations work, look at the intervals to see how they appear in multiple locations.

The following songs all feature some type of maj7 chord.

"Across the Universe" by The Beatles

"Band on the Run" by Wings

"Best of My Love" by the Eagles

"Californication" by Red Hot Chili Peppers

"Don't Know Why" Norah Jones

"Dreams" by Fleetwood Mac

"Dust in the Wind" by Kansas

"Hold Your Head Up" by Argent

"One" by U2

"You've Got a Friend" by James Taylor

Book III

Getting to Know Guitar Theory

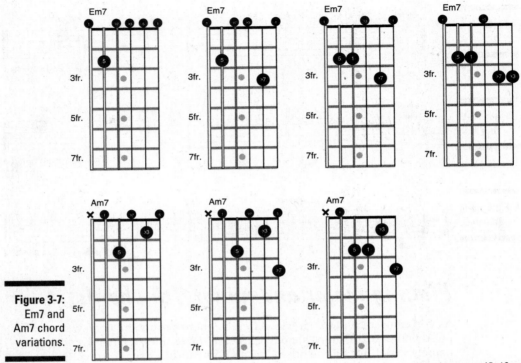

Figure 3-7:
Em7 and
Am7 chord
variations.

As you work through the song lists in this chapter, keep in mind that some examples may include other types of chords in addition to the chords that pertain to the particular list. You get introduced to more chord types as you progress through the chapter. You may want to revisit the songs in each list after you finish this chapter.

The following songs all feature some type of m7 chord:

"Black Water" by The Doobie Brothers

"Cold Shot" by Stevie Ray Vaughan

"Daughters" by John Mayer

"Fly Like an Eagle" by Steve Miller Band

"It's Too Late" by Carole King

"Let's Stay Together" by Al Green

"You Ain't Seen Nothin' Yet" by Bachman-Turner Overdrive

Playing dominant 7th chords

The three major chords in the major scale occur on the 1st, 4th, and 5th scale degrees. You know these chords by number as I, IV, and V. In the key of G, these chords are G, C, and D. You may expect them all to make similar major 7th chords, but they don't. G and C have a major 7th, but D has a flat or minor 7th.

A major triad with a minor 7th is technically called a *dominant 7th,* but, and this is where things get confusing, it's simply referred to as a *7th.* You always have to specify major 7th chords as maj7, but you can simply use "7" to label dominant 7ths. In other words, if a 7 by itself follows a letter name, then that chord is dominant (a major triad with a minor 7th). So in the G major scale, the three major chords with 7ths become Gmaj7, Cmaj7, and D7.

The dominant 7th chord naturally occurs on chord V in the major scale.

Dominant 7th chords are extremely common. Some of the most popular forms along with their intervals are in Figure 3-8. Keep in mind that you can move these shapes around to produce dominant 7th chords for other notes.

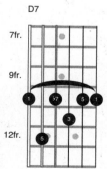
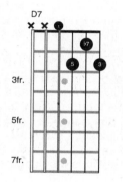
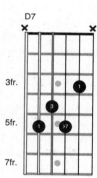
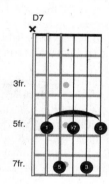
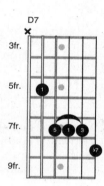

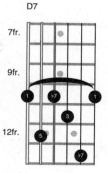

Figure 3-8: D dominant 7ths.

Illustration courtesy of Desi Serna

The following songs all feature some form of dominant 7th chord:

"Alive" by Pearl Jam

"Born On the Bayou" by Creedence Clearwater Revival

"Brown Eyed Girl" by Van Morrison

"Couldn't Stand the Weather" by Stevie Ray Vaughan

"Crossroads (Live at Winterland)" by Cream

"Get Down Tonight" by K.C. and the Sunshine Band

"Margaritaville" by Jimmy Buffet

"Papa's Got a Brand New Bag" by James Brown

"Wild Honey Pie" by The Beatles

Playing minor 7th flat 5 chords

The 7th scale degree produces a chord that requires a little extra explanation. As a triad, it has a root, 3rd, and ♭5th; it's called a *minor ♭5*. Add a 7th and it becomes a *minor 7♭5*. For example, the F♯ in the G major scale becomes F♯m7♭5. You see how to form a m7♭5 chord with the root on the 5th string in Figure 3-2 and with the root on the 6th string in Figure 3-3.

You can also call the minor ♭5 a *diminished triad,* because a ♭5th is also called a *diminished* 5th. Add a 7th and it becomes a *half-diminished* chord. So F♯m7♭5 can also be called F♯ half diminished (F♯°). Why is it only *half* diminished? Because a fully diminished chord, also called a *diminished 7th*, actually has a double flat 7th (♭♭7). Just keep in mind that a diminished triad and a full diminished chord are not completely the same thing. In fact, this book calls the 7th triad in the major scale m♭5 to avoid confusing it with a full diminished chord.

The following songs feature a m7♭5 chord (that is, half diminished). Some of them have other types of 7 chords mixed in, too.

"Change the World" by Eric Clapton

"I Will Survive" by Gloria Gaynor

"Smooth" by Santana

"Still Got the Blues" by Gary Moore

Working with 2nds and 9ths

There are many types of chords that include 2nds and 9ths, but the three that you're most likely to encounter are sus2, add9, and 9 chords. You start with the sus2 chord, a chord that has its 3rd replaced or suspended by a 2nd.

Sus2 chords

Sus2 chords are stacked 1-2-5 or some combination thereof. The two most common sus2 chord shapes are based on A and D in the open position, as shown in Figure 3-9, with numbers representing intervals. Notice that neither chord has a 3rd. For this reason, the chords are called sus and the 2nds are still called 2nds even though they extend more than an octave away from the chord roots. You can move these shapes up and play them as full or partial barre chords to produce sus2 chords for other notes.

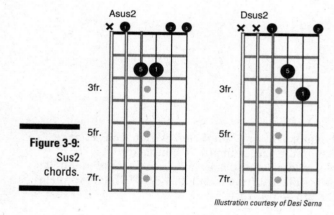

Figure 3-9: Sus2 chords.

Illustration courtesy of Desi Serna

Book III

Getting to Know Guitar Theory

Add9 chords

Technically, an add9 is a 2nd that's extended in the next register and added to a chord that still retains its 3rd. It's supposed to be stacked 1-3-5-9, with the 9th above the 3rd, but you occasionally see it stacked differently on guitar. You may also hear and see this chord identified as an add2. You see common add9 examples in Figure 3-10.

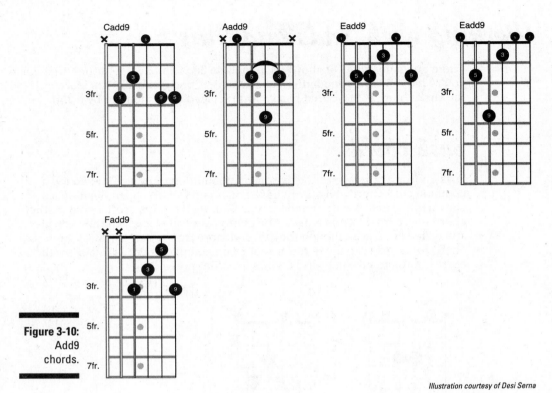

Figure 3-10: Add9 chords.

Illustration courtesy of Desi Serna

Note: Major chords with major 7ths are called *maj7*. When a chord name includes *maj* along with a number other than 7, it's implied that a 7th is also present. For example, a Gmaj9 chord is a Gmaj7 with an added 9th. It's formula is 1-3-5-7-9. (This is different from a Gadd9, 1-3-5-9, which is a plain major triad with an added 9th — no 7th.)

Minor chords with 2nds and 9ths

2nds and 9ths are more likely to be added to major chords, but you occasionally see them in minor chords, too. When a minor 3rd is replaced with a 2nd, the chord is still called a sus2. After all, its formula is still 1-2-5. For example, Am, 1-♭3-5, becomes Asus2, 1-2-5. If you add a 2nd or 9th but retain the minor 3rd, the chord is called minor add9 and is usually written as m(add9). Chords written as m(add9) are some combination of 1-♭3-5-9. Figure 3-11 shows a few examples.

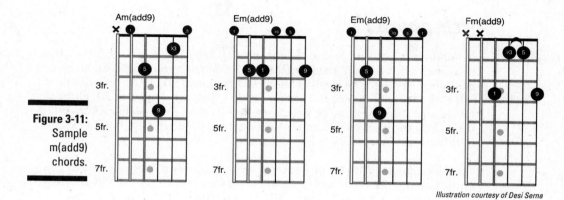

Figure 3-11:
Sample
m(add9)
chords.

Illustration courtesy of Desi Serna

Note: Minor chords with minor 7ths are called *m7*. When a chord name includes *m* along with a number other than 7, it's implied that a 7th is also present. For example, an Em9 chord is an Em7 with an added 9th. Its formula is 1-♭3-5-♭7-9. (This is different from an Em(add9), 1-♭3-5-9, which is a plain minor triad with an added 9th, no 7th.)

Here is a list of songs that each feature at least one major or minor chord as either a sus2 or add9:

"Black Diamond" by Kiss

"Castles Made of Sand" by Jimi Hendrix

"Every Breath You Take" by The Police

"Fire and Rain" by James Taylor

"If I Had $1,000,000" by Barenaked Ladies

"Message in a Bottle" by The Police

"Talkin' 'Bout a Revolution" by Tracy Chapman

"What I Am" by Edie Brickell and the New Bohemians

"Wonderwall" by Oasis

Sus2 and add9 chords naturally occur on all but chords iii and vii in the major scale. In music theory, Roman numerals (I, II, III, IV, and so on) represent both the degrees of the major scale and the chord quality of each chord. Uppercase Roman numerals represent major chords, and lowercase numerals represent minor chords. See Book III Chapter 4 for a detailed explanation of chords written in Roman numerals.

9th chords

In addition to add9 and m(add9) chords, you see chords like G9, C9, and D9 in music. When a chord name includes a 9 that isn't preceded by *add, m,* or anything else, then the implied chord is a *dominant* 9th, which is a dominant 7th chord with a 9th (see the earlier section "Playing dominant 7th chords" for details). The formula for 9th chords is 1-3-5-♭7-9. It naturally occurs on chord V in the major scale and is the only type of chord with both a 7th and 9th that regularly occurs in popular music.

Just as dominant 7th chords are represented by only a 7, dominant 9th chords are marked only with a 9. Guitar players frequently use 9th chords, especially in blues music. Figure 3-12 shows a few of the most common shapes. With the G9 shapes, the root notes used for tracking are on the 6th string (shown in the white dots) and not usually played.

As you play complex chords, it's not always possible or practical to include all chord tones. As a result, you often leave some chord members out, as seen with the G9/B and G9/F in Figure 3-12, both of which omit the root.

The following songs all feature 9th chords:

"Come On (Part II)" by Jimi Hendrix

"Cult of Personality" by Living Colour

"Jeff's Boogie" by Jeff Beck

"Oye Como Va" by Santana

"Play that Funky Music" by Wild Cherry

Note: Extended dominant chords are dominant 7th chords with extensions added. They include the 7th and all extensions leading up to the number in the chord name. So D11 is 1-3-5-♭7-9-11 and D13 is 1-3-5-♭7-9-11-13. Because guitar players can't stack chords like this, if these chords occur at all, they're played as fragments with some chord members left out.

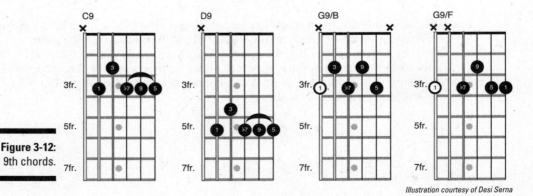

Figure 3-12:
9th chords.

Illustration courtesy of Desi Serna

Working with 4ths and 11ths

By far the most common type of 4th chord that you encounter is a sus4, where a 4th replaces the 3rd and a chord is stacked 1-4-5. On occasion, a 4th is added and the 3rd is retained, in which case you view the formula as either 1-3-4-5 or 1-3-5-11 and call it either add4 or add11.

Sus4 chords

Figure 3-13 includes a handful of sus4 chords in various keys. Sus4 chords naturally occur on chords I and V (see Book III Chapter 4 for more on Roman numeral chords). You can also move these shapes up the neck and use them as full or partial barre chords. The F shape is one example of a barre chord; it's actually a partial E form.

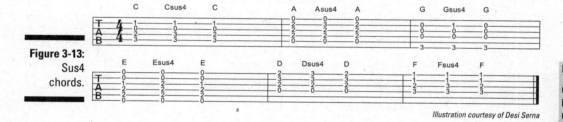

Figure 3-13:
Sus4
chords.

Illustration courtesy of Desi Serna

Book III

Getting to Know Guitar Theory

In a major scale, sus4 chords occur on the 1st and 5th degrees. For example, the G major scale produces both a Gsus4 and a Dsus4. You may expect the other major chord in the key, C, to also produce a sus4 chord, but it doesn't. When you count from C in the G major scale, its 4th is F♯, a half step higher than a perfect 4th interval. The 4th degree in the major scale always has a ♯4th. You often hear this naturally raised interval in a song's melody, but you don't usually hear it in the guitar chords. In fact, even though the 4th chord in a key technically has a ♯4th, guitarists are far more likely to use a regular (perfect) 4th on it instead, probably not knowing the difference.

Add4 chords

Figure 3-14 offers a few examples of add4 chords, which can also be called add11 depending on how the chords are stacked and your preference. Notice that the Cadd4, stacked 1-4-5-1-3, keeps its 3rd, E (the 1st string open). Likewise, the Gadd11, stacked 1-3-5-1-11-1, keeps its 3rd, B (2nd fret of the 5th string). The Dadd4, stacked 1-3-4-1-5, is a type of C form moved up two frets without barring.

Figure 3-14:
Add4
chords.

Play the Dadd4 in Figure 3-14 with the 1st string open and it becomes Dadd4(add9). The 1st string, E, is a 9th to D.

The following songs feature some form of sus4 or add4:

"All Shook Up" by Elvis Presley

"Brass in Pocket" by The Pretenders

"Pinball Wizard" by The Who

"Closer to Fine" by Indigo Girls

"Eye of the Tiger" by Survivor

"Margaritaville" by Jimmy Buffet

"Signs" by Tesla

"Stairway to Heaven" by Led Zeppelin

"What I Like About You" by The Romantics

"Yellow Ledbetter" by Pearl Jam

Playing 6th Chords and Blues Shuffles

A 6th chord is some combination of 1-3-5-6 (see Figure 3-15). If a 6th extends beyond the 7th, it's still called a 6th unless a 7th is also present in the chord, in which case it's called a major 13th.

The following songs feature 6th chords:

"Bad Moon Rising" by Creedence Clearwater Revival

"Brass in Pocket" by The Pretenders

"Laughing" by The Guess Who

"Lenny" by Stevie Ray Vaughan

"Lie in Our Graves" by Dave Matthews Band

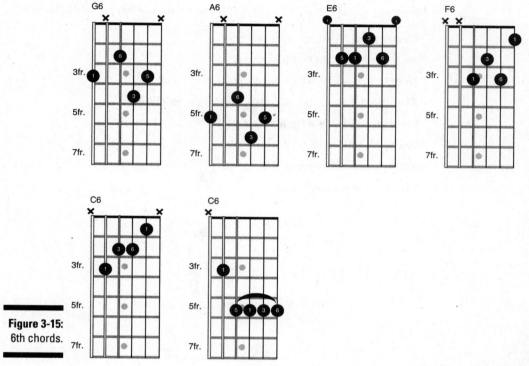

Figure 3-15: 6th chords.

Illustration courtesy of Desi Serna

Book III

Getting to Know Guitar Theory

By far the most common use of 6ths on guitar is when guitarists play the so-called "blues shuffle" or "boogie-woogie" that accompanies many rock, rockabilly, and blues songs. In a blues shuffle, a root and 5th are alternated with a root and 6th, as shown in Figure 3-16. Here, the progression is A-D-E-A, I-IV-V-I in A major. On these major scale degrees, 6ths occur naturally.

Figure 3-16: Blues shuffle with 6ths.

Illustration courtesy of Desi Serna

Watch Video Clip 23 to see and hear the 6ths example from Figure 3-16.

The following songs are all good examples of using a blues shuffle with 6ths:

"Glory Days" by Bruce Springsteen

"Jet Airliner" by Steve Miller Band

"Johnny B. Goode" by Chuck Berry

"Keep Your Hands to Yourself" by Georgia Satellites

"Red House" by Jimi Hendrix (bass)

"Rocky Mountain Way" by Joe Walsh

"Taking Care of Business" by Bachman-Turner Overdrive

"Truckin'" by Grateful Dead

Chapter 4

Playing Chord Progressions by Numbers

In This Chapter

▶ Progressing to chord progressions, using the major scale

▶ Numbering chords in a key with Roman numerals

▶ Visualizing chord patterns on the fretboard

▶ Playing through popular chord progressions

▶ Access the audio track and video clips at www.dummies.com/go/guitaraio/

Have you ever wondered what it means to play a "one, four, five"? Why do some guitarists seem to pick up on new chord changes so easily, almost knowing what's coming next in a song the first time through? What's the trick to transposing a song to a new key quickly and easily without having to fuss with key signatures and notes and rebuilding chords?

In music, different songs often use the same types of chord changes. On the fretboard, these chord changes make patterns that guitarists visualize and follow by number. The chords and numbers are based on the triads and degrees of the major scale talked about in Book III Chapter 3.

The neat thing about using patterns is that all keys look and feel the same. Numbers stay the same from key to key, too. You can pick up a chord progression (or series) from one key and move it to another as easily as moving a chord shape or scale pattern.

In this chapter, you play by numbers, using some of the most recognizable chord progressions in popular music. You find out how to identify the chords of any key instantly and reproduce chord progressions in new positions in the snap of a finger.

Listen to Audio Track 47 to hear sample chord progressions and get an overview of this chapter.

Drawing Chord Progressions from the Major Scale

A *chord progression* is any series of chords used in a piece of music. For example, the chord progression to "Wild Thing" by The Troggs is A-D-E-D. Chords can go together in all sorts of ways, but they're usually drawn from a scale — specifically, the major scale.

You use the major scale to stack groups of three intervals called *triads* (see Book III Chapter 1 for everything you need to know about triads). These triads harmonize the scale and form chords. Each scale degree produces a different chord and number. The sequence of major and minor chords found in the major scale looks like this:

1-2-3-4-5-6-7

Major-minor-minor-major-major-minor-minor♭5 (also called a *diminished triad;* see Book III Chapter 1)

Using the key of G as an example, the major scale chords are

G-A-B-C-D-E-F♯

1-2-3-4-5-6-7

G-Am-Bm-C-D-Em-F♯m♭5

Play through this key by using the standard barre chords shown in Figure 4-1.

Figure 4-1: Major scale chords in G.

Illustration courtesy of Desi Serna

Using Roman Numerals to Represent Chords

In traditional music theory, Roman numerals (I, II, III, IV, and so on) represent both the degrees of the major scale and the chord quality of each chord. Uppercase Roman numerals represent major chords, and lowercase numerals represent minor chords. Table 4-1 lists the Roman numerals that represent chords, along with the major/minor sequence of the major scale and a sample key of G major.

Table 4-1	Roman Numerals Used to Represent Chords			
Chord Number	Uppercase Roman Numeral	Lowercase Roman Numeral	Major/Minor Sequence of the Major Scale	G Major Scale
1	I	i	I	G
2	II	ii	ii	Am
3	III	iii	iii	Bm
4	IV	iv	IV	C
5	V	v	V	D
6	VI	vi	vi	Em
7	VII	vii	vii♭5	F#m♭5

Visualizing Numbers on the Fretboard

Figure 4-2 shows the number pattern made by the G scale on the fretboard. Notice that the chords in this pattern are the same chords shown in Figure 4-1. Guitarists come to know this pattern very well because songs regularly use chord progressions that move through it in predictable ways.

Book III

Getting to Know Guitar Theory

G major scale

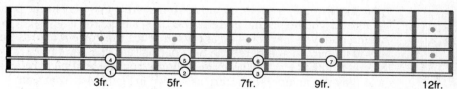

G major scale Roman numerals

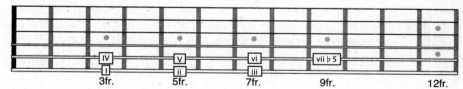

G major scale chords

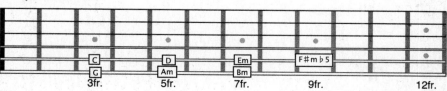

Figure 4-2: Major scale chord pattern in G.

Illustration courtesy of Desi Serna

Hear and see the chord pattern from Figure 4-2 played by watching Video Clip 24.

This chord pattern is the basis for the first half of this chapter and needs to be memorized now. While you play through it, call out each chord number as you play it. As you rehearse, try the following different combinations:

1. **Play chords I through vi forward and backward.**

2. **Play just the majors (I, IV, and V) forward and backward.**

3. **Play just the minors (ii, iii, and vi) forward and backward.**

4. **Alternate between the 6th and 5th strings by playing I-IV, ii-V, and iii-vi.**

Most progressions are based on the first six chords of the major scale, so you can disregard the seventh chord, vii♭5, and leave it out of the patterns. The minor triad with a flattened 5th is also called a *diminished triad*. The diminished triad is not to be confused with or used in the same way as full diminished and diminished 7th chords.

Transposing to New Keys

After you memorize the G major chord pattern from the preceding section, you can instantly play the chords in any new key simply by moving to a different position. For example, move the whole chord pattern up two frets and play in the A major scale. Or move up four frets and play in the B major scale. Wherever you begin this pattern, the 1st scale degree is your key. No matter which note you start on, you always produce the correct chords for that scale if you follow the numbers. The best part is that you don't have to concern yourself with the actual notes and chords you use; just pick a starting point and play the numbered pattern as shown in Figure 4-3. That's all!

With this chord pattern, all keys look and feel the same. The notes and chord names aren't even in in Figure 4-3 because you should think in terms of numbers. Just keep track of the note on your starting point — chord I. Notice that this pattern also works with I and IV as open chords in the key of E.

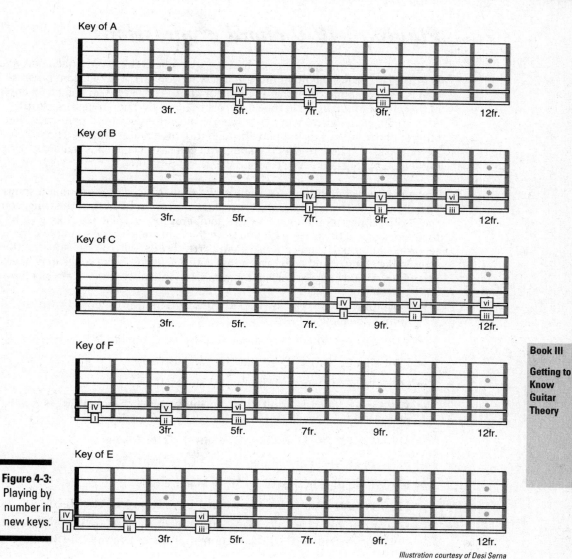

Figure 4-3:
Playing by
number in
new keys.

Key of A

Key of B

Key of C

Key of F

Key of E

Illustration courtesy of Desi Serna

Book III

**Getting to
Know
Guitar
Theory**

Playing Common Chord Progressions

You use the numbered chord pattern to put together chord progressions. This is where you get into playing by numbers. Songs can center on any number (chord) and combine numbers (chords) in any order and any amount. The most basic progression uses just the major chords, numbers I, IV, and V.

Playing I-IV-V chord progressions

By far the most common type of chord progression is the I-IV-V (that's *one, four, five,* in case the Roman numerals are throwing you off). A *I-IV-V chord progression* is any combination of the three major chords in a key. You find an example of this chord progression in the song "Wild Thing" by The Troggs. Its chords, A, D, and E, are I, IV, and V in the A major scale. Start the chord pattern at the 5th fret of the 6th string and play through the three major chords. That's it! If anyone asks you how to play the song, you can say, "Oh, it's just an ordinary I-IV-V in A. No big deal." You'll sound like a real pro.

The following list mentions just a few of the thousands of other common songs based on I-IV-V. To play through these, find the scale note on the 6th string, start the chord pattern, and then follow the numbers. You can also play along with the recordings of these songs, if you have them. In some of the examples, the recorded guitar parts may not use plain barre chords, but you can still practice strumming along using the barre chords in the pattern. These songs may have other chords and progressions in them too, but the main sections are as follows:

- **I-IV-V in A:** "Stir it Up" by Bob Marley, "When the Sun Goes Down" by Kenny Chesney

- **V-I-IV-I in A:** "What I Like about You" by The Romantics

- **I-IV-I-V in G:** "Brown Eyed Girl" by Van Morrison

- **I-IV-V-IV in G:** "Hang on Sloopy" by The McCoys

- **V-IV-I in G:** "Magic Carpet Ride" by Steppenwolf, "Seven Bridges Road" by the Eagles, "Sweet Home Alabama" by Lynyrd Skynyrd

- **I-IV-I-V in F:** "The Lion Sleeps Tonight" by The Tokens

- **I-IV-V in F:** "Twist and Shout" by The Isley Brothers

- **I-IV-V-IV in F:** "The Joker" by Steve Miller Band

- **I-IV-V-IV in B♭:** "Walking on Sunshine" by Katrina and The Waves

- **Mix of I-IV-V in E:** "I Love Rock 'n' Roll" by Joan Jett and the Blackhearts, "I Wanna Be Sedated" by the Ramones, "Walk of Life" by Dire Straits

You can form major and minor chords in other ways besides the standard barre chords used in this chapter. But using a different type of chord shape doesn't change a chord progression. For example, G-C-D is always I-IV-V, whether you use standard barre chords, open chords, or something else.

Playing major chord progressions

When a song centers on a major chord, it's called a *major chord progression.* Notice that in the previous song list the actual order of the chords varies. Also, some examples, like "What I Like about You" by The Romantics, don't even start on chord I. With the chord pattern you're using, progressions can center on any chord. Major chord progressions typically center on chord I or V, but IV is also an option.

Adding minor chords ii, iii, and vi

In the next group of lists, you see chord progressions that incorporate the minor chords in the pattern ii, iii, and vi. These examples are in different scales, so be sure to position the chord pattern with chord I on the right starting note. As you play through these progressions, remember to call out the numbers while you're at it.

- ✔ **ii chord:** "Heaven" by Los Lonely Boys (I-ii G with guitars tuned down one half-step to E♭), "One Night at a Time" by George Strait (I-ii-IV A), "Upside Down" by Jack Johnson (I-ii and I-ii-IV-V E), "What's Up?" by 4 Non Blondes (I-ii-IV A)

- ✔ **iii chord:** "All She Wants to Do Is Dance" by Don Henley (V-I-iii-IV G), "Do You Believe in Love" by Huey Lewis and the News (I-iii-IV-V B), "The Weight" by The Band (I-iii-IV A)

- ✔ **vi chord:** "Earth Angel (Will You Be Mine)" by The Penguins (I-vi-IV-V B♭), "Every Breath You Take" by The Police (I-vi-IV-V A♭), "Hit Me with Your Best Shot" by Pat Benatar (Mix of I-IV-V-vi E), "Hurts So Good" by John Mellencamp (I-V-vi-IV A), "I'm Yours" by Jason Mraz (I-V-vi-IV B), "Stand by Me" by Ben E. King (I-vi-IV-V A), "When I Come Around" by Green Day (I-V-vi-IV G)

Book III

Getting to Know Guitar Theory

Playing minor chord progressions

When a song centers on a minor chord, it's called a *minor chord progression*. It can be any progression that centers on chord ii, iii, or vi in the major scale. The following song examples all start and center on a minor chord. The major scales that these progressions are based in are indicated in parentheses. For example, "Black Magic Woman" is vi-ii-iii in the F major scale, so position the chord pattern to start on F. Find out more about minor chord progressions in Book III Chapter 5.

"All Along the Watchtower" by Jimi Hendrix (vi-V-IV-V E with guitars tuned down one half-step to E♭)

"Black Magic Woman" by Santana (mix of vi-ii-iii F)

"Evil Ways" by Santana (ii-V F)

"Layla (Unplugged)" by Eric Clapton (vi-IV-V F)

"Livin' on a Prayer" by Bon Jovi (vi-IV-V G)

"Moondance" by Van Morrison (ii-iii G)

"Oye Como Va" by Santana (ii-V G)

"Paranoid" by Black Sabbath (vi-V-I-IV G)

"Rockin' in the Free World" by Neil Young (vi-V-IV G)

"Who Will Save Your Soul" by Jewel (ii-IV-I-V G)

Starting Numbers on the 5th String

In this section, you build a new chord pattern that starts on the 5th string. The chords and scale degrees are still drawn from the major scale. The numbers stay the same, too. But the pattern looks and feels different because chords I, ii, and iii are placed on the 5th string, whereas the others — IV, V, and vi — get moved over to the 6th string. This pattern doesn't line up as nicely as the last one, but it's used just as much and needs to be played. Starting on the 5th string gives you better access to some keys by allowing you to play them in more comfortable positions. You start in the key of C with chord I at the 3rd fret of the 5th string, as shown in Figure 4-4. This example also includes the vii♭5 chord so you can complete the scale, but it won't be used once you begin playing chord progressions.

Figure 4-4: Major scale chords in C.

Illustration courtesy of Desi Serna

Figure 4-5 shows what the chords from Figure 4-3 look like as a fretboard pattern. You focus on using only the first six chords on the fretboard because vii♭5 is rarely, if ever, used.

The chords shown in Figure 4-5 are exactly the same as the C chords in the pattern that begins at the 8th fret of the 6th string from the previous section. The only difference is that you play in a different position. Take a moment to play through this pattern forward and backward while calling out the numbers as you go.

Generally speaking, you use this new chord pattern in keys that would reach too high on the fretboard when based on the 6th string. For example, in the keys of B, C, and D, it's difficult to reach up to the iii and vi chords. Plus, barre chords near the 12th fret are voiced too high — that is, they sound too high-pitched for most rhythm playing. In Figure 4-6, you move this pattern around and play in some different keys. Notice that the same pattern also works in the key of B, using an open E chord on IV. You always need to think about using open strings!

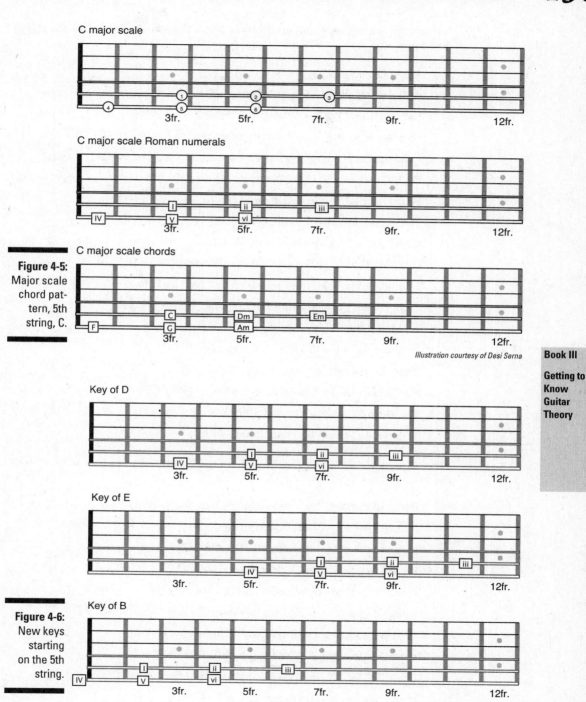

C major scale

C major scale Roman numerals

C major scale chords

Figure 4-5:
Major scale chord pattern, 5th string, C.

Illustration courtesy of Desi Serna

Key of D

Key of E

Figure 4-6:
New keys starting on the 5th string.

Illustration courtesy of Desi Serna

Key of B

Book III

Getting to Know Guitar Theory

The following songs are all variations of I-IV-V that work well in the 5th string chord pattern:

"Angel Of Harlem" by U2 (I-IV-V C)

"Authority Song" by John Mellencamp (I-IV-V D)

"Baba O'Riley" by The Who (I-V-IV F)

"Bad Moon Rising" by Creedence Clearwater Revival (I-V-IV D)

"Crimson and Clover" by Tommy James and the Shondells (I-V-IV B)

"Do Ya" by Electric Light Orchestra (I-V-IV D)

"Feliz Navidad" by Jose Feliciano (IV-V-I D)

"The First Cut Is the Deepest" by Sheryl Crow (I-V-IV D)

"Good Lovin'" by The Rascals (I-IV-V-IV D)

"Hold My Hand" by Hootie and the Blowfish (I-IV-V B)

"I Could Never Take the Place of Your Man" by Prince (I-V-IV C)

"I Still Haven't Found What I'm Looking For" by U2 (I-IV-V D♭)

"A Life of Illusion" by Joe Walsh (I-IV-V D)

"Nothing but a Good Time" by Poison (V-IV-I D)

"Twist and Shout" by The Beatles (I-IV-V D)

"She's So Cold" by The Rolling Stones (V-I-IV-V C)

"Southern Cross" by Crosby, Stills & Nash (V-IV-I D)

"Yellow Ledbetter" by Pearl Jam (I-V-IV E)

The next list of songs includes examples with minor chords that work well in the 5th string chord pattern:

"Beast of Burden" by The Rolling Stones (I-V-vi-IV E)

"Blessed Be Your Name" by Matt Redman (I-V-vi-IV B)

"Dy'er Mak'er" by Led Zeppelin (I-vi-IV-V C)

"Friend of God" by Israel Houghton (I-vi-ii-I D)

"Jessie's Girl" by Rick Springfield (I-V-vi-IV-V-I D)

"Heard It in a Love Song" by Marshall Tucker Band (I-iii-IV-V D)

"How Great Is Our God" by Chris Tomlin (I-vi-IV-V D♭)

"Lean on Me" by Bill Withers (I-ii-iii-IV, IV-iii-ii-I C)

"Let It Be" by The Beatles (I-V-vi-IV, I-V-IV-I C)

"Louie, Louie" by The Kingsmen (V-I-ii-I D)

"Runaround Sue" by Dion (I-vi-IV-V D)

"Two Princes" by Spin Doctors (I-vi-V-IV D)

"Unchained Melody" by The Righteous Brothers (I-vi-IV-V C)

"Under the Bridge" by Red Hot Chili Peppers (I-V-vi-iii-IV E)

"With or Without You" by U2 (I-V-vi-IV D)

"You Are the Woman" by Firefall (I-iii-ii-V D)

This next list has songs that not only use minor chords but center on one, mostly chord vi, creating minor keys:

"Californication" by Red Hot Chili Peppers (vi-IV C)

"Don't Fear the Reaper" by Blue Oyster Cult (vi-V-IV-V C)

"Horse with No Name" by America (ii-iii D)

"Maria, Maria" by Santana (vi-ii-iii C)

"Otherside" by Red Hot Chili Peppers (vi-IV-I-V C)

"The Thrill Is Gone" by B.B. King (vi-ii-vi-IV-iii-vi D)

Playing Chord Progressions with Open Chords

Book III

Getting to Know Guitar Theory

You can use the two chord patterns covered in this chapter to track chord progressions in the open position too, although doing so takes some extra work and requires that you identify the actual note name of each chord.

To play in the key of G using common open chords, visualize the 6th string chord pattern starting on G at the 3rd fret (Figure 4-2) and replace each barre chord with an open chord. Here's how:

1. **Visualize the 1st barre chord, the I chord (G), but play an open G chord instead.**

2. **Visualize the 2nd chord, the ii chord (Am), but play an open Am instead.**

3. **Because there's no open chord iii (Bm), play Bm at the 2nd fret of the 5th string close to the open position instead.**

4. **Use common open chords to play chords IV, V, and vi (C, D, and Em).**

5. **Play through all the chords forward and backward, calling out the numbers as you go.**

Follow along with your eye using the 6th string chord pattern even though you're not using its barre chords.

Watch Video Clip 25 for a demonstration on how to play by number in the open position.

After you get the hang of playing like this in G, you can move the chord pattern and use open chords in other keys like F and A. When you do this, play open chords when you can and use the barre chords to fill in the rest, staying as close to the open position as possible. For example, in the key of F, you can play the Am, C, and Dm as open chords, but you have to use the barre chords to play the rest. In the key of A, you can play A, D, and E as open chords, Bm and C#m at the 2nd and 4th frets of the 5th string, and F#m at the 2nd fret of the 6th string.

Do the same thing with the 5th string chord pattern starting in the key of C. In C, you can play all the chords as open chords except for F, which guitarists usually play as a partial barre chord when it's paired with open chords. Move the chord pattern and use open chords in other keys; just remember to stay as close to the open position as possible when you need to fill in with barre chords.

After you get the hang of playing in the open position, you can revisit any of the song lists in this chapter and try working out the progressions using open chords. When you do, call out the numbers as you go so that in time you know your way around the open position by number as well as you do the barre chord patterns.

Chapter 5

Identifying Tonics, Keys, and Modes

In This Chapter

▶ Getting familiar with tonics

▶ Defining relative major and relative minor

▶ Identifying modes and parent major scales

▶ Renumbering chords and progressions

▶ Comparing scale formulas and structures

▶ Access the audio track and video clips at www.dummies.com/go/guitaraio/

*W*hen musicians say that a song is in the "key of" this or that, they can mean a few different things. They may be referring to the primary pitch or chord that the music centers on, the major scale that the notes and chords are drawn from, or the mode that everything is based on.

In this chapter, you get to know the different types of keys associated with music, and you find out how to renumber chords and progressions to reflect the modes of the major scale. You also gain a little insight into key signatures, an element of standard written notation.

Although this chapter gets a bit technical, don't be discouraged. Analyzing keys, modes, and songs helps you discover new things about the inner workings of music. This, in turn, makes you a better player, composer, and improviser. The information in this chapter also helps you as you work with other topics throughout the book.

Listen to Audio Track 48 to get an idea of what this chapter is all about.

Understanding the Relationship between Major and Minor Scales

Every piece of music has a tonal center called a *tonic*. The tonic is the primary pitch or chord that everything else revolves around. It's where a piece of music sounds resolved or complete and usually where the music begins and ends.

Generally speaking, the tonic also determines a song's *key*. There are two basic types of music tonalities and keys: major and minor. If a piece of music centers on a major chord, then it's considered to be in a major key. If music centers on a minor chord, it's in a minor key. For instance, if a song centers on a G chord, you say it's in the *key of G*. Similarly, when an Em chord is the center, you call it the key of E minor.

Traditionally, music has been taught as being in either the major or minor scale. The good news is if you know the major scale, then you also know the minor scale. The minor scale is drawn from the 6th degree of the major scale. Start any major scale on its 6th degree and you have a minor scale. For example, the 6th degree in the G major scale is E. The E minor scale is simply the notes of G major starting on E, as you see here:

G major scale

1-2-3-4-5-6-7

G-A-B-C-D-E-F♯

E minor scale

1-2-3-4-5-6-7

E-F♯-G-A-B-C-D

The relationship between the major and minor scales (and between the 1st and 6th chords) is often described as being *relative*. For example, in the key of G, I and vi are G and Em. G major is the *relative major* of E minor, and E minor is the *relative minor* of G major. This relative relationship holds true in all keys. In the key of C, for example, the I chord is C major and the vi chord is A minor. They, too, are relative major and minor chords and scales. In written music, relative major and minor keys actually share the same key signature.

Just as you use G major scale notes to play the E minor scale by starting on the 6th degree, you use G major scale chords to play in the key of E minor. The following list shows the chords for both the G major scale and its relative minor, E minor. Notice how the E minor scale features the very same chords, starting on the 6th degree:

G major

1-2-3-4-5-6-7

G-Am-Bm-C-D-Em-F♯m♭5

E minor

1-2-3-4-5-6-7

Em-F#m♭5-G-Am-Bm-C-D

As discussed in Book III Chapter 4, the major scale chords are represented with Roman numerals that look like this:

I-ii-iii-IV-V-vi-vii♭5

Rearrange the major scale with the 6th degree in the first position and you get this sequence:

vi-vii♭5-I-ii-iii-IV-V

Numbering the Relative Minor

The major scale has seven degrees, with a triad built on each one. In music, uppercase Roman numerals represent major chords, and lowercase Roman numerals represent minor chords, as you can see in this example:

1-2-3-4-5-6-7

I-ii-iii-IV-V-vi-vii♭5

You may recognize this example as the major scale. After all, in music, you use the major scale as your starting place for naming chords, scale degrees, and intervals. From this perspective, the pattern of whole steps and half steps between the scale degrees of the major scale are what you think of as the naturally occurring ones.

If the distance between any two scale degrees changes for some reason, you can reflect this change with an *accidental* — typically a sharp or a flat. For example, a flattened 3rd scale degree is written ♭3 and is a half step (semitone) lower than the one found in a regular major scale. A sharpened 4th, #4, raises the 4th scale degree by a half step, and a flattened 7th, ♭7, lowers the 7th by a semitone . . . you get the idea.

When numbering scale degrees, you always regard the tonic as 1. Because the tonic in the E minor scale is E, you count the E as 1 and renumber everything else from there, as you see here:

E minor

1-2-♭3-4-5-♭6-♭7

E-F#-G-A-B-C-D

i-ii♭5-♭III-iv-v-♭VI-♭VII

Em-F#m♭5-G-Am-Bm-C-D

Keep in mind that the notes and chords of E minor are still the same as G major. The only difference is that you've rearranged the chords to begin with E. Don't forget to adjust the Roman numerals to match the new order. Because the major/minor sequence changes if you count the E as 1, you adjust the case of the Roman numerals to reflect the correct chord quality for each scale degree. For example, the 1st chord is now minor, so you have to write it with a lower-case Roman numeral: i. The 3rd chord changes from minor (iii) to major (III), and so on.

Accounting for any interval changes

When you renumber chords from the tonic, you also need to indicate any changes to the intervals between the chords. Compare the original G major scale with the new E minor scale:

> **G major**
>
> 1-2-3-4-5-6-7
>
> G-A-B-C-D-E-F♯
>
> I-ii-iii-IV-V-vi-vii♭5
>
> G-Am-Bm-C-D-Em-F♯m♭5
>
> **E minor**
>
> 1-2♭3-4-5♭6♭7
>
> E-F♯-G-A-B-C-D
>
> i-ii♭5♭III-iv-v♭VI♭VII
>
> Em-F♯m♭5-G-Am-Bm-C-D

Major scale intervals are what you think of as the naturally occurring ones. In the major scale, the distance from the 1st to 3rd degrees is two whole steps, better known as a major 3rd. But when you start counting from E, the distance from 1 to 3 is only one and a half steps, better known as a minor or flattened 3rd. As a result, the 3rd degree is preceded by a flat sign (♭3), as is its chord (♭III). For the same reason, the 6th and 7th degrees and chords are also flattened (♭6 and ♭7, ♭VI and ♭VII).

In Figure 5-1, you see what G major looks like on the fretboard as both scale degrees and Roman numeral chords, followed by the same notes and chords numbered to reflect E minor. Notice in the last diagram that you end up playing the same chords either way.

You can see a brief demonstration on playing in G major and E minor by watching Video Clip 26.

G major scale

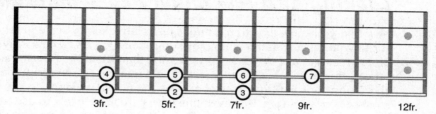

G major scale Roman numerals

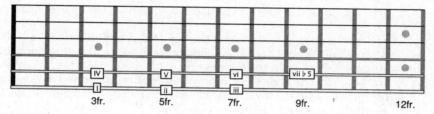

E minor scale

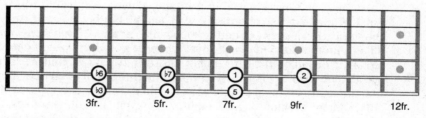

E minor scale Roman numerals

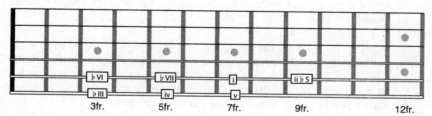

Same chords either way

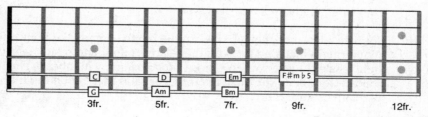

Figure 5-1:
G major
and E minor
scales and
chords.

Book III

**Getting to
Know
Guitar
Theory**

Looking at a few minor key song examples

Now that you know how to renumber the relative minor scale to reflect its starting point, consider a minor key song example, "Livin' on a Prayer" by Bon Jovi. It features the chord progression Em-C-D. In the G major scale, this progression is vi-IV-V. Of course, you could number this progression by the chord positions in G major; after all, G is the *parent major scale,* the scale that E minor is drawn from. However, musicians are more likely to use a number system that puts the tonic chord, Em, in the first position. If you go by the chord positions in the E minor scale, the progression becomes i-♭VI-♭VII. That's *one, flat six,* and *flat seven,* in case the Roman numerals are throwing you off.

For another example, consider the key of C. A minor is relative to C major where C and A are I and vi. To play the A minor scale, simply use the notes of C major, but start on the 6th degree, A. Likewise, use the C major chords, but start on Am. Use Figure 5-2 to play this relative major and minor scale on the fretboard. Notice that this new key starts the relative major on the 5th string, a pattern introduced in Book III Chapter 4.

Take the song "Maria Maria" by Santana, which uses the chords Am, Dm, and Em. In C major, these chords are vi, ii, and iii, but because the Am chord is the tonic, the chords are better known as i, iv, and v. That's *one, four,* and *five,* all as minor chords. In major keys, the most popular types of chord progressions are based on the three major chords I, IV, and V. Similar progressions are also popular in minor keys, where the three chords all appear as minor: i, iv, and v; this type of progression is called a *minor one-four-five.* Santana's "Black Magic Woman" is also a minor i-iv-v, only in a different key. It uses the chords Dm, Gm, and Am, which are vi, ii, and iii from the F major scale. When you renumber everything counting from the relative minor, Dm, the chords become i, iv, and v.

You can identify relative major and minor keys by using the two types of chord patterns shown in Figures 5-1 and 5-2 (which you also find in Book III Chapter 4). Wherever you move these patterns on the fretboard, chords I and vi are always the relative major and minor. Want to know the relative minor for B? Play a major scale chord pattern starting on B and then move to chord vi. That's the relative minor — always! Want to know the parent major scale for C♯m? Play C♯m on the fretboard, count it as vi, and then move to chord I. That's the relative major — always!

Here are a few more songs based in the relative minor. For your reference, numbering is included for both the relative minor and relative major. You may find it easier to work out the chord progression by number in a familiar major scale pattern first (shown in parentheses) and then renumber it according to its relative minor tonic.

C major scale

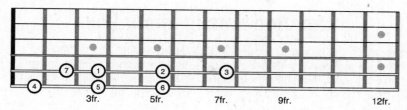

C major scale Roman numerals

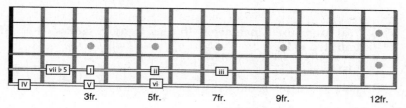

A minor scale

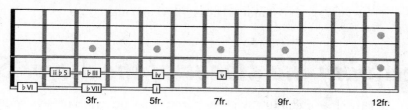

A minor scale Roman numerals

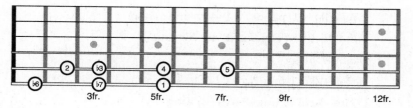

Same chords either way

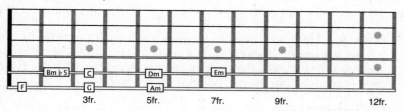

Figure 5-2: C major and A minor scales and chords.

Illustration courtesy of Desi Serna

Book III

Getting to Know Guitar Theory

Implied flats in minor keys

In minor keys, the flattened scale degrees, such as the 3rd and 6th, are often assumed rather than specifically mentioned or written. For example, in the key of E minor, a musician may refer to the G as the 3rd of the key without specifying that it's the flattened 3rd. Likewise, the three chord may be written simply as III with the minor key itself implying that it's ♭III. The same is true for ♭VI and ♭VII, so you may hear and see them simply referred to as VI and VII.

"All Along the Watchtower" by Jimi Hendrix (guitars tuned down one half step to E♭)

C♯m-B-A-B

i-♭VII-♭VI-♭VII in C♯ minor (vi-V-IV-V in E major)

"Layla" by Eric Clapton

Dm-B♭-C-Dm

i-♭VI-♭VII-i in D minor (vi-IV-V-vi in F major)

"Smells like Teen Spirit" by Nirvana

F5-B♭5-A♭5-D♭5

i-iv-♭III-♭VI in F minor (vi-ii-I-IV in A♭ major)

"The Thrill Is Gone" by B.B. King

Bm-Em-Bm-G-F♯m-Bm

i-iv-i-♭VI-v-i in B minor (vi-ii-vi-IV-iii-vi in D major)

Identifying the Modes of the Major Scale

Relative major and relative minor aren't the only types of keys you can have in music. In fact, any degree in the major scale can function as the tonic (or key) and serve as the starting place in the scale, so because the major scale has seven degrees, it also has seven possible starting points, or *modes*.

In a major scale, three degrees produce major triads and chords — I, IV, and V — so any one of these can be the mode of a piece of music. The major scale also has three degrees that produce minor chords — ii, iii, and vi — and each one of these can also be the mode of a piece of music.

Notice the 7th scale degree isn't mentioned as a modal option. The 7th chord in the major scale has a minor-flat-five quality (diminished triad), which has a dissonant and unresolved sound. The instability of its sound makes it impractical to base a piece of music on it.

Each mode of the major scale is identified by a Greek name:

- ✔ Ionian (I)
- ✔ Dorian (ii)
- ✔ Phrygian (iii)
- ✔ Lydian (IV)
- ✔ Mixolydian (V)
- ✔ Aeolian (vi)
- ✔ Locrian (vii♭5)

Ionian (I)

Ionian is the first mode of the major scale — when the 1st scale degree functions as the tonic. Because it centers on a major chord (I), it's considered a major key. It's better known as the *plain* or *relative major scale,* and it's one of the most commonly used modes. Refer to Figure 5-1 to see how to view the fretboard in Ionian mode. Just think *major scale.*

Any type of chord progression that's based in a major scale and centers on chord I is Ionian mode. Some chord progression and song examples include

Book III

Getting to Know Guitar Theory

"Twist and Shout" by The Beatles

D-G-A

I-IV-V in the D major scale.

D Ionian (better known as simply D major)

"Stir It Up" by Bob Marley

A-D-E

I-IV-V in the A major scale

A Ionian (better known as simply A major)

"The Lion Sleeps Tonight" by The Tokens

F-B♭-F-C

I-IV-I-V in the F major scale

F Ionian (better known as simply F major)

"Wonderful Tonight" by Eric Clapton

G-D-C-D

I-V-IV-V in the G major scale

G Ionian (better known as simply G major)

Dorian (ii)

Dorian is the second mode of the major scale — when the 2nd scale degree functions as the tonic. Because it centers on a minor chord (ii), it's considered a minor key. Although this type of minor scale isn't as common as Aeolian mode (the natural or relative minor, covered soon) it does come up from time to time, so you need to look out for it.

In the same way that you renumber the relative minor, you can renumber all the modes of the major scale, starting from their tonics to reflect their unique interval structures and chord qualities. Here's what happens to the G major scale when you reorganize its notes and chords, beginning with the 2nd degree, A, to produce A Dorian mode:

G major

1-2-3-4-5-6-7

G-A-B-C-D-E-F♯

I-ii-iii-IV-V-vi-vii♭5

G-Am-Bm-C-D-Em-F♯m♭5

A Dorian

1-2♭3-4-5-6♭7

A-B-C-D-E-F♯-G

i-ii♭III-IV-v-vi♭5♭VII

Am-Bm-C-D-Em-F♯m♭5-G

Notice how the interval structure changes from G major to A Dorian. When you start the scale from the 2nd degree, it has a flattened 3rd and 7th. Also, the Roman numerals change to reflect the new chord qualities of each degree.

In Figure 5-3 you see how A Dorian looks on the fretboard, using the G major scale chord pattern that begins on the 6th string. In this example, you see G major first and then the same notes and chords reorganized starting on A. You can move this pattern around the fretboard and produce Dorian mode in other keys.

You can see a brief demonstration on playing in A Dorian by watching Video Clip 27.

The example in Figure 5-3 is just a starting point. You can play in A Dorian mode anywhere on the fretboard by using G major scale notes and chords and centering on the 2nd degree, A.

Modes are thought of as their own scales too. You can think of the Dorian scale either as a major scale with a flattened 3rd and 7th or as a minor scale with a major 6th. Its most defining characteristic is the major 6th because minor scales usually have a flattened 6th. Having the major 6th changes how the Dorian scale sounds melodically. It also changes the chord structure. The major 6th makes Dorian's 4th chord major, something that doesn't occur in a natural minor scale. The major 6th also makes the 2nd chord in Dorian mode minor with a perfect 5th, allowing for i-ii chord progressions.

Here are a few sample chord progressions and songs based on the 2nd degree of the major scale. Numbering is included for both the mode and the parent major scale (the common major scale that the mode is drawn from). You may find it easier to work out the chord progression by number in a familiar major scale pattern first (shown in parentheses) and then renumber it according to its modal tonic.

"Oye Como Va" by Santana

Am7-D9

i-IV in A Dorian (ii-V in the G major scale)

"Moondance" by Van Morrison

Am7-Bm7

i-ii in A Dorian (ii-iii in the G major scale)

"Who Will Save Your Soul" by Jewel

Am-C-G-D

i-♭III-♭VII-IV in A Dorian (ii-IV-I-V in the G major scale)

"Evil Ways" by Santana

Gm-C

i-IV in G Dorian (ii-V in the F major scale)

"Horse with No Name" by America

Em-F♯m11

i-ii in E Dorian (ii-iii in the D major scale)

Book III

Getting to Know Guitar Theory

In addition to using the patterns shown in Figure 5-3, you may also find yourself playing Dorian mode while in the chord pattern that begins on the 5th string. Figure 5-4 shows you how to reorganize the C major scale to fit with its 2nd mode, D Dorian. "Another Brick in the Wall (Part II)" by Pink Floyd has chord changes based in D Dorian in this position. You can also move this pattern around the fretboard to produce Dorian mode in other keys.

You refer to modes by their tonic pitch and Greek name. So *A Dorian* means the tonic pitch is A and it's the 2nd scale degree in the major scale. If A is 2, then G must be 1 and the parent major scale. *G Dorian* means the tonic pitch is G and it's the 2nd degree in the major scale. If G is 2, then F is 1 and the parent major scale. Because mode names don't indicate the parent major scale, you have to figure them out on your own.

G major scale

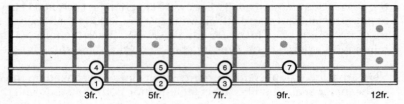

G major scale Roman numerals

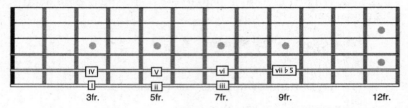

A Dorian mode

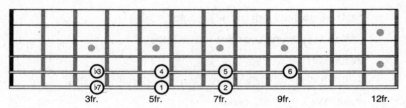

A Dorian mode Roman numerals

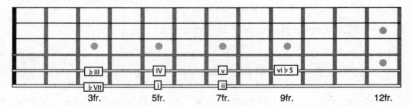

Same chords either way

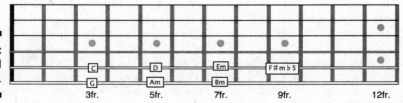

Figure 5-3:
G major and
A Dorian.

Illustration courtesy of Desi Serna

C major scale

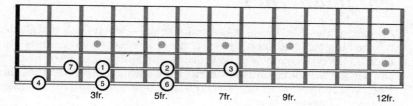

C major scale Roman numerals

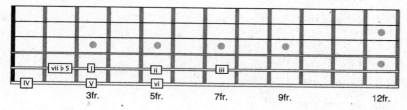

D Dorian mode

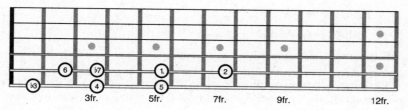

Book III

Getting to Know Guitar Theory

D Dorian mode Roman numerals

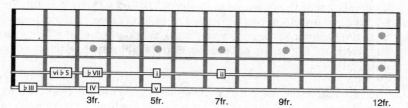

Same chords either way

Figure 5-4:
C major and
D Dorian.

Illustration courtesy of Desi Serna

Phrygian (iii)

Phrygian is the third mode of the major scale — when the 3rd scale degree functions as the tonic. It's considered a minor key because it centers on a minor chord. This type of minor scale is pretty uncommon, but some heavy metal artists use it for its dark, unusual sound. Here's what happens to the G major scale when you reorganize its notes and chords, beginning with the 3rd degree, B, to produce B Phrygian mode:

G major

1-2-3-4-5-6-7

G-A-B-C-D-E-F♯

I-ii-iii-IV-V-vi-vii♭5

G-Am-Bm-C-D-Em-F♯m♭5

B Phrygian

1♭2♭3-4-5♭6♭7

B-C-D-E-F♯-G-A

i♭II♭III-iv-v♭5♭VI♭vii

Bm-C-D-Em-F♯m♭5-G-Am

Phrygian is a type of minor scale with a flattened 2nd as its most defining characteristic. Figure 5-5 shows how B Phrygian comes from its parent major scale, G.

Remember that the example in Figure 5-5 is just a starting point. You can play B Phrygian anywhere on the fretboard as long as you use notes and chords from the G major scale and center on B. When playing in B Phrygian, most guitarists opt to put the chords Bm and C right next to each other on the same string.

You can also move the pattern in Figure 5-5 around the fretboard to play Phrygian mode in other keys. Figure 5-6 shows how E Phrygian is taken from its parent major scale, C. This example puts you into a chord pattern that begins on the 5th string. You can move this pattern around to play in other Phrygian keys, too. In E Phrygian, guitarists seem to prefer playing off of the open 6th string, putting an E5 and F5 right next to each other.

Here are some sample chord progressions and songs based on the 3rd degree of the major scale. You may find it easier to work out the chord progression by number in a familiar major scale pattern first (shown in parentheses) and then renumber it according to its Phrygian tonic.

G major scale

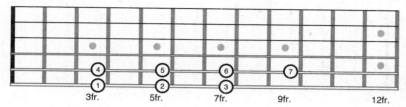

3fr. 5fr. 7fr. 9fr. 12fr.

G major scale Roman numerals

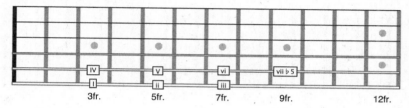

3fr. 5fr. 7fr. 9fr. 12fr.

B Phrygian mode

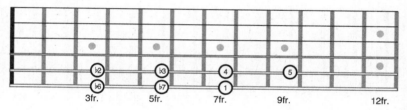

3fr. 5fr. 7fr. 9fr. 12fr.

B Phrygian mode Roman numerals

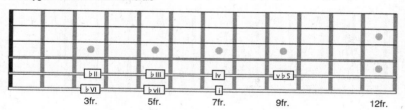

3fr. 5fr. 7fr. 9fr. 12fr.

Same chords either way

Figure 5-5:
G major and
B Phrygian.

3fr. 5fr. 7fr. 9fr. 12fr.

Illustration courtesy of Desi Serna

Book III

Getting to Know Guitar Theory

C major scale

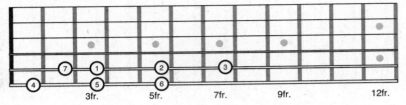

C major scale Roman numerals

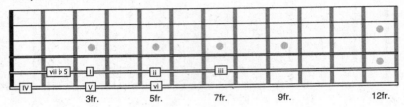

E Phrygian mode

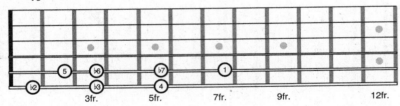

E Phrygian mode Roman numerals

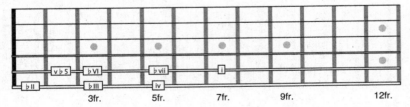

Same chords either way

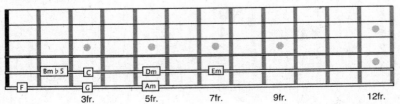

Figure 5-6:
C major and
E Phrygian.

Illustration courtesy of Desi Serna

"The Sails of Charon" by Scorpions

B5-C5

i-♭II in B Phrygian (iii-IV in the G major scale)

"Remember Tomorrow" by Iron Maiden

Em-F

i-♭II in E Phrygian (iii-IV in the C major scale)

"War" by Joe Satriani (guitars tuned down one half step to E♭)

E5-F5

i-♭II in E Phrygian (iii-IV in the C major scale)

"Symphony of Destruction" by Megadeth

F5-E5

♭II-i in E Phrygian (IV-i in the C major scale)

Though this progression starts on the ♭II chord, F5, the i chord, E5, is functioning as the tonic in the song example.

Songs don't always stay in one key. Some of the songs listed in this chapter have certain modal sections but then move on to other keys. For example, "War" by Joe Satriani starts in E Phrygian but then cycles through other types of keys from there. Similarly, "Moondance" by Van Morrison starts in A Dorian but then changes to other modes.

Book III

Getting to Know Guitar Theory

Lydian (IV)

Lydian is the fourth mode of the major scale — when the 4th scale degree functions as the tonic. Because it centers on a major chord, it's considered a major key. Rarely do you hear a song that's completely in Lydian mode. Instead, this mode usually occurs only temporarily in a song, until the music moves to a more stable tonic like I. Here you see what happens to the G major scale when you reorganize its notes and chords, beginning with the 4th degree, C, to produce C Lydian mode:

G major

1-2-3-4-5-6-7

G-A-B-C-D-E-F♯

I-ii-iii-IV-V-vi-vii♭5

G-Am-Bm-C-D-Em-F♯m♭5

C Lydian

1-2-3-♯4-5-6-7

C-D-E-F♯-G-A-B

I-II-iii-♯iv♭5-V-vi-vii

C-D-Em-F♯m♭5-G-Am-Bm

The most defining characteristic of Lydian mode is its sharpened 4th, which is why many musicians think of it as a major scale with a sharpened 4th. In Figure 5-7, you see C Lydian taken from its parent major scale, G.

You can play C Lydian anywhere on the fretboard as long as you use notes and chords from the G major scale and center on C. You can also move the pattern in Figure 5-7 around the fretboard to play Lydian mode in other keys.

Figure 5-8 puts you in a new major scale pattern that begins on the 5th string. Here, the parent major scale is C and the mode is F Lydian. Again, this is just a starting point. You find the same notes and chords elsewhere on the fretboard, and you can move this pattern around to play in other keys.

Here are a few sample chord progressions and songs based on the 4th degree of the major scale:

"Dreams" by Fleetwood Mac

Fmaj7-G6

I-II in F Lydian (IV-V in the C major scale)

"Just Remember I Love You" by Firefall

Fmaj7-G6

I-II in F Lydian (IV-V in the C major scale)

"Jane Says" by Jane's Addiction

G-A

I-II in G Lydian (IV-V in the D major scale)

"Here Comes My Girl" by Tom Petty

A-B

I-II in A Lydian (IV-V in the E major scale)

"Man on the Moon" by R.E.M.

C-D

I-II in C Lydian (IV-V in the G major scale)

"Hey Jealousy" by Gin Blossoms

D-E-F♯m-E

I-II-iii-II in D Lydian (IV-V-vi-V in the A major scale)

"Space Oddity" by David Bowie

Fmaj7-Em

I-vii in F Lydian (IV-iii in the C major scale)

G major scale

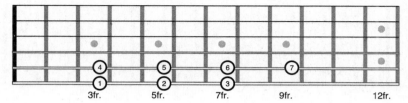

G major scale Roman numerals

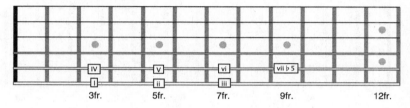

C Lydian mode

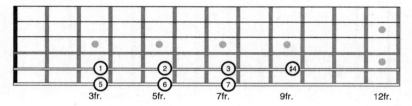

C Lydian mode Roman numerals

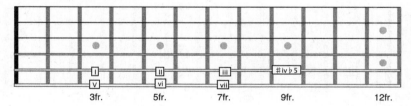

Same chords either way

Figure 5-7:
G major and
C Lydian.

Illustration courtesy of Desi Serna

Book III

Getting to Know Guitar Theory

C major scale

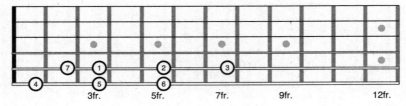

C major scale Roman numerals

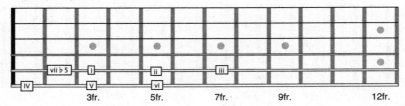

F Lydian mode

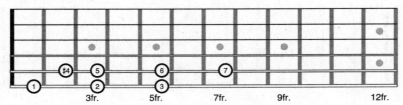

F Lydian mode Roman numerals

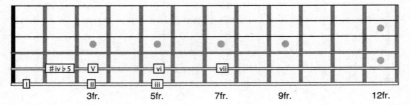

Same chords either way

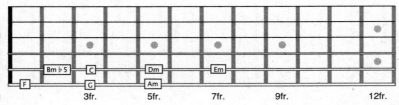

Figure 5-8:
C major and
F Lydian.

Illustration courtesy of Desi Serna

Mixolydian (V)

Mixolydian is the fifth mode of the major scale — when the 5th scale degree functions as the tonic. It centers on a major chord, so it's considered a major key. It's also called the *dominant scale* because the 5th degree of the major scale is named the dominant pitch (see Book III Chapter 6) and forms a dominant 7th chord. This mode is fairly common, almost as much as the relative major and minor. Here you see what happens to the G major scale when you reorganize its notes and chords, beginning with the 5th degree, D, to produce D Mixolydian mode:

G major

1-2-3-4-5-6-7

G-A-B-C-D-E-F♯

I-ii-iii-IV-V-vi-vii♭5

G-Am-Bm-C-D-Em-F♯m♭5

D Mixolydian

1-2-3-4-5-6♭7

D-E-F♯-G-A-B-C

I-ii-iii♭5-IV-v-vi♭VII

D-Em-F♯m♭5-G-Am-Bm-C

Mixolydian mode is often thought of as a major scale with a flattened 7th, its most defining characteristic. Mixolydian also features a ♭VII chord, a major chord one whole step below the tonic. Figure 5-9 shows D Mixolydian taken from its parent major scale, G.

You can play D Mixolydian anywhere on the fretboard as long as you use notes and chords from the G major scale and center on D. You can also move the pattern in Figure 5-9 around the fretboard to play Mixolydian mode in other keys.

Figure 5-10 puts you in a new major scale pattern that begins on the 5th string. Here the parent major scale is C and the mode is G Mixolydian. Of course, you find the same notes and chords elsewhere on the fretboard, so you can move this pattern around to play in other keys, too.

Book III

Getting to Know Guitar Theory

G major scale

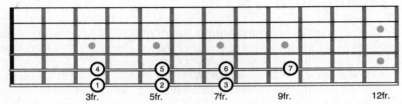

G major scale Roman numerals

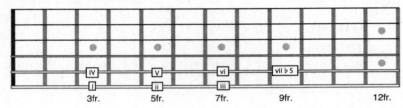

D Mixolydian mode

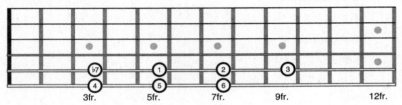

D Mixolydian mode Roman numerals

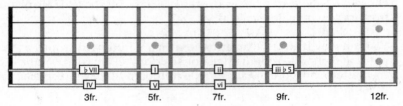

Same chords either way

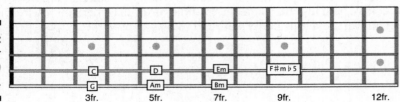

Figure 5-9:
G major
and D
Mixolydian.

Illustration courtesy of Desi Serna

C major scale

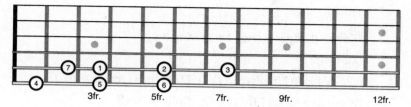

C major scale Roman numerals

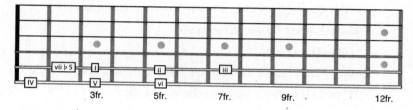

G Mixolydian mode

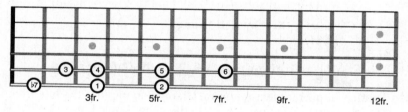

G Mixolydian mode Roman numerals

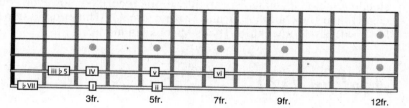

Same chords either way

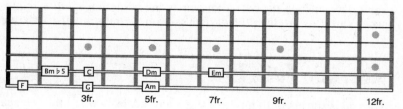

Figure 5-10:
C major
and G
Mixolydian.

Illustration courtesy of Desi Serna

Book III

Getting to Know Guitar Theory

Here are some sample chord progressions and songs based on the 5th degree of the major scale:

"Seven Bridges Road" by the Eagles

D-C-G-D

I♭VII-IV-I in D Mixolydian (V-IV-I-V in the G major scale)

"Southern Cross" by Crosby, Stills & Nash

A-G-D-A

I♭VII-IV-I in A Mixolydian (V-IV-I-V in the D major scale)

"Louie Louie" by The Kingsmen

A-D-Em-D

I-IV-v-IV in A Mixolydian (V-I-ii-I in the D major scale)

"What I Like about You" by the Romantics

E-A-D-A

I-IV♭VII-IV in E Mixolydian (V-I-IV-I in the A major scale)

"Cinnamon Girl" by Neil Young

D-Am7-C-G

I-v♭VII-IV in D Mixolydian (V-ii-IV-I in the G major scale)

Another important feature of the Mixolydian mode is the minor chord on the 5th degree. You hear it used in the song "Louie Louie" by The Kingsmen. Many musicians mistake this song for being a common I-IV-V chord progression in A major. If you listen carefully to the recording, however, you can clearly hear the chords A, D, and *Em,* not E major. This progression is actually I-IV-v with a minor v chord. That's Mixolydian mode!

Aeolian (vi)

Aeolian is the sixth mode of the major scale — when the 6th scale degree functions as the tonic. Because it centers on a minor chord, it's considered a minor key. In fact, it's better known as the *natural* or *relative minor scale.* You work with this mode in the earlier section "Numbering the Relative Minor."

Locrian (vii♭5)

Locrian is the seventh mode of the major scale — when the 7th scale degree functions as the tonic. As mentioned earlier, the 7th chord in the major scale has a minor-flat-five quality (diminished triad), which produces a dissonant and unresolved sound. Not many (any?) songs use it, so there's no need to spend time on it here. Nevertheless, it's still considered a type of minor key.

Key Signatures and Common Discrepancies

Generally, major keyed songs center on the 1st degree of the major scale, while minor keyed songs center on the 6th degree. However, you can also center music on one of the other major scale degrees. As a result, you can't assume that a major key is always Ionian or that a minor key is always Aeolian.

Looking past the key signature to figure out a song's mode

Here's where things get tricky. Although the major scale has multiple modes, musicians generally think of and notate music as being in only the relative major and relative minor, even when another mode is being used. So songs in the major modes (Ionian, Lydian, and Mixolydian) are all treated as if they were plain major, or in Ionian mode, while songs in the minor modes (Dorian, Phrygian, and Aeolian) are all treated as if they were natural minor, or in Aeolian mode.

Music publishers generally disregard the mode and write everything as if it were in a plain major or natural minor key, going off of the tonic chord. For example, if a piece of music centers on a G chord, it's notated with a key signature reflecting the G major scale even if it's really G Lydian or G Mixolydian. Likewise, if a piece of music centers on an Em chord, it's notated with a key signature reflecting E natural minor even if it's really E Dorian or E Phrygian. Then any necessary *accidentals* (sharps, flats, or natural signs) are used for notes that fall outside of the key signature. As a result, you receive no initial instruction that the music you're reading is based in a scale other than the scale reflected in the key signature. This isn't a problem for sight-readers; they're used to playing everything off the page anyway, accidentals and all. But if you want to know how a piece of music was composed or if you plan to improvise a guitar solo, you need to understand the real parent major scale being used.

Take the song "Seven Bridges Road" by the Eagles, for example. The primary chord progression is in D Mixolydian mode. The notes and chords are from the G major scale (G-A-B-C-D-E-F♯), and the 5th scale degree, D, functions as the tonic. Because the tonic chord is D, music publishers notate the song as if it were in a plain D major key signature, which includes two sharps, F♯ and C♯. Then every time a C-natural note occurs in the music, both in the melody and in the chords, they specially mark it with a natural sign (♮) to cue you not to use the C♯ note reflected in the key signature (see Figure 5-11).

Figure 5-11:
D
Mixolydian
with D
major key
signature.

Illustration courtesy of Desi Serna

If Figure 5-11 were written with a key signature for G major, you wouldn't need any accidentals. But, alas, things are never that easy.

Publishers often use the same technique when a piece of music is in Lydian; they write it as if it were plain major and then rely on accidentals to make any necessary changes. For example, C Lydian, which is drawn from the G major scale, is written with a key signature of C, implying the plain C major scale. Then a sharp sign appears each time an F♯ occurs throughout the music.

The same thing happens in minor keys, too. Take, for example, "Oye Como Va" by Santana. This song centers on an Am chord and is said to be in the key of A minor. However, saying *A minor* implies *A natural minor,* the relative minor of C major. That's incorrect. A natural minor features an F-natural and produces a Dm chord. But this song features F♯s and D major chords. The parent major scale is really G major. Nevertheless, you usually see this song marked with a key signature of A minor with sharp signs next to all the F notes used in the score (see Figure 5-12). ***Note:*** If Figure 5-12 were written with a key signature for G major, you wouldn't need any accidentals. You can expect to see the same technique used with Phrygian; it's notated as natural minor and then corrected with accidentals.

Figure 5-12:
A Dorian
with A
minor key
signature.

Illustration courtesy of Desi Serna

Considering some common discrepancies in music notation

Although the practice of notating music as if it were plain major or natural minor is standard procedure for music publishers, you occasionally come across a score that truly reflects the mode. For example, if a song is in A

Dorian mode, the score may actually use the key signature for G major, its true parent major scale. The score may also include a performance note, such as "A minor tonality" or "A Dorian mode," to clue you into the fact that the G scale is being used although the G note isn't the tonic. Likewise, if a song is in A Mixolydian mode, you may see the key signature for D major and a note such as "A major tonality" or "A Mixolydian mode."

You may occasionally come across these kinds of scores that actually tell it like it is, but they're definitely not the norm. So don't count on them! Instead, get used to examining the elements of every piece of music to determine whether it's really using the scale reflected in the key signature.

Here are a few other important issues to keep in mind as you work through different pieces of music to determine their modes and scales:

- **Modes aren't always properly identified in music circles.** If you ask musicians what key "Oye Como Va" by Santana is in, most of them will say A minor. Although Dorian mode is a type of minor key, you know there's more to it than that. Unfortunately, musicians usually refer to only the initial tonic of a song and leave all the other details, including modes, up to you to figure out.

- **Some musicians always name the key after the first chord, even if it isn't the true tonic.** For example, "Sweet Home Alabama" by Lynyrd Skynyrd is tonally centered around a G chord, and most of the guitar solos are based on G major pentatonic. Nevertheless, many guitar players say that the song is in the key of D simply because the chord progression starts on a D chord.

- **Some musicians identify a key without considering its major or minor quality.** For example, many musicians would say that "Black Magic Woman" by Santana and "Twist and Shout" by The Beatles are both in the key of D. You just have to know that one is minor and the other is major because the songs have two completely different parent major scales.

- **Some musicians think about the key based on the notes in the melody rather than on the chords.** For example, the vocal melody in "Give Me One Reason" by Tracy Chapman outlines notes from F♯ minor played over an F♯ major chord. For this reason, a musician, particularly a singer, may think that the song is in the key of F♯ minor when it's really in F♯ major.

- **Some guitar players confuse the key of a song with the type of pentatonic scale they're playing.** "Pride and Joy" by Stevie Ray Vaughan is tonally centered around an open E major chord (guitars tuned down a half step to E♭). Nevertheless, much of the guitar solos are based on an E minor pentatonic scale, leading some guitar players to say that the song is in the key of E minor.

Book III

Getting to Know Guitar Theory

✔ **Some pieces of music don't even have a complete parent major scale.** They simply focus on a tonic by means of some basic intervals, though not enough to piece together full chords, a chord progression, or an entire major scale. You see this technique in the songs "Boom Boom" by John Lee Hooker, "Voodoo Child (Slight Return)" by Jimi Hendrix, and "Whole Lotta Love" by Led Zeppelin. All three songs use mostly minor pentatonic scales. Likewise, in some hard rock and heavy metal songs, you see power chords and chromatic steps without any parent major scale represented in the chords, the chord progression, or even the melody itself.

Comparing Scale Formulas and Structures

A *scale* or *chord formula* is its pattern of steps and intervals. For example, a major triad is 1-3-5. A major scale is 1-2-3-4-5-6-7. The following tables compare the different scale formulas of the major scale modes that are used for keys and chord progressions. Don't worry about memorizing all the tables; just use them as a tool to help you better understand the relationship between the modes and their structures and the major scale.

Table 5-1 compares the interval structure for the six main modes of the major scale. (Locrian mode isn't included because it's more of a theoretical mode.) The relative major and relative minors are used the most and are considered to be plain, natural scales. Roman numerals are included so you can see how the major and minor chord sequences relate to the major scale.

Table 5-1	Modes and Interval Structures		
Degree/ Chord	**Mode Name**	**Interval Structure**	**Roman Numeral Sequence**
I	Ionian (plain major)	1-2-3-4-5-6-7	I-ii-iii-IV-V-vi-vii♭5
ii	Dorian	1-2-♭3-4-5-6-♭7	i-ii-♭III-IV-v-vi♭5-♭VII
iii	Phrygian	1-♭2-♭3-4-5-♭6-♭7	i-♭II-♭III-iv-v♭5-♭VI-♭vii
IV	Lydian	1-2-3-♯4-5-6-7	I-II-iii-♯iv♭5-V-vi-vii
V	Mixolydian	1-2-3-4-5-6-♭7	I-ii-iii♭5-IV-v-vi-♭VII
vi	Aeolian (natural minor)	1-2-♭3-4-5-♭6-♭7	i-ii♭5-♭III-iv-v-♭VI-♭VII

Table 5-2 shows you what all these chords look like when you build out each mode in the sample scale of A major.

Table 5-2	Building Each Mode in the Scale of A Major
Mode Name	*Chords*
A Ionian (plain major)	A-Bm-C#m-D-E-F#m-G#m♭5
B Dorian	Bm-C#m-D-E-F#m-G#m♭5-A
C# Phrygian	C#m-D-E-F#m-G#m♭5-A-Bm
D Lydian	D-E-F#m-G#m♭5-A-Bm-C#m
E Mixolydian	E-F#m-G#m♭5-A-Bm-C#m-D
F# Aeolian (natural minor)	F#m-G#m♭5-A-Bm-C#m-D-E

Finally, Table 5-3 provides a chart of parallel modes. Here, the term *parallel* means different scales that all center on the same primary pitch. In the comparison in this table, the tonic pitch remains A for each mode. You compare A major to A Dorian to A Phrygian and so on. The parent major scale is different in each example here.

Table 5-3	Parallel Modes with A as the Tonic	
Mode Name	*Chords*	*Parent Scale*
A Ionian (plain major)	A-Bm-C#m-D-E-F#m-G#m♭5	1st mode of A major scale
A Dorian	Am-Bm-C-D-Em-F#m♭5-G	2nd mode of G major scale
A Phrygian	Am-B♭-C-Dm-Em♭5-F-Gm	3rd mode of F major scale
A Lydian	A-B-C#m-D#m♭5-E-F#m-G#m	4th mode of E major scale
A Mixolydian	A-Bm-C#m♭5-D-Em-F#m-G	5th mode of D major scale
A Aeolian (natural minor)	Am-Bm♭5-C-Dm-Em-F-G	6th mode of C major scale

Seeing the chords of parallel modes like this gives you an idea of how many options you have when approaching a composition in the key of A. What key of A are you going to use? A major or A minor? Plain A major, Mixolydian, or Lydian? Natural A minor, Dorian, or Phrygian?

Chapter 6

Dominant Function and Voice Leading

● ●

In This Chapter

▶ Getting to know the functions of dominant 7th chords

▶ Playing sample chord progressions

▶ Leading from one chord voicing to another

▶ Access the audio track and video clips at www.dummies.com/go/guitaraio/

● ●

T he *dominant chord* (or the chord built on the 5th degree of a scale) is a fairly important chord in music because its structure and tendency toward the tonic chord really help define the tonal center of a progression. In this chapter, you get to know dominant chords and find out how to use them in your music. You also take a look at secondary dominants, which allow you to use the dominant sound to strengthen a progression toward chords other than the tonic. In addition, you discover the ins and outs of voice leading.

Listen to Audio Track 49 to hear examples of dominant function and voice leading plus get an idea of what this chapter is all about.

Chord Function and the Dominant Chord

The word *dominant* refers to two things in guitar theory:

✔ The first is the 5th degree of the major scale, named the *dominant.*

✔ The second is a major triad with a minor 7th, called the *dominant 7th chord,* which naturally occurs on the 5th scale degree.

The chord function on V is the most important example of this. Because it's built on the 5th scale degree, or the dominant note, the V chord has what's sometimes called a *dominant function*. In a chord progression like I-V, the dominant chord has a sense of movement, or instability, that makes the progression want to continue leading back to the tonic, chord I. You can intensify this leading quality of V by adding a 7th to the chord, making V7, or a *dominant 7th chord*. Every major scale has a naturally occurring V7 chord: G7 in C major, D7 in G major, A7 in D major, and so on. Figure 6-1 gives you a sample I-V7 chord progression in C.

Figure 6-1:
I-V7 chord
progression.

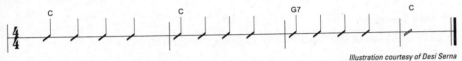

Illustration courtesy of Desi Serna

Musicians also use the dominant 7th chord for its sound quality, or color. You hear this use in blues-based music, where the dominant 7th sound is a huge part of its style. These *static dominant 7th chords*, as they're called, don't necessarily need to resolve to a tonic chord.

There are a couple reasons why V resolves so well on I. Understanding these reasons requires you to examine the intervals within a V chord to see how they relate to chord I. This involves taking a look at the leading tone and the tritone.

Naming notes, scale degrees, and chords

The notes of a scale are usually numbered 1st, 2nd, 3rd, and so on. You use Arabic numbers when you're talking about the notes themselves and Roman numerals when you're talking about the chords built on those notes. So in C major, *3* or *the 3rd* is the note E, and *iii* is the chord E-G-B.

The different scale degrees also have names. *Dominant* refers to the 5th scale degree. For example, G is the dominant of C major, and B is the dominant of E major. Here's a complete list of the names for the different scale degrees:

1. Tonic

2. Supertonic

3. Mediant

4. Subdominant

5. Dominant

6. Submediant

7. Leading note or leading tone

You can also call the V chord a dominant chord. For example, the dominant chord of C major is G-B-D.

Leading with the leading tone

As a listening experiment, play up a major scale, starting from the tonic note, but instead of playing a full octave, stop on the 7th scale degree. Using C major as an example, play up the scale from C to B and hold on the B. The scale sounds incomplete: The B *wants* to lead back to the C to sound complete. This is why the 7th scale degree is also called the *leading tone* or *leading note* of a scale.

If you turn to the pitches of the V chord, you find that it contains the leading tone of its parent scale, which is one of the reasons why it has such a strong tendency toward I. For example, the V chord of C major is G. The G chord is made up of the pitches G, B, and D — its root, 3rd, and 5th. The 3rd of the chord is a B, the leading tone of C major.

Tension rises with a tritone

To intensify the tendency for V to lead to I, simply add a 7th to the chord, making V7. This added pitch comes from the 4th degree of a major scale. The interval from the 4th to the 7th of a major scale is an *augmented 4th,* while the interval from the 7th back up to the 4th is a *diminished 5th.* Both of these intervals are made up of three whole tones and can be called *tritones,* which, not surprisingly, means *three tones.* Examples of tritones are B-F in C major and G♯-D in A major.

When you play these examples of tritones, you can hear that a tritone is a fairly unstable, or dissonant-sounding, interval. As a matter of fact, it sounds so unstable that when it appears in a chord like V7, the chord itself has a strong tendency to move to a more stable one. For example, the B and F of G7 want to move to the C and E of C, and the G♯ and D of E7 want to move to the A and C♯ of A.

Figure 6-2 shows two versions of a G7 chord, with the tritones shaded in black. Follow each one of these chord shapes with a C chord and you hear resolution.

Playing songs with dominant function

Some songs are based on simple progressions that contain only the I and V chords (also known as the tonic and dominant chords). Songs like "You Never Can Tell" by Chuck Berry, "Jambalaya" by Hank Williams, and "Achy Breaky Heart" by Billy Ray Cyrus are all good examples of this basic chord progression. Play any one of these songs and stop on the V chord. Notice that the music doesn't sound complete or resolved, but as though it wants to continue back to chord I. That's an example of dominant function.

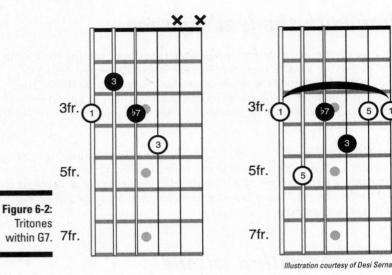

Figure 6-2:
Tritones
within G7.

Illustration courtesy of Desi Serna

In traditional uses, the V7-I progression appears to close a section or phrase of music (see Figure 6-3).

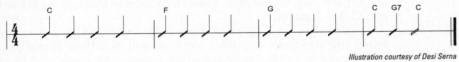

Figure 6-3:
Closing
progression.

Illustration courtesy of Desi Serna

PLAY THIS! ▶

Watch Video Clip 28 to see a demonstration of a closing progression.

You hear many examples of functioning dominant 7th chord progressions in traditional folk songs. Think of songs like "Skip to My Lou," "Shortnin' Bread," "Go Tell Aunt Rhody," "Down in the Valley," "Clementine," and "Buffalo Gals." Figure 6-4 shows a folk song example in the style of "He's Got the Whole World in His Hands." If you know the words, sing along.

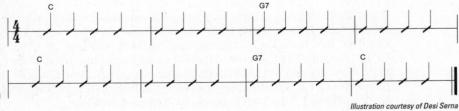

Figure 6-4:
"He's Got
the Whole
World in His
Hands."

Illustration courtesy of Desi Serna

You can figure out the chords to most two-chord folk songs simply by singing or humming the melody while playing along with I and V7 in any key. Just pick a key, any key, and try it. For example, in the key of C, I and V7 are C and G7; in the key of G, I and V7 are G and D7. You can also try D and A7, E and B7, or F and C7.

"Twist and Shout" by The Beatles is a great example of a V7 chord that has a dominant function. After the guitar solo, you hear six measures of the dominant 7th chord sung one note at a time by each of the band's members. The root of the chord, A, appears in the first measure, followed by the 3rd, C♯, in measure 2, the 5th of the chord, E, in measure 3, and finally the 7th, G, in measure 4. After two more measures of climactic, rock 'n' roll screaming, this musical tension resolves to the I chord, D, and the music continues on.

Secondary Dominants

The relationship between the tonic and dominant chords in music is so strong that composers sometimes use a dominant function on chords other than the tonic, like on the ii chord or perhaps even the V chord itself. These non-tonic-but-still-dominant chords are called *secondary dominants*. You recognize them in chord progressions as major chords where you're expecting minor ones and especially as dominant 7th chords where you're expecting simple triads.

For an example, look at the C major progression: C-Am-Dm-G7. A common variation on this progression is C-Am-D7-G7, as shown in Figure 6-5. You would normally expect a D minor chord rather than a D7 chord in C major, but if you think about this progression, you can see that the D7 chord is the dominant 7th of G.

Book III

Getting to Know Guitar Theory

Figure 6-5: Secondary dominant C-Am-D7-G7.

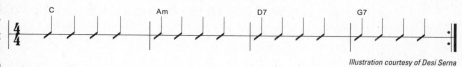

Illustration courtesy of Desi Serna

Drawing attention to some common secondary dominants

Musicians use secondary dominants on almost any chord in a key to provide some variety to a progression and to give some temporary focus to another chord. For example, the D7 chord in Figure 6-5 has a different sound quality than a simple D minor chord, which is what you normally find in the key of C. Because the chord has a dominant function, it draws attention to the following G7 chord. It's as if the chord progression temporarily changes keys to G.

You can lead to almost any chord with its own dominant. A chord's dominant is a major chord or dominant 7th chord that's a 5th away from the chord itself. Building on the example in Figure 6-5, you could lead to D with A7, which is five steps away from D, the interval of a 5th, as shown in Figure 6-6.

Figure 6-6:
Secondary
dominants
C-A7-D7-G7.

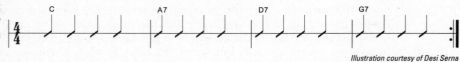

Illustration courtesy of Desi Serna

To see and hear the secondary dominant from Figure 6-6, watch Video Clip 29.

Keep going! The 5th of A is E, and an E7 chord can lead to any type of A chord. Figure 6-7 shows an example of E7 leading to A7 in a series of dominant 7th chords that begins on E7 and moves to C.

Figure 6-7:
Secondary
dominants
C-E7-A7-
D7-G7.

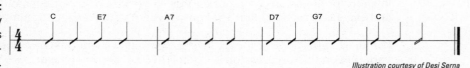

Illustration courtesy of Desi Serna

Another common secondary dominant progression is I7-IV. In C major, this progression is C7 moving to F. An example of this secondary dominant's use is in the larger progression F-G-C-C7-F-G-C that you see in Figure 6-8. The progression is in C major, but the C7 chord is functioning as a dominant 7th of the F chord.

Figure 6-8:
I7 sec-
ondary
dominant.

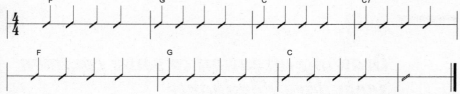

Illustration courtesy of Desi Serna

The most common secondary dominants are the ones you see here — those that lead to I, ii, IV, V, and vi. Musicians generally don't use secondary dominants that lead to vii♭5, and although V7 of iii is possible, it isn't very common.

Thinking of secondary dominants as mini key changes

A secondary dominant is really just an altered version of an existing chord. This change to the chord is to create a dominant 7th. What gives it its secondary dominant function is that it leads to another chord a 5th below. So the I chord is altered to I7 to create movement toward IV, the ii chord is altered to II7 to highlight V, and so on.

In this way, secondary dominants are like mini key changes. Think of the chord progression in C major where G7 leads to C. This is a common V7-I progression in C major. But what if these two chords appeared in F major, as in the progression F-Dm-G7-C? Although the progression as a whole is in F major (I-vi-II7-V), the G7 chord has notes in it that don't belong to this key but instead belong to C major. For your solos to work in this chord progression, you have to start out in F major and then switch patterns to C major when you reach the G7 chord. Finally, when the C chord sounds, you have to switch back to F major patterns.

G7 is the dominant 7th chord of C major. When G7 appears in any key other than C and leads to a C chord, it's a secondary dominant. The same is true for any other functioning dominant 7th chord.

When playing over a secondary dominant, you need to switch to its parent major scale. Take another look at the secondary dominants progressions shown in Figures 6-5 through 6-7:

Book III

Getting to Know Guitar Theory

- ✔ **Figure 6-5 is I-vi-II7-V7 in C.** The D7 chord belongs to the key of G. Use G major patterns over D7 and then return to C major on the G7 chord. When you play G major patterns over the D7 chord, you're actually playing in D Mixolydian, the dominant scale.

  Switching scales like this is no easy task! For the most part, you hear solos played over progressions like this only in jazz and country styles.

- ✔ **Figure 6-6 is I-VI7-II7-V7 in C.** The A7 chord belongs to the key of D, and D7 belongs to the key of G. Use D major patterns over A7 and G major patterns for D7. Return to C major on the G7 chord. A D major scale over A7 results in A Mixolydian mode, or an A dominant scale. Here, you have to switch scales twice.

- ✔ **Figure 6-7 is I-III7-VI7-II7-V7-I in C.** E7 belongs to A major, A7 belongs to D, and D7 belongs to the key of G. Think *dominant scale* over each dominant 7th chord. That is, for each dominant 7th chord, play its parent major scale.

Switching scales over secondary dominants can be quite a challenge, but fortunately, making the switch isn't always necessary. With the right note selection, you can stay in one scale and avoid any troublesome notes — refer to the "Aura Lee" example in Figure 6-9. Notice that the melody remains in the key of C even though secondary dominants appear in the progression. Notice that the song uses an F note over an A7 chord even though the F isn't part of the A dominant scale.

"Aura Lee" is an old American Civil War song that Elvis Presley adapted for his hit single "Love Me Tender." The traditional version has several secondary dominants.

Figure 6-9: Aura Lee.

Illustration courtesy of Desi Serna

Most traditional guitar methods include songs and exercises that are based on very simple V7-I chord progressions, where the dominant 7th chord is a functioning dominant 7th. For example, every song that has written-in chord progressions in *Mel Bay's Modern Guitar Method Grade 1* (the blue book) includes dominant 7th chords.

A note on reading music

To be honest, books like *Mel Bay's Modern Guitar Method,* the granddaddy of all guitar methods, are more about learning how to read standard musical notation than learning how to play guitar. Nevertheless, these books are worth the time and effort it takes to work through them because reading music is a useful skill to have.

Learning how to read notes and rhythms can influence how you think about music and play the guitar even when you don't have any sheet music in front of you. You don't have to be able to read like a concert violinist; just focus on the basics. Learn up to at least the point where you can count and play sixteenth notes.

Although secondary dominants work best when they're dominant 7th chords, in some cases, they can be simple major chords. This approach works when you're altering a chord that's originally minor. For example, if you adjust a ii chord to II, it becomes a secondary dominant of V. If you change iii to III, it becomes a secondary dominant of vi. For I to work as a secondary dominant of IV, however, you have to adjust the chord to I7.

When you see II-V or VI-ii, the first chord in the progression is a secondary dominant. Another possible secondary dominant is III-vi. Sometimes, however, it's useful to think of this particular progression as V-i in the relative minor key with the major V chord a result of the harmonic minor scale.

Although approaching the progressions in this section as a lead guitarist may be challenging, playing the chord progressions themselves isn't hard at all. Plus, after you get a handle on what secondary dominants are, you begin to recognize how common they are in popular music. With some careful listening, you can hear that players often don't even attempt to solo over them. What a relief!

Book III

Getting to Know Guitar Theory

Songs that use secondary dominants

The following songs all feature chord progressions that make use of a secondary dominant either as a dominant 7th chord or, in some cases, a major chord on a minor scale degree. Secondary dominants are in parentheses:

"Act Naturally" by The Beatles (Chorus: II chord leads to V)

"Every Breath You Take" by The Police (Chorus: II chord leads to V)

"Faith" by George Michael (Chorus: II chord leads to V)

"Heart of Glass" by Blondie (Chorus: II chord leads to V)

"Hello Mary Lou" by Ricky Nelson (Chorus: III chord leads to vi and II chord leads to V)

"Hey Good Lookin'" by Hank Williams (Verse: II chord leads to V)

"Hey Jude" by The Beatles (Verse: I7 chord leads to IV)

"Honky Tonk Women" by The Rolling Stones (Verse: II chord leads to V)

"Margaritaville" by Jimmy Buffett (Verse: I7 chord leads to IV)

"Out of My Head" by Fastball (Chorus: I7 chord leads to IV; verse and chorus: II chord leads to V)

"Patience" by Guns N' Roses (Verse: II chord leads to V)

"Running on Faith" by Eric Clapton (Verse: I7 chord leads to IV)

"The Star-Spangled Banner" (U.S. national anthem) (Verse: II chord leads to V)

"That'll Be the Day" by Buddy Holly (Verse: II chord leads to V)

"The Way" by Fastball (Verse: VI chord leads to ii)

Note: Because the progression in "The Way" is in a minor key, you can renumber it to a I chord leading to iv.

Voice Leading

In music composition, *voice leading* is the technique of writing smooth transitions from one chord to another, using common tones between chords and stepwise motion between their different pitches. Voice leading allows composers to take advantage of relationships between chords when connecting them in order to create more melodic lines.

You can see an example of voice leading in the chord progression C-E7-F-G-C. With the pitches of these chords, you have a stepwise musical line G-G♯-A-B-C. The 5th of the C chord, G, moves to the G♯ of E7, then to the A of the F chord, then to the B of G, and finally to the C of the C chord. This voice leading explains why an E7 chord can lead well into an F chord, even though these chords don't have a V-I relationship. Figure 6-10 voices this line in the higher part of the chords to clearly show it. In practice, you may not actually play the chords with these specific chord shapes.

Figure 6-10:
Voice
leading
C-E7-F-G-C.

Illustration courtesy of Desi Serna

To see and hear the voice leading example from Figure 6-10, watch Video Clip 30.

Again, there's no V-I relationship between E7 and F. The chords are actually III7-IV in C major. But the voice leading makes it work anyway.

The defining musical features of many songs owe their greatness, at least in part, to similar III7-IV voice-leading techniques. For example, "Imagine" by John Lennon, "Don't Look Back in Anger" by Oasis, "Space Oddity" by David Bowie, and "The Air That I Breathe" by The Hollies all feature an E7 chord leading to F in the key of C. "The Way" by Fastball has C#7 leading to D in the key of A, and "Interstate Love Song" by Stone Temple Pilots has G# leading to A in the key of E.

A few more examples don't necessarily involve a dominant 7th chord. Look for similar lines, both *chromatic* (moving up or down in half steps) and *diatonic* (moving through the major scale), in the music you're playing. Voice-leading techniques are easy to recognize when they happen in the bass part. A good example is a progression like the one shown in Figure 6-11. You can hear this progression in the opening to "Stairway to Heaven" by Led Zeppelin. If you've ever wondered why these chords fit together so well, take a look at the chromatic bass line that moves down the 4th string.

Figure 6-11: Bass voice leading — Round 1.

Illustration courtesy of Desi Serna

Book III

Getting to Know Guitar Theory

Another clear example of voice leading in the bass part is shown in Figure 6-12. Here, the bass line descends from A to E. Notice the half step movement from G to E. Led Zeppelin uses this kind of progression in the song "Babe I'm Gonna Leave You," and The Beatles use something similar in their song "While My Guitar Gently Weeps."

Figure 6-12: Bass voice leading — Round 2.

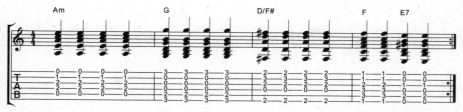

Illustration courtesy of Desi Serna

You see a similar descending chromatic bass line over the changes G-D/ F#-F-C/E-E♭maj7 in the verse of "Plush" by Stone Temple Pilots.

Hearing voice leading with the progression I-Imaj7-I7-IV is also fairly common. In C major, the chords are C-Cmaj7-C7-F, and they're often connected with the descending chromatic line C-B-B♭-A — C from the C chord, B from Cmaj7, B♭ from C7, and A from the F chord. Here the voice leading is internal, placed within the chords, not in the bass. Figure 6-13 voices the chords with this line by moving along the 3rd string. You hear a similar chord progression in "Something" by The Beatles.

Figure 6-13:
I-Imaj7-
I7-IV voice
leading.

Illustration courtesy of Desi Serna

One final example is the progression I-Imaj7-I6-I, or C-Cmaj7-C6-C, in C major. Here, the voice leading is purely diatonic, that is, sticking with the major scale. These chords are linked together with the descending line C-B-A-G. "Jingle Bell Rock" by Bobby Helms connects its chords with a similar progression. See Figure 6-14.

Figure 6-14:
I-Imaj7-
I6-I voice
leading.

Illustration courtesy of Desi Serna

Book IV
Rock Guitar

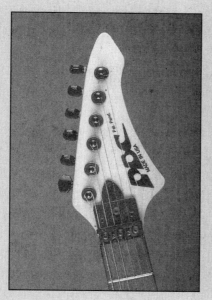

Contents at a Glance

Chapter 1: I Know, It's Only Rock Guitar, but I Like It 285

Differentiating Between Rock and Acoustic Guitar . . . It Ain't Just Volume......... 286
Knowing the Essentials: The Power Trio 290
Accessorizing Your Guitar 298

Chapter 2: Playing Lead 301

Taking the Lead 301
Playing Single Notes 304
Starting at the Bottom: Low-Note Melodies 311
Going to the Top: High-Note Melodies 312
Playing in Position 313
Jamming on Lower Register Riffs 315
Making It Easy: The Pentatonic Scale 316
Playing the Pentatonic Scale: Three Ways to Solo 317
Improvising Leads 321

Chapter 3: Groovin' on Riffs 323

Getting Your Groove On: Basic Riffs 324
Playing Two Notes Can be Better than One: Double-Stops 330
Combining Single-Note Riffs and Chords 331

Chapter 4: Going Up the Neck and Playing the Fancy Stuff 333

Going Up the Neck 334
Playing in Position 337
Using the Moveable Pentatonic Scale 338
Changing Your Position 341
Knowing Where to Play 343
Bringing Down the Hammer-ons 347
Having Pull with Pull-offs 348
Slippin' into Slides 349
Bending to Your Will 351
Sounding a Vibrato That Makes You Quiver 354

Chapter 5: The Care and Feeding of Your Electric Guitar 355

Using the Tools of the Trade 356
Changing Strings 359
Cleaning the Parts of Your Guitar 366
Setting Up Your Guitar to Optimize Performance 368
Troubleshooting Guide 373
Storing Your Guitar 374

Chapter 1

I Know, It's Only Rock Guitar, but I Like It

In This Chapter

▶ Hearing the difference between electric guitar and acoustic guitar tone

▶ Discovering the inner-workings of the electric guitar

▶ Knowing the essential components of the electric guitar sound

▶ Getting the gear that goes with your guitar

▶ Access the audio track at www.dummies.com/go/guitaraio/

*R*ock guitar does not have a dignified history in music.

It doesn't come from a long lineage of historical development where composers such as Bach, Beethoven, and Brahms wrote lovingly for it, composing concertos and sonatas highlighting its piquant and gentle qualities. It was not played in the great European concert halls or in the parlors of fine households.

Not only was rock guitar unknown to the great composers of the ages, but they couldn't have even conceived of such a thing, even in their worst nightmares. (Imagine what they would have made of an Ozzy Osbourne concert — a nightmare no matter which century you hail from!) Indeed, even if they could have heard, through some sort of time travel, an electric guitar banging out the riff to "Satisfaction," they would have hardly recognized it as music.

Rock guitar is a modern, mid-20th-century invention, a phenomenon of the post-electronic age. It has no memory of a bygone era when youth was respectful of elders, music was a polite pursuit, and musicians gave a rusty E string about social acceptance. It's for people who like their music loud, in your face, electric, and rebellious, and who owe no debt to history. Rock guitar is probably not the wisest choice of instruments to tackle if you want to garner acceptance from the music community.

So, if you want respect, take up the flute. But if you want to set the world on fire, attract throngs of adoring fans, and get back at your parents to boot — pick up an electric guitar and wail, baby, wail, because rock guitar will change your life.

First, though, you gotta learn how to play the thing.

Differentiating Between Rock and Acoustic Guitar . . . It Ain't Just Volume

When you see someone flailing away on rock guitar — on TV, in a film, or at a live concert — be aware that what you're seeing tells only part of the story.

Sure, someone playing rock guitar is holding an instrument with six strings, a neck, and a body — qualities that describe the instrument that classical guitarist Andrés Segovia played — but the sound couldn't be more different. That difference in sound is the key to understanding rock guitar. What's important is not the leather, the hair, the onstage theatrics, the posturing, the smoke bombs, or the bloody tongues, but the *sound* coming from that guitar.

It was the sound of the electric guitar, so different from that of its predecessor, the acoustic guitar, and placed in the hands of some early, forward-looking visionaries, that forced a cultural change, a musical modification, and a historical adjustment to the way we experience popular music. Songwriters had to write differently, recording engineers had to record differently, and listeners had to do a major attitude adjustment to get their ears around it. Heck, people even had to learn new dances.

But what makes the sound of an electric guitar so different from an acoustic one? If you didn't think about it, you might say, well, *volume*. Rock guitar is just a whole lot louder than its acoustic counterpart. Although that might be true most of the time, volume alone is not what makes rock guitar unique. True, rock is listened to at high volumes — its message tastes better served up loud — but volume is a by-product, an after-effect, not what makes rock different or what drives it.

To become familiar with the qualities of the electric guitar, try this simple test. Listen to Track 50. As you listen, turn the volume down so that it's quiet, very quiet — quieter than you'd normally listen to music, rock, or otherwise. You'll hear that the guitar sounds, well, just different. In fact, if you have to strain a little bit to make out that what you're hearing is a guitar at all, you'll be aware that the *tone* (the quality, or character of the sound, independent of its pitch and volume), in spite of the low volume, doesn't sound like the guitar your camp counselor strummed around the campfire.

To really understand rock guitar, you need to explore some of its qualities *other* than volume. Don't worry, though. We get back to volume eventually.

Sound quality, or timbre

When guitarists "electrified" their acoustic guitars, they originally intended to give the guitar a fighting chance in the volume department. Unsatisfied with the results of placing a microphone in front of the guitar, they sent the guitar's sound to a speaker by placing a magnetic element called a *pickup* under the guitar's strings.

Players quickly found, however, that, unlike a microphone, a pickup didn't just make the sound louder, it *changed* the tone too. But how? It wasn't that obvious, but it was tangible.

The basic differences between a guitar coming out of a pickup and a guitar playing into a "mike" (slang for microphone) are:

- The sound is smoother and less woody.
- The sound is more electronic, with purer-sounding tones, like that of an organ.
- The sound has a less defined life cycle, or *envelope* — a beginning, middle, and end. These stages, so clear in the sound of a plucked acoustic guitar string, are blurred together in an electric guitar.

Signal

When progressive-minded guitarists of the 1930s and '40s first put electro-magnetic elements under their strings to "pick up" their vibrations and send them along a wire to an amplifier, they did a lot more than increase the volume — though they didn't know it at the time. They were on their way to creating one of those "happy accidents" so common in art and science (and this was a little of both, really).

Originally, jazz guitarists playing in the big bands of the day were merely seeking a way to cut through all the din of those blaring horns and thundering drums. The mellow guitar, regarded by most other musicians as a mere parlor instrument with dubious stage presence, was no match for the louder brass and percussion instruments. The banjo had a sharp, cutting quality and was better at projecting on the bandstand, but its tone was falling out of fashion in favor of the more full-bodied, versatile tone of the guitar. Problem was, the guitar just wasn't that loud, so something had to be done.

Slapping on heavier-gauge (thicker) steel strings helped (an improvement over nylon strings), but it still wasn't enough. Placing a microphone in front of the guitar, as was done for vocalists, worked somewhat, but was cumbersome, and the mike picked up the surrounding sound as well as the guitar.

To avoid these problems, someone got the idea to put a magnetic element just underneath the strings to carry the signal electronically to an amplifier. Because the strings were metal — specifically, electrically conductive magnetic metal — the sound of the strings traveled electronically through the pickup (so called because it "picked up" the sound of the vibrating string), down the attached wire, into a portable amplifier, and then out of a speaker.

The electric guitar was born. But getting from electrification to rock-and-roll nirvana was still a bit of a journey. It would be some time before guitarists would recognize the monster they had spawned in the unholy union of electricity and acoustic guitar.

Distortion and sustain

When the six-string Dr. Frankensteins of the 1930s and '40s were electrifying their guitars, they weren't envisioning what Jimi Hendrix would do decades later at Woodstock and Monterey. Just like the well-meaning doctor in Mary Shelley's novel, early electronic guitar designers were wholesome and good. They wanted to reproduce the sound of the acoustic guitar as faithfully as possible. Fortunately for us, they failed miserably. But electronics' loss was music's gain, because even though the electric guitar sound was nothing like the acoustic sound — or the acoustic guitar sound as heard through a microphone — it had a very pleasing, and musically useful, quality.

The effort to produce an exact amplified match of the original acoustic guitar failed primarily because it introduced *distortion* (an untrue representation of the sound) into the sound. The louder the sound, or the more the guitar "worked" the electronic circuitry, the more distorted the sound got. As the electronic signal "heated up," the sound became *fuzzier* (where the high frequencies became more muted), and the tone generally *warmed up* (sounding more rounded and less brittle). All this distortion increased the *sustain* (the tendency for the tone to ring indefinitely at the same level), which was noticeable in even the lowest of volumes.

Distortion, normally a bad thing in just about any other electronic endeavor, had a beneficial, musical effect for guitar tone. As the guitar became thought of more and more as a lead instrument, guitarists found they could work the distortion factor to their advantage. A louder guitar wasn't just louder — it had a different, *better* tonal quality than a guitar coming out of the same apparatus, but at a lower volume.

This *timbre* (a fancy musical term for tone, or sound quality), distortion, and increased sustain took the plunkiness out of the guitar's tone, and made it more smoothly melodic — more like the buzzy, reedy qualities of, say, a saxophone or a blues vocalist, which is why so many early rock guitarists cut their musical teeth on the blues. Whereas the guitar had formerly been a rhythm instrument, owing to its clipped sound, rapid decay (the quality of a sound to die away), and strident tone, the "electronic" guitar now had properties more suited to melody-making. The guitar was poised to step out of the background and up to the spotlight itself. All it needed was some brave souls to tame this new sonic monster.

Oh yes, and volume

Of course, electrifying a guitar did accomplish what it set out to do — make the guitar louder. Although it needed an electronic crutch, in the form of amplification through an external apparatus, this system of pickups, wires, and a portable amplifier (where the guitarist didn't need to rely on the auditorium's sound engineer) gave guitarists the freedom to play in all sorts of styles — melodic, rhythmic, and chordal — and freed them from the "rhythm section ghetto."

An excellent example of an early electric guitarist who realized and exploited the newfound qualities of the electric guitar was jazz guitarist Charlie Christian. It's important to note that even though Christian was not a rock player (rock didn't exist in the 1920s and '30s), he is worshipped by electric guitarists everywhere — from blues to jazz to rock — as being an incredible visionary for realizing the power of the electric guitar's tone.

Some people may claim that Christian was, in part, responsible for inventing the electric guitar pickup, but this is just a myth. But he certainly did his part to popularize the "pickup-configured" electronic guitar, and he is one of its best early practitioners, because he recognized — and exploited through his musical genius — its sustain qualities.

After the guitar could play as loud as the other, more charismatic instruments (such as the trumpet and saxophone), it wasn't long before the guitar would become a featured instrument, both from a personality perspective as well as an instrument for solo exhibitionism.

Book IV

Rock Guitar

Listening examples

You can talk all you want about the tone of the electric guitar, but the best way to understand its tonal qualities is to listen to some classic examples. Led Zeppelin's "Stairway to Heaven" is not only a classic song, it's one of the best illustrations of the differences between electric and acoustic guitar.

The song begins with a plaintive vocal by Robert Plant, accompanied by a Renaissance-sounding acoustic guitar. The accompaniment gradually builds, and then at 6:42 guitarist Jimmy Page launches into the solo section with an opening *phrase* (a musically complete passage or thought of any given length) that sums up the essence of the electric guitar in just two short measures. Listen to the first note, which seems to hang in mid-air and *sing* — as if powered by its own set of lungs. The rest of the solo is a tour de force of technique, phrasing, and tone, but it's that opening *riff* (a self-contained musical phrase) that grabs you.

Another well-known example is the electric guitar solo section of the Eagles' "Hotel California," played by Joe Walsh and Don Felder. This back-and-forth solo is given plenty of room to breathe by the accompaniment. The gliding quality you hear at the end of Walsh's first short phrase (the fifth note in the opening sequence) is a *string bend,* where you stretch the string by pushing it out of its normal alignment causing the pitch to rise. Listen to how the note, again, *sings.* This singing quality, broken down to its component attributes, has a smooth sound (timbre); a reedy, fuzzy quality that does not resemble the plucked sound of the acoustic guitar (distortion); and an elongated, non-decaying volume and intensity (sustain).

These examples are both in the melodic vein. Things really get weird when guitarists started abandoning melody altogether and chose to exploit timbre, distortion and sustain for their own purpose. Jimi Hendrix was one of those who took distortion and sustain to the *n*th degree.

Knowing the Essentials: The Power Trio

A burning question for most aspiring rock guitarists is, "Since I have an electric guitar here, does that mean I also have to have an amp?"

Yes, you do need an amplifier. Just as you can't hear a scream without ears, so, too, can you not hear a guitar without its amplifier and speaker (in guitar terms, an "amplifier" can refer to the amplifier circuitry *and* the speaker, which are often housed in the same box).

Electric guitars can have the biggest, most-powerful, nuclear-charged pickups on board, but without an amp, the guitar will make no more noise than if the pickups were absent completely.

Sounds unbelievable, but it's true. No amp, no electric guitar sound. Anytime you see somebody walking around with an electric guitar, you can bet he or she is looking for an amp. Therefore, you must have at least two elements to even be audible on the electric guitar — the guitar itself and the amp (plus a wire, or cable, or cord, to attach the electric guitar to the amp.

Realistically, however, guitarists these days routinely introduce a third element into the signal chain (as the path from the originating guitar pickups to the terminating amp speaker is known): intermediary electronic gizmos known as *effects*. These typically sit between a guitar and an amp, and connect to each other with short cords, via in and out *jacks* (the electronic term for sockets, or something you can insert plugs into). Effects are like a VCR that goes between your cable box and your TV because they pass the signal through, but perform their own magic on the signal.

This section covers the three essential components in rock guitar playing: the electric guitar, the amplifier, and electronic effects devices.

The electric guitar

The electric guitar is the principal player in the three-part system that comprises the rock guitar sound.

Whether it has a natural mahogany finish or is painted Day-Glo green with purple lightning bolts across the body, all electric guitars have common properties. Like a "regular," or acoustic, guitar, an electric guitar has a neck and a body, six strings, and tuning keys on the top of the neck that allow you to tighten or loosen the strings to the desired pitch — the process known as tuning.

Unlike the acoustic guitar, though, an electric guitar sports *pickups* (electromagnetic devices that "sense" the strings' vibrations and create a small current), knobs, and switches for controlling the pickups, and possibly other hardware (such as a *bar*, described in the following bulleted list) that acoustic guitars don't have.

Figure 1-1 shows the various parts of the electric guitar.

Book IV

Rock Guitar

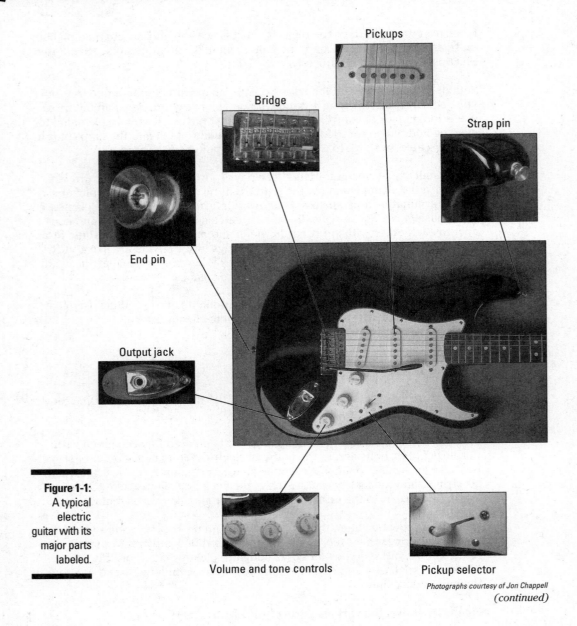

Pickups

Bridge

Strap pin

End pin

Output jack

Figure 1-1:
A typical
electric
guitar with its
major parts
labeled.

Volume and tone controls

Pickup selector

Photographs courtesy of Jon Chappell
(continued)

(continued)

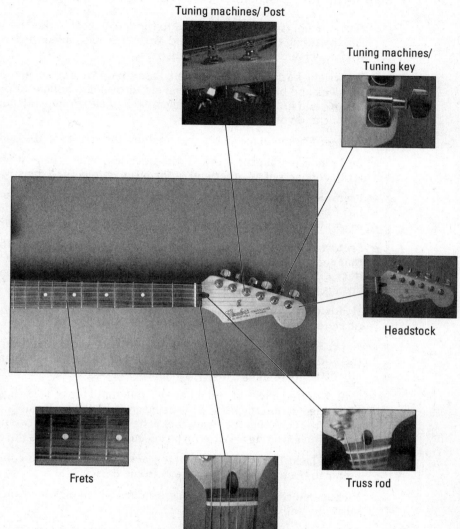

Tuning machines/ Post

Tuning machines/
Tuning key

Headstock

Frets

Nut

Truss rod

Here are the functions of the various parts of the electric guitar.

- ✔ **Bar:** A metal rod or arm attached to the bridge that varies the string tension by tilting the bridge back and forth. It is also called the tremolo bar, whammy bar, vibrato bar, or wang bar.

- ✔ **Body:** The large, shapely wooden mass that provides an anchor for the neck and bridge. The body can either be solid, hollow, or partially hollow, and houses the bridge assembly and electronics (pickups as well as tone and volume controls).

- ✔ **Bridge:** The metal assembly that anchors the strings to the body.

- ✔ **End pin:** A metal post screwed into the body, where the rear end of the strap connects. The other end of the strap connects to the strap pin.

- ✔ **Fretboard:** A flat, plank-like piece of wood that sits atop the neck and has frets embedded in it. This is where you place your left-hand fingers to produce notes and chords. It is also known as the fingerboard.

- ✔ **Fret(s):** 1) Thin metal wires or bars running perpendicular to the strings that shorten the effective vibrating length of a string, enabling it to produce different pitches. 2) A verb describing the action of pressing the strings to the fretboard.

- ✔ **Headstock:** The section that holds the tuning machines and provides a place for the manufacturer to display its logo.

- ✔ **Neck:** The long, club-like wooden piece that connects the headstock to the body. Some guitarists like to wield their guitars like clubs, and usually do so by holding them by the neck.

- ✔ **Nut:** A slotted sliver of stiff nylon or bone that stops the strings from vibrating beyond the neck. The strings pass through the slots on their way to the tuners in the headstock. The nut is one of the two points at which the vibrating area of the string ends. (The bridge is the other.)

- ✔ **Output jack:** The insertion point, or jack, for the cord that connects the guitar to the amplifier or other electronic device.

- ✔ **Pickup selector:** A switch that determines which pickup or pickups are currently active.

- ✔ **Pickups:** Bar-like magnets that create the electrical current that the amplifier converts into musical sound.

- ✔ **Strap pin:** Metal post where the front, or top, end of the strap connects. The strap pin is screwed into either the guitar's back (as on a Gibson Les Paul) or into the end of one of the "horns" (as on a Fender Stratocaster). The other end of the strap connects to a corresponding pin, the end pin.

✔ **Strings:** The six metal wires that, drawn taut, produce the notes of the guitar. Although not strictly part of the actual guitar (you attach and remove them at will), strings are an integral part of the whole system, and a guitar's entire design and structure revolves around making the strings ring out with passion and musicality (and don't forget volume!).

✔ **Top:** The face of the guitar's body. The top is often a cosmetic or decorative cap that overlays the rest of the body material.

✔ **Trussrod:** An adjustable steel rod that can be rotated using a special wrench and which helps keep the neck straight. You gain access to the rod through a hole in the headstock or at the base of the neck.

✔ **Tuning machines:** Geared mechanisms that raise and lower the tension of the strings, drawing them to different pitches. The string wraps tightly around a *post* that sticks out through the top, or face, of the headstock. The post passes through to the back of the headstock, where gears connect it to a *tuning key*. Tuning machines are also known as tuners, tuning pegs, tuning keys, and tuning gears.

✔ **Volume and tone controls:** Knobs that vary the loudness of the guitar's sound and its bass and treble frequencies.

The amplifier

The amplifier is an all-electronic device with no moving parts (except for its knobs and switches, which control the volume and tone of the incoming signal). You might think that those rather pedestrian-looking, geometrically plain boxes that do nothing but a lot of internal electrical processing are functional and necessary, but not particularly sexy (well, not by electric guitar standards, anyway). Amp lore, however, is every bit as epic and mythological as guitar lore. Entire subcultures (that all, curiously, seem to have an Internet newsgroup devoted to their cause) are devoted to assessing, proselytizing, and otherwise pondering the mysteries and myths of the perfect guitar amplifier.

In any quest for the perfect tone, you must have an amp in the equation, and the history and contributions of such legendary amp manufacturers as Fender, Marshall, and Vox are an inextricable part of the rock and roll gear legacy. Plus, an amp gives you a place to set your drink when you go onstage.

Figure 1-2 shows the various parts of an electric guitar amplifier.

Book IV

Rock Guitar

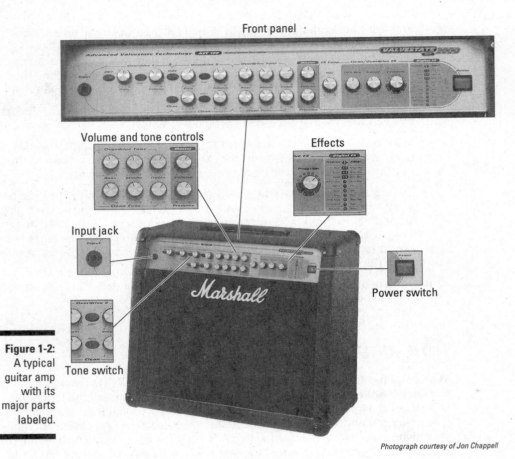

Front panel

Volume and tone controls

Effects

Input jack

Power switch

Figure 1-2: A typical guitar amp with its major parts labeled.

Tone switch

Photograph courtesy of Jon Chappell

Here are the functions of the various parts of the guitar amplifier.

- **Cabinet:** The box that houses the speaker and electronic components. It is typically made of plywood or pressure-treated wood and encased in a durable protective covering.

- **Effects:** Many modern amps also include onboard digital signal processing, such as reverb, delay, chorus, and flange.

- **Front panel** or **face plate:** The metal plate through which knobs and switches protrude to protect the controls that sit just below the surface.

- **Grille cloth:** The mesh-like fabric, usually made of a synthetic weave, that allows sound to pass through, but keeps foreign, and potentially harmful, objects (such as the toe of a boot) away from sensitive speaker surfaces.

- **Input jack:** The socket where you put the cord from your electric guitar, or the cord from the output of the last effect in your signal chain.
- **Power switch:** A switch that turns the amp on and off.
- **Tone switch:** Two-position, or toggle, switches (not rotary or continuous) that provide additional tonal control.
- **Volume and tone controls:** Rotary knobs that provide continuous control over the outgoing signal.

Effects

The newest member of the triumvirate of principal players is the group whose members are electronic effects. These self-contained units range in size anywhere from a cigarette pack to a small furnace. The size and range of most effects, though, falls between a bar of soap and a VCR deck.

Understanding pickups and amplification

Vibrating strings produce the different tones on a guitar. You must be able to hear those tones, however, or you face one of those if-a-tree-falls-in-a-forest questions. For an acoustic guitar, hearing it is no problem because it provides its own amplifier in the form of the hollow sound chamber that boosts its sound . . . well, acoustically.

An electric guitar, on the other hand, makes virtually no acoustic sound at all. (Well, a tiny bit, like a buzzing mosquito, but nowhere near enough to fill a stadium or anger your next-door neighbors.) An electric instrument creates its tones entirely through electronic means. The vibrating string is still the source of the sound, but a hollow wood chamber isn't what makes those vibrations audible. Instead, the vibrations disturb, or modulate, the magnetic field that the pickups — wire-wrapped magnets positioned

underneath the strings — produce. As the vibrations of the strings modulate the pickup's magnetic field, the pickup produces a tiny electric current.

If you remember from eighth-grade science, wrapping wire around a magnet creates a small current in the wire. If you then take any magnetic substance and disturb the magnetic field around that wire, you create fluctuations in the current itself. A taut steel string vibrating at the rate of 440 times per second creates a current that itself fluctuates 440 times per second. Pass that current through an amplifier and then a speaker, and you hear the musical tone A. More specifically, you hear the A above middle C, which is the standard absolute tuning reference in modern music — from the New York Philharmonic to Daft Punk.

Figure 1-3 shows four of the most common electronic effects used by rock guitarists.

Figure 1-3:
Four common electronic effects used by guitarists (left to right): digital delay, chorus, distortion, wah-wah.

Photograph courtesy of Jon Chappell

Here are the functions of four effects commonly used by guitarists.

✔ **Digital delay:** Creates an echo by digitally recording the signal and playing it back at adjustable times after the principal signal has sounded.

✔ **Chorus:** Creates a thick, swirly effect by simulating the sound of two or more guitars playing in tandem, but not quite with the exact tuning or timing.

✔ **Distortion:** Simulates the sound of an amp that's played too loud to handle a signal cleanly. Distortion devices are used for their convenience, so that the guitarist doesn't have to constantly adjust the amp controls to get a distorted sound.

✔ **Wah-wah:** A foot-pedal rocked by the guitarist's foot, that creates a tonal variation that resembles a horn with a mute, or a human voice saying the phrase "wah wah" (thus the name).

Accessorizing Your Guitar

You may also want to acquire some other useful components, including various accessories that all serve to make rock guitar playing a little easier. Figure 1-4 shows an assortment of guitar accessories.

Figure 1-4:
Clockwise
from top
left: picks,
strap, cord,
electronic
tuner, bat-
teries, capo,
slide, extra
strings, peg
winder, wire
cutters.

Photograph courtesy of Jon Chappell

In no particular order, following is a list of accessories, and their descriptions, that go with the well-heeled rock guitarist.

Picks

An optional item for acoustic guitarists, a pick is a requirement for playing rock guitar. Sometimes referred to as a *plectrum*, a pick is a small triangular- or teardrop-shaped piece of thin plastic or nylon, about the size of a quarter, that's held between the thumb and index finger of the right, or strumming, hand. When you strum a chord or pluck a note, you use your pick to make contact. You can buy guitar picks (there's no distinction between an electric guitar and acoustic guitar picks) at any music or CD store, in a variety of colors, shapes, and thickness (called gauges). Buy 'em by the bucketful, because you'll lose, break, give away, and squander plenty in your guitar-playing career.

Straps

A strap is also an absolute necessity, but under only one condition: if you plan to play while standing. Straps *can* be used while sitting, but that's a matter of personal preference. Most people interested in playing rock guitar, however, want to stand for at least some of that time (especially if you plan to perform). A strap is always a good thing to have rolled up and tucked away in your guitar case, even if you do most of your playing sitting down.

Straps come in all materials, from leather to fabric to space-age mesh, so you will certainly be able find one that suits your sense of fashion. You can even have a custom-made strap with your initials or name emblazoned on the side that faces the audience. Looks great for television.

Cords

A cord, or cable, is the technical term for the wire, or lead, that connects electric guitars to amps and other components, so you need at least one. If you use one electronic effects device you'll need two — one to connect the guitar to the effect's input, and one to connect the effect's output to the amp. If you have two effects, you'll need three cables; three effects, four cables, and so on. But whether you use effects or not, carrying an extra cable with you is always a good idea (like straps, cables can be coiled up and unobtrusively stashed in a guitar case). An extra cable is cheap insurance indeed; a bad cable can silence you.

Tuners

A tuner is a device that helps you to tune your instruments. It won't turn the pegs for you, but its meters tell you when a string is flat or sharp with much more accuracy that your ear can — even if you have perfect pitch. And what's the definition of perfect pitch, you ask? Why, that's when you can toss a banjo into a dumpster without hitting the sides. Read more about tuning in Book I Chapter 1.

Chapter 2

Playing Lead

· ·

In This Chapter

▶ Learning scales, arpeggios, and lead patterns

▶ Reading notation

▶ Practicing riffs

▶ Improvising good solos

▶ Access the audio tracks at www.dummies.com/go/guitaraio/

· ·

*L*ead guitar is the most spectacular and dazzling feature of rock guitar playing. Lead guitar can embody emotions that run the gamut from mournful and soulful to screaming, frenzied abandon — sometimes in the same solo. Whereas riffs are grounded, composed, and can manifest their power through their unflinching solidity, lead is beckoned by the music to launch into divinely inspired flights of fancy, to be forever soaring.

The greatest lead guitarists, from Eric Clapton and Jimi Hendrix to Eddie Van Halen and Steve Vai, have all been able to soar, but they have also all been disciplined masters of their instruments. They resolved the ultimate artistic paradox: total freedom through total control.

As you begin developing the basic technique for playing lead, never forget that your playing possesses the potential for evoking enormous emotional power. And kick over a few amplifiers while you're at it too!

Taking the Lead

You must play many before you can play one, Grasshopper.

This probably fake saying certainly applies to rock guitar playing, because you need to learn to play chords (note groupings of at least three notes) before you can learn single-notes — the stuff of leads.

Actually, you don't *have* to learn chords before lead, but in rock guitar it's a good idea, at least from a technical standpoint, because when playing rhythm you don't have to be as precise with your right-hand motions. Most beginning guitarists find striking multiple strings easier than plucking individual ones.

But the time has come to venture into the world of single-note playing, where you pick only one string at a time, and which string you play is critical. Single-note playing also involves a lot more movement in the left hand.

Single-note playing provides a variety of musical devices. Four of the most important ones for playing rock include:

- **Melody:** A major component of single-note playing on the guitar is melody. *Melody* can be the composed tune of the song played instrumentally, or it can be an improvised break or solo, using the melody as the point of departure.

- **Arpeggio:** An *arpeggio* is when you play a chord one note at a time, so, by definition, it's a single-note technique. You can use arpeggios as an accompaniment figure or as lead material, as many hard rock and heavy metal guitarists have done. Lead guitarists burn up many a measure just by playing arpeggios in their lead breaks, and the results can be thrilling.

- **Riff:** A *riff* is a self-contained musical phrase, usually composed of single notes and used as a structural component of a song or song section. A riff straddles the line between melody and rhythm guitar, because it contains elements of both. A riff is typically repeated multiple times and serves as a backing figure for a song section.

  Think of the signature riffs to the Beatles' "Day Tripper" and "Birthday," the Rolling Stones' "Satisfaction," Aerosmith's "Walk This Way," Cream's "Sunshine of Your Love," Led Zeppelin's "Whole Lotta Love" and "Black Dog," Ozzy Osbourne's "Crazy Train," and Bon Jovi's "You Give Love a Bad Name." These are all songs based on highly identifiable and memorable riffs.

  Riffs aren't always composed of just single notes. Deep Purple's "Smoke on the Water" and Black Sabbath's "Iron Man" are actually composed of multiple-sounding notes (power chords) moving in unison. And two or more guitars can play riffs in harmony too. The Allman Brothers and the Eagles are famous for this.

- **Free improvisation:** This isn't a recognized technical term, but a descriptive phrase of any lead material not necessarily derived from the melody. Free improvisation doesn't even have to be melodic in nature. Wide interval skips, percussive playing, effects used as music, and melodic note sequences (such as patterns of fast repeated notes, or even one note) can all contribute to an exciting lead guitar solo or passage.

The terms *lead*, *melody*, *single line*, *riff*, *solo*, and *improv* are all types of single-note playing and are often used interchangeably. The phrase "single-note playing" is a little cumbersome, so you can refer to any playing that is not rhythm playing as lead playing, even if it's to indicate playing a riff.

Strictly speaking, lead playing is the *featured* guitar, which is usually playing a single-note-based line. But it doesn't always have to be playing only single notes; it could be playing *double-stops*, which are two notes played together. Also, the designation *lead guitar* helps to distinguish that guitar from the other guitar(s) in the band playing rhythm guitar.

Sometimes the featured guitar can consist of a strummed chordal figure. The guitar break in Buddy Holly's "Peggy Sue" and the opening riff to the Who's "Pinball Wizard" are two standout examples of the rhythm guitar taking a featured role.

The yin and yang of rhythm and lead

If a band has two guitarists, a logical division of duties is to have one guitarist play rhythm and the other play lead. Often, the better guitarist will be the lead guitarist. Sometimes, however, dividing the duties this way is not necessarily for reasons of musical talent, but because the rhythm guitarist is the principal songwriter (as in the case of Tom Petty and Metallica). And in many bands with two guitarists, the divisions of lead and rhythm are not clearly defined, as in the case of Lynyrd Skynyrd, the Allman Bros., and Judas Priest. In the following list, however, the duties between lead and rhythm are clearly separated.

Group	Rhythm	Lead
The Beatles	John Lennon	George Harrison
The Rolling Stones	Keith Richards	Brian Jones/Mick Taylor/Ron Wood
The Kinks	Ray Davies	Dave Davies
Grateful Dead	Bob Weir	Jerry Garcia
AC/DC	Malcolm Young	Angus Young
Creedence Clearwater Revival	Tom Fogerty	John Fogerty
Aerosmith	Brad Whitford	Joe Perry
Kiss	Paul Stanley	Ace Frehley
Tom Petty	Tom Petty	Mike Campbell
The Cars	Ric Ocasek	Elliot Easton
The Clash	Joe Strummer	Mick Jones
Def Leppard	Steve Clark	Phil Collen
Bruce Springsteen	Bruce Springsteen	Nils Lofgren
Metallica	James Hetfield	Kirk Hammett
Guns N' Roses	Izzy Stradlin	Slash

Book IV

Rock Guitar

Holding the pick

You don't need to hold the pick any differently for lead playing than you do for rhythm playing. Have the tip of the pick extending perpendicularly from the side of your thumb, and bring your hand close to the individual string you want to play.

You may find yourself gripping the pick a little more firmly, especially when you dig in to play loudly or aggressively. This is fine. In time, the pick becomes almost like a natural extension of one of your fingers.

Attacking the problem

The sounding or striking of a note, in musical terms, is called an *attack*. It doesn't necessarily mean you have to do it aggressively, it's just a term that differentiates the beginning of the note from the sustain part (the part that rings, after the percussive sound).

To attack an individual string, position the pick so that it touches or is slightly above the string's upper side (the side toward the ceiling) and bring it through with a quick, smooth motion. Use just enough force to clear the string, but not enough to sound the next string down.

This motion is known as a downstroke (see Book II Chapter 4 for more on downstrokes and upstrokes). When playing lead, you usually strike only one string. To play an upstroke, simply reverse the motion. In rock guitar, rhythm guitarists tend to favor downstrokes. Downstrokes are more forceful and are generally used to accentuate notes to play even, deliberate rhythms. Alternating downstrokes and upstrokes is called *alternate picking* (covered later in this chapter) and is essential for playing lead guitar.

Playing Single Notes

Single-note playing requires less arm movement than playing chords does, because most of the energy comes from the wrist. You may be tempted to anchor the heel of the right hand on the bridge, which is okay, as long as you don't unintentionally dampen the strings in the process.

As you move from playing notes on the lower strings to notes on the higher strings, your right-hand heel will naturally want to adjust itself and slide along the bridge. Of course, you don't *have* to anchor your hand on the strings at all, either; you can just let your hand float roughly in the area above the bridge.

Even when you play loud and aggressively, your right-hand movements should remain fairly controlled and contained. When you see your favorite rock stars on stage flailing away, arms wildly windmilling in circular motions of large diameters, that's rhythm playing, not single-note playing.

You'll start with some easy exercises for learning to play single notes on the guitar. Then the chapter moves on to things that actually sound cool and are fun to play.

Single-note technique

Using all downstrokes, play the music in Figure 2-1 (if you need a refresher on reading music, see Book I Chapter 4). These are six passages, each on separate strings that require you to play three different notes. All the melodies are in quarter notes, which means the notes come one per beat, or one per foot tap if you're tapping along in tempo.

The trick here is to play single notes on individual strings accurately, without accidentally hitting the wrong string. You don't have to play any fancy rhythms or down- and upstroke combinations, you just have to hit the desired string cleanly. Obviously, it's harder to do that on the interior strings (2nd, 3rd, 4th, 5th) than on exterior ones (1st, 6th).

Try playing the music by yourself (without listening to Track 51, starting at 00:00), counting (and tapping) out a bar of tempo before you begin to play. After you think you've mastered the exercise and can play it without stopping or making a mistake, try playing it along with Track 51.

Book IV

Rock Guitar

Figure 2-1:
Quarter-note melodies on each of the guitar's six strings in open position.

(Continued)

(Continued)

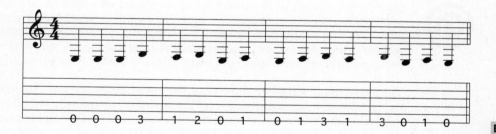

Each exercise is written in a different feel (as evidenced by the recording on Track 51), but don't let that throw you. As long as you count out the quarter notes with the count-off on the audio track (heard as the percussive click of the struck hi-hat cymbals, as a drummer would do when counting off a song) and focus on playing smooth, one-note-per-foot-tap notes, you should do fine.

The next exercise is a bit harder, because it requires you to switch strings as you play. When you play the examples in Figure 2-2 try to go between the strings smoothly, without breaking the rhythm, and without varying your dynamics (the intensity of your pick attack) as you switch strings. Listen to this one on Track 51, starting at 1:12.

Figure 2-2:
A quarter-
note melody
played
across
different
strings.

As a guitarist, you not only have to focus on keeping the rhythm steady between bars, but also when switching strings.

Alternate picking in downstrokes and upstrokes

Let's double the pace, shall we, by introducing eighth notes into your playing. Keep in mind that in rhythm playing, you can often play eighth notes by just speeding up your downstroke picking. But in lead playing, you must always play eighth notes using the technique called *alternate picking*.

Alternate picking requires you to follow a simple rule: Downbeat notes are played with downstrokes; upbeat notes are played with upstrokes. Sounds mundanely simple, but in practice, maintaining this strict alternating pattern while crossing — and even skipping — strings can be difficult. Still, alternate picking works, even when it seems illogical, or at least inefficient, and virtually every guitarist on the planet who plays with any facility uses alternate picking.

The alternate-picking technique doesn't care whether you have to cross strings or not. In an eighth-note melody, the alternate-picking technique requires that the downbeat notes take downstrokes and the upbeat notes (the ones that fall in between the beats) take upstrokes.

Using scales

By definition, a scale proceeds in stepwise motion. Scales are the dreaded instruments of musical torture wielded by Dickensian disciplinarians (like your fourth-grade piano teacher), but they do serve a purpose. They are a great way to warm up your fingers within a recognizable structure and they reveal available notes on the fingerboard within a key.

Plus, playing scales provides a familiar-sounding melody (*do re mi fa sol la ti do*) that yields a certain satisfaction upon correct execution — at least until you've done them two or three billion times and you can't stand it anymore.

But for now, try an ascending, contiguously sequenced set of natural notes in the key of C beginning on the root (the first degree of the scale or chord) — a C major scale.

Playing in the majors

Figure 2-3 (Track 52 at 00:00) is a one-octave C major scale in eighth notes. Note that the pick-stroke indications are given for the first two beats, and then the term *sim.* (which is short for *simile*, or "in the same fashion") tells you to continue on in the same way.

Left-hand fingerings are also provided in the standard music notation staff. The idea is not that you sight read all this stuff — the notes, the right- and left-hand indications, and so forth — but that you learn this passage and play it whenever you feel like warming up, playing a C scale. Or you can just play the scale when inspiration waits in the wing space of your mind, mute and mocking, and you can't think of anything else musically cohesive to play.

Figure 2-3:
A one-octave C major scale, ascending and descending.

Now for another scale that's musically about the same, but in a different key, and somewhat harder to play. Figure 2-4 (Track 52 at 0:14), a two-octave G major scale, ascending and descending. What makes it harder is the left-hand fingering: You use all your left-hand fingers for this scale, in a four-fret span.

Keep your left hand fairly stationary above the strings, and let your fingers stretch and reach for their correspondingly numbered fret (the 1st, or index, finger plays the 1st fret; the 2nd, or middle, finger, plays the 2nd fret; and so forth). As your hand becomes more agile, your finger span will widen and you will be able to reach the frets comfortably while keeping your left hand almost perfectly stationary.

Book IV

Rock Guitar

Figure 2-4:
A two-
octave G
major scale,
ascending
and
descending.

A minor adjustment

Every major scale has a corresponding minor scale, the *relative minor,* which you can play in its entirety using the same key signature. In any major key, the natural minor scale (so called because you can play it naturally, with no altering of the major-scale notes) begins at the 6th degree.

So in the key of C, the 6th degree would be A (remember the musical alphabet only goes up to G). Figure 2-5 (Track 52 at 0:35) is a one-octave minor scale, in eighth notes, starting on the open 5th string, A.

Figure 2-5:
A one-
octave A
minor scale.

Skips

Skips are melodic movements of non-contiguous letter names, such as A, C, E, G, B. Skips can be of any interval and don't have to follow the notes of a chord. So all arpeggios are skips, but not all skips are arpeggios. Figure 2-6 (Track 52 at 0:49) shows an Am7 arpeggio. The notes of the chord are played one after the other: A-C-E-G.

Figure 2-6:
An Am7
arpeggio.

Combining steps and skips

Most melodies are composed of a mix of stepwise motion and skips, and sometimes melodies can include an arpeggio (such as in the army bugle calls "Taps" and "Reveille"). Scales are a series of notes organized by key, where you play the notes in order, ascending and/or descending. Arpeggios can be skips in any order, but are limited to the notes of the chord.

Starting at the Bottom: Low-Note Melodies

For some reason, all traditional guitar method books start with the guitar's top strings and work their way down to the low strings. But in the true rebellious spirit of both rock and roll and the *For Dummies* series, this section starts at the bottom.

The impetus for so many of the world's greatest melodies, riffs, and rock rhythm figures have low-born origins (from a guitar perspective, anyway). Think of all the classic riffs already mentioned in this chapter — "Smoke on the Water," "Iron Man," "Day Tripper" — and how many of them are low-note riffs.

In that spirit, try Figure 2-7 (Track 53 at 0:00), which is a low-note melody, in the style of a classic-rock riff. Note how it almost revels in its own subterranean girth. Spinal Tap would be proud.

Book IV

Rock Guitar

Figure 2-7:
A rocking low-note melody, exploiting the low strings of the guitar.

Figure 2-8 (Track 53 at 0:11) is another melody, more nimble than the one in Figure 2-7. This one moves in steady eighth notes and features some unexpected changes in direction. It also contains melodic skips, which in this case is an arpeggio because it outlines the notes of an A minor chord.

Figure 2-8:
A low-note melody in moving eighth notes.

Going to the Top: High-Note Melodies

Lead playing typically exploits the upper registers of the guitar, where melodic material is most naturally situated. Before you get really high up on the neck, play the melodic example in Figure 2-9 (Track 53 at 0:23) to hear the guitar's upper registers cut through the rhythm section's din.

Figure 2-9:
A high-note melody in open position.

If your guitar sounds twangy instead of smooth and creamy, try increasing the distortion factor of your sound. See Book IV Chapter 1 for information on how to dial up a more distorted sound if necessary.

Playing in Position

So far you've played all of your melodies and exercises in the lower regions of the neck, between the 1st and 4th frets. This is where it's easiest to place the notes that you see written on paper onto frets of the guitar neck.

But the guitar has many more frets on the neck than just the first four. Playing in the lowest regions of the neck is where you play most of your low-note riffs, a lot of chords, and some lead work, but the bulk of your lead playing takes place in the upper regions of the neck for two reasons:

- ✔ The higher on the neck you are, the higher the notes you can hit. The guitar is sort of a low instrument, because the notes you read on the treble clef actually sound an octave lower on the guitar. For this reason, it's a good idea to get as far up the neck as possible if you want to distinguish yourself melodically, above the low end rumble of basses, drums, and, of course, other guitars playing rhythm in the lower range.

- ✔ The strings are more flexible and easily manipulated by the left hand on the higher frets, which means you have better expressive opportunities for bends, vibrato, hammer-ons, pull-offs, slides and other expressive devices (all of which are covered in Book IV Chapter 4).

Open position

Playing in open position is where you've spent your time thus far — by *design*. When you have complete command of the entire neck and you can play anywhere you can find the note, playing in open position will be a *choice*. In other words, you'll play in open position only because you want to, because it suits your musical purpose.

Rock guitar uses both open position and the upper positions (the positions' names are defined by where the left-hand index finger falls) for the different musical colorings they offer. By contrast, jazz guitar tends to avoid open position completely, and folk guitar uses open position exclusively. But rock uses both, and so you need to understand the strengths offered by both open position and the upper positions.

Book IV

Rock Guitar

Moveable, or closed, position

Playing in a *moveable position* allows you to take a passage of music and play it anywhere on the neck. If you play a melody on all fretted strings, as in a barre chord (incorporating no open strings), it doesn't matter if you play it at the 1st fret or the 15th. The notes will preserve the same melodic relationship. It's sort of like swimming: After you learn the technique of keeping yourself afloat and moving, it doesn't matter if the water is five feet or five miles deep — except five-mile deep water is probably colder.

A moveable position is also called *closed position,* because it involves no open strings. After you play anything on all-fretted strings, you have created a great opportunity to slide it anywhere on the neck and have it play exactly the same — except of course that you're apt to find yourself in another key. (Book II Chapter 3 has more on open, movable, and barre chords.)

The best part is that you can move closed-position melodies around — instantly transposing their key, something that no piano player, trumpet player, or flute player can do easily, and they will be eternally jealous of you.

To demonstrate a moveable position, first take your two-octave G major scale and play exactly the same pitches, but place them on all fretted strings. Figure 2-10 (Track 54) is a two-octave G major scale in 2nd position. It's 2nd position because the lowest fret played defines the position's name, and here it's the 2nd fret.

Figure 2-10: A two-octave G major scale in 2nd position.

Try sliding your hand up and down the neck, playing the scale in different positions. Doing so will *transpose* your G major scale into other keys.

Jamming on Lower Register Riffs

The best thing about the lower register of the guitar is its powerful bass notes. You simply have no better arsenal for grinding out earth-shattering, filling-rattling, brain-splattering tones than the lower register of the guitar, and so this is where 99 percent of all the greatest riffs are written.

Start off with a classic riff in quarter notes, called, variously, boogie-woogie, boogie, or walking bass. Figure 2-11 (Track 55) is a classic boogie figure using only the notes of the chord — plus one, the sixth degree — in a fixed pattern for each chord. Its repetition is its strength. Your ears want to hear the same pattern for each of the chords, so infectious is the sound!

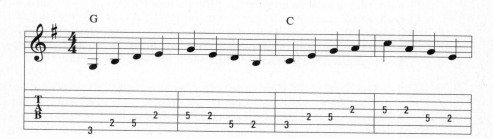

Figure 2-11: A classic walking-bass boogie-woogie riff in G.

Book IV

Rock Guitar

Making It Easy: The Pentatonic Scale

The major and minor scales may be music-education stalwarts, but as melodic material they sound, well, academic when used over chord progressions. Rock guitarists have a much better scale to supply them with melodic fodder: the pentatonic scale.

The pentatonic scale is not the only scale available for playing rock lead, but it is the most widely used *and* easiest to learn. The beauty of this scale is that it sounds great over every chord change in a key, and you can begin to make music with it almost immediately. The pentatonic scale is to the rock guitarist what anesthesia, the printing press, and the cordless screwdriver are to modern civilization — an indispensable entity without which life would be much more difficult.

As its name implies, the *pentatonic scale* contains five notes, which is two notes shy of the normal seven-note major and minor scales. This creates a more open and less linear sound than either the major or minor scale. The pentatonic scale is also more ambiguous, but this is a good thing, because it means that it's harder to play "bad" notes — notes that, although they're within the key, may not fit well against any given chord in the progression. The pentatonic scale uses just the most universal note choices.

The first scale you'll learn here is the A minor pentatonic. A minor pentatonic can be used as a lead scale over chord progressions in A minor, C major, and A blues ("blues" can imply a specific, six-note scale, as well as a chord progression). It also works pretty well over A major and C blues. Not bad for a scale that's two notes shy of a major scale.

Figure 2-12 (Track 56) is a neck diagram outlining a pentatonic scale form in 5th position. The neck is positioned as if you're facing an upright guitar that is laid on its side, to your left. So it looks like tablature in the sense that the first string is on top, but it's a schematic of the actual neck instead of the tab staff. On the audio track, it's played from top (the 1st string, 8th fret) to bottom (6th string, 5th fret) in quarter notes. Try playing it, and don't worry about playing along in rhythm with the audio track — the track is just there so you can make sure you're in the right position hitting the right notes.

Figure 2-12:
A neck diagram showing the pentatonic scale in 5th position.

5th fret   8th fret

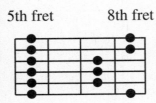

In the neck diagram in Figure 2-12, just as in a tab staff, the 1st string is the top line. Also, this is not a chord, but all the available notes for the pentatonic scale. The left-hand index finger plays all the notes that occur at the fifth fret; the ring finger plays all the seventh-fret notes; and the little finger plays all the eighth-fret notes. In this particular scale pattern, the middle finger doesn't play at all.

Playing the Pentatonic Scale: Three Ways to Solo

In this section you learn to play one pentatonic scale pattern in three different musical contexts:

- A progression in a major key
- A progression in a minor key
- A blues progression

You can use just one pattern to satisfy all three musical settings. This is an unbelievable stroke of luck for beginning guitarists, and you can apply a shortcut, a quick mental calculation, that allows you to instantly wail away in a major-key song, a minor-key song, or a blues song — simply by performing what is essentially a musical parlor trick. This is a great quick-fix solution to get you playing decent-sounding music virtually instantly.

As you get more into the music, however, you may want to know why these notes are working the way they do. But until then, it's just time to jam.

Place your index finger on the 5th fret, 1st string. Relax your hand so that your other fingers naturally drape over the neck, hovering above the 6th, 7th, and 8th frets. You are now in 5th position ready to play.

Work to play each note singly, from top to bottom, so that you get your fingers used to playing the frets and switching strings. Don't worry about playing downstrokes and upstrokes until you're comfortable moving your left-hand fingers up and down the strings, like a spider walking across her web.

Now try Figure 2-13 (Track 57 at 0:00), which is a descending scale in C pentatonic major in eighth notes, beginning with your left-hand little finger on the 1st string, 8th fret.

This particular pentatonic pattern allows you to keep your left hand stationary; all the fingers can reach their respective fret easily without stretching or requiring left-hand movement.

Figure 2-13: A descending eighth-note C pentatonic major scale.

Now that you've played the scale, try it in a musical context. This is where you witness the magic that transpires when you play the same notes over different feels in different keys. Let the games begin!

Pentatonics over a major key

Figure 2-14 (Track 57 at 0:11) is a C major progression in a medium-tempo 4/4 groove. The written solo is a mix of quarter notes and eighth notes comprised of notes from the C major pentatonic scale, moving up and down the neck. The left channel of the audio track has the rhythm instruments, and the right channel features the lead guitar. As soon as you get the idea about how the lead sounds, dial it the existing lead guitar and try to play the melody against the recorded rhythm sound by yourself. Then check your work by dialing back in the right channel and see how close you got.

Figure 2-14: Solo in C major over a medium-tempo 4/4.

Pentatonics over a minor key

And now, as Monty Python once said, for something completely different. Or is it? In Figure 2-15 (Track 57 at 0:35), the feel changes (to a heavy back-beat 4/4), the key changes (to A minor), but you still play the same notes. Notice the strikingly different results.

Figure 2-15: An A minor solo over a heavy backbeat 4/4.

Pentatonics over a blues progression

And now, incredibly, a different groove again that will work with the same scale. Figure 2-16 (Track 57 at 0:52) is an up-tempo blues shuffle in A. Note that the eighth notes in this example swing — that is, they are to be played in a long-short scheme. Make it cry.

In the next section, you don't have to master any music at all. You get to make up your own.

Figure 2-16: An A blues solo over an up-tempo shuffle.

Improvising Leads

In rock, jazz, and blues, improvisation plays a great role. In fact, being a good improviser is much more important than being a good technician. It's much more important to create honest, credible, and inspired music through improvisation than it is to play with technical accuracy and perfection.

The best musicians in the world are the best improvisers, but they are not necessarily the best practitioners of the instrument. About the only thing that competes with the ability to improvise a good solo is the ability to write a song.

You're going to take a collection of notes and turn it into music. To do this, use the 5th-position pentatonic scale you learned earlier in this chapter to play over. Figure 2-17 (Track 58) is a slow, gutbucket blues shuffle in A. Don't forget to swing those eighth notes and remember the blues credo: You don't have to feel bad to play the blues . . . but it helps.

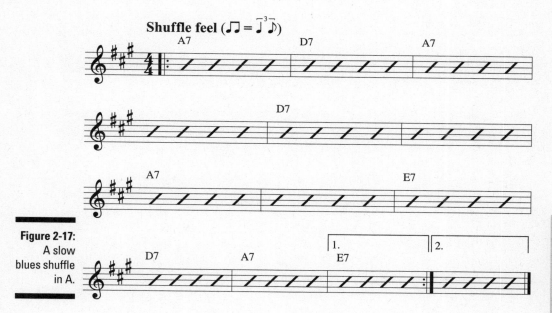

Figure 2-17:
A slow
blues shuffle
in A.

Book IV

Rock Guitar

Improvising is, at the same time, one of the easiest things to do (just find your notes and go) and one of the hardest (try to make up a meaningful melody on the spot). The more note choices you have, the more vocabulary you'll be able to pull from to express your message.

The pentatonic scale is a great way to start making music immediately, but plenty of other scales exist to help you in your music making. And you still have to listen to other guitarists for ideas. Go outside any scale you use to get unusual notes, and learn passages of classic solos on recordings to see what makes them tick. Above all, you must develop you own sense of phrasing and your own voice.

Chapter 3

Groovin' on Riffs

· ·

In This Chapter

▶ Working out with riffs

▶ Doing double-time with double-stops

▶ Combining riffs and chords

▶ Playing rhythm figures

▶ Access the audio tracks at www.dummies.com/go/guitaraio/

· ·

Riffs are often the most memorable component of a rock and roll song and can form the perfect bridge between a chord progression and a melodic lead phrase. Although technically a short, self-contained musical phrase, a riff is much, much more than that. A riff sticks in your head long after you forget the lyrics — and even the melody — and at a noisy party, it is the riff that makes a song instantly recognizable when you can't quite make out the rest of the music. In many cases, the riff is the backbone of the song, and the rhythm, melody, and chords are all derived from the riff.

In this chapter, you venture deep into riff territory to see where rock and roll *lives* and discover why riffs themselves are such a vital and inextricable component of rock and roll. This chapter also talks about two other rock staples: the *power chord* and the *double-stop*. (See Book II Chapter 3 for more on power chords, and Book II Chapter 5 for more on double-stops.) Then the chapter shows you how to combine riffs, power chords, and double-stops into full-blown, fully realized *rhythm figures*. Rhythm figures embody the total approach to rhythm guitar. Virtually any strumming or single-note technique you can come up with can be pressed into rhythm-guitar service and incorporated into a rhythm figure.

Getting Your Groove On: Basic Riffs

Riffs that exploit the lower register of the guitar are a good place to start. Make sure you strike only one string at a time, but that your pick strokes carry the same confidence and power that they had when playing chords. Even if the riffs sound familiar, make sure you execute the rhythms and articulations precisely as written; don't let your ears allow you to gloss over the tricky parts.

Half-note and whole-note riffs

A riff doesn't have to be flashy to be memorable. Figure 3-1 (Track 59 at 0:00), in the style of the band Black Sabbath, uses only half notes and whole notes to create an eerie, menacing effect.

Figure 3-1: A powerful-sounding riff using only half notes and whole notes.

You can give fretted notes with long values (half notes and whole notes) more life by applying left-hand vibrato to them. Gently pull and release the string (causing it to bend slightly) very rapidly, causing the note to waver. Vibrato helps give slower notes more intensity. A wavy line (〰) placed above the note tells you to apply vibrato, as seen in Figure 3-1.

Eighth-note and quarter-note riffs

Other than slow riffs created from half notes and whole notes, the simplest riffs to play are formed from the straightforward, non-syncopated rhythmic units of quarter notes and eighth notes. Figures 3-2 and 3-3 (Track 59 at 0:11 and 0:19) are riffs that mix quarter notes and eighth notes. Be sure to observe the pick-stroke indications for downstrokes (⊓) and upstrokes (∨).

Note the presence of F♯ in the key signature of Figures 3-2 and 3-3. This means that all Fs are sharped and that the key is either G major or E minor. So even though these two riffs don't contain any Fs, the key signature tells us that the examples are in E minor, which we know because the riffs gravitate to and around the root note, E. (Book III Chapter 5 has more on key signatures.)

Figure 3-2:
A riff comprised of mostly quarter notes, with one eighth-note pair.

Figure 3-3:
A riff comprised of mostly eighth notes, with one quarter note on beat 2 to break up the motion.

Now try the boogie riff in Figure 3-4 (Track 59 at 0:27), which is comprised of mostly quarter notes, but with a couple of shuffle eighth notes thrown in to give the groove an extra kick. The tempo is fairly bright here, so watch that you execute the long-short rhythm of the shuffle eighth notes correctly.

Figure 3-4:
A boogie shuffle in quarter notes, with a few eighth notes thrown in.

Book IV

Rock Guitar

Riffs that consist of all eighth notes create a sense of continuous motion and can really help propel a song along. Figure 3-5 (Track 59 at 0:37) is in all eighth notes, and note how easily the end of the measure leads into the beginning of the second measure, creating a seamless sound. Note, too, the presence of the B♭ and D♯ — two chromatic, or "out of key," notes in E minor.

Figure 3-5:
A steady-eighth-note riff in E minor, with two chromatic notes, B♭ and D♯.

Whereas Figure 3-5 is a simple one-bar riff that repeats over and over, Figure 3-6 (Track 59 at 0:45) is a longer steady-eighth-note phrase that goes for two measures before repeating.

Figure 3-6:
A two-bar riff in steady eighth notes.

Because riffs are short and self-contained, they can be easily *looped*, or repeated back to back with no break. All the riffs presented in this chapter can be played seamlessly, and you're encouraged to play multiple repetitions until you execute the notes flawlessly — both from a technical standpoint (no missed or *fluffed* notes, no buzzing) as well as a rhythmic one. Pay particular attention when *rounding the corner* (going from the end of the riff back to the beginning). The barrier preventing a smooth transition can be more psychological than technical.

It's one thing to maintain a steady, consistent delivery for two bars. It's quite another to stay solid over bars upon bars or minutes upon minutes of playing the same riff within a groove. So repeat the riffs in this chapter in a loop fashion; that is, play them numerous times until you're sure you've got the long-term as well as the short-term consistency considerations under control.

Or at least repeat the riffs until you can't stand it anymore. Either way, it's good training for playing with any band claiming the Allman Brothers, the Grateful Dead, or Phish as an influence.

Sixteenth-note riffs

A sixteenth-note riff doesn't have to be fast or syncopated just because it contains sixteenth notes. Figure 3-7 (Track 59 at 0:57) is a riff that builds up speed by going first through quarter notes, then eighth notes, then sixteenths. Does this riff sound familiar?

Figure 3-7:
A riff that steps through quarter, eighth, and sixteenth notes.

Many hard rock and heavy metal riffs are based in sixteenth notes, including the infamous *gallop* pattern. Figure 3-8 (Track 59 at 1:12) is a gallop riff that takes you on a wild ride. Buckle up — or should that be saddle up?

Figure 3-8:
A hard rock/ heavy metal gallop riff based on eighth and sixteenth notes.

Book IV

Rock Guitar

Then again, sometimes a riff written in sixteenth notes is just plain doggone fast, such as the hard-rock groove in Figure 3-9 (Track 59 at 1:23). Be sure to observe the alternate-picking indications in this example.

Figure 3-9:
A fast
sixteenth-
note-based
riff in a hard-
rock style.

Eighth-note syncopation

Technically, playing a syncopated riff is no harder than playing a non-syncopated riff; it's just trickier to read in printed music. Remember: Syncopation is accenting the off-beat —the unexpected. The more experience you have with syncopation, the more you can learn to recognize typical syncopation patterns. So you don't have to count your brains out with every dot and tie that appears — you can use your memory to help you. Syncopation is not intentionally designed to trip you up (although it may seem like that at first); it's there to put a kick into the music. Learn a few patterns and combinations, and you'll start to recognize them when they reappear. Memorizing a vocabulary of pre-existing syncopation patterns helps so that you don't have to reinvent the wheel every time you encounter a syncopated rhythm.

A great example of eighth-note syncopation occurs in the first line of the Beatles song "Eleanor Rigby." If you tap your hand or foot in time and sing, or say in rhythm, the words "Eleanor Rigby picks up the rice in the church where a wedding has been," you notice that the words "Rigby," "rice," "church," "wedding," and "been" all fall on the offbeat.

Figure 3-10 (Track 59 at 1:33) is a steady eighth-note figure where only the last eighth note in the bar is syncopated — here, through the use of a tie that binds it to the first note of the next measure. This particular syncopation device is called an *anticipation,* because it anticipates the downbeat, or first — and strongest — beat, of the measure. In fact, an anticipation is such a common and cool-sounding syncopation device that often players will introduce it even when it's not written into the music. It's one of the those rock and roll situations where something can be justified simply because "it's a feel thing."

Figure 3-10:
An eighth-note riff with beat 1 anticipated, or tied over from beat four-and-a-half.

Now, double your syncopation efforts and put anticipations before beat 3 (the beginning of the second half of the bar) as well as beat 1, in Figure 3-11 (Track 59 at 1:46).

Figure 3-11:
An eighth-note riff with anticipations on beats 1 and 3.

Finally, Figure 3-12 (Track 59 at 1:58) is an ultra-syncopated figure where none of the notes in bar 2 fall on the beat; they all fall in between. The band Deep Purple wrote the riff to their classic hit "Smoke on the Water" using a similar syncopation scheme.

Book IV

Rock Guitar

Figure 3-12:
A highly syncopated eighth-note riff.

The melody to the Beatles' "Eleanor Rigby" is highly syncopated, as already mentioned. In the same scheme as used in Figure 3-11, beats 1 and 3 are anticipated throughout the verse section.

Playing Two Notes Can be Better than One: Double-Stops

Stuck in a categorical netherworld between single notes and power chords is the two-note phenomenon known as the double-stop. A *double-stop* is simply two notes played simultaneously — on adjacent strings or separated by one to four (the maximum) strings in-between. The term comes from violin lingo, where a finger pressing a string to the fingerboard — remember the violin has no frets — is called a *stop*. So two stopped strings constitute a double-stop.

Because it is obviously not a single note, and because a chord requires at least three notes, the double-stop wanders between the two camps like some musical double agent — sometimes masquerading as a chord, sometimes exhibiting single-note properties. As such, it's a tremendously useful tool in rhythm guitar playing. Because of its facile properties, you can use it for lead playing, too, which is discussed in Book IV Chapter 2.

Right now, though, you'll employ double-stops in a rhythm context. A two-note power chord is technically a double-stop, because it's two strings played together. But conceptually, guitarists don't really think of power chords as double-stops. Figure 3-13 (Track 60 at 0:00) is more of a true double-stop, especially in its usage here. Note how its movement — between the fretted and open strings — is much easier to execute and less clunky than, say, switching between two chords (such as A and G) in the same tempo. Yet the double-stop movement still retains a chord-like sound and feel.

Figure 3-13: A moving double-stop figure, used as a chordal device.

Note that you've crept up, register-wise on the guitar. You're now not playing just low notes, but have moved to the midrange of open position.

Figure 3-14 (Track 60 at 0:10) is a chord progression based on A, D, and E minor, but the ascending double-stop movement lends a nice melodic, quasi-single-line feel to the passage. In this case, the double-stops are not on adjacent strings, as in Figure 3-11. Here, they have a string separating them (the open 3rd string, G), so you have to "pinch" the 2nd and 4th strings with your right-hand middle finger, or, if you want to employ a little fingerstyle action, the middle or index finger and thumb.

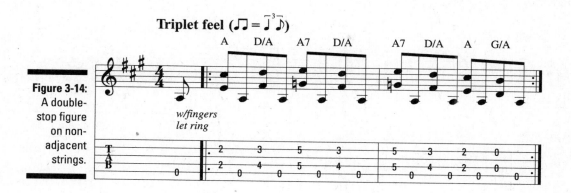

Figure 3-14: A double-stop figure on non-adjacent strings.

If you accidentally let the middle string (the open G) ring while playing Figure 3-14, you notice it doesn't sound half bad. So try playing the open G string intentionally, either by plucking all three strings, or by strumming the three interior strings (4th, 3rd, and 2nd) with your pick. The unchanging bass note (the open A string) sounded against changing ones (in this case the ascending double-stops) is called a *pedal tone*, or just a *pedal*, in music. Usually a pedal is the bass note, less often it's the highest note, but sometimes it's in the middle.

Combining Single-Note Riffs and Chords

Although lead guitar is a studied craft with an established orthodoxy (that is, you can buy books on the subject), rhythm guitar is a universe without any rules. No one can say for sure what makes up a good rhythm guitar part, but you sure know one when you hear it. The best rhythm players in rock — such as Pete Townshend, Eddie Van Halen, and Keith Richards, just to name a few — all play in a style that's hard to label or analyze. But part of that indefinable magic comes from the fact that these guitarists don't limit themselves to just chords when playing rhythm guitar. They mix a healthy dose of single notes into their playing.

Although he was known for his fiery leads and stage antics (such as playing with his teeth and lighting his guitar on fire), Jimi Hendrix was a superb rhythm player. In his ballads, notably "Little Wing" and "The Wind Cries Mary," Hendrix plays lovely Curtis-Mayfield-inspired R&B chords that sound like a cross between gospel, country, and piano figures. Hendrix also played his share of double-stops, too.

Figure 3-15 (Track 61) is a hard rock progression that mixes power chords, open position chords, and single notes into one cohesive part. Note how it builds up dramatic power by starting slow and becoming increasingly active.

Book IV

Rock Guitar

Figure 3-15: A hard rock progression mixing chords and single notes.

The squiggly vertical lines in bar 2 of Figure 3-15 tell you to draw the pick across the string in a quick arpeggio, creating a *kerrrang* sound. Experiment to see just how long you can drag out the strums without losing the sense of the rhythm.

Don't be discouraged if you can't make the riffs in this chapter sound exactly like the versions you hear on the audio tracks. As long as you can play the correct pitches in the specified rhythm, you're doing fine. You have to find your own style.

Chapter 4

Going Up the Neck and Playing the Fancy Stuff

In This Chapter

▶ Playing up the neck and playing in position

▶ Playing the movable pentatonic scale

▶ Playing hammer-ons and pull-offs

▶ Getting expressive with slides, bends, and vibrato

▶ Access the audio tracks at www.dummies.com/go/guitaraio/

To sound like a true rock and roller and to share the stratospheric heights frequented by the legions of wailing guitar heroes, you must learn to play up the neck. Actually, you need to learn how to *think* up the neck.

Playing up the neck requires both a theoretical approach and a technical adjustment. In fact, it's probably a little harder on the brain (at least at first) to figure out what to play than it is for the fingers to fall in line. Those smart-alecky digits, which acclimate very quickly, just prove the old saying, "the flesh is willing but the spirit is weak." Or something like that.

Rock players play up the neck a lot — a whole lot. Many rock players play way, way up the neck, higher than any folk-based music would dare venture, and beyond the usual range of many jazz players. In many folk-based and singer-songwriter-type songs, you often don't have to play beyond open position at all. In rock, though, playing up the neck is essential, especially for lead playing. Playing up the neck also allows you to play the same notes many different ways. Barre chords also allow you to use chords of the same name but which appear in different parts of the neck. To suddenly glimpse what it's like to have a command of the entire fretboard is a very exciting and empowering feeling.

Playing the guitar expressively — with passion, feeling, and an individual voice — is how you evolve from merely executing the correct pitches and rhythms to actually playing with *style*. In rock guitar playing, the technical approach to expressive playing involves varied approaches to *articulation,* or the way in which you sound the notes. Hammer-ons, pull-offs, slides, and bends are all different articulations to connect notes together smoothly.

In addition to attacking, or sounding, the notes, you can add expression to already-sounded notes with *vibrato,* which adds life to sustained notes that would otherwise just sit there like a head of brown lettuce. You can also apply *muting,* where you shape the *envelope* (the beginning, middle and end) of individual notes, giving them a tight, clipped sound.

Applying varied articulations is how you play and connect notes on the guitar. It's what gives music a sense of continuity and coherence. If you master articulations and can weave them seamlessly into an integrated playing style, you can convince your guitar to do almost anything: talk, sing, cry, and even write bad checks.

Going Up the Neck

You are now leaving the relatively safe haven of open position for the great unknown — that vast uncharted sea of wire and wood they call (cue dramatic music) . . . the upper frets! It's time to unbolt those training wheels, cut the apron strings, loose the surly bonds of earthbound music, and fly high. You're going up the neck into the wild blue yonder.

Playing up the neck opens up a whole new world of possibilities for playing rock guitar music. If you know only one way to play an A chord — or to play a riff one way when you hear an A chord — then all your music will have a certain sameness about it. But if you have the entire neck at your disposal, can play A chords in several different places, can form lead lines in four or five places, and have opinions and associations on what effect you'll produce when you choose one over the other — then you're tapping the true potential of the possibilities the guitar neck has to offer.

Choking up on the neck

Let's start with some known chord forms that you can move up and down to good musical effect over an open-D-string pedal (see the explanation of *pedal* in Book IV Chapter 3).

Figure 4-1 (Track 62 at 0:00) is a rhythm figure that pits an open D string against some chord forms that move up and down the neck. Notice that forms themselves are the familiar D, Dm, Dm7, and D7 shapes. But they move around the frets, rather than staying in one place. Be sure to carefully observe the fret-number indications.

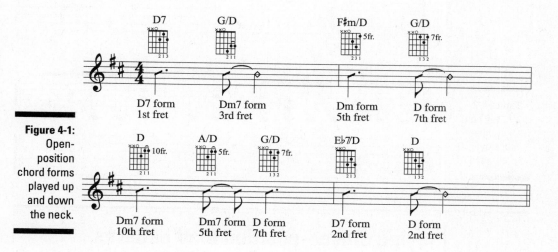

Figure 4-1: Open-position chord forms played up and down the neck.

Conveniently, you can refer to these forms by their open-position shapes: D, Dm, Dm7, and D7. But these forms don't necessarily *sound* like those chords, because they've been moved or transposed. When they're moved out of their original, open position, they produce a different-sounding chord. Be aware of the difference between a D *shape* and a D *chord*. A D *shape* played at the 7th position actually sounds like a G chord — because it *is* a G chord. Chords are named by their sound, not the shape used to create them.

Playing double-stops on the move

Now move to the interior of the guitar's strings and play a rhythm figure comprised of moving double-stops on adjacent strings. Figure 4-2 (Track 62 at 0:13) is a hard-rock figure that creates drama by moving a series of melodic-oriented double-stops up and down two strings, the 3rd and the 4th, over an open-A pedal. This is a great exercise to get your eyes and left hand used to accurately playing the up-the-neck frets.

Because Figure 4-2 creates an interplay between the open A string and the moving double-stops, try increasing that sense of delineation by applying palm mutes (stopping the ringing of the strings with your right hand) to the open A string and accents to the fretted double-stop notes. You can hear this effect on the audio track.

Book IV

Rock Guitar

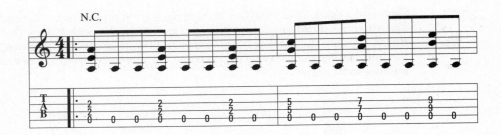

Figure 4-2:
Moving double-stops over an A pedal.

Playing closed-position lead patterns

Playing in *closed* position means you employ no open strings to play your chords, melodies, or riffs. That might seem like a restriction, but it actually frees you from the tyranny of open position, allowing you to transpose instantly and easily. But getting comfortable playing all fretted strings takes a bit of an adjustment.

When you first learn the guitar, the open strings are like spin doctors to your politically incorrect blunders: They can shield your most embarrassing gaffes by running sonic interference. The open strings will ring through clearly while your fingers struggle with a tough chord change, muffling and buzzing their way to coherence.

But in up-the-neck playing, if you relax your left hand — even for the briefest moment — the sound disappears. So you have to be really sensitive to what's happening on both sides of the notes — the attack as well as the cut-off (the point your finger leaves the current fret to go do something else). And without the benefit of open strings, you have to actively work to get the notes to connect to each other smoothly. You do that by employing legato.

Letting notes ring for their full term is called playing *legato*, and after guitarists no longer have ringing strings to provide the sonic glue, achieving legato turns from a passive let-it-just-happen affair into a concerted effort.

So as you begin playing up the neck, in closed position, keep an ear out for making the notes ring for their full value. Don't let a note stop ringing until it's time for the new note to take over. Often that's as simple as leaving full pressure on your finger before releasing it at the last possible moment to play a new note on the same string (if the next note is lower), or placing an additional finger down on the same string (if the next note is higher).

Learning to play patterns that employ no open strings has big-time benefits. Playing all-fretted patterns presents a clear advantage in one respect: The pattern can be transposed easily.

After you've gotten a feel for what it's like to move around the neck, you can see that not only won't you get hurt, but also it's kind of cool to do. The next section shows some movable lead patterns that will get you sounding and thinking like a pro in no time.

Playing in Position

Guitarists don't just go up the neck because it's higher up there (although that's sometimes a desired result — to produce higher-pitched notes), they do so because a certain position gives them better access to the notes or figures they want to play. Going to a certain zone on the neck, to better facilitate playing in a given key, is called *playing in position*. Book II Chapter 5 also discusses playing in position.

Positions defined

A *position* is defined as the lowest-numbered fret the left-hand index finger plays in a given passage. So to play in 5th position, place your left hand so that the index finger can comfortably fret the 5th fret on any string. If your hand is relaxed and the ball-side of the ridge of knuckles on your left-hand palm is resting near the neck, parallel to it, your remaining fingers — the middle, ring, and little — should be able to fret comfortably the 6th, 7th, and 8th frets, respectively. Figure 4-3 shows a neck diagram outlining the available notes of the C major pentatonic scale in 5th position.

Figure 4-3: The available frets in 5th position.

5 fr.   12 fr.

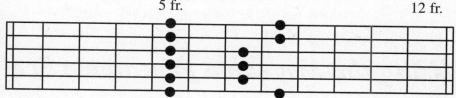

Book IV

Rock Guitar

A firm position

The next question is what specific benefits playing in position brings — other than allowing you access to higher-pitched notes not available in open position? The answer is that certain positions favor certain keys, scales, figures, or styles, better than other positions do. Following are the three most common criteria for determining the best position in which to play a given passage of music:

- ✔ **Key and pitch class:** The chief way to determine which position to play a certain piece of music in is by its key. To use the example in Figures 4-3 and 4-4, 5th position favors the major keys of C and F. If you have melodic material in the key of C or F, you'd be well advised to first try playing it in 5th position. Chances are, you'd find the notes fall easily and naturally under your fingers. Their relative minors A minor and D minor also fall very comfortably in 5th position. This is no accident, because these minor keys share the same key signature, which means they use exactly the same *pitch class* (a term you learn in music school for collection of notes, not necessarily in any given order) as their major-key counterparts.

  The pitch class of the C major and A minor pentatonic scale is A C D E G. The order of the notes changes depending on the context. For example, in the key of C, where the root is C, the notes read C D E G A. In A minor, A is the root, so the notes are ordered as A C D E G. After you start to play, however, the order becomes unimportant.

- ✔ **From a scale:** A scale can be derived from a key, but often the scale you want isn't extracted from a traditional major or minor key. For example, the blues scale is one of the most useful scales in rock, but it's not pulled from an existing, major or minor key. So C *blues* is better played out of 8th position, not 5th.

- ✔ **From a chord:** Sometimes you may not care anything about scales or keys because you find a chord whose sound you can manipulate by pressing down additional fingers or lifting up existing fingers to create a cool chord move. The technical term for this is *a cool chord move*, and often the movement doesn't involve melodic or scalar movement, just a neat way to move your fingers that results in a nice sound.

Using the Moveable Pentatonic Scale

Probably the greatest invention ever created for lead rock guitarists is the pentatonic scale. Its construction and theory have spawned countless theoretical discussions, but for rock guitar purposes, it just sounds good.

Staying at home position

The main position for the pentatonic scale is in 5th position. This is the home position of the pentatonic scale in C major or A minor. For simplicity's sake, this section uses one scale, A minor, for pentatonic studies for the remainder of this chapter. Most of the same qualities discussed can be applied to C major as well. Figure 4-4 is the A minor pentatonic scale in 5th position, shown in tab and a vertically oriented diagram.

Figure 4-4:
The A minor pentatonic scale in its home, or 5th, position.

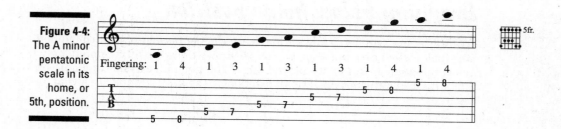

Although this scale looks to be positioned fairly high up the neck, only two of its notes — the 8th-fret C and 5th-fret A, both on the 1st string — are out of range in open position. The rest of the pitches can be found in other places in open position. For example, the 8th fret on the 2nd string is a G, which is the same G as the 1st string, 3rd fret — a note that's easily played in open position. So as you step through these notes in 5th position, be aware that you can play almost all of those same pitches in an open-position location as well.

The next step is to learn the various ways to play the same scale but in a different position, starting on a different note. This is known in music as an *inversion*. An inversion of something (a scale, a chord) is a different ordering of the same elements.

Going above home position

After the home position, you may feel restless and yearn to break out of the box. To extend your reach, learn the pentatonic scale in the position immediately above the home position. Figure 4-5 is a map of the A minor pentatonic scale in 7th position.

Figure 4-5:
Notes of the A minor pentatonic scale in 7th position.

Book IV

Rock Guitar

REMEMBER

These are exactly the same notes (except the highest note, the 1st string, 10th fret, which is out of the home position's range) as those found in 5th position.

Dropping below home position

To apply some symmetry in your life, learn the pentatonic scale form immediately below the home position. Figure 4-6 shows the scale form immediately below the home position. It's played out of 2nd position and has one note on the bottom that the 5th position doesn't have, the low G on the 6th string, 3rd fret.

Figure 4-6:
The 2nd-position A minor pentatonic scale.

Take a moment and see what you've accomplished so far. You can now play one scale, the A minor pentatonic, in three different positions: 2nd, 5th (the home position), and 7th. If you look at the neck diagram with all three patterns superimposed on the frets, it looks like Figure 4-7. It's presented in two ways: as three separate but interlocking patterns (triangles, dots, and squares), and the union of those patterns, the notes available (as just dots).

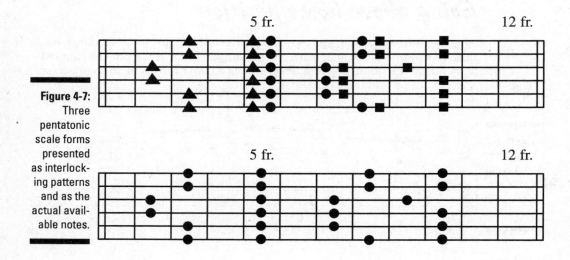

Figure 4-7:
Three pentatonic scale forms presented as interlocking patterns and as the actual available notes.

Chord licks, lead licks

In rock, a *lick* is a short, self-contained melodic phrase. This may sound suspiciously close to the definition of a riff, but there is a slight difference. While "riff" and "lick" are often used interchangeably, most guitarists agree that a riff is a repeated figure that can be used to form the basis of a song, while a lick is more of a melodic snippet, fleeting in nature, and is not generally used to form the basis of a rhythm figure.

Like riffs, licks are usually single-note affairs. But sometimes a lick can be chord based. If the distinction between a riff and a lick is a little fuzzy on the single-note front, it's even more obscure when dealing with chords. In other words, there's not much difference from a chord-based riff and a chord-based lick. It's sort of like distinguishing between good tequila and bad tequila: It's hard to do because the best tequila you've ever had in your life doesn't taste a whole lot different than the worst tequila you've ever had in your life.

Nevertheless, in an effort to pigeonhole, classify, and label all things musical, some famous chord-based licks throughout the history of rock and roll include the Doobie Brothers' "Listen to the Music" and "Long Train Running," Jimi Hendrix's "Hey Joe," "The Wind Cries Mary," and "Little Wing," and Led Zeppelin's "Stairway to Heaven" (the section right before the line "Ooh, and it makes me wonder").

Note how the patterns "dovetail," or overlap: The bottom of the 5th position acts as the top of the 2nd position, and the top of the 5th position acts as the bottom of the 7th position.

Changing Your Position

What's cool about playing up the neck is how often you get to shift positions while doing it. And make no mistake, shifting is cool. You get to move your whole hand instead of just your fingers. That looks really good on TV.

You're ready to try some real licks.

Book IV

Rock Guitar

Licks that transport

Just like life, a lick can start you out in one location and take you to another unexpected place — often with delightful results. Figure 4-8 (Track 63 at 0:00) begins in 5th position, but quickly shoots up to 7th and finishes in 8th position with a bluesy flourish. The added chromatic note here is the flat five in A minor, E♭, which is called a *blue note* (so named because it is the note that creates a sad or blue sound). The left-hand fingering indications will help you to play this smoothly.

Figure 4-8:
A short blues lick starting in 5th position and ending up in 8th position.

Adding E♭ to the A minor pentatonic scale creates a six-note scale called the *blues scale* (see the chapters in Book V for much more about blues music). In A, the blues scale is A C D E♭ E G. The numeric formula (the "interval recipe," if you will) for the blues scale is:

1 ♭3 4 ♭5 5 ♭7

The ♭5 can also be written as a ♯4, the ♭5's *enharmonic* equivalent. So applying this formula to a C major scale (C D E F G A B) produces C E♭ F G♭ G B♭, the C blues scale.

Of course, you can start high and end low — which might be bad in the world of finance or investments, but is perfectly fine in music. Figure 4-9 (Track 63 at 0:09) is a lick that begins in 5th position and takes an unexpected dip into 2nd position for some low-end gravity.

Figure 4-9:
A lick that dips down to 2nd position to get some "big bottom."

From the depths to the heights

For the ultimate exercise in shifting, try Figure 4-10 (Track 63 at 0:18), which starts in 2nd position, goes through 5th position, then 7th, and finally winds up in 9th — ending on a high, 12th-fret E on the 1st string.

Figure 4-10: An ascending line that progresses through three position shifts.

Remember that although you've gone through different positions, various ways to shift, and five versions of the pentatonic scale, you've never left the key of C major/A minor.

Knowing Where to Play

After you get your hand moving comfortably around the neck, and you have a solid foundation in the A minor pentatonic scale and its different positions, try playing the pentatonic scale in its various forms in different keys. To do that, you must know how to place the scale patterns on the different regions of the neck.

Associating keys with positions

Some keys just fall more comfortably in certain positions than in others, so this section starts with the obvious, default positions for three common keys. Remember, any pentatonic scale satisfies two (related) keys: a major and its relative minor, or a minor and its relative major, depending on your orientation.

G positions

The home position for G major falls in open position or 12th position (which is exactly an octave higher). Because these are two extremes of the neck (and the open-position version defeats the purpose of this exercise), you might try to play G-based stuff out of 7th position. Figure 4-11 (Track 64 at 0:00) is a riff in 7th-position G major pentatonic (with one out-of-key note, the A♭ in bar 1), and its corresponding neck diagram.

Book IV

Rock Guitar

Figure 4-11:
A riff in
7th-position
G major
pentatonic.

F positions

F is a common key for blues, especially if you jam with horn players. Figure 4-12 (Track 64 at 0:08) is a bluesy riff in F major, with an added flat 3, A♭. This riff sits well in 7th-position F major pentatonic. Note that because F is one whole step down from G, its five pentatonic scale positions are the same as the key of G, but shifted down two frets.

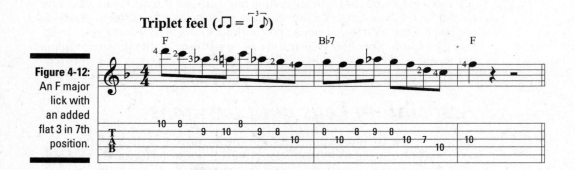

Figure 4-12:
An F major
lick with
an added
flat 3 in 7th
position.

Note that even though this lick is in 7th position, it's in F, not G, and so uses a different pentatonic scale form than the 7th-position form designated for G or E minor.

F minor positions

The key of F minor (and its relative major, A♭) is the interval of a major 3rd (4 frets) lower than our dearly beloved A minor, so all of its pentatonic scale positions are shifted down four frets, relative to A minor. Its home position falls in 1st position, which means all subsequent positions are up from that.

So even though the A minor example had a position lower than the home position, in the F minor example, that lower position gets "rotated" up the neck to the 10th position.

Figure 4-13 (Track 64 at 0:18) is an earthy minor riff that takes advantage of its low position on the neck — the lowest possible closed-position pentatonic scale.

Figure 4-13:
A low riff in
1st-position
F minor
pentatonic.

Placing positions

One great advantage to the guitar is that after you learn one pattern, in any key, you can instantly adapt it to any other key without much thought at all. Unlike piano players, flute players, and trombonists — who have to transpose and remember key signatures to play the same phrase in another key — guitarists just have to shift their left hand up or down the neck a few frets. But the pattern — what you actually play — remains the same.

It's as if you wanted to learn a foreign language, but instead of learning new words for all the nouns and verbs you know in English, you simply had to raise or lower your voice. Speak in a high, squeaky voice, and you're talking French. Say the same words in a deep, booming voice and you're conversing in Chinese. That's what transposing is like for the guitarist. That's how lucky you are.

To help you know which positions are good for which keys, look at Figure 4-14. This table is by no means exhaustive and by no means the final word on where to place your pentatonic positions. It merely gives you a jumping off point to know in what general vicinity to put your hands to improvise in, say, the key of A♭.

Book IV

**Rock
Guitar**

Major/minor key	Pentatonic pattern/fret #	Chord forms
A major/F# minor	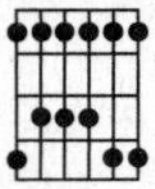 2nd fret	G/Em
B♭ major/G minor	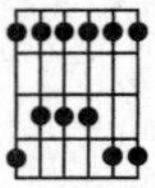 3rd fret	G/Em
B major/G# minor	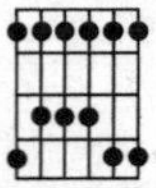 4th fret	G/Em
C major/A minor	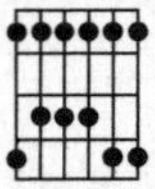 5th fret	G/Em
D♭ major/B♭ minor	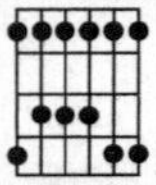 6th fret	G/Em
D major/B minor	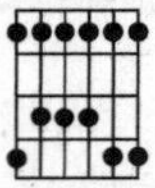 7th fret	G/Em
E♭ major/C minor	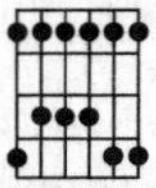 8th fret	G/Em
E major/C# minor	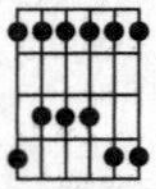 9th fret	G/Em
F major/D minor	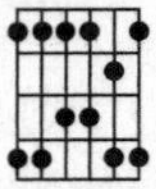 5th fret	C/Am
G♭ major/E♭ minor	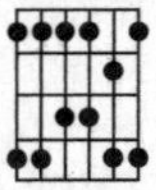 6th fret	C/Am
G major/E minor	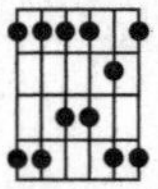 7th fret	C/Am
A♭ major/F minor	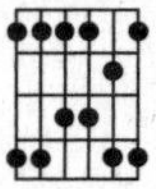 1st fret	G/Em

Figure 4-14:
A table showing the 12 keys and their relative minors, the fret number, appropriate pentatonic pattern, and chord form.

Putting the five positions into play

After you learn the pentatonic scale in five positions, you are more than 90 percent there, technically. The next hurdle is more mental than anything else. You simply have to be able to calculate where to play any given key, and which pentatonic pattern best suits your mood. Here are some exercises you can do to limber up your brain, learn the fretboard, and become acquainted with the differing characteristics offered by the five pentatonic positions:

- ✔ **Work out in different keys, spot transpose.** Don't just always play in A minor and C. Jam along to the radio, which often has strange (at least for guitarists) keys.

- ✔ **Arpeggiate the chords you're playing over.** All scale positions have associated chord forms. Try arpeggiating (playing one at a time) the notes of the chord whenever that chord comes up in the progression. This is a great way to break up linear playing, and it forces you to think of the notes of the chord, rather than playing memorized patterns.

- ✔ **Work out in different positions.** It's one thing to work out in different keys. It's another to work out in different positions. Make sure you mix it up with respect to positions as well as keys.

We're all human and we tend to favor routines and like to tread familiar ground. With pentatonic scale patterns, the comfort zone lies in the home position and the ones immediately above and below. Make an effort to treat all positions equally, however, so you can breeze through them on an ascending or descending line, without hesitating about where the correct notes are.

Bringing Down the Hammer-ons

A *hammer-on* is a left-hand technique where you sound a note without picking it. This makes a smoother, more legato connection between the notes than if you picked each note separately. In the notation, a *slur* (curved line) indicates a hammer-on.

To play a hammer-on, pick the first note and then sound the second note by fretting it with a left-hand finger — *without* re-picking the string. Figure 4-15 (Track 65 at 0:00) shows two examples of a hammer-on from a fretted note.

Book IV

Rock Guitar

Figure 4-15: A hammer-on from a fretted note.

You can play hammer-ons in a variety of ways: from an open string to a fretted string, as double-stops, and in succession, or multiple times, where a hammer-on follows another hammer-on. But the technique is the same; you always sound the hammered notes by slamming down a left-hand finger (or fingers) without re-picking them with the right hand.

Idiomatic licks are musical phrases in a particular technique or style. Figure 4-16 (Track 65 at 0:07) shows a passage using different types of hammer-ons in a blues-rock groove.

Figure 4-16: Various hammer-ons in a blues-rock groove.

The opening lick to Eric Clapton's "Layla" features a series of hammer-ons that gives the passage a facility and fluidity not possible if each note were to have been individually picked. Open strings help make this lick ring out and, along with the hammer-ons, give it an ultra-legato sound.

Having Pull with Pull-offs

A *pull-off* enables you play two consecutive descending notes by picking once with the right hand. To play a pull-off, pick the first note and then pull the fret-ting finger off to sound the lower note (another fretted note or an open string). Figure 4-17 (Track 65 at 0:16) shows two pull-offs: one from a fretted note to another, lower fretted note, and a double pull-off, where two successive notes are sounded.

Figure 4-17: Two kinds of pull-offs to fretted notes.

Like hammer-ons, you can apply pull-offs in several different situations: You can pull off to either an open string or a fretted one; you can pull off two notes at a time (a double-stop pull-off); or you can have consecutive pull-offs (one after the other, with no picked note in between). You can even pull-off in a chordal context, in a reciprocal motion to hammering on within a chord position.

Figure 4-18 (Track 65 at 0:23) shows different pull-offs in a musical context.

Figure 4-18:
Several different types of pull-offs.

Sometimes getting a clear, clean attack on a pulled note is difficult. If you find you can't get the second note to speak clearly, try "peeling" the finger off to the side as you sound the second note, rather than lifting it straight up. This enables you to create a sort of "left-hand pick" and provides a sharper attack to the second note.

Slippin' into Slides

Slides are one of the most expressive techniques available to guitarists because they allow you to sound the notes *in between* your two targets, or principal notes. Slides give your playing a slippery sound, and can help you produce an even more fluid sound to your lines than hammer-ons and pull-offs. To play a slide, pick the note and then, while keeping pressure on the fretted finger, slide it up or down the string length to the second note. Do not pick the second note. Figure 4-19 (Track 65 at 0:34) shows how a slide connects two notes.

Book IV

Rock Guitar

Figure 4-19:
A slide lets you connect two notes without picking the second one.

In addition to using slides to connect two notes, you can also employ them to enter into and slide off of individual notes, for a horn-like sound.

In addition to slides that connect two notes, you can play two other types of slides, known variously as *indeterminate slides,* and *scoops* (for ascending, and going into a note) and *fall-offs* (for descending and going out of a note). These slides decorate single, individual notes, and imbue them with the vocal- and horn-like characteristics where notes begin and end with a slight pitch scoop and fall-off.

Figure 4-20 (Track 65 at 0:41) begins with an indeterminate slide and ends with a fall-off, and in between are ascending and descending slides. Note that you can use a slide to facilitate a position shift.

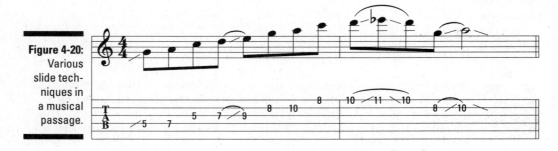

Figure 4-20:
Various slide techniques in a musical passage.

Slide guitar

Many rock players love the sound of slides so much that they explore the style of playing called *slide guitar,* where the notes are *stopped* (they're not *fretted* in the traditional sense, but stopped at different points along the string length to produce different pitches) with a physical device called, appropriately enough, a *slide.* Slide guitar involves playing different notes and chords using a glass or metal cylinder placed over the left-hand ring or little finger. You can play both rhythm and lead using a slide, though it's usually best employed on lead breaks. Great rock slide players include Johnny Winter, Duane Allman, Danny Gatton, Bonnie Raitt, Warren Haynes, and the Wallflowers' Michael Ward.

Bending to Your Will

Bending strings is probably the most important of all the articulation techniques available to a rock guitarist. More expressive than hammer-ons, pull-offs, and slides, a *bend* (the action of stretching the sounding string across the fretboard with a left-hand finger, raising its pitch) can turn your soloing technique from merely adequate and accurate to soulful and expressive.

Because the pitch changes in a truly continuous fashion in a bend (rather than in the discrete, fretted intervals that hammers, pulls, and slides are relegated to), you can really access those "in-between" notes available to horns, vocalists, and bowed stringed instruments. What's more, you can control the rhythm, or travel, of a bend — something you can't do with a hammer-on or pull-off. For example, you can take an entire whole note's time to bend gradually up a half step; or you can wait three and a half beats and then bend up quickly during the last eighth note's time; or you can do any of the infinitely variable ways in between. How you bend is all a matter of taste — and your personal expressive approach.

To play a bend, pick a fretted note and push (toward the 6th, lowest, string) or pull (toward the 1st, highest, string) the string with your left-hand fretting finger so that the string stretches, raising the pitch. Figure 4-21 (Track 66 at 0:00) shows two types of typical bends in 5th position, on the 3rd string, 7th fret.

Figure 4-21: Two ways to bend on the 3rd string, 7th fret.

If you find it difficult to bend with one finger, try "backing up" the bending finger with another finger behind (toward the nut) it. For example, if you use your 3rd finger to bend (as you would when in 5th position and bending the 3rd string, 7th fret), you can use your 2nd, 1st, or even both your 2nd and 1st fingers help push the string.

To bend successfully and without pain, your strings must be of a light enough gauge that they will stretch easily as you push your fretting finger sideways. Electric guitars take gauges light enough to do this, whereas acoustic guitars usually don't. Also, the sustain factor in electric guitars allows the note to ring

Book IV

Rock Guitar

longer as the bend is applied, yielding a more dramatic effect. You also must practice bending in tune, where your bends go up exactly the interval the notation dictates (a quarter step, a half step, a whole step, and so on). In the notation, the distance of the bend is indicated by pitches in the music staff connected by angled (not curved) slurs, whereas tab uses numerals and curved arrows.

Figure 4-22 (Track 66 at 0:07) shows a passage mixing two types of bends: an immediate, or instantaneous, bend and a bend in rhythm.

Figure 4-22:
An immediate bend and a bend in rhythm.

Bend and release

In addition to the standard bend, where you push or pull a string to raise its pitch, you can play other bends to create different effects, such as a continuous up-and-down pitch movement through a bend and release.

Figure 4-23 (Track 66 at 0:16) shows a *bend and release*, which consists of a picked note, a bend up, and then a release of that bend, which produces three distinct notes, but where only the first one is picked. Note the rhythm of the bent notes and that the notes change in sync with the chord changes.

Figure 4-23:
A bend and release in rhythm, in sync to chord changes.

Pre-bend

Another variation of the standard bend produces a "downward bend" effect through a pre-bend and release, where the pitch appears to drop. A *pre-bend* is where you bend the note and hold it in its bent position *before* picking it. This allows you to then release the note after it's picked, creating the illusion that you're bending downward. This is sometimes called a "reverse bend," although that's technically a misnomer. You can only bend in one direction, with regards to pitch: up. By letting the listener hear the pre-bent note first, however, and then executing the release, you give the impression that you're bending (especially if you do it slowly) downward. Because pre-bends are a little trickier to set up, they are not as common as normal, ascending bends. But they are extremely powerful expressive devices and should be employed wherever you desire to create a "falling-pitch" effect.

Figure 4-24 (Track 66 at 0:23) shows a good example of how to use a pre-bend and release to fall into a note from above. Again, the note choice is dictated by the chord progression going on above it.

Figure 4-24:
Three ways to use a pre-bend and release over chord changes.

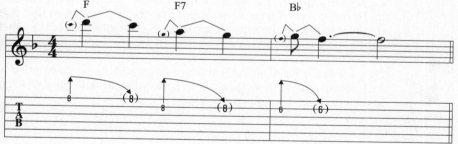

The hardest part about performing a pre-bend is not technical but musical: You must bend up to the starting note — and it must be in tune — without your being able to hear it first. Because you can perform bends on a variety of different strings, on many different frets, and to different intervals (for example half-steps, whole steps, minor 3rds, and major 3rds), the pre-bend distances are all different. Still, through practice, you can learn to "feel your way" to an in-tune pre-bend and achieve remarkably consistent results.

Book IV

Rock Guitar

Sounding a Vibrato That Makes You Quiver

Vibrato is that wavering, quivering quality that an opera singer or a power-ballad vocalist adds to a sustained note to give it a sense of increased energy or life. Some guitarists, such as Eric Clapton, are renowned for their expressive vibrato technique. The notation indicates a vibrato by placing a wavy line over a note. You can create a vibrato several ways:

- By bending and releasing a fretted note rapidly ("fingered" vibrato)
- By giving your whammy bar a shake
- By applying electronic vibrato, through an external effect

The bend-and-release, fingered approach to vibrato is the most common, controllable, and expressive, because, naturally, you use your fingers to execute it. To play a vibrato this way, bend and release the fretted string rapidly, causing the note's pitch to quiver. You determine the speed and intensity (how fast and how far you bend the note to achieve the wavering effect) by the context in which the vibrato appears. Slower music usually dictates a shallow and slow vibrato; faster music urges you to bend faster, so that the vibrato is detectable before the note changes pitch. The intensity of the vibrato is how subtle or obvious you want the effect to appear, independent of the speed.

Figure 4-25 (Track 67 at 0:00) shows a fingered vibrato, over a tied whole note. The notation indicates vibrato with a wavy line appearing above a note head and continuing through its duration.

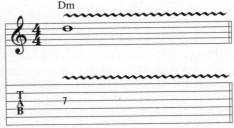

Figure 4-25: A vibrato executed with the left-hand fingers.

Guitarists often play a descending fall-off type of slide after a long held note with vibrato. Another trick is to allow a note to sound without vibrato, then to add some vibrato. This *delayed vibrato* is a standard technique for vocalists.

Chapter 5

The Care and Feeding of Your Electric Guitar

••

In This Chapter

▶ Using guitar-adjusting tools

▶ Changing your strings

▶ Keeping your guitar clean and performing a setup

▶ Troubleshooting

▶ Storing your guitar and amp

••

A guitar — like any other machine — is subject to wear and tear: The strings go bad, or they break; climate changes shrink and swell the wood; moving parts wear out, and so forth. These afflictions and deteriorations can prevent you from properly expressing yourself with your instrument and can increase your tendency to express yourself in other, less printable, ways. If you want to keep your guitar on the straight and narrow, you should know how to perform some basic maintenance and repairs.

As you grow more comfortable playing the guitar, your sensitivity to its touch and response increases, so when little things go out of whack, you notice them more. Your ears develop too, so sometimes the guitar just won't sound right — even when it feels okay — and this too is a sign you may need to perform some adjustments. As you become more intimate with your guitar, you find its workings are demystified: You're no longer afraid to go, "This doesn't feel right. What if I turned this doohickey a notch . . . hey! It's better!" Gaining greater knowledge and increased confidence with the workings of your guitar as you play it is a natural process. You never know, however, when you might be stuck somewhere — or flat broke — and must or want to perform these guitar repairs yourself. And when you do the job yourself, you not only save money, but you gain a deeper understanding of the workings of your guitar. So put down your pick and pick up your tools! This chapter shows you what tools you need and how to use them.

Using the Tools of the Trade

Before attempting any tweaks on your guitar, you should acquire, lay out, or otherwise assemble certain tools specific to guitar maintenance and repair. Don't worry — you won't have to renovate your garage and find a new home for your car: The tools you need for the repairs described in this chapter should fit into a small pouch or the accessories compartment of a gig bag.

If you're at all uncomfortable with any of the procedures described in this chapter, stop, and take the instrument to a qualified repairperson.

The basics

You can use the tools shown in Figure 5-1 for the day-to-day maintenance tasks: changing strings, cleaning the guitar, and making minor setup adjustments (discussed later in this chapter). Clockwise from top left, those tools are: guitar polish, soft cloth, Allen wrenches, wire cutters, reversible screwdriver, and string winder.

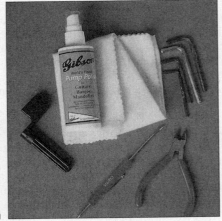

Figure 5-1: Basic tools every guitarist should have.

Photograph courtesy of Jon Chappell

Don't leave home without the important items shown in the following list:

- ✔ **Soft cloth:** You use this for everything from wiping down the strings after you play to polishing the guitar. Keep the cloth clean and dry. You can use a cotton diaper, because it's absorbent, doesn't shed its fibers, and is tailor made for absorbing bodily fluids. But any absorbent material that won't shred and shed will suffice. Chamois (pronounced "shammy") is a traditional favorite for polishing-cloth material.

✔ **Guitar polish:** Although you can apply common furniture polish to your guitar's neck and body, the stuff tends to leave an oily film over the hardware and strings. You don't want your licks to be that slick. Guitar polish, available at most music stores, doesn't muck up the hardware, and still protects the wood. Plus, it comes in small containers that fit easily in your guitar case.

✔ **String winder:** Although not an absolute necessity, these plastic wonders save time when you must tighten or loosen strings with multiple wrappings. Most winders also double as a tool for removing the bridge pins on acoustic guitars.

✔ **Allen wrenches:** One of the most vital guitar adjusting tools is also one of the easiest to misplace — do yourself a favor and buy a multi-wrench set. You use Allen "keys" to adjust bridge saddles, fasten locking nuts and bridge pieces, and tighten or loosen neck truss rods.

✔ **Needle-nose pliers/wire cutters:** Use these for everything from cutting off old strings to tightening and loosening nuts and bolts.

✔ **Phillips and flathead screwdrivers:** You use a screwdriver to vary a pickup's height, tighten the tuning keys, adjust bridge saddles, and remove and replace parts like pickguards, jackplates, and pickup covers. A reversible screwdriver offers you both types of blades on one shank, but is often less versatile than a set of both kinds. If you keep your flathead screwdriver clean, it can also double as a cheese knife when the club owner lets the band visit the buffet table on their break, but doesn't provide silverware. (Most if not all musicians can operate cutlery when pressed.)

Power user tools

In addition to the kit described under "The basics," the well-equipped guitarist may add some or all of the following tools to his or her arsenal:

✔ **Soldering iron:** This is good for fixing and connecting electronic parts like pickups, potentiometers ("pots," for short, or just "controls" — the contraptions that sit under the knobs), switches, and jacks. A low-wattage soldering iron often works best, because it won't damage the surrounding components by overheating them. Most guitar wiring is very basic, so even if you've never soldered before, you can fix simple problems, such as a broken solder joint or a disconnected lead, without worrying too much that you'll cause any harm.

✔ **Rosin core solder:** It flows more easily than acid core solder, and makes a more solid contact with guitar parts. You don't need to know the specifics about its composition, so just look on the label or ask the hardware store clerk if you're not sure what to buy.

Book IV

Rock Guitar

- ✔ **White glue:** You can use the familiar "white" glue (you know, the stuff with the cow on the bottle that you used in grade school) to fix a chipped nut (assuming you're lucky enough to find both pieces) or a small wood chip in neck or body. Fixing a chip right when it happens will guarantee the best fit (wood changes over time). Be careful when gluing your guitar, though. Excess leakage on the finish can leave a nasty spot if it's allowed to dry.

- ✔ **Spare wire:** Sometimes you can't work with the existing parts when a wire breaks, often because the lengths are too short or the repair area is inaccessible. So a length of insulated single-strand copper wire can often help you to create a makeshift shunt, or bridge.

- ✔ **Contact cleaner:** Electronic parts, such as pots and switches, can corrode, and moisture, dirt and grime, which can result in crackling or other noise. Contact cleaner, available at your local electronic megastore, can rid your electronic components of pollution and improve their performance.

- ✔ **Flashlight and tweezers:** Carry a flashlight and tweezers, because these come in handy for any "surgical operations." Plus, you can take the splinters out of your drummer's feet when you play those summer gigs on the boardwalk.

- ✔ **Light vise or clamp:** Use this for holding individual components together while the glue dries or the solder sets. Most guitar parts are light, so a small portable vise or a clamp should do the trick. Having a vise around can also come in handy when you're renegotiating your contract with the record label.

- ✔ **Soldering accessories:** Stock up on alligator clips, sponges (for absorbing drips), and flux (a material that helps solder adhere to a surface). Every soldering surgeon keeps a supply of these. An alligator clip can hold together a broken-wire connection when you don't have time to break out the soldering kit.

- ✔ **Files:** You can use small files to make adjustments to the nut slots; you use larger files (with caution) to trim rough edges on frets or other metal parts. A file can also help you break out of the slammer after your raucous festival gig in Des Moines.

- ✔ **Sandpaper and steel wool:** Use this for smoothing out frets and other parts after filing. And there's no truth to the rumor that swallowing a sheet of 200-grit helps you sing like Rod Stewart.

Change 'em now!

Here are ten reasons why you need to change your strings *now:* (1) Guitar sounds dull; (2) Guitar won't stay in tune; (3) Intonation — the guitar's ability to produce the correct pitch at various points on the neck — is off, even though the neck is correctly aligned; (4) Strings are hard to play; (5) Strings break; (6) Strings show fraying around the winding. This can lead to breakage, which always occurs at the climax of your show-stopping solo; (7) Strings are mismatched: maybe you had to use a heavier E string than your string set calls for — that's okay for one gig, but now that you're home, it's time to change the lot of 'em; (8) You can't remember the last time you changed your strings; (9) Strings have become dirty or rusted; (10) Strings older than lead singer.

Changing Strings

Most guitarists change their strings about as often as drummers change their socks — in other words, not often enough. Old strings can sound dull, go out of tune, and break more easily. An old saying goes, "There's nothing in the world better than an old guitar with new strings." So change your strings like a corrupt politician votes: early and often. (See Book I Chapter 3 for more on changing strings.)

Choosing the right strings

Before you can change strings, you must decide what type of strings to use on your guitar. Strings come in various sizes (called gauges) and are made of a variety of materials. The chart in Figure 5-2 shows some typical sets. The first two strings (the high E and B) are always *plain,* or unwound — without a center core and a spiral wraparound material; the bottom three are always wound. The 3rd string can be plain *or* wound; rockers usually choose a plain 3rd because it's easier to bend, but there are styles — like authentic '50s rockabilly — where a wound 3rd works best.

The individual strings included in a set will vary by manufacturer — one brand might mate an .011 (pronounced "eleven") first string with a .015 ("fifteen") second, whereas another might use an .011 and a .014 for the same two strings. And brand names don't always tell the whole story: Some manufacturers call medium gauges things like "Power Gauge" and "Blues/Jazz Rock Gauge." Why? Wouldn't you rather be a power blues rocker than a medium? If you're unsure when presented with the gauge's name, you can ask for a set by naming just the manufacturer and the first string, as in, "I'd like a set of D'Addario elevens." Gauges for each string in a set are printed on the packaging, too.

String Set Name	1	2	3	4	5	6
Ultra Light	.008	.010	.015	.022(w)	.032(w)	.039(w)
Super Light	.009	.011	.017	.024(w)	.032(w)	.042(w)
Light	.010	.013	.017	.026(w)	.036(w)	.046(w)
Medium	.011	.014	.018	.028(w)	.038(w)	.049(w)
Medium Heavy	.012	.016	.024(w)	.032(w)	.042(w)	.052(w)
Heavy	.013	.017	.026(w)	.036(w)	.046(w)	.056(w)

Figure 5-2: Sets of electric guitar string gauges. The *w* stands for wound string.

Many rock-oriented electric guitars come from the factory strung with super-light strings, such as .009s ("nines"). Lighter-gauge strings make the guitar easier to play, which is a good thing on the sales floor. If you have a light touch and like to bend the strings, the .009s will serve you well; for an even lighter touch, you might try .008s.

But heavier strings offer a more powerful tone — and they stand up better to aggressive playing. You can compensate for the increased string tension (the heavier the string, the tighter they feel to your fingers on the neck) by tuning the guitar down by a half or whole step. Stevie Ray Vaughan used heavy strings and tuned down — his top string was a .013, and he tuned down a half step to E♭, though his reasons were musical, not tactile. Other players who tuned down include Jimi Hendrix, Led Zeppelin, Guns N' Roses, and heavy metal rockers Pantera and Korn — who often tune down a whole step or more.

When you change the string tension on your guitar, as you do when putting on a different-gauge string, you may have to adjust the intonation, action, and truss rod (discussed in detail later in the chapter). If you're inexperienced — or if this is the first time the guitar has undergone a radical string-tension change — take the guitar to a professional repairperson.

Removing the old strings

Before you can put on new strings, you must first remove the old. This statement may seem obvious, but still it raises a few questions that you must answer before you begin.

What kind of bridge does your guitar have?

Electric guitars come with a variety of bridges: both fixed and floating. A fixed bridge, as its name implies, doesn't move. A floating bridge allows you to move it up or down, by pressing down or pulling up an attached arm or bar. With a floating bridge you can create pitch-wavering effects that can range from subtle, shimmering vibrato to dramatically wide vibrato and "dive-bomb" effects. For some styles of music, like heavy metal, a floating bridge is essential. But as far as changing strings, the type of bridge you have can influence your approach to taking off the strings.

A *fixed bridge* doesn't mean that it "ain't broken," but that it stays in place at all times, so feel free to take all the strings off at once. This makes it easier to clean and inspect the fingerboard, frets, and other hardware. Guitars with fixed bridges include Telecasters, "hardtail" Stratocasters, and many Gibson models, like the Les Paul, SG, Explorer, and Flying V.

Floating bridges fall into two categories: tension and vibrato (also erroneously called "tremolo," probably because the abbreviation *trem* sounds cooler than *vib*). In either case, the strings play a role in holding the bridge in the correct position.

Here are the differences between the two types of floating bridges:

- *Tension* bridges are similar to the ones found on violins — the bridge sits freely atop the body, held down by the downward tension of the taught strings passing over it. If you remove all the strings at once, the bridge will come off the guitar. This won't damage the bridge or the guitar, but — assuming your guitar was set up correctly in the first place — you must put the bridge back exactly where it was *before* you removed the strings. Otherwise, the intonation and action can go out of whack.

- *Vibrato* (or *whammy*, or *tremolo*) bridges are secured to the body by a combination of screws and springs. The bridge rocks on a fulcrum (the center point of a lever), its movements adding or reducing string tension (and increasing or decreasing the pitch). The springs offset the string tension so that the bridge can rest in a neutral position. It's like a tug of war — if one side pulls too hard, you'll find yourself in the mud. Floyd Rose is a designer who created a popular floating bridge system that bears his name. A Floyd Rose is the bridge of choice great for manic metal manipulations.

When you remove a string (or worse, *break* one in the middle of a set) on a floating bridge, the springs pull the bridge back, closer to the body, making the rest of the strings go sharp. If you replace and retune the missing string right away, this isn't much of a problem — the guitar will regain its balance, so to speak. But if you remove more than one string at a time, or replace the old string with one of a different gauge, you can be in for some serious tuning problems. Strings that are way out of tune — or purposely detuned — will also displace the tension, putting the guitar out of tune.

If you simply *must* take off all the strings on a vibrato-type floating bridge, use a shim between the bridge and body to keep the bridge stationary. This keeps the bridge more or less in position while you clean the neck and frets, and then restringing doesn't become a tuning nightmare. If you change the string gauge (thickness), you'll have to adjust the spring tension — tighter if you increase the gauge, looser if you decrease the gauge. That adjustment is covered in a little in more depth later in this chapter.

Not all vibrato systems use a floating design. Some, like the Bigsby (found on many old Gretsch models), have a fixed bridge with spring-loaded tailpiece. The vibrato bar moves the tailpiece to change the pitch. Bigsby-type systems don't offer the same range of pitch changing as their floating counterparts, but when you change strings, you can treat them like a conventional fixed bridge.

What kind of tuning system does your guitar have?

Not all guitar tuners and tuning systems (which can involve the nut and/or the bridges as well) work in the same way, so your technique for removing strings will vary. Restringing may not seem like a "technique" when you're in your living room, but if you break a string in the middle of a set, you'll find that your "string-winding chops" are just as important as your vibrato. Following is a list of two different tuning systems:

- **Standard (non-locking) tuner system:** Unwind the string part way — after it's loose, you can usually pull it away from the headstock by grabbing the string with your right hand and yanking it off the post. You can also snip old strings off with a wire cutter.

- **Locking system:** With a locking system you must "unlock" the string before you can remove it. Locking systems come in two types: 1) The *locking nut/bridge systems,* such as the Floyd Rose, which clamp down on the strings at the bridge and the nut. You must loosen the clamps in both places (usually with an Allen wrench or a screwdriver) to replace the string. 2) *Locking tuners,* such as the ones shown in Figure 5-3, are simpler because they use standard, non-locking bridges. A small clamp inside the tuning machine keeps the string in place so you don't have to wind the string multiple times around the post to keep it from slipping. A thumbscrew on the back of the tuner opens and closes the clamp. Provided you have opposable thumbs, no additional tools are required.

Figure 5-3:
A Sperzel locking tuner uses a vise-like clamp to hold the string.

Photograph courtesy of Jon Chappell

Putting on the new strings

Attaching new strings requires three steps:

1. Threading the string.

2. Wrapping the string.

3. Winding, tuning, and stretching out the string.

Threading the string

With most electric guitars, you thread the string through the tailpiece, or — if the bridge and tailpiece are combined into one unit — the bridge.

On some models, such as the Fender Stratocaster shown in Figure 5-4, you thread the string through the back of the guitar. Others, like the Gibson SG shown in Figure 5-5, have a tailpiece mounted on the top of the guitar. Although you encounter many variations on both string-through and surface-mounted bridges, the procedure for threading the string will be similar.

The string goes in pointy end first; a cylinder at the other end (called a *ball*) fits into a slot in the tailpiece. The ball holds the string in place and prevents it from slipping through.

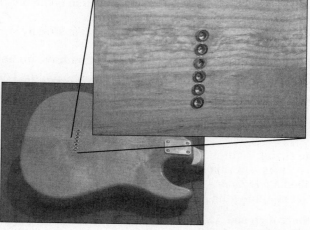

Figure 5-4: Many guit- ars — such as the Fender Stratoca- ster — have string- though-body designs.

Photograph courtesy of Jon Chappell

Book IV

Rock Guitar

Figure 5-5:
A Tune-
O-Matic
bridge (A)
with a stop
tailpiece (B).

Photograph courtesy of Jon Chappell

Locking bridge systems, such as the Floyd Rose, require a different string-ing technique. Rather than passing the string through a tailpiece, you must clamp it down at the bridge, using a screw mechanism. Then you pass the string through a locking nut, which uses another clamp system. Though stringing with the locking system is more complicated and requires more time, because the string is locked in two places — at the nut and at the bridge — it also offers the highest tuning stability. For music that involves dramatic or wild whammy-bar antics, a locking system is the only way to go.

Here's the stringing process in a locking bridge system step by step:

1. **Snip off the ball end (or buy special strings that have no ball ends).**

2. **Clamp the string in the bridge, using the appropriate tools (usually Allen wrenches, but these will vary depending on the actual model).**

3. **Loosen the nut clamp and pass the string through the nut to the tuning machine.**

4. **Wrap the string.** Tighten it until it's close to the desired pitch. Then set the micro tuner — a small tuner that's mounted on the bridge, some-times called a *fine tuner* — to a half-way position, so you have some leeway in fine tuning the guitar.

5. **Clamp the nut closed.** Use the micro tuner to finish getting the guitar in tune. Repeat steps 1–5 for each string. Once you're clamped off, the micro (or *fine*) tuners are the only way to tune the string without loosen-ing the nut clamp.

The micro tuner allows you to make only minor adjustments in pitch. If you've turned the micro tuner all the way in either direction and your string is *still* out of tune, you need to unclamp the string at the nut, adjust the tuning by using the headstock tuning keys, and re-clamp the string. Don't forget to reset the micro tuner to its midpoint before completing your tuning process with the tuning machines.

Some locking bridge systems use a modified pass-through design, instead of the "clip and clamp" configuration mentioned earlier. These offer a special slot at the end of the bridge that accommodates the ball end of the string, so you don't have to snip the ball off, which saves you a step.

Wrapping or winding the string

The method for winding, or wrapping, the string around the tuning peg is simple but vital. A good winding technique is critical to ensure tuning stability in your guitar.

For conventional tuning machines, follow these steps:

1. **Pull the string from the bridge toward the tuning machine.** Pull tight, ensuring that the ball end is secure in the bridge or tailpiece, with no slack at the bottom end.

2. **Guide the string to the correct tuning peg and inset the string through the post hole.** Leave enough slack so that the string can wrap around the tuning post. With thicker, wound strings, two inches should suffice; with thinner unwound strings, leave about four inches. If the string has too little slack, it won't grip the post properly. Too much slack (especially on wound strings) causes the string to overlap the post, which may result in slippage.

3. **Bend the string at the tuning post.** You actually *kink* (fold or crease) the string in the opposite direction you wind it. Correct winding direction depends on the type and position of the tuning machines. For inline, or six-on-a-side, tuners like the ones in Figure 5-6a, the strings go counterclockwise around the peg as you face the headstock. For split, or three-by-three tuners like the ones in Figure 5-6b, the bass side tuners go counterclockwise, while the treble side tuners go clockwise.

4. **Turn the tuning key to wrap the string.** Use your free hand to hold the string in place near the tuning key. Allow for moderate tension in the string between the post and your hand as you wind the tuner. This creates a tighter wrap and prevents slippage.

5. **As the string tunes up, guide it into the nut slot.** Keep applying pressure.

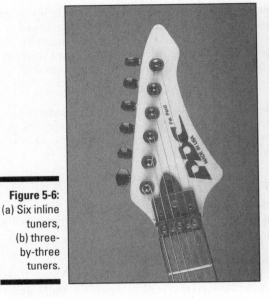 

Figure 5-6:
(a) Six inline tuners, (b) three-by-three tuners.

Photograph courtesy of Jon Chappell

6. **Stretch out the string.** Slippage is one of the leading causes of tuning problems. The string seems tight on the post, but there's actually some hidden slack that can cause the string to go out of tune when you play (especially if you bend the strings or use a vibrato bar). Prevent this by stretching out the string. Pull firmly but gently along the length of the string, raising it directly above the fretboard. After a couple of solid, steady pulls, check the tuning. If the string is flat, retune and repeat. After several tries, the string will stop going flat when you pull it. Congrats: You've removed all the slack. You are now free to beat your guitar to death without worry (at least with regard to tuning, that is).

7. **Clip the excess string.** Go as close to the tuning peg as possible. Alternatively, you may leave a small amount of excess and wrap this around the string.

Cleaning the Parts of Your Guitar

You may not want to hear this, but the most destructive force your guitar will encounter is you. Your hands sweat, depositing moisture, oil, corrosive chemicals, and — unless you have Howard Hughes's compulsion for hand washing — dirt on the strings, wood, and hardware. That's not to mention environmental hazards like dust, beer, cigarette smoke (which, despite your own clean-living habits, are unavoidable if you play gigs), and drool from the bass player. Fortunately, basic guitar cleaning is easy and fast. Most jobs take just a couple of minutes and restore your guitar to a like-new luster.

You can minimize dirt/drool buildup by always storing the guitar in its case. Always close the lid and engage at least one of the clasps.

The strings

Use a soft cloth to wipe down the guitar after each performance. As you do, take a moment to check the nut and bridge pieces for grunge. Wipe each string individually all the way around — this will prolong its life. Do this every time you play.

The body, fingerboard, and hardware

With the strings on, apply guitar polish to a soft cloth and rub liberally on the body, neck, and fingerboard (you can slip the cloth under loosened strings to get better contact with the wood). Use a dry portion of the cloth to buff the guitar. You can also clean the hardware with the soft cloth; use a Q-Tip to reach crevices, like string slots and the area under the string saddles. Try to avoid getting polish on the strings; it can make them feel as oily as a politician's handshake.

The frets

Remove the strings. Wipe down the frets with a soft cloth. To remove grime and other buildup, use a piece of light (0000) steel wool and carefully push the wool over each fret, horizontally across the neck. Use a light touch to avoid wearing down the fretwire.

Be careful not to scratch the wood with the steel wool. Always sand in one direction, and proceed very slowly, so that your hand doesn't slip and brush against the wood.

Inspect the frets for pits and gouges. You can rub out small pits with the steel wool or light sandpaper. Deeper gouges are best left to a qualified repairperson.

The constant pressure of the string pressing against the fret wears a groove in the fret. When the fret surface is perfectly flat, the string hits it in random (although in a small area) places, spreading the "damage" around. After a groove develops, however, the string goes for that place every time — like your tongue finding the hole of a newly missing tooth — hastening the wear. So filing out dips — before they become grooves — is essential for prolonging fret life.

Book IV

Rock Guitar

The electronics

Dirty switches, jacks, and pots can make your guitar sound like a bowl of Rice Krispies — snap, crackle, and pop. You can often eliminate these unwanted noises with a good cleaning.

Cleaning pots

Follow this simple three-step process and you should be able to eradicate most minor problems caused by dirt or rust:

1. **Remove the outer knob.** Plastic knobs are usually held on by just friction. Use a flathead screwdriver to gently pry the knob off its post. Metal knobs are often held in place by a small screw. Loosen the screw and pull the knob off.

2. **Spray contact cleaner into the pot.**

3. **Turn the pot back and forth a few times to spread the cleaner over the contact.**

Cleaning switches and jacks

Switches and jacks are not always as accessible as pots. On some guitars, you must remove either the pickguard or the jack plate to get at the switch. After you have accessed the part, though, the cleaning technique is the same: Use only as much contact cleaner as you need to get the job done.

Setting Up Your Guitar to Optimize Performance

It's a well-guarded secret, but guitars are made primarily of wood. As time goes by, various factors — moisture, temperature, string tension, and even your playing — make the wood expand and contract, warp, and move around. Your guitar's performance suffers as a result. Before you play it again, Sam, it's time for a *setup* — a thorough adjustment over of your guitar's key components. You can have a professional repairperson do your setup for you, but you can also perform many of the tasks involved in a setup yourself. That way, you get to learn a little more about what makes your guitar tick — and how to set that ticker just how you like it.

Warning signs

You know it's time for a setup if the

- Intonation is off.
- Action is too high.
- Guitar buzzes when you fret a note.
- Strings "fret out" — stop vibrating and buzz as you bend them.
- Frets feel sharp along the edges.
- Neck appears warped.

Fortunately, you can solve many of these problems yourself.

Intonation

Intonation is often confused with tuning, but intonation refers to a guitar's pitch accuracy up and down the neck (not the strings' open-tuning status, which is a function of tuning). You can test intonation by playing a harmonic at the 12th fret, then fretting a note in the normal fashion at the same place. Use a tuner to measure the difference between the notes (for more on using tuners, see Book I Chapter 1 — to adjust intonation, you want to use a very good tuner). When you perform the harmonic test, one of three things will occur:

- The two notes match, meaning the string is intonated correctly.

- The fretted note is *sharper* than the harmonic, meaning the string is too "short." Use a screwdriver or Allen wrench to move the saddle *away* from the nut (usually a clockwise turn).

- The fretted note is *flatter* than the harmonic, meaning the string is too "long." Use a screwdriver or Allen wrench to move the saddle *closer* to the nut.

Most electric guitars let you adjust intonation for each string separately, although some (like the vintage Telecaster) put two or more strings on one saddle. Turn the screws carefully — the screws can strip easily, especially when the saddle is under tension from the string.

If you've reached the end of the screw, and the string is *still* not intonated correctly, it's time to call in the cavalry (or in this case, your guitar tech).

WARNING!

Book IV

Rock
Guitar

Action

Action refers to the height of the strings relative to the fretboard. You may want a high-action social life (that's why you took up the guitar in the first place, right?), but most guitarists prefer low or moderate action on their instruments.

Low action is best for a light touch because it takes less effort to fret the strings — thus facilitating speedy playing. But low action can make the guitar buzz under a heavier hand (because the strings come into more contact with the frets), which is why many blues players opt for higher action. Slide players who rarely fret the guitar with their fingers prefer very high action, which lets the side move freely without interference from the frets.

Whether your action is low, high, or somewhere in the middle, it should be consistent up and down the neck. Measure the action by placing an accurate gauge on the frets in several places on the neck. The distance between the string and the fret should be about the same at each point you measure. A standard measurement for low action is 5/64" at the 12th fret.

If you want to measure the action of the guitar independent of the nut's influence, capo the first fret and then measure the string's distance from the fretboard at various places. The capo removes the nut's contribution to the action and can help you better isolate the location of your action problem.

The easiest action adjustment is to raise and lower the bridge (or individual string saddles). Some bridges, such as the Tune-O-Matic in Figure 5-7, have thumbscrews on the bass and treble sides instead of saddle screws. These let you raise overall action but offer less precise control over individual strings.

Figure 5-7:
Adjust the action on a Tune-O-Matic bridge with side-mounted thumbscrews.

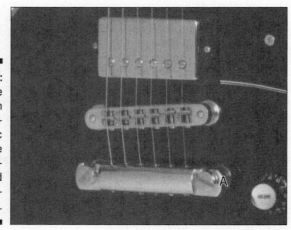

Photograph courtesy of Jon Chappell

If your bridge has individual saddles, use an Allen wrench to turn the screw clockwise to raise the action, counterclockwise to lower it. Be sure to raise both sides of the saddle to the same height.

The position of a floating tremolo bridge can also affect the action. Adjust the bridge tension *before* you adjust the string saddles.

If the action is too high at the nut, adjusting at the bridge may not solve the problem. You can use a small file to trim down the string slots in the nut. If action is too low at the nut, you may need to replace the nut.

Unlike adjusting bridge saddles, filing the nut is a destructive act that can't be undone. If you're in doubt, take the guitar to a qualified tech.

Truss rod

If the action is higher or lower in the middle of the neck than at either end, the neck is probably warped, or curved. This sounds ominous, but it's not uncommon — especially during seasonal changes. A change in string gauge can also cause the neck to warp.

When the neck warps, you can straighten it with an adjustment of the truss rod — the metal rod that runs inside your neck from the headstock to the body.

A simple quarter turn with an Allen wrench in either direction (tightening the truss rod to correct a curve away from the strings, loosening the rod to correct a curve into the strings) is fine to alleviate slight misalignments, but beyond that, and unless you know what you're doing, a truss rod adjustment is best left to a professional.

Bridge spring tension

Correct spring tension is one of the keys to getting the best performance out of a floating bridge system. The springs counteract the pull of the strings, holding the bridge in a neutral position. For most players, the ideal bridge position is 1/4–1/2 inches off the guitar's body, because this allows you to both raise and lower the pitch with the vibrato arm.

If the springs are too loose, the bridge will sit too high, adversely affecting intonation and action. If the springs are too tight, the bridge will make contact with the body. When the bridge is in this position, you can't raise the pitch with the bar.

Book IV

Rock Guitar

Some players actually prefer a little body contact with their bridge because they feel that it improves tuning stability.

Anytime you change string gauges, you must adjust spring tension by removing the backplate.

The following list describes the procedure for adjusting spring tension:

1. **Turn the guitar over and unscrew the backplate that covers the springs and bridge.** (Most guitarists leave this off permanently because the backplate can get in the way when you change strings.)

2. **The springs are attached in two places: at the *claw* at the top of the cavity, and to holes at the back of the bridge, as shown in Figure 5-8.** The claw is attached to the body with two screws. Tighten the screws to increase string tension by turning clockwise. Loosen tension by turning the screws counterclockwise.

These screws can be very tight; be careful not to strip them.

Figure 5-8:
Vibrato springs connect bridge to a claw that's mounted in the guitar's body.

Photograph courtesy of Jon Chappell

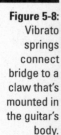

You can further increase tension — and change the feel of your vibrato bridge — by adding or subtracting springs. Most bridges can take from two to five springs. The more springs, the tighter the bridge. You have to apply more energy to your vibrato bar, but the benefit is: a loose bridge can move when you rest your hand on it or bend a string with your fretting hand (causing the rest of the strings to get out of tune). If this happens, add a spring.

Fixing minor wiring problems

Rock and roll is more than a half-century old, and the electric guitar's basic wiring hasn't changed much since the days of "Rock Around the Clock." Buddy Holly's tech (if he even had one) could probably fix your Strat without so much as a look at the owner's manual. So, with some basic soldering chops, you should be able to repair most minor wiring problems yourself.

Output jack

The output jack is one of the first things to break on a guitar (it sees a lot of action, after all). Fortunately, it's also the easiest to repair. Use a socket wrench to unscrew the jack and check for loose wires.

Pots, pickups, and switches

Pots, pickups, and switches can also go bad. They're harder to get at than the output jack, but they're usually easy to repair. If your guitar has rear-mounted controls (you'll find these on Les Pauls and other models), you can access the connections without removing the strings and pickguard. Sadly, Strats and other models with front-mounted controls require that you take off the strings before working on the electronics. Although the connections can vary depending on the specific capabilities of the individual components, you should be able to find your way around with an assist from a good wiring diagram (when in doubt, contact the guitar or pickup manufacturer).

Troubleshooting Guide

Many seemingly insurmountable problems often have a simple and quick solution. The troubleshooting guide in Table 5-1 should cover most of the basic problems. It doesn't offer the obvious troubleshooting standbys like "Make sure your guitar is plugged in" and "Make sure your amp is turned on," because surely you don't need to hear *those*.

Book IV

Rock Guitar

Table 5-1	Troubleshooting Guide	
Symptom	*Possible Cause*	*Solution*
Buzzing	Action too low	Adjust bridge saddles
		Adjust truss rod
		Adjust action at the nut
High action on the upper frets	Bridge saddles set too high	Lower bridge saddles

(continued)

Table 5-1 *(continued)*

Symptom	Possible Cause	Solution
High action in the middle or top of neck	Neck is warped	Adjust truss rod
Guitar won't stay in tune	Strings too old	Replace strings
		Replace cheap tuners
Floating bridge up too high	Spring tension is too loose	Tighten vibrato bar springs
Floating bridge too close to guitar body	Spring tension too tight	Loosen vibrato springs
No output	Bad output jack	Remove jack, check wiring
Scratchy output	Bad volume or tone pots or switches	Spray pots and switches with contact cleaner
Amp has no output	Bad connection between guitar and amp	Replace guitar cable
		Replace fuse
	Blown fuse	Replace tube
	Bad tube	Replace speaker
	Blown speaker	
Amp whistles, rings, or sounds distorted	Bad tube	Replace tube
	Blown speaker	Replace speaker
Crackling sound, signal cuts out	Bad cable or patch cord	Replace
		Replace battery
Low output, diminished sound, unwanted distortion	Bad battery or power supply (effects)	

Storing Your Guitar

You can take great care of your guitar while it's with you, but all of your due diligence will be for naught unless you store the guitar properly. As mentioned earlier, wood is sensitive to changes in the environment, and these changes can cause some serious problems for your guitar. The following steps should save you from quite a few headaches — and repair bills.

✔ **Always store the guitar in its case.** Gigbags are fine for short-term storage, but nothing protects the wood, hardware, and strings like a good hard-shell case, which can keep the neck stable and blocks dust, moisture, and your adorable nephew who got your guitar confused with his soccer ball. Remember to latch the case — otherwise, you (or your nephew) may pick it up and spill your guitar to the floor.

✔ **Avoid temperature extremes.** Store your instrument in a temperate space (like your house) and avoid places that can get very hot or very cold, like the trunk of your car, an unheated garage, attic, or warehouse (like those self-storage facilities), your fridge, or your oven.

✔ **Keep the guitar in moderate humidity.** Spaces that are too damp can make the wood swell. Spaces that are too dry can make the wood shrink and crack. Combat dampness by inserting desiccant (available at most hardware stores) in your guitar case. Combat dryness with a guitar humidifier or a moist sponge. You don't have to loosen the strings when storing the guitar or checking it on an airplane, as is commonly believed.

✔ **Check your guitar regularly.** Even if your instrument (or your playing career) is in hibernation for a while, it's a good idea to look things over every now and then. Who knows — the sight of your well-preserved guitar may inspire you to play.

Book V
Blues Guitar

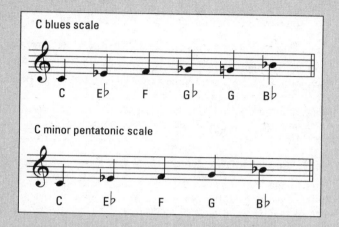

Contents at a Glance

Chapter 1: Introducing the Blues and Playing Blues Rhythm 379

Beyond the Delta: Defining the Blues Guitar Sound.....................................380
Strumming Along 383
Mixing Single Notes and Strumming...386
Shuffling the Beats with Syncopated Strumming 389
Muting: Stopping the String from Ringing 391
Copying the Classics: Plucking Fingerstyle Blues......................................394
The Right Hand's Bliss: Different Rhythm Styles to Play............................394

Chapter 2: Blues Progressions, Song Forms, and Moves 405

Blues by the Numbers...405
Recognizing the Big Dogs: Primary Key Families and Their Chords.............406
The Structure of a Blues Song, Baby 407
Applying Structures to Keys 415
Accessorizing the 12-Bar Blues: Intros, Turnarounds, and Endings 421
High Moves 423

Chapter 3: Musical Riffs: Bedrock of the Blues 427

Basic Single-Note Riffs..427
Double the Strings, Double the Fun: Two-Note Riffs (or Double-Stops) 431
High-Note Riffs, the Bridge to Lead Guitar..434
Mastering the Rhythm Figure 440

Chapter 1

Introducing the Blues and Playing Blues Rhythm

In This Chapter

▶ The roots of blues guitar

▶ Mixing up your playing with downstrokes and upstrokes

▶ Applying syncopation to your sound and discovering different muting techniques

▶ Checking out some classic fingerstyle blues and playing different grooves and feels

▶ Access the audio tracks at www.dummies.com/go/guitaraio/

The guitar and blues go together like apple and pie. The guitar allows you to sing along with yourself (try that with a flute), and singing was the way the blues started. And it's much easier to bring out on the front porch than a piano. It's cheaper to own (or make yourself) than many other instruments, and that helped bring the blues to many poor folks — the people who really had the blues.

As the blues developed, guitar makers adopted features that helped bring out the qualities of the blues to even better effect. An electric guitar is played with two hands and leaves your mouth free to sing (as an acoustic does), but electric guitar strings are thinner and easier to *bend* (stretching the string while it's ringing, producing a rise in pitch), and electronic amplification helps project the guitar's sound out into the audience of (often raucous and noisy) blues-loving listeners.

Because the blues was concentrated in the rural South, in the time before musical instruments adopted electricity, the earliest blues guitar music was played on acoustics. The "Delta blues" style was the first recognized style of the blues and consisted of strummed and plucked acoustic guitars with chords formed the same way as in other forms of folk music.

Chords (explored in the chapters in Book II) don't by themselves convey anything meaningful. They're just raw building materials of music — until you arrange and play them in a certain way. For guitarists, that playing part is done by the right hand. By playing chords with the right hand in a certain tempo, rhythm, and strumming pattern, you enter into the world of rhythm guitar — an indispensable part of the blues.

Beyond the Delta: Defining the Blues Guitar Sound

Blues guitar can take many forms. It's grown dramatically since its humble beginnings in the southern United States. Blues players of this time were largely self-taught (and often illiterate), and one of the easiest ways to create different chords was to tune the guitar to an open chord, such as G major or E major, and then use a metal or glass slide (a pocket knife or bottle neck) to change chords. In both slide and fretted guitar styles, guitarists would emphasize the driving rhythm of the blues by thumping out steady bass notes on the low strings with their thumb while in turn, or simultaneously, fingerpicking upper strings to sound out chords, melodic riffs, and fills.

Playing simple chords to back up a blues singer is still a form of blues guitar — as is playing chords with a slide. You can't help but sound bluesy when you move a slide from one position to another to play the different chords in a song — especially if you do it expressively. But beyond this, you can ascribe certain musical hallmarks to the blues that don't make you play any more soulfully but provide you with a deeper understanding when you hear the blues.

The following sections break down the elements of the blues into four musical concepts. Keep in mind that these concepts are the main ones and there are certainly more, but thinking of and listening to the blues while considering these criteria helps in your understanding of this sometimes elusive music form. You may not be able to define the blues, but you know it when you hear it. Or as Sonny Terry says:

Sometimes I want to holler,

Sometimes I want to shout,

Sometimes I want to cry,

But I wonder what about.

I think I got the blues.

The method to the music: Chord progressions

What defines a blues song is the way chords are put together, or the *chord progression*. Although there's such a thing as a jazz chord, there's not really a blues chord (but don't worry, there's no such thing as a classical chord, either). But if you put certain chords together in a certain way, you can definitely have a blues chord progression. The most common blues progression is the 12-bar blues, covered in Book V Chapter 2.

Chords used in blues include major and minor triads (simple, three-note chords), dominant 7th chords — triads with the flatted (lowered by a half step) 7th added, and sometimes even jazz chords (with complex-sounding names like G13♭9/♭5).

The guitarist's language of melody

The blues definitely has a harmonic and melodic language, and even a scale named after it: the 6-note blues scale. If music is described as *bluesy*, it usually means that the melody borrows or enlists notes from the blues scale (nicknamed *blue notes*) rather than the standard major and minor scales that make up other, non-blues styles.

The blue notes are the minor third, flatted fifth, and minor seventh.

Figure 1-1 shows the C major scale with the blue notes appearing below their unaltered counterparts.

Figure 1-1:
The C major scale with blue notes.

C major:	C	D	E	F	G	A	B	(C)
Blue notes:			E♭		G♭		B♭	

When playing the blues, guitarists incorporate aspects of both the major scale and the blue notes to come up with two new scales of their own: the 6-note blues scale and the 5-note minor pentatonic scale (covered in detail in Book IV Chapter 2). Figure 1-2 shows both scales in letter names and in music notation.

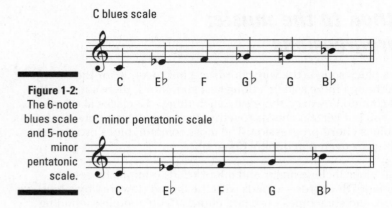

Figure 1-2:
The 6-note blues scale and 5-note minor pentatonic scale.

Playing blues expressively

One of the best things about the blues — and a huge relief to beginning guitarists — is that the blues isn't all that hard to play, technically speaking. Playing lead or rhythm in most blues songs requires only intermediate technique. What is harder to do — in fact, you never stop figuring out how to do it better — is to play *expressively*. Expression in the blues is what turns craft into art. A lot of the following techniques of expression are covered in detail in Book IV Chapter 4. Here are ways to make your music more bluesy:

✔ **Use bent notes.** Bent notes are notes where the pitch is raised slowly upwards in a continuous fashion, and this element is closely identified with the blues.

✔ **Make your music shake.** Vibrato is a technique that makes the notes of the music quiver by using left-hand finger wiggling, which gives blues a signature sound. B.B. King is well known for his expressive and soulful vibrato. Because much of the blues is set to medium tempos, players hold notes for long periods of time. Vibrato is a great way to bring notes to life, so they don't just sit there.

✔ **Give it some slide.** If you don't hit notes straight on and rather slide into notes from above and below, you give music a bluesy feel and breathe some life into your notes. Guitarists often draw their inspiration from vocalists and horn players (saxophone, trumpet, trombone, and so on), who exercise the slide technique on a regular basis.

✔ **Slur your notes.** Connecting notes through slurs — where you don't restrike the second note with the right hand — is a good way to loosen up your playing in the typical way a blues player does.

✔ **Allow the rhythm to flow.** Blues also allows a certain rhythmic liberty to be taken with melodies and especially letting the melody notes deliberately fall after, or behind, the beat. Backphrasing is actually more of a rhythmic alteration, or rubato, but it's generally thought of as a phrasing technique. It's been described as lazy, devil may care, or cavalier — but whatever, it sure makes the notes sound more bluesy.

The groove that sets the pace

Groove is often used informally to mean "on the mark" or "in sync with," but the term refers to the meter, rhythmic feel, tempo, and the instruments' role in providing the accompaniment, or backing figures. Several different grooves exist within the blues:

✔ A shuffle is a type of groove that uses triplet eighth notes with the emphasis on sounding just the first and third notes played at a medium tempo. "Sweet Home Chicago" is an example of a song in a shuffle groove.

✔ A slow 12/8 blues (the "12/8" refers to the time signature) is another type of groove that's also based on three-note groups, but the tempo is slower and all three notes of the beat are pronounced. "Stormy Monday" is a song in a slow 12/8 feel.

✔ A straight-four groove is where the eighth notes are evenly spaced apart, rather than in the long-short scheme of a shuffle. "Johnny B. Goode" is in a straight four, and so is Junior Wells's "Messin' with the Kid."

✔ Jump is another groove that's an uptempo shuffle, but it requires a slightly different approach in phrasing and rhythm, Like Louis Jordan's "Caldonia."

Given the infinite forms of expression the blues takes, it's nice to know that at least from a technical standpoint, only a few grooves need to be mastered to play most of the blues music out there.

Strumming Along

Book II Chapter 4 covers different right-hand playing styles, including strumming. This section is a refresher, applied in particular to the blues. One of the most basic ways you can play chords is with a strum. Strumming involves taking your right hand and, with a pick, thumb, or the back of your fingernails, brushing it across several or all the strings, sounding them simultaneously. A strum can be slow, fast, hard, or gentle, or any of the infinite shadings in between. When you strum, bring your hand from the top of the guitar (closest to the ceiling) to the bottom (toward the floor) in one motion, striking the strings along the way.

Stroking down

You may not have thought of basic strumming as "executing a downstroke," but that's what you're doing when you go to naturally strike the strings on a guitar. When you get to more complex strumming patterns — especially ones involving syncopation — you distinguish between downstrokes and upstrokes (see the next section). But for now, focus on the more popular and prevalent downstroke strum.

A downstroke (indicated with the symbol ⊓) is played with a downward motion of the pick, toward the floor — the way you naturally strike a guitar. You can strum multiple strings or pick an individual string with a downstroke.

. . . And stroking up

An upstroke (indicated by the symbol V) is played upward, toward the ceiling, in the opposite direction of a downstroke. So instead of dragging your pick down toward the floor, as you did in a downstroke, you start from a position below the first string and drag your pick upward across the strings, from first to sixth.

In an upstroke, you don't need to worry about hitting all the strings. The top three or four strings are usually sufficient. For example, when playing an E chord with an upstroke, you don't have to strum the strings all the way from the first to the sixth, just up to about the third or fourth string. There are exceptions to this rule, but generally, in the blues, you don't hit as many strings on an upstroke strum as you do in a downstroke.

Upstrokes don't get equal playing time as downstrokes do. You typically use upstrokes only in conjunction with downstrokes, but you use downstrokes by themselves fairly often in blues playing.

Combining down and up

In certain fast lead passages, upstrokes alternate with downstrokes, making them appear in virtually equal numbers. For fast eighth notes, the strict observance of upstrokes following downstrokes is called *alternate picking* and is the key for playing fast leads smoothly. So for now, practice upstrokes as they occur in their natural state — in an eighth-note rhythm in between downstrokes (see the section "Eighth-note striking, twice per beat," later in this chapter).

Striking to a beat

Regardless of whether your hand moves up or down when it strikes the strings, the important thing to remember is that you're striking in a rhythm — or in sync with the beat. If you strike the strings once per beat, you're playing quarter notes. If you play two strokes per beat, you're playing in eighth notes, which come twice as fast as quarter notes. (Book I Chapter 4 has a lot more on quarter notes, eighth notes, and beyond.)

Quarter-note striking, beat by beat

Figure 1-3 (Track 68 at 0:00) shows two bars of an E chord with quarter-note slashes. You play four strums for each bar for a total of eight strums. The quarter notes tell you that the strums occur once per beat. Listen and play along with the audio track, and before long, your sound can sound just like the recording.

Figure 1-3: Strumming an E chord in quarter notes for two bars.

Eighth-note striking, twice per beat

Eighth notes come twice as frequently as quarter notes, in the same tempo, or two for every beat, instead of one. Instead of the previously used slashes, you now face slashes with stems (the vertical lines attached to the slash noteheads — not the round, normal noteheads) and beams (the horizontal lines that connect the stems). Quarter notes have just a stem attached to them; eighth notes have stems with beams connecting them to each other.

For the eighth notes that appear in Figure 1-4 (Track 68 at 0:12), you strum twice as fast (two per beat) as you do for the quarter notes (one per beat). You can do this easily with downstrokes at most blues tempos, which are slow to moderate (between 60–160 beats per minutes (BPM) on your metronome). To make things interesting, change chords and introduce A and B7 into the mix. Note that in the figure, the last note of each bar is a quarter note, which gives you a little more time than two eighth notes would for changing chords.

Figure 1-4:
Eighth-note and quarter-note strums in down-strokes.

Figure 1-5 (Track 68 at 0:25) combines downstrokes and upstrokes in an eighth-note rhythm. As you practice this passage, keep a relaxed, free-swinging, up-and-down arm motion going. Also work to get equal emphasis on the downstrokes and upstrokes. You may notice that your downstrokes naturally include more and lower strings, while the upstrokes play just the top strings and fewer of them. That's perfectly natural.

Figure 1-5:
Strumming up and down in quarter and eighth notes.

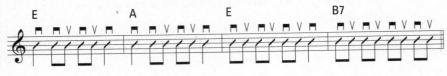

At a moderate tempo, you can easily play Figure 1-5 with all downstrokes, but that variation gives the figure a different feel — more driving and intense. It may be a subtle difference, but playing an eighth-note figure in all downstrokes — versus playing it with alternating downstrokes and upstrokes — is a musical choice, not a technical consideration.

Mixing Single Notes and Strumming

Downstrokes and upstrokes are used for playing single notes as well as for strumming. Combining single notes with strums is an important part of rhythm guitar playing and gives the guitarist more options than just strumming. For example, a piano player doesn't plunk down all her fingers at once every time she plays, and guitarists shouldn't have to strike all the strings every time they bring their picks down (or up, for that matter).

Separating bass and treble: The pick-strum

Separating the bass and treble so they play independently is a great way to provide rhythmic variety and introduce different textures into your playing. In the pick-strum pattern, the pick refers to picking the single bass note, and the strum refers to the upper-string chord that follows. Both the pick and the strum are played with the pick in downstrokes.

Figure 1-6 (Track 69) is a simple pick-strum pattern that's used in many folk blues and country blues songs. This notation mixes single notes (which appear with normal, rounded noteheads) and rhythm slashes (with the narrower, elongated noteheads).

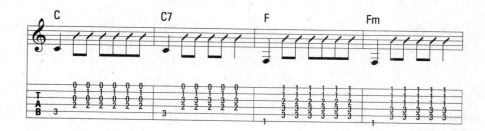

Figure 1-6: Bass-and-chord pick-strum pattern for country blues.

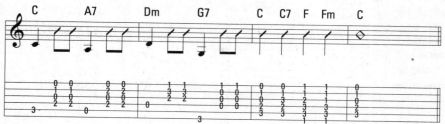

Playing common pick-strum patterns

Most strumming patterns in blues are either all strums or a pick-strum combination, and which approach you use depends on the instruments in your ensemble at the time. A pick-strum approach is good for solo playing or if you're the only rhythm instrument, because the bass notes fall on different parts of the measure than the chord parts.

If you're playing solo guitar, you play a lot more pick-strum patterns. In a band setting, you usually have a bass player who handles the bass duties, and it's more appropriate to play all strumming patterns, so as not to get in the bass's way. The following sections include other pick-strum patterns for the most common blues feels.

Two-beat or cut shuffle

The two-beat or cut shuffle is sometimes referred to as a *boom-chick* pattern because the bass note and chords alternate, as shown in Figure 1-7 (Track 70). A two-beat feel is common in other forms of music (Dixieland and big-band jazz, polka, samba, and country), but it has its place in the blues, too.

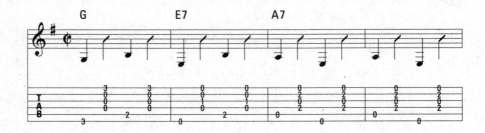

Figure 1-7: Two-beat or cut shuffle feel alternates bass notes with chords.

The 12/8 groove

The 12/8 groove is the slowest pattern of the blues, so it helps to have the bass note play twice on beats one and three, while the chords play on beats two and four, as shown in Figure 1-8 (Track 71).

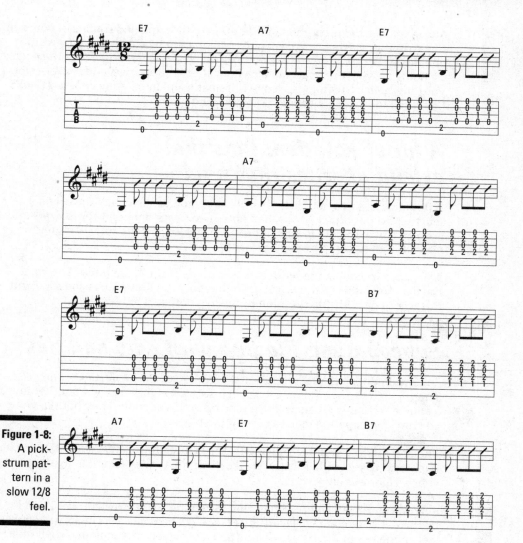

Figure 1-8: A pick-strum pattern in a slow 12/8 feel.

Shuffling the Beats with Syncopated Strumming

After you develop a feel strumming in different combinations of eighths, quarters, and sixteenth (which come four per beat, or twice as fast as eighth notes), you can increase the rhythmic variation to these various groupings by applying syncopation.

Syncopation is the disruption or alteration of the expected sounds of notes. In blues rhythm playing, you can apply syncopation by staggering your strum and mixing up your up- and downstrokes to strike different parts of the beats. By doing so, you let the agents of syncopation — dots, ties, and rests — steer your rhythmic strumming to a more dramatic and interesting course. (Book I Chapter 4 talks in detail about dots, ties, and more.)

A bit of notation: Dots that extend and ties that bind

A dot attached to a note increases its rhythmic value by half the original length. So a dot attached to a half note (two beats) makes it three beats long. A dotted quarter note is one and a half beats long or the total of a quarter note plus an eighth note.

A tie is a curved line that connects two notes of the same pitch. The value of the tied note adds to the original, so that only the first note is sounded, but the note is held for the duration of the two notes added together.

Syncopation: Playing with dots and ties

So how do dots and ties actually make syncopation in a musical context? There are two progressions — one in a straight-eighth feel and another in a shuffle — that you can practice playing in this section. They both have common syncopation figures used in the blues.

The normal flow of down- and upstrokes is interrupted in syncopation, so it's important to remember which stroke direction to play a note to avoid getting your strums out of sync.

In both Figures 1-9 and 1-10, pay close attention to the downstroke (2) and upstroke (4) indications. Figure 1-9 (Track 72 at 0:00) is a straight-eighth-note feel, in the key of A. The use of dots and ties signals a syncopated rhythm. If the tied figures present a problem, practice the figure by first ignoring the ties (in other words, play the tied note).

Figure 1-9:
Straight-eighth pro-gression in A that uses common syncopation figures.

Figure 1-10 (Track 72 at 0:16) is in a shuffle feel in the key of A. A shuffle rhythm divides the quarter note into two eighth notes, but the first eighth note is held longer than the second, producing a swinging, lilting feel. The same syncopation scheme appears here as it did in Figure 1-9, but the shuffle feel makes it fall in a slightly different place in the beat.

Figure 1-10:
Shuffle in A that uses common syncopation figures.

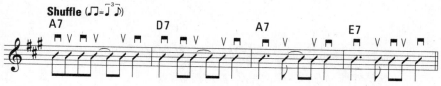

Muting: Stopping the String from Ringing

Listen to blues rhythm guitar and you hear that it's not one repetitive wall of sound, but an open, varied sound with breathing room and subtle breaks. It's these breaks that prevent the chord strums from running into each other and creating sonic mush. The little gaps in sound keep a strumming figure sounding crisp and controlled.

To create a rhythm guitar part with some breathing space between the notes, you need to stop the strings from ringing momentarily. We're talking very small moments here — much smaller than can be indicated by a rest symbol in the music. You can stop the strings instantly with the left hand — letting the left hand go limp is the best and quickest way to stop a string from ringing — far faster and more controlled than anything you can do with the right hand.

This left-hand technique may seem out of place in a chapter devoted to the right hand, but it belongs here because it's a coordinated effort between the two hands, which can only occur when the right hand plays.

Muting the sound between two chords (left hand)

To get the left hand to mute (indicated by an X notehead) the in-between sound between any two chords, just relax slightly the fretting fingers enough to release pressure on the fretted strings. The strings instantly deaden, completely cutting off the sound. If your right hand keeps going in the established strumming pattern, you produce a satisfying thunk sound as the right hand hits all these deadened strings.

The muted strings intermixed with the sounding strings create a percussive and syncopated rhythm. Allowing your left hand to mute means you don't have to stop and start your right hand to produce syncopation. You can keep it going uninterrupted, in alternating down- and upstrokes.

Simulating syncopation with left-hand muting

Left-hand muting gives you the means to control the strings' sound. Figure 1-11 (Track 72 at 0:32) is technically a straight-ahead down-up eighth-note strum in the right hand. But because you employ left-hand muting, the sound seems to cut off in just the right places, creating a syncopated sound. Your right hand isn't performing true syncopation, because it's playing straight through. It's just that some of the notes don't come through audibly.

Figure 1-11:
Strumming
pattern that
employs
left-hand
muting to
simulate
syncopation.

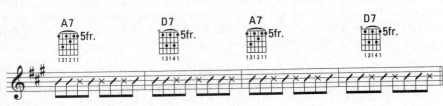

Guitarists seem to develop left-hand muting naturally, almost as if it wasn't a technique you had to learn but a way of playing that evolves. So don't try to analyze it too much, or slow your playing down as you're learning; just strum and relax and tighten your left hand in the context of a medium-tempo groove. Eventually, your two hands sync up without even thinking about it.

Muting the sound of a note (right hand)

Right-hand muting is a technique entirely separate from left-hand muting and produces a totally different effect. When you mute with your right hand, you still hear the pitch and tone of the vibrating string but in a subdued way — more like a true mute, in the musical sense. Right-hand muting keeps the string from ringing freely and reduces the volume and ringing of your strings while still maintaining drive and intensity. This technique is a great way to add dramatic variation to your playing.

Two ways to play the right-hand mute include the following:

- **Palm mute:** The palm mute is another name for the right-hand mute and is executed by resting the heel of your right-hand on the strings just above the bridge. If you place your hand too far forward, you completely deaden the strings, so place it just forward enough of the bridge that the strings still sound a little but are dampened. Keep your hand in position through the duration of the strum.

- **Accent:** The accent is the opposite of a palm mute: It highlights a strike and lets the resulting sound ring out. To accent a chord, just strike it harder than usual and allow the strings to ring free. The result is that the accented strum stands out above all the rest. An accent is indicated with a > just above or below the notehead.

Palm mutes are usually applied to only one or two strings, because the right hand is restricted when you rest it directly on the strings above the bridge. Figure 1-12 (Track 73) is a rhythm figure where you strike only the lowest two strings of the chord during the palm mutes and the upper strings on the accents. Play this progression by using all downstrokes to add intensity.

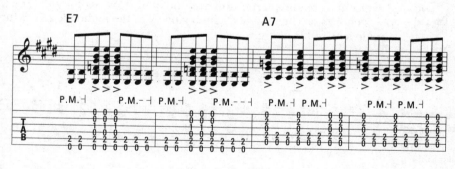

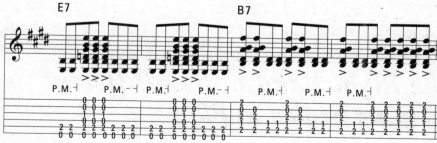

Figure 1-12: Rhythm figure with palm mutes and accents.

Copying the Classics: Plucking Fingerstyle Blues

If you want to make money playing the blues, you should probably get yourself an electric guitar and play it with a pick (make sure to practice the styles presented in the following section). But if you want insight into the roots of the blues, grab an acoustic and play it fingerstyle. Acoustic finger-style blues is a wonderful tradition, populated with such immortal figures as Robert Johnson, Skip James, Lightnin' Hopkins, Mance Lipscomb, Leadbelly, Mississippi John Hurt, Reverend Gary Davis, John Hammond, Rory Block, Roy Book Binder, Bob Brozman, Jerry Reed, and Chet Atkins.

Early solo blues guitar players quickly realized that separating the thumb and fingers was a great way to get the bass line going independent of the chords and riffs above it. So acoustic fingerstyle blues is best played with an inde-pendent thumb. And more than just using the thumb to hit the bass notes while the fingers brush the treble strings, independent thumb means that the thumb and fingers can play separate musical roles — almost like a mini rhythm section. The thumb can be the bass player, and the fingers can pro-vide chords like the guitar's traditional role.

Figure 1-13 (Track 74) shows a basic fingerstyle pattern where the thumb drives out a steady quarter note rhythm on the low strings, and the thumb plays chords on the offbeats. Listen closely to the audio file to capture the shuffle feel in this figure.

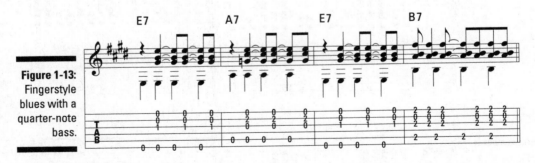

Figure 1-13: Fingerstyle blues with a quarter-note bass.

The Right Hand's Bliss: Different Rhythm Styles to Play

Blues consists of a few different feels, and if some songs sound like others (as some people say), it's partly because of the relatively few feels. Table 1-1 is a list of the common blues feels and well-known songs written in that feel (and if you don't know these songs, find them and listen to them).

Table 1-1		Blues Songs by Feel
Feel	**Song**	**Artist**
Shuffle	Sweet Home Chicago	Robert Johnson, The Blues Brothers
	Blue Suede Shoes	Carl Perkins, Elvis Presley
	Midnight Special	Leadbelly
	Hide Away	Freddie King, Eric Clapton, Stevie Ray Vaughan
12/8	Stormy Monday	Allman Brothers, T-Bone Walker
	Red House	Jimi Hendrix
	At Last	Etta James
	The Sky Is Crying	Elmore James, Stevie Ray Vaughan
Two-beat	Maybellene	Chuck Berry
	Got My Mojo Working	Muddy Waters
	I Found a New Baby	Charlie Christian
Straight-four	The Thrill Is Gone	B.B. King
	Killing Floor	Howlin' Wolf, Mike Bloomfield, Jimi Hendrix
	Crossroads	Robert Johnson, Cream
	Born Under a Bad Sign	Albert King, Cream
16 feel	Hard to Handle	Otis Redding, Black Crowes
	Little Wing	Jimi Hendrix, Stevie Ray Vaughan
	Mary Had a Little Lamb	Buddy Guy, Stevie Ray Vaughan

The shuffle groove

The shuffle groove is certainly the most common feel in blues — more common than the straight-four and slow 12/8 feel. There's one small hurdle to get over: A shuffle feel uses a triplet-based rhythmic division, where each quarter note is divided into eighth-note triplets. The typical melodic division is two eighth notes, where the first note is held for the duration of the first two notes of the triplet, and the second eighth note is the third note of the triplet. This yields a lopsided, lilting feel in the eighth-note flow that's the heart of the shuffle sound.

Figure 1-14 (Track 75) is a progression in a shuffle feel. Practice while listening to the audio track on this one to make sure you get the sound of the shuffle.

Figure 1-14: The shuffle feel is the most common groove in the blues.

(continued)

(continued)

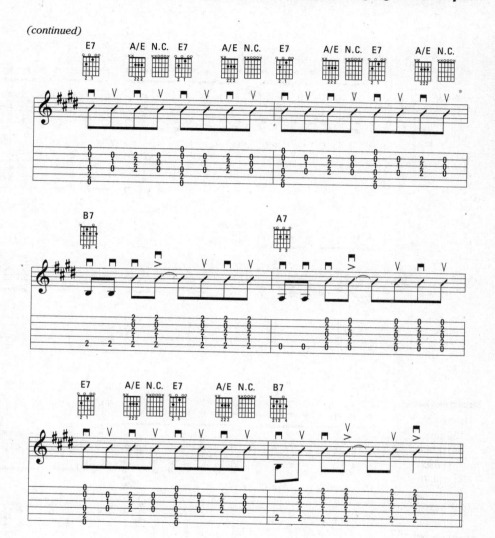

The driving straight-four

The straight in straight-four refers to the eighth notes being evenly spaced, just as they are in most normal music forms you encounter. The four is four-four time, which is the most common time signature for blues. This explanation may sound mundane, except when you consider that most blues is in a shuffle feel, so the word straight indicates that you're doing something a little uncommon for the blues. Figure 1-15 (Track 76) shows a driving straight-four groove.

Figure 1-15: Straight-four feel is used for a more driving, rock-based sound.

(continued)

(*continued*)

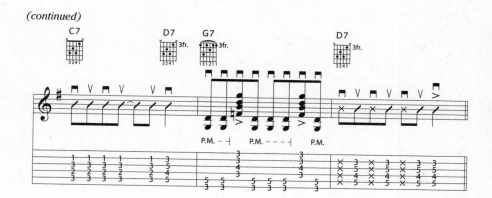

The slow 12/8, with groups of three

The slow part of the slow 12/8 feel is easy to grasp. The 12/8 is related to the shuffle, because a shuffle is a four-four feel based on triplet divisions of eighth notes. But in 12/8, the feel is slower, and the individual eighth notes (they're not triplets, because their grouping of three is built into the time signature) are given more prominence.

Don't be intimidated by the 12/8 part of this feel. There are twelve eighth notes to the bar, and each eighth note gets one beat. In practice though, the eighth notes are grouped in four units of three each. So it's a lot like 4/4 time with eighth-note triplets on every beat. If it's a slow blues, and you can hear note-groupings of three, it's probably a 12/8 feel.

Famous blues songs in 12/8 include T-Bone Walker's "Stormy Monday," covered by the Allman Brothers on their *Live at the Fillmore* album. Figure 1-16 (Track 77) is a passage in the style of "Stormy Monday."

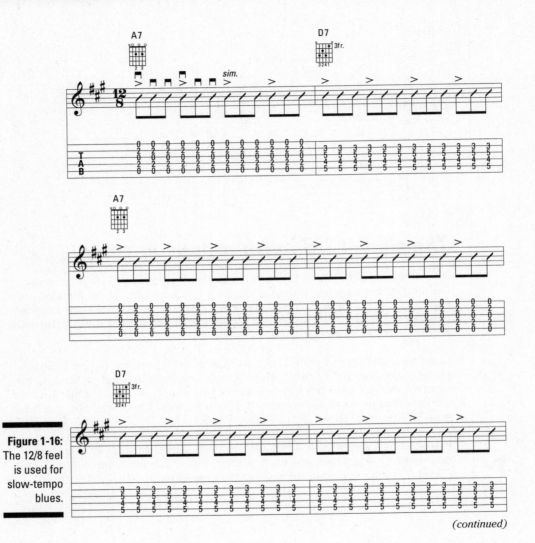

Figure 1-16:
The 12/8 feel is used for slow-tempo blues.

(continued)

(continued)

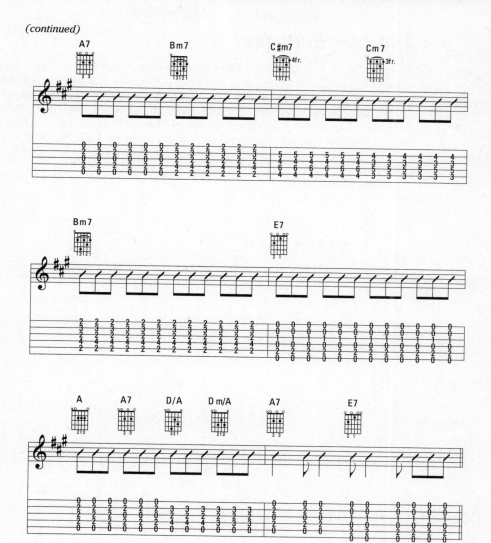

The two-beat feel

The two-beat feel came to the blues from Dixieland and big-band jazz and from novelty tunes. The lively pace of this style makes you want to jump, unlike the more sedate blues grooves. The two-beat feel, also called cut time or cut shuffle, is characterized by a pronounced boom-chick, boom-chick feel, where the *booms* are bass notes (usually alternating between the root and the fifth of the chord), and the *chicks* are the chords, shown in Figure 1-17 (Track 78).

Figure 1-17: The two-beat feel is used for more lively blues.

The slow and funky 16 feel

More modern blues grooves include the 16 feel, which has a slower tempo but funkier sound due to the sixteenth-note subdivisions. (James Brown's "I Feel Good" and "Papa's Got a Brand New Bag" are classic examples of sixteenth-note based funk.) "Hard to Handle," written by Otis Redding and covered by the Black Crowes, is a famous example of 16-feel blues. Figure 1-18 (Track 79) is medium tempo, funky groove in a 16 feel.

Book V

Blues Guitar

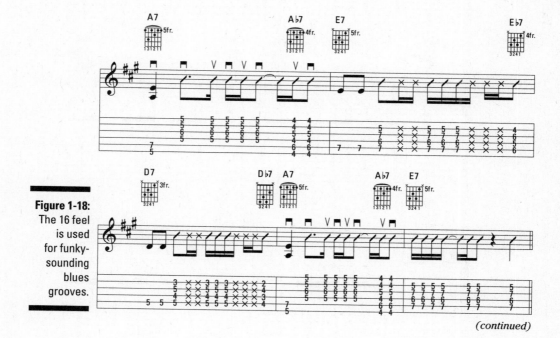

Figure 1-18: The 16 feel is used for funky-sounding blues grooves.

(continued)

(continued)

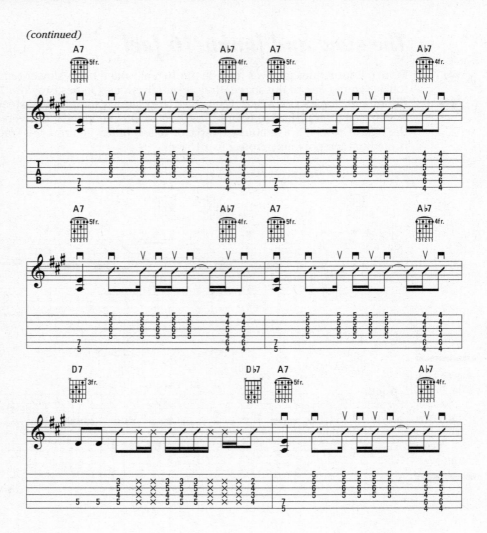

Chapter 2

Blues Progressions, Song Forms, and Moves

- -

In This Chapter

▶ Distinguishing the primary key families and their chords

▶ Recognizing the structure of a blues song

▶ Playing the 12-bar blues

▶ Access the audio tracks at www.dummies.com/go/guitaraio/

- -

*B*lues is a welcoming, beckoning music for both listener and performer that says, "Join in and start contributing!" Its repetition and call-and-response qualities — derived from its forebears, the work song and field holler — make it easy for people to join in a song on the fly. Musicians can grasp the form quickly, and listeners have an expectation that's set up by each phrase, which is then satisfied by the lyrics or the chord progression. Best of all, these simple, infectious, and ingenious devices that make the blues so relatable are easy to understand and master, and are covered in this chapter.

Blues by the Numbers

You can learn music a lot quicker if you associate chords and keys by their numerical equivalents. Book III Chapter 4 goes into this in detail, but here is a short recap. In any key, the root or tonic (the tone that names the key or chord) becomes one, and subsequent pitches become two, three, four, and so on. These numbers are expressed in Roman numerals. So in the key of C, the numbers are broken down like this:

▶ C is I

▶ D is II

▶ E is III

▶ F is IV, and so on

As keys change, so do the letter names, but the *numbers*, or relationships, remain the same, allowing you to treat all keys equally. The number system works well for building chords by intervals, too, but in the blues, you're more concerned with chords formed on the notes of the scale of a key.

If you memorize the chord formula in numbers (and in the blues, you are usually only concerned with chords I, IV, and V), then you can figure out the progression in any key because the numbers — and therefore the relationships — don't change, even if the letters do. And the more experienced you become, the more your ears take you to the right chord without having to memorize anything! But the numbers reveal the underlying structure, and are important in understanding the function of the chords.

Musicians often refer to chords by their numerical designation instead of their actual letter name. For example, when a musician says, "In that song, listen to what B.B. does when he goes to the IV chord," you know exactly where in the song that is (bar five). If the musician had said, "When B.B. goes to the D chord," you'd have to know what key he was in first, and you or the story-teller may not have that information. By viewing music through numbers, the key is irrelevant. Or more precisely, the key can change, but the function doesn't, and that's the important point of the exercise.

Recognizing the Big Dogs: Primary Key Families and Their Chords

You'll surely notice that certain chords seem to cluster together. If you think of these chords by their numerical assignments, or function, you see this phenomena is common to all keys. In every key, the main chords are the one, four, and five, represented by the Roman numerals I, IV, and V. These groupings of I, IV, V are known as *families*. It's a virtual certainty that whatever other chords you may find in a song, you always have a I, IV, and V. And many songs — especially blues songs — have only these three chords.

Here's an example of how to figure out the I, IV, and V of different keys:

✔ In the key of A, A is the I chord.

- Count on your fingers up to your fourth finger, saying the letters of the alphabet as you go, and you find that, in A, the IV chord is D.

- The V chord, then, is E.

✔ In the key of C, C is the I chord.

- The IV chord is F.

- And the V chord is G.

Try it yourself with other keys, starting on I with the letter that names the key (in the key of G, G is I, and so on). Table 2-1 shows common blues keys and their I, IV, and V chords. There are other keys, of course, but the ones in Table 2-1 are the most commonly used keys for blues guitar.

Table 2-1	The I, IV, and V Chords in Common Blues Keys		
Key	*I*	*IV*	*V*
A	A	D	E
C	C	F	G
D	D	G	A
E	E	A	B
F	F	B♭	C
G	G	C	D

For guitarists, some keys and chords lend themselves certain movements that sound especially good for the blues; other keys are less successful. The following section mixes up the keys to help get you familiar with the different families. But the blues is most accommodating to the keys of E and A, especially when using open-position chords, and most blues songs are in E or A.

The Structure of a Blues Song, Baby

It's time to give your hands some direction — to organize sounds into chord progressions and song forms. These larger organizing principles make the blues come alive and build a meaningful experience for the player and the listener. In this section, you take the shorter phrases of the right-hand patterns (covered in Book V Chapter 1) and make them into actual songs.

A *song* is made up of a chord progression. The song's *form* and *chord progression* are concepts that can be used almost interchangeably, with chord progression describing more often the harmonic architecture of the song. Many people can recognize a song form — such as the 12-bar blues — but as a guitarist, you need to know the corresponding chord progression that makes up that 12-bar form (covered in the next section). And you need to be able to identify the actual chords as well as any variations to that form. In the blues, the progression is written in stone — it's part of what makes the blues the blues. So, when it comes to the blues, the progression is synonymous with the form. In fact, saying *the blues* implies a 12-bar structure with the chords falling at specific bars within that structure.

A chord progression isn't the only aspect of a song, but it's a pretty important one, because it forms the framework that supports the other elements: melody, lyrics, riffs, and the solo sections (something guitarists care deeply about).

Playing the 12-bar blues

The 12-bar blues is by far the most popular form for the blues. It consists of 12 measures and observes a particular scheme, as shown in Figure 2-1.

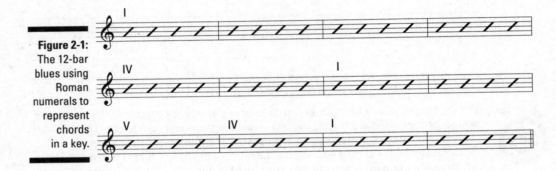

Figure 2-1: The 12-bar blues using Roman numerals to represent chords in a key.

Again, Roman numerals are handy because the progression is the same in every key. For example, if you play blues in E, then E is the I chord, A is the IV chord, and B or B7 is the V chord. So with the corresponding letters substituted for the Roman numerals, the progression looks like Figure 2-2 (Track 80 at 0:00).

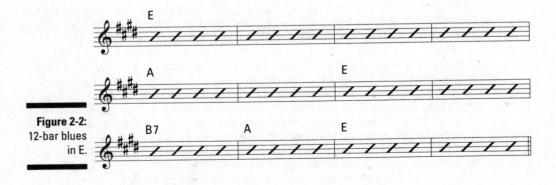

Figure 2-2: 12-bar blues in E.

B7 often replaces B because B7 is the easier of the two chords to play. Technically, you could play B as a barre chord on the second fret. But playing either B7 or B is acceptable for this case. (Book II Chapter 2 covers 7th chords.)

Because the slashes in the music leave some interpretation in what you're playing, try the following exercise with shuffle eighth notes in alternating downstrokes and upstrokes. You hear this version on the audio track (Track 80), so see if you can match the rhythm of the performance on the audio.

If you're a little shaky on the eighth-note strum for Figure 2-2, try first playing this blues with quarter-note downstrokes (covered in Book I Chapter 4). Don't worry, you're still in sync with the audio track, but the guitar on the track strums two chords to your one. After you can play that comfortably, try playing with eighth-note downstrokes in a shuffle feel. And after that, try the alternate-picking approach, which is discussed in Book V Chapter 1.

The quick four

The *quick four* is a variation on the 12-bar blues that occurs in the second bar, where you go to a IV chord — for example, A in the key of E — for one bar, and go back to the I chord for two bars. The quick four, as shown in Figure 2-3 (Track 80 at 0:37), provides an opportunity for variation and interest in an otherwise unbroken stretch of four bars of the same chord.

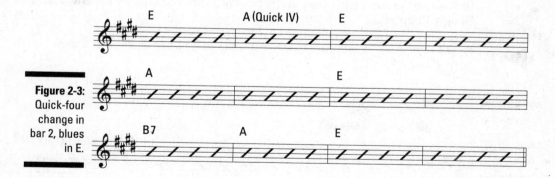

Figure 2-3: Quick-four change in bar 2, blues in E.

The quick four happens just about as often as not in blues songs. Some songs that use the quick-four method include "Sweet Home Chicago" and "Hide Away." Songs such as "Hound Dog" and "Johnny B. Goode" don't use this variation. Most blues guitarists don't think too much about whether a song has a quick four. They just look at someone else in the band who knows more than they do to see if they're going to make that move in bar two or not.

The quick four happens very soon after you start the song, so if you're at a jam session, or are playing along with a song for the first time, you must be on your toes to anticipate its use. If you miss it the first time, just nod and grimace and remember to switch for the rest of the song.

The turnaround

The *turnaround* refers to the last two bars of the progression, which point the music back to the beginning. At the end of the 12-bar blues, you can repeat the progression or end it. Most of the time you repeat the progression to play additional verses and solos. To help get the progression ready for a repeat, you employ a turnaround that sets up the repeat. At the most basic level, you can create a turnaround by just substituting a V chord for the I chord in the last bar — bar 12.

Practically all songs (blues or otherwise) end on a I chord (the tonic chord of the key), so the substitution of the V chord creates a strong pull that brings the song back to a I chord, which occurs at bar 1 of the progression. When the V chord occurs at the end of the progression, it tells musicians and listeners "we're going back around again." Although the most basic application of a turnaround is just playing a V chord in the last bar, to most guitarists, a turnaround presents an opportunity to play a riff or lick. (Riffs are covered in Book V Chapter 3.)

Figure 2-4 (Track 81) shows the last four bars of a 12-bar blues with a turnaround bar added .

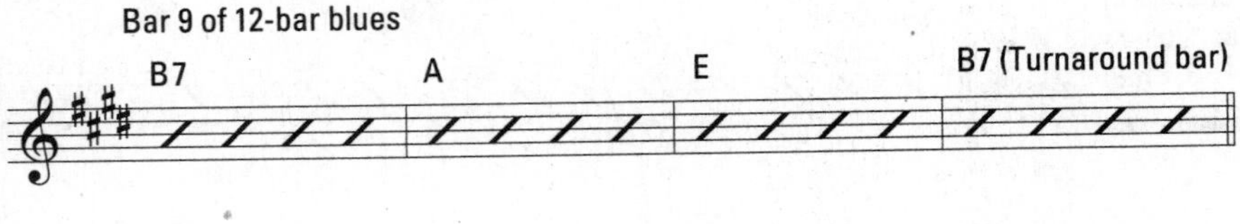

Figure 2-4:
The turnaround is the V chord in the last bar.

Bar 9 of 12-bar blues

B7   A   E   B7 (Turnaround bar)

The 12-bar blues in song

If you're wondering how musical charts and symbols relate to the actual songs (melody and lyrics), here's the quick version:

- The 12-bar blues breaks down neatly into three lines of four bars each. These three lines correspond to the vocal phrases.

- The vocal scheme of the blues is A-A-B. Each letter represents a sentence, complete thought, or phrase of the lyric.

- Think of any 12-bar blues, such as "Hound Dog," "Stormy Monday," "Kansas City,"

"St. Louis Blues," "Easy Rider," or "Corrina, Corrina." Each song has three lines per verse, with the first line repeated.

Even though the first vocal line is repeated, it doesn't sound repetitious, because the chords underneath the lyric and melody change, which provides interest. You can actually sing any of these songs along to any 12-bar progression.

In written music or fake books, you may see the V chord in the turnaround bar with parentheses around it. This method is shorthand for saying that you use the turnaround optionally or whenever you decide to repeat the progression. When you want the progression to end, you ignore the parentheses and continue playing the I chord from the previous bar.

Slow blues

Slow blues is usually a 12-bar blues played in 12/8 time, using three strums to the beat. Because of the slower tempo, there's often more opportunity to put in additional chords — especially ninth chords, which are a common slow-blues hallmark (for more on ninth chords, see Book III Chapter 3).

Figure 2-5 (Track 82) is a slow 12-bar blues in 12/8 time with its own moves added — moves that consist of adding chords a whole step higher before the main ones. But it's still a 12-bar blues. You can hear a lot of this quality in the playing of T-Bone Walker.

One irony of slow blues is that although the tempo is slower than a shuffle, and the changes come more slowly and are therefore more manageable, the lead playing is often very intricate, especially with regard to rhythm. If you ever get a chance to see transcribed guitar solos in print, look at the ones in a slow 12/8. The notation can get quite hairy!

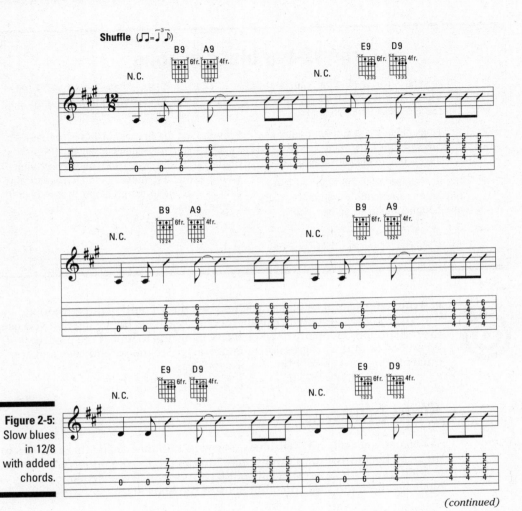

Figure 2-5:
Slow blues
in 12/8
with added
chords.

(continued)

(continued)

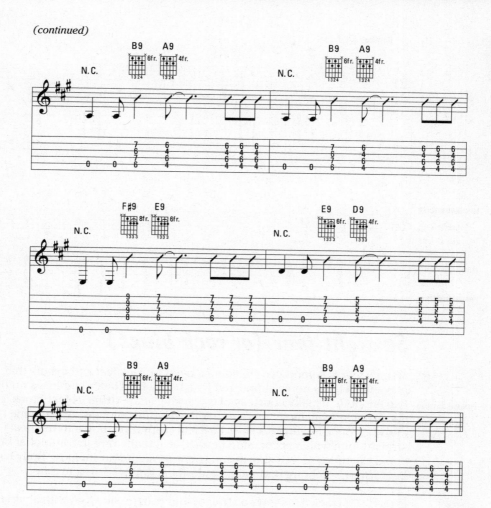

The 8-bar blues

The 8-bar blues is four bars shorter than the 12-bar blues, but the 8-bar blues doesn't really follow a strict form the way the 12-bar blues does. The 8-bar blues encompasses several feels, tempos, and qualities — often an 8-bar blues has more chords in it than just the basic I, IV, and V, making it more "songlike" than a 12-bar blues.

Figure 2-6 is an 8-bar blues played with a bass-strum pattern by using a variety of chords.

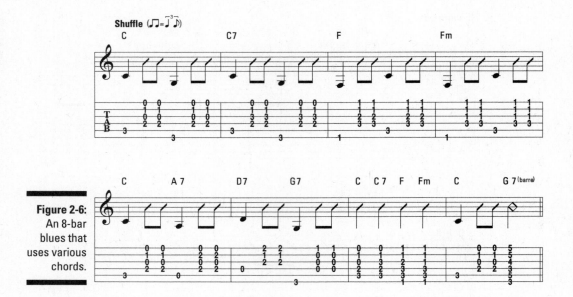

Figure 2-6:
An 8-bar
blues that
uses various
chords.

Straight-four (or rock blues)

Straight-four is sometimes called *rock blues* or rock feel and means that you play even eighth notes supported by a heavy backbeat (emphasis on beats two and four, usually courtesy of a cracking snare drum). Most blues is in a *non*-straight feel, meaning it's either in a shuffle (a long-short scheme that derives from triplets) or a slow 12/8 feel (with three notes to the beat). So a straight-four, which is common in rock, is actually rare in traditional blues. Some examples of well-known songs in a straight-four include "Roll Over Beethoven," "Johnny B. Goode," and Albert King's "Crosscut Saw."

Figure 2-7 (Track 83) shows a straight-four progression in A with a variation on the 5-to-6 move (also called the *Jimmy Reed*, covered in the next section). This variation has the moving voice occasionally going up to the flat seven (which would be G in the A chord, C in the D chord, and D in the E chord).

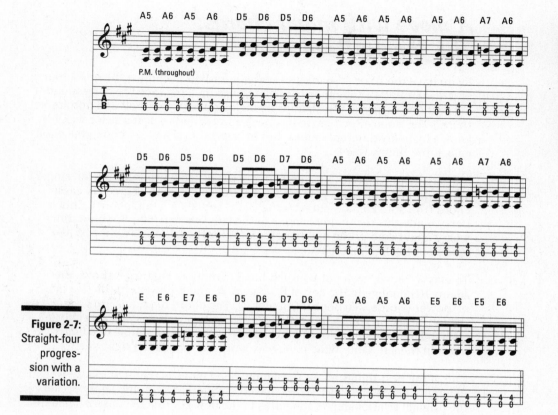

Figure 2-7:
Straight-four progres-sion with a variation.

Applying Structures to Keys

Although every key is treated equally when discussing function and music theory (see "Blues by the Numbers" earlier in this chapter), the reality is that different keys and chords on the guitar present different moves. What you can do easily in E, you may not be able to do in G, and G has other options that E may not have. These variations are a delight (and frustration!) of play-ing the guitar. Each key has something idiomatic that can't be performed comfortably or convincingly in another key. Composers and musicians write and play songs in different keys to exploit these little differences that each key provides.

A move with many chords: The Jimmy Reed move

If you have the basic 12-bar blues under your belt, including the quick four and turnaround bar, it's time to shake things up a bit. (See the corresponding sections earlier in the chapter if you look under your belt and nothing's there.) The Jimmy Reed move has been a blues and rock staple forever. It's known by many different names, but because this is a blues book, this book calls it the Jimmy Reed.

The Jimmy Reed move — named after the Chicago harmonica player, singer, and guitarist — involves going from the fifth to the sixth degrees in each chord (the note E in a G chord is the sixth, and it's A in a C chord). Chuck Berry made this technique famous in the late '50s and '60s. For now, don't worry about converting numbers to notes for the I, IV, and V chords; just figure out the left-hand part.

To play a "move," you put your left hand in motion. Figure 2-8 shows the Jimmy Reed move in the key of E, using E, A, and B power chords (for more on power chords, see Book II Chapter 3). The chord diagrams are given above the tab, allowing you to think of this move in two ways: as an extra chord inserted in between the ones you already know or as a simple one-finger move in the left hand. Whichever way works for you is the right one!

One of the best things about the Jimmy Reed move is that it works so well in different chords and keys. When played in different keys, the figure preserves the original relationship of the notes in the new key, but because it's in a different key, it just sounds, well, different. Not better or worse, perhaps, just different — and still very cool! It's like singing "Happy Birthday" in the key of G or E♭: You can recognize the melody in any key setting — but the Jimmy Reed move is so much hipper than "Happy Birthday."

Jimmy's move in G

If you had to play in the key of G, and you wanted to throw in the Jimmy Reed move, it would look like Figure 2-9 (Track 84). This move has a different character and is a little easier to play than the same move in E. The chord diagrams in the figure are presented above the staffs, so you can view the move as either a new chord inserted between the ones you already know or as just simply moving a finger over to play a previously open string on beats two and four.

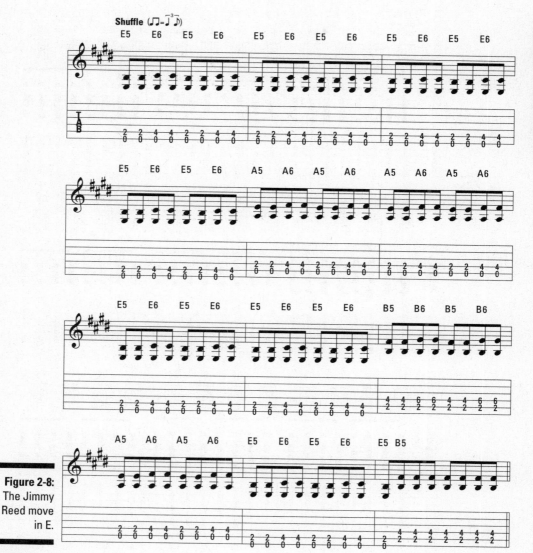

Figure 2-8:
The Jimmy
Reed move
in E.

In the blues move in G, you have to mute the open string that your finger just left to play the new chord (indicated by an X in the chord diagram).

Jimmy's move in A

In A, the move travels up the neck of the guitar to grab the IV and V chords (shown in Figure 2-10 — listen to it on Track 85). This sound is very rock and roll (in a good way), and has a less folky character than the G progression. The blues move in A has an entirely different feel than the same move in G, yet they're only one letter away — the basis for Chuck Berry's sound and for much of the "boogie" rock and roll played by rockabilly artists of the '50s, '60s, and today.

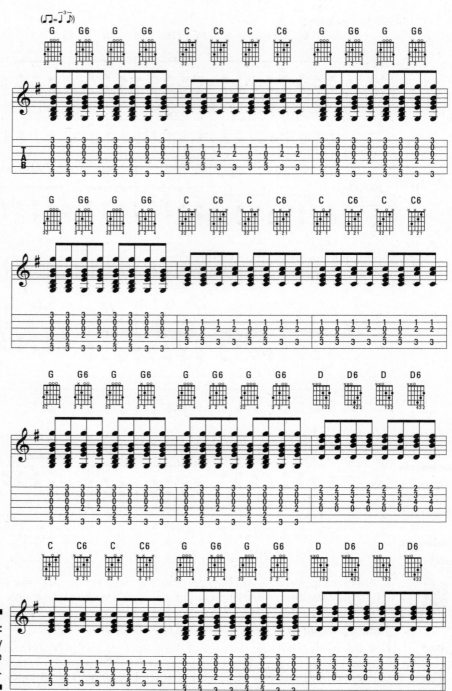

Figure 2-9:
The Jimmy Reed move in G.

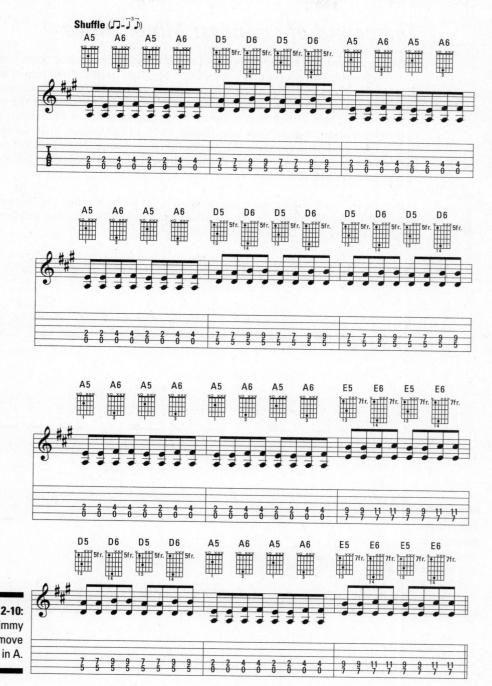

Figure 2-10: The Jimmy Reed move in A.

The sound of sadness: Minor blues

Minor keys in music sound sad or menacing or mysterious, and what better way to give the blues a double dose of trouble than to put it in a minor key? Putting the blues in minor also provides some variety. A minor blues doesn't say much about the form, only that it uses minor chords instead of the usual major or dominant 7th chords. A minor blues can be a 12-bar blues with minor chords or a straight-eighth (or non-shuffle feel), 16-bar format (instead of the more common 12-bar format). "St. James Infirmary" and "The Thrill Is Gone" are two minor blues songs. "The Thrill Is Gone" is a popular format for more contemporary blues.

Figure 2-11 (Track 86) shows a progression more along the lines of this song. Notice the addition of minor 7th chords, which help give a jazzier feel (see Book II Chapter 2 for more on minor 7th chords).

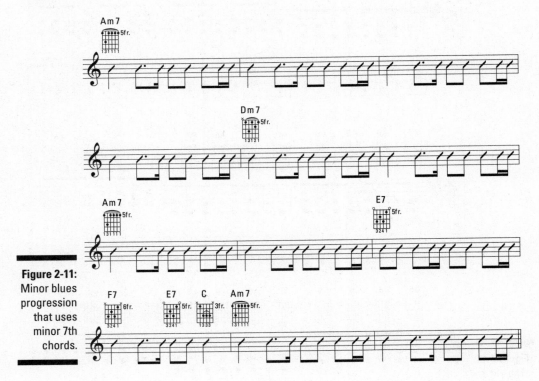

Figure 2-11: Minor blues progression that uses minor 7th chords.

Accessorizing the 12-Bar Blues: Intros, Turnarounds, and Endings

Intros (short for introductions), *turnarounds*, and *endings* are all enhancements to the 12-bar blues. They're used to steer the song toward repeats or resolutions and are all related. Countless variations exist for these three devices, and they're often reworked versions of each other, where the only difference is how they end.

Intros

An intro often features a solo lick by the guitar, piano, or other instrument (think of "That'll Be the Day" by Buddy Holly). But sometimes the whole band plays the intro, and the guitar is expected to play rhythm guitar (licks and riffs are covered in Book V Chapter 3). Intros often borrow from their turnaround cousins, because the whole idea is to set up the I chord and the beginning of the progression — the same duties that the turnaround has.

Track 87 at 0:00 is a basic two-bar intro. The rhythm features a syncopation and then a held note, which creates a musical space (or hole) before the downbeat of the 12-bar progression. This space allows room for a vocal or instrumental melodic pickup — a phrase that starts before bar one.

Figure 2-12 (Track 87 at 0:08) is a four-bar intro that is just the last four bars of the 12-bar blues. This intro is popular and is often announced by a musician saying, "Let's bring it in from the V," or "Let's walk it down from the V."

Figure 2-12:
Four-bar intro.

Turnarounds

As you may recall, a turnaround bar is a bar that substitutes a V chord for a I chord in the last bar of the progression — bar 12 in a 12-bar blues (see "Playing the 12-bar blues" earlier in this chapter). A true, full turnaround is, at minimum, a two-bar phrase that goes from the I chord to the V chord. Note: Entire books could be written on just turnarounds, but I'm only going to cover a few rhythm approaches in this section.

Figure 2-13 (Track 87 at 0:22) shows a simple two-bar turnaround using the Jimmy Reed move and syncopation.

Figure 2-13:
Two-bar turnaround.

Figure 2-14 (Track 88 at 0:00) shows a more elaborate turnaround using one chord for every two beats or five different chords in all: C, C7, F, Fm, and G7 — all in the space of two bars.

Figure 2-14:
Two-bar turnaround with chord changes every two beats.

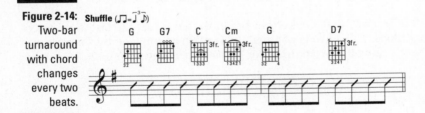

Figure 2-15 (Track 88 at 0:10) is a variation of Figure 2-14, with a chromatic move in the last part. It's also in an unusual key — B♭.

Figure 2-15:
Two-bar turnaround with chromatic movement.

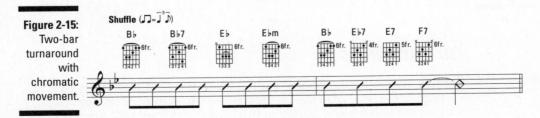

Endings

Endings are closely related to turnarounds, except for the last part of the last measure. The last measure terminates on a I chord of some type.

Figure 2-16 (Track 89 at 0:00) shows an ending that a slow blues often uses — a 9th chord for the final chord of the piece.

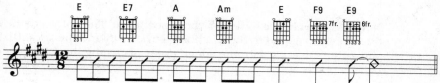

Figure 2-16:
Typical ending for a slow blues.

Figure 2-17 (Track 89 at 0:13) is an ending that's typical for medium-tempo shuffle tunes.

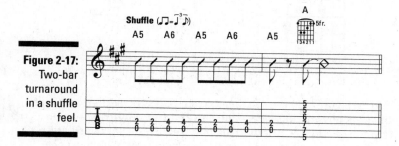

Figure 2-17:
Two-bar turnaround in a shuffle feel.

High Moves

You can play moves on the higher strings, too. These strings often involve the same notes played on the lower strings (the fifth and sixth of the chord featured in the Jimmy Reed move — discussed earlier), but when played up high, it sounds more like a riff than a chord figure. That creates a bridge between chord figures and riffs and licks (explored in Book V Chapter 3). Think of these new, higher moves as chord forms added to your basic eighth-note strumming. As you play these added chords, notice that the sound produces a melodic motif.

Figure 2-18 shows the first high-note move in the key of E. The two added chords are E7 chords with your 4th finger of the left hand playing notes on the 2nd string.

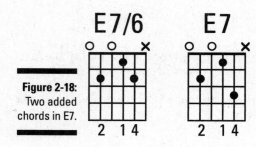

Figure 2-18: Two added chords in E7.

Now add two chords to the A7 chord sequence. The notes are the same relative ones you added to the E7 chord — the sixth and the seventh. Figure 2-19 shows the fingering with the added notes played by the 4th finger of the left hand.

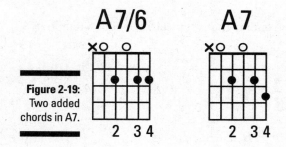

Figure 2-19: Two added chords in A7.

For the B7 chord, in Figure 2-20 the 4th finger again plays the added note, but because the finger is already in place — on the 2nd fret, 1st string — you must move it up to the 3rd fret briefly. This may seem a bit awkward at first, and the stretch between your 4th and 3rd fingers may take a while to get smoothly, but it will come in time.

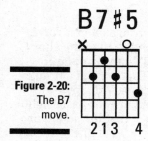

Figure 2-20: The B7 move.

Figure 2-21 (Track 90) shows all three moves in a 12-bar blues. If some of the moves seem difficult, or come too fast, try leaving them out at first. As long as you don't break the rhythm in your right hand and you change left-hand chords where you're supposed to, the blues still sound fine. That's the beauty of the blues: You can play any variation on the basic structure — from simple to complex — and it always sounds good!

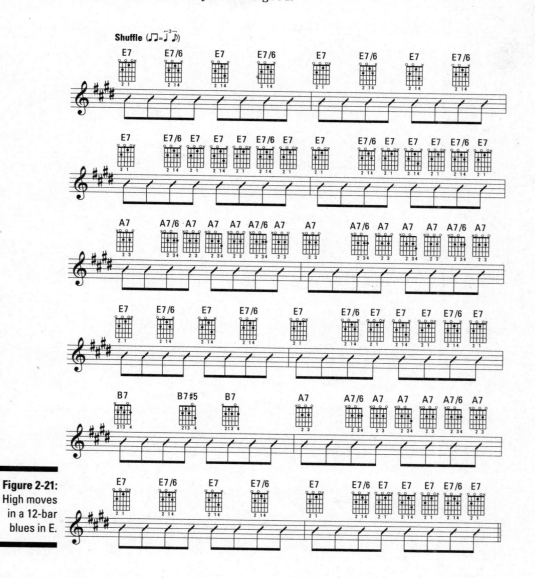

Figure 2-21:
High moves
in a 12-bar
blues in E.

Chapter 3

Musical Riffs: Bedrock of the Blues

In This Chapter

▶ Mastering the basics: Single-note riffs

▶ Exploring double-stop riffs

▶ Shooting for high-note riffs

▶ Taking your skills to the next level: Mastering rhythm figures

▶ Access the audio tracks at www.dummies.com/go/guitaraio/

*I*t can be tough to find your own blues voice because you can't spontaneously improvise the blues any more than you can improvise baroque or bebop; you have to learn the vocabulary. And the vocabulary for blues includes licks and riffs.

Although related to chords, riffs aren't tethered to chords the way the rhythm-based approach is. It's always good to know where your riffs spring from — especially if they're derived out of a chord form. But you don't need to grab a chord first to play a riff. In this chapter, you play riffs with a liberated left hand.

When you learn chords, strumming, double-stops, and single-note riffs, you have most of the ingredients necessary to start really developing as a player. In the blues, it's always a delicate balance between cloning the greats and doing your own thing.

Basic Single-Note Riffs

A *riff* is a self-contained musical phrase, and it can be used to form the basis for a song. Riffs are the bridge between chords and lead guitar. Riffs are usually based on single notes, but they can involve double-stops (two notes played simultaneously) and bits of full-chord playing.

You may hear the terms *riff* and *lick* used interchangeably in your blues guitar career. A riff is more of a structural, repeatable phrase, and a lick may well be a cliché — that is, it's a self-contained lead figure that doesn't necessarily have structural importance (like those short, snappy melodic phrases played by blues and country guitar-players between vocal lines).

The signature guitar parts in the Stones' "Satisfaction" and the Beatles' "Day Tripper" are classic examples of riffs. In blues, the crisp, ascending, horn-like melodic bursts in Freddie King's "Hide Away" are riffs, as is the repeating pattern in Bo Diddley's "I'm a Man."

In the next few sections, you look at riffs in order of increasing rhythmic activity, starting with quarter notes, advancing through eighth notes (the straight, shuffle, and triplet varieties), and moving to the more complex 16-note-based and syncopated riffs (which involve eighths and sixteenths). Just as you do when playing chords, you must play riffs with a solid and consistent approach to articulation (attack), rhythm, and dynamics (overall loud and soft) to help keep the drive in the guitar part.

Use a metronome to help keep yourself playing along with the beat, and use a combination of your ears and muscle memory to make sure you strike the strings with the same force for achieving consistent dynamics.

For the low-down bass notes:
Quarter-note riffs

You may think you can't do much to groove hard with boring ol' quarter notes, but the quarter note drives a lot of boogie-woogie bass lines. Boogie-woogie and blues are close cousins, and you can always throw in a boogie bass as a variation to almost any medium- to uptempo shuffle. Figure 3-1 (Track 91 at 0:00) shows a common quarter-note boogie pattern that you can play easily with just downstrokes.

Figure 3-1:
Boogie-
woogie bass
line in
quarter
notes.

The big daddy of riffs: Eighth-note riffs

Most riffs in blues are eighth-note based, so there's a wide range of music you can play in an eighth-note groove. But to start off, jump into eighth-note riffs by taking quarter-note riffs (from Figure 3-1) and doubling them up — that is, play two notes per beat instead of one. Figure 3-2 (Track 91 at 0:16) is a boogie-bass pattern in shuffle eighth-notes.

Figure 3-2: Boogie bass line with double-struck eighth notes.

Another popular riff is the stop-time feel. It features the low notes of the guitar. The entire band plays a figure in unison and stops at the downbeat of each measure in the phrase, like in "Blue Suede Shoes." This approach is used famously in the Muddy Waters tunes "Mannish Boy" and "Hoochie Coochie Man." A tribute to the stop-time riff is featured in Figure 3-3 (Track 91 at 0:32).

Figure 3-3: Stop-time riff in eighth notes.

Figure 3-4 (Track 92 at 0:00) shows a riff in the style of Freddie King's "Hide Away" — one of the most recognizable eighth-note riff-based songs in the blues repertoire.

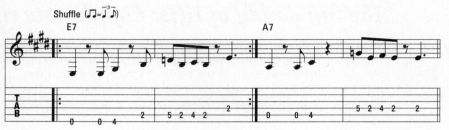

Figure 3-4:
Eighth-note
riff in the
style of
Freddie
King's "Hide
Away."

Adding a little funk: 16th-note riffs

Funky blues usually sound that way because sixteenth notes are in the mix. In a sixteenth-note groove, the tempos tend to be moderate. But because the beats use sixteenth-note subdivisions, the groove sounds quite active. Often the bass line and drums (particularly the hi-hat) employ sixteenth notes to lend support to the scratchings laid down by the guitar.

Figure 3-5 (Track 92 at 0:21) is a sixteenth-note riff on the low strings that you play with strict alternate (down-up-down-up) picking.

Figure 3-5:
Sixteenth-
note riff,
using
alternate
picking.

Throwing rhythm for a loop: Syncopated eighth-note riffs

Although syncopation isn't a huge influence in the blues (compared to, say, jazz, R&B, and funk), it's used sometimes and is always a welcome treat.

Figure 3-6 (Track 92 at 0:32) shows a syncopated blues line consisting of a dotted eighth, a tie, and sixteenth notes.

Figure 3-6:
Eighth-note
riff featuring
common
syncopation
figures.

If you're practicing the syncopation in Figure 3-6 and it gives you trouble at first, try practicing the line without the tie (so you're playing both notes in the tie). Then, when you're confident with the figure, practice the tie by letting the note ring through.

Double the Strings, Double the Fun: Two-Note Riffs (or Double-Stops)

Riffs aren't restricted to single notes. This section explores double-stops, a technique that doesn't strictly involve single notes. The term *double-stop* means *two strings*.

A double-stop applies to all string instruments when two notes are stopped or played together. Even when guitarists don't have to fret a string, they still refer to simultaneous two-string playing as double-stops. Double-stop playing also implies moving in lockstep — and even performing bends, slurs, and vibrato (check out Book IV Chapter 4 for more on that fancy stuff) on two strings at once.

Part of the versatility of a two-note figure is that it can be played on any two strings — low, high, and in the middle — all for a slightly different effect. When you get tired of playing chords and single-note leads, a two-note riff can be just the ticket to give your playing (and your listeners) a much-needed dose of dual-string diversity.

The *5-6 riff* is a blues-rhythm hallmark of going from the fifth to the sixth degree in a chord (E to F# in an A chord) and is technically a double-stop, although the string motion doesn't proceed in parallel motion. But the right-hand coordination is the same: You strike two strings as if they're one every time your right hand comes in contact with the strings. The 5-6 riff is also known as the Jimmy Reed move, which is covered in Book V Chapter 2.

The following sections cover two 5-6 riffs, each in a different feel.

Straight feel

Straight-eighth notes are unusual in blues. But in blues-rock, classic rock and roll, and rockabilly — all closely related to the blues — the straight-eighth feel rules. Straight eighths are spaced equally apart, whereas shuffle eighths follow a long-short scheme.

Book V Chapter 2 tackles the basic 5-6 move, but Figure 3-7 (Track 93 at 0:00) shows an expanded version that uses linear movement instead of the more static, back-and-forth 5-5-6-6-5-5-6-6. Also think of the riff to Roy Orbison's (and later Van Halen's) "Oh, Pretty Woman" for a classic straight-eighth approach to a low-note riff.

Figure 3-7:
Expanded
version of
the classic
5-6 move
in straight
eighths.

Many eighth-note riffs sound equally good in a shuffle or straight-eighth feel. And in many early rock and R&B recordings, such as Chuck Berry's "Johnny B. Goode" and "Carol," you can actually hear some instruments playing straight eighths and others playing shuffle eighths! Try the passage in Figure 3-7 in a shuffle feel to see if it translates. Some riffs will work, and some won't. You don't really know until you try, and there's no harm in that, even when it doesn't work out.

Shuffle, or swing, eighths

Most blues are in a shuffle feel, and shuffle-based eighth-note riffs (also called swing eighths) are the most popular blues riffs. Countless tunes employ eighth-note riffs, including such hits as "Dust My Broom" and "Sweet Home Chicago."

Figure 3-8 (Track 93 at 0:13) shows a classic shuffle rhythm that employs swing eighths and the occasional eighth-note triplet.

Figure 3-8:
Variation
on the
5-6 move
in swing
eighths.

Figure 3-9 (Track 93 at 0:28) is an eighth-note riff with the melody weaving in and out of the low and high strings. This riff, once mastered, is tons of fun to play because it takes your left hand up and down and makes you look like you're really moving on those strings.

Figure 3-9:
Expanded
version of
the classic
5-6 move.

Figure 3-10 (Track 94) brings together chords, double-stops, swing eighth-notes, and eighth-note triplets. Practice this at various tempos to make sure you're playing all the elements with equal precision and command.

Figure 3-10: Progression fusing chords, single notes, and double-stops.

High-Note Riffs, the Bridge to Lead Guitar

A *high-note* riff is very close — in words and in music — to a lick (see "Basic Single-Note Riffs" early in this chapter for more on these two terms). So, just forget the whole idea of strictly defining terms in such a forgiving and nonjudgmental form as the blues. But if you're mastering all that low-note stuff, you deserve to see what awaits you when you ascend the cellar stairs into the sunshine of high-note, melodic-based playing.

Keith Richards's borrowed trademark: Quick-four riffs

A *quick-four* (in this section) refers to a double-stop riff that you play on the 2nd and 3rd strings within a measure of a I or IV chord. (Don't get this quick-four confused with the kind of *quick four* that happens in bar two of a 12-bar blues, covered in Book V Chapter 2.) When you play this riff during a chord, you create a temporary IV chord.

The Rolling Stones' Keith Richards carved out a very successful career exploiting this riff, and he learned from the great American blues masters. Figure 3-11 (Track 95) shows a four-bar phrase where the quick-four riff is applied at the end of each bar of an E and A chord.

Figure 3-11:
The quick-four move over open position E and A chords.

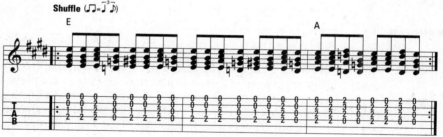

Keith Richards's signature riffs in Stones classics like "Brown Sugar," "Honky-Tonk Women," and "Start Me Up" are actually in open-G tuning, which makes the quick-four easier to access. Open tunings in G, A, D, and E were used extensively by prewar acoustic guitarists — such as Charlie Patton, Son House, and Robert Johnson — especially for slide playing.

Intro, turnaround, and ending riffs

Intros, turnarounds, and ending riffs fill out the chord structure with melodic figures. As you play the figures in this section, try to hear the underlying structure — the rhythm guitar in your mind — playing along with you. You can play the chords according to the chord symbols above the music, but in this case the symbols identify the overall harmony and don't tell you what to actually play at that moment.

Intro, turnaround, and ending riffs have very similar DNA, so they can be mutated ever so slightly to change into the others. The figures in this section provide examples that you can easily adapt and add your own flavor to, so take a stab at converting the intro in Figure 3-12 into an ending that borrows from Figure 3-17. These practices get you used to taking other people's ideas and fashioning them into your own. That's how pre-existing riffs and licks get turned into an individual and original voice.

Intro riffs

Figure 3-12 (Track 96 at 0:00) is a snappy, triplet-based intro riff. The lower voice descends while the top voice stays fixed. Try playing this riff fingerstyle or with a pick and fingers.

Figure 3-12: Triplet-based intro riff in E.

Figure 3-13 (Track 96 at 0:11) is related to Figure 3-12 in that the lower voice descends against a fixed upper-note. But here, the notes are played together as double-stops for a more obvious and dramatic harmonic clash of the two notes. This blues lick and the one in Figure 3-14 are borrowed from a famous pop song — Johnny Rivers's version of Chuck Berry's "Memphis." Play this lick fingerstyle or with pick and fingers.

Figure 3-13: Double-stop intro riff in E.

The varying motion of the riff in Figure 3-14 (Track 96 at 0:21) makes it unpredictable and dramatic. The figure shows an all-single-note riff in triplets, ending in a B7 chord that comes on beat two. The melody here changes direction often and can be a little tricky at first. But you'll can get the hang of it with some practice. The last note of the melody, low B, is actually the root of the B7 chord that you play one moment later. So play that B with your left-hand 2nd finger.

Figure 3-14: Melodic intro riff based on all triplet eighth notes.

Turnaround riffs

Figure 3-15 (Track 96 at 0:30) can be used as an intro or a turnaround, but here it's cast as a turnaround. This is a double-stop riff in A with a descending lower voice, reminiscent of the playing of Robert Johnson.

Figure 3-15: Descending double-stop turnaround riff in A.

Figure 3-16 (Track 97 at 0:00) is a wide-voiced double-stop riff where the voices move in contrary motion (the bass ascends while the treble descends). This riff is great for any fingerstyle blues in E because it highlights the separation of the bass and treble voices — a signature feature of the fingerstyle approach.

Figure 3-16: Turnaround riff in E featuring contrary motion.

If the double strikes in the bass give you trouble at first, try playing them as quarter notes, in lock step with the treble voice.

Figure 3-17 (Track 97 at 0:12) is an open-chord turnaround riff in C — the key for fingerpicking country blues like Mississippi John Hurt. The last chord is a treat: a jazzy G7 augmented (where the fifth of the chord, D, is raised a half step to D♯), which gives the progression a gospel feel with a little extra flavor.

Combining single notes and chords

One way to get the best of both worlds — the lead and rhythm worlds, that is — is to combine single notes and chords. Many blues players don't make clear distinctions between chord playing, riff playing, or lead playing. Their technique just melds aspects of all these approaches into one cohesive style. And many of them do this while singing! Here are two examples:

✔ Stevie Ray Vaughan was a master of this style. He created full-sounding, active, and infinitely varied parts under his vocals as well as when he was just vamping along with the band.

✔ Eddie Van Halen, when in rare blues mode (as opposed to his tapping, metal rock-god mode), was also an excellent practitioner of the integrated single-note-and-chord approach.

Today's students of the guitar tend to look at rhythm versus lead guitar as a black-and-white issue. But the history of blues shows that, until the advent of modern rock (from about the late '60s and beyond), players didn't really think of guitar-playing in those terms.

Be sure to also listen to the traditional players who sang and accompanied themselves on guitar:

✔ Robert Johnson

✔ John Lee Hooker

✔ Mississippi John Hurt

You hear the best examples of how to combine single notes and chords in those players' styles, and the musical playing is some of the best you may ever hear.

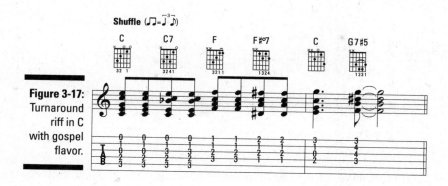

Figure 3-17: Turnaround riff in C with gospel flavor.

Ending riffs

Ending riffs are similar to both intros and turnarounds, except ending riffs terminate with the I chord, not the V.

Figure 3-18 (Track 97 at 0:22) is a triplet-based riff in sixths, where the second string isn't played. You can play this riff with just the pick, but it's easier with fingers or a pick and fingers. The open B string on the last triplet of beat one gives you a bit of a head start to get your hand up the neck to play the F9 and E9 ending chords.

Figure 3-18: Triplet-based ending riff.

Figure 3-19 (Track 97 at 0:33) is a low note ending in E, using triplet eighths and a double-stop descending form. This riff is meaty and doesn't sound too melodic because it has more of a low, walking bass feel.

Figure 3-19: Low-note ending riff in E using triplets and double-stops.

Figure 3-20 (Track 98) is something completely different: a ragtime or country-blues progression in A. The more complex-sounding chords and the voice leading (where each note resolves by a half or whole step to the closest chord tone) give the riff a tight, barbershop sound. You hear this type of progression in the playing of the great country-blues fingerstyle-players like Mance Lipscomb, Fred McDowell, Mississippi John Hurt, Reverend Gary Davis, and Taj Mahal.

Figure 3-20: Triplet-based riff featuring sixths.

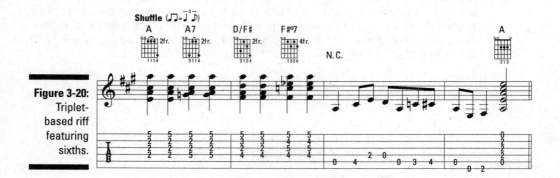

Mastering the Rhythm Figure

After you have a handle on the components of rhythm guitar — left-hand chords, right-hand strums, riffs, and combinations thereof — it's time to put them all together in various ways.

In this section, you master the rhythm figure, which combines all the components of rhythm guitar: left-hand chords, right-hand strums, riffs, and combinations of the three. In some musical circles, a rhythm figure — usually longer than a riff — describes any repeatable passage of music that forms the basis for a song or section of a song.

Rhythm figures can be as simple as a quarter-note chord strum, an eighth-note boogie pattern, or a wild hybrid containing everything but the kitchen sink, as evidenced by the complex, integrated rhythm work of Magic Sam, Freddie King, Jimi Hendrix, and Stevie Ray Vaughan.

Figure 3-21 (Track 99) is a 12-bar blues that uses chords, single-note bass runs (to bring you in and out of those chords), and single-note riffs that go into flights of blues fancy.

Figure 3-21:
Rhythm groove over a 12-bar blues in E.

Book VI
Classical Guitar

Acoustic guitar   Classical guitar

Contents at a Glance

Chapter 1: Introducing the Classical Guitar 445

Classical Guitar: One Term, Two Meanings, and a Bit of History............................446
How a Classical Guitar Is Physically Different from Its Peers.................................447
Beyond Physique: Other Unique Attributes of Classical Guitar...............................450
Situating Yourself to Play...452
Approaching the Strings with Your Hands...459

Chapter 2: Playing Easy Pieces in Open Position 467

Coordinating Contrapuntal Music: Layered Melodies...468
Melody and Accompaniment: Using All Your Fingers..472
Playing Easy Pieces in Different Textural Styles...474

Chapter 3: Combining Arpeggios and Melody 481

Grasping the Combination in Context...481
Going Downtown: Melody in the Bass..482
Moving Uptown: Melody in the Treble..485
Mixing Up Your Melodic Moves: The Thumb and Fingers Take Turns.....................488
Playing Pieces That Combine Arpeggios and Melodies...491

Chapter 1

Introducing the Classical Guitar

In This Chapter

▶ Defining the term *classical guitar*

▶ Surveying the classical guitar's history in music

▶ Noting the differences between a classical guitar and other guitar types

▶ Holding the guitar

▶ Fretting and stroking the strings

*I*n the right hands, the classical guitar can produce some of the most beautiful sounds in all of music. With it, a skilled performer can create miniature moments of intimate tenderness or stirring sagas of grandeur and passion. One reason the classical (or any) guitar is capable of wide-ranging textures and emotions is that it's one of the few stringed instruments that can play chords and single notes with equal ease. And many people credit its special emotive powers to the fact that the performer uses both hands to touch the strings directly to make a sound, allowing him to coax out the softest melody or to vigorously ring out triumphant, full-voiced chords. The tonal variations you can achieve on a guitar played in the classical way rival the colors of the entire symphony orchestra. Even the great Beethoven agreed, calling the guitar "a miniature orchestra in itself."

This chapter starts off with the very basics, explaining the two different connotations associated with classical guitar to give you a solid understanding of what you're reading about in the first place. (Many people may not realize that simply playing a classical piece on a guitar doesn't necessarily qualify as classical guitar!) You then get a side-by-side comparison of the classical guitar and its traditional acoustic counterpart, exploring their differences in physique as well as in technique and musical requirements. After that, the chapter gets you poised and ready to play classical guitar with the proper posture, hand positions, and approach to the instrument.

Classical Guitar: One Term, Two Meanings, and a Bit of History

The first thing you have to sort out is just what's meant by the term *classical guitar*. It can describe both a type of instrument and a style of music played on that instrument. When referring to the instrument itself, you're talking about a guitar that has a particular design and construction, is made of certain materials, and requires playing techniques that are unique to this type of guitar, as compared to other guitars. To mine the depths of all the tonal and textural richness that await you in the world of classical guitar music, you must employ those specific right- and left-hand techniques, which together comprise the *classical guitar style*.

This chapter focuses exclusively on the techniques that get you playing the classical guitar style — using a nylon-string classical guitar and stroking the strings with your right-hand fingers. Doing this empowers you to play the music written by the great classical composers throughout history.

The guitar is a relatively young instrument, having evolved to its present form in the 19th century. As such, it doesn't have the rich body of music available for it that, say, the violin does, which has been around for more than 500 years. But the classical guitar has been industrious in the way it has "borrowed" music from other instruments to claim as its own. As a result, studying classical guitar means that in addition to playing music written for the guitar, you'll play a lot of music that wasn't written for the guitar in the first place, nor written by a composer who would recognize the instrument you hold in your hands. But that's just part of the adventure of being a guitarist; you have to be somewhat of a pioneer with your instrument.

Nowadays composers write for the instrument all the time, ensuring its continued place in the field of serious musical instrument study. Many guitarists, associations, and organizations commission well-known composers to write compositions for the guitar in the same way that wealthy benefactors commissioned Beethoven and Mozart to write symphonies and sonatas.

Some well-known composers from the 20th century who've written for the guitar include Heitor Villa-Lobos, Luciano Berio, Benjamin Britten, Elliott Carter, Peter Maxwell Davies, William Walton, Alberto Ginestera, Ástor Piazzolla, and Leo Brouwer. If you think of the classical guitar as playing just the work of the great masters or having an undeniably "Spanish sound," check out what modern musical thinkers are cooking up for the classical guitar all the time.

After taking a while to come into its own historically, the classical guitar is now a permanent member of the classical music community. Classical guitar is taught in universities and conservatories, it's a frequent program entry for concert and recital halls, and it's found readily in new recordings by major classical music record companies. As far as music for the guitar goes, however, it's definitely in the minority, at least in terms of music that gets heard by the public at large — with rock and pop being the major players in this arena.

How a Classical Guitar Is Physically Different from Its Peers

A classical guitar is like every other guitar in overall physique. And like other types of acoustic guitars, the classical guitar produces its sound *acoustically* — that is, without the aid of amplification — unlike the Stratocaster of Jimi Hendrix, which must be played through a guitar amplifier (though you can amplify the acoustic sound of a classical guitar with a pickup or microphone).

All classical guitars are in a sense acoustic guitars. But not all acoustics are classical.

Sometimes the best way to know what something is and what makes it special is to know what it isn't. Check out Figure 1-1, which shows a classical guitar alongside a popular traditional acoustic model. Then read through the following list, which sums up some of the major differences between them:

- **A classical guitar uses nylon strings.** All other acoustics used for unplugged purposes are built for steel strings. And you can't just swap out a set of nylons in your steel string and start playing Bach. The parts that connect the strings to the guitar are built differently, and you'd have a tough time securing a nylon string onto a steel-string guitar. Nylon strings have a gentler sound that suits classical guitar music better than the steel variety.

  Some people use the adjective *folk* to mean any unamplified guitar, so it's always a good idea to clarify whether they mean the nylon-string (classical) or steel-string variety — assuming they're aware of the difference. The guitars played by James Taylor, Paul Simon, Bob Dylan, Joni Mitchell, Neil Young, and Sheryl Crow are all *steel-string acoustics,* though some folk, pop, and jazz musicians do play their brand of music on a classical guitar, including jazz guitarist Earl Klugh and, somewhat improbably, country music legend Willie Nelson.

Figure 1-1:
A classical
guitar (right)
with an
acoustic
steel-string
model
alongside it.

Acoustic guitar   Classical guitar

Illustration © John Wiley & Sons, Inc.

Though the instrument is officially known as a *classical guitar,* other nicknames have sprung up that have come to refer to the "instrument played by classical guitarists." Some of these names include *nylon-string guitar, Spanish guitar,* and *gut-string guitar.*

✔ **A classical guitar has only one body size.** Acoustic guitar bodies vary widely with regard to size and shape, with names like *jumbo, dreadnought, orchestra model,* and *grand auditorium* to help you keep track of them all. It's much easier with classical guitars — they're all the same size and they all feel exactly alike when you hold them. So anything you learn on one classical guitar will transfer over to any other without a major adjustment.

✔ **A classical guitar has no cutaway.** Many acoustic guitars have a scoop on the *treble* (toward the skinny, higher-pitched strings) side of the upper bout that allows upper-fret access for the left hand. On a classical guitar, the body is symmetrical.

✔ **A classical guitar neck is wider than the necks on most steel strings and joins the body at the 12th fret.** Steel-string necks are skinnier to facilitate strumming with a pick, and most modern-style steel-string necks join the body at the 14th fret. The wider frets of the classical guitar accommodate playing with the right-hand fingers, and tradition dictates the 12-fret union of neck and body (although some classical guitarists lament the more limited range of a 12-fret neck).

✔ **A classical guitar has no pickguard.** A pickguard helps protect the soundboard from the ravages of a pick. But because you don't play classical guitar with a pick, the pickguard is unnecessary and is left off to expose more of the wooden surface. In flamenco guitars, though, a clear protective plate (called a *golpeador*) is added to protect the top from the percussive taps a performer is sometimes required to play as part of the style.

✔ **A classical guitar has no fret markers.** Acoustic guitars have inlay patterns both on the fingerboard and on the side of the neck. Sometimes these inlays can be quite elaborate, even gaudy. But classical guitars shun such showy displays and present the fingerboard in its natural, unadorned state. Occasionally, a classical guitar may have a single dot fret marker on the side of the neck.

✔ **A classical guitar never has the following images painted or stickered onto its surface:** skulls, lightning bolts, flames, your girlfriend's name, or slogans like "Honk if I'm playing too fast."

Book VI

Classical Guitar

Antonio Torres: Inventor of the modern classical guitar

Plucked string instruments have been around since ancient times, but the shape that all modern classical guitar makers follow was established by a *luthier* (the term for guitar maker) named Antonio Torres (1817–1892), who lived in Spain and built guitars in the middle of the 19th century. Up until that time, a classical guitar could be found in a range of sizes, which affected the tuning and your entire approach to playing the instrument. For the guitar to be accepted, it had to be standardized, and Torres did that. In fact, an 1863 Torres-made guitar is almost indistinguishable from ones built today. One of the most important things Torres did was establish the string length at 650 millimeters, which hasn't changed. The string length

has helped to determine other things, like the body proportions, the neck length, and the guitar's overall dimensions. Many bold makers have tried alternate shapes and materials and added strings, but no one has successfully improved on the basic design of Torres's creation.

Modern improvements have been made, of course, especially in the manufacturing process and in some of the materials (such as synthetic substitutes for the bone or ivory nut and saddle, and better alloy chemistries for the metal tuning parts). But the woods and design have remained largely unchanged since Torres codified them back in the mid-1800s.

Beyond Physique: Other Unique Attributes of Classical Guitar

You may find yourself in a position of trying to explain to someone what's different about the classical guitar when compared to other types of guitar music or guitar playing styles. (You may even want to be clear on what you're getting into yourself!) Sure, the most fundamental difference is that classical guitar is acoustic and played on a nylon-string guitar, but you could say that about other styles and other performers. (Willie Nelson is just one famous example of a nonclassical nylon-string guitar player.) So you have to dig deeper into the essence of classical guitar.

The next section explores some of these key differences — in terms of the physical approach to the instrument — between classical guitar and other acoustic guitar styles.

Player's form and technique

Classical guitar requires that you hold the guitar in a certain way and position your hands in ways that are different from those of other styles of music. Using these positions makes playing pieces easier, especially when you have to play up the neck or play notes with certain right-hand strokes in order to achieve the fuller tone of classical guitar music. The most important factors are how you hold the guitar, how you place your hands in playing position, and how your right-hand fingers pluck the strings.

The way you hold the instrument

You can hold an acoustic guitar a number of different ways: balanced on your right leg, balanced on your left leg (either between your legs or with your left leg crossed over your right), or dangling from a strap when you're standing up. But the classical guitar is played only in a sitting position, supported by the left leg — either with the left foot elevated or with a special support device (a cushion or frame) between the inner thigh and the guitar's body.

Hand positions

In other styles, you can position the right hand in a number of ways, and no one will correct you (as long as you sound good and aren't doing anything wrong). But in classical guitar, you must hold your right-hand fingers perpendicular to the strings, without touching any other part of the guitar (the top, the bridge). You must also position the left hand so that the hand knuckles (the ones farthest from the fingertips) are parallel to the strings, not sloped away from the strings at the little finger, which some styles allow. And in classical guitar, the left-hand thumb stays braced at the center of the back of the neck or can move toward the high strings, if necessary. But it should never be seen coming up from the bass-string side of the instrument, as you can do in some fingerpicking styles.

Playing style: No picks allowed

To produce sounds on the guitar, you pluck the strings with the fingers of the right hand at a position over the sound hole (actually, the ideal position is not directly over the hole, but a little closer to the bridge than the fingerboard). With the left-hand fingers, you change the pitches of the notes by pressing the strings to the fretboard — a process known as *fretting* — which shortens the strings' vibrating length at a particular fret. (Violinists and other bowed string players don't have frets, so they refer to pressing fingers to the fingerboard as *stopping* the string, a term guitarists sometimes use, too.)

Book VI

Classical Guitar

Unlike other forms of guitar playing, in classical guitar, you don't use a pick, or plectrum. (If you play with a pick in another guitar life, leave it at the door when you come into the world of classical guitar!) All the sounds produced by the right hand are created by the unadorned fingers, using the tips with a combination of the fleshy pad and a bit of fingernail (except in the rare cases where you strum downward, "brushing" the strings). The fingernail must extend slightly over the fingertip, and the guitarist must therefore maintain longer nails on the right hand than guitarists who play with a pick, or those who choose to fingerpick with just the flesh of the fingers.

Though classical guitar is played by "picking with the fingers," the term *fingerpicking* isn't used, as it sometimes is with other styles. And don't ever call a serious classical guitarist a "fingerpicker."

Musical knowledge and skills

Beyond perfecting the techniques necessary to execute classical music flawlessly (or getting ever nearer to that goal), classical guitarists develop their music-reading skills to cover more repertoire. And having more and more pieces under your belt means you can perform for longer periods of time and with more variety when entertaining listeners. The best classical guitarists are also technically superior to players of lesser abilities (a quality that's not necessarily true in, say, pop music). The following sections outline why classical guitarists focus on improving their reading, mastering repertoire, and honing their technical skills.

The importance of reading music

You can play many types of music without reading a single note of music. Certainly some of the best rock, blues, and folk players don't read music well or even at all, and it doesn't hamper their creative or technical abilities. But classical guitar relies on learning pieces, and the fastest, most efficient way to play through and memorize written music is, obviously, to be able to read music well. That doesn't mean you have to sight read at a level where you can play the music perfectly and up to tempo the first time, but you should be able to read well enough to get a sense of the piece.

The value of mastering repertoire

If you play the classical guitar, you play *pieces* — classical compositions or arrangements written out from start to finish, with the exact notes you're to play and often the way to play them (with indications for articulations, dynamics, and expression). You have to know written, composed music from start to finish, and most of the time you have to play it from memory.

The focus on technical skill, virtuosity, and musicianship

Other styles of music may focus on aspects such as the originality of the material or the inspired results of an improvisation. But in classical guitar, the primary focus is on technical mastery of the instrument. You work and work at improving your skill constantly your whole musical life, and your prowess is measured by how well you play standard pieces of repertoire. Simply put, classical guitarists are measured in the same way athletes are: The best classical guitarists are the most demonstrably technically proficient over their rivals.

One measure of technical proficiency is virtuosity — the ability to play extraordinarily difficult pieces with complete confidence, ease, and mastery. Along with technical prowess comes the not-so-showy quality called *musicianship*, which is understanding and executing the music with great accuracy, authority, and expression. In this way, the classical guitar has more in common with other classical instruments than it does with other styles of guitar music.

Now, if all this sounds like a lot of rules and that these rules may somehow restrict you in some way, take heart. The opposite is true. You'll find that the differences between classical technique and other techniques (or no discernible approach to technique at all!) actually enable you to play notes more comfortably, easily, and with greater speed, accuracy, control, and range of expression. It may seem like a lot of do's and don'ts at first, but just as in ballet, architecture, and other art forms, you need to master the basic skills to open up a world of possibilities. To achieve total freedom of expression in playing classical guitar music, you first need to gain total control.

Situating Yourself to Play

Your first step in getting ready to play classical guitar is to make sure you're holding the instrument correctly and with your hands in the proper position. Unlike other styles of guitar playing, where common sense and comfort are often the only guidelines, classical guitar requires you to hold and position the instrument in certain ways, because they allow you to play more smoothly and to master more difficult fingerings you may encounter. But though these requirements are specific, they're not difficult or restrictive in any way.

In proper position, a classical guitar makes contact with four points on your body. This allows you to keep a firm hold on the guitar while your hands enjoy the mobility they need to play freely. The four contact points support the guitar as follows (see Figure 1-2):

1. **Resting on the left leg.** This one's easy, because gravity does all the work! Set the guitar on your raised left leg (or use a support, explained in the section "Supporting the guitar: Leg position") and proceed to the other points from here.

2. **Braced against the right leg.** The lower side of the guitar presses against the inner thigh of the right leg. You can move your leg around a bit if you feel the corner (the spot where the back and sides meet at a 90-degree angle) digging into your thigh in an uncomfortable way.

3. **Touching the chest.** The back of the guitar, just behind the bass side of the upper bout, should lightly touch the center of your chest.

4. **Lightly touching your right arm.** Your right arm rests, but doesn't press tightly, on the side. Avoid pushing the underside of the forearm into the guitar's top, as that may impede its ability to vibrate and project sound.

Figure 1-2: How to hold the guitar according to the four pressure points.

Photograph courtesy of Jon Chappell

Taking your seat

Unlike other styles of playing where you can stand or sit, classical guitar is always played from a seated position. You never stand (or kneel, or lie on your back, as some showoff rock guitarists do), and you never use a strap. In fact, a classical guitar doesn't even have the strap pins you often find built into other types of acoustic guitars.

Before you sit down just anywhere to hold the guitar, you should know that classical guitar prohibits certain types of seating arrangements. For one, you can't plop down on the living room couch or a beanbag chair. These two locations, as comfortable as they are for reading or messing around with *other* types of guitar, can't put you in the proper playing position for dealing with classical guitar technique. What you need is a sturdy, armless chair (which rules out easy chairs and desk chairs with arms). Any kind of armless chair will do the job, including a dining room chair, a straight-back chair, or even a folding chair.

The chair you use should be relatively comfortable so that you can spend long periods there without getting uncomfortable or risking strain or stiffness. If you use a normal metal folding chair, you may want to add a pad or cushion for comfort, as you may be spending a good deal of time in that chair — especially if you want to get really good!

Supporting the guitar: Leg position

Another thing you have to attend to, after you find the appropriate chair, is a means to elevate your left foot off the floor about 4 to 6 inches, a trick you can easily accomplish with a footstool that's specially built for the classical guitarist. They're not very expensive (about $25), and you can buy them at any music store. If you don't have a footstool yet, just use a couple of hardcover books.

So to get started, find yourself a sturdy armless chair and sit toward the edge. Sit up straight with your legs slightly apart so that you can set the waist of the guitar on your left leg. Place your foot on the footstool (or whatever improvised platform you have) and look straight ahead. Your position should look similar to that shown in Figure 1-3.

An alternative to raising your leg is to use a specially made *support* or *cushion* on your left leg, which raises the guitar to the proper playing position while allowing you to keep both feet on the floor. Advocates of the support claim that it's better for your back because it doesn't require you to lift one leg in a sitting position, which causes strain. Figure 1-4 shows this alternate method, using an adjustable support that braces against the inner thigh and cradles the guitar by means of a curved piece that matches the contour of the side of the guitar's body.

Some guitarists alternate the support with the footstool, which mixes it up for the body, preventing them from having to maintain one position for too long. A guitarist may, for example, practice for two hours using the support, and then practice another hour with the footstool. Or she may choose to rehearse with the support and perform with the footstool. This may be the best approach, because the support is more comfortable over long periods of time.

Figure 1-3:
Seated in the playing position, with the left leg elevated.

Photograph courtesy of Jon Chappell

Book VI

Classical Guitar

Figure 1-4:
The support offers an alternative means of raising the guitar to playing position without elevating the left foot.

Photograph courtesy of Jon Chappell

Embracing the guitar: Arm support

Classical guitarists don't invest in all the doodads and gadgetry available for other types of guitarists, but occasionally, a device or accessory comes along that becomes part of the classical guitarist's bag of tricks. In addition to the support, another common external device you find is the *arm rest*. This fits on the guitar's side, on the bass side of the lower bout, directly under where the right arm sits, as shown in Figure 1-5. The arm rest lifts the forearm off the guitar's top, allowing the top to vibrate freely. Without the arm rest, the right arm inevitably touches the top, even if the guitarist is careful to maintain light contact only. Because the arm rest prevents direct contact between the arm and the guitar, it also serves to prevent wear to the finish from sweat and from friction caused by the arm rubbing against the top and side (especially on instruments with thin tops). Some arm rests lift the right arm off the instrument entirely, which is a benefit to big and tall players, as it helps them maintain good posture and prevents them from having to hunch over the instrument.

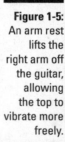

Figure 1-5:
An arm rest lifts the right arm off the guitar, allowing the top to vibrate more freely.

Photograph courtesy of Jon Chappell

Placing your hands correctly

When you're in the proper sitting position and feeling comfortable, it's time to turn your attention to your hands. Classical guitar technique requires a specific way to position your right and left hands when playing the guitar, so this section takes things one hand at a time to get you ready to play your first notes in the correct classical guitar way.

For now, all you're going to do here is *place* your hands in the proper position for playing. Don't worry just yet about actually making sounds or playing notes. This is simply a check to make sure that your hands fall on the guitar in a natural, comfortable, and correct way.

The right hand

Assuming you're seated with the guitar balanced on your left leg (as discussed in the earlier sections, "Taking your seat" and "Supporting the guitar: Leg position"), place your right hand so that it hovers above the strings over the sound hole. Actually, don't center your hand directly over the sound hole, but slightly to the right of it, in the direction of the bridge. Figure 1-6 shows how your right hand should look when placed correctly.

Book VI

Classical Guitar

Figure 1-6: Placing the right hand over the strings, over the sound hole but a little toward the bridge.

Photograph courtesy of Jon Chappell

Let your right forearm touch the edge of the guitar on the bass side of the lower bout. Your hand should be loose and relaxed, with your wrist bent, or angled, in a way to cause the fingers, if you were to outstretch them, to fall perpendicular to the strings, as shown in Figure 1-7. In some playing situations, you may relax this "absolutely perpendicular" approach, allowing your hand to look like the position back in Figure 1-2.

You should be able to pivot your right elbow so that your right hand pulls away from the guitar without the guitar moving or going out of balance.

Try wiggling your fingers in the air above the strings. If you feel tension in your forearm muscle, you may be pressing your arm against the guitar's top too tightly. You don't need to hold the guitar in place with your right arm, so try lightening up a bit. The right arm and hand should almost float above the guitar and strings. And no part of your right hand should rest on the top of the guitar. All your fingers should dangle freely above the strings. Make sure your shoulders are relaxed as well.

Figure 1-7:
Angling your
right hand
so that the
fingers fall
perpendicu-
lar to the
strings.

Photograph courtesy of Jon Chappell

The left hand

When your right hand is in position, turn your focus — and your head — to points leftward. With the guitar balanced on your left leg, open your left hand slightly by separating the thumb from the fingers. Then slip your left hand around the neck and place your thumb on the center of the neck's back, allowing it to rest lightly there. Position your left-hand fingertips to press down the strings on the top of the fingerboard. Figure 1-8 shows how your left hand should look from the back.

Figure 1-8:
The left
hand placed
on the
neck, with
the thumb
centered on
the neck's
back.

Photograph courtesy of Jon Chappell

Turning your attention to the fingerboard side of the neck, check to see that the hand knuckles (the ones farthest from the fingertips) are more or less parallel to the strings. Don't worry about pressing any strings yet; for now just get your hand in position. Figure 1-9 shows the fingers arched and ready to press down on the strings.

Figure 1-9:
The left-hand fingers ready to press down on the strings.

Photograph courtesy of Jon Chappell

Book VI

Classical Guitar

A good check to see if the guitar is well-balanced is to take your left hand completely away from the guitar. The guitar shouldn't move at all, as you don't use the left hand to support the neck.

Approaching the Strings with Your Hands

In classical guitar, left-hand techniques are intuitive and natural — not that much different from left-hand techniques used in other types of guitar playing. In contrast, right-hand techniques are very specific and have to be learned, and they require you to not only position your hand so that the fingers strike the strings at a perpendicular angle but also to execute the notes using specific plucking methods, or strokes, called the free stroke and the rest stroke. This section walks you through these left-hand and right-hand techniques.

Fretting the strings: Left-hand form

Pressing the strings to the fretboard with the left-hand fingers is known as *fretting,* and it's the way guitarists change pitches on the strings. To fret a string, use a left-hand finger to press the string down to the fingerboard with just enough pressure to cause the string to ring clearly (without buzzing or muffling).

To fret the strings as effectively and efficiently as possible, don't place your finger squarely in the middle of the two fret wires; you play a little closer to the higher fret (the one closer to the bridge). This gives you better leverage when pressing down on the string, meaning that it requires less strength to produce a strong, pure sound. Pressing closer to the higher fret helps eliminate buzzing, too.

When fretting a note, approach the string from above, rather than from the side, to get the maximum downward pressure against the fretboard, and keep your fingers rounded (not flat or hyper-extended) by curling your knuckles. This best marshals your finger strength to the tip, where it provides the most effective fretting. Curving your fingers also helps you avoid accidentally touching adjacent strings. And you may be relieved to know that the left-hand fingernails can be kept short! In fact, if you're accustomed to having long left-hand fingernails, you'll have to trim them back to be flush or below the fingertips for the best results.

Figures 1-10 and 1-11 show proper left-hand fretting technique.

Figure 1-10: The left hand placed correctly on the fingerboard.

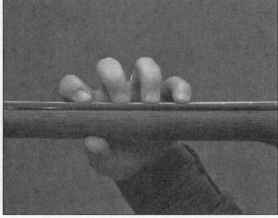

Photograph courtesy of Jon Chappell

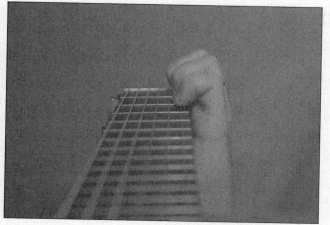

Figure 1-11: Keeping the fingers curved and approaching the string from above to achieve the best sound.

Photograph courtesy of Jon Chappell

A classical guitarist's guide to nail filing

After you acquire the proper tools and your right-hand nails are long enough to give you some raw material to work with, follow these steps to shape and finish them so that they can enhance your classical guitar tone:

1. Use the coarse surface of the file or emery board to get the nails into a basic rounded shape. If you're using a multi-surface emery board, start with the roughest-feeling grit. File down excess length and then shape the nail's edge to follow the contour of the fingertip in a symmetrical oval. Check your progress frequently by holding your outstretched fingers in front of you, parallel to the wall, with your fingertips at eye level. Make sure to file in one direction. Going back and forth can encourage tearing of the nails.

2. In addition to filing the edge of the nail, drag the file between the nail and the fingertip to round out any rough surface on the underside of the nail.

3. When the shape is curved and even, switch to a finer grit to smooth out any rough edges left by the coarser surface. Eliminating snags or rough spots will make your sound smoother as well as prevent snagging on clothing and other fabrics, which can cause the nail to tear.

4. When you've filed the nails smooth, try using fine grit sandpaper (600 or finer) or the emery board's finishing surface to make the nails even smoother, giving them an almost polished feel that protects them for longer periods between maintenance.

Preparing to pluck: Right-hand form

Though you don't have to start out with long right-hand fingernails, sooner or later you have to grow and maintain them to be able to effect the tonal variations necessary for classical guitar playing. All classical guitarists agree that combining the nail with the fleshy part of the fingertip to pluck the string is essential in deriving the full spectrum of tonal colors and achieving the wide dynamic range required for classical guitar music.

Preparing your right-hand fingernails for action

To get "good guitar nails," let your right-hand fingernails grow so that they extend about 1/16 inch beyond the tip. This measurement is only an estimate, so your nails can be longer or shorter, as long as you're able to get some of the nail in contact with the string when you pluck it. You may find it easier to keep your nails shorter as you're first learning to use them, allowing them to grow longer as you develop control. Many players like to have a slightly longer thumbnail for added bass note authority.

It's not enough just to have long fingernails. They also have to be properly shaped — that is, they should follow the shape of your fingertip — and you should keep them smooth and free of nicks and chips. To keep your finger-nails at a consistent length and shape, you need to care for them on a regular basis and to invest in some "fingernail paraphernalia." A two-sided diamond nail file and a multi-surface emery board are good options. For more on nail care, see the nearby sidebar, "A classical guitarist's guide to nail filing."

Making a beautiful sound: The nail-flesh tone

Anyone who studies classical guitar spends long hours perfecting the devel-opment of the nail-flesh tone, as it's such an inherent part of classical guitar technique and tone. Being able to combine the nail with the flesh (as shown in Figure 1-12) by angling the finger so that both tip and nail catch the string, in combinations that provide near-infinite degrees of tonal shading, is what makes the guitarist's palette of right-hand sounds so rich.

Stroking the strings: Basic right-hand technique

The *free stroke* is the classical guitar name for the stroke that you probably perform naturally if you already pluck the guitar strings with your fingers. In a free stroke, your fingers and thumb pluck the string in an outward motion, away from the top of the guitar, leaving them "free," or dangling in the air, above the strings and poised to strike again.

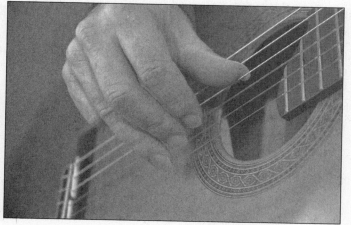

Book VI

Classical Guitar

Figure 1-12:
How to pluck to achieve the classical nail-flesh tone.

Photograph courtesy of Jon Chappell

The *rest stroke* is what classical guitar players use to produce strong, expressive, and powerful notes — more powerful than those that can be obtained by the free stroke. The "rest" part refers to the finger coming to a stop, or rest, on the next string in the direction of the stroke. Rest strokes are played with the fingers more often than the thumb and enable you to give notes more power and volume than a free stroke yields. But rest strokes are a little less nimble than free strokes, so you use them on notes that aren't moving too quickly.

The free stroke

Playing the free stroke doesn't involve any specific trick or technique. It's a very natural way to play the guitar, and the way all styles of fingerpicking (not just limited to the classical style) are performed. In fact, if you think about it too much, you may cause it to sound overly deliberate. Just pluck the string and do it several times to ensure an easy, natural approach.

To play a free stroke, place the index finger of your right hand on the open 1st string. With a brisk motion, bending from the finger knuckle, pluck the string by drawing the finger toward the palm and slightly upward (being careful not to strike the 2nd string as you do) so that your finger ends up above the strings dangling freely, as shown in Figure 1-13.

Repeat the process until you can play several plucks in a row smoothly. (Be sure that you're striking only the intended string and not the adjacent string.) After you're comfortable playing free strokes with your index finger, play free strokes several times in a row using your middle finger. Then repeat the process with your ring finger.

You almost never use the little finger of the right hand in classical guitar, so after you can play free strokes with your index, middle, and ring fingers by themselves, try playing free strokes with the three fingers in combination. For example, try playing index, middle, index, middle; then index, middle, ring, index, middle, ring; then middle, ring, middle, ring; and finally, index, ring, index, ring.

Figure 1-13:
Play a free stroke by plucking the 1st string and leaving your finger above the strings, poised to strike again.

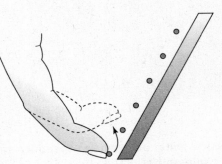

Illustration © John Wiley & Sons, Inc.

Playing a free stroke with the thumb is just like playing a free stroke with the fingers, except that you move in the opposite direction. To play a free stroke with your thumb, place it on the 6th string. Then push through the string, plucking it, and bring your thumb slightly upward toward your palm so that you don't strike the 5th string. Your thumb should end up above the strings, as shown in Figure 1-14.

Figure 1-14:
The motion of the free stroke played by the thumb.

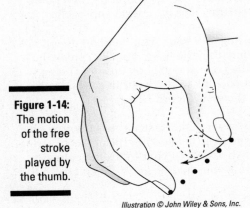

Illustration © John Wiley & Sons, Inc.

The rest stroke

A rest stroke always means coming to rest on the next adjacent string in the direction of the stroke. For the fingers, this means the next lower string in pitch (or next higher-numbered string). For example, if you play a rest stroke on the 2nd string, your finger rests on the 3rd string. Rest strokes must always have a "place to park" after you play the string. Sometimes this creates a problem if you have to play the string underneath with the thumb or another finger, or if that string must be allowed to ring out from being previously plucked. In those cases, you must use a free stroke, even if a rest stoke would be a more musical choice.

To play a rest stroke, plant your right-hand index finger on the open 1st string. Then, in one motion, draw it back, plucking the string and following all the way through until your finger is stopped by the 2nd string. Be sure you don't play through the 2nd string; if you do, you're plucking too hard. To better adopt the rest-stroke motion, it may help to think of drawing or pulling the finger downward into the guitar, rather than away from the guitar, as you do in a free stroke. Figure 1-15 shows the motion of the rest stroke.

Book VI

Classical Guitar

Figure 1-15:
The right-hand index finger playing a rest stroke on the 1st string and then stopping, or resting, on the 2nd string.

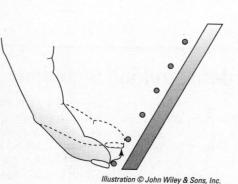

Illustration © John Wiley & Sons, Inc.

Because the rest stroke has this extra condition of a "landing string," it's a little more limited in its use than a free stroke is. For example, you can't use the rest stroke for arpeggios. But for bringing out a solo melody, nothing beats the expressive power of a rest stroke!

Playing rest strokes with the thumb is rare, though you sometimes play them this way in order to bring out a solo bass line or low-note melody. In case you do need to play one, you should know that the principles for playing a rest stroke with the thumb are the same as with the fingers, except that your thumb moves in the opposite direction (toward the floor instead of the ceiling). To play a rest stroke with the thumb, plant your thumb on the open 6th string. Then push your thumb so that it plucks the 6th string and follows through to the 5th string, where it stops. See Figure 1-16 for the motion of the thumb rest stroke.

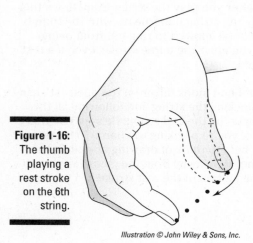

Figure 1-16:
The thumb
playing a
rest stroke
on the 6th
string.

Illustration © John Wiley & Sons, Inc.

The birth of modern stroking technique

Because they imbue classical guitar music with its unique flavor, you may think the rest stroke and nail sound were always there — preordained, like some version of the "Ten Commandments of Classical Guitar" or something. But the rest stroke is only a recent practice and one largely promoted by Andrés Segovia's mentor, Francisco Tárrega (1852–1909). The rest stroke gave guitarists a much more powerful way to extract notes from the guitar than the free stroke could muster. And while Segovia adopted, embraced, and perfected Tárrega's rest stroke, he differed with him regarding the use of right-hand fingernails.

Tárrega and many others of the time were strongly opposed to using the nails. Emilio Pujol, a famous guitarist, composer, and Tárrega champion, thought the sound was "conical, pungent, and nasal," whereas the flesh-only sound "possesses an intrinsic beauty . . . as might be the notes of an ideally expressive and responsive harp." But Segovia persevered and ultimately won out. It's a good thing, too, as, without the use of the nail, the guitarist can't produce a sharp, percussive attack. And when playing the wide range of classical guitar music, we guitarists need to be able to play bright, crispy sounds as well as soft, mellow ones.

Chapter 2

Playing Easy Pieces in Open Position

In This Chapter

▶ Exploring counterpoint

▶ Mastering melody and accompaniment

▶ Practicing pieces in different textures

▶ Access the audio tracks at www.dummies.com/go/guitaraio/

In this chapter the fun begins, because you get to play honest-to-goodness pieces of music. The pieces here are all rather easy to play. Where they differ is in texture.

These pieces make use of lots of open strings — and as any guitarist knows, an open string is easier to play than a fretted one. They contain no notes played above the 5th fret. Even though fretting a note at the 6th fret is technically no more difficult than playing a note at the 4th fret, people learning to read music on the guitar customarily begin with the lower frets and find playing music in low positions the easiest. And open strings and low positions naturally go together, because scales and chords played in low positions often include open strings in their very makeup. (The higher you go on the neck, the less likely you are to encounter those easy-to-play open strings.) Finally, the pieces here include no difficult fingering techniques such as barres or slurs.

Lemon sorbet and rice pudding are both desserts, but one is light and smooth while the other is thick and chunky; that is, they have different textures. Musical compositions have texture, too. Some sound light and airy (a flute duet, for example) while others sound heavy and dense (a funeral march played by a full orchestra). Texture can also refer to how the notes of a composition relate to each other. For example, are they played one at a time or all together? Do they work with each other or against each other? And how densely layered is the piece? Is it written for two instruments or 50? The classical guitar is such a versatile instrument that it can create a myriad of textures all by itself.

Coordinating Contrapuntal Music: Layered Melodies

Sometimes composers create music by combining individual melodies that are independent of each other yet sound good together. Music containing independent melodies is known as *counterpoint* — or, to use the adjective, *contrapuntal* music. Often (but not always), a contrapuntal piece includes nothing but those melodies; that is, no instrument plays any actual chords. If a chord does occur, it's because the various melodies happen to meet at a certain point and coincidentally (perhaps accidentally) produce one, not because the composer decided to put a chord there.

The simplest contrapuntal music is music that has two parts. That is, it contains just two melodies, usually a high one (often called the *treble,* or *treble part*) and a low one, which can sometimes be thought of as a bass line. J. S. Bach's two-part inventions (which he wrote for the keyboard) are well-known examples of two-part counterpoint. But how can you tell, you may wonder, whether the low melody part is a true bass line or simply a low melody line? One answer is that it makes no difference what you prefer to call it. But perhaps a better answer is that it depends on how the low part sounds. For example, a low part made up of long sustained notes, or of many repeated notes, can be considered a bass line, whereas a low part that moves a lot, as a melody does, can be thought of as part of the contrapuntal fabric (that is, as one of the independent melodies).

In classical guitar music, you always play the low part (whether you choose to call it a bass line or a low melody) with your thumb and the high part(s) of your fingers. By the way, in contrapuntal guitar compositions you rarely see more than two melodies combined, because playing more than two independent parts on the guitar is technically quite difficult. However, the upper melody can often be thickened with double-stops.

Another term for counterpoint is *polyphony,* which comes from the Greek and literally means "many voices." So, contrapuntal music (music containing a number of independent melodies) can also be referred to as *polyphonic* music.

Playing two melodies in sync rhythmically

The easiest way to start playing counterpoint is with music that contains only two lines (melodies) that happen to be in the same rhythm. Now, you can understandably argue that because they're in the same rhythm, the melodies aren't truly independent of each other — and you'd be right. But for now, concentrate on how your fingers and thumb work together to play two melodies without having to worry about executing independent rhythms. The exercise that follows gives your thumb and fingers a workout without taxing your rhythmic sense.

PLAY THIS!

In Figure 2-1 (Track 100 at 0:00), a two-part arrangement of the famous Christmas carol "O Little Town of Bethlehem," play all the low notes with your thumb, and use any comfortable combination of *i* (index) and *m* (middle) for the top *voice* (part, or melody). Because the thumb and one of the fingers sometimes must play on adjacent strings (making a rest stroke impossible), use all free strokes on this one.

WARNING!

Pay special attention to places where the thumb and finger play on adjacent strings. That's where the free stroke follow-throughs may cause your thumb and finger to bump into each other. But if you watch your right-hand position (that is, if you keep your right hand perpendicular to the strings), your thumb should extend well to the left of your fingers, and bumping shouldn't be a problem.

Book VI

Classical Guitar

Figure 2-1: "O Little Town of Bethlehem" played with thumb and fingers together.

Opposing forces: Separating the thumb and fingers rhythmically

Music whose parts are all played in the same rhythm can become boring fast. In this section, your thumb and fingers play melodies that are truly independent; that is, they're independent in rhythm as well as in pitch.

The tricky part of playing two independent melodies is that you have to keep track of two rhythms at the same time, which, until you get used to it, is sort of like rubbing your stomach and patting your head. Just make sure to count the required number of beats in each measure properly. For example, in 3/4 time, even though you see what may look like six beats (three in the upper part and three in the lower), count the beats simultaneously for a total of three, not six. And keep in mind that if you have trouble counting any of the rhythms, you can listen to the audio tracks for help.

Figure 2-2 (Track 100 at 0:23) comes from a *minuet* (a ballroom dance) by an unknown composer of the late 17th century. This arrangement (adaptation for guitar) is especially easy to play because of the numerous open strings in the bass part. Play this exercise using free strokes and with any comfortable combination of right-hand fingers.

Figure 2-2: Minuet in A Minor played with thumb and fingers separated rhythmically.

Thickening the upper part by adding double-stops

The exercise in the previous section is pretty, but it doesn't sound especially full because it consists of only two single-note parts. In this section, you thicken the texture by adding some *double-stops* (two notes played together) to the upper part. Actually, if you play a double-stop in the upper part along with a bass note, you're playing three notes at once — a chord! And chords help classical guitar pieces sound full. Playing three notes at once isn't especially difficult. Just make sure to keep your right hand relaxed and your fingers nicely aligned. Depending on the strings involved, you can play the top notes of the chords with *i-m* (index-middle), *m-a* (middle-annular, or ring), or *i-a* (index-annular).

Book VI

Classical Guitar

Figure 2-3 (Track 100 at 0:43) comes from a *gavotte* (a French dance popular in the 18th century) by German-born composer and organist George Frederick Handel (1685–1759), who, along with J. S. Bach, was the giant of music's Baroque era. This piece is good for practice because it offers a little of everything: single notes, double-stops (pinches), and three-note chords, with a nice variety of string combinations on those chords (that is, sometimes the strings that make up a chord are adjacent or close together; other times they're far apart).

Figure 2-3: Gavotte in A played in contrapuntal style with texture thickened by chords.

Melody and Accompaniment: Using All Your Fingers

In this section, you play pieces in which a single melody predominates. What makes this style — which we call *melody and accompaniment* — tricky is that while the melody is nothing but single notes, the accompaniment can take any form at all: full chords, double-stops, or anything that the composer (or an arranger) dreams up. Here you need to contend with, among other things, four-note chords and conflicting rhythms.

The technical term for music with one main melody (and accompaniment) — especially when the melody and accompaniment are in the same rhythm — is *homophony,* which comes from the Greek and literally means "same sound." So you can also refer to music in melody-and-accompaniment style as *homophonic* music.

Matching rhythm between accompaniment and melody

The simplest way to play melody-and-accompaniment style is to play the accompaniment in the same rhythm as the melody — an approach known as *block chord* style, or *block* style. It's simple because it allows you to concentrate on playing chords without concerning yourself with conflicting rhythms (that may exist between the melody and accompaniment).

When playing block style, even though you're playing nothing but chords, bring out the top note of each chord so that the listener hears those top notes as the melody. You can't use rest strokes to bring out the top notes, however, because the lower adjacent string is also being played and needs to ring out. So accentuate the top notes simply by plucking them slightly louder than the other notes of the chord.

Figure 2-4 (Track 100 at 0:59), an arrangement of the famous Christmas carol "O Christmas Tree," combines the melody and accompaniment in a series of simple three-note chords. For the right hand, play all free strokes and use *p-i-m, p-m-a,* or *p-i-a,* depending on the strings involved and on what feels comfortable to you.

Figure 2-4:
"O Christmas Tree" played in three-note block chord style.

Book VI

Classical Guitar

Normally in printed classical guitar music, notes taken by the thumb are written with their stems pointing down from the note head (and this arrangement could have been notated that way). However, because the thumb and fingers play in the same rhythm, indicating separate voices (with up and down stems) is unnecessary. Nevertheless, make sure to play the bottom note of each three-note chord with your thumb.

Getting creative with the flow: Two parts, two rhythms

Now let's break away from block style to examine melody and accompaniment the way it most often appears — with the rhythm of the accompaniment *not* paralleling that of the melody. In other words, the accompaniment has its own rhythm. But whereas in counterpoint a melody is supported by another melody, in melody-and-accompaniment style the melody is supported by, well, an accompaniment — and that means an accompaniment that's mainly chordal in nature. So, in this section you play music that contains melody and chords, but because their rhythms are different, the music seems to nicely flow along.

In melody and accompaniment playing (whether block style or normal, "flowing" style), bring out the top notes so the listener will discern them as a melody.

Figure 2-5 (Track 100 at 1:18) comes from an *andante* (a piece played at a moderately slow tempo) by Spanish guitar composer and virtuoso Fernando Sor (1778–1839). Although the melody and accompaniment are in different rhythms, they're rather simple, so you shouldn't have difficulty combining them.

Figure 2-5: Andante in E Minor played in flowing, melody-and-accompaniment style.

Playing Easy Pieces in Different Textural Styles

The four pieces in this section — in different styles and by a variety of composers — sound like what they are: real guitar performance pieces. These are pieces that you can play for your friends (or your parents or your date, as the case may be) and duly impress them with your talent and skill. Here's some useful information about the pieces to help you along:

✔ **Minuet in G (Track 101):** This minuet, a ballroom dance of the 18th century by German composer and organist J. S. Bach (1685–1750), wasn't originally written for guitar, but because of its beauty and simplicity, it's performed by guitarists with great frequency. The piece is rather famous, too. As explained by the character Mr. Holland in the 1995 film *Mr. Holland's Opus,* it was used as the basis for the 1965 pop hit "A Lover's Concerto," by the Toys.

Notice that when one voice is rhythmically active (playing eighth notes), the other is relatively inactive (playing longer notes), and that the active part sometimes switches from voice to voice. This type of interplay (with fast notes against slow ones and with the active rhythm moving from voice to voice) is typical of Bach's music and of contrapuntal music in general. And that's a good thing, not only because it makes the music interesting but also because on the guitar it's easier to play one actively moving voice than two. You'll find that as you play this piece, if you focus on the rhythm of the active part, the rhythm of the other part seems to automatically take care of itself.

✔ **Air in A Minor (Track 102):** *Air* is another word for melody or song, and this one was written by the preeminent English Baroque composer Henry Purcell (1659–1695). The arrangement offers single notes, pinches, and chords — and a nice variety of string combinations on those chords.

Note that in measure 9, beat 3, the upper voice moves so low that it actually converges with the bass. Although that note has stems pointing both up and down, implying that it can be taken by either the thumb or a finger, you'll find it easier to take with the thumb. Also notice that in bars 3 and 4 the fingering is tricky because the first finger must suddenly jump from the 2nd string down to the 6th and then up to the 3rd. You may find it helpful to isolate those two measures for special practice.

✔ **"America (My Country 'Tis of Thee) (Track 103)":** This arrangement uses many four-note chords in block style. When playing four-note chords, keep your hand in a steady but relaxed position and let all the motion come only from the thumb and fingers. But the arrangement also contains three-note chords, and pinches — and a couple of single notes to boot! In other words, a little of everything, so it's a good piece for practice. As always, use the thumb for all notes with stems down. For notes with stems up, use whichever fingers feel most natural (but with four-note chords always fingered *p-i-m-a*).

✔ **Andante in G (Track 104):** This andante was composed by Fernando Sor, and it offers some nice interplay between melody and accompaniment. Pay special attention to the rests; that is, don't let a note before a rest continue to ring into the beat the rest falls on. If that note happens to be fretted (measure 5, beat 3, for example), simply release the left-hand finger pressure to stop the note from sounding. But if the string is open (measure 13, beat 3, for instance), you need to lightly touch it with a finger (of whichever hand feels more natural) to stop it from sounding. You'll find that as you become proficient, your hands automatically stop strings from sounding when necessary without even having to think about it.

As usual, take advantage of all guide finger opportunities, as in measures 7, 9, 10, 15, and 16. Measures 15 and 16, in fact, are a guide finger extravaganza. You use two guide fingers at the same time (fingers 1 and 2), making it a "double guide finger," and those fingers guide your hand down the neck twice in a row (from 3rd position to 2nd, then from 2nd position to 1st), making it a "double double guide finger"!

Book VI

Classical Guitar

Minuet in G

Air in A Minor

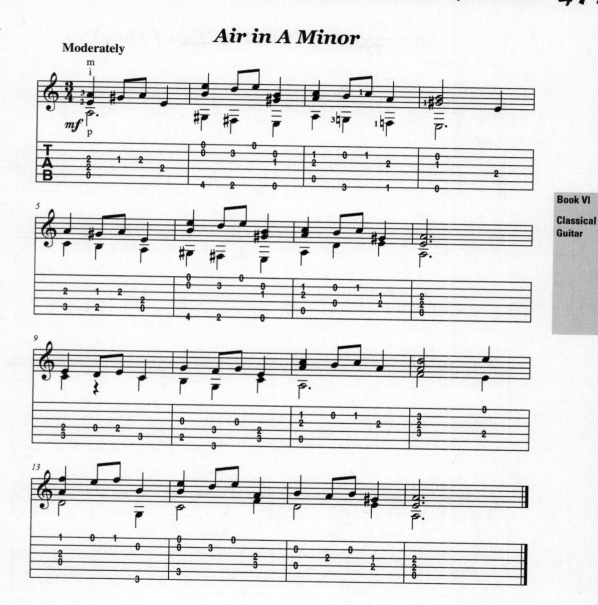

Book VI

Classical
Guitar

America (My Country 'Tis of Thee)

Andante in G

Chapter 3

Combining Arpeggios and Melody

In This Chapter

▶ Understanding how arpeggios combine with melodies

▶ Combining arpeggios with melodies in the bass and in the treble

▶ Shifting the melody between the thumb and fingers

▶ Practicing pieces with arpeggios and melodies

▶ Access the audio tracks at www.dummies.com/go/guitaraio/

*P*erhaps nothing is more satisfying to a classical guitarist than a composition that deftly combines *arpeggios* (chords played one note at a time) and melodies. And the reason is simple: To a listener, the piece sounds intricate and advanced (sometimes even virtuosic), yet typically, it's not very difficult to play. So, with such pieces, you can amaze (or at least impress) your friends — without being a Segovia.

This chapter shows you how melody and arpeggios work together quite simply to create beautiful pieces, and we show you how to play them with ease.

Grasping the Combination in Context

Combining a melody with an arpeggio is often a matter of simply playing the notes you're already fingering (rather than having to play additional notes) — the melody's notes are usually contained within the arpeggio itself. Also, when you play an arpeggio, all or many of the chord's notes are either open strings or are already held down (as a chord) by your left hand. Your right-hand fingers, too, are already in position — each resting in preparedness against its respective string. In other words, your hands hardly move for the duration of each chord!

How, you may wonder, can you simultaneously play notes with various values (that is, quarter notes, whole notes, eighth-notes, and so on) and keep them from sounding like a blur of overlapping pitches while also letting them all ring out as long as possible in each measure? The answer is that you actually play the notes at different levels of loudness — or, perhaps, different levels of emphasis. You do that by giving more *oomph* to some notes than to others.

The human touch (your touch, as determined by your understanding of the notes' roles and interactions) imparts the proper textural feel to the listener — and that's what makes playing such pieces so exciting. If you give the right amount of emphasis to the respective notes (even merely psychologically), the effect comes across to the listener, who hears the music not as just a blur of overlapping pitches but as a melody, an accompaniment, and a bass line. The technique for doing that varies, depending on whether you play the melody with your thumb or fingers.

As always when playing arpeggios, hold down your left-hand fingers as a chord whenever possible and for as long as possible. And keep the motion of your right hand to a minimum by resting your fingers ahead of time against the strings they need to play in each arpeggio. For example, before playing an A minor arpeggio (as in measure 1 in Figure 3-1), your thumb should be resting against the 5th string, your index finger against the 3rd string, and your middle finger against the 2nd string. While playing each arpeggio, your right hand itself doesn't move; only your fingers and thumb move as they strike their respective strings.

The sections that follow present exercises that allow you to combine arpeggios with melodies in the bass (played by the thumb) and the treble (played by the fingers), and explores ways to draw the melody out of the background and into the limelight, where it belongs.

Going Downtown: Melody in the Bass

The melody of a classical guitar piece, though usually played by the fingers on the high strings (in the treble), is sometimes played by the thumb on the low strings (in the bass). (This concept applies to the piano, too, by the way. The right hand plays the melody of most pieces, though for a different effect, the melody can be placed in the left hand.)

You may find it easier to combine arpeggios with a melody played by your thumb than by your fingers. For one thing, your thumb usually plays *on* the beat (rather than between the beats, as the fingers do). For another, you have no decisions to make about *which* finger plays the melody; that is, your thumb, acting alone, plays nothing but the melody notes while your fingers play nothing but the accompaniment (the higher notes of each arpeggio).

Don't worry about having to hunt down the melody in a piece. The melody usually reveals itself soon enough when you start to play, just in the way the composer or arranger wrote the notes. (Sometimes the written music itself even offers clues, such as giving the melody its own stem direction.) After you're able to hear where the melody falls, you can work to bring it out further, using slightly stronger strokes on the melody notes themselves. Or, if the piece has no melody at all (which sometimes happens in short passages between melodic phrases), you hear that, too, and give no emphasis to any particular notes.

Playing a bass melody within arpeggios

How do you bring out the notes when the melody is in the bass line? Just play them a little louder (striking them a little harder) than the other notes, and make sure the other notes are consistent with each other in loudness.

Figure 3-1 is an exercise that offers you an opportunity to practice the basic technique of combining arpeggios with a bass melody without having to worry about any of the complicated rhythms or unusual left-hand fingerings that real-life pieces may contain.

Note that the first note of each triplet group has a downward stem (in addition to an upward stem). Those downward stems tell you not only to play those notes with your thumb but also to play them as quarter notes; in other words, to let them ring throughout the beat.

Now, alert reader that you are, you may point out that one of the rules of arpeggio playing is that all the notes of an arpeggio should ring out (rather than be stopped short) — so all those bass notes would sound as quarter notes anyway. And you're right. So in reality, those downward stems on the first note of each triplet group tell you not only to play them with the thumb and to let them ring out but also to bring out those thumb notes so that a listener hears them as an independent melody.

Measure 2 presents an interesting right-hand fingering dilemma. Normal, or typical, right-hand position has the index finger assigned to the 3rd string, the middle finger to the 2nd, and the ring finger to the 1st. Also, you generally try not to move the right hand itself, if at all possible. For those reasons, you'd expect to use fingers *m* and *a* to play the top two notes of the D minor arpeggio.

But another rule of arpeggio playing says that you should use the strongest fingers whenever possible — and the combination of *i* and *m* is stronger than that of *m* and *a*. So, according to that rule, you should use *i* and *m* for the top two strings (even though you have to move your right hand across the neck a bit). Hence the dilemma.

The important point is that when you have a situation in which those right-hand fingering rules conflict, the "strong fingers" rule takes precedence over the "minimize motion" rule, and thus we indicate in measure 2 that you play the top two notes of the D minor arpeggio with *i* and *m*.

Figure 3-1 (Track 105) presents no technical difficulties, but for best results, follow the left-hand fingering carefully, and keep the rhythm as steady and even as possible.

Book VI

Classical Guitar

Figure 3-1:
Arpeggio
exercise
with melody
in bass.

Practicing making a bass melody stand out

Figure 3-2 (Track 106) is taken from a study by early 19th-century Spanish guitar virtuoso Dionisio Aguado. It features a single right-hand pattern throughout (*p-i-m-i*) and a uniform rhythm. That's what makes it easy to play. But at the same time, the study is somewhat challenging for a few reasons.

p-i-m-a: What it stands for

When you see fingerings that specify *p, i, m,* or *a,* remember that each one stands for a particular finger. The letters don't quite match up with our English words for fingers because they actually stand for the Spanish words for the fingers.

Here's what p-i-m-a stands for:

p: "*Pulgar*" in Spanish, *thumb* in English

i: "*Indice*" in Spanish, *index* in English

m: "*Medio*" in Spanish, *middle* in English

a: "*Anular*" in Spanish, *ring* in English

Figure 3-2: Study in A Minor, with the melody in the bass.

First, the notes are sixteenth, which means that they move along rather briskly. So start out by practicing slowly, then gradually increase the tempo. Second, the bass notes — because they're all chord tones that occur at the beginning of each four-note group — have a tendency to sound like nothing more than simply the first note of each arpeggio. So it's your job to make them especially melodic; that is, bring them out forcefully — but smoothly and sweetly — so that a listener hears a "tune" in the bass. Finally, you play some of the notes on strings you may not expect. Check out measure 2, beat 4, for example, where, in order to preserve the right-hand pattern (and flow), you play the C on the 3rd string, and the repeated E's alternate between the 2nd and 1st strings.

For ease of playing, pay special attention to the left-hand fingering (and especially to the guide finger indications). And for an effective performance, keep the rhythm as even as possible.

Moving Uptown: Melody in the Treble

Melodies in the bass are a bit easier to combine with arpeggios than are melodies in the treble. However, arpeggio pieces with melodies in the treble are actually more common than those with melodies in the bass, and in this section we look at the technique you use to play such pieces.

Playing arpeggios with the melody in the treble rather than the bass can be a bit trickier for a few reasons, as the following list explains:

- ✔ **Question of fingering:** Technically, any given melody note can be taken with any available finger — *i, m,* or *a* — and it's often up to you to decide which to use. (See nearby sidebar for a refresher on the *p-i-m-a* system.)

- ✔ **Use of the ring finger:** Because the *i* and *m* fingers usually play accompaniment notes on the inner strings, the *a* finger takes many melody notes. The problem is that the melody notes must be emphasized, but the ring finger is the weakest.

- ✔ **Question of right-hand technique:** As explained in the sections that follow, you have more than one way to bring out a treble melody from an arpeggio, and it's up to you to decide which technique to use.

- ✔ **Use of rest strokes:** Whereas you play arpeggios with a melody in the bass with free strokes only, you generally combine rest strokes and free strokes when you play arpeggios with a melody in the treble.

- ✔ **Complexity of notation:** Standard music notation for arpeggio pieces with a melody in the treble often requires the indication of three separate parts, or *voices* — one each for the melody, the accompaniment (usually filler notes on the inner strings), and the bass. Normally, stem directions tell you which notes belong to which part (for example, notes with stems up are melody and notes with stems down are bass). Depending on the musical context (or sometimes simply on the amount of available space), the accompaniment notes may be stemmed either down (sometimes making them hard to distinguish from bass notes) or up (sometimes making them hard to distinguish from melody notes). Sometimes, at the whim of a composer or arranger, the melody and accompaniment notes are combined into a single voice (as a continuous flow of upstemmed eighth notes, for example), and it's up to you, using your ear, to discover the real melody.

Although the aforementioned potential complications may cause you concern, remember that most arpeggiated pieces — even those with the melody in the treble — aren't difficult to play. That's because, as stated, in such pieces, the left hand generally holds down a chord, and the melody notes themselves are often contained within that chord.

To bring out the melody in the treble, you have to make it either louder than, or different in tone from, the other notes. You can do this simply by

- ✔ Making the melody notes sound stronger than the others by playing them with rest strokes (and the accompaniment notes with free strokes). You can also try the techniques in the following bullets, but this technique — the use of rest strokes for melody notes — is generally used by classical guitarists, and it's the one you should strive to perfect.

- ✔ Striking the melody notes harder than the others (as you do when you bring out a bass melody with the thumb).

✔ Making the melody notes brighter-sounding than the others by using more nail when you strike them (that is, if you play with a combination of flesh and nail, use more nail than flesh on the melody notes, and more flesh than nail on the accompaniment notes).

Playing a treble melody within arpeggios

Figure 3-3 (Track 107) is an exercise that allows you to combine a treble melody with a series of arpeggios. Note that you play the melody in quarter notes (indicated by upward quarter-note stems), that the bass notes are whole notes (and thus must ring throughout each measure), and that the accompaniment notes are eighth-note triplets, which, though they're written as short notes, should also ring out (according to the general rules of arpeggio playing).

Practice Figure 3-3 using rest strokes on all the melody notes. Start out playing slowly (but evenly), then gradually increase your speed. Follow the left-hand fingerings to ensure that you can hold down each chord with your left hand for as long as possible. If necessary, listen to Track 107 to hear how the piece works rhythmically and how the separate voices interact.

Book VI

Classical Guitar

Figure 3-3: Arpeggio exercise with melody in treble.

Practicing making a treble melody stand out

Figure 3-4 (Track 108) comes from a study by late 19th-century Spanish guitar virtuoso Francisco Tárrega. It employs a consistent right-hand pattern throughout: *p-i-m, a-m-i, a-m-i, a-m-i.* Play all the melody notes as rest strokes with the ring finger.

Note that the bass notes sustain throughout each arpeggio, but in measure 3, fingering requirements force you to stop the bass from ringing one beat early (as the finger that plays the bass note, the first finger, is suddenly needed on the 1st string to play the last melody note of the measure).

Figure 3-4: Study in C, with the melody in the treble.

Mixing Up Your Melodic Moves: The Thumb and Fingers Take Turns

Not all arpeggiated passages are as straightforward as those you encounter earlier in this chapter — where the melody occurs consistently in either the treble or bass part. In some cases the melody moves back and forth between the treble and bass, and in others the treble and bass parts contain melodic motion simultaneously. Fortunately, the playing of such pieces requires no new techniques, but it does require a heightened awareness (on your part) of where the melody is and how to bring it out.

Playing a shifting treble-and-bass melody within arpeggios

In Figure 3-5 (Track 109), from measure to measure, the melody alternates between the treble and bass. In the odd-numbered measures, which have the melody in the treble, bring out the melody (the upstemmed notes) with rest strokes. For the even-numbered measures, which have the melody in the bass, bring out the melody (the downstemmed notes) by giving the first note of each triplet a little more *oomph* than the other notes.

Book VI

Classical Guitar

Figure 3-5: Arpeggio exercise with melody alternating between treble and bass.

Note that the melody note that occurs on the third beat of each measure is a *dissonance* (that is, it's not a member of the chord being arpeggiated), but that it passes smoothly from one chord tone to another. For example, in measure 1, in which an E minor chord (made up of the notes E, G, and B) is arpeggiated, the F♯ on beat 3 functions as a *passing tone* (a dissonance that, in stepwise motion, passes between, and thus fills the gap between, two chord tones — in this case, G and E). Also note, as a point of interest, that each bass melody is a repetition, but two octaves lower, of the treble melody that precedes it. Repetition imparts structural unity and thus a sense of balance to a composition.

Practicing making a shifting melody stand out

Figure 3-6 (Track 110) is an excerpt from a waltz from the guitar method of early 19th-century Italian guitar composer and virtuoso Ferdinando Carulli. A glance at the music reveals that the melody begins in the bass (measures 1 and 2) and moves to the treble (measures 3 through 5).

In measures 3 and 4, note that in the written notation, for the sake of simplicity, the composer combined the melody (the upstemmed notes on the beats: F♯-G-F♯, G-F♯-G) and the accompaniment notes (the open B's) into a single voice. What you need to realize is that although the melody notes are written as eighths, you render them in performance as quarters.

In Figure 3-5 you play a dissonance known as a passing tone. In Figure 3-6, Waltz in E Minor presents another type of dissonance: the neighboring tone. A neighboring tone is a non-chord tone that, in stepwise motion, follows a chord tone and then returns to it (with the word *neighboring* obviously coming from the idea that, being just one step away from the chord tone, the dissonant note is like the chord tone's next-door neighbor). For example, in measure 3 you arpeggiate a B chord (B-D♯-F♯), and the G on beat 2 follows and then returns to the chord tone F♯. Because G is above F♯ in the scale, it's called, specifically, an upper neighbor. In the following measure you arpeggiate an E minor chord (E-G-B), and the F♯ on beat 2 (following and then returning to G) is a lower neighbor.

Figure 3-6: Waltz in E Minor, with the melody alternating between the bass and treble.

Book VI

Classical Guitar

Playing Pieces That Combine Arpeggios and Melodies

Unlike simple arpeggio-and-melody practice exercises, which generally feature easy left-hand fingerings or consistent right-hand patterns, real-life pieces often contain complications in the form of some not-so-easy fingerings and not-so-consistent patterns. This section offers, for your practice and enjoyment, pieces by classical guitar masters that combine arpeggios with melodies — one with the melody in the bass, one with the melody in the treble, and one with a melody that moves between the treble and bass. Here's some information to help you with the pieces:

> ✔ **Ländler in D (Track 111):** A *ländler* is an Austrian folk dance in 3/4 time (or a musical piece to accompany such a dance), and this one was composed by 19th-century Hungarian guitar virtuoso Johann Kaspar Mertz.
>
> Play notes with stems both up and down (generally on beats 1 and 3 in the first section and on each beat in the second) with the thumb, and bring them out as a melody (and remember to hold down all the notes of each measure as a chord whenever possible).

In measures 13 through 20, you play only a single note after each bass note, and so the patterns aren't true arpeggios. That is, an arpeggio is a "broken chord," and a chord, by definition, contains three or more notes. However, in that section, if you think of each beat as a two-note "chord," then you can see that you're still playing in arpeggio style (meaning that the thumb and fingers alternate).

In two-note arpeggio figures (as in measures 13 through 20), your thumb, of course, plays all the bass notes. You play the treble notes, if they change pitch from beat to beat, by alternating between *i* and *m*. But if the pitch of the treble notes remains constant, as in this instance, you usually play the notes with just one finger — either *i* or *m* (depending on which strings your thumb plays and how close they are to the treble string in question). Try measures 13 through 20 first using *i* for all the open E's and then using *m*, and see which fingering you prefer.

✔ **"Romanza" (Track 112):** This is one of the all-time most famous classical guitar pieces; virtually every classical guitarist encounters it and plays it at some time or another. It is known by several titles, including "Romanza," "Romance," "Spanish Romance," and "Romance d'Amour." In most collections that include it, the composer is said to be anonymous, which may lead you to believe that the piece was written hundreds of years ago. Actually, the piece isn't nearly that old, and the identity of the composer isn't so much unknown as it is in *doubt,* or in *dispute;* a number of composers have claimed authorship of this piece.

As indicated, play all the melody notes with the *a* (ring) finger, and bring them out by emphasizing, or accenting, them slightly. Even though *a* may be the weakest finger, it's charged with the important work of carrying the melody here.

What makes this piece relatively easy is the great number of open strings (as is typically the case with pieces in the key of E minor). What makes it difficult (besides the many barre chords) are the left-hand stretches in measures 10, 27, and 28. Isolate those measures and practice them separately, if necessary. And what makes the piece interesting (besides its inherent beauty) is the shift from the minor to the major key in the second section (at measure 17), and then the return to the minor key after measure 32. Note the double-sharp in measure 20, which tells you to play the note *two* frets higher than the natural version.

✔ **Andante in C (Track 113):** Just as Carulli did with Waltz in E Minor in Figure 3-6, so too did early 19th-century Italian guitar virtuoso Matteo Carcassi combine the melody and accompaniment notes into a single part. But whereas in the Carulli piece it's obvious which notes are melody and which are accompaniment, this piece has a certain amount of ambiguity. Sometimes, as in the first two full measures, it's easy to discern the melody: It's made up of the notes that occur at beats 1, 2, and 4 (and which you should render in performance as a quarter note, a half note, and a quarter). But in the next measure, is the A on beat 4 melody or accompaniment? And in the measure after, are the final three notes (G, F, and D) melody or accompaniment? Only Carcassi could answer definitively, but because you can't ask him, it's up to you, the performer, to answer such questions by bringing out (or not bringing out) those ambiguous notes accordingly.

If you look at the piece's second section (measures 10 through 17), you see that the upper voice contains a melody (albeit intermingled with accompaniment notes in the same voice) and that the bass part also moves melodically. This really gives you an opportunity to practice your melody/arpeggio chops (or to display them, as the case may be). All at once you have to decide which of the upstemmed notes you consider the real melody notes, to bring out those notes from the notes that function merely as accompaniment, and to also bring out the separate melody that occurs in the bass!

Book VI

Classical Guitar

Because Carcassi's notation leaves some unanswered questions, you may wonder why he didn't employ three separate voices in his notation — one for the upper melody, one for the filler (accompaniment) notes, and one for the bass line. He could have, and some pieces are so notated. However, the risk is that the notation is so complicated that it's counterproductive. That's why Carcassi chose to notate the piece as he did. But that doesn't mean a different composer may have notated it as three separate voices.

Ländler in D

Moderately slow

Book VI

Classical Guitar

D.C. al Fine

Romanza

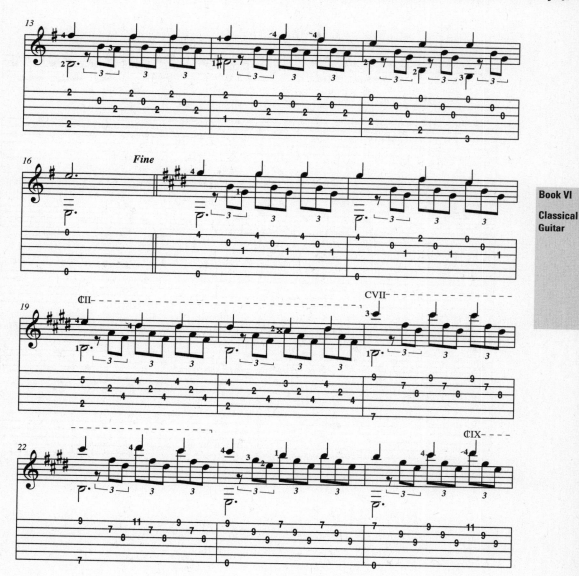

Andante in C

D.S. al Fine

Book VII
Exercises: Practice, Practice, Practice

Contents at a Glance

Chapter 1: Putting the Major Scales to Use in Your Playing 503

Practicing Five Major Scale Patterns 504
Applying Your Scale Work to Actual Pieces of Music 513

Chapter 2: Adding Major Scale Sequences to Your Repertoire 517

Practicing Major Scale Sequences...518
Putting Your Sequence Skills to Work with a Few Songs..............................526

Chapter 3: Tackling the Three Minor Scales .531

Familiarizing Yourself with Natural Minor Scales..532
Raising the Bar with Melodic Minor Scales 540
Harmonizing with Harmonic Minor Scales..549
Playing Pieces Using the Three Minor Scales 557

Chapter 4: Building Finger Independence with Chord Exercises . . .561

Practicing Inversion Patterns...562
Playing Chord Progressions...580
Practicing Pieces that Use Chord Progressions 582

Chapter 1

Putting the Major Scales to Use in Your Playing

In This Chapter

▶ Playing major scales using five patterns

▶ Performing pieces using the major scales

▶ Access the audio track at www.dummies.com/go/guitaraio/

*P*racticing scales may sound boring, but it's a discipline that guitarists use to perfect their technique, especially their right-hand technique. Think about this: Classical guitar great Andrés Segovia recommended practicing scales two hours a day! For guitarists who use a pick, rather than their fingers and nails, these scales are an excellent medium to work on alternate picking.

Most music is based on scales. So if you learn and memorize where the scale patterns and positions are, your fingers will know what to do when you see a scale in music. Playing whole passages of notes becomes automatic.

So how do you get to such a place? By taking common scale patterns and playing them repeatedly until you know them cold. "Practice makes perfect," the saying goes, and it's true. You not only memorize the notes through repeated playings, but you gradually increase the strength and elasticity of your fingers, which allows you to play more difficult music later on. Sound like exercise? Well, it is, except that it's exercise for your fingers and your brain. And just like swimming, running, or biking, you need to do it several times a week to improve. For learning guitar, it's best to practice every day, even if you can manage only a little on some days.

In this chapter, you discover five patterns for playing the major scale. Each pattern has its own particular advantages, which we touch on along the way. At the end of the chapter, you get a real piece of music to play.

After you memorize each fingering pattern in this chapter, simply move it up or down the neck to a different starting note to produce other major scales. The familiar *do, re, mi, fa, sol, la, ti, do* sound (think Maria von Trapp and The Sound of Music here) stays the same, but as you switch positions, the key, or letter name, of the scale changes.

Practicing Five Major Scale Patterns

You can play major scales in position (meaning that the left-hand fingers cover four consecutive frets and that the position is named for the fret played by the 1st finger) by applying five unique fingerings. So, with 12 major scales and five fingering options for each scale, you're looking at 60 major scales in position. All of these options are what make the guitar so incredibly cool. You can play a lot of music by simply memorizing five patterns, and you can play it many different ways — according to the best pattern for the situation or by changing keys easily while maintaining a pattern. These options also show why you need to practice: There's a lot to master!

As you practice, play each major scale from low to high, slowly, loudly, and deliberately at first to help develop the muscles in your hand and fingers — similar to the way athletes might lift weights. Then play it faster and lighter to more closely approach how the music is actually played in performance. Just be sure to maintain your starting tempo and dynamic level (loudness) throughout the scale.

Major scale pattern #1

Major scale pattern #1 starts with the 2nd finger on the 6th string (see Figure 1-1, Track 114 at 0:00). Notice that the first note of the exercise has a fingering indication in the music staff. What we're talking about is the small 2 to the left of the A notehead. This indicator tells you to use your left-hand 2nd finger to play that note. Keep in mind that the 2nd finger is actually one fret higher than the name of the position (which is always defined as the fret number that the 1st finger plays). Practice this pattern as many times as you need to in order to feel comfortable playing it.

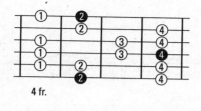

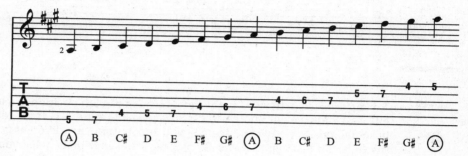

Figure 1-1:
An A major
scale in 4th
position in
both a neck
diagram and
in music
and tab.

Book VII

**Exercises:
Practice,
Practice,
Practice**

PLAY THIS!

After you can adeptly finger this pattern in all keys, practice it in rhythm using the exercise shown in Figure 1-2 (Track 114 at 0:35). This exercise is in the key of G major in 2nd position and in ascending and descending eighth notes. Play it in a steady beat (using a metronome or a foot tap) and try to make the music flow. The exercise may be "just a scale," but you can still make it musical by employing accents (striking the string slightly harder on certain notes, usually on the beat), and varying the length of the notes from sustained (called legato) to crisp and clipped (staccato).

Figure 1-2:
Practicing in the key of G major in 2nd position and in ascending and descending eighth notes.

Try major scale pattern #1 in the key of B♭ major in 5th position in ascending and descending eighth-note triplets, as shown in Figure 1-3 (Track 114 at 0:54). In actual music (versus just scales), you encounter many types of rhythms, not just eighth notes. So playing scales in triplets helps you mix things up a bit, rhythmically speaking. Try to give your triplets a skipping or lilting feel.

Figure 1-3:
Pattern #1 in the key of B♭ major in 5th position.

Figure 1-4 (Track 114 at 1:11) shows major scale pattern #1 in the key of C major in 7th position in ascending and descending sixteenth notes. This exercise brings you back to even numbers (from the triplets of the previous exercise), but the notes now come four to the beat instead of two. So play these sixteenth notes a little faster than you would play eighth notes. This way you get used to playing quickly as well as moderately.

Figure 1-4:
Pattern #1 in the key of C major in 7th position.

Major scale pattern #2

Major scale pattern #2 starts with the 4th finger on the 6th string and includes one out-of-position note on the 4th string. An out-of-position note is one that doesn't fall within the four-fret span defined by the position and that requires a stretch to play. You must stretch up (higher on the neck, toward the bridge) with your 4th finger to reach this note, because it occurs one fret above where the finger naturally falls.

Wherever these patterns contain out-of-position notes, pay special attention, because these spots are where you might play a wrong note or just have trouble playing the right one correctly. If you can't perform the out-of-position note correctly, try isolating the passage with the problem note and playing it a few times by itself. Then play the whole pattern from start to finish.

Figure 1-5 shows major scale pattern #2 in the key of C major in both a neck diagram and in music and tab format. Note that in addition to the starting finger next to the first note in the music (a 4 to the left of the notehead), another fingering indication is included where an out-of-position note occurs (a 4 next to the 4th-string note B at the 9th fret). Throughout this book, fingerings are indicated for any out-of-position notes, including subsequent notes if there's a chance you might use the wrong finger. Figure 1-5 is just such a case! Practice this pattern as many times as you need to in order to make all the notes sound smooth and effortless. When you use the correct fingerings automatically, you know you're on the right track.

After you can successfully finger this pattern in all keys, practice it in rhythm. Figure 1-6 shows major scale pattern #2 in the key of B♭ major in 3rd position in ascending and descending eighth-note triplets. Don't be afraid of the flats in the key signature of this exercise. Usually guitar music is written in "guitar-friendly" keys, which contain sharps in the key signature. But because you're learning patterns that can be moved around and played in any key with equal ease, a flat key is no more difficult than a sharp key or a key with no flats or sharps at all!

Book VII

**Exercises:
Practice,
Practice,
Practice**

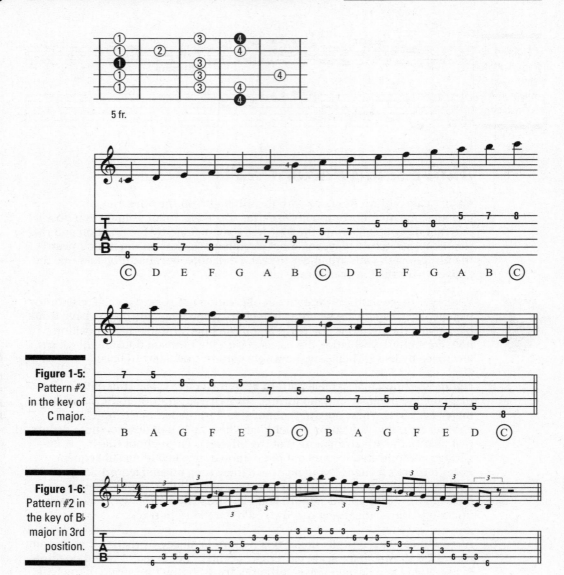

Figure 1-5: Pattern #2 in the key of C major.

Figure 1-6: Pattern #2 in the key of B♭ major in 3rd position.

Major scale pattern #3

Patterns #1 and #2 have a range of two octaves, going from bottom to top. Major scale patterns #3, #4, and #5, on the other hand, span a bit less than two octaves. Playing just a single octave may seem a bit short, so in these patterns, as well as other patterns that span less than two complete octaves, we go as high as the position will allow.

Figure 1-7 shows major scale pattern #3, which starts on the 5th string (not the 6th as in patterns #1 and #2). The pattern is in the key of D major and is shown in both a neck diagram and in music and tab format. Notice that in addition to the starting finger next to the first note in the music (a 2 to the left of the note-head), we include the fingering for the out-of-position note (a 1 next to the 1st-string note G at the 3rd fret). In this stretch, unlike the stretch of pattern #2, you reach down (toward the nut) instead of up. This move helps you get used to stretching in both directions. Practice this pattern as many times as you need to in order to feel as confident starting a scale on the 5th string as you do on the 6th string.

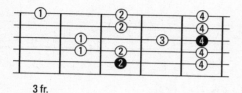

3 fr.

D E F# G A B C# D E F# G A B

Book VII

Exercises: Practice, Practice, Practice

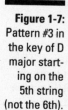

Figure 1-7: Pattern #3 in the key of D major starting on the 5th string (not the 6th).

A G F# E D C# B A G F# E D

After you can confidently play this pattern starting on any 5th-string note, practice it in rhythm with Figure 1-8 which shows major scale pattern #3 in the key of F major in 7th position in ascending and descending sixteenth notes. Because this exercise is in sixteenth notes (which are relatively fast compared to eighth notes or triplets), play it slowly at first to make sure the notes come at a steady rate. After that you can gradually speed up.

Figure 1-8:
Pattern #3 in the key of F major in 7th position.

Major scale pattern #4

Like pattern #3, major scale pattern #4 also begins and ends on the 5th string. This time, though, your starting finger is the 4th finger. The good news is that this position has no out-of-position notes (hooray!). So if you feel up to it, you can play the exercises using major scale pattern #4 with a little more brio (that's music-speak for speed) than the patterns that require stretches.

Figure 1-9 shows major scale pattern #4 in the key of F major in both a neck diagram and in music and tab format. Because this pattern is in the middle of the neck and has no out-of-position notes, you may want to jump right in and play a little faster. Whenever you try an exercise a little faster than you normally would, take a moment to prepare. Then play the entire exercise completely. Don't get into the habit of making "false starts," which is an indication that your fingers are ahead of your brain.

When you're ready, try the exercise shown in Figure 1-10 in rhythm. This figure shows major scale pattern #4 in the key of G major in 7th position. This exercise is an easy one. It's up the neck (where the frets are nicely snuggled together for comfortable playing), it's in eighth notes (which are a little easier to play than triplets or sixteenth notes), and there are no out-of-position notes to stretch for. So try playing this exercise fast from the get-go. You may surprise yourself by playing a lot faster than you think you can. Just be sure whenever you play fast that you don't rush (or play ahead of the tempo). When something seems easy, it's tempting to keep accelerating until you reach your limit. But you have to stay with the tempo established at the outset.

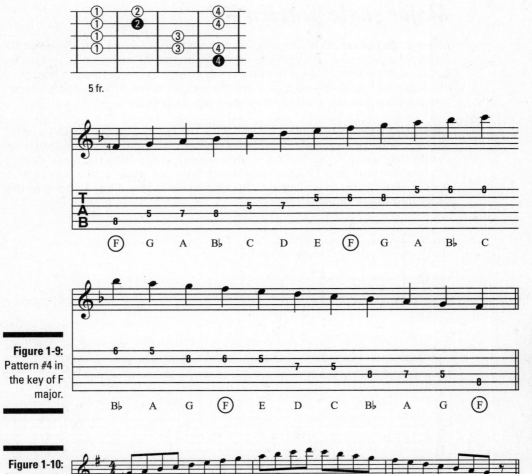

Figure 1-9:
Pattern #4 in the key of F major.

Figure 1-10:
Pattern #4 in the key of G major in 7th position.

Book VII

**Exercises:
Practice,
Practice,
Practice**

Major scale pattern #5

Major scale pattern #5 is a four-string pattern whose lowest note is on the 4th string. The pattern starts with the 1st finger on the 4th string and includes an out-of-position note that occurs on the 4th string. You have to stretch your 4th finger higher on the neck (toward the bridge) to reach this note, because it occurs one fret above where the finger naturally falls.

Figure 1-11 shows major scale pattern #5 in the key of G major in both a neck diagram and in music and tab format. The stretch for the out-of-position note comes right away — on the first string you play — so watch out for it. First practice the stretch in isolation and then try the full pattern. Play this pattern as many times as you need to in order to get it sounding as strong as the other four major scale patterns.

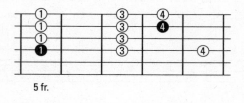

5 fr.

Figure 1-11:
Pattern #5
in the key of
G major.

Figure 1-12 shows major scale pattern #5 in the key of A♭ major in 6th position in ascending and descending eighth-note triplets. Start with your 1st finger on the 4th string, 6th fret. Sixth position presents a moderately difficult stretch on the 4th string.

Figure 1-12:
Pattern #5 in
the key of A♭
major in 6th
position.

Applying Your Scale Work to Actual Pieces of Music

Okay, so you've practiced, and now you realize that playing scales on a guitar is about as interesting as watching paint dry, right? Well, don't you drop your flatpick and grab knitting needles just yet. You've made it to the fun part where you get to use your scale-playing prowess to play actual music — you know, songs! It's a reward to you for all the effort you've put in so far.

After you get the five major scale patterns "under your fingers" (musician lingo for knowing them cold), you can make those patterns work for you. It bears repeating that most music is made up of scales. And although you may not encounter a lot of music that runs a scale from bottom to top and back down again in eighth notes, you will play many pieces that contain passages of scale segments — the same material you practice here. When you run across a passage that's similar to a scale you've practiced, it's like the music almost plays itself. You can go into a kind of automatic pilot and enjoy listening to the music as it goes by.

As you practice scales more and more, you'll find that playing passages of stepwise notes becomes easier and more natural. Scales are an efficient way to practice the notes contained in a song — even if the melody doesn't lay them out in a strict, regular fashion. In fact, most music isn't laid out in a strict, regular way because it would be boring and sound like, well, scales. So while practicing scales may not prepare you for a particular piece of music, it's the best way to prepare yourself equally well for most music. The following sections include two pieces of music whose melodies are made up of primarily major scale passages.

Book VII

Exercises:
Practice,
Practice,
Practice

"The First Noël"

"The First Noël" is a Christmas carol that you probably know, so you can use your familiarity with it to help ensure that you're playing the song correctly — hitting the right pitches in the correct rhythms.

You use two major scale patterns to play "The First Noël": major scale patterns #1 and #4. To begin, put your hand in 2nd position (with your left-hand 1st finger hovering above the 2nd fret). Then place your left-hand 3rd finger (your ring finger) on the starting note F♯ at the 4th string, 4th fret. Now you're ready to play.

Notice in Figure 1-13 at bar 8 you switch positions, jumping up to 9th position between beats 2 and 3. Try to let that half note ring for as long as possible before making the jump, but don't be late for beat 3! This mid-measure jump allows you to play the chorus of the second phrase an octave higher. The song doesn't really do that, but we thought we'd make it more interesting for you. Plus it gives you a workout in different positions.

After playing eight bars in the upper octave, shift your hand back to 2nd position at bar 16 to finish out the last eight bars. Note that the last bar, like the first pickup bar, is incomplete. It contains two beats, which allows it to even out the one-beat bar that starts the song. You can repeat the song by mentally stitching together the first bar and the last as if the whole song were a repeatable loop.

Figure 1-13: "The First Noël" is a good song to practice scales on.

Book VII

Exercises: Practice, Practice, Practice

Chapter 2

Adding Major Scale Sequences to Your Repertoire

In This Chapter

▶ Playing major scale sequences using five major scale patterns

▶ Applying sequences to actual pieces of music

▶ Access the audio track at www.dummies.com/go/guitaraio/

I f you've practiced the five major scale patterns presented in the last chapter (Book VII Chapter 1) — and drilled them into your conscious-ness — it's time to have some fun with them, don't you think? Instead of going up and down and up and down (and up and down), in this chapter you get to mix things up by playing sequences. Sequences are musical pat-terns — not finger patterns like the ones you memorized to learn your scales (uh, you did memorize those, didn't you?).

Playing sequences not only makes practicing more interesting and less pre-dictable, but it also makes you feel like you're playing real music — that is, pattern-based songs with repeated gestures. Many melodies get their "memo-rableness" from their sequences, which make them different enough to be interesting, but predictable enough to become recognizable. It's a delicate balance, but all great melodies have some repetition to them in the form of sequences, which you can explore in this chapter.

Just as you did in your scale work in Chapter 1 in Book VII, familiarize yourself with the sequences in this chapter and then move them up and down the neck to produce other major scale sequences in different keys.

Practicing Major Scale Sequences

Unlike scales, which run in the same direction for long stretches, *sequences* change direction often and may at first seem a little trickier than scales. But you can make them more manageable by discovering the *scheme* (or pattern), which reveals itself in the first few notes you play. Learning the pattern can help you better anticipate the direction changes and find the starting note of the new sequence. You may have to start off practicing sequences a little slower than you would scales, but you'll soon find that learning the sequence helps your brain keep up with your fingers, allowing you to play faster.

You should always play the ascending and descending sequences as a pair. In other words, always begin the descending sequence immediately after you finish the ascending one. Doing so will help you maintain a sense of ascending and descending symmetry in your music.

Major scale sequences using pattern #1

Major scale pattern #1 is an ascending two-octave scale that starts on the 6th string and contains no *out-of-position notes* (notes that don't fall within the four-fret span defined by the position and that require stretches by the 1st and 4th finger to play). Even though you have no stretches to contend with, you still may want to start out slowly as you play this pattern. After all, the notes change direction often and are quite different from the "one-way" motion (all up and then all down) of scale playing.

Figure 2-1 (Track 115 at 0:00) features ascending and descending four-note sequences. In the ascending version, between bars 5 and 6, you must use the same finger (the 4th in this case) to play two notes in a row, across two strings. This may feel awkward at first, so feel free to supply your own alternate fingering in these cases. For example, try flattening out your 4th finger into a *mini-barre* (a partial barre that covers just two or three strings), or try substituting your 3rd finger for the note played on the 3rd string. Just be sure to get back into position as soon as you can after employing an alternate fingering. And remember the old saying, "You can break the rules as long as you know the rules first."

Figure 2-2 (Track 115 at 0:53) shows ascending and descending sequences in the key of G in 2nd position. This exercise includes a wide skip after every sixth note, sometimes requiring you to jump over a string in the process. Practice these wide skips across two strings so you can play them with the same smoothness as you play a step on the same string. One trick that helps ensure smooth skip execution is to look ahead in the music slightly to help you anticipate the next interval.

Book VII

**Exercises:
Practice,
Practice,
Practice**

Figure 2-1:
Ascending
and
descending
four-note
sequences.

Major scale sequences using pattern #2

Major scale pattern #2 starts with the 4th finger on the 6th string and includes an out-of-position note on the 4th string. Stretch your 4th finger up (toward the bridge) to play this note, because it occurs one fret above (higher on the neck) the note the 4th finger would normally play. Be sure to play stretch notes with the same smoothness as you play the in-position notes.

Figure 2-2: Ascending and descending sequences in the key of G in 2nd position.

Figure 2-3 shows ascending and descending sequences in the key of C in 5th position. The sequences are three notes in one direction followed by a change in the opposite direction of one step. These frequent changes of direction require you to glue your eyeballs to the page to make sure you handle the twists and turns of the melodic line.

TIP

Note that bar 2 of this figure indicates the fingering for notes 3, 4, and 5 as *4, 3, 4* — as dictated by major scale pattern #2. In reality, however, most guitarists would play this passage with fingers 4, 2, 4. That fingering is a little easier on your hand with regard to stretching, but you have to be careful not to get out of position. When you find other opportunities in this book for alternate fingerings, you're welcome to use them. Just be sure you can get back on track for the rest of the sequence using the correct fingers according to the scale pattern.

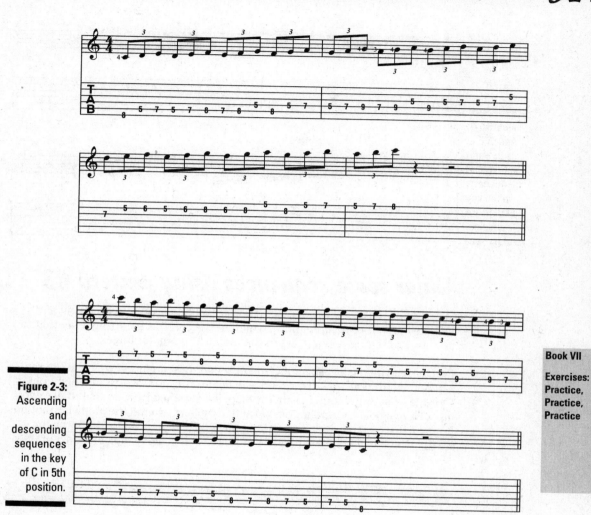

Figure 2-3:
Ascending
and
descending
sequences
in the key
of C in 5th
position.

Book VII

**Exercises:
Practice,
Practice,
Practice**

Figure 2-4 shows ascending and descending sequences in the key of B♭ in 3rd position. These sequences contain no skips and are in sixteenth notes, so try playing them at a fairly brisk clip. Just because you're *practicing* these sequences doesn't mean you shouldn't be playing fast — even if the music is still new or unfamiliar to you. Real music is often played fast, so at times you should practice fast, too.

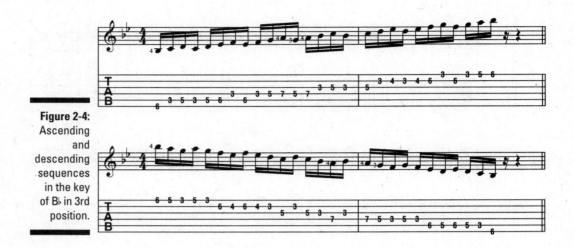

Figure 2-4:
Ascending and descending sequences in the key of B♭ in 3rd position.

Major scale sequences using pattern #3

Major scale pattern #3 starts with the second finger on the 5th string and includes an out-of-position note, which occurs on the 1st string. Play this note by stretching down (toward the nut) with your 1st finger.

Practice the following ascending and descending sequences, which are in the key of D in 4th position. The exercise in Figure 2-5 starts with a skip right out of the gate — so watch out. Isolate the skip, if necessary. Beyond that, these exercises have a healthy amount of skip activity in and around the stepwise motion. It may help to memorize this pattern quickly. Then you can focus on the fretboard, which can help you play the mixture of skips and steps more accurately.

Figure 2-5:
Ascending and descending sequences in the key of D in 4th position.

Figure 2-6 shows ascending and descending sequences in the key of F in 7th position. There's only one skip in this sequence, which occurs immediately at the beginning. So work on speed and smoothness by playing at brighter tempos. In the ascending version in bar 2, consider an alternate fingering, such as flattening out your fourth finger to play both notes 13 and 14 at the 10th fret. In the descending version, try the same approach at bar 1 between notes 13 and 14.

Figure 2-6: Ascending and descending sequences in the key of F in 7th position.

Book VII

Exercises: Practice, Practice, Practice

Major scale sequences using pattern #4

Major scale pattern #4 starts with the 4th finger on the 5th string and contains no out-of-position notes. So feel free to play these exercises with a swift and light feel, if you like.

In Figure 2-7 you see ascending and descending sequences in the key of F in 5th position. Because of the way the guitar's strings are tuned (in fourths, mostly), this sequence has many same-fret hops between strings (first seen in the ascending version between notes 4 and 5). So you have plenty of opportunities to swap out mini-barres for these cases. You have permission to use them at will.

Figure 2-8 shows ascending and descending sequences in the key of G in 7th position. Only the last note of each sequence is approached by a skip (and a small one at that, a third). So try playing these up to (or nearly up to) tempo right from the get-go. Playing new music fast and accurately is a skill you can develop, and this is a good sequence to try that approach on.

Figure 2-7:
Ascending
and
descending
sequences
in the key of
F in 5th
position.

Major scale sequences using pattern #5

Major scale pattern #5 starts on the 4th string and includes an out-of-position note on the 4th string. Remember, this stretch comes right away — on the first string you play, and you have to reach up (toward the bridge) with your fourth finger to play the out-of-position note.

Figure 2-9 includes ascending and descending sequences in the key of G in 5th position. These sequences are fairly easy sequences to play for three reasons:

- ✔ The same-direction nature of the melody
- ✔ The absence of skips
- ✔ As luck would have it, the lack of any same-fret string-hopping situations

Put your metronome on *presto* — if you dare.

Figure 2-10 shows ascending and descending sequences in the key of B♭ in 8th position. This sequence has just one skip, but it occurs immediately — between the first and second notes. You can breathe easy after that, however, because the remaining notes are stepwise, including the note that connects one sequence to the next.

Book VII

Exercises: Practice, Practice, Practice

Figure 2-8: Ascending and descending sequences in the key of G in 7th position.

Figure 2-9: Ascending and descending sequences in the key of G in 5th position.

Figure 2-10: Ascending and descending sequences in the key of B♭ in 8th position.

Putting Your Sequence Skills to Work with a Few Songs

The two pieces in the following sections feature melodies that are based on sequences. In these songs, you'll also see scalar passages. After all, most music that contains sequences also includes scale-like material. But don't think of these songs as exercises or sequences. They're songs! Sure you're supposed to practice them, but the idea is to have fun while doing it. Simply recognizing that these songs are made up of sequences will increase your appreciation of them, deepen your understanding of their structure, and make them easier to play.

"Oh, Them Golden Slippers"

When you look at the beginning of "Oh, Them Golden Slippers," notice the elements that give you clues to the song's character: tempo marking, time signature, key signature, and dynamics.

"Oh, Them Golden Slippers" has two parts, and you may recognize the first part as the melody to the children's song "Polly Wolly Doodle All the Day." Yes, this children's song actually derives its melody from the early American folk song about valuable footwear.

"Oh, Them Golden Slippers" is played in A major, starting with major scale pattern #2 in 2nd position. (If you need a refresher on any of this information, refer to Chapter 1 in Book VII.) This song (shown in Figure 2-11) uses two scale patterns, one for each section. Use major scale pattern #2 for the first section, and remember that it has one out-of-position note occurring on the 4th string. Use pattern #1 (and enjoy the fact that it contains no out-of-position notes) for the second section, which begins after the second ending. Also, note that because "Oh, Them Golden Slippers" is played down the neck (in the lower frets), the frets are wider, making stretches a little more difficult.

Book VII

Exercises:
Practice,
Practice,
Practice

TIP

A difficult stretch occurs in bar 5, beat 4, where you have to reach out of position to play the 4th string, 6th fret (G#). Just make sure you can get back into position for the next note — the 3rd string, 2nd fret (A) — which is the last note of the bar.

At the second ending of the first section, the music has a quarter rest at the end of the bar. You can use this rest as a way of silently switching positions for the next section, which is played using major scale pattern #1 in 4th position.

"We Wish You a Merry Christmas"

"We Wish You a Merry Christmas" is a great example of a sequential melody. The sequences present themselves in neat little two-bar phrases right from the beginning.

"We Wish You a Merry Christmas" (shown in Figure 2-12) is played in the key of F, using major scale pattern #5 in 3rd position. From bars 3 to 4 and in bar 8, there's some 1st finger string hopping, but the real challenge occurs at bars 5 and 6, where the 3rd finger really has to leap around.

Figure 2-11: "Oh Them Golden Slippers" is an old American folk song.

At the position change in bar 9 (to major scale pattern #4 in 5th position), you may notice that you don't actually have to release your 4th finger to play the first note dictated by the new position's fingering (the C at the 3rd string, 5th fret). So you can actually change positions after the text in the score tells you to. Little tricks like these help guitarists to play more *legato* (smoothly) where the notes connect or blend into one another slightly (versus *staccato,* where the notes sound separated and slightly choppy). These tricks also help musicians find economy in their hand movements that may not always be written into the music.

Figure 2-12: "We Wish You a Merry Christmas" is a good song for practicing sequences.

Book VII

Exercises: Practice, Practice, Practice

Chapter 3

Tackling the Three Minor Scales

In This Chapter

▶ Practicing natural, melodic, and harmonic minor scales using five patterns

▶ Performing pieces using the three minor scales

▶ Access the audio tracks at www.dummies.com/go/guitaraio/

*E*ven though major scales rule the cosmos (see Book VII Chapters 1 and 2), life would be pretty dull without their darker counterparts: minor scales. Minor scales and minor keys are sometimes described as "sad," "foreboding," "mysterious," "haunting," and even "creepy." But minor scales can also be quite beautiful, and most music — even if it's in a major key — uses some minor material to convey a richer message.

As a guitar student studying and perfecting scales, you have three different versions of minor scales that you must tackle. With the major scale, you have only one. The three minor scale flavors are called *natural, melodic,* and *harmonic.* They all have the characteristic "mournful" quality, which is characterized by the flatted 3rd degree (meaning, the third note of the scale is a half-step lower than in the major scale). However, some of their other notes are altered (namely, the 6th and 7th degrees of the scale), depending on the musical context. The three pieces at the end of this chapter each explore a different minor scale. For now, though, don't worry about altered degrees and such; just focus on getting the notes under your fingers. This chapter helps you do exactly that.

If you're looking for even more practice, remember that after you memorize each scale's fingering pattern, you can simply move it up or down the neck to different starting notes to produce and practice other minor scales. That way, you can hear how the minor scale sounds in all 12 keys using just one pattern — instead of learning 11 new ones.

Familiarizing Yourself with Natural Minor Scales

Even though a minor scale produces a decidedly different musical mood than a major scale, you treat it the same way when you sit down to practice. It's not like you have to be nicer to a minor scale because it seems so gloomy. Approach minor scales with the same vigor and positive attitude as major scales; they can take it.

As far as placing your fingers on the frets and playing your right hand in rhythm, minor scales are no different from major scales. The only wrinkle is that there are three types of minor scales (compared to just one major scale), so you have more information to keep track of. And that means you may have to spend a little more time memorizing them.

Compared to the major scale — the familiar *do, re, mi, fa, sol, la, ti, do,* or playing from C to C using all white notes on the piano — the natural minor scale has three notes that are different: the 3rd, the 6th, and the 7th degrees. These notes are flatted, or lowered a half-step. So a C natural minor scale would be C, D, E♭, F, G, A♭, B♭, C.

Play each of the following natural minor scale patterns slowly, loudly, and deliberately at first to build strength and confidence in your fingers. Then try playing it faster and lighter to better simulate how you'll play minor scales in actual pieces of music. Just be sure to maintain your starting tempo and dynamic level (loudness) throughout each scale.

Natural minor scale pattern #1

Natural minor scale pattern #1 starts with the 1st finger on the 6th string. As you play this scale pattern, watch for the out-of-position note that occurs on the 4th string. (An *out-of-position note* is a note that doesn't fall within the four-fret span defined by the position and that requires a stretch by the first or 4th finger to play it.) You must stretch up (toward the bridge) with your 4th finger to reach this note, because it occurs one fret above (higher on the neck) where the finger naturally falls.

Figure 3-1 (Track 116) shows an A natural minor scale in 5th position in both a neck diagram and in music and tab format. Take a look at the standard notation for a moment to see that we indicate both the starting finger (a *1* at the first note for the 1st finger) and the fingering for the out-of-position note (a *4* next to the B on the 4th string, 7th fret). Use the figure to memorize this scale's fingering pattern and then practice it until you feel comfortable playing it. Practice this pattern several times slowly to make sure you can hear the notes that produce the minor quality as well as to get your fingers comfortable with playing a new scale.

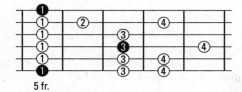

Book VII

**Exercises:
Practice,
Practice,
Practice**

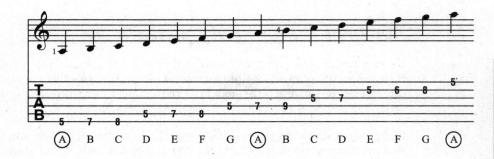

Figure 3-1:
A natural
minor
scale in 5th
position.

Now try your hand at the exercise in rhythm shown in Figure 3-2, which is in the key of B minor in 7th position.

Figure 3-2:
A rhythm
exercise in
B minor in
7th position.

Be sure not to unduly emphasize the out-of-position note (4th string, 11th fret). Some guitar players fall into the bad habit of musically stressing the difficult parts, such as stretches and position shifts. The out-of-position note here is like any other note in the scale and should blend in. The listener shouldn't be aware that the guitarist is doing something difficult.

Natural minor scale pattern #2

Natural minor scale pattern #2 starts with the 4th finger on the 6th string and includes an out-of-position note on the 1st string. Because this note occurs one fret below (lower on the neck) where the finger naturally falls, you must stretch down (toward the nut) with your 1st finger to reach it.

In Figure 3-3 you find the neck diagram and corresponding music and tab for natural minor scale pattern #2 in the key of C minor. Notice that in the standard notation we include both the starting finger (4th finger) and the fingering where the out-of-position note occurs (a *1* next to the A♭ on the 1st string, 4th fret). Practice this pattern so you can play the out-of-position note as smoothly as you play the other notes of the scale.

When you're ready, try playing this pattern in rhythm. The exercise in Figure 3-4 is in the key of A minor in 2nd position. Notice that the out-of-position note occurs on the F on the 1st string, 1st fret. Because this stretch occurs low on the neck, where the frets are wider, you really have to have your left hand warmed up. Try isolating the passage that occurs between bar 1, beat 4, and bar 2, beat 2, and play it eight times, or until you get used to the stretch.

Figure 3-3:
Minor scale pattern #2 in C minor.

Figure 3-4:
A rhythm exercise in A minor in 2nd position.

Book VII

Exercises: Practice, Practice, Practice

Natural minor scale pattern #3

Natural minor scale pattern #3 starts with the 1st finger on the 5th string (not the 6th, as in the previous two patterns) and includes no out-of-position notes. Sometimes it takes a little more "aim" to place a finger on the 5th string because it's an inside string (that is, not on the edge of the neck like the 6th string, which is easier to find by feeling your way around). So just before you're ready to put your finger down, make sure you're eyeballing that 5th string.

In Figure 3-5, you see the neck diagram and corresponding music and tab for natural minor scale pattern #3 in the key of D minor. Because this pattern includes no out-of-position notes — which can slow you down because they take extra effort — you can try taking this pattern a little faster than you normally would. Be careful not to rush it and make mistakes, though. Practice this pattern until you feel you know it well enough to play it in a steady tempo with no mistakes.

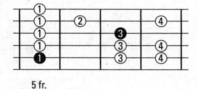

5 fr.

Figure 3-5: Minor scale pattern #3 in D minor.

Now try the rhythm exercise in Figure 3-6, in the key of E minor in 7th position. Be sure to play the sixteenth notes evenly and smoothly at first. Then, if you like, try *accenting* (striking slightly harder) the first note of each beat group. Applying accents helps to delineate the beat, which adds drive to your music.

Figure 3-6:
A rhythm exercise in E minor in 7th position.

Natural minor scale pattern #4

Natural minor scale pattern #4 starts on the 5th string with the 4th finger and includes an out-of-position note on the 1st string. In Figure 3-7, you can see the neck diagram and corresponding music and tab for natural minor scale pattern #4 in the key of F minor. Notice that in the standard notation, in addition to the starting finger (4th finger), we put in the fingering where the out-of-position note occurs (a *1* next to the A♭ on the 1st string, 4th fret).

You may find it difficult at first to lead off a scale with the 4th finger, because it's traditionally a weaker and "less confident" finger than the 1st or 2nd finger (the fingers that begin natural minor scale patterns #1 and #3). So practice the beginning of this pattern (just the first three or four notes) a few times to make sure you kick it off steadily and confidently before playing the rest of the pattern.

When you're ready to try this pattern in rhythm, check out Figure 3-8, which is in the key of D minor in 2nd position. In this rhythm exercise, notice that an out-of-position note occurs on the F on the 1st string, 1st fret.

A stretch to the 1st fret is a wide one, so try measuring it first by placing your 4th finger on the 2nd string, 5th fret. While still holding your 4th finger down, reach up and place your 1st finger on the 1st string, 1st fret, and hold that down, too. That's the span your hand will have to make when you encounter the reach in bar 2. This measuring routine should help you remember how far to stretch when the time comes, and it's a little quicker than isolating the passage containing the stretch.

Book VII

Exercises: Practice, Practice, Practice

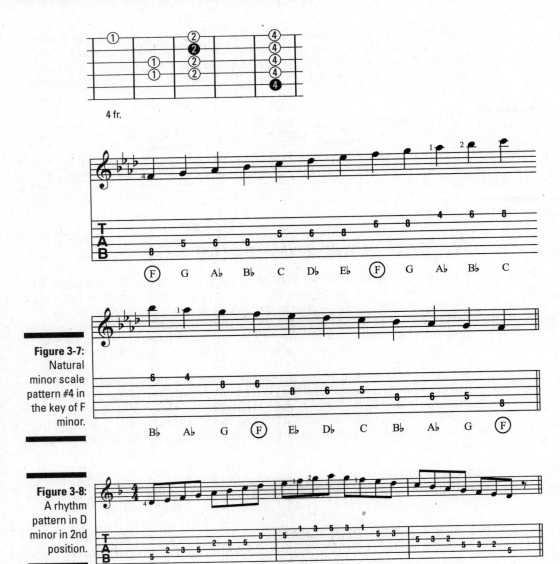

Figure 3-7: Natural minor scale pattern #4 in the key of F minor.

Figure 3-8: A rhythm pattern in D minor in 2nd position.

Natural minor scale pattern #5

Natural minor scale pattern #5 starts with your 1st finger on the 4th string and includes no out-of-position notes. Figure 3-9 shows a neck diagram and corresponding music and tab for natural minor scale pattern #5 in the key of G minor. Because this pattern begins on an inside string (away from the easily accessible edges of the guitar), you may want to practice placing your 1st finger quickly on the starting note. The good news is that you're back to beginning a scale with a strong finger — the 1st. Practice grabbing the starting note at different points on the neck, naming each starting note as you do, and then play through the pattern at least four times to memorize the fingering.

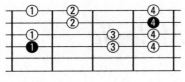

5 fr.

Book VII

Exercises: Practice, Practice, Practice

Figure 3-9: Natural minor scale pattern #5 in G minor.

Figure 3-10 provides a rhythm exercise in the key of A minor in 7th position. To help emphasize the sound of a triplet, play the first note in each group of three with a slight accent — that is, strike it a little harder than you do the surrounding notes.

Figure 3-10:
A rhythm
exercise in
A minor in
7th position.

Raising the Bar with Melodic Minor Scales

Compared to the major scale (for example, C, D, E, F, G, A, B, C in the key of C), the ascending melodic minor scale has only one note that's different: the 3rd, which is flatted. So an ascending C melodic minor scale would be C, D, E♭, F, G, A, B, C. The descending melodic minor is the same as the natural minor scale, and so it has three notes that are different: the 3rd, 6th, and 7th degrees. These are flatted, so a descending C melodic minor scale would be C, B♭, A♭, G, F, E♭, D, C.

The raising of the notes on only the ascending version is said to make the scale more elegant. Much Baroque and Classical music — undoubtedly elegant — often includes melodic minor scales.

Because the 6th and 7th notes are sometimes raised and sometimes not, the melodic minor scale can be somewhat tricky to memorize. But that difficulty is also what makes it interesting. After all, you simply have more notes available than with the other major and minor scales. Practice the melodic minor scale as you would the natural minor scale, but do be aware of the two scale degrees that are different (the 6th and 7th) on the ascending version. Don't make these notes obvious by hitting them harder, either. Give the raised and unraised notes equal emphasis.

Melodic minor scale pattern #1

Melodic minor scale pattern #1 begins on the 6th string with the 1st finger. Figure 3-11 (Track 117) shows the neck diagram and corresponding music and tab for the pattern. Because the melodic minor scale has two forms — one for ascending and one for descending — two neck diagrams are shown side by side.

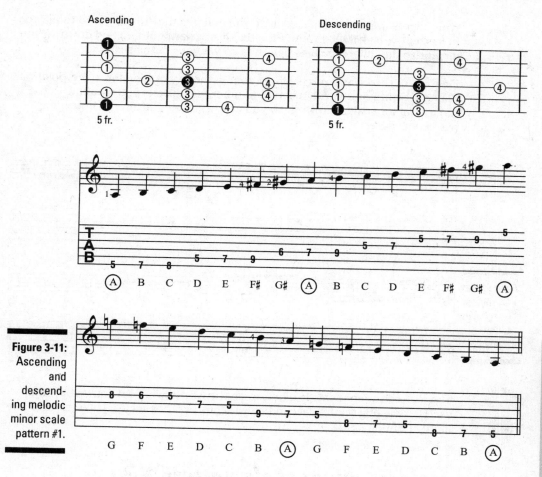

Figure 3-11: Ascending and descending melodic minor scale pattern #1.

The ascending form of the melodic minor scale pattern #1 includes out-of-position notes on the 5th, 4th, and 2nd strings. The descending form includes just one out-of-position note, on the 4th string. The fingerings for these notes are indicated in the standard notation. Between the ascending and descending versions you have a fair amount of stretching to do here, so make sure you're limbered up before trying this one.

Because only the top part of the scale (between the 6th and octave notes) presents the raised and unraised notes, you need to isolate the passage from the high E (2nd string, 5th fret) to the high A (1st string, 5th fret), ascending and descending. Play the passage eight times in a row at a slow tempo before trying the exercise from the beginning. As you memorize the scale, make sure

Book VII

Exercises: Practice, Practice, Practice

your fingers don't get confused as to which notes they're supposed to play on the ascent versus the descent. Practice this pattern both up and down so you memorize the difference between the two versions of the scale.

Figure 3-12 shows an exercise in rhythm in the key of G minor in 3rd position. Play the eighth notes with a light and quick feel, just as you would with the natural minor scale, and work so you can negotiate the altered notes here with equal ease.

Figure 3-12:
A rhythm
exercise in
G minor in
3rd position.

The melodic minor scale is different on the way down. So if you've become used to coasting on the descending versions of other scales, you'll have to pay more attention here.

Melodic minor scale pattern #2

Melodic minor scale pattern #2 starts with the 4th finger on the 6th string and includes two out-of-position notes. One of these notes occurs when ascending (on the 4th string) and one occurs when descending (on the 1st string).

Figure 3-13 shows the neck diagrams in ascending and descending forms along with the corresponding music and tab for melodic minor scale pattern #2 in the key of C minor. Notice that in the standard notation, in addition to the starting finger (4th finger), there are fingerings where the out-of-position notes occur. So not only is the scale different depending on the direction you're going, but the out-of-position notes change as well. Melodic minor scales are really two scales under one name. That means two times the effort to learn, but two times the possibilities for musical variety! Practice this pattern along with natural minor scale pattern #1, if you want; they're identical in their descending versions.

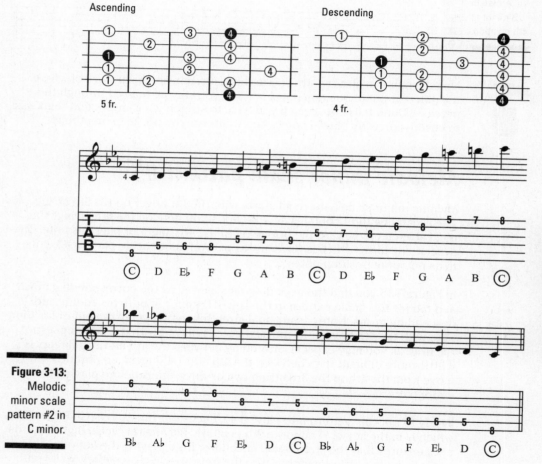

Figure 3-13:
Melodic minor scale pattern #2 in C minor.

Book VII

**Exercises:
Practice,
Practice,
Practice**

After you have the pattern down pat, use the rhythm exercise shown in Figure 3-14 as practice. This exercise is in the key of B minor in 4th position.

Figure 3-14: A rhythm exercise in B minor in 4th position.

Melodic minor scales require you to think, stretch, and keep track of where the different out-of-position notes fall. Are you staying relaxed through this process? Don't tense up, even if you have to stretch your fingers and think fast to ensure correctly played notes. And whatever you do, keep breathing!

Melodic minor scale pattern #3

Melodic minor scale pattern #3 starts with the 1st finger on the 5th string. The ascending form contains an out-of-position note on the 4th string. You must stretch up (toward the bridge) with the 4th finger to play this note. The descending form, which is the same as natural minor scale pattern #3, contains no out-of-position notes.

In Figure 3-15 you find the neck diagrams as well as the corresponding music and tab for this scale pattern in the key of D minor in both ascending and descending forms. Note the unusual stretch here: You play the out-of-position note with the 4th finger, but the next note is played with the 2nd finger (not the first, as you may expect). Stretching between the 4th and 2nd fingers is a little more difficult than between the 4th and 1st fingers, so practice the move from the 4th to the 3rd string two or three times before playing the entire pattern.

Ready to put this pattern into play? If so, check out the exercise in Figure 3-16, which is in the key of F♯ minor in 9th position. Playing this scale higher up the neck ensures that the stretch you encounter from playing the out-of-position notes is made a little easier because the frets are closer together. So if you have any say in the matter, always opt to head north to play this scale. Your fingers will thank you for it.

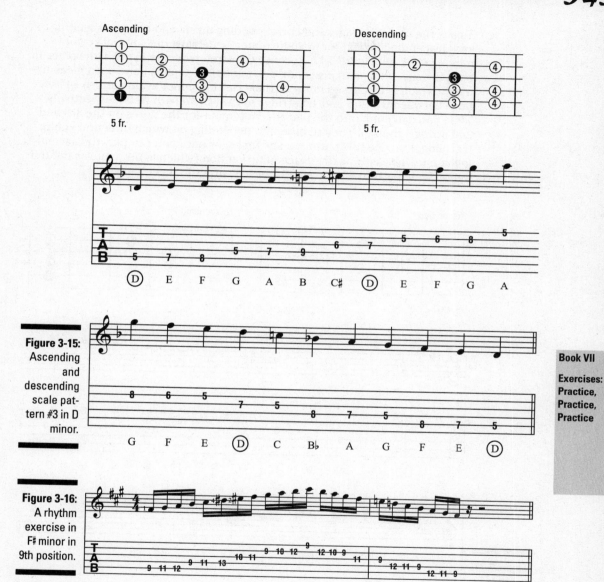

Figure 3-15:
Ascending and descending scale pattern #3 in D minor.

Figure 3-16:
A rhythm exercise in F# minor in 9th position.

Melodic minor scale pattern #4

Melodic minor scale pattern #4 starts with the 4th finger on the 5th string and includes an out-of-position note on the 1st string in both the ascending and descending forms.

To see the neck diagrams and corresponding music and tab (in ascending and descending forms) for melodic minor scale pattern #4 in the key of F minor, check out Figure 3-17. Because the stretch occurs in the same place in both the ascending and descending versions, do a quick hand-span measurement (which is discussed in the earlier "Natural minor scale pattern #4" section) between the 2nd and 1st strings at the 8th and 4th frets, respectively. Then you can jump into the pattern. Watch out for the notes on the 3rd and 2nd strings, though. They're different, depending on which direction you're traveling. Practice this pattern a few times, or until you can play the ascending version as easily as the descending version (which is the same as natural minor scale pattern #4, a scale discussed earlier in this chapter).

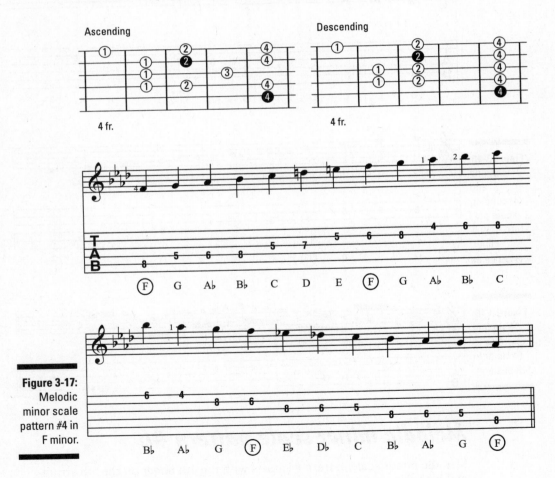

Figure 3-17: Melodic minor scale pattern #4 in F minor.

Now take a look at Figure 3-18, which provides a rhythm exercise in the key of E minor in 4th position. Notice that an out-of-position note occurs on the G on the 1st string, 3rd fret. As melodic minor scales go, this pattern is relatively accessible because its stretch occurs in only one spot (on the 1st string). Practice the stretch first to get your fingers limbered up, and then focus on the differences between the ascending and descending version, which requires a limber brain.

Figure 3-18: A rhythm exercise in E minor in 4th position.

Melodic minor scale pattern #5

Melodic minor scale pattern #5 begins with the 1st finger on the 4th string and includes no out-of-position notes in either the ascending or descending versions. In Figure 3-19, you can see the neck diagram and corresponding music and tab in ascending and descending form for melodic minor scale pattern #5 in the key of G minor. Use the figure to memorize this scale's fingering pattern, and practice it several times to ensure that the notes are equally smooth and even in either direction.

When you have pattern #5 memorized, use Figure 3-20 to practice it in rhythm. This exercise is in the key of B♭ minor in 8th position.

B♭ minor is an unusual key for the guitar, because it contains five flats. Guitarists generally find themselves in sharp keys (such as G, D, A, and E), which are considered more favorable to the instrument. (This relates to the open strings of the guitar being the *tonics,* or starting notes, of sharp keys.) And when guitar players do have to play in flat keys, they're more comfortable with keys that have only a few flats (such as F, B♭, and E♭, which have one, two, and three flats, respectively). But one of the advantages of movable scale patterns is that they let you explore uncharted territory (including keys with lots of flats) without having to learn any new patterns.

Note: The ascending version of the melodic minor is sometimes used in both directions, especially in jazz, but examples can be found in Bach as well.

Book VII

Exercises: Practice, Practice, Practice

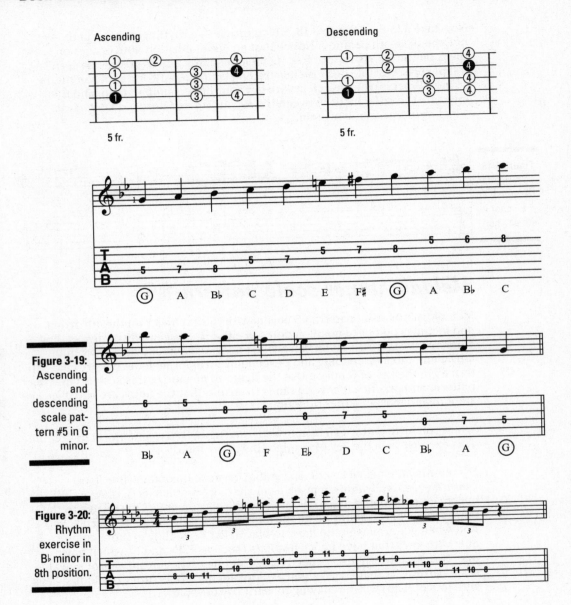

Ascending

Descending

5 fr.

5 fr.

G A B♭ C D E F♯ G A B♭ C

Figure 3-19: Ascending and descending scale pattern #5 in G minor.

B♭ A G F E♭ D C B♭ A G

Figure 3-20: Rhythm exercise in B♭ minor in 8th position.

Harmonizing with Harmonic Minor Scales

Compared to the major scale, the harmonic minor scale has two notes that are different: the 3rd and the 6th degrees. These are flatted, so a C harmonic minor scale would be C, D, E♭, F, G, A♭, B, C.

Consider the harmonic minor scale alongside its other minor scale brethren. The harmonic minor is different from the natural minor in that the 7th degree is raised a half-step. This is true whether the scale is ascending or descending. This raising of the 7th degree gives the scale's melody a strong pull from the 7th degree to the top of the scale. It also allows for the formation of a dominant 7th chord in the harmony (for example, an E7 chord in the key of A minor). For these reasons, the scale is called the "harmonic" minor. After all, it allows more desirable chords to be formed from it.

Raising the 7th degree produces a colorful "skip" in the melody between the unraised 6th and the raised 7th. Some people think this skip isn't very scale-like, but the harmonic minor has a tart flavor and sounds Middle Eastern (think snake-charmer music). The harmonic minor scale is the same ascending and descending, so it should be a little easier to memorize. Practice all five patterns of the harmonic minor scale until you can play them as smoothly — skip and all — as you do the natural and melodic minor scales.

Harmonic minor scale pattern #1

Harmonic minor scale pattern #1 is an A harmonic minor scale in 5th position, starting with the 1st finger on the 6th string.

Figure 3-21 (Track 118) shows the neck diagram as well as the corresponding music and tab. This pattern has out-of-position notes on the 4th and 2nd strings. Included are fingerings for these notes in the standard notation. The stretch that occurs on the 2nd string, between the 2nd and 4th fingers, is unusual, so practice playing just the 2nd string notes two or three times before playing the rest of the pattern. Keep in mind that you have another stretch to contend with, too — on the 4th string between the 3rd and 4th fingers. But this is the kind of stretch you're used to, so it shouldn't present an additional problem, as long as you're prepared for it.

Try the rhythm exercise in Figure 3-22, which is in the key of C minor and in 8th position. Before you begin playing, notice where the out-of-position notes fall, and be sure to observe the fingering indications.

As an option, you can play fingers 1, 2, and 4 on the 4th string (instead of fingers 2, 3, 4). This eliminates the stretch that occurs between the 3rd and 4th finger, which some people find uncomfortable.

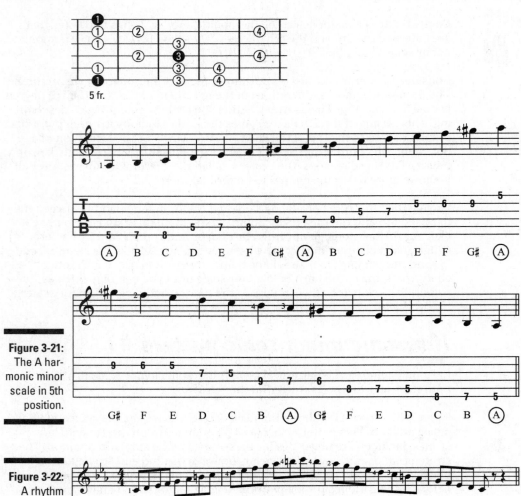

Figure 3-21:
The A harmonic minor scale in 5th position.

Figure 3-22:
A rhythm exercise in C minor in 8th position.

Harmonic minor scale pattern #2

Harmonic minor scale pattern #2 starts with the 4th finger on the 6th string and includes out-of-position notes on the 4th and 1st strings. You stretch up (toward the bridge) with the 4th finger to reach the out-of-position note on the 4th string, and you stretch down (toward the nut) with the 1st finger to reach the out-of-position note on the 1st string.

Figure 3-23 shows the neck diagram and corresponding music and tab for harmonic minor scale pattern #2 in the key of C minor. In the standard notation, in addition to the starting finger (4th finger), You'll find the fingerings where the out-of-position notes occur. Use these figures to familiarize yourself with the fingering pattern, and then play it until you know it cold.

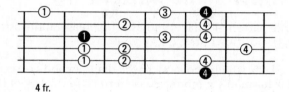

4 fr.

Book VII

Exercises: Practice, Practice, Practice

Figure 3-23: Harmonic minor scale pattern #2 in C minor.

To practice this pattern in rhythm, check out Figure 3-24, which is in the key of D minor in 7th position. Accent the first note of each triplet to help keep your place in the measure.

Figure 3-24:
A rhythm exercise in D minor in 7th position.

Harmonic minor scale pattern #3

Harmonic minor scale pattern #3 starts with the 1st finger on the 5th string and includes no out-of-position notes. Lucky you!

Take a look at Figure 3-25, which shows the neck diagram and corresponding music and tab for harmonic minor scale pattern #3 in the key of D minor. Be careful that you don't overemphasize the note that's played with the 2nd finger on the 3rd string (the raised 7th). In trying to memorize the sound and fingering of the three different minor scales, it's pretty obvious that the 7th note of the scale is the one that adds the "flavor." But you should work to make the attack as even as the rest of the notes of the scale. To ensure that you aren't applying undue emphasis to any particular note, practice this pattern in its entirety every time you play it (without isolating specific passages), and work to make each note equal in volume.

When you have pattern #3 under your belt, practice it in rhythm. To do so, consult Figure 3-26, which is in the key of B minor in 2nd position. Playing a pattern that has no stretches and is the same ascending as descending sounds like an opportunity to give it the gas. Practice this exercise at a bright tempo, but be careful that you don't flub the notes because your fingers are going too fast for your brain. Just because you find a scale to be technically easy doesn't mean you won't make a mistake due to a lapse in concentration.

Harmonic minor scale pattern #4

Harmonic minor scale pattern #4 starts with the 4th finger on the 5th string and includes an out-of-position note on the 1st string. You must stretch down (toward the nut) with the first finger to play it.

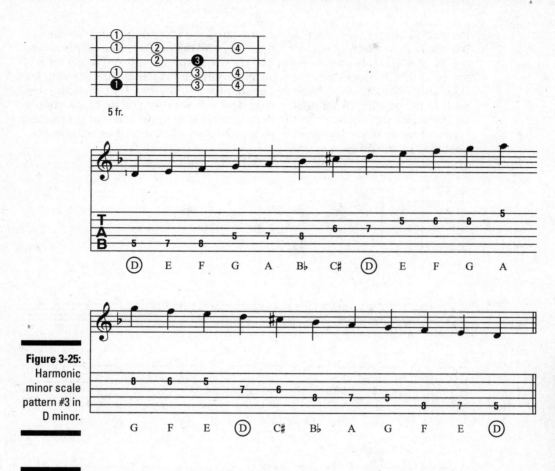

Figure 3-25:
Harmonic minor scale pattern #3 in D minor.

Book VII

**Exercises:
Practice,
Practice,
Practice**

Figure 3-26:
A rhythm exercise in the key of B minor in 2nd position.

Figure 3-27 shows the neck diagram and corresponding music and tab for harmonic minor scale pattern #4 in the key of F minor. The 1st-finger note on the 1st string creates a two-fret stretch between the 1st and 2nd fingers. Be aware of this unusual stretch as you approach the 1st string. To limber up for the out-of-position note before you encounter it in rhythm, try practicing this pattern descending (from the top note down) first. After you do that a couple of times, practice the scale in the normal ascending approach four times, or however many times you need to memorize the fingering and feel comfortable playing the notes.

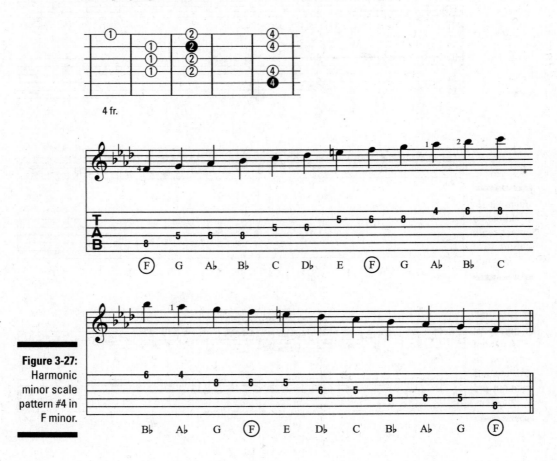

Figure 3-27: Harmonic minor scale pattern #4 in F minor.

When you're ready for some practice, try your hand at the exercise in Figure 3-28, which is in the key of G minor in 7th position. When playing eighth notes in 4/4 time, the most important beat is beat 1. The next most important is beat 3, followed by beats 2 and 4. Can you play a right-hand articulation approach that reflects that? Don't make the changes in volume between the accented notes and the unaccented ones too drastic, or it becomes harder to play an even, steady rhythm.

Figure 3-28:
A rhythm exercise in G minor in 7th position.

Harmonic minor scale pattern #5

Harmonic minor scale pattern #5 starts with the 1st finger on the 4th string and includes no out-of-position notes.

To see the neck diagram and corresponding music and tab for harmonic minor scale pattern #5 in the key of G minor, refer to Figure 3-29. Because this pattern has no stretches to contend with, it's rather easy to play. So try doing something different: Focus on your right hand. If you normally use a flatpick, try playing the notes smoothly and evenly by alternating your right-hand index and middle fingers. Conversely, if you play fingerstyle, try picking up a flatpick for this one. (Come on, it won't kill you to do it! And your classical guitar teacher doesn't even have to know.) In either case, approaching an exercise from a different perspective often helps you solidify your own internal rhythmic sense, so when you go back to the way you would normally play, you'll find new confidence.

When you're ready, practice the pattern using Figure 3-30, which is in the key of F# minor in 4th position. Have you ever played in the dark or with your eyes closed? It's a great way to test your muscle memory, and performing this experiment on a scale with no out-of-position notes is a good place to start. It's also the acid test for seeing whether you *truly* have a pattern memorized. Try closing your eyes right now, and see how well you do going up and down one time slowly and steadily. No peeking!

Figure 3-29: Harmonic minor scale pattern #5 in G minor.

Figure 3-30: A rhythm exercise in F# minor in 4th position.

Playing Pieces Using the Three Minor Scales

Playing minor scales prepares you for the vast underworld of music that forsakes major-key optimism and chooses to express itself in darker tones. Just as you need both sunshine and rain to make flowers grow, so too do you need a little minor among the major to make your musical garden flourish.

In this section, you get to see what minor-scale music is all about: three major-league compositions, each using a different minor scale. One piece is an old traditional carol, one is from the great Baroque composer George Frideric Handel, and one is attributed to the Renaissance. Enjoy your musical journey to the dark side!

"God Rest Ye Merry, Gentlemen"

Despite the fact that "God Rest Ye Merry, Gentlemen" is in a minor key, it's quite spirited and uplifting. The key signature has no sharps or flats, so you may think that the song is in C major. But it's actually in A minor, which shares the same key signature and notes as C major. (Now you see why A minor is known as the *relative* minor of C major). This song is composed of almost all quarter notes, so you can take it at a pretty brisk tempo. The song uses just one pattern, natural minor scale pattern #5, in 7th position, starting with the 1st finger.

Even though the song is arranged using all one scale pattern, some of the intervals and direction changes can be tricky. Try playing the song by ear (close the book or look away from the music). No peeking, now! See how well you do at picking out the correct notes. Even when you know the pattern cold, "God Rest Ye Merry, Gentlemen" (Figure 3-31) can be difficult to perform completely accurately because of some of the intervals.

Handel's "Allegro"

The opening statement in this piece is just an ascending scale. However, you may not even realize it because of the way it's disguised with different rhythms. The faster notes in bars 5 through 7 are all just descending scale segments, but do note how beautiful they sound.

Book VII

Exercises: Practice, Practice, Practice

Figure 3-31: "God Rest Ye Merry, Gentlemen" may be minor, but it's lively.

Handel's "Allegro" (Figure 3-32) uses the melodic minor scale pattern #4 in 7th position, starting with the 4th finger. It's in the key of G minor and written in *cut time* (2/2), which is indicated with a C and a vertical line "cutting" it in half. This symbol tells you to count the half note, not the quarter note (as you're used to doing with songs in 4/4 and 3/4), as one beat. Because you count the half note as the beat, the measure is felt in 2 (with two beats to the bar).

In bar 3 of this piece, you see two accidentals in the music: an E natural and an F♯. These accidentals indicate that those notes have been raised as the melodic minor commands. In bar 5, the melody descends, so the melodic minor scale again requires that the E♭ and F — raised on the way up to E natural and F♯ — be in their natural state, as F and E♭, which agrees with the key signature. The natural and flat signs are in bar 5 just as a gentle reminder not to play the wrong notes. The melody has a nice way of building here, using slow notes in the beginning and working up to the eighth-note passages in bars 5 through 7.

Brightly, in 2

Figure 3-32: Handel's "Allegro" uses melodic minor scale pattern #4 in 7th position.

"The Three Ravens"

If you're old enough, you may recognize "The Three Ravens" (Figure 3-33) from the Peter, Paul, and Mary version of this folk song. The key signature in the music tells you that this song is in F minor, but because you're using the harmonic minor scale, every instance of the note E will be E natural, not E♭ as indicated by the key signature.

Because the harmonic scale here is in 1st position and you have some out-of-position notes to play, you have a pretty serious case of finger stretching ahead of you. So first play bars 1 and 2 in isolation. This bit of practice allows you to execute the stretch in both an ascending and descending context. Practicing these stretching parts ensures that they don't take you by surprise when you try to play the whole piece.

Book VII

Exercises: Practice, Practice, Practice

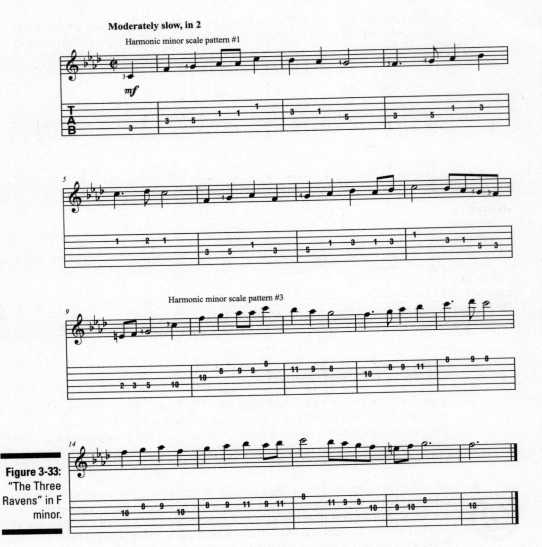

Figure 3-33: "The Three Ravens" in F minor.

Chapter 4

Building Finger Independence with Chord Exercises

In This Chapter

▶ Playing patterns using outside and inside chords

▶ Putting together a series of chords

▶ Performing pieces with chord progressions

▶ Access the audio tracks at www.dummies.com/go/guitaraio/

Chords are the rhythm guitar *yin* to the lead guitar *yang*. In most musical settings, single-note playing is supported by some sort of chord-based accompaniment. The great thing about the guitar is that it can play chords or single-note leads with equal awesomeness — try doing that with a flute or saxophone. But, because the guitar plays chords as well as single notes, it's important that you keep your chording *and* melody skills up to snuff. This chapter addresses chord playing.

As with the single-note exercises, the chord forms presented in this chapter are movable — meaning they contain no open strings. So after you can play a chord form comfortably, try moving it around the neck to play different chords. Doing so changes the letter name of the chord (for example, from A to C) but keeps the quality of the chord (major, minor, and so on) the same.

You can play the chords in this chapter a number of different ways with the right hand, including plucking the individual strings with your fingertips, brushing the strings with the backs of your fingernails, and striking the notes with a pick. But whether you pluck or strum with the right hand, your left-hand approach is the same. Your fingers on your left hand must fret the notes in a way that allows the strings to ring clearly, and they must be able to change chords — that is, get off the old chord and grab the new chord — quickly and imperceptibly (or close to it, anyway). At a performance tempo.

The exercises in this chapter are designed to help get your fingers moving independently. The bountiful number of useful examples also helps you build up strength in the process.

Practicing Inversion Patterns

Chords come in many different guises; even chords with the same name can be played in various ways. For example, you can play an F major chord on the guitar in exactly one billion and seven ways. Okay, that's a *bit* of an exaggeration. But you can find lots of chord options on the neck.

The first way you can narrow down the F major chord choices is to organize them by the low-to-high order of their notes. An F major chord is spelled F-A-C, bottom note to top. But the notes A-C-F and C-F-A are also F chords. Any chord with the combination of the notes F, A, and C constitutes an F chord, but if the lowest note of the chord is anything but an F, it's called an *inversion* of F. So you get an F (with an F on the bottom), its first inversion (with an A on the bottom), and its second inversion (with a C on the bottom).

In addition to the order of notes from bottom to top, you can also group chords by which strings they're played on. For example, you can play a chord using all six strings (as you do with a basic open E), just the top five strings, just the top four strings, or any other combination of strings.

 Playing all six strings may make the guitar sound full and complete in one setting, but it's not always appropriate — especially if you're playing in a band or with other instruments. (Playing all six strings all the time can sound too full and can muddy up the texture and crowd out other instruments, such as the bass.) Sometimes four-string chords are just right.

Two groups of four-string chords are called *outside chords* and *inside chords*:

- ✔ **Outside chords:** Outside forms refer to the top four strings closest to the outside, or edge, of the fretboard. Outside chords don't include bass notes and are good for melody playing and a higher harmonic part.

- ✔ **Inside chords:** Inside forms — at least for the purposes of this chapter (the term can have other meanings) — are the 2nd, 3rd, and 4th strings (which are insulated from the outside of the neck by surrounding strings) and a 6th string for a low note. Inside chords, which include a bass note, produce a deeper, fuller sound. Good for when there's no bass player.

Because the chord explorations start at the 1st fret, F was chosen to name the chords. But all the forms presented in this chapter are movable, so when you practice playing them at different frets, the letter name will change. For example, if you play the chords two frets higher than where they are in the figures, you'll produce G chords of various qualities. F is an efficient way to present all the different forms. But we don't favor F any more than G or B♭ or F♯. (Okay, F is a little friendlier than F♯, but only because the key of F♯ has six sharps.)

As with practicing scales and arpeggios, play each chord exercise in this chapter slowly, loudly, and deliberately at first, making sure you can hear all the strings that are supposed to ring — and none of the strings that aren't! Then play the exercise faster and with a lighter touch. Just be sure to maintain your starting tempo and dynamic level (loudness) throughout each exercise.

Patterns using outside chords

Figure 4-1 shows the neck diagram and the corresponding music and tab for the three forms of an outside-string F major chord. Remember that when you practice these exercises, the *X*s in the chord diagrams mean that those strings aren't played. So avoid striking or plucking them with your right hand.

In all the rhythm examples that follow for outside chords, strum each chord lightly in quarter notes (one strum per beat) and avoid playing the lowest two strings of the guitar.

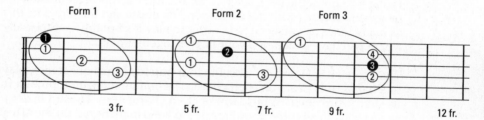

Book VII

**Exercises:
Practice,
Practice,
Practice**

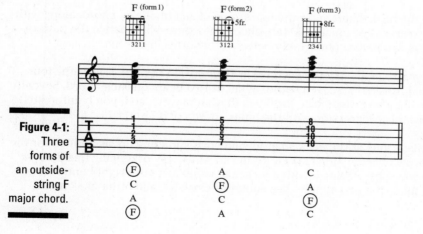

Figure 4-1:
Three forms of an outside-string F major chord.

Now try the rhythm exercise in Figure 4-2, which uses the outside forms of F, played two to a bar, or two beats on each chord.

Figure 4-2:
A rhythm
exercise
for outside
F major
chords.

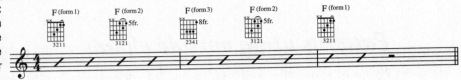

When going from the first form to the second, keep your 3rd finger on the string as you slide up the neck. That way, you only have to reposition two other fingers (rather than all three). Apply the same "common finger" approach between the fourth and fifth chords in the exercise.

Figure 4-3 shows the neck diagram for the three forms of an outside-string F minor chord along with the corresponding music and tab. Practice this pattern as many times as you need to in order to play it smoothly — especially form 3, where you have to squeeze your fingers together a bit.

The exercise in Figure 4-4 uses the four outside forms of F minor, played two to a bar, or two beats on each chord. The common finger approach that you use in the previous exercise works like a charm here: The 3rd finger plays the same string in all three chord forms. So keep it anchored on the 4th string as you move your hand up and down the neck.

To see the neck diagram for the four forms of an outside F7 chord, along with the corresponding music and tab, check out Figure 4-5. Practice the pattern until you can move comfortably between the forms in rhythm.

When you're ready, try the exercise in Figure 4-6 in rhythm. It uses the four outside forms of F7, played two to a bar, or two beats on each chord. Seventh chords are a favorite choice for blues rhythm players, so if you're interested, practice this progression with the blues chords of B♭7 and C7.

Now take a look at the neck diagram and corresponding music and tab for the four forms of an outside Fm7 chord in Figure 4-7. Try practicing this pattern in two ways: by playing it with a pick, and using just your right-hand fingers. Try to make the two approaches sound as close to each other as you can.

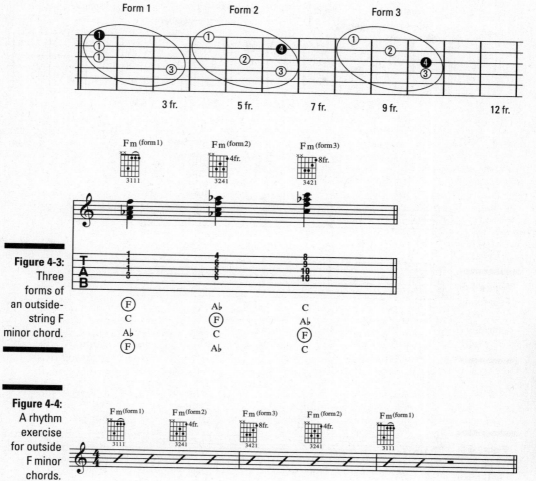

Figure 4-3: Three forms of an outside-string F minor chord.

Figure 4-4: A rhythm exercise for outside F minor chords.

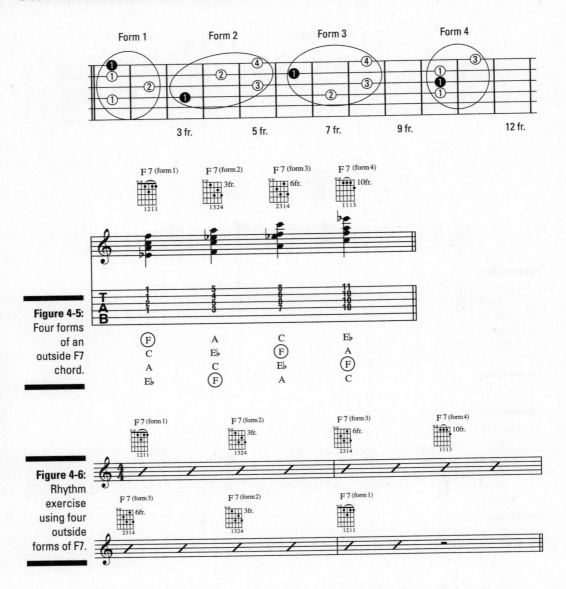

Figure 4-5: Four forms of an outside F7 chord.

Figure 4-6: Rhythm exercise using four outside forms of F7.

Figure 4-8 shows an exercise using the four outside forms of Fm7, played two to a bar, or two beats on each chord. Outside minor 7th chords are quite common in the jazz guitar style known as *chord melody,* so work for a smooth, even, and mellow sound as you play these chords. Imagine yourself jamming alongside a stand-up bass and a drummer using brushes.

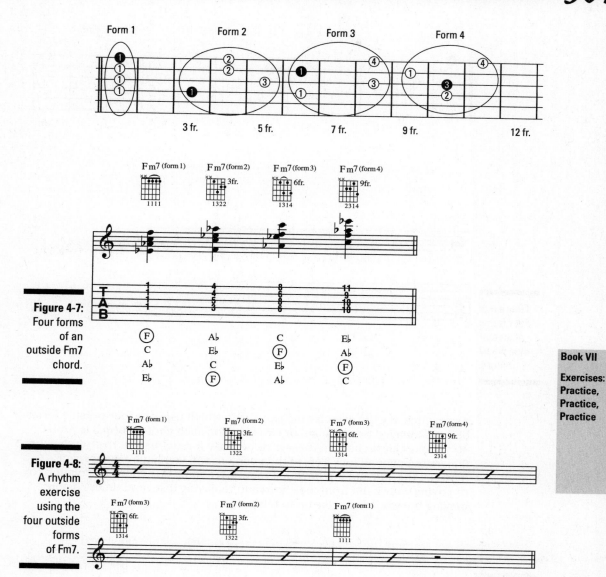

Figure 4-7:
Four forms of an outside Fm7 chord.

Figure 4-8:
A rhythm exercise using the four outside forms of Fm7.

Book VII

Exercises: Practice, Practice, Practice

Figure 4-9 illustrates the neck diagram and corresponding music and tab for the four forms of an outside Fmaj7 chord. Practice this pattern until you're completely comfortable with the four-fret spread among your left-hand fingers in form 3.

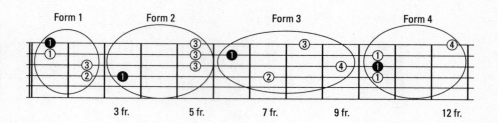

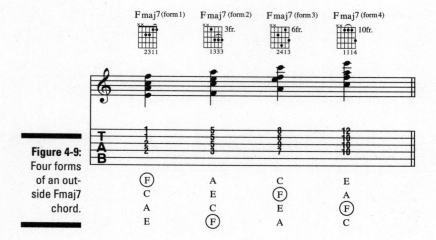

Figure 4-9: Four forms of an outside Fmaj7 chord.

As practice, try the exercise in Figure 4-10, which uses the four outside forms of Fmaj7, played two to a bar, or two beats on each chord. Form 3 is probably the trickiest chord in this series because it requires you to stretch your fingers out over all four frets in the position, and you have a wide space between the 2nd and 3rd fingers. Practice grabbing this chord in isolation (by removing your hand from the chord and replaying it several times) before playing the whole exercise up to tempo.

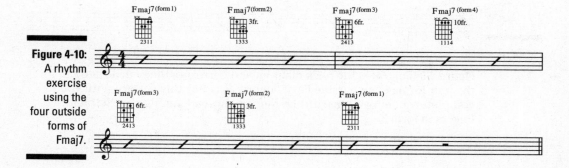

Figure 4-10: A rhythm exercise using the four outside forms of Fmaj7.

In Figure 4-11, you see the neck diagram for the four forms of an outside F#m7♭5 chord along with the corresponding music and tab. Practice this pattern slowly at first and as many times as you need to until you have it memorized. Then, when you get "off book," work on playing it faster.

Now try your hand at the exercise in Figure 4-12, which uses the four outside forms of F#m7♭5, played two to a bar, or two beats on each chord. Except for the first and last chords, every chord in this exercise is played with a barre. Be sure to check your barre notes (by playing the individual strings one at a time, slowly) to make sure they're all ringing out clearly and with no buzzing.

To see the neck diagram and corresponding music and tab for the three forms of an outside-string F#dim7 chord, check out Figure 4-13. Songs using the diminished 7th chord sometimes have you playing several forms in quick succession, so make sure you can play this at a fairly fast tempo.

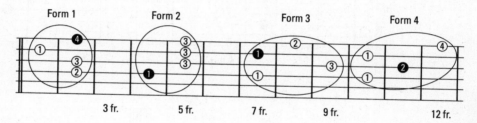

Book VII

Exercises: Practice, Practice, Practice

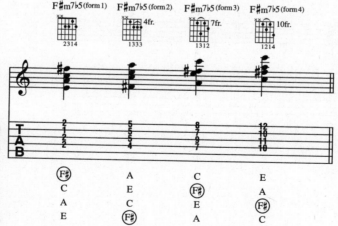

Figure 4-11: Four forms of an outside F#m7♭5 chord.

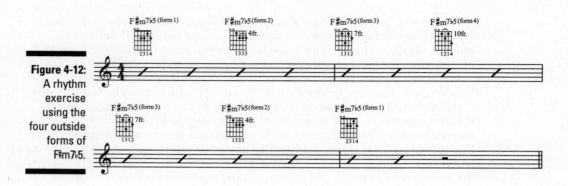

Figure 4-12: A rhythm exercise using the four outside forms of F#m7b5.

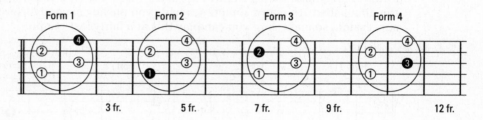

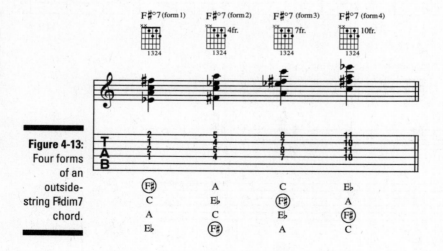

Figure 4-13: Four forms of an outside-string F#dim7 chord.

When you're ready to finish off your outside chord practice, take a look at Figure 4-14, which shows an exercise in rhythm using the four outside forms of F♯dim7, played two to a bar, or two beats on each chord. The diminished chord form has the same fingering for all of its inversions. So you get a free pass here and have to learn only one form, which you can slide up and down the neck with abandon. Because your fingers don't have to switch strings, try playing this example at a brighter tempo than you normally would.

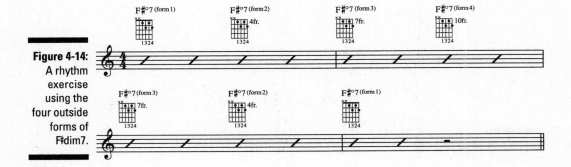

Figure 4-14: A rhythm exercise using the four outside forms of F♯dim7.

Patterns using inside chords

Figure 4-15 shows the neck diagram and corresponding music and tab for the three forms of an inside F major chord. Remember that the *X*s in the chord diagrams indicate that those strings aren't played. Practice this pattern as many times as you need to in order to get it to flow smoothly and so there's no trace of that 5th string ringing through.

In the case of inside chords, it's difficult *not* to strike the 5th string when strumming (either with the backs of the fingernails or with a pick). So you should mute, or deaden, the string by allowing a left-hand finger to lightly touch it, which will prevent it from ringing out. This muting action is usually done by the finger that's fretting the 6th string. For the 1st string, simply relaxing the left hand so the underside of the fingers touch the string lightly is enough to prevent it from ringing out.

You can practice this muting technique in Figure 4-16, which uses the three inside forms of F, played two to a bar, or two beats on each chord. Strum each chord lightly in quarter notes (one strum per beat), and avoid or mute the 5th and 1st strings of the guitar (indicated with *X*s in the chord diagrams).

Book VII

Exercises: Practice, Practice, Practice

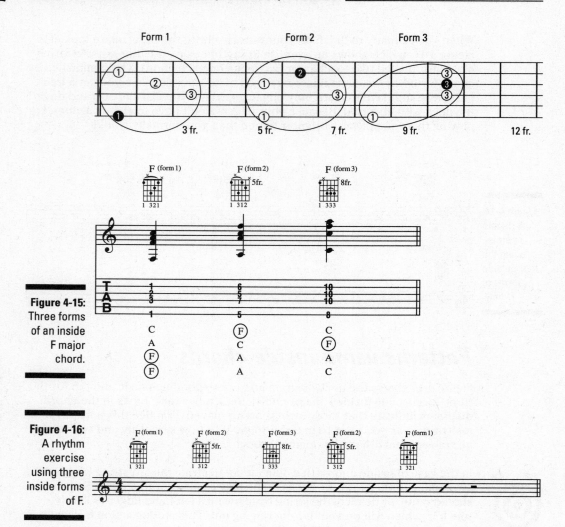

Figure 4-15:
Three forms of an inside F major chord.

Figure 4-16:
A rhythm exercise using three inside forms of F.

Figure 4-17 shows the neck diagram and corresponding standard notation and tab for the three forms of an inside F minor chord. You can practice this pattern by keeping the 3rd and 1st fingers in the same basic shape as you change chords; they never leave the string they're on, and they're always one fret apart from each other.

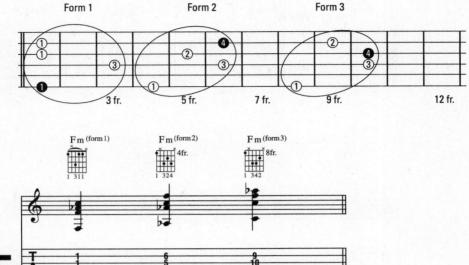

Figure 4-17: The three forms of an inside F minor chord.

When you're ready, try Figure 4-18's exercise in rhythm, which uses the three inside forms of F minor, played two to a bar, or two beats on each chord. You may have trouble muting the 5th string (which isn't supposed to sound) on form 1. So for this exercise, try plucking the strings with your right-hand fingers rather than strumming them with a pick.

Figure 4-18: A rhythm exercise using three inside forms of F minor.

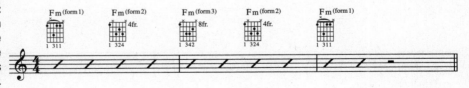

Now take a look at the neck diagram and corresponding music and tab for the four forms of an inside F7 chord, shown in Figure 4-19. Make sure you can blend all the notes together with your right-hand attack and that no one note stands out. Practice this pattern so you can change smoothly between the chords that use barres (forms 1 and 4) and those that don't (forms 2 and 3).

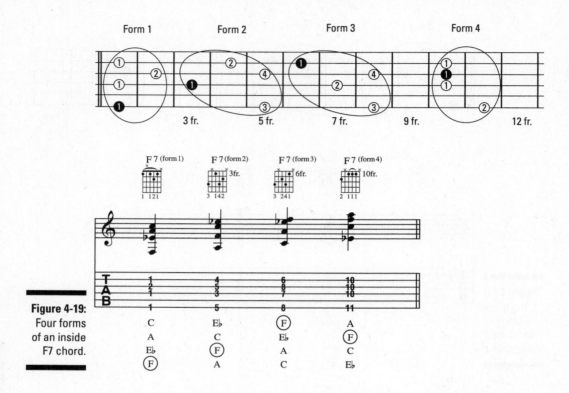

Figure 4-19:
Four forms
of an inside
F7 chord.

Give the exercise in Figure 4-20 a try. It uses the four inside forms of F7, played two to a bar, or two beats on each chord. Some guitarists, especially jazz players, like to use an alternate fingering for form 1. Try playing this chord with your 1st finger (not barred) on the 6th string, 2nd finger on the 4th string, 4th finger on the 3rd string, and 3rd finger on the 2nd string. If you prefer this fingering to the barred version, you may be a jazzbo!

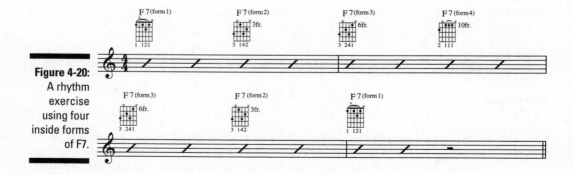

Figure 4-20:
A rhythm
exercise
using four
inside forms
of F7.

Here in Figure 4-21 is the neck diagram and corresponding music and tab for the four forms of an inside Fm7 chord. Practice this pattern using two versions of form 1: the one indicated in the pattern, and an alternate form with the 2nd finger on the 6th string and a 3rd-finger mini-barre for strings 4, 3, and 2.

Figure 4-22 shows an exercise using the four inside forms of Fm7, played two to a bar, or two beats on each chord. Most experienced guitarists (jazz and rock players alike) play form 1 with the 2nd finger on the 6th string and the 3rd finger (barred) across the 4th, 3rd, and 2nd strings, described in the previous paragraph. Playing the chord this way helps you to better keep the 5th string from sounding. Try form 1 the two-finger way, and if it seems awkward at the 1st fret, move it up to the middle of the neck.

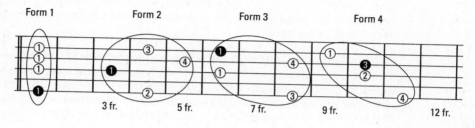

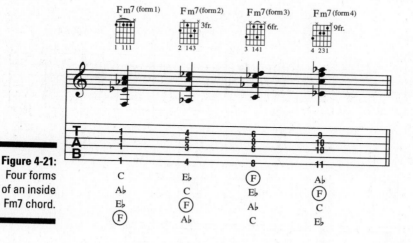

Figure 4-21: Four forms of an inside Fm7 chord.

Book VII

Exercises: Practice, Practice, Practice

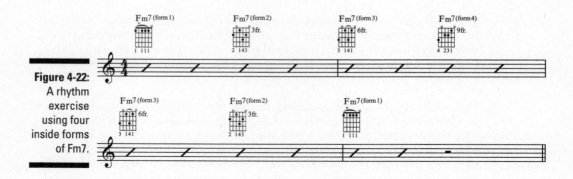

Figure 4-22: A rhythm exercise using four inside forms of Fm7.

To see the neck diagram and corresponding music and tab for the four forms of an inside Fmaj7 chord, check out Figure 4-23. Practice form 2 first in isolation because it has a stretch between the 2nd and 1st fingers. Then try the exercise in its entirety.

Figure 4-24 is an exercise using the four inside forms of Fmaj7, played two to a bar, or two beats on each chord. Between forms 3 and 4 you have an opportunity to make the chord change even smoother by leaving your 3rd finger on the 6th string as you move up and down the neck. Just be sure to relax the 3rd finger so it doesn't make a sliding sound on the string as you change positions.

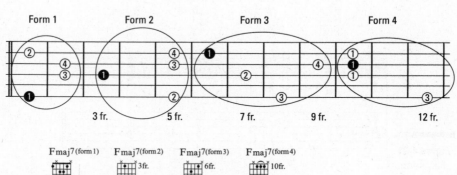

Figure 4-23: Four forms of an inside Fmaj7 chord.

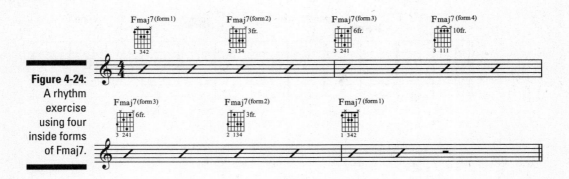

Figure 4-24:
A rhythm
exercise
using four
inside forms
of Fmaj7.

Figure 4-25 shows the neck diagram and corresponding music and tab for the four forms of an inside F#m7♭5 chord. Practice this pattern several times or until you master the three mini-barres that occur in this exercise.

As practice, try the exercise in Figure 4-26, which uses the four inside forms of F#m7♭5, played two to a bar, or two beats on each chord. A very cool "common finger" chord change occurs between forms 2 and 3. Both the 2nd and 1st fingers stay on the same strings as they move to the new form. But the 1st finger goes from playing a single note on the fingertip to playing a barre on the flat part. So be sure to flatten out your 1st finger slightly as you move. To become familiar with this efficient finger movement, try isolating these two chords (that is, practice changing between the two forms a number of times before playing the whole exercise).

Figure 4-27 shows the neck diagram and corresponding music and tab for the four forms of an inside F#dim7 chord. Your fingering doesn't change when moving among the four forms here, so work for speed and accuracy as you shift this pattern up and down the neck in three-fret increments.

To practice, you can try the exercise in Figure 4-28, which uses the four inside forms of F#dim7, played two to a bar, or two beats on each chord. Just as in the outside forms earlier in the chapter, the inside form of the diminished 7th chord is the same for all four forms.

Book VII

**Exercises:
Practice,
Practice,
Practice**

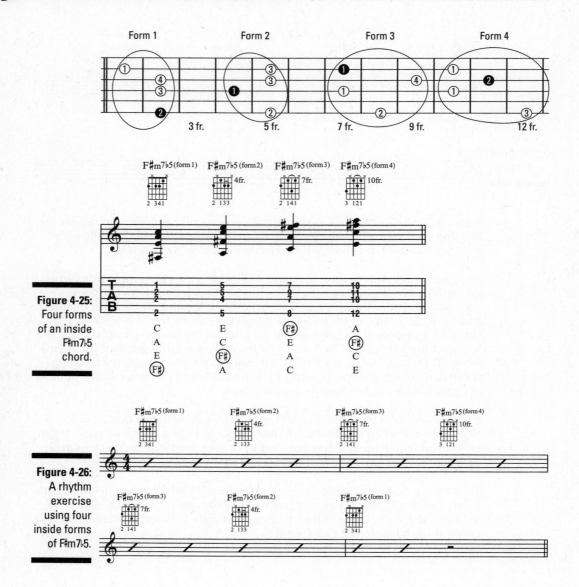

Figure 4-25:
Four forms
of an inside
F#m7♭5
chord.

Figure 4-26:
A rhythm
exercise
using four
inside forms
of F#m7♭5.

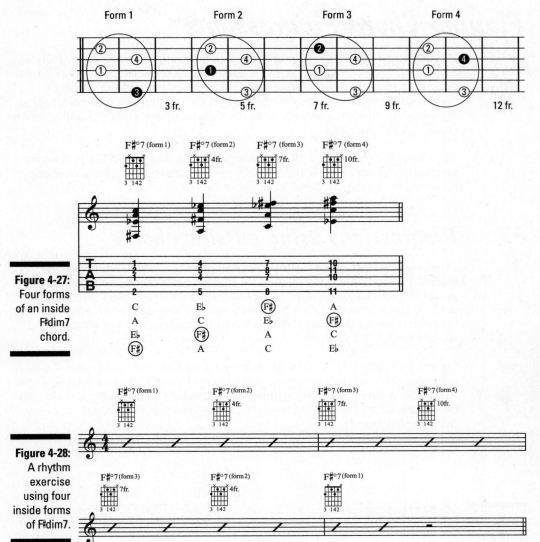

Figure 4-27: Four forms of an inside F#dim7 chord.

Figure 4-28: A rhythm exercise using four inside forms of F#dim7.

Book VII

Exercises: Practice, Practice, Practice

As if having the same forms didn't make things easy enough, try the alternate, three-finger version of the chord: Barre the 4th and 2nd strings with your 1st finger. Then play the 6th string note with your 2nd finger and the 3rd string note with your 3rd finger. Many guitarists find this fingering faster to grab than the one presented (especially after they become better at playing barre chords). Try both versions and decide for yourself, however.

Playing Chord Progressions

Playing chords by themselves or organized by string assignment is a good way to get your fingers in shape. But in actual musical situations, you play chords according to another organizing principle: a chord progression. A *chord progression* is merely a series of chords that go together in a musically logical fashion — to support a melody or as the framework for a jam or improvisation (such as the 12-bar blues).

The chord progressions in the following sections may sound like real and familiar songs, and they should. That's because many songs have used the following progressions either in whole or in part.

Progressions using outside chords

Outside chord forms use the top four strings of the guitar (which are the highest pitched), and they're good for rhythm parts when you have a bass player in your midst (or when you're joined by a pianist who's playing low notes in the left hand). Outside chord forms are also nice when you want the brighter sound of the higher strings to cut through — the way a mandolin sounds when it plays rhythm.

Figures 4-29 (Track 119) and 4-30 show two chord progressions, each of which uses nine different outside forms, played two to a bar. Play the chord progressions both *legato* (letting the strings ring out as long as possible) and *staccato* (where the strings are muted by the release of your fretting fingers) to create two different moods.

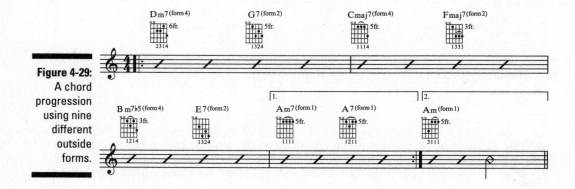

Figure 4-29: A chord progression using nine different outside forms.

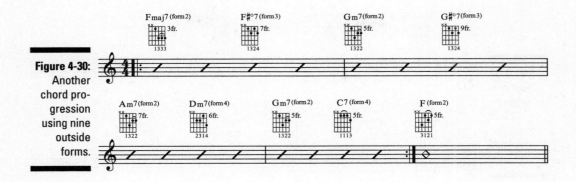

Figure 4-30: Another chord progression using nine outside forms.

Progressions using inside chords

In this book, inside chords feature the 6th string as part of the chord, separated widely from the next highest note because of the skip of the 5th string. The presence of the low note in inside chords means that the inside chords provide a nice bottom, or bass part, which is good for solo guitarists, guitarists playing with other instruments but without a bass player, or accompanists backing up a singer.

Take a look at Figures 4-31 (Track 120) and 4-32, which show two chord progressions, each using nine different inside forms, played two to a bar. To help get the 6th string note to ring a little more clearly, try separating it from the rest of the chord by plucking it a little harder than the rest of the strings, or by playing the bass note with your right-hand thumb and the rest of the chord with your index, middle, and ring fingers. For extra practice, try playing just the bass note on beats 1 and 3 and just the upper three strings of the chord on beats 2 and 4.

Book VII

Exercises: Practice, Practice, Practice

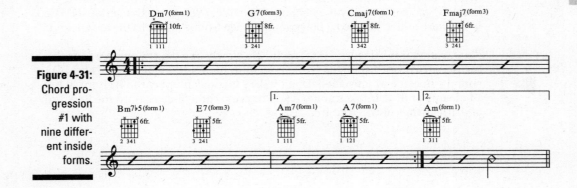

Figure 4-31: Chord progression #1 with nine different inside forms.

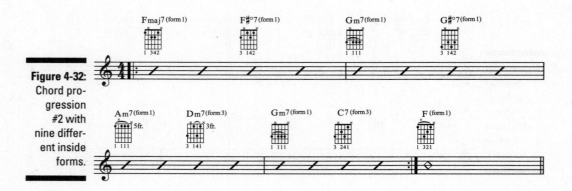

Figure 4-32: Chord progression #2 with nine different inside forms.

Practicing Pieces that Use Chord Progressions

Seventh chords are great for playing jazz and jazzy types of arrangements, so we selected two songs to jazzify in the following sections: One is a traditional folk ballad, and the other is a standard by Jerome Kern. The first song has you working with outside chords, and the second one gives you an inside look at inside chords.

Putting outside chords to use with "Danny Boy"

The lovely Irish ballad "Danny Boy" is actually based on an old traditional melody called "Londonderry Air." And if you've ever checked out the *derrières* in London, you can see why they changed the title. *[Rim shot.]* But seriously. The lyrics were added later, as a poignant message from a father to his absent son.

Play "Danny Boy" (Figure 4-33, Track 121) slowly and gently, and try to make the one-beat chord changes (which occur in bars 8, 9, 11, 12, 14, 15, and 16) sound smooth and unrushed. Don't worry if you can't play the F chord in bar 14 cleanly at first; it takes some effort to cram three fingers onto the 2nd, 3rd, and 4th strings at the 10th fret.

Figure 4-33: Outside chords in "Danny Boy."

Book VII

Exercises: Practice, Practice, Practice

Try this alternate fingering if you're having trouble: Use your 3rd finger to barre the 2nd, 3rd, and 4th strings at the 10th fret, lifting it just enough to allow the 1st string (fretted by the 1st finger) to ring. It's tricky, but you may find it easier than using four separate fingers so high on the neck.

Playing inside chords in "Look for the Silver Lining"

Jerome Kern wrote "Look for the Silver Lining" for an all-but-forgotten musical called *Sally,* but most people who know this call to optimism are familiar with the versions sung by Judy Garland or jazz trumpet great Chet Baker.

Play this song (Figure 4-34, Track 122) moderately slowly, and try to let the chords that last only one beat (such as the Am7 and D7 chords in bar 1) sound as legato as the chords that receive two beats.

The trick to this piece is making quick and efficient motions *between* chord changes without affecting the ring-out of the chord strum itself. You need to change chords quickly, but you must also allow the chords to sound for their full duration.

Figure 4-34:
Inside chords in "Look for the Silver Lining."

Appendix A

96 Common Chords

● ●

*H*ere are chord diagrams for 96 of the most widely used chords. The chords are arranged in 12 columns from C to B, for all 12 notes of the chromatic scale. Each of the eight rows shows a different quality — major, minor, 7th, minor 7th, and so on. So if you're looking at a piece of music that calls for, say, a Gsus4 chord, go over to the eighth column from the left and then down to the sixth row from the top.

Left-hand fingerings appear immediately below the strings (1 = index, 2 = middle, 3 = ring, and 4 = little). An *O* above a string means to play the open string as part of the chord; an *X* above a string indicates it isn't part of the chord and shouldn't be played. A curved line means to play the dots (fretted notes) immediately below the line with a barre.

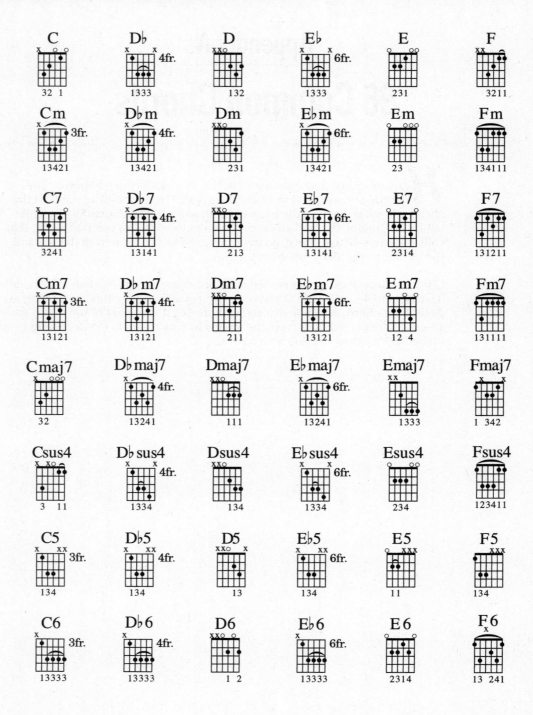

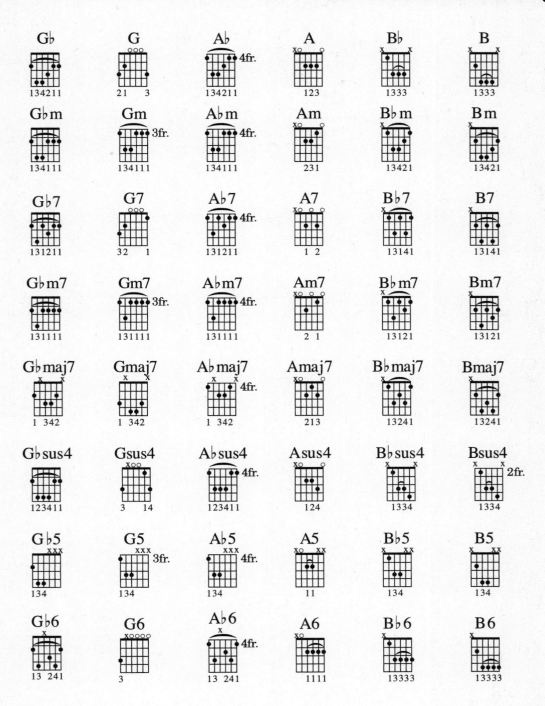

Appendix B

Accessing the Video Clips and Audio Tracks

• •

Sometimes, reading about a concept and trying to practice it just don't cut it — you need to see it or hear it, too. Wherever you see the "PlayThis!" icon in this book, you'll find references to a video clip or audio track that demonstrates various musical pieces, songs, exercises, scales, and the like. Several of the audio tracks play a tune for your reference, so you can see the printed music and hear it at the same time. This appendix provides you with a handy list of all the video clips and audio tracks referenced throughout the book.

So, where *are* these audio tracks and how do you get them? Like so much else in life, they're on the Internet — at www.dummies.com/go/guitaraio/.

Discovering What's on the Video Clips

Table B-1 lists all the video clips that accompany each chapter.

Table B-1		Video Clips
Track Number	*Chapter*	*Description*
1	Book I Chapter 1	The 5th-fret tuning method
2	Book I Chapter 2	Fretting correctly on the fingerboard
3	Book I Chapter 2	How to pick correctly
4	Book I Chapter 2	Forming an E chord step-by-step
5	Book II Chapter 1	Chord progression in the key of A
6	Book II Chapter 1	The motion of the downstrokes and upstrokes

(continued)

Table B-1 *(continued)*

Track Number	Chapter	Description
7	Book II Chapter 1	Chord progression using G-family chords
8	Book II Chapter 1	Chord progression using C-family chords
9	Book II Chapter 2	Right-hand strumming motion
10	Book II Chapter 2	Playing Dm7, Em7, and Am7
11	Book II Chapter 2	Checking 1st finger position
12	Book II Chapter 5	One-octave C-major scale in 2nd position
13	Book II Chapter 5	Orienting the left hand for playing in 7th position
14	Book II Chapter 5	The Segovia shift in the C major scale
15	Book II Chapter 5	Ascending motion of the left hand and correct fingering
16	Book II Chapter 5	Playing in 3rds in open position
17	Book III Chapter 1	Playing octave shapes
18	Book III Chapter 1	Playing in 3rds
19	Book III Chapter 1	Building and playing triads
20	Book III Chapter 1	Playing major scale chords in G
21	Book III Chapter 2	Playing your first CAGED form — C
22	Book III Chapter 3	7th chords in G
23	Book III Chapter 3	Blues shuffle with 6ths
24	Book III Chapter 4	Major scale chord pattern in G
25	Book III Chapter 4	Playing by number in the open position
26	Book III Chapter 5	G major and E minor scales and chords
27	Book III Chapter 5	Playing in A Dorian
28	Book III Chapter 6	Demonstrating a closing progression
29	Book III Chapter 6	Secondary dominants C-A7-D7-G7
30	Book III Chapter 6	Voice leading C-E7-F-G-C

Discovering What's on the Audio Tracks

Table B-2 lists all the audio tracks that accompany each chapter, along with any figure numbers if applicable. You also find several backing and play-along tracks to help you with your practice.

Table B-2		Audio Tracks
Track Number	**Chapter**	**Description**
1	Book I Chapter 1	Open string tuning reference
2	Book II Chapter 1	Simple chord progressions in the keys of A, D, G, and C
3	Book II Chapter 1	"Kumbaya"
4	Book II Chapter 1	"Swing Low, Sweet Chariot"
5	Book II Chapter 1	"Auld Lang Syne"
6	Book II Chapter 1	"Michael, Row the Boat Ashore"
7	Book II Chapter 2	"Home on the Range"
8	Book II Chapter 2	"All Through the Night"
9	Book II Chapter 2	"Over the River and Through the Woods"
10	Book II Chapter 2	"It's Raining, It's Pouring"
11	Book II Chapter 2	"Oh, Susanna"
12	Book II Chapter 3	A typical power-chord progression
13	Book II Chapter 3	A progression using A-based major barre chords
14	Book II Chapter 3	Chord changes to Bob Dylan's "Lay Lady Lay"
15	Book II Chapter 4	Strumming an E chord in quarter notes
16	Book II Chapter 4	An eighth-note progression using right-hand downstrokes
17	Book II Chapter 4	An easy 4/4 strum in eighth notes using downstrokes and upstrokes
18	Book II Chapter 4	Strumming in quarter and eighth notes for different intensity levels
19	Book II Chapter 4	A medium-tempo R&B progression using sixteenth notes

(continued)

Table B-2 *(continued)*

Track Number	Chapter	Description
20	Book II Chapter 4	Eighth-note shuffle in G
21	Book II Chapter 4	A boom-chick pattern in a bouncy country-rock progression
22	Book II Chapter 4	Separating the bass notes from the treble chord forms with Led Zeppelin-ish feel
23	Book II Chapter 4	A moving bass line over a chord progression
24	Book II Chapter 4	A common rock figure using eighth-note syncopation
25	Book II Chapter 4	A common rock figure using eighth- and sixteenth-note syncopation
26	Book II Chapter 4	Left-hand muting to simulate syncopation
27	Book II Chapter 4	A rhythm figure with palm mutes and accents
28	Book II Chapter 4	An eighth-note 5-6 progression using all downstrokes and a moving left hand
29	Book II Chapter 4	Fingerstyle arpeggios
30	Book II Chapter 4	A straight-ahead 4/4 groove in the style of The Eagles
31	Book II Chapter 4	A two-beat country groove with bass runs
32	Book II Chapter 4	A medium tempo funky groove in a 16-feel
33	Book II Chapter 4	A heavy metal gallop using eighths and sixteenths
34	Book II Chapter 4	A typical Reggae backup pattern highlighting the offbeats
35	Book II Chapter 4	A song in 3/4, featuring a moving bass line
36	Book II Chapter 5	Three examples of patterns to help build up the left hand
37	Book II Chapter 5	"Simple Gifts"
38	Book II Chapter 5	"Turkey in the Straw"
39	Book II Chapter 5	C major scales in double-stops

Track Number	Chapter	Description
40	Book II Chapter 5	"Aura Lee"
41	Book II Chapter 5	"The Streets of Laredo"
42	Book II Chapter 5	"Double-Stop Rock"
43	Book III Chapter 1	Notes, steps, octaves, and intervals
44	Book III Chapter 1	Chord construction, triads, chords, and the harmonized major scale
45	Book III Chapter 2	Some examples of the CAGED system in action
46	Book III Chapter 3	Some examples of chord tones and extensions
47	Book III Chapter 4	Sample chord progressions
48	Book III Chapter 5	Identifying tonics, keys, and modes
49	Book III Chapter 6	Examples of dominant function and voice leading
50	Book IV Chapter 1	Sound quality of the electric guitar
51	Book IV Chapter 2	Quarter-note melodies
52	Book IV Chapter 2	Octave scales and arpeggios
53	Book IV Chapter 2	Various melodies
54	Book IV Chapter 2	A two-octave G major scale in 2nd position
55	Book IV Chapter 2	A classic walking-bass boogie-woogie riff in G
56	Book IV Chapter 2	Pentatonic scale played from high to low
57	Book IV Chapter 2	Solos
58	Book IV Chapter 2	A slow blues shuffle in A
59	Book IV Chapter 3	Lots of riffs
60	Book IV Chapter 3	Double-stop figures
61	Book IV Chapter 3	A hard rock progression mixing chords and single notes
62	Book IV Chapter 4	Rhythm figures and double-stops
63	Book IV Chapter 4	Blues licks
64	Book IV Chapter 4	Bluesy riffs
65	Book IV Chapter 4	Hammer-ons, pull-offs, and slides
66	Book IV Chapter 4	Various bends

(continued)

Table B-2 *(continued)*

Track Number	Chapter	Description
67	Book IV Chapter 4	Vibrato
68	Book V Chapter 1	Striking to a beat
69	Book V Chapter 1	A bass-and-chord pick-strum pattern for country blues
70	Book V Chapter 1	Two-beat or cut shuffle feel alternates bass notes with chords
71	Book V Chapter 1	A pick-strum pattern in a slow 12/8 feel
72	Book V Chapter 1	Examples of syncopation
73	Book V Chapter 1	Rhythm figure with palm mutes and accents
74	Book V Chapter 1	Fingerstyle blues with a quarter-note bass
75	Book V Chapter 1	A progression in a shuffle feel
76	Book V Chapter 1	A driving straight-four groove
77	Book V Chapter 1	12/8 feel for slow-tempo blues, a la The Allman Brothers
78	Book V Chapter 1	The two-beat feel used for more lively blues
79	Book V Chapter 1	Medium tempo, funky groove in a 16 feel
80	Book V Chapter 2	12-bar blues and quick-four variation
81	Book V Chapter 2	The last four bars of a 12-bar blues with a turnaround bar
82	Book V Chapter 2	Slow 12-bar blues in 12/8 time
83	Book V Chapter 2	Straight-four progression with a variation
84	Book V Chapter 2	The Jimmy Reed move in G
85	Book V Chapter 2	The Jimmy Reed move in A
86	Book V Chapter 2	Minor blues progression that uses minor 7th chords
87	Book V Chapter 2	A four-bar intro and two-bar turnaround
88	Book V Chapter 2	Two-bar turnarounds
89	Book V Chapter 2	Slow blues ending
90	Book V Chapter 2	High moves in a 12-bar blues in E

Track Number	Chapter	Description
91	Book V Chapter 3	Boogie-woogie bass lines
92	Book V Chapter 3	Eighth- and sixteenth-note riffs
93	Book V Chapter 3	Two-note riffs
94	Book V Chapter 3	Progression fusing chords, single notes, and double-stops
95	Book V Chapter 3	Keith Richards riff
96	Book V Chapter 3	Intro riffs
97	Book V Chapter 3	Turnaround and ending riffs
98	Book V Chapter 3	A ragtime or country-blues progression in A
99	Book V Chapter 3	Rhythm groove over a 12-bar blues in E
100	Book VI Chapter 2	Layered melodies
101	Book VI Chapter 2	Minuet in G
102	Book VI Chapter 2	Air in A Minor
103	Book VI Chapter 2	"America (My Country 'Tis of Thee)"
104	Book VI Chapter 2	Andante in G
105	Book VI Chapter 3	Arpeggio exercise with melody in bass
106	Book VI Chapter 3	Study in A Minor, with the melody in the bass
107	Book VI Chapter 3	Arpeggio exercise with melody in treble
108	Book VI Chapter 3	Study in C, with the melody in the treble
109	Book VI Chapter 3	Arpeggio exercise with melody alternating between treble and bass
110	Book VI Chapter 3	Waltz in E Minor, with the melody alternating between the bass and treble
111	Book VI Chapter 3	Ländler in D
112	Book VI Chapter 3	"Romanza"
113	Book VI Chapter 3	Andante in C
114	Book VII Chapter 1	Major scale pattern #1
115	Book VII Chapter 2	Ascending and descending sequences

(continued)

Table B-2 *(continued)*

Track Number	Chapter	Description
116	Book VII Chapter 3	A natural minor scale in 5th position
117	Book VII Chapter 3	Ascending and descending melodic minor scale pattern
118	Book VII Chapter 3	The A harmonic minor scale in 5th position
119	Book VII Chapter 4	Chord progression using nine different outside forms
120	Book VII Chapter 4	Chord progression with nine different inside forms
121	Book VII Chapter 4	Outside chords in "Danny Boy"
122	Book VII Chapter 4	Inside chords in "Look for the Silver Lining"

Customer Care

If you have trouble downloading the companion files, please call Wiley Product Technical Support at 800-762-2974. Outside the United States, call 317-572-3994. You can also contact Wiley Product Technical Support at `http://support.wiley.com`. Wiley Publishing will provide technical support only for downloading and other general quality control items.

To place additional orders or to request information about other Wiley products, please call 877-762-2974.

Index

• *Symbols and Numerics* •

♭ (flat symbol), 168, 170
♮ (natural sign), 62
♯ (sharp symbol), 168, 170
> (accent mark), 68
· (augmentation dot), 65
· (*staccato* dot), 68
1st finger position, 100, 592
3 (triplet) notation, 64
3rds. *See* triads
4/4 time
  audio track, 593
  overview, 132
5-6 move
  audio track, 594
  eighth-note progressions, 138–139
  song examples, 138
5-6 riff (Jimmy Reed move)
  audio track, 596
  key of A, 417–419
  key of G, 416–417
  overview, 416, 432
5-note minor pentatonic scale, 381–382.
    See also pentatonic scale
5th-fret tuning method, 14–16, 591
6-note blues scale, 342, 381–382
6th string/5th string associations
  grouping notes, 170–172
  octave pitches, 173
  overview, 166–168
7th chords
  blues sound, 95, 272
  dominant, 95–98, 219–220,
    271–272
  Em7, Am7 variation diagrams, 218
  major scale diagrams, 213–214
  major/minor barre scale diagrams, 215
  open position chord diagrams, 216

overview, 78
  song examples, 217–218
  static dominant, 272
  video demonstration, 592
7th notes
  adding to chords, 213–217, 272–273
  double flat, 220
  flattened, 244, 250, 261
  implied notation, 223
8-bar blues, 413–414
9th chords, 224
12/8 groove. *See also* rhythm styles
  exercises, 388–389, 400–401
  overview, 383
  slow 12/8 feel, 399–401, 596
12-bar blues
  audio track, 596
  endings, 423
  high-note moves, 423–425
  intros, 421
  overview, 407–408
  quick four variation, 409–410
  slow blues, 411–412
  song examples, 411
  turnarounds, 410–411, 421–422
16-feel. *See also* rhythm styles
  exercises, 143, 403–404
  funky groove audio tracks, 594, 596
  funky groove usage, 403
  overview, 143, 403

• *A* •

A (augmented intervals), 182
a (right-hand ring finger) notation, 71
A chords
  diagrams, 79, 111, 589
  power chord diagrams, 112
  progression demonstration, 591

A Dorian chords
  diagram, 250
  video demonstration, 592
A7 chord, 97, 111, 216–217, 589
accelerando (accel.), 67
accent mark (>), 68
accenting notes
  audio track, 594
  muting versus, 137–138
  overview, 87
accentuation, 87
accidentals, 62
acoustic guitars
  acoustic-electrics, 9
  anatomy of, 8–10
  archtop, 39
  blues music, 379, 394
  electric versus, 7–8
  electrifying, 287–288
  nylon versus steel strings, 25, 48,
    52–53, 288
  picking versus fingerstyle, 26
  steel strings, 55–56, 288
  stringing, 48–51
action, 25
Adagio, 67
add9 chords
  diagrams, 222
  overview, 221
Aeolian tonic mode
  fretboard patterns, 245, 247
  overview, 264
  song examples, 246–248
A-family chords
  exercises, 80
  fingering, 78–79
  overview, 78
  strumming, 79–81
A-form barre chords
  audio track, 593
  B♭ diagram, 120
  B♭7 diagram, 122
  B♭7sus diagram, 122
  B♭m diagram, 122
  B♭m7 diagram, 122
  B♭maj7 diagram, 122
  moving technique, 121
  overview, 119–120

power-chord counterparts, 120
  progressions, 121
  variations, 121–122
Aguado, Dionisio, 484
"Air in A Minor"
  arrangement, 475, 477
  audio track, 597
"All Through the Night"
  arrangement, 101, 104
  audio track, 593
"Allegro" (Handel), 557–559
Am chord, 84, 111, 589
Am7 chord
  diagrams, 99, 111, 214–218, 589
  video demonstration, 592
Amaj7 chord, 100, 111, 217, 289
"America (My Country 'Tis of Thee)"
  arrangement, 475, 478
  audio track, 597
amplification, 12–13
amplifiers
  anatomy of, 296–297
  blues music, 379
  illustration of, 296
  overview, 290–291, 295
  physics explanation, 297
Andante, 67, 474
"Andante in C"
  arrangement, 493, 499–500
  audio track, 597
"Andante in E minor", 474
"Andante in G"
  arrangement, 475, 479
  audio track, 597
anticipation, 328
arpeggio chords
  audio tracks, 594, 597
  fingerstyle advantage, 139–140
  linear playing versus, 347
  overview, 302
  practice scales, 311
  skips versus, 311
arpeggio melodies
  accenting notes, 486–487
  "Andante in C", 493, 499–500
  audio track, 597
  bass melodies, 482–485
  bass versus treble, 485

fingering technique, 481–483
"Ländler in D", 491, 494–495
melody combinations, 481
"Romanza", 492, 496–498
textures, 481–482
treble melodies, 485–488
treble/bass shifts, 488–491
"Waltz in E Minor", 491
articulation
bending, 290, 334
expressive playing, 334
hammer-ons, 313, 334
muting, 334
pull-offs, 313, 334
slides, 313, 334
vibrato, 8, 294, 313, 324, 334
articulation symbols, 67–68
attacking notes, 304
audio tracks
accessing, 2–4
overview, 3–4
track numbers/descriptions,
494–496
tuning with, 19
augmentation dot (·), 65
augmented intervals (A), 182
"Auld Lang Syne"
arrangement, 89, 92
audio track, 593
G-family chords, 85
"Aura Lee"
arrangement, 158, 160
audio track, 594

• B •

B7 chord, 98, 111, 589
Bach, J. S., 471
back of guitar, 8
backphrasing technique, 383
balance, 22
bar. See barre chords
bar (electric guitar), 8, 294
bar lines
double, 68
overview, 60–61
playing instructions, 80–81

barre chords. See also A-form barre
chords; E-form barre chords
buzzing, 99
exercises, 121–122
F-family chords, 86
major/minor scale diagrams, 213–214
moving technique, 117
notations on staff, 72
open chord counterparts, 122
overview, 115
playing up the neck, 333
progressions, 121–122
technique suggestions, 115
two-string, 99
Bartolini pickups, 42
bass line melodies
arpeggio melodies, 482–485
"Study in A minor", 485
treble/bass shifts, 488–491
"Waltz in E Minor", 491
bass lines
audio tracks, 594
classical guitar technique, 468
counterpoint versus, 468
descending chromatic progressions, 281–282
examples, 187
moving bass line, 132–133
thumb technique, 482
treble separation advantages, 132
bass runs
definition, 143
two-beat feel audio example, 594
bass strings, 27–28
bass-chord pattern, 131–132
beats. See also notes; progressions
accenting notes, 505, 537
arpeggio notes, 482–483
audio tracks, 596
counting/tapping, 65
independent rhythm challenges, 470
last bar completion, 514
metronome use, 428
mid-measure jumps, 514
pickup measures, 88
striking in rhythm, 385–386
syncopation, 87, 390–391
tie notes, 86

bends
  acoustic versus electric guitars, 351–352
  articulation, 334
  audio tracks, 595
  bend and release, 352
  blues music, 379, 382
  overview, 290
  pre-bend technique, 353
  string gauge, 351–352
  technique, 351
  vibrato technique, 354
Bb barre chord, 120
Bb chord, 111, 589
Bb7 barre chord, 122
Bb7sus barre chord, 122
Bbm barre chord, 122
Bbm7 barre chord, 122
Bbmaj7 barre chord, 122
Bill Lawrence pickups, 42
blue notes, 341, 381
bluegrass guitars, 37
blues. *See also* I-IV-V chord progressions;
    shuffle rhythm; strumming
  5-6 move, 138
  5-note minor pentatonic scale, 381–382
  7th chords, 78, 95, 272
  8-bar structure, 413–414
  9th chords, 224
  12/8 groove, 383, 388–389, 399–401, 596
  12-bar structure, 407–408
  audio tracks, 595, 596
  backphrasing technique, 383
  bending notes, 379, 382
  blue notes, 341, 381
  blues scale, 342, 381–382
  blues shuffle style, 227
  chord progressions, 381
  common feels, 395
  definition, 380
  double-stops, 158–159
  electric guitar effect on, 289
  electric versus acoustic guitars, 379, 394
  fingerstyle, 394
  guitar models associated with, 37
  improvisation, 321
  Jimmy Reed move, 416–419
  jump rhythm, 383

  minor 7th chord progressions, 420
  minor keys, 420
  overview, 271, 379–380
  picking, 26
  playing in position, 152
  primary key families, 406–407
  slide use, 380, 382
  slurring use, 382
  song structure, 407–408
  straight-four, 414–415
  techniques, 382–383
  vibrato use, 382
blues rhythm styles
  12/8 groove, 399–401
  12-bar blues, 408—409
  16-feel, 403–404
  audio tracks, 596
  listing, 395
  quick-four, 409–410
  shuffle groove, 395–397
  straight-four, 397–398
  two-beat feel, 402
blues shuffle
  overview, 227
  video demonstration, 592
blues-rock music
  5-6 move, 138–139
  audio track, 594
Bm chord, 111
body caps, 40
body of guitar, 8, 294
boogie-bass pattern, 429–430
boogie-woogie
  6th chord use, 227
  audio tracks, 595, 597
  lower register riffs, 315
  practice riff, 325
  quarter-note riffs, 428
boom-chick pattern
  audio track, 594
  exercises, 388, 402
  overview, 131–132
  three feel, 145
bouts, 22
bridge
  description, 9, 294
  illustration of, 292

bridge pins, 9
buying guitars
   construction quality, 38–40
   cosmetics, 43
   criteria, 35–36
   materials, 41–42
   online versus retail stores, 44, 46–47
   personal decisions, 34–35
   shopping choices, 44–47
   style/model choices, 36–38
   workmanship, 42–43
buzzing
   avoiding, 24
   eliminating during two-string barre, 99
   overview, 32

• *C* •

C (ceja; cejilla) barre notation, 72
C chords
   diagrams, 84, 111
   progression demonstration, 592
C form. *See* CAGED system
C7 chord, 96, 111, 588
CAGED system
   A minor form, 208
   audio track, 595
   C form arpeggio pattern, 191–192
   C form barre chords, 191–192
   C form chord voicings, 195–198
   C minor form, 207
   D form, 205–207
   D minor form, 209
   E form, 202–204
   E minor form, 209
   G form, 201–202
   G minor form, 208
   overview, 189
   video demonstration, 592
calluses, 80–81
capos, 191
Carcassi, Matteo, 493
Carulli, Ferdinando, 490
C-family chords
   exercises, 87
   fingering, 85–86

overview, 85
strumming, 86–87
chord diagrams
   A, 79, 111, 589
   A5, 589
   A6, 227, 589
   A7, 97, 111, 217, 589
   Aadd9, 222
   A♭, 589
   A♭5, 589
   A♭6, 589
   A♭7, 589
   A♭m, 589
   A♭m7, 589
   A♭maj7, 589
   A♭sus4, 589
   Am, 84, 111, 589
   Am7, 99, 111, 214–218, 589
   Am(add9), 223
   Amaj7, 100, 111, 217, 589
   Asus2, 221
   Asus4, 225, 589
   B, 589
   B5, 589
   B6, 589
   B7, 98, 111, 589
   B♭, 111, 589
   B♭5, 589
   B♭6, 589
   B♭m, 589
   B♭m7, 589
   B♭maj7, 589
   B♭sus4, 589
   Bm, 111, 589
   Bm7, 214–217, 589
   Bm7(♭5), 217
   Bmaj7, 589
   Bsus4, 589
   C, 84, 111, 588
   C5, 588
   C6, 227, 588
   C7, 96, 111, 588
   C9, 224
   Cadd4, 225–226
   Cadd9, 222
   Cm7, 588

chord diagrams *(continued)*
Cmaj7, 100, 111, 214–217, 588
C♯m7, 217
C♯m7(♭5), 217
Csus4, 225, 588
D, 79, 111, 588
D5, 588
D6, 588
D7, 96, 111, 216, 219, 588
D9, 224
Dadd4, 225–226
D♭, 588
D♭5, 588
D♭6, 588
D♭m, 588
D♭m7, 588
D♭maj7, 588
D♭sus4, 588
Dm, 86, 111, 588
Dm7, 99, 111, 214–215, 588
Dmaj7, 100, 111, 217, 588
Dsus2, 221
Dsus4, 225, 588
E, 79, 111, 588
E5, 588
E6, 227, 588
E7, 98, 111, 217, 588
Eadd9, 222
E♭, 588
E♭5, 588
E♭6, 588
E♭7, 588
E♭m, 588
E♭m7, 588
E♭maj7, 588
E♭sus4, 588
Em, 82, 111, 588
Em7, 99, 111, 214–218, 588
Em(add9), 223
Emaj7, 588
Esus4, 225, 588
F, 86, 111, 588
F5, 588
F6, 227, 588
F7, 588
Fadd9, 222

Fm, 588
Fm7, 588
Fm(add9), 223
Fmaj7, 100, 111, 217
F♯m7, 217
F♯m7♭5, 215–216
Fsus4, 225, 588
G, 82, 111, 589
G5, 589
G6, 227, 589
G7, 96, 111, 217, 589
G9/B, 224
G9/F, 224
Gadd11, 225–226
G♭, 589
G♭5, 589
G♭6, 589
G♭7, 589
G♭m, 589
G♭m7, 589
G♭maj7, 589
G♭sus4, 589
Gm, 589
Gm7, 589
Gmaj7, 214–217, 589
G♯m7(♭5), 217
Gsus4, 225, 589
open chords, 29
open versus fretted strings, 29
overview, 28
tonic numbering system, 244–245
chord numbers
5th string chord progressions, 236–239
fretboard visualization, 231–232
I-IV-V chord progressions, 234, 236–239
major chord progressions, 234–235
minor chord progressions, 235–236
open position chords, 239–240
overview, 230–231, 405–406
Roman numeral representations,
230–231, 235
transposing, 232–233
video demonstration, 592
chord practice. *See* inversions
chord progressions. *See* progressions
chord tones, 211–212

chords. *See also* 7th chords; barre chords; CAGED system; inversions; moveable chords; progressions; rhythm styles; triads
  A-family, 78–81
  arpeggio style, 302
  blues progressions, 381
  capo use, 191
  C-family, 85–87
  chord formulas, 268
  common tones, 84
  counterpoint technique, 471
  definition, 28
  D-family, 81–83
  dominant, 271
  dominant 7th, 95–98, 219–220, 271
  double-stop properties, 330
  E-form barre, 116–119
  extended dominant, 224
  extensions, 212–213
  families, overview, 77
  fingering technique, 78
  fingering techniques, 561
  G5 notation, 113
  G-family, 84–85
  grabbing, 110
  half diminished, 220
  key/chord form listing, 346
  major and minor 7th, 217–218
  major versus minor, 78
  members, 190
  minor, staff notation, 81
  minor 7th, 98–99
  moveable, 113
  numbered patterns, 229–232
  open position, 29, 110–111
  parallel tonics mode chart, 269
  pattern recognition, 229
  pattern visualization, 231–232
  plucking, 31
  positions, 114
  qualities of, 78
  riffs, bridging with, 323
  Roman numeral use, 230–231
  root notes, 166
  secondary dominants, 275–280
  shapes versus, 335
  strumming, 31
  technique demonstration, 591
  tonic mode build chart, 269
  transposing, 148, 150, 232–233
  V7 chords, 272
  voicing, 98, 190, 200
chorus effect, 298
chromatic notes, 326
chromatic scales, 281
classical guitar genre. *See also* counterpoint; textures
  barre notation, 72
  contrapuntal (polyphonic) music, 468–471
  definition of, 446
  fingering notation, 70–72, 139–140
  free stroke/rest stroke, 28
  guitar models associated with, 37
  history, 446–447
  memorizing compositions, 452
  minor scale usage, 540
  music notation usage, 59
  musicianship (accuracy), 452
  music-reading requirements, 451–452
  overview, 445
  playing in position, 150–151
  special strokes, 28
  standard music notation, 59
  tablature staff viewpoint, 74
  tempo headings, 67
  virtuosity, 452
classical guitars. *See also* counterpoint
  acoustic guitars versus, 447–449
  arm rest use, 456
  body shape/size, 448
  chair selection, 454
  counterpoint fingering technique, 468–469
  design differences, 25
  footstool versus support (cushion), 454–455
  free stroke, 462–464
  fretboard differences, 449
  fretting technique, 460–461
  golpeador (protective plate), 449

classical guitars *(continued)*
  hand positions, 25–26, 450
  history of, 446–447
  inventor of, 449
  left hand placement, 458–459
  leg position, 454
  little finger usage, 464
  nail filing guide, 461–462
  nail-flesh tone development, 462–463
  neck differences, 448
  plucking technique, 462
  plucking versus picking, 451
  posture/playing position, 21–22, 452–453
  rest stroke, 465–466
  right hand placement, 457
  sitting position, 454
  string differences, 447
  stringing, 10, 48
  texture creation, 467
clefs, 60
Cmaj7 chord, 100, 111
Coda, 68
common time, 132
common tones, 84, 98
construction quality of guitars
  appointments, 43
  body caps, 40
  hardware, 41–42
  neck types, 40
  overview, 36
  pickups/electronics, 42
  solid versus laminated wood, 40
  wood types, 41
  workmanship, 42–43
contrapuntal music. *See* counterpoint
counterpoint
  "Andante in E minor", 474
  bass lines versus, 468
  block versus flowing styles, 472–473
  double-stops, 471
  fingering techniques, 468–469, 472–473
  "Gavotte in A", 471
  homophonic sound, 472
  independent rhythms, 470, 473–474
  matching rhythms, 472–473
  melody and accompaniment style, 472–473

"Minuet in A Minor", 470
"O Christmas Tree", 473
"O Little Town of Bethlehem", 469
  overview, 468
  rhythms in sync, 468–469
country music
  audio tracks, 594, 596–597
  bass-chord pattern, 131
  double-stops, 156
  guitar models associated with, 37
  picking, 26
  playing in position, 152–153
  secondary dominant chords, 277
  two-beat feel, 143, 594
crescendo (cresc.), 68
cut shuffle. *See* boom-chick pattern
cut time, 143. *See also* 4/4 time

D chord, 79, 111, 588
D7 chord, 96, 111, 210, 216, 588
damping, 137. *See also* muting
"Danny Boy"
  arrangement, 582–584
  audio track, 598
D.C. al Coda, 68
D.C. al Fine, 68
decrescendo (decres.), 68
D-family chords
  exercises, 83
  fingering, 81–82
  overview, 81
  strumming, 83
diatonic scales, 281
digital delay effect, 298
dim (diminished intervals), 182
dim. (diminuendo), 68
DiMarzio pickups, 42
diminished 7th chords, 220
diminished intervals (dim), 182
diminuendo (dim.), 68
dissonance
  7th scale degree, 248
  Locrian mode, 264
  passing versus neighboring tones, 490
  tritones, 273

distortion
adjusting sound quality, 313
overview, 288–289
power chords, 112
special effect, 298
Dm chord, 86, 111, 588
Dm7 chord
diagrams, 99, 111, 214–215, 588
video demonstration, 592
Dmaj7 chord, 100, 111, 217, 288
dominant 7th chords. *See also* secondary
dominant chords
B7, 98, 111, 589
C7, 96, 111, 588
chromatic versus diatonic progressions,
281–282
D7, 96, 111, 216, 219, 588
E7, 98, 111, 217, 588
G7, 96, 111, 217, 589
overview, 95–96, 271
popular songs, 220–221
song examples, 220, 274–275
sound quality/color, 272
V7, 272
voice leading, 280
Dorian tonic mode
fretboard patterns, 252–253
overview, 250
song examples, 251
dots. *See also* ties
augmentation, 65
definition, 390
note extension, 390–391
staccato, 68
syncopation notation, 133–134
double-flat 7th notes, 220
double-stop riffs. *See also* Jimmy Reed
move
examples, 156
overview, 427–428, 431
shuffle eighths, 433–435
straight feel, 432
"Double-Stop Rock"
arrangement, 159, 162
audio track, 594

double-stops
across versus up and down
the neck, 594
audio tracks, 594, 595
"Aura Lee", 158, 160
chord progression example, 331
chord/single-note properties, 330
country music, 156
definition, 147
"Double-Stop Rock", 159, 162
exercises, 157–158, 330–331
moving on the neck, 156–157
overview, 156, 330
practice songs, 158–162
right-hand technique, 330–331
"The Streets of Laredo", 159, 161
downstrokes
alternate picking, 150, 304, 308
audio track, 593
combining with upstrokes, 126–130
demonstration, 591
eighth-note strumming, 124–125
exercises, 125–126, 306–307, 308
music notation, 124–125
overview, 124
tempo decisions, 126–127
upstrokes versus, 126, 304
driving straight-four groove
audio track, 596
overview, 397–398
D.S., 68
duration
overview, 63
rests, 63, 66
symbols indicating, 64–65
tie symbol, 64
Dylan, Bob, 122, 593
dynamic markings, 67

E chord
audio track, 593
diagrams, 79, 111, 588
fingering, 31–32

E7 chord
  diagrams, 98, 111, 217, 588
  two-finger versus four, 97–98
The Eagles
  audio track, 142
  I-IV-V song examples, 234
  major 7th chord usage, 99
  minor 7th chord song example, 217
  Mixolydian mode example, 265
  riff harmonies, 302
  straight-four feel, 142
  three-feel song example, 144–145
E-form barre chords
  fingering, 116
  G minor, 118
  G7, 118
  G7sus, 119
  Gm7, 118
  moving technique, 117–119
  power chords included, 120
  variations, 117–119
8-bar blues, 413–414
eighth note triplets, 64
eighth notes
  audio tracks, 594
  rock syncopation patterns, 134–135
  symbol for, 64
eighth rests, 65
eighth-note progressions
  5-6 move, 138–139
  audio tracks, 593, 594
eighth-note riffs
  audio track, 597
  overview, 429–430
eighth-note shuffle
  audio track, 594
  song chart, 130
  triplet formation, 128–129
eighth-note strumming
  audio tracks, 593, 597
  notations on staff, 125
  overview, 124–125
electric guitars. *See also* amplifiers;
    electronic effects
  accessories for, 298–300
  acoustic versus, 7–8, 286–287

anatomy of, 8–10, 292–295
arpeggio style, 302
Charlie Christian's popularization of, 289
cleaning, 366–368
free improvisation, 302
history of, 286–288
learning chords before lead, 302
modifying acoustic guitars, 186–188
music community acceptance, 285
overview, 290–291
pentatonic scale, 316–320
picking, 26
playing melody, 302
riffs, 302–303
solid-body, 39
sound quality, 286–289
string bending, 290, 334
string choices, 360
string type, 288
stringing, 55–57
tone versus volume, 286–287
tuning, 57
volume, 289
volume/tone controls, 10
electrical cords and cables,
    299–300
electronic effects
  description, 297
  overview, 291
  types of effects, 298
electronic tuners, 18–19
Em chord
  diagrams, 82, 111, 588
  video demonstration, 592
Em7 chord
  diagrams, 99, 111, 214–218, 588
  video demonstration, 592
EMG pickups, 42
end pin
  description, 9, 294
  illustration of, 292
ending brackets, 68
endings
  audio track, 597
  overview, 423
  riffs, 439–440

enharmonic equivalents, 342
exercises. *See also* practice songs
  A-family chords, 80
  barre chords, 121–122
  C-family chords, 87
  D-family chords, 83
  double-stops, 157–158
  downstrokes, 125–126
  fingerstyle, 140
  G-family chords, 85
  position playing, 149–152
  position shift, 150–151
  power chords, 114
  rhythm styles, 142–145
  scales, 149–152
  shuffle rhythm, 129
  strengthening, 151–152
  strumming, 124–129
  syncopation, 136, 138
  upstrokes, 126
expression symbols, 67–68
expressive playing, 382
extended dominant chords, 224

● *F.* ●

f (forte), 67
F barre chord, 116
F chord, 86, 111, 588
facility, 110
fall-offs, 350
families, chord, 77. *See also* chords
feels. *See* rhythm styles
Fender Stratocaster, 37–38, 40, 45–46
ff (fortissimo), 67
5th string/sixth string associations
  grouping notes, 170–172
  octave pitches, 173
  overview, 166–168
5th-fret tuning method, 14–16, 591
Fine, 68
finger strengthening exercises, 24, 151–152
fingerboard. *See* fretboard
fingering. *See also* barre chords; *names of*
    specific chords
  A-family chords, 78–79
  arpeggio bass melodies, 483–485

arpeggio technique, 481–482,
  486–487
arpeggio treble melodies, 486–488
audio track, 594
buzzing, 24
C-family chords, 85
chord techniques, 78, 561
contrapuntal music, 468–470
D-family chords, 81–83
dominant 7th chords, 95–98
G-family chords, 85
guide finger notation, 71
independent movement, 394,
  468–470, 561
inside strings, 536
left-hand notation, 70
major 7th chords, 100
minor 7th chords, 99
out-of-position notes, 527,
  532–534
overview, 24, 70
pentatonic scale, 316–317
right-hand notation, 71
strengthening exercises, 151–152
string choices, 71–72
fingernail length, 461–462
fingerpicking
  calluses, 80–81
  overview, 27–28, 30–31
  picking versus, 26
  thumb versus fingers, 27–28
fingerstyle
  arpeggio chords, 139–140
  arpeggio melodies, 481–485
  audio tracks, 594, 596
  blues music, 394
  calluses, 80–81
  exercises, 140
  finger notation, 139–140
  fingering technique, 139–140
  overview, 139
  pentatonic scale, 316–317
  right-hand position, 26
  strengthening exercises,
    151–152
"The First Noël", 514–515
1st finger position, 100, 592

Fishman pickups, 42
5-6 move
  audio track, 594
  eighth-note progressions, 138–139
  song examples, 138
5-note minor pentatonic scale, 381–382.
    See also pentatonic scale
5-6 riff (Jimmy Reed move)
  audio track, 596
  key of A, 417–419
  key of G, 416–417
  overview, 416, 432
fixed-source tuning
  overview, 16
  with piano, 17–18
flats
  implied flats, 248
  overview, 62
  sharps versus, 181
  symbol for, 168–170
floating bridges
  overview, 42
  restringing, 361–362
  setting up, 57–58
  tuning, 58
Floyd Rose system
  overview, 42
  setting up, 57–58
fluffed notes, 326
Fmaj7 chord, 100, 111, 588
folk songs
  7th chord progressions, 274–275
  guitar models associated with, 37
foot stools, 22
forte (f), 67
fortissimo (ff), 67
4/4 time
  audio track, 593
  overview, 132
free stroke
  arpeggio bass melodies, 486
  fingerpicking, 28
  overview, 462
  technique, 463–464
fretboard
  6th string/5th string associations, 166–168
  Aeolian tonic mode patterns, 245, 247

chord number visualization, 231–232
cleaning, 367
description, 9, 294
Dorian tonic mode patterns, 252–253
interval diagrams, 176–180
Lydian tonic mode patterns, 259–260
Mixolydian tonic mode patterns, 262–263
note tracking, 166
pattern recognition, 165, 229
pattern visualization, 231–232
Phrygian tonic mode patterns, 255–256
whole steps versus half steps, 168–172
frets
  cleaning, 367
  description, 9, 12, 294
  half-steps, 12
  illustration of, 293
  overview, 13–14
fretting
  chord diagrams, 29
  classical versus electric techniques,
    25–26
  grouping notes, 170–172
  left hand technique, 13, 24–25, 591
  octave pitches, 172–176
  octave shapes, 173–176
  open versus fretted strings, 14
  overview, 11–12, 24
funky groove
  7th-chord usage, 78, 95
  audio tracks, 594, 596
  sixteenth note groove, 430
  song examples, 141

• G •

G chords
  diagrams, 82, 111, 589
  progression demonstration, 592
G clef (treble clef), 60
G minor barre chord, 118
G5 chord, 113, 589
G7 barre chord, 118
G7 chord, 96, 111, 217, 589
G7sus barre chord, 119
gallop pattern riffs, 327
gapless joints, 43

"Gavotte in A" (Handel), 471
G-family chords
  exercises, 85
  fingering, 84
  overview, 84
  strumming, 84–85
Gibson Les Paul, 37–38, 45–46
Gm7 barre chord, 118
Gmaj chord
  diagram, 589
  video demonstration, 592
"God Rest Ye Merry, Gentlemen", 557–558
golpeador, 449
grabbing chords, 110
grooves. *See* rhythm styles
guide finger notation, 71
guitar foot stools, 22
guitar language, 30
guitar maintenance. *See also* guitar setup;
    stringing
  cleaning, 366–368
  electrical system, 368, 373
  overview, 355
  proper storage, 374–375
  tools, 356–358
  troubleshooting, 373–374
guitar notation. *See* music notation
guitar setup
  action adjustments, 370–371
  bridge spring tension adjustments,
    371–372
  electrical problems, 373
  intonation adjustments, 369
  overview, 368
  troubleshooting, 373–374
  truss rod adjustments, 371
  warning signs, 369
guitar tab. *See* tablature staff
guitars. *See also* construction quality of
    guitars
  acoustic versus electric, 7–8
  action, 25
  anatomy of, 7–10, 22
  buying criteria, 35–36
  buying strategies, 34–35, 44–47
  cleaning, 366–368

electronic emulation, 42
  model choices, 36–38
  piano versus, 71–72
  pitch, 63
  playing positions, 21–23
  posture techniques, 21
  practice suggestions, 82
  slide guitars, 350
  style choices, 37–38
  temperature/humidity issues, 375
  upgrading strategies, 38–39
guitar-specific notation, 70–71

• *H* •

half notes, 64
half rests, 64
half-note riffs, 324
half-steps
  sharps and flats, 181
  whole steps versus, 168–172
hammer-ons
  articulation, 334
  audio track, 595
  definition, 347
  idiomatic licks, 348
  music notation, 347
  playing in position, 313
  technique, 348
Handel, George Frederick
  "Allegro", 557–559
  "Gavotte in A", 471
Hanon, 152
hard rock
  audio tracks, 595
  mixed-style progression, 331–332
  sixteenth-note riffs, 327–328
hardware, 41–42
harmonics. *See also* minor scale harmonics
  enharmonic pitches, 170
  intervals, 178–179
  power chords, 112
harmonizing, 182–183
headstock
  description, 9, 294
  illustration of, 293

heavy metal gallop. *See also* rhythm styles
  audio track, 594
  overview, 144
Hendrix, Jimi
  electric guitar history, 288
  rhythm styles, 331
high-note moves
  E7, A7, B7 diagrams, 424
  exercises, 425
  overview, 423
high-note riffs, 434–435
history of guitars, 1
"Home on the Range"
  7th chord usage, 97
  arrangement, 101, 103
  audio track, 593
homophonic sound, 472

● **/** ●

i (right-hand index finger) notation, 71
I-IV-V chord progressions
  The Eagles song examples, 234
  overview, 234
  patterns, 237
  primary key families, 406–407
  song examples, 238–239
improvisation
  overview, 302
  pentatonic scale, 321–322
intervals. *See also* pitch
  1 through 7, 177–178
  3rds, 178–179
  4ths, 180
  5ths, 179–180
  6ths, 178–179
  harmonics, 178–179
  inverted, 178, 180
  overview, 12, 176
  qualities list, 182
  sharps and flats, 181
  tonic structure comparison, 268
intonation, 36
intros
  audio tracks, 596
  overview, 421
  riffs, 435–437

inversions. *See also* progressions
  barre chords, 579
  definition, 190
  inside chords, 562, 571
  inside F7 chord, 573–574
  inside Fm chord, 572–573
  inside Fm7 chord, 575–577
  inside Fmaj chord, 571–572
  inside Fmaj7 chord, 576–577
  inside F♯dim7 chord, 577–579
  inside F♯m7♭5 chord, 577–578
  outside chords, 562, 564
  outside F7 chord, 564, 566
  outside Fm chord, 564–565
  outside Fm7 chord, 566–567
  outside Fmaj chord, 563, 564
  outside Fmaj7 chord, 567–568
  outside F♯dim7 chord, 569–571
  outside F♯m7♭5 chord, 569–570
  overview, 562
Ionian tonic mode
  overview, 249
  song examples, 249
"It's Raining, It's Pouring"
  arrangement, 102, 106
  audio track, 593

● **J** ●

jazz
  electric guitars and, 289
  guitar models associated with,
    36–39
  improvisation, 321
  major 7th chords, 78
  minor 7th chords, 78
  picking, 26
  playing in position, 152, 313
  secondary dominant chords, 277
  shaping octaves, 173
Jimmy Reed move (5-6 riff)
  audio tracks, 596
  key of A, 417–419
  key of G, 416–417
  overview, 416, 432
jump rhythm, 383

• K •

Kahler floating bridge system, 57
Kern, Jerome, 584
key signature
    determining, 267
    major versus minor, 267
    overview, 63
    tonic mode errors, 265–266
keys. *See also* chords; tonics
    audio tracks, 595
    description, 77
    F position association, 344
    Fm position association, 344–345
    G position association, 343
    listing, 346
    mid-song changes, 257
"Kumbaya"
    A-family chords, 81
    arrangement, 88, 90
    audio track, 593

• L •

Lace pickups, 42
"Lay Lady Lay" (Dylan), 593
"Ländler in D"
    arrangement, 491, 494–495
    audio track, 597
ländlers, 491
lead melody, 26
lead playing
    arpeggio style, 302
    closed-position advantages, 336
    double-stops, 330
    featured guitar, 303
    free improvisation, 302
    improvisation, 321–322
    left-hand liberation, 138
    lower register riffs, 315
    low-note scales, 311–312
    overview, 301
    pentatonic scale, 316–320
    picking, 26, 302, 304–305
    playing in position, 152
    practice scales, 309–312, 314–315,
        318–321
    rhythm versus, 303
    riffs, 302–303, 315
    right hand control, 123
    secondary dominant chords, 279
    single-note technique,
        304–305
    walking bass, 315
leading notes/tones
    overview, 273
    voice leading, 280–282
Led Zeppelin
    audio tracks, 594
    moving bass line, 132–133
    straight-ahead rock rhythm, 132
ledger lines, 62, 70
left hand
    5-6 move, 138–139
    7th position orientation, 592
    arpeggio melody techniques, 486
    ascending motion demonstration, 592
    attack versus cut-off, 336
    audio tracks, 594
    chord fingering, 109–110
    classical fretting, 25–26
    electric guitar fretting, 25
    fingering notations, 71
    fretting technique, 13, 24–25
    hammer-on technique, 347–348
    high-note practice, 312
    lead playing, 138
    liberating, 138–139
    position playing, 149
    pull-off technique, 348–349
    slides, 349–350
    strengthening, 24
left hand/right hand instructions
    overview, 2, 16
    sitting position, 22
left-hand muting
    implying (simulating) syncopation,
        136–137, 392
    overview, 136

legato (*ligado*)
  slurs, playing with, 67
  staccato versus, 505, 528
  techniques, 336
licks
  playing up the neck, 341–342
  riffs versus, 341
locking Sperzels (tuners), 41
Locrian tonic mode, 264
"Look For the Silver Lining" (Kern)
  arrangement, 584–585
  audio track, 598
looping, 326
low positions
  ease of playing, 467
  examples, 344–345, 476–479
L.R. Baggs pickups, 42
Lydian tonic mode
  fretboard patterns, 259–260
  overview, 257–258
  song examples, 258

• M •

M (major intervals), 182
m (minor intervals), 182
m (right-hand middle finger) notaion, 71
major 7th chords
  diagrams, 215–216
  overview, 99
  song examples, 217
major intervals (M), 182
major scales. *See also* intervals; tonics
  7th chord locations, 216
  audio track, 597
  Dorian mode, 250–253
  Ionian tonic mode, 249
  minor scale relationship, 242
  modes, 248–249
  overview, 513, 517
  pattern #1, 504–507, 505, 506, 507, 518–519
  pattern #2, 508, 519–522
  pattern #3, 508–509, 509, 510, 522–523
  pattern #4, 510, 511, 523–524
  pattern #5, 512, 513, 524–526

positions, 503
  practicing, 503–504
  relative minor versus, 242–243
  song examples, 220, 514–515, 526–529
  video demonstration, 592
measures
  overview, 60–61
  pickup measures, 88
  playing instructions, 81
Mel Bay's Modern Guitar Method Grade 1, 278–279
melody. *See also* arpeggio melodies; counterpoint
  arpeggio chords combinations, 481
  audio track, 597
  blues rhythm techniques, 383
  bridging with riffs, 323
  classical thumb playing, 482
  overview, 302
  skips/steps combinations, 311
Mertz, Johann Kaspar, 491
metronomes, 428
mezzo-forte (*mf*), 67
mezzo-piano (*mp*), 67
mf (*mezzo-forte*), 67
"Michael, Row the Boat Ashore"
  arrangement, 89, 93
  audio track, 593
  C-family chords, 87
minor 7♭5 chord, 220
minor 7th chords
  diagrams, 99, 218
  overview, 98
  song examples, 217, 218
minor 7th flat 5 chord
  overview, 220
  song examples, 220
minor chords
  notation, 81
  overview, 81
minor intervals (m), 182
minor scale harmonics
  audio tracks, 598
  baroque and classical use of, 540
  harmonic scale, 549, 549–550, 551–552, 552–555, 555–556

melodic scale, 540, 540–542, 542–544,
    544–545, 545–547, 547–548
natural scale, 532, 532–534, 534–535,
    536–537, 537–538, 539–540
overview, 531, 540
song examples, 557–560
minor scales
    7th chords, 98–99
    7th intervals, 214–217
    Aeolian tonic mode, 243–248, 264
    key signature versus tonic modes, 267
    major scale relationship, 242–243
    minor 7th diagrams, 218
    Phrygian tonic mode, 254
    Roman numerals, 243–244
    song examples, 246–248
"Minuet in A Minor", 470
"Minuet in G"
    arrangement, 474–476
    audio track, 597
minuets, 470
Mixolydian tonic mode
    fretboard patterns, 262–263
    overview, 261
    song examples, 264–265
model choices, 37–38
Moderato, 67
modes. *See* tonics
moveable chords
    barre chords, 117
    name versus quality, 561
    playing in position, 148, 314
    power chords, 113
    transposing, 148, 314
moving bass line
    3/4 time song examples, 145
    audio tracks, 594
    Led Zeppelin style, 132–133
    music notation, 133
    overview, 132
moving left hand
    5-6 move examples, 138
    audio track, 594
    eighth-note progression exercise, 139
    left hand liberation, 138

mp (*mezzo-piano*), 67
music notation
    advantages of, 59
    andante, 67
    Arabic numbers, 272
    arpeggio chords, 332
    arpeggio treble melodies, 486
    bar lines, 60–61
    bending, 352
    chord diagrams, 28–29
    chord names, 272
    common discrepancies, 266–268
    common time, 132
    dots, 65–68, 133–134, 390–391
    downstrokes, 124–125
    dual arrangements, 2
    duration symbols, 63–66
    expression/articulation symbols, 67–68
    finger notations, 484
    fingering notation, 70–72, 139–140,
        473, 484
    flags, 125, 128
    flat symbol, 168–170
    guitar-specific, 70
    hammer-ons, 347
    implied notation, 48, 223
    key signature, 63, 265–266
    learning to read, 279
    ledger lines, 62, 70
    left-hand muting, 136
    melody indication, 482
    moving bass line, 133
    note symbols, 61–63, 66
    open strings, 29
    overview, 28
    palm mute, 137–138
    pentatonic scale, 316–317
    performance notes, 266–267
    pick-stroke indicators, 309
    pitch symbols, 64–65
    pre-bends, 353
    rhythm slashes, 124
    Roman numerals, 223, 272
    scale degree names, 272
    sharp symbol, 168–170

music notation *(continued)*
  sharp/flat/natural/accidental notes, 62
  staff memory aids, 61
  staff overview, 60
  standard notation, 59
  static dominant, 272
  stems and beams, 125
  strumming symbols, 125
  syncopation, 390–391
  ties, 390–391
  tonic numbering system, 242–245, 247
  treble clef, 60
  upstrokes, 125
  vibrato, 324, 354
  x notation, 185
music scales
  alternate picking, 150
  degree names, 272
  exercises, 149–152
  leading notes/tones, 273
  major scale, 176–177
  position shift, 150–151
  tonic structure comparison, 268
  transposing, 150
  triads, 182–187
muting
  accenting versus, 137–138
  audio tracks, 594, 596
  avoiding, 24
  clipping notes, 334
  damping, 137
  implying (simulating) syncopation,
      136–137, 392, 594
  inside chords, 5th string, 571
  left-hand muting, 136–137, 392
  overview, 32
  right-hand muting, 137–138, 144, 335,
      392–393

● *N* ●

natural notes, 166
natural sign (♮), 62
neck
  construction types, 40
  description, 10, 294

9th chords, 224
notes. *See also* bends; fretboard; fretting
  6th string/5th string associations,
      166–168
  definition/description, 61
  duration symbols, 63–66
  eighth-notes, 124–125
  flags, 125, 128
  fluffing, 326
  grouping, 170–172
  mathematical relationships, 66
  natural, 62, 166
  out-of-position, 532
  pedal tones, 331
  pitch symbols, 61–63
  quarter notes, 124, 126–127
  roots, 166
  sixteenth notes, 127–128
  staff memory aids, 61
  stems and beams, 125
  string bending, 290, 334
  whole steps versus half steps, 168–172
numbers, in guitar notation
  barre indication, 72
  with circles, 71–72
  without circles, 70–71
nut
  description, 10, 29, 294
  illustration of, 293
nylon-string guitars. *See also* classical
      guitars
  fretting adjustments, 25–26
  stringing, 52–54
  tuning, 55

● *O* ●

"O Christmas Tree", 473
"O Little Town of Bethlehem", 469
octave pitches
  4th string/3rd string, 174
  6th string/5th string, 172
  audio tracks, 595
  beyond 12th fret, 175–176
  overview, 172
  three strings apart, 175

octave shapes
  4th string/3rd string, 174
  6th string/5th string, 173–174
  beyond 12th fret, 175–176
  fingering, 173–174
  overview, 172
  three strings apart, 175
  video demonstration, 592
"Oh, Susanna"
  arrangement, 102, 107
  audio track, 593
one-octave scales, 592
open position chords
  barre chord counterparts, 122
  diagrams, 111
  notations on staff, 29
  overview, 110
open strings
  definition, 14
  ease of playing, 467
  learning advantages, 467
  music examples, 469–471, 474, 476–479
  music notation, 29
out-of-position notes, 532
output jack
  description, 10, 294
  illustration of, 292
"Over the River and Through the Woods"
  arrangement, 101–102, 105
  audio track, 593

● *p* ●

P (perfect intervals), 182
p (*piano*), 67
p (right-hand thumb) notation, 71
palm mute (P.M.). *See* right-hand muting
patterns. *See* playing in position;
    strumming
pedal tones, 331
peg winders, 52
pentatonic scale
  above home position, 339–340
  advantages, 316
  Amin, 316
  audio track, 595

  below home position, 340
  choosing positions, 347
  Cmaj (descending), 317–318
  exercises, 318, 319
  home position, 338–339
  improvisation, 321–322
  overview, 316
  pattern/fret listing, 346
  practice song, 319–320
  transposing, 347
perfect intervals (P), 182
performance notes, 266–267
Peter, Paul, and Mary, 559–560
Phrygian tonic mode
  fretboard patterns, 255–256
  overview, 254
  song examples, 257
pianissimo (pp), 67
piano (p), 67
pianos
  guitar versus, 71–72
  tuning with, 17–18
picking
  acoustic versus electric, 26
  alternate strokes, 150, 304, 308
  anchoring, 304–305
  attacking notes, 304
  classical guitar versus electrics/
    acoustics, 451
  combining upstrokes/downstrokes,
    126–130
  downstrokes versus upstrokes, 304
  exercises, 306–307, 308
  fingerstyle versus, 26
  grip style, 304
  lead playing, 302
  pick gauges, 27
  pick-holding technique, 26–27
  scales, 309
  single-note technique,
    304–305
  strumming motion, 27, 31
  technique demonstration, 591
picks
  grip style, 304
  overview, 299

pick-strum pattern
  12/8 groove, 388–389, 596
  audio track, 596
  overview, 131, 387
  two-beat shuffle, 388–389
pickup selector
  description, 10, 294
  illustration of, 292
pickups
  description, 13, 294
  electrifying acoustic guitars, 287
  illustration of, 292
  overview, 10
  quality considerations, 42
pitch. *See also* intervals
  definition, 61, 168
  description, 11
  half-steps, 12
  harmonics, 112, 170
  octave pitches, 172–176
  sharps and flats, 168–170
  staff memory aids, 61
  symbol listing, 61–63
  unison, 172
  whole steps versus half steps, 168
  written versus actual, 63
pitch pipes, tuning with, 18
playing by number. *See* chord numbers
playing in position. *See also* left hand;
    pentatonic scale; right hand
  advantages of, 337–338, 345
  best position determination, 338
  key/position associations, 343–345
  mixing exercises, 347
  picking, 26
  position, defined, 337
  posture techniques, 21
  scale patterns, 504
  transposing, 347
playing up the neck
  artistic possibilities, 334
  barre chord use, 333
  closed-position advantages, 336
  legato techniques, 336
  moving double-stops, 335–336
  moving licks, 341–342
  overview, 333

palm mute/accented chord
    combination, 335
  playing in position, 337–338
  shapes versus sounds, 335
  sus4 shapes, 225
plectrum. *See* picking
plucking
  chords, 31
  two-hand cooperation, 11–12
P.M. (palm mute). *See* right-hand muting
polyphony. *See* counterpoint
position playing. *See also* practice songs;
    strumming
  audio tracks, 594, 595
  blues, 152
  country music, 152–153
  definition, 114
  exercises, 149–152
  finger assignments, 148
  jazz, 152
  lead playing, 152
  low position examples, 476–479
  moveable (closed) position, 314
  open position chords, 313
  open string examples, 476–479
  open strings versus, 148
  rock, 152
  strengthening exercises, 151–152
  transposing advantages, 148
  upper region advantages, 313
posture techniques
  left shoulder relaxation breaks, 24
  value of, 21
power chords
  5th-string versus 6th-string, 113–114, 117
  audio track, 593
  exercises, 114
  G5 notation, 113
  harmonics, 112
  moving technique, 113
  overview, 111–112
pp (pianissimo), 67
practice songs. *See also* exercises
  7th chords, 101–107
  "All Through the Night", 97, 101, 104
  "Allegro", 557–559
  "Auld Lang Syne", 85, 89, 92

"Danny Boy", 582–584
double-stops, 158–162
"The First Noël", 514–515
"God Rest Ye Merry, Gentlemen", 557–558
"Home on the Range", 97, 101, 103
"It's Raining, It's Pouring", 100, 102, 106
"Kumbaya", 81, 88, 90
"Ländler in D", 491
"Look For the Silver Lining", 584–585
"Michael, Row the Boat Ashore", 87, 89, 93
"Oh, Susanna", 100, 102, 107
"Oh, Them Golden Slippers", 527
oldies progressions, 94
"Over the River and Through the Woods", 98, 101–102, 105
position playing, 153–155
strumming, 90–93
"Swing Low, Sweet Chariot", 83, 89, 91
"We Wish You a Merry Christmas", 527–529
practicing
    five major scale patterns, 503–504
    major scale sequences, 518
    recommendations, 82
progressions. *See also* chord numbers; I-IV-V chord progressions; triads
    5th string patterns, 236–239
    12-bar blues, 407–411
    A-family chords, 81
    audio tracks, 593, 594, 595, 596, 598
    barre chords, 121–122
    basic chords, 88–93
    bass line separation, 132–133
    blues, 319–320, 381
    chromatic versus diatonic, 281
    closing demonstration, 592
    closing diagram, 274
    D-family chords, 83
    dominant functions, 273–274
    double-stop example, 330–331
    F-family chords, 87
    folk songs, 274–275
    G-family chords, 85
    ii, iii, and vi pattern, 234
    I-IV-V chord pattern, 234

inside chords, 581–582
I-V7 progressions, 272
major chord patterns, 234–235
major key (pentatonic), 318
major scale, 230
minor blues, 420
minor chord patterns, 235–236
minor key (pentatonic), 319
numbered patterns, 229–232
oldies, 94
open chord patterns, 239–240
outside chords, 580–581
overview, 80, 407, 580
pattern recognition, 229
pentatonic scale, 316–317
secondary dominant chords, 275–276
song examples, 273–274
technique demonstration, 591–592
turnarounds, 410–411
V7-I progressions, 273–274
Pujol, Emilio, 466
pull-offs
    articulation, 334
    audio tracks, 595
    playing in position, 313
    technique, 348–349

● *Q* ●

quarter notes
    audio tracks, 593, 595
    strumming overview, 124
    symbol for, 64
    upstroke/downstroke strumming, 126–127
quarter rests, 64
quarter-note riffs, 428

● *R* ●

R&B
    audio track, 593
    sixteenth note progressions, 127–128
reggae. *See also* rhythm styles
    audio track, 594
    overview, 144
    song examples, 142

relative minor scale
  Aeolin mode, 264
  major scale versus, 242–243
  relative major versus, 310
  renumbering major modes, 243–246
relative tuning, 14–16
repeat signs, 68
rest stroke
  arpeggio treble melodies, 486–487
  finger position, 28
  finger technique, 465
  overview, 465
  thumb technique, 465–466
rests
  eighth, 65
  half, 64
  observing, 66
  overview, 63
  quarter, 64
  sixteenth, 65
  whole, 64
rhythm
  definition, 26
  lead versus, 303
  right hand control, 13
  strumming motion, 27
rhythm figures
  audio track, 596
  D string audio file, 595
  exercises, 441
  overview, 440–441
  shapes versus chords, 335
rhythm slashes, 30–31
rhythm styles. *See also* strumming
  16-feel, 143
  audio track, 142
  blues, 383
  blues music feels, 395
  double-stops, 330–331
  electric guitar effect on, 289
  exercises, 142–145
  grooves listing, 141–142
  heavy metal gallop, 144
  reggae, 144
  shuffle rhythm, 128–130, 227, 319–320, 383

straight-four feel, 142, 383
three-feel, 144–145
two-beat feel, 143
Richards, Keith
  audio track, 597
  quick-four riffs, 435
riffs
  audio tracks, 595, 597
  boogie rhythm, 325
  boogie-woogie, 315
  bridging melodies and chords, 323
  double-stop, 156, 427–428, 431–435
  eighth-note, 324–327, 429–430, 597
  eighth-note syncopation, 327–329
  endings, 439–440
  examples, 186
  exercises, 329
  gallop pattern, 327
  half-note, 324
  harmonies, 302
  high-note, 312, 434–435
  intros, 435–437
  licks versus, 341
  looping, 326
  low-note, 311–312
  overview, 302–303, 323, 427–428
  quarter-note, 324–327, 428
  quick-four, 435
  rock music, 323
  rounding the corner, 326
  shuffle eighth, 433–434
  single-note, 427–431
  single-note/chord combination,
    331–332, 438
  sixteenth-note, 327–328, 430, 597
  turnarounds, 437–439
  vibrato with, 324
  whole-note, 324
right hand. *See also* picking
  arpeggio melody techniques, 486–487
  audio track, 594
  double-stop technique, 330–331
  downstrokes, 124–125, 304
  fingering notations, 71
  fingerpicking, 27–28

fingerstyle position, 26
guide finger notation, 71
lead playing, 123
low-note scales, 311–312
muting, 137–138
picking, 26–27
playing in time, 124
practice scales, 309–312, 314–315,
    318–321
practice songs, 306–308
rhythm/tempo/speed control, 13, 379
strumming, overview, 123–124
upstrokes, 125–126, 304
right hand/left hand instructions
    overview, 2, 16
    sitting position, 16
right-hand muting
    accented chord combination, 138, 393
    double-stop exercise, 336
    heavy metal gallop rhythm, 144
    muting exercise, 393
    overview, 137, 392–393
    palm muting, 393
    playing up the neck, 335
ritardando (*rit.*; *ritard.*), 67
rock guitars. *See also* amplifiers; electronic
    effects
    accessories for, 298–300
    acoustic versus, 7–8, 286–287
    anatomy of, 8–10, 292–295
    arpeggio style, 302
    Charlie Christian popularization of, 289
    chords, learning before lead, 302
    cleaning, 366–368
    free improvisation, 302
    history, 286–288
    melody, playing, 302
    modifying acoustic guitars, 186–188
    music community acceptance, 285
    overview, 290–291
    pentatonic scale, 316–320
    picking, 26
    playing in position, 313
    riffs, 302–303
    solid-body, 39
    song examples, 290

sound quality, 286–289
string bending, 290, 334
string type, 288
stringing, 55–57
tone versus volume, 286–287
tuning, 57
volume, 289
volume/tone controls, 10
rock lead. *See* lead playing
rock music
    5-6 move, 138
    barre chords, 115
    boom-chick pattern, 131
    double-stops, 156, 158–159
    floating bridges, 57
    guitar models associated with,
        38–39
    heavy metal gallop rhythm, 144
    improvisation, 321–322
    left-hand muting, 136
    picking, 26, 139
    playing in position, 152
    playing up the neck, 333
    power chords, 111–112, 179
    riffs, 323
    shuffle rhythm, 128
    straight-four feel, 142
    syncopation, 133–135
    three-feel rhythm, 144–145
    whammy bars, 57
rockabilly, 227
Roman numerals
    advantages over key names, 408
    barre chords, 72
    chord representations, 230–231
    major scale mode changes, 250
    minor scale numbers, 243–244
"Romanza"
    arrangement, 492, 496–498
    audio track, 597
root notes
    6th string/5th string associations,
        166–168
    overview, 166
rosettes, 43
rounding the corner, 326

• S •

saddle, 10
scale patterns. *See* major scales
scales. *See also* major scales; minor scale
  harmonics
  5-note minor pentatonic, 381–382
  alternate picking, 150
  Am, 310
  Am7, 311
  Amin, 316, 319
  ascending and descending, 309–310
  audio tracks, 594, 595
  blues, 342, 381–382
  chromatic versus diatonic, 281
  Cmaj (one octave), 309
  Cmaj (pentatonic), 317–318
  definition, 311
  degree names, 272
  exercises, 149–152
  Gmaj, 310
  high-note riffs, 312
  leading notes/tones, 273
  low-note riffs, 311–312
  major scale, 176–177
  moveable position, 314
  pick-stroke indicators, 309
  position shift, 150–151
  tonic structure comparison, 268
  transposing, 150, 314–315
  triads, 182–187
  warm-up exercises, 308–309
scoops, 350
secondary dominant chords
  7th versus major chords, 279
  diagrams, 276
  exiting chord alterations, 277
  overview, 275
  song examples, 278–280
  video demonstration, 592
Segovia, Andrés, 150–151, 466
Segovia shift
  overview, 150–151
  video demonstration, 592
semitones, 168

7th chords
  blues sound, 95, 272
  dominant, 95–98, 219–220, 271–272
  Em7, Am7 variation diagrams, 218
  major scale diagrams, 213–214
  major/minor barre scale diagrams, 215
  open position chord diagrams, 216
  overview, 78
  song examples, 217–218
  static dominant, 272
  video demonstration, 592
7th notes
  adding to chords, 213–217, 272–273
  double flat, 220
  flattened, 244, 250, 261
  implied notation, 223
Seymour Duncan pickups, 42
shapes. *See also* octave shapes
  6th forms, 227
  7th forms, 215–217
  9th forms, 224
  A-based barre chords, 119–120
  add4 forms, 226
  add9 forms, 222
  Am form, 208
  C form, 195–198
  CAGED system, 189
  chord inversions/voicings, 190
  chords versus, 335
  Cm form, 207
  connecting to notes, 166, 176
  D form, 205–207
  Dm form, 209
  dominant 7th chords, 219
  E form, 202–204
  Em form, 209
  A form, 198–200
  G form, 201–202
  Gm form, 208
  intervals, 178–179
  minor add9 forms, 223
  moving on the neck, 118
  navigating with, 165
  pentatonic scale, 338–340
  sus2 forms, 221

sus4 forms, 225
triad diagrams, 184–185
sharp symbol (♯), 168–170
sharps
flats versus, 181
overview, 62
shuffle eighth riffs
examples, 433
exercises, 434
overview, 433
shuffle rhythm. *See also* rhythm styles
blues shuffle example, 227
definition, 383
exercises, 129, 396–397
overview, 128, 395
practice songs, 319–320
song examples, 130
straight eighths versus, 128, 130
sides of guitar, 10
signal response, 42
simile (sim.), 83, 125, 309
"Simple Gifts", 154, 594
single-note riffs
eighth-note, 429–430
overview, 427–428
quarter-note, 428
sixteenth-note, 430
syncopated eighth-note, 430–431
sitting position
classical technique, 22
picking posture, 26
standing versus, 21
6-note blues scale, 342, 381–382
16-feel. *See also* rhythm styles
audio tracks, 594, 596
exercises, 143, 403–404
funky groove usage, 403
overview, 143, 403
sixteenth notes
audio track, 593
funky blues usage, 430
progressions, 127–128
symbol for, 64
sixteenth rests, 65
sixteenth-note riffs
audio track, 597
overview, 430

6th string/5th string associations
grouping notes, 170–172
octave pitches, 173
overview, 166–168
skips, 311
slide guitars, 350
slides
articulation, 334
audio tracks, 595
blues, 380, 382
overview, 349
playing in position, 313
scoops versus fall-offs, 350
slow 12/8 feel
audio track, 596
exercises, 400–401
overview, 399
slow blues
audio tracks, 595, 596
endings, 423
exercises, 412–413
overview, 411
slurs
blues music, 382
overview, 67
solo, 303
song styles. *See names of specific styles*
songs. *See also* exercises; practice songs
7th chords, 101–102
basic chords, 88–93
oldies progression, 94
personalized style, 88
Sor, Fernando, 474
sound hole, 28
sound production
fretting, 11
string length/tension, 11
two-hand cooperation, 11–12
sound quality
amplifiers, 287, 297
distortion, 288–289
electric guitars, 287–289
electric versus acoustic, 286–287
electronic effects, 297–298
envelope blurring, 286–288

sound quality *(continued)*
  sustain, 288
  timbre, 287, 289
  tone, 287
  volume, 289
staccato
  definition, 528
  legato versus, 505, 528
  technique, 580
staccato dot (·), 68
staff
  advantages of, 73
  bar lines, 60–61
  classical viewpoint of, 74
  eighth-note strumming, 125
  fretboard, relating to, 69
  guitar tab versus standard notation, 30
  ledger lines, 62, 70
  measures, 60–61
  memory aids, 61
  numbers, meaning of, 70–72
  overview, 30, 60
  pitch symbols, 61–63
  rhythm slashes, 30–31
  standard notation versus, 73
  string notations, 30
  tablature versus, 73
standard music notation. *See* music
    notation
standing position
  sitting versus, 21
  strap use, 23
steps
  audio track, 595
  skip/step combinations, 311
  whole versus half, 168
straight-ahead rock rhythm
  audio track, 594
  overview, 132
straight-eighth feel
  blues usage, 420
  overview, 432
  reggae usage, 144
  shuffle rhythm versus, 238
  song examples, 130, 432
  syncopation, 390

straight-four feel. *See also* rhythm styles
  audio tracks, 142, 596
  blues music, 383
  driving straight-four groove, 397–398
  The Eagles style, 142
  exercises, 398–399, 415
  Jimmy Reed move, 414–419
  overview, 142, 397
  song examples, 414
strap pin
  description, 10, 294
  illustration of, 292
straps, 299–300
"The Streets of Laredo"
  arrangement, 159, 161
  audio track, 594
striking in rhythm. *See also* strumming
  eighth notes, 385–386
  quarter notes, 385
string bending
  articulation, 334
  overview, 290
stringing
  acoustic guitars, 48–51
  electric guitars, 55–57
  floating bridge issues, 361–362
  frequency, 55
  nylon versus steel strings, 48, 52–53
  nylon-string guitars, 52–54
  overview, 47–48
  removing, 48, 360–361
  threading new string, 363–365
  trimming excess, 55
  tuning after, 52, 55, 57
  tuning system issues, 362
  winding/wrapping technique, 365–366
strings
  bending, 290, 334, 351–353
  choosing, 359–360
  chord diagrams, 29
  cleaning, 367
  note choices, 71–72
  numbering, 13
  nylon string fretting, 25–26
  nylon versus steel, 25, 48, 52–53, 288
  open versus fretted, 14

overview, 10, 295
reasons for changing, 359
remembering order of, 13
tablature notation, 30, 74–75
tensility, 47
treble, 28
upper versus lower, 15
x notation, 185
strumming. *See also names of specific chords*; rhythm styles
accenting, 137
A-family chords, 79
audio tracks, 593, 594
boom-chick pattern, 131–132
C-family chords, 86–87
combination tempo, 127
D-family chords, 83
dominant 7th chords, 95–98
downstrokes, 124–125, 384, 591
downstroke/upstroke combination, 126–137, 384–385
eighth notes, 124–125, 385–386
exercises, 124–129
G-family chords, 84–85
intensity level variation, 307
left hand liberation, 138–139
left hand versus strumming hand, 2
left-hand muting, 136
major 7th chords, 100
minor 7th chords, 96–98
motion, 31
moving bass line, 132–133
overview, 27, 123–124
pick-strum patterns, 131, 387–389
playing in time, 124, 385–386
quarter notes, 124, 126–127, 385
right hand demonstration, 592
right-hand muting, 137–138
shuffle rhythm, 128–130
single-note/chord combination, 386
sixteenth notes, 127–128
syncopation, 87
upstrokes, 125–126, 384, 591
"Study in A minor", 485
"Study in C", 488
support arm, 22

sus2 chords, 221
sus4 chords, 225
sustain, 288–289
"Swing Low, Sweet Chariot"
   arrangement, 89, 91
   audio track, 593
   D-family chords, 83
syncopation
   anticipation, 328
   audio tracks, 594, 596
   dot and tie notation, 133–134, 390–391
   eighth-note examples, 328–329
   example, 89
   exercises, 136, 138
   features listing, 134
   left-hand muting, 136–137, 392
   overview, 87, 133, 390
   playing with, 134–135
   riffs, 328–329
   right-hand muting, 137–138, 392–393
   syncopated eighth-note riffs, 430–431

• *T* •

Tárrega, Francisco, 466, 488
tablature staff. *See* staff
taper knobs, 42
tapping/counting beats, 65
tempo heading, 67
tensility, 47
textures
   "Air in A Minor", 475, 477
   "America (My Country 'Tis of Thee)", 475, 478
   "Andante in G", 475, 479
   arpeggio melodies, 482
   example pieces, 474–475
   "Minuet in G", 474–476
   overview, 467
3rds. *See* triads
"The Three Ravens" (Peter, Paul, and Mary), 559–560
3/4 time. *See* three-feel
three-feel. *See also* rhythm styles
   audio track, 594
   overview, 144–145
   song examples, 145

ties. *See also* dots
  definition, 390
  overview, 65
  syncopation notation, 133–134, 390–391
timbre, 287, 289
time signature, 65, 88
To Coda, 68
tone/volume controls
  description, 10
  illustration of, 292
tonics
  audio tracks, 595
  Greek naming system, 251
  initial chord progression versus, 267
  initial tonic versus modes, 267
  interval structure comparison, 268
  key signature errors, 265–266
  Locrian mode, 264
  Lydian mode, 257–260
  major/minor identification, 246
  major/minor scale relationship, 242–243
  mid-song changes, 257
  Mixolydian mode, 261–264
  mode build chart, 269
  numbering systems, 242–245
  overview, 242–243, 248
  parallel mode chart, 269
  parent major scale computation, 251
  Phrygian mode, 254–257
  song examples, 246–248
top of guitar, 10, 295
Torres, Antonio, 449
transposing
  number patterns, 232–233
  playing in position, 148, 314
  scales, 150, 314–315
treble clef (G clef), 60
treble melodies
  bass/treble shifts, 488–491
  difficulties with, 486
  exercise, 487
  overview, 485
  Study in C, 488
treble strings, 28
triads. *See also* progressions
  chord sequences, 187
  diminished, 232

  major, 183–184, 186
  minor, 184–185
  overview, 182–183
  video demonstration, 592
triplet notation, 64
tritones
  diagrams, 274
  overview, 273
trussrod
  description, 295
  illustration of, 293
tuners
  description, 10
  illustration of, 293, 366
  overview, 295, 300
  winding/wrapping new strings,
   365–366
tuning
  5th-fret method, 14–16
  audio tracks, 19, 593
  electronic tuners, 18–19
  fixed-source method, 16–19
  floating bridge systems, 57–58
  frequency, 13
  locking Sperzels, 41
  peg winders, 52
  with piano, 17–18
  with pitch pipe, 18
  relative versus fixed source, 14, 16
  sharp versus flat, 18–19
  stringing issues, 52
  with tuning fork, 18
tuning forks, 18
tuning machines
  description, 10
  illustration of, 293
  overview, 295, 300
"Turkey in the Straw", 155, 594
turnarounds
  audio tracks, 596, 597
  examples, 421–422
  overview, 410–411
  riffs, 437–439
12/8 groove. *See also* rhythm styles
  exercises, 388–389, 400–401
  overview, 383
  slow 12/8 feel, 399–401, 596

12-bar blues
  audio tracks, 596
  endings, 423
  high-note moves, 423–425
  intros, 421
  overview, 407–408
  quick four variation, 409–410
  slow blues, 411–412
  song examples, 411
  turnarounds, 410–411, 421–422
two-beat feel. *See also* rhythm styles
  audio track, 596
  country groove audio example, 594
  overview, 143
two-beat shuffle. *See* boom-chick pattern

• U •

unison pitches, 172
upbeats. *See* upstrokes
upstroke symbol, 83
upstrokes
  alternate picking, 150, 304, 308
  combining with downstrokes, 126–130
  demonstration, 591
  downstrokes versus, 126, 304
  eighth-note strumming, 126–127
  exercises, 126
  music notation, 125
  tempo decisions, 126–127
  upbeat playing, 126

• V •

V7-I progressions, 274
vibrato
  audio tracks, 596
  blues music, 382
  definition, 354
  delayed vibrato, 354
  music notation, 324
  playing in position, 313
  playing with riffs, 324
  technique, 324
  vibrato bar, 8
  whammy bar use, 294

video clips
  accessing, 2–4
  track numbers/descriptions, 491–492
  website access, 3–4
voice leading
  audio tracks, 595
  chromatic versus diatonic, 281
  descending chromatic bass lines, 281–282
  diagram, 280
  internal versus bass, 282
  overview, 280
  song examples, 281–282
  video demonstration, 592
voicing, 98, 190, 200
volume/tone controls
  description, 10, 295
  illustration of, 292

• W •

wah-wah effect, 298
waist (guitar), 22
walking bass
  audio track, 595
  overview, 315
"Waltz in E Minor", 491
warm-up exercises, 308–309
websites
  audio/video tracks, 2–4
  extra book content, 4
  Wiley Publishing, 598
whammy bars
  floating bridge mechanism, 42
  floating bridge setup, 57–58
  string changing, 48
  vibrato, 354
whole notes
  symbol for, 64
  vibrato, playing with, 324
whole rests, 64
whole steps
  description, 12
  half-steps versus, 168–172
whole tones, 168
wood grades, 41

About the Authors

Jon Chappell is a multi-style guitarist, transcriber, and arranger. He attended Carnegie-Mellon University, where he studied with Carlos Barbosa-Lima, and he then went on to earn his master's degree in composition from DePaul University, where he also taught theory and ear training. He is a competition-winning flatpicker and fingerpicker, specializing in acoustic music.

Chappell was formerly editor-in-chief of *Guitar* magazine, founding editor of *Home* magazine, and musicologist for *Guitarra*, a classical magazine. He has played and recorded with Pat Benatar, Judy Collins, Graham Nash, and Gunther Schuller, and he has contributed numerous musical pieces to film and TV. Some of these include *Northern Exposure*; *Walker, Texas Ranger*; *All My Children*; and the feature film *Bleeding Hearts* directed by actor-dancer Gregory Hines.

In his book publishing career, Chappell has served as associate music director of Cherry Lane Music where he has transcribed, edited, and arranged the music of Joe Satriani, Steve Vai, Steve Morse, Mike Stern, and Eddie Van Halen, among others. He has more than a dozen method books to his name and is the author or co-author of *Guitar For Dummies* (Wiley), *Rock Guitar For Dummies* (Wiley), *Blues Guitar For Dummies* (Wiley), *Classical Guitar For Dummies* (Wiley), *Build Your Own PC Recording Studio* (McGraw-Hill), and the textbook *The Recording Guitarist: A Guide for Home and Studio* (Hal Leonard).

Mark Phillips is a guitarist, arranger, and editor with more than 30 years in the music publishing field. He earned his bachelor's degree in music theory from Case Western Reserve University, where he received the Carolyn Neff Award for scholastic excellence, and his master's degree in music theory from Northwestern University, where he was elected to Pi Kappa Lambda, the most prestigious U.S. honor society for college and university music students. While working toward a doctorate in music theory at Northwestern, Phillips taught classes in theory, ear training, sight-singing, counterpoint, and guitar.

During the 1970s and early '80s, Phillips was director of Popular Music at Warner Bros. Publications, where he edited and arranged the songbooks of such artists as Neil Young, James Taylor, the Eagles, and Led Zeppelin. Since the mid-'80s he has served as director of music and director of publications at Cherry Lane Music, where he has edited or arranged the songbooks of such artists as John Denver, Van Halen, Guns N' Roses, and Metallica, and has served as music editor of the magazines *Guitar* and *Guitar One*.

Desi Serna, hailed as a "music-theory expert" by *Rolling Stone* magazine, is a guitarist and the author of the very popular *Fretboard Theory* line of guitar instructional material. He's known for his hands-on approach to music theory, and his emphasis on popular music. Desi honed his craft through decades of guitar teaching, performing, and publishing. He operates his own guitar theory website, where he posts online guitar lessons and discusses various music-theory–related topics with his community of followers. He lives near Toledo, Ohio, with his wife and two daughters.

Publisher's Acknowledgments

Acquisitions Editor: David Lutton

Editor: Corbin Collins

Technical Editor: Alexander "Sandy" Williams

Art Coordinator: Alicia B. South

Project Coordinator: Melissa Cossell

Special thanks to W. R. Music Service for some of the music engraving

Cover Image: ©iStockphoto.com/Brigida_Soriano